Microsoft®

Internet Explorer Resource Kit

Microsoft Press

PUBLISHED BY
Microsoft Press
A Division of Microsoft Corporation
One Microsoft Way
Redmond, Washington 98052-6399

Library of Congress Cataloging-in-Publication Data
Microsoft Internet Explorer Resource Kit / Microsoft Corporation.
     p. cm.
   Includes index.
   ISBN 1-57231-842-2
   1. Microsoft Internet Explorer.   2. Internet (Computer network)
  3. World Wide Web (information retrieval system)   I. Microsoft
Corporation.
  TK5105.883.M53M536   1998
  005.7'13769--dc21   97-43135
                                                CIP

Printed and bound in the United States of America.

1 2 3 4 5 6 7 8 9 QMQM 3 2 1 0 9 8

Distributed to the book trade in Canada by Macmillan of Canada, a division of Canada Publishing
Corporation.

A CIP catalogue record for this book is available from the British Library.

Microsoft Press books are available through booksellers and distributors worldwide. For further
information about international editions, contact your local Microsoft Corporation office. Or contact
Microsoft Press International directly at fax (425) 936-7329. Visit our Web site at
mspress.microsoft.com.

Macintosh, QuickTime, and TrueType fonts are registered trademarks of Apple Computer, Inc. Indeo is
a trademark of Intel Corporation. ActiveX, DirectSound, DirectX, FrontPage, IntelliSense, Microsoft,
Microsoft Press, MS-DOS, PowerPoint, Visual Basic, Visual C++, WebBot, Win32, Windows, the
Windows logo, Windows NT, and the Windows Start logo are registered trademarks and Active Channel,
Active Desktop, ActiveMovie, Authenticode, DirectAnimation, JScript, the Microsoft Internet Explorer
logo, MSN, NetMeeting, NetShow, Outlook, Visual InterDev, Visual J++, and Visual SourceSafe are
trademarks of Microsoft Corporation.

Other product and company names mentioned herein may be the trademarks of their respective owners.

Acquisitions Editor: Casey Doyle
Project Editor: Stuart J. Stuple

Contributors

Project Lead:	Craig Beilinson
Managing Editor:	Helen Kaplow
Lead Technical Writers:	Randy Grandle
	Bruce Bartram
	William French III
Technical Contributors:	Kim Akers
	Joe Belfiore
	Robert Bennett
	Scott Berkun
	Eric Berman
	Greg Blaum
	Chris Brown
	Chris Carper
	Christine Chang
	Micheal Dunn
	Castedo Ellerman
	Brent Ethington
	Joe Herman
	Scott Johnson
	Timothy Johnson
	Loren Kohnfelder
	Luanne LaLonde
	Ken Ong
	Srivatsan Parthasarathy
	Hadi Partovi
	Brent Ponto
	Toni Saddler-French
	Kathryn Schmidt
	Thad Schwebke
	Maryanne K. Snyder
	Robert Stewart
	Kevin Unangst
	Michael Wallent
	Tom Yaryan

Contents

Appendixes

Welcome to the Microsoft Internet Explorer 4 Resource Kit

Microsoft® Internet Explorer 4 integrates the power of the computer and the exciting content on the Internet to give users a compelling Web experience. Internet Explorer 4 integrates Web tasks into a proven and popular user interface that makes use of current investments in training and solves key customer issues. Internet Explorer 4 is the next step in Microsoft's vision of "information at your fingertips"; finding and using information should be easy, regardless of how, or where, it is stored.

For corporations, Internet Explorer 4 is designed to make users more productive and to ease migration to intranets, while allowing administrators complete control of Web browser management and design. For users, it provides a much richer Web experience, delivers full-featured communication capabilities, and makes finding information on the Internet or an intranet easier than ever. For developers, Internet Explorer 4 offers support for full interactivity and cutting-edge content, while reducing bandwidth constraints.

The Microsoft Internet Explorer 4 Resource Kit is written for system administrators and information systems (IS) professionals. It provides the information required for understanding, customizing, deploying, and supporting Internet Explorer 4 in their organizations. This resource kit is a technical and planning resource that supplements the information included with the Internet Explorer 4 product and the Microsoft Internet Explorer Administration Kit (IEAK). For information about how to use specific Internet Explorer 4 features, see the Help system supplied with the software. For more information about Internet Explorer 4, see the Internet Explorer Web site at **http://www.microsoft.com/ie/**.

What's New in Microsoft Internet Explorer 4

This section gives a brief description of some of the most interesting and exciting new features and functionality in Microsoft Internet Explorer 4. Internet Explorer 4 delivers innovation in nine key areas that correspond to nine parts in this book:

1. **Easy installation.** Internet Explorer 4 Active Setup offers a powerful solution to the challenges associated with current Internet-based installation programs. The new, modular approach used by Internet Explorer 4 conserves bandwidth and offers users a faster, more versatile installation experience.

2. **Best browser.** Having a great experience on the Web starts with the browser. Internet Explorer 4 contains a variety of improvements that make browsing the Web easier, faster, and more productive so that users can find the information they need.

3. **True Web integration.** Internet Explorer 4 integrates the Internet into every aspect of personal computing—the desktop, file folders, the local network, and even the **Start** menu. The Windows® Desktop Update provides users with a single metaphor for exploring and searching for information. Information from the Internet or an intranet becomes a seamless part of the desktop, and browser-like navigation becomes available in every view. Whether looking at a local hard disk, a local area network (LAN) network drive, or a Web site on an HTTP server, the same navigation toolbar provides functionality for going backward and forward, marking favorite locations, and searching for desired information. Because the same menus and navigation toolbar accomplish similar tasks in different scenarios, users need to learn only one navigational model; thus, the cost of training and supporting users is reduced.

4. **Webcasting.** The built-in Webcasting features in Internet Explorer 4 provide the broadest range of intelligent "push" and "pull" solutions for optimized information delivery. Users can subscribe to any Web site, schedule Internet Explorer 4 to automatically check for updated content on that site, be notified when content changes, and even set Internet Explorer 4 to automatically download updated content for offline viewing. In addition, users can target Web page downloads to the Active Desktop so that they can view their content as desktop wallpaper, as a screen saver, in a desktop ticker, or in a desktop Web window. Using the new Channel Definition Format (CDF), it's easy for content providers or corporate administrators to create custom Active Channels that deliver personalized information to users' desktops in an efficient, effective format.

5. **Complete communication and collaboration.** Internet Explorer 4 offers a complete, scalable suite of integrated tools for communication and collaboration. These include electronic mail, news, conferencing, broadcasting, authoring, and publishing tools. This suite of tools is tightly integrated to ensure consistency across all components in the suite and to provide an easy way to switch between them or other applications you may want to use. Built-in extensibility also makes it easy to integrate third-party clients.

6. **A great publishing platform.** Internet Explorer 4 supports a wide range of new features that publishers can use to create interactive, exciting Web pages based on the newest Internet technologies and standards. Using this set of technologies, Web authors can produce more attractive content while taking up less bandwidth. They can develop business applications that deliver more value and create a more rewarding Web experience. A new object model exposes every element of an HTML page to the content developer. This enables the creation of pages where each page attribute—whether a single word, text style, or a graphic object—can respond to user interaction at run time so that Web pages don't require an entire refresh. Thus, Web page effects finally rival the great performance of multimedia CD-ROM titles. And, Microsoft has again designed the fastest, most reliable, and fully compatible Java support on the market; and delivers a new Java security model that allows users to run powerful, interactive Java applications without having to worry about harm to their computers.

7. **Enhanced security and privacy.** Internet security is a primary concern of every user and corporation on the Internet today, and Internet Explorer 4 is the safest, most secure browser on the Internet today. It supports more of today's emerging and existing security standards, such as Authenticode™, Java permission-based security, Secure Sockets Layer (SSL), and Private Communication Technology (PCT). In addition, Internet Explorer 4 introduces new security enhancements, including Authenticode 2.0 technology and the innovative use of security zones. Security zones provide an easy interface for dividing the Internet or an intranet into safe and unsafe regions, each with its own security settings. Administrators can pre-configure security zone settings, providing better safeguards for corporate users and intranets.

8. **Better accessibility.** Internet Explorer 4 introduces a number of advances that make the Web more accessible to computer users with disabilities. In particular, several features allow users to customize the appearance of Web pages to meet their own needs and preferences. Internet Explorer 4 also includes the best features of Internet Explorer 3, including the ability to navigate the Web using the keyboard. Users without disabilities may also be interested in many of these options as ways to customize colors and fonts to their own tastes or to save time by using keyboard shortcuts.

9. **Expanded deployment and accessibility.** A corporation can begin to realize intranet cost reduction by deploying Internet Explorer 4 using the setup functionality provided in the IEAK. The IEAK allows a system administrator to build a custom package that includes all the specific configuration settings mandated within a corporation. Such an Internet Explorer 4 installation package can also include additional components that need to be installed along with Internet Explorer 4, making it easier for corporations to deploy multiple applications to all desktops at the same time as deploying Internet Explorer 4.

The specific advantage of the IEAK is that it builds Internet Explorer installation packages for all intranet platforms and completely eliminates all end-user setup choices and options, ensuring that all users within an organization experience hands-free setup with the exact same application configuration for Internet Explorer 4 and additional components. Part 9, "Deployment and Maintenance," provides extensive deployment planning, implementation, and maintenance information for Internet Explorer 4.

Easy Installation with Active Setup

Internet Explorer 4 Active Setup is an innovative solution to the challenges of current Internet-based installation programs. Before Internet Explorer 4, all browsers were installed by downloading a single, large, monolithic package. If the download failed, it had to be restarted from the beginning of that large file. If a connection to a server was dropped during download, Setup could not resume and none of the data downloaded could be used.

An executable file cannot run until it has been completely downloaded, so large Setup packages are unable to check system requirements in advance. Users may wait a long time only to find out that they have to free up disk space and try again. A single, monolithic file does not give you control over which components will be installed. If you don't want all the components included in a monolithic package, time is wasted downloading unwanted data, and disk space is wasted storing that data.

Internet Explorer 4 uses a modular approach to solve the problems with previous browser Setups. Internet Explorer Setup is based on an ActiveX® engine called Active Setup, which runs on the client. The process begins with a small Setup package. This self-extracting file can be downloaded to the computer using an existing browser, or it can be copied directly to a computer with no existing browser. Because the file is only 400 kilobytes in size, it downloads very quickly and can fit on a single floppy disk. This file is all that is needed to initiate the installation of Internet Explorer 4. It contains the bare minimum code necessary to give the client Internet access and provide a basic level of file download capabilities.

This small Setup package also allows Setup to collect information about the host computer before the download begins. Active Setup uses this information to intelligently manage the download of Internet Explorer cabinet (.cab) files and make installation as efficient and problem free as possible.

After all the needed user and system information has been gathered and you have selected from the available Microsoft distribution servers on the Internet, the necessary .cab files are downloaded. Because Setup has already inventoried any Internet Explorer components already on the system and has already asked you which components are desired, it knows to download only the .cab files needed. After all the .cab files have been successfully downloaded, Active Setup is complete.

Best Browser

A powerful browser can help your organization reap the important benefits the Web has to offer. As the Internet increases in utility and complexity, more and more computer users have come to rely on Internet Explorer to help them make the most of Internet advancements. Ease-of-use innovations and enhanced personalization features in Internet Explorer 4 truly give users the Web on their terms, or "the Web the way you want it." Internet Explorer 4 also offers key underlying technologies for Web developers.

Internet Explorer 4 contains a variety of improvements that make browsing the Web easier, faster, and more fun than ever before. Part 2, "Configuring the Browser," provides detailed information about the features and functionality of the Internet Explorer 4 browser; a few key features are highlighted here.

AutoComplete

The Address bar in Internet Explorer 4 automatically completes addresses for you, based on sites you've already visited. By filling in long, complicated URLs automatically, AutoComplete makes it easier for you to type in URLs and reduces the opportunity for typographical mistakes. AutoComplete also automatically adds prefixes and suffixes to Internet addresses.

As an extension of the AutoComplete feature, you can right-click the Address bar to have Internet Explorer 4 provide a list of available completions for a partial URL.

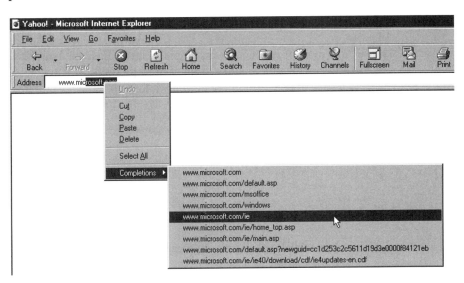

Navigation History on Back and Forward Buttons

Instead of pressing the **Back** button over and over again to go to a site you visited earlier, you now click the drop-down arrow next to the **Back** or **Forward** button to see a list of your current navigation history. From that list, you can quickly go to the pages you need.

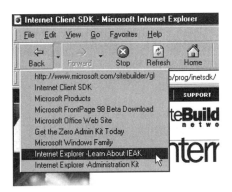

Explorer Bars

The Explorer bar is an innovation exclusive to Internet Explorer 4 that makes it dramatically easier to navigate the Web. Explorer bars for Search, Favorites, History, and Active Channel™ view make it easier to find the sites you need, visit your favorite pages, return to the places you've been, and access the information you use most often. When you select an Explorer bar by clicking its button on the Internet Explorer toolbar, a special pane slides in on the left side of Internet Explorer content window. When you click a link on an Explorer bar, the corresponding page opens in the main content window, so your links are still visible while the content is displayed. To remove the Explorer bar from your desktop, click its **Close** button.

For example, the Search bar displays search results independent of the main browser area. When you rest the pointer over a result, Internet Explorer also displays a summary of the site in a ToolTip. When you select a site from the results list, the site appears in the main browser area, keeping the Search bar available for future searches. The results list remains in the Search bar, so if you need to visit a different site that the search engine revealed, you can easily move from result to result without repeatedly using the **Back** button to return to the search results page. Internet Explorer 4 also preserves the state of the search, so if you click the **Search** button again during the same session, the results of the previous search appear. This way, you easily can move the Search bar out of the way and then bring it back when you need it.

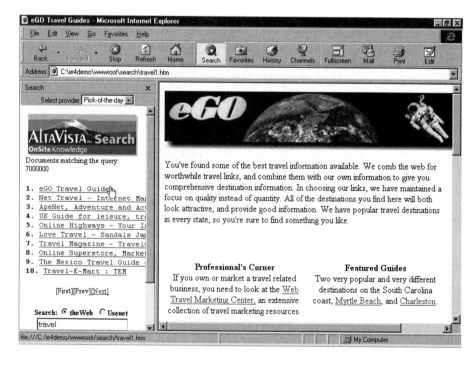

Offline Browsing

When users want to go to a favorite site on the company intranet or on the Web, it's not always convenient to connect to the network or to their Internet service provider (ISP). With offline browsing, users can view sites without these connections. For example, users can browse offline while using their laptop computers at locations where Internet access is not available. Or users can find it helpful to browse offline at home when they don't want to tie up their only phone line. Some users may even prefer to browse offline at the office when server traffic is heavy and load time is slow. (Offline browsing is faster than browsing online.)

Internet Explorer 4 makes offline browsing possible by automatically caching every site you visit when online. All Web pages you access, as well as files related to those pages (such as graphic files), are stored on your hard disk so that they can be viewed later without an active Internet connection. To begin browsing offline, select **Work Offline** from the **File** menu in Internet Explorer and select any page from the History bar. The History bar automatically sorts your visited Web pages by date and then by site, so it's easy to see where you've been in the past, whether you're online or offline.

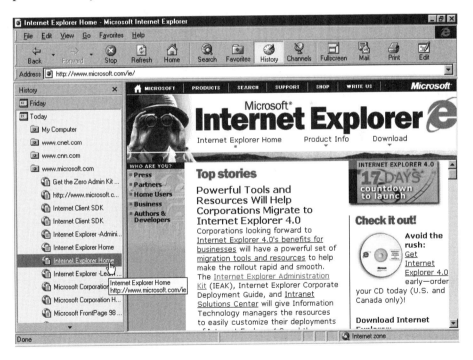

In addition, you can use the Webcasting technology in Internet Explorer 4 to schedule your browser to automatically check a Web site for changes since your last visit and download any new or updated content so that you're always browsing the most up-to-date information, even when offline. (For more information about Webcasting, see Part 4, "Information Delivery: Webcasting.")

True Web Integration

Until now, business computer users got their information from two distinct worlds: the online world of the Internet and the "local" world of company networks and systems. But, as the Internet advances to permeate users' everyday computing experience, the integration of Web features and functionality with the desktop operating system is an idea that has become increasingly important and valuable.

For this reason, Internet Explorer 4 provides true Web integration with the Windows Desktop Update, a set of features that integrate the Internet into every aspect of personal computing—the desktop, file folders, the network, and even the **Start** menu. Part 3, "True Web Integration: Windows Desktop Update," describes how true Web integration works in Internet Explorer 4, details the features included in the Windows Desktop Update, and explains how you can use these features to create a richer, more streamlined, and more productive working environment in your organization. A few key features are outlined here.

Start Menu and Taskbar

The **Start** menu and taskbar provide an anchor on the Windows desktop, giving users one center for starting and switching tasks. In Internet Explorer 4, these elements are extended to integrate Internet and intranet tasks into a user interface that many users have already mastered. For example, an address bar allows users to enter any Web address or file path directly from their Windows taskbar, eliminating the need to switch back and forth between the file folder window (Windows Explorer) and the browser window (Internet Explorer). This concept is called Single Explorer, and it offers consistent navigation at the same time as it provides flexible functionality.

When using the Windows 95 and Windows NT® operating systems, users know they can use the **Start** button to access almost everything. Inside the Web browser, they know they can rely on their **Favorites** menu to get to their commonly used sites. In Internet Explorer 4, these ideas are combined and the **Favorites** menu attached to the **Start** button, so users can now get to their favorite sites quickly—without having to launch their Web browser first.

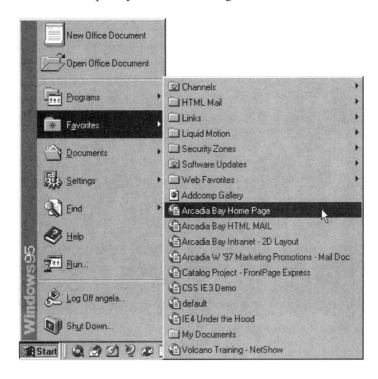

Following the same logic, the Internet Explorer 4 taskbar provides access to a wide array of Internet-focused functions, permitting users to get to the information they need quickly and conveniently. With Internet Explorer 4, the taskbar has become extensible to support expandable, dockable, and layered browser toolbars. In addition, custom toolbars can contain any sort of content, including application shortcuts or even Web pages.

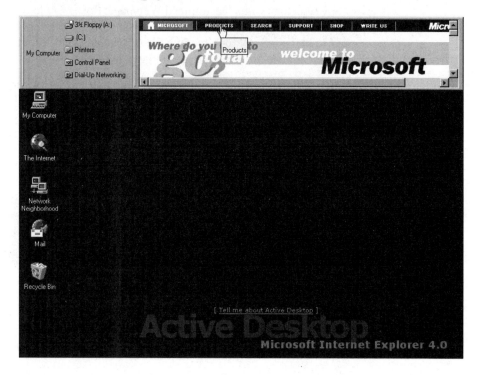

Web View

Internet Explorer 4 opens up the user interface so that you can customize any folder (on a floppy disk, on a local hard disk, or on a server) with HTML. The Web View feature extends the original views in Windows 95 (Large Icons, Small Icons, List, and Details) with a fifth view that can represent the contents of any directory with a customized Web page. For example, when viewing a public folder on a network, users today just see a list of files and folders. They need to know to look for a readme file (if one exists) to see what is present in those directories and where to go for help.

With Internet Explorer 4, administrators can set up these folders with Web views so that users can see a Web page with HTML, Java, or ActiveX controls that richly describe the contents of that folder, or whatever information the administrator decides to provide. With Web View, administrators can extend the user interface of Windows with the simplicity of HTML.

For example, a typical directory on a public server may appear this way to a user:

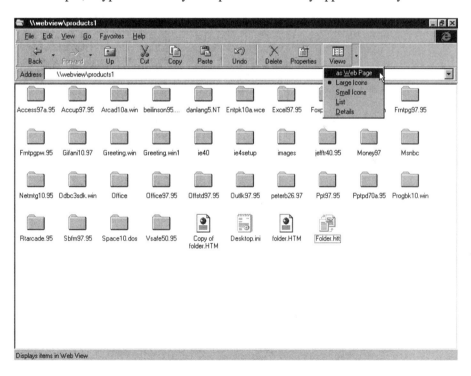

However, administrators can dramatically enhance the appearance of that directory by implementing an HTML Web view. The window in the following illustration is displaying the exact same directory, but Web View has been activated.

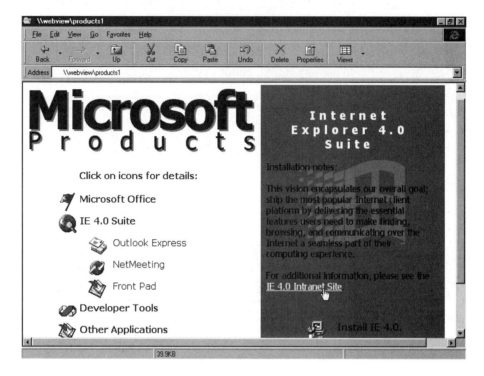

Web View Wizard

The Web View Wizard makes it easy for users and network administrators to create a custom Web view (based on HTML) for any folder, whether it is local or on a network share, without requiring a Web server. Any Internet Explorer 4 user who views that folder will see the customized Web view instead of the usual, nondescript list of files and folders. By default, the wizard will use FrontPage® Express to help create the Web view, but Internet Explorer 4 can be customized to use any HTML editor.

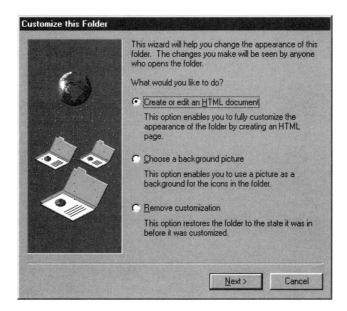

Active Desktop

The Active Desktop interface brings the Web right to users' desktops with HTML wallpaper, screen savers, and Active Desktop items. Now you can use a Web page as desktop wallpaper or as a screen saver, complete with graphics and links to your favorite files and URLs. ActiveX objects, JavaScript, and Visual Basic® Scripting Edition (VBScript) can be used to add even more functionality. Active Desktop items, which are essentially miniature Web pages that reside on the desktop, complement this functionality. They can be used to provide information such as news headlines, weather, traffic information, and stock quotes. For users, adding an Active Desktop item can be as simple as pointing and clicking. For system administrators, creating an Active Desktop item is as easy as creating a Web page.

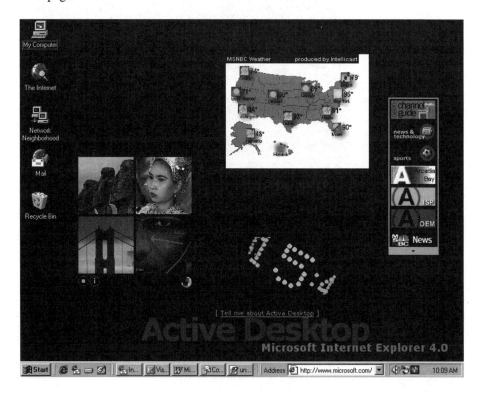

The flexibility of the Active Desktop interface allows intranet administrators to use "push" and "smart pull" technologies to make information and resources directly accessible from users' desktops, and to customize that information for specific user groups. The Active Desktop turns users' desktops into dynamic, personalized, live Web "bulletin boards" that regularly update with the latest content, for quick access online or offline. Such custom configurations can be easily managed using the IEAK.

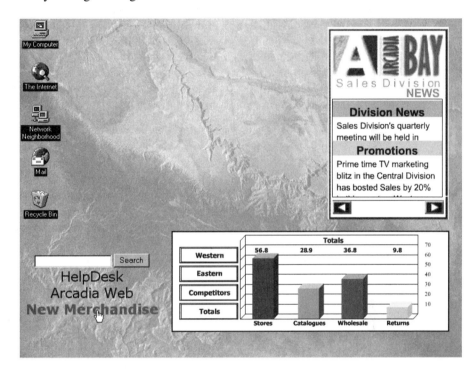

Webcasting

The information delivery architecture in Internet Explorer 4 enables new ways for Web content or applications to reach end users, using the new "push" and "pull" technologies, which are collectively referred to as *Webcasting*. Webcasting is the automated delivery of personalized, up-to-date information to users' desktops. Internet Explorer 4 provides a mechanism for end users to schedule recurring monitoring, or crawling, of Web sites and automatic downloading of updated information. These advanced features for pulling content allow online users to receive notification when content changes, and they allow mobile workers to view favorite Web content even when they work offline. In addition, the information delivery architecture allows intranet administrators to set up servers that push content to corporate employees via bandwidth-efficient multicast protocols.

Why introduce a new model of information delivery on the Web? Because traditional Web browsing poses several problems for end users and the organizations that support them. Currently, most Internet and intranet sites require users to manually browse for useful information and then frequently revisit the sites for updated content. This process is time-consuming for users and bandwidth-consuming for the network, as the same pages are repeatedly downloaded. For mobile workers, the problem is exacerbated by painfully slow dial-up connections.

To address these problems, Internet Explorer 4 provides three Webcasting options that allow you to take the best advantage of this new technology, based on your current business needs and technology investments. By automatically tracking updates to Web content, Webcasting can help minimize the time users spend searching the Web for up-to-date information, while ensuring that the latest information is automatically delivered to the people who need it. In addition, Webcasting can reduce the bandwidth necessary to deliver updated content on the Web by reducing the amount of redundant information that is downloaded and by operating at off-peak network load periods, rather than the peak load periods often used with manual browsing. Part 4, "Information Delivery: Webcasting," describes the three types of Webcasting and explains how to incorporate these information delivery technologies into your organization. A brief overview is outlined here.

Basic Webcasting

Using basic Webcasting, users can subscribe to any existing Web site and have Internet Explorer 4 automatically visit and crawl the site on a scheduled basis to check for updated content. Internet Explorer 4 can check the site up to three levels deep; when content changes, Internet Explorer 4 notifies users—either by a gleam on their Favorites lists or by e-mail. Internet Explorer can also automatically download updated content for offline use. Site subscription can be thought of as "smart pull" technology.

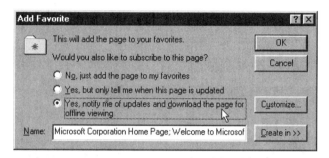

Managed Webcasting

Similar to basic Webcasting, managed Webcasting also works through a subscription process, except that users subscribe to publisher-specified Active Channels; an Active Channel™ delivers a defined range of Web content. This can be thought of as "programmed pull." Users can check for updates on specific types of content and can accept a publisher's predefined update schedule or specify their own custom schedule. When channel content changes, Internet Explorer notifies the user of changes and can be set to download only the requested content for viewing offline.

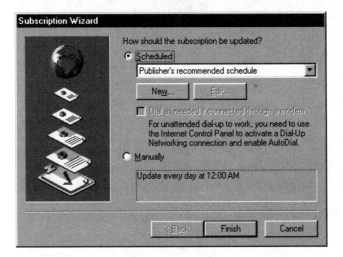

Active Channels allow Web site authors to optimize, personalize, and more fully control how a site is Webcast, and adding a Channel Definition Format (CDF) file is the only step required to convert any existing Web site into an Active Channel. Using CDF, it's easy to design Active Channels, Active Desktop items, or channel screen savers for your intranet to efficiently deliver business information to users' desktops.

After a user subscribes to an Active Channel, Internet Explorer will automatically add the subscribed channel logo to the Channel bar on the Active Desktop and in the browser, making the Web site more prominent and more easily accessible.

Here is the Active Channel bar directly on the desktop.

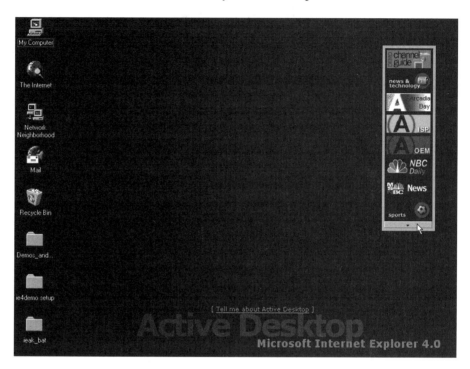

Here is the Active Channel bar inside Internet Explorer 4.

True Webcasting

True Webcasting, or "true push" technology, uses multicast add-ons such as Microsoft NetShow™ 2.0 to deliver bandwidth-efficient multimedia information to users' desktops. Organizations can use true Webcasting to automatically push updated information to subscribers at scheduled periods. (For more information, see Chapter 19, "NetShow.")

Complete Communication and Collaboration

Collaboration across the Internet is one of the most exciting, avidly discussed topics today. Microsoft is committed to a complete communication and collaboration suite of tools, and the Internet Explorer 4 suite provides a solution for whatever Internet-based communication needs users have. Using its modular installation program or the IEAK, users and administrators can set up only the pieces they need or take advantage of the flexibility of the Internet Explorer suite and integrate it with their existing software solutions.

The Internet Explorer suite allows seamless integration from one application to the next because the applications are all tightly integrated and have been developed with a common menu and toolbar. This simplifies training, because a user who learns one application in the suite already has a head start in learning the next one.

The Internet Explorer 4 suite contains these components for communication and collaboration across the Internet or local intranet:

- Outlook™ Express for e-mail and newsgroups
- NetShow for broadcasting
- NetMeeting™ for conferencing and application sharing
- FrontPage Express for Web authoring
- Personal Web Server for Web publishing

Outlook Express

E-mail has become one of the most popular and effective ways for people to communicate, both in business and in their personal lives. Unfortunately, most e-mail has been limited to text-only messages, perhaps with attachments. Internet Explorer 4 allows an entirely new type of standards-based messaging, opening the door to greater richness and detail. Outlook Express supports full HTML, so you can create e-mail messages with the color and functionality of Web pages without knowing HTML.

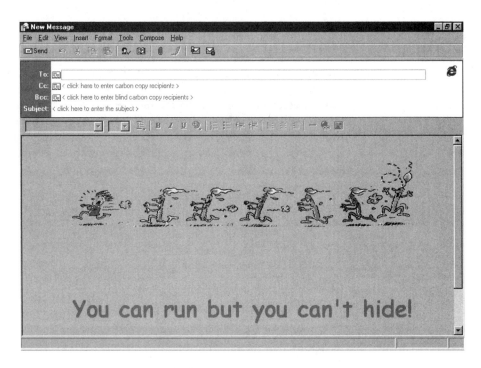

You can even send full Web pages from the Internet as part of your e-mail message.

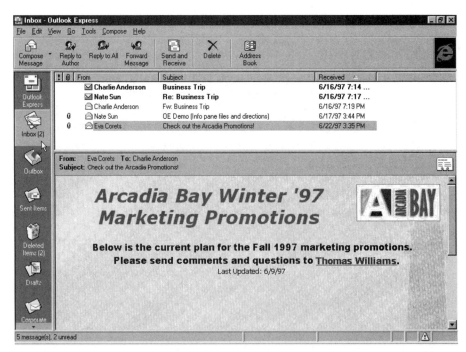

In addition, Outlook Express provides users with powerful mail management features, more efficient e-mail and newsgroup use, enhanced security, and full support for Internet standards and technologies. Outlook Express is flexible enough to meet the diverse e-mail needs of users with dial-up Internet access through an ISP and users who work on a LAN based on Internet standards such as Simple Mail Transfer Protocol (SMTP), Post Office Protocol 3 (POP3), Internet Mail Access Protocol 4 (IMAP4), or Lightweight Directory Access Protocol (LDAP).

NetShow

NetShow brings the power of broadcasting to the desktop. With NetShow, Web content comes alive with interactive content, including audio, illustrated audio (images and sound), and video. It includes both client and server components to add the power of traditional broadcasting systems – audio and video – to HTTP. NetShow harnesses Internet technologies and the power of Windows NT server to transform Web communications into a richer and more effective medium: the network show.

NetMeeting

Microsoft NetMeeting is a powerful tool that enables real-time communications and collaboration over the Internet or intranet, providing standards-based audio, video, and multipoint data conferencing support. From a Windows® 95-based or Windows NT 4-based desktop, users can communicate over the network with real-time voice and video technology. They can share data and information with many people through true application sharing, electronic whiteboard, text-based chat, and file transfer features. NetMeeting helps organizations communicate more effectively, thus increasing productivity for their users. Also, NetMeeting helps organizations reduce their support burden by providing real-time application sharing features so that help-desk staff can remotely resolve user problems more quickly and efficiently.

Designed for corporate communication, NetMeeting supports international communication standards for audio, video, and data conferencing. With NetMeeting, people can connect by modem, ISDN, or LAN using the TCP/IP protocol, and communicate and collaborate with users of NetMeeting and other standards-based, compatible products. In addition, support for system policies in NetMeeting makes it easy for administrators to centrally control and manage the NetMeeting work environment.

FrontPage Express

While HTML has made it possible for many people to become Web publishers, it is still not a particularly intuitive language. For this reason, Microsoft FrontPage Express has been included as a component of the Internet Explorer suite. Based on the full-featured Microsoft FrontPage 97 Web authoring and management tool, FrontPage Express features a graphical interface that makes creating HTML pages as easy as creating a document in a word processor.

FrontPage Express allows users to create their own Web pages in a what-you-see-is-what-you-get (WYSIWYG) environment, without knowing HTML. FrontPage Express includes all the features of the FrontPage 97 editor, except for premium features such as Active Server Pages and some of the WebBot® components that rely on specific server extensions. WebBot components from FrontPage 97, such as Include, Search, and Time-Stamp, are still included, however.

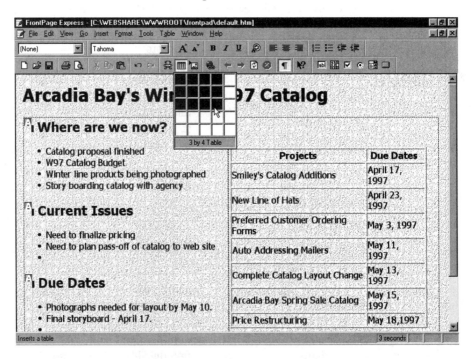

Personal Web Server

As millions of users flock to the Internet for information and entertainment, many decide that they also want to share information with the world. Personal Web Server turns any Windows 95 or Windows NT 4 computer into a Web server, enabling easy publication of Web pages. The simplicity of this tool makes the Personal Web Server perfect for home users, schools, and corporate workgroups.

A Great Publishing Platform

The implementation of Internet standards is crucial to enhancing the Web experience. Now users can view and listen to real-time broadcasts, watch videos, run ActiveX controls and Java applets, and play interactive, multiplayer games on the Web. All of this can be experienced with Internet Explorer 4 because of the browser's extensive support for Internet standards and because it includes support for innovative underlying technologies such as Dynamic HTML, ActiveX, and Java. For more information, see Part 6, "Authoring for Internet Explorer 4."

Dynamic HTML

Limitations of current browser technology often require authors using HTML to choose between interactivity and speed. After a page is loaded, changing the display or content of the page typically requires that the entire page be reloaded. Or, depending on how extensive the changes are, additional pages may have to be retrieved from the server. To address that limitation, Internet Explorer 4 includes several new features collectively called Dynamic HTML. These features provide the client-side intelligence and flexibility to enable HTML authors to create interactive pages that dynamically change the display and content of a page entirely on the client machine, without requiring additional server resources. Dynamic HTML enables HTML authors to create innovative Web sites with interactive pages without having to pay a performance penalty. In addition, by reducing requests from the server, Dynamic HTML also reduces server load, thus improving performance.

ActiveX

For those who need more power than Dynamic HTML offers, Internet Explorer 4 provides enhanced support for ActiveX controls. ActiveX controls are software components that provide interactive and user-controllable functions. Small and versatile, they open a wide range of opportunities for creating attractive and effective Web content. Internet Explorer 4 presents a set of new opportunities for control and script engine developers. Controls can now be faster, smaller, and more integrated than ever before.

Java

You can also use Java to extend the capabilities of Dynamic HTML and create even more interactive, exciting Web content. While Internet Explorer 3 brought the fastest, most reliable, and fully compatible Java support to the market, Internet Explorer 4 goes even further, taking Java support to the next level. Java applets not only run faster than in Internet Explorer 3, but also you can optimize Java applets to take full advantage of all the features and speed of the Windows 95 and Windows NT operating systems. In addition, Internet Explorer 4 introduces a Java security model that allows you to run powerful, interactive Java applications without harming your organization's computers or threatening its privacy.

Active Scripting

With its support for active scripting, Internet Explorer 4 provides fast, comprehensive, language-independent script-handling capability. Users can view Web pages that use any popular scripting language, including Visual Basic Scripting Edition (VBScript) and JScript™ development software. Internet Explorer scripting support allows authors to develop pages that can ask questions, respond to queries, check user data, calculate expressions, link to other programs, and connect to ActiveX controls, Java applets, or anything else you specify. In addition, Internet Explorer 4 complies with the new Internet scripting standard specified by the European Computer Manufacturers Association (ECMA). Compliance to Internet standards helps ensure that the Web content and active scripting you develop for Internet Explorer 4 will run seamlessly across a wide range of platforms and products.

Enhanced Security and Privacy

Microsoft Internet Explorer 4 provides a full range of security features to help system administrators manage Internet and network security in their organizations. Internet Explorer 4 also provides features to help ensure user privacy. Part 7, "Security and Privacy," describes the security and privacy features of Internet Explorer 4 and explains how these features can be used to help protect the individuals and information in your organization.

Security Zones

Internet Explorer 4 introduces security zones, an innovative approach to secure browsing that offers greater management control and flexibility. Security zones allow users to divide the Internet and intranet into four groups of trusted (safe) and untrusted (unsafe) areas and to designate that specific Web content belongs to these safe and unsafe areas. This Web content can be anything from an HTML file, a graphic, an Active X control, a Java applet, or an executable program. After zones of trust have been established, browser security levels can be set for each zone.

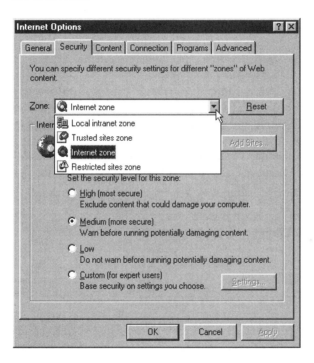

Certificate Management

To verify the identity of individuals and organizations on the Web and to ensure content integrity, Internet Explorer 4 uses industry-standard digital certificates and Microsoft Authenticode 2.0 technology. Together with security zones, these can be used to control user access to online content based on the type, source, and location of the content. For example, system administrators can use security zones in conjunction with certificates to allow users to have full access to Web content on their intranet but limit users' access to Web content from restricted sites located on the Internet.

Trust-Based Security for Java

Internet Explorer 4 provides trust-based security for Java, which is a cross-platform security model for Java that provides fine-grained management of the permissions granted to Java applets and libraries.

Content Ratings

System administrators can control the types of content that users can access on the Internet by using the Internet Explorer 4 Content Advisor. You can adjust the content rating settings to reflect what you think is appropriate content in four areas: language, nudity, sex, and violence.

User Privacy

Internet Explorer 4 supports a wide range of Internet protocols for secure information transfers and financial transactions over the Internet or an intranet. Internet Explorer 4 also provides a variety of features to help users ensure the privacy of their information. For example, Microsoft Wallet is an "electronic wallet" where users can securely store and access private information such as credit card numbers, digital certificates, and digital keys for easy and private online transactions.

Conventions Used for This Guide

The following terms and text formats are used throughout this guide.

Convention	Meaning
Bold	Indicates the actual commands, words, or characters that you type or that you click in the user interface.
Italic	Indicates a placeholder for information or parameters that you must provide. For example, if the procedure asks you to type a *file name*, you type the actual name of a file.
Path\File name	Indicates a Microsoft Windows file system path or registry key—for example, Templates\Normal.dot. Unless otherwise indicated, you can use a mixture of uppercase and lowercase characters when you type paths and file names.
`Monospace`	Represents examples of screen text or code text.

PART 1

Installation of Internet Explorer 4

Part 1 describes the components, processes, and options for installing Internet Explorer 4 on Microsoft® Windows 95 and Windows NT® 4 operating systems, and offers troubleshooting tips. Internet Explorer 4 is also available for Windows 3.1, Windows for Workgroups, and the Macintosh®. For more information about Internet Explorer 4 on these platforms, please refer to the documentation for the specific version you are using.

Chapter 1: Installation Requirements and Issues

This chapter outlines the system requirements for installing Internet Explorer 4 on the Windows 95 and Windows NT operating systems. Issues that may impact the successful installation of Internet Explorer are also discussed.

Chapter 2: Phase 1 - Active Setup

Internet Explorer 4 Active Setup offers an innovative solution to the challenges associated with current Internet-based installation programs. This chapter explains the modular approach used by Internet Explorer 4, which conserves bandwidth and offers users a faster, more versatile installation experience. The chapter guides you through the Active Setup process, step by step.

Chapter 3: Phase 2 - ACME Setup

ACME Setup is the process of extracting, installing, and registering program files on the user's computer, and making the necessary configurations to the system. The processes of the ACME Setup are described in detail here.

Chapter 4: Automated Installation (Hands-Free Mode)

This chapter describes how to install Internet Explorer 4 with a minimum of user prompts. Administrators can use the default settings specified in the Setup program or use the command prompt to choose their own options for installation. Automatic configuration is also explained.

Chapter 5: User Profiles

User profile settings allow multiple users to use a single installation of Internet Explorer while retaining unique, individual settings for each user. This is useful for situations where multiple users share a workstation and for storing roaming settings for mobile users.

Chapter 6: Adding and Removing Components After Setup

After installing Internet Explorer 4, it is possible to further customize the installation by adding new components or removing existing components. This chapter explains how to update your version of Internet Explorer to be sure you're using the latest software.

Chapter 7: Uninstalling Internet Explorer

This chapter describes the processes involved in uninstalling Internet Explorer 4. The files and registry entries that are used for uninstallation are described in detail.

Chapter 8: Configuring Connection Settings

The Internet Connection Wizard (ICW) lets users configure an Internet connection. Users can choose an existing Internet service provider (ISP) account or create a new one. They can establish a connection using either a modem or a local area network (LAN).

C H A P T E R 1

Installation Requirements and Issues

In this chapter

Understanding System Requirements

System Requirements for Internet Explorer 4:

Component	Requirements
Processor	486/66 or better
Operating System	Windows 95, OSR2, or Windows NT 4.0 with SP3
Memory	Windows 95: 8 MB minimum, 16 MB with Active Desktop
	Windows NT: 16 MB minimum, 24 MB with Active Desktop
Disk Space	40 MB for a minimal installation (52 MB with .cab files)
	51 MB for a standard installation (67 MB with .cab files)
	64 MB for a full installation (89 MB with .cab files)
Peripherals	A mouse and a modem or network interface card

At least 70 MB of free disk space is required on the Windows partition if installing to another partition.

For troubleshooting purposes, it is suggested that you add 5 MB to each of the above numbers.

For Setup to run on a computer running Windows NT, Service Pack 3 (SP3) for Windows NT must be installed. If SP3 is not on the system, Setup will fail, with a message that informs the user that SP3 must be installed before Internet Explorer can be installed.

In addition, a user must have administrative privileges to install or uninstall on a Windows NT operating system. This includes having administrative privileges the first time you start your computer after installing or uninstalling. If the Temporary Internet Files cache is on an NTFS volume, all users will need full rights to the folder.

Understanding Installation Issues

Please read through the following issues before installing Internet Explorer 4.

Diskless workstations

A user cannot set up Internet Explorer to run from a network disk. The **Download only** option supports downloading to a network disk, but not running from a network disk.

Coexisting with previous versions of Internet Explorer

It is *not* possible to have Internet Explorer 3 and Internet Explorer 4 coexist on the same computer. Internet Explorer 3 will be restored if Internet Explorer 4 is uninstalled.

Because some clients of MSN™, the Microsoft Network, are based on Internet Explorer 3, MSN users will need to upgrade their MSN client software to MSN version 4 when they install Internet Explorer.

Coexisting with Netscape browsers

Internet Explorer may coexist with any Netscape browser. Although Setup detects the presence of Netscape, there is nothing in the Setup user interface to reflect this. You do not get the choice to upgrade over Netscape and replace it with Internet Explorer. Internet Explorer adopts Netscape user settings at the time of installation. For more information, see Chapter 34, "Planning the Deployment," in Part 9, "Deployment and Maintenance."

Installing on a dual-boot computer

Multiple installations of Internet Explorer 4 on a single computer are not supported. If you plan multiple installations, you should install them to separate operating systems on separate disks or partitions. Internet Explorer provides full support for user profiles so that multiple users of a computer may use a single installation. (See Chapter 5, "User Profiles," for more information.)

Although it is not supported, the Internet Explorer core can be shared on the same disk in separate folders. However, the add-ons always install to the Program Files directory of the Windows disk. If you have Windows NT and Windows 95 installed on the same disk, the add-ons have to be shared. This can cause problems if you uninstall from one operating system, because then you can't uninstall the add-on from the other operating system.

Installing on a system with no browser

For Active Setup to work on a system with no browser installed, a working Dial-Up Networking connection to an ISP must be created before Setup is run. If the distribution server can be accessed on the local intranet, no pre-configuration is required.

Can't reinstall Windows 95 (or OSR2) over Internet Explorer 4

Once Internet Explorer has been installed on a system, the operating system may not be reinstalled without first uninstalling Internet Explorer. Users will get a warning message if they try to do so, but they may ignore the warning. Doing so will result in a mismatch of files and registry settings that will render the system unbootable. The resolution to this state can be found in Appendix B or in the Knowledge Base, in the "Reinstalling Internet Explorer 4" section. You can access the Microsoft Knowledge Base at **http://www.microsoft.com/support/**.

Can't remove Windows Desktop Update during a reinstall

When reinstalling Internet Explorer over itself, you cannot remove the Windows Desktop Update during the reinstall. You can, however, *add* the Windows Desktop Update during a reinstall. For instructions on removing Windows Desktop Update after installation, see Chapter 6, "Adding and Removing Components After Setup."

Can't change the Setup folder during a reinstall

When reinstalling, Active Setup will place the cabinet (.cab) files in the existing Setup folder and will not give you an opportunity to specify a different folder.

Failed trust check

When installing Internet Explorer, all the components in the installation checklist may quickly fail. This may be caused by a corrupt .cab file in the Setup folder (to identify, check file sizes) or a bad version of Wintrust.dll. The .cab file can be replaced by another download.

The log file can be used to see if trust check failed. If it has, there are a variety of possible resolutions:

- Install the Authenticode™ 2 update.
- Rename Wintrust.dll before launching IE4Setup.exe again.
- Add the following key to the registry to disable the trust check:

  **HKEY_LOCAL_MACHINE\Software\Microsoft\Active Setup\
  "DisableCheckTrust"="y"**
- Try renaming Digsig.dll and Schannel.dll.

For information about additional issues related to installation and uninstallation of Internet Explorer 4, see Appendix B.

C H A P T E R   2

Phase 1: Active Setup

In this chapter

Note Active Setup is needed only to install Internet Explorer from the Internet, not from a compact disc. If you are installing from a compact disc, skip this chapter, and begin reading at Chapter 3, "Phase 2: ACME Setup."

Understanding Active Setup

Internet Explorer 4 Setup is an innovative solution to the challenges of current Internet-based installation programs. Before Internet Explorer, all browsers were installed by downloading a single, large, monolithic package. If the download failed, it had to be restarted from the beginning of that large file. If a connection to a server was dropped during download, Setup could not resume, and none of the data downloaded could be used.

An executable file cannot run until it has been completely downloaded, so large setup packages are unable to check system requirements in advance. Users may wait a long time, only to find out that they have to free up disk space and try again. A single, monolithic file does not give you control over what components will be installed. If you don't want all the components included in a monolithic package, time is wasted downloading unwanted data, and disk space is wasted storing that data.

Internet Explorer uses a modular approach to solve the problems with previous browser setups. Internet Explorer Setup is based on an ActiveX™ engine called Active Setup, which runs on the client. The process begins with a small setup package. This self-extracting file can be downloaded to the computer, using an existing browser, or it can be copied directly on to a computer with no existing browser. Only 400 kilobytes in size, it downloads very quickly or fits on a single floppy disk. This file is all that is needed to initiate the installation of Internet Explorer. It contains the bare minimum code necessary to give the client Internet access and provide a basic level of file download capabilities.

This small setup package also allows Setup to collect information about the host computer before the download begins. Active Setup uses this information to intelligently manage the download of Internet Explorer .cab files and make installation as efficient and problem-free as possible.

After all the needed user and system information has been gathered, and you have selected from the available Microsoft distribution servers on the Internet, the necessary .cab files are downloaded. Because Setup has already inventoried any Internet Explorer components already on the system and has already asked you which components are desired, it knows to download only the .cab files needed. Once the .cab files have all been successfully downloaded, Active Setup is complete.

The next phase of Internet Explorer 4 Setup uses the traditional ACME Setup engine used by most Microsoft products. This process follows the typical methodology of an ACME-driven installation using a collection of .cab files. The only difference in this case is that the .cab files are in a folder on the local hard disk, rather than on a removable disk or network disk.

Downloading and Extracting IE4Setup.exe

To install Internet Explorer from the Internet, you must first establish a connection to a download site (such as **http://www.microsoft.com/ie/**) with whatever browser is currently installed. From this site, you will download IE4Setup.exe. IE4Setup.exe may also be copied to the computer from a network connection or a removable disk (for unsupported custom installations). Note that if you choose to save IE4Setup.exe to your hard disk when downloading IE4Setup.exe, you will need to manually launch it from your local disk to begin Active Setup.

Understanding Language Considerations

From the download site, you will be asked to select the language version of Internet Explorer you want. Internet Explorer is language-specific. For example, the English version of Internet Explorer will only run properly on English-language-based operating systems. If you have accidentally installed the English version over a non-English-language-based operating system, you can use only limited Internet Explorer functionality. You will not be able to use the Active Desktop™ interface or access Active Channels™, for instance.

Users are not informed if they pick a language that is different from their current shell. (It is assumed that users will choose the correct language.) Setup checks to see if the chosen language matches the currently installed operating system. If it doesn't match, you will get an error saying that the Windows Desktop Update shell will not be installed, and the option to choose the Windows Desktop Update will not be displayed during setup. This error is also displayed if you try to install the wrong language version of the shell from the add-on page. The Windows Desktop Update and the add-on page are discussed later in this chapter.

For troubleshooting information on languages, see "Shell Integration Not Enabled After Installing Internet Explorer" in Appendix B.

Understanding Cabinet Files in Internet Explorer 4

For a number of years, Microsoft has been using cabinet (.cab) files to compress software that was distributed on diskettes. Originally, these files were used to minimize the number of diskettes shipped with packaged product. Today, .cab files are used to reduce the file size and the associated download time for Web content that is found on the Internet or corporate intranet servers. The .cab file format is a nonproprietary compression format, also known as MSZIP, that is based on the Lempel-Ziv data-compression algorithm.

Cabinet files and ActiveX controls can be digitally signed when they are created. A digital signature provides accountability for software developers by associating a given file with a software vendor. Authenticode™ is the name of the client-side technology that reads the digital signatures of .cab files and ActiveX controls and prompts the user with the name of the software vendor before downloading them. (For more information about digital signatures and Authenticode, see Part 7, "Security and Privacy.") There is Visual Basic Scripting Edition (VBScript) that checks the computer for the presence of Authenticode 2.0 and presents the prompt if Authenticode 2.0 files are not found. It is best if you download Authenticode 2.0 and then reboot before installing Internet Explorer 4.

WExtract is a new technology that expands what we can do with .cab files. WExtract gives a .cab files the ability to create a temporary directory, self extract, and then automatically launch a process using an .inf file (in which case a GenInstall is executed) or an executable file. The launched .inf or .exe file can be contained in the .cab file. In the case of IE4Setup.exe, WExtract expands into the files needed to run Active Setup and automatically launches the Setup Wizard. When the process is complete, the temporary directory containing the extracted contents of the .cab file is automatically deleted.

During the course of a successful installation, users will never realize that IE4Setup.exe is actually many files. This is because the extracted files are placed in a special temporary folder that is automatically removed from the user's system after installation has finished or been canceled.

The Setup Wizard creates the folder C:\Temp\Ixp000.tmp and extracts into it. The following files are extracted into the C:\Temp\Ixp000.tmp folder:

File Name	Byte Size	Description
IE4Setup.inf	40,088	This is the master .inf file for Active Setup. It identifies the other settings files, contains all the registry keys updated during installation, and tells Setup how and when to install components.
Homepage.inf	1,594	Contains information for setting the default home page in the registry.
Content.inf	23,337	Contains language version information for Channel Guide selection.
Wininet.dll	291,600	Core Setup file, provides ActiveX support on non-IE systems.
Urlmon.dll	166,160	Provides HTTP services on non-IE systems. (OSI Application layer).
IE4Wzd.exe	124,672	The Active Setup Wizard.
Advpack.dll	79,824	The Setup engine, it extracts .cab files and changes registry keys.
Inseng.dll	58,528	The Active Setup engine, it controls installing components.
Jobexec.dll	42,688	Parses the .cif file and gives instructions to Inseng.dll
Globe.ani	6,300	Animation for the Setup screens.
IE4Setup.hlp	12,734	Setup Help file.
W95inf16.dll	2,272	Companions to Advpack.dll used for thunking.
W95inf32.dll	4,608	Companions to Advpack.dll used for thunking.
IE4.txt	26,643	The Internet Explorer readme file containing the latest product issues.
This.txt	331	A text document describing the purpose of the setup folder.
License.txt	11,026	Microsoft Internet Products License Agreement.

If you cancel the Setup Wizard at any time, the C:\Temp\Ixp000.tmp folder is deleted before Active Setup quits. You will only see this folder if Active Setup quits unexpectedly and the folder is not deleted.

Downloading IE4Setup.exe

▶ **To download IE4Setup.exe using Internet Explorer 3**

1. If Authenticode 2.0 is not on the computer, install it, and then restart the computer before continuing. See **http://www.microsoft.com/ie/security/** to download Authenticode 2.0.

2. Download IE4Setup.exe from **http://www.microsoft.com/ie/ie40/download/**.

3. While following the instructions from the download site, choose a download server that is close to you.

4. In the **Internet Explorer** dialog box that appears when you begin the download, select the **Save it to disk** option, and then click **OK**.

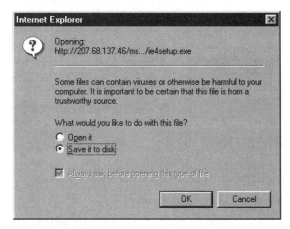

5. In the **Save As** dialog box, specify the root directory of C:\ as the target path, and then click **Save**.

6. Using a file management tool, such as Windows Explorer, create the folder C:\Savepack, and copy (do not move) IE4Setup.exe from C:\ to the C:\Savepack folder.

7. Delete any files in the C:\Windows\Temp folder.

8. From the command prompt, type the following to extract the .cab file but suppress its execution:

   C:\IE4Setup /c

9. When you get the following prompt, type **C:\Windows\Temp**.

```
Internet Explorer 4.0 Setup                    _ □ ✕

Please type the location where you want to place the extracted files.

[                                      ]   Browse...

                          OK        Cancel
```

From the C:\Windows\Temp folder, support engineers can check for corruption and attempt an installation by running IE4Wzd.exe, which was suppressed by using the **/c** switch.

Tip   To be sure the Setup package has not been customized, support engineers troubleshooting Setup should verify the size of IE4Setup.exe.

Note   For a full list of WExtract command line switches that can be used on IE4Setup.exe, refer to Appendix A.

Understanding System Checks

When IE4Setup.exe is executed, it extracts and prepares the system to run Active Setup by performing a series of system checks and installing the files needed to run Phase 2, ACME Setup. The progress of the installation is recorded in a log file that is automatically created in the Windows directory. This file can be useful for troubleshooting installation problems.

IE4Setup.exe performs the following system checks:

- **Operating system**   Checks the version of the operating system (Version.dll). If Windows NT 3 is detected, a Setup failure message will be displayed, stating that Setup will only run on Windows NT 4.

- **Version**   Checks to see if a previous version of Internet Explorer is installed on Iexplore.exe and Shadocvw.dll.

- **OLE**   OLE is initialized.

- **The Shell**   Shell32.dll is checked for its version and its language version (409 is the code for English).

- **Smart Recovery**   Checks for a previous failed installation of Internet Explorer.

- **Encryption Check**   Internet Explorer 4 contains two versions of Schannel.dll: one is an update for domestic 128-bit encryption, and the other supports exportable 40-bit encryption.

  The 128-bit domestic version of Schannel.dll is encrypted using 128-bit encryption, so it is impossible to hack it in without already having 128-bit encryption. This allows Internet Explorer to be shipped out of the country, without worrying about encryption export laws, policies, or procedures.

  To upgrade Internet Explorer from 40-bit encryption to domestic 128-bit encryption, the update may be downloaded from **http://www.microsoft.com/**.

  Both versions of Schannel.dll support Server Gated Cryptography (SGC). SGC is different from straight 128-bit encryption. SGC 128-bit encryption is implemented as an extension to the standard SSL 3.0 protocol. A 128-bit SSL session is set up only if the server presents a special SGC certificate; otherwise, a 40-bit session is used. (For more information about SGC, see Chapter 28, "Digital Certificates.")

If the version check fails, you will get a message stating that the version of the browser cannot be determined, and setup will not continue. If Internet Explorer is the installed browser, just rename Shdocvw.dll and IExplore.exe.

The following files are loaded directly into memory from the IXP000.tmp folder:

- Advpack.dll
- W95inf16.dll
- W95inf32.dll

The following files are copied from C:\Temp\Ixp000.tmp to the C:\Windows\System folder and registered:

- Wininet.dll
- Urlmon.dll
- Jobexec.dll
- Inseng.dll

Wininet.dll and Urlmon.dll are not copied if a released version of Internet Explorer 3 was the previous browser and the existing files pass the check.

Understanding the Active Setup Log File

The Active Setup Log.txt file is a log of the entire Active Setup process from the moment IE4Setup.exe is executed until the download of the last .cab file is complete. When IE4Setup.exe is executed, Active Setup Log.txt is created in the C:\Windows folder. If an Active Setup Log from a previous Internet Explorer Setup session exists, it is renamed to Active Setup Log.bak.

The log begins with the date and time Active Setup was launched and ends with the date and time it successfully downloads the last .cab file. As the user goes through the Setup Wizard, logging entries are continually written to this file. It is the most informative log file for determining what caused a download failure and when the failure occurred. Most entries logged in this file are also written to the registry.

The following HResult error codes indicate the download phases in which an error occurred. This can help to determine exactly what Setup was doing when it failed and also give an idea of the cause:

HResult Error Code	Download Phase
0	Initializing (Making a temp folder, checking disk space)
1	Dependency - (Checking for all dependencies)
2	Downloading (Server to download folder)
3	Copying (Download folder to temp installation folder)
4	Retrying (Restarting download due to timeout or some other download error)
5	Checking Trust
6	Extracting
7	Running (.inf or .exe)
8	Finished (Installation complete)
9	Download finished (Downloading complete)

The following are other common error codes:

- **80100003.** During install, one or more files are missing from download folder.
- **800b*xxxx*.** Anything starting with 800b is a trust failure.
- **800C*xxxx*.** Anything starting with 800C is a Urlmon failure (for example, 800C005 - file or server not found, 800C00B - connection timeout).
- **8004004.** User canceled.

Using the Setup Wizard

After extraction, IE4Setup.exe automatically launches the Setup Wizard, IE4Wzd.exe, unless you suppressed it earlier. If you did, you can run it from the command prompt by typing **C:\Windows\Temp\IE4Wzd** and pressing ENTER. To control the wizard, you can use the following command-line switches:

Command-line Switch	Description
/m:[0|1|2]	Specifies the installation option (default is **1**)
/I:[y|n]	Specifies whether to install the integrated desktop or not (default is **y**)
/r:n	Disables SoftBoot
/v	Skips version check

For a full list of WExtract command-line switches that can be used on IE4Setup.exe, refer to Appendix A.

Note All the dialog boxes in this chapter show the default settings.

After performing the system checks, the Setup Wizard walks the user through the Active Setup. The rest of this section details the Setup Wizard dialog boxes, explains what actions are being performed "behind the screens," and offers relevant, administrative information related to each screen, such as corresponding registry keys.

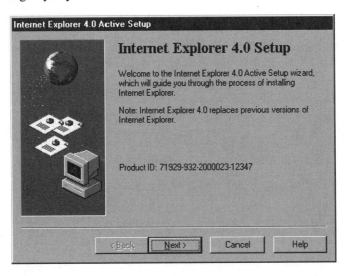

The Setup Wizard uses the Times New Roman font, Timesbd.ttf, installed on the system, for the titles. If this font does not exist, the System font will be used.

End-User License Agreement

The License agreement text comes from License.txt. At this time, the version of any installed ActiveX support files is checked, including Wininet.dll, Urlmon.dll, Shdocvw.dll, and Shlwapi.dll. Trust files are checked: Wintrust.dll, Digsig.dll, Inseng.dll, and Jobexec.dll. If these files need updating, Active Setup does so using the AXControl.Register section of the IE4Setup.inf to install and register them:

**HKEY_LOCAL_MACHINE\SOFTWARE\Microsoft\IE4\SETUP\
"ActiveXFiles"="C:\ WINDOWS.95\SYSTEM\…"**

Download Options

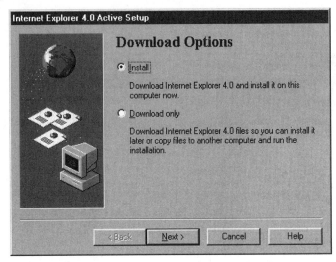

This option specifies whether Setup should stop after the download phase or continue on into the installation phase. The download option is recorded in the following log, where Install=1, Download=2:

```
Setup Options :[1|2]:
```

A preliminary space check is done on all partitions, and free space is logged. The text string, "Microsoft Corporation," corresponding to the digital signature of each .cab file, is added to the Trust Database in the registry so that users do not get security warnings during download:

HKEY_CURRENT_USER\Software\Microsoft\Windows\CurrentVersion\ WinTrust\Trust Providers\Software Publishing\Trust Database\...

Installation Options

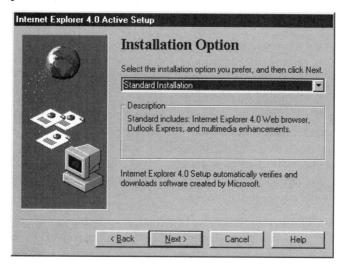

This dialog box offers the following installation options:

Option	Disk Space	.cab File Size	Components
Browser Only	40 MB	12 MB	Internet Explorer core, Java VM, DirectShow™ (DirectX® mini, DirectDraw™, DirectAnimation™), and ActiveMovie™.
Standard	51 MB	16 MB	Internet Explorer, Outlook™ Express, Connection Manager, Internet Connection Wizard, Java VM, Microsoft Interactive Music Control, DirectShow, ActiveMovie, VDO Player, Microsoft Wallet, and Web fonts.
Full	64 MB	24.3 MB	Internet Explorer, Outlook Express, NetMeeting™, NetShow™, FrontPage™ Express, Web Publishing Wizard, Chat 2.0, Connection Manager, Internet Connection Wizard, Java VM, Microsoft Interactive Music Control, DirectShow, ActiveMovie, VDO Player, Real Player, Indeo™ 5, Microsoft Visual Basic® 5.01 Runtime, Microsoft Wallet, and Web fonts.

The installation option is recorded in the log, where Standard= 0, Enhanced=1, and Full=2:

```
Setup mode selected :[0|1|2]:
```

The installation option is also recorded in the registry:

HKEY_LOCAL_MACHINE\SOFTWARE\Microsoft\Active Setup\ InstallInfo\"Setup mode"="2"

The IE4Setup.inf contains a list of all possible components and the mode numbers that correspond to each. Active Setup will install only those components whose Setup mode flag corresponds to the installation option selected by the user. For example, a component that would be installed in all three options would have the flag: Modes="012", whereas a component that would only install in the Full Installation option would have the flag, "Setup mode"="2".

Minimal installation is not a valid option when installing from a compact disc. Only the Standard Installation and Full Installation options are available. This is to ensure that the new Internet Connection Wizard is installed.

Windows Desktop Update

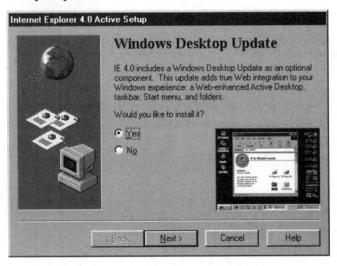

This dialog box allows users to choose if they want to install the Windows Desktop Update (integrated browser). For more information about the Windows Desktop Update, see Part 3, "True Web Integration." You will not see this dialog box if the Windows Desktop Update is already installed. If you do see it and click **No**, the example image will change to the following:

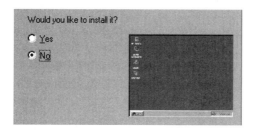

The option is recorded in the log, where the default is **Yes**:

Integrated Browser : [0|1]:

The option is also recorded in the registry:

HKEY_LOCAL_MACHINE\SOFTWARE\Microsoft\Active Setup\ InstallInfo\"Integrated Shell"="1"

If you choose **Yes**, one of the following additional .cab files will be downloaded, which contains all the files required for the Windows Desktop Update:

- IE4Shl95.cab for Windows 95 systems
- IE4Shlnt.cab for Windows NT systems

If you choose not to install Windows Desktop Update at this time, you can add it later. This process requires reconnection to a download site to get IE4Shl*xx*.cab, even if the file exists in the Setup folder.

Jobexec.dll will parse the AddInstallShell.win section of the IE4Setup.inf when installing the Integrated Shell, otherwise the No_Integrated_Shell section is used.

Active Channel Language

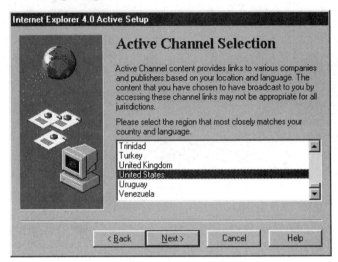

At this point, the user has already chosen the language version of the product when downloading IE4Setup.exe. This dialog box only relates to Active Channels™. It gets its information from Content.inf.

Setup performs a language check on Shell32.dll (409=English).

The choice is registered in the log:

```
Content selected:United States:
```

This choice determines the version of Chl*xx-xx*.cab (English example: Chlen-us.cab) that will be downloaded. This file is a collection of the default channels also known as the Channel Guide.

Destination Folder

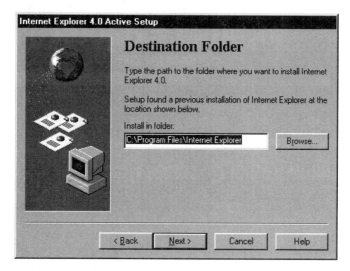

This dialog box specifies the location of the folder to which the .cab files will be downloaded. The default is to create this folder on the partition with the most free disk space. This dialog box is displayed only if a Setup folder does not exist. When reinstalling Internet Explorer, you will not see this dialog box.

The path is recorded in the registry as:

HKEY_LOCAL_MACHINE\SOFTWARE\Microsoft\Active Setup\ InstallInfo\"Download Dir"="C:\Internet Explorer 4.0 Setup"

HKEY_LOCAL_MACHINE\SOFTWARE\Microsoft\Active Setup\Download Directories\"C:\Internet Explorer 4.0 Setup"="1"

The path is also recorded in the log:

```
Download Dir: C:\Internet Explorer 4.0 Setup
```

Note that no connectivity is required up to this point.

Errors

If there is not enough disk space for the chosen installation option on the partition specified, the following error message will be displayed:

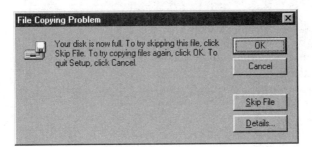

This is a rough-estimate disk-space check. It is not as accurate and is more forgiving than the final disk-space check. The C:\Temp folder and Temporary Internet Files folder are not automatically cleared to free up disk space, but it's a good idea to do this manually before installing Internet Explorer.

Distribution Server List Download

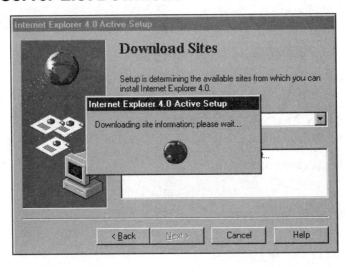

An HTTP GET request for IE4sites.dat is sent to the address specified in the IE4Setup.inf:

```
[Strings]
url="http://www.microsoft.com/…"
```

The IE4sites.dat file is a table of download locations. It contains four fields: region, language, friendly name, and URL. The language-specific Setup package determines which language version of IE4Sites.dat is pointed to in the IE4Setup.inf.

The C:\Windows\Msdownld.tmp folder is created. The IE4Sites.dat is downloaded to the C:\Windows\Temporary Internet Files folder and is used to display the list of download servers. The location of the site list is copied to the registry from IE4Setup.inf:

HKEY_LOCAL_MACHINE\SOFTWARE\Microsoft\Active Setup\ Jobs\Job.IE4\"DownloadSiteURL"="http://…/ie4sites.dat"

Errors

There is a potential for Proxy errors at this point.

Urlmon.dll uses the existing proxy settings in the following registry key to connect to the site specified:

HKEY_CURRENT_USER\Software\Microsoft\Windows\CurrentVersion\ Internet Settings\"ProxyServer"="*data*"

HKEY_CURRENT_USER\Software\Microsoft\Windows\ CurrentVersion\InternetSettings\"ProxyEnable"="01 00 00 00"

If the system was configured to use an ISP that uses proprietary proxy settings, Setup may be unable to find and adopt those proxy settings.

The **Advanced** button gives the user the following convenient interface to edit the registry keys that Setup uses to find the proxy server:

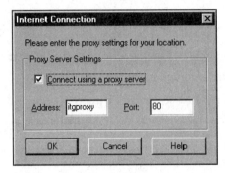

Even though proxy settings are adopted correctly, server-side problems with the proxy server, download server, or network traffic could prevent the successful download of IE4sites.dat. It is suggested that the connection be retried a few times before changing the proxy settings.

Download Sites

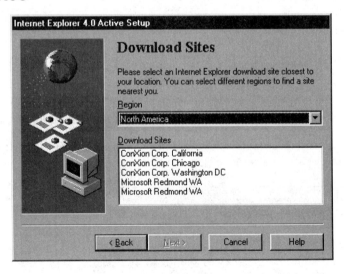

The subfolder C:\Windows\Msdownld.tmp\Ase000.tmp is created. The selected download region is recorded in the log:

```
Selected region: North America:
```

The IE4sites.dat is sorted by region, and only sites for the selected region are displayed in the user interface. The selected download region and all corresponding URLs are recorded in the registry:

HKEY_LOCAL_MACHINE\SOFTWARE\Microsoft\Active Setup\ Jobs\Job.IE4\"DownloadSiteRegion"="North America"

HKEY_LOCAL_MACHINE\SOFTWARE\Microsoft\ActiveSetup\ Jobs\Job.IE4\URLList

http://mschus.www.conxion.com/msdownload/ie4/rtw/x86/en/ cab = "ConXion Corp. Chicago"

http://mssjus.www.conxion.com/msdownload/ie4/rtw/x86/en/ cab = "ConXion Corp. California"

http://msvaus.www.conxion.com/msdownload/ie4/rtw/x86/en/ cab = "ConXion Corp. Washington DC"

http://207.68.137.46/msdownload/ie4/rtw/x86/en/ cab = "Microsoft Redmond WA"

Note   This registry key is deleted at the end of Active Setup. The download sites are listed with the protocol that Active Setup will use to connect to the distribution server. FTP is slightly faster than HTTP.

The selected download site and its corresponding URL are also recorded in the registry:

HKEY_LOCAL_MACHINE\SOFTWARE\Microsoft\Active Setup\ Jobs\Job.IE4\DownloadSiteURL

Note   The keys in **HKEY_LOCAL_MACHINE\SOFTWARE\Microsoft\ Active Setup**, previously mentioned in this chapter, are not actually written until the **Next** button on the **Download Sites** dialog box is clicked.

The .Cab Information File

As soon as the user selects the download site, a GET request for IE40cif.cab is sent to the URL corresponding the chosen distribution server. IE40cif.cab is downloaded to the Internet Explorer 4 Setup folder. It is immediately copied to C:\Windows\Msdownld.tmp\Ase000.tmp, where it self-extracts to a single file, IE40.cif.

The IE40.cif file contains instructions for downloading the .cab files and installing the components they contain. It includes a separate section for each component. Each section contains the name and size of the .cab file, the amount of disk space needed to install that component, a dependency (all components are dependent on the successful installation of the Internet Explorer core files), and more.

Final Disk-Space Check

At this point, Active Setup has enough information to perform a final disk-space check, including:

- The amount of free space on each partition.
- The list of components required for the selected installation option (from the IE4Setup.inf).
- The target location to which the .cab files will be downloaded.

And now that the IE40.cif has been downloaded, Active Setup can use the size information it contains for each component to be installed. The size of each component included in the selected option is added up. This number is compared the amount of free disk space on the target partition.

Errors

If the connection to the distribution server fails to be established or is dropped at any point during the download phase of Setup, the following connection error will be displayed:

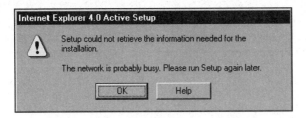

A simple traffic issue may cause this. Just clicking **OK**, going back to the previous dialog box, and clicking **Next** until a connection is made may solve the problem.

A corrupt IE40.cif will prevent any component from installing. The best way to recover from this situation is to choose a different distribution server to get a new IE40cif.cab.

Preparing Setup

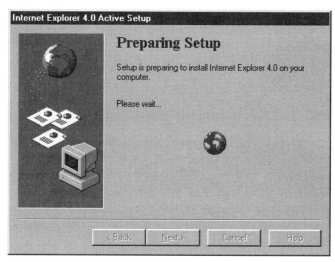

A connection is established to the download site. Active Setup logs the time that JobExec.dll begins parsing IE4Setup.inf and IE4.cif for jobs (instructions about which .cab files to download based on the chosen installation option). Each job with the appropriate mode flag is executed, and its corresponding .cab file is downloaded.

The Filelist.dat, IE4Setup.dir, and IE4Setup.ini are created in the C:\Internet Explorer 4 Setup folder. They log the .cab files as they are successfully downloaded and track which files are contained in the Setup folder. Because the Setup folder could contain Internet Explorer files for both Windows NT and Windows 95 operating systems, .cab file version information is also kept here.

At this point, C:\Internet Explorer 4 Setup should contain:

- Filelist.dat
- IE40cif.cab
- IE4Setup.dir
- IE4Setup.ini

The C:\Windows\Temporary Internet Files folder is created.

Downloading to Your Computer

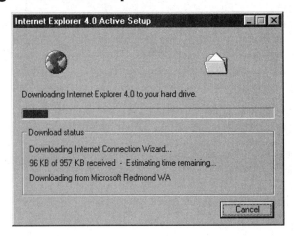

Active Setup provides the user with valuable download information, including a progress bar, bytes received, approximate download time in minutes, and the name of the selected download site. Download time is calculated using .cab file size information in the .cif file and an evaluation of the connection speed. For each .cab file, the following occurs:

1. A dependency check is done (by Jobexec.dll).
2. The download takes place.
3. A CheckSum is performed, and the size of the file is then recorded in Filelist.dat.

   A trust check is performed against its digital signature.

Active Setup has the ability to shift servers during an installation to maintain maximum throughput or recover from a down distribution site. If a connection times out, Setup will try to connect to the next download site in the list and pick up where it left off. If a connection to that site cannot be established, Setup will ask you if you wish to abort the installation or try again.

Errors

Most problems that may be encountered at this point will be related to a trust issue. Perhaps a newer version of Wintrust.dll is needed. Problems may also be encountered in a reinstallation scenario if the wrong version of Inseng.dll or Jobexec.dll is running.

.Cab File List

After the download phase of a full installation, the contents of the C:\Internet Explorer 4 Setup folder should look like the following list, plus these four files that existed prior to download phase:

- IE4Setup.dir (created)
- Filelist.dat (created)
- IE40cif.cab
- IE4Setup.ini (created)

Component	File Name	Byte Size	Description
Core Components			
Browser Only Install			
Standard Install			
Full Install			
ActiveMovie	Amov4ie.cab	512,263	
DirectAnimation	Axa.cab	802,557	
	Branding.cab	10,608	Setup information from the IEAK
Channel Guide	Chlen_us.cab	154,779	
DirectDraw® Extensions	Dxddex.cab	33,166	
DirectX® Layering	Dxmini.cab	339,279	
Web Fonts	Fontcore.cab	627,056	
Front Pad	Fpesetup.cab	1,386,589	

Component	File Name	Byte Size	Description
Internet Connection Wizard	Icw95.cab	315,605	
	IE4.txt	26,643	The Internet Explorer readme file
	IE4_s1.cab	1,427,294	
	IE4_s2.cab	1,458,534	
	IE4_s3.cab	1,458,534	
	IE4_s4.cab	1,458,534	
	IE4_s5.cab	1,313,010	
	IE40cif.cab	14,614	The .cab information file
	IE4data.cab	329,575	
Integrated Desktop	IE4shlxx.cab	800,014	Where x = 95 or NT (optional)
Java Support	IEjava.cab	26,057	
Indeo™ 5	Ir50_32.cab	483,521	
Java Support	Javi386.cab	2,892,161	
Outlook Express	Mailnews.cab	1,472,540	
Microsoft NetMeeting	Mnm2095.cab	1,885,958	
Microsoft Chat	Mschat2.cab	875,227	
Internet Music Control	Msmus_1.cab	176,434	
Visual Basic® Support	Msvbvm50.cab	704,015	
Microsoft Wallet	Mswallet.cab	314,493	
Microsoft NetShow	Nsie4.cab	1,545,651	
Real Player	R32msie4.exe	1,226,680	
	Setupw95.cab	526,607	
	Thisfo~1.txt	331	Text explaining the setup folder
VDO Live	Vdolive.cab	141,175	
Microsoft Publishing Wizard	Wpie4x86.cab	364,605	

You may notice that .cab files IE4_s1.cab through IE4_s5.cab actually have multiple .cab files inside them. The .cab files need to be signed for download security checking, but ACME Setup doesn't work with signed .cab files, so the signed .cab files are downloaded and extracted into unsigned .cab files that ACME Setup can use. This also gives the bonus of separating the process of building a working component from the signing process. The compact disc contains the same signed .cab files that are downloaded to the Setup folder during an installation from the Web.

When the last .cab file has successfully downloaded, the following things occur:

- The Ase000.tmp folder is deleted, but the C:\Windows\Msdownld.tmp folder remains.
- The success string is written to the Active Setup Log.txt:

  `"Install Engine - Download complete"`

- IE4Setup.exe is moved into the C:\Internet Explorer 4 Setup folder, and the original is deleted.

If the **Download only** option was selected in the **Download Options** dialog box, the user will see this message:

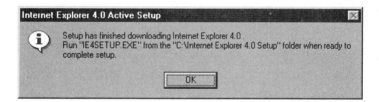

The Setup Wizard will stop here. To begin installing Internet Explorer in this case, you must manually execute IE4Setup.exe.

If the **Install** option was selected in the **Download Options** dialog box, the user will see this message:

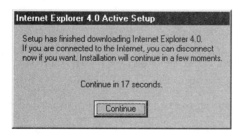

In this case, Setup gives you 30 seconds to disconnect from the Internet before proceeding to the installation phase.

For information on Active Setup registry keys not mentioned yet, refer to Appendix A.

Understanding Smart Recovery

Smart Recovery is the feature that allows Setup to recover from interrupted Internet downloads. Smart Recovery allows Setup to pick up where it failed previously, rather than starting over from the beginning.

When rebooting or relaunching, Setup will check the log files, registry, and IE4Setup.ini to determine if a previous installation attempt was incomplete. If so, the following dialog box is displayed:

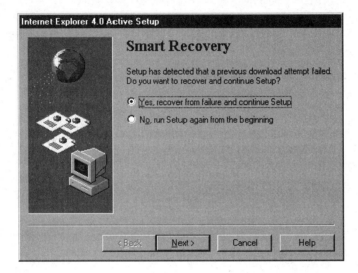

The status of the two phases of setup are logged in the registry, where 0 = not started, 1 = started, 2 = finished:

HKEY_LOCAL_MACHINE\SOFTWARE\Microsoft\Active Setup\ InstallInfo\"Download"={0|1|2}

HKEY_LOCAL_MACHINE\SOFTWARE\Microsoft\Active Setup\ InstallInfo\"Install"={0|1|2}

Smart Recovery and IE4Setup.exe use this information to identify the state of the system.

C H A P T E R   3

Phase 2: ACME Setup

Installing Internet Explorer 4 on Your Computer

The next phase of Internet Explorer 4 Setup uses the traditional ACME Setup
engine used by most Microsoft products. Users who are installing Internet
Explorer from a compact disc begin the installation process here.

Note If, in the Active Setup part of the installation process, the **Download Only**
option was chosen in the **Download Options** dialog box, you must now manually
launch ACME Setup by running IE4Setup.exe again. Because the state of the
system may have changed since Active Setup completed the .cab file download,
or a new user may be launching ACME Setup, some portions of Active Setup are
repeated. The system checks are performed again, and the first several user
options are gathered again, as described in "Using the Setup Wizard" in Chapter
2. If the **Install** option was chosen in the **Download Options** dialog box, then
earlier dialog boxes are not displayed, because it is unlikely the system or user
has changed since Active Setup.

Destination Folder

The first prompt for user input is the target folder for the installation. (If the
Install option was chosen prior to downloading the .cab files, this dialog box
is not displayed.)

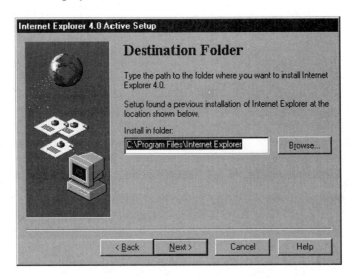

When upgrading a previous version of Internet Explorer, the installed location is used.

The installation folder is recorded in the registry. The default is C:\Program Files\Internet Explorer.

HKEY_LOCAL_MACHINE\SOFTWARE\Microsoft\Active Setup\ InstallInfo\"Install Dir"="C:\Program Files\Internet Explorer"

For a list of ACME 3.0 Setup command-line switches, see Appendix A.

Items Are Being Installed

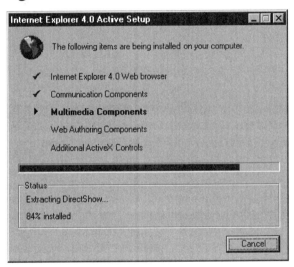

ACME Setup first copies files, makes registry changes, and then registers .ocx files and .dll files. A check is performed on IExplore.exe to see if there is an existing installation of Microsoft Internet Explorer. Before the Internet Explorer core files are installed, Setup backs up existing files and configuration information needed to restore the system to its pre-Setup state during an uninstall. This data is moved into IE4bak.dat, and the IE4bak.ini is created.

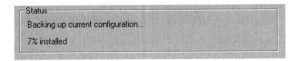

Then the .cab files are expanded and installed. The following steps are performed for each component:

1. **Trust check.** The .cab is found in the Setup folder, and the signature is checked for Authenticode trust verification.

2. **CheckSum.** If trust check is not available, a file size CheckSum is done on the .cab file, based on information in the .cif file. If it fails, the user is prompted to download the .cab file again.

3. **Extraction.** The .cab file is extracted to C:\Windows\Msdownld.tmp\Ase000.tmp.

4. **Install.** Files are moved from Ase001.tmp to C:\Program Files\ Internet Explorer\Setup and C:\Windows\System.

The configuration is updated in the registry.

Errors

If any components fail to install, a red X appears next to that component, rather than a check mark. All components are dependent on the core Internet Explorer files. If the core components are not installed successfully, all remaining components will immediately fail, and a red X will appear next to all the items in the install list. If any component fails to install, the following error message is displayed after the last component has installed or failed:

Low disk space or an inaccurate determination of free disk space, a file still in use, an invalid system configuration, or insufficient system requirements can cause this error. It can also be caused by a corrupt .cab file (to identify, check file sizes) or a bad .cif file. This can be resolved by moving IE4Setup.exe to the root, deleting the Setup folder, and re-running the download portion of Setup. This can also be caused by an Authenticode failure.

If Setup is interrupted while ACME setup is updating the OLE files, Smart Recovery will be unable to recover, because the OLE files will not initialize at startup, and the system becomes unbootable. The operating system will need to be reinstalled. The point at which the OLE files are being updated changes, based on the installation option. For example, Full Installation is between approximately 18% and 25%.

Understanding System.1st Backup

If Windows Desktop Update is installed, the registry is backed up as follows:

- The old desktop files are backed up to the file, Integrated Browser.dat, and the corresponding Integrated Browser.ini is created.
- Additionally, for Windows 95 and OSR2, the original System.1st is also backed up and stored in the Integrated Browser.dat.
- A command that copies System.dat to C:\System.1st is added to the **RunOnce** key of the registry. System.dat will be copied to C:\System.1st at the next reboot or when SoftBoot processes the **RunOnce** key.

If the original System.1st is not present during the install of the new shell, the new System.1st will not be created. Note that it does not check the validity of the System.1st file. A dummy System.1st will be enough to trigger the backup.

In the case of low disk space, the creation of the new System.1st will be skipped in order to ensure the successful installation of the new shell.

Because a new System.1st may not be created in some circumstances, you will want to verify its creation before using it to replace the registry. Do this by viewing the Integrated Browser.ini file. If System.1st was updated, it will be listed in this file usually at the second entry.

Configuring the System

As the Setup Wizard configures your system, you'll see this screen:

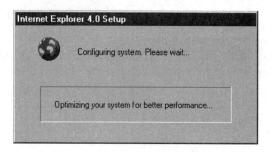

In the subwindow of this screen, you will see three phases:

- Closing all programs
- Optimizing your system for better performance
- Preparing to run Internet Explorer 4

Shortcuts are also updated while this dialog box is displayed.

There are three log files associated with the processes behind the Configuring System screen:

- **SoftBoot Log.txt.** Logs the SoftBoot process.
- **RunOnceEx Log.txt.** Logs the registration of .dll files.
- **Bind List Log.txt.** Logs problems during binding.

Completing Installation

A successful installation will end with this dialog box:

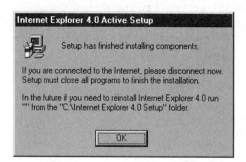

Emergency Repair Disk on Windows NT

After Internet Explorer is successfully installed on Windows NT 4, the backup of the registry that stored on the Emergency Repair Disk (ERD) becomes obsolete. To remedy this, setup will prompt the user to update or create a new ERD.

After rebooting a computer running Windows NT, a final Setup dialog box is displayed as the final changes are made to the system.

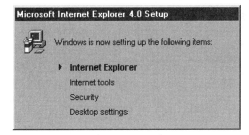

The Welcome Screen

The first time the browser is run, it will try to connect to the default Welcome screen. The URL for the Welcome screen is written from the Homepage.inf:

**HKEY_CURRENT_USER\Software\Microsoft\Internet Explorer\
Main\"Start Page"="http://home.microsoft.com/"**

Understanding the IE4 Setup Log File

IE4 Setup Log.txt is the log file for the ACME Setup phase of Internet Explorer 4 installation. It is found in the C:\Windows folder along with the other Internet Explorer log files. If an installation is interrupted during this second phase, this log is part of what tells Smart Recovery where to pick up.

IE4 Setup Log.txt logs the following:

- The time installation begins.
- The successful completion of each step, with one of the following flags:
  - Succeeded
  - Failed
  - Completed successfully
  - Incomplete
- The time the current configuration backup information is saved.
- The backup files placed in IE4bak.dat.
- The files moved from C:\Windows.95\Msdownld.tmp\Ase001.tmp to \Program Files\Internet Explorer\Setup and Windows95\System.
- The successful creation of the following new directories:
  - Program Files\Internet Explorer: Succeeded
  - Program Files\Internet Explorer\Setup: Succeeded
  - Program Files\Common Files: Succeeded
  - Program Files\Common Files\Microsoft Shared: Succeeded
  - Program Files\Common Files\Microsoft Shared\TextConv: Succeeded
  - Windows\Help\Frames: Succeeded
  - Windows\Help\Topics: Succeeded
  - Windows\System\ShellExt: Succeeded
- Registry key change instruction JobExec finds.
- The country code information, which is added to the Telephon.ini.
- The time the log is completed.

"Safe = 1" or "Safe = 0" in the last section of the log describes when it's safe to quit ACME Setup. "Safe = 1" means it's safe. This tells JobExec if it needs to complete a process before responding to a click of the **Cancel** button.

The Telephon.ini file stores the settings for all TAPI-enabled programs, such as Fax and Dial-Up Networking. If Telephon.ini is deleted and regenerated by running Tapiini.exe, it will no longer contain the country code information added to it during the Internet Explorer installation.

Understanding SoftBoot

Normally, when a Setup program runs, it modifies registry keys and replaces files. As long as those keys and files are not in use, this can be done on the fly. A Setup program that needs to modify registry keys and files that are in use, however, writes the instructions for key modifications and file replacements to the Wininit.ini, then prompts the user to reboot the system. During reboot, the Wininit.exe processes the instructions in the Wininit.ini. Then Runonce.exe processes instructions in the **RunOnce** branch of the registry. Finally, the system is loaded, and control is given to the user.

SoftBoot is a way to update the registry and new files without actually rebooting. SoftBoot only works on Windows 95 and OSR2 systems. When installing on Windows NT, the system must always be restarted.

Since SoftBoot is trying to simulate a reboot, it must first take full control of the system. Using information in the Softboot.inf, it closes down running programs. The Softboot.inf contains a listing of programs and processes and instruction for closing them. Processes are listed in the Softboot.inf by section. Each section defines how the process should be terminated. The sections are defined in Appendix A.

Once all running processes have been successfully closed, SoftBoot takes control of the system. At this point, the user cannot use ALT+TAB to focus the system away from Setup. It then executes the instructions in the Wininit.ini, updating registry keys and replacing files. If no errors occur during this process, the Wininit.ini is cleared of entries.

The Wininit.ini is only cleared if all instructions are executed successfully. If any error is encountered, the contents in the Wininit.ini are left so that Wininit.exe will have a chance to do its job upon reboot.

If SoftBoot is unable to close any running programs, the user will see one of the following two messages:

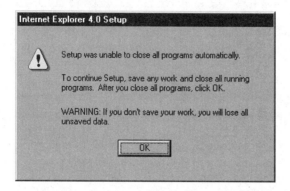

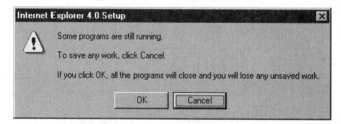

SoftBoot also runs any time Windows Desktop Update is installed or uninstalled separately.

Errors

The way that Setup closes programs may prevent them from saving recent changes or cause them to hang.

Troubleshooting SoftBoot is unnecessary. Because the Wininit.ini entries are not cleared until after SoftBoot is successful, simply rebooting after a SoftBoot failure allows Windows 95 to handle the registry updates as it normally would.

To solve .dll registration problems, use the command below to unregister the .dll files. The entries will re-register automatically upon the next reboot:

regsvr32 /u *filename***.dll**

CHAPTER 4

Automated Installation (Hands-Free Mode)

In this chapter

Using Automated Installation

To run the Setup executable file hands-free, using Setup's defaults, save IE4Setup.exe to your disk, and then type **ie4setup /q**.

This will install Internet Explorer 4 in quiet mode. Setup will bypass the license agreement, will use the Full Installation option, and will install the Windows Desktop Update. You will only be prompted to pick the region and download location. Setup defaults will automatically upgrade to the same folder of any previous Internet Explorer version.

System administrators may want users to run in quiet mode with a different set of defaults. For example, you may want a different install folder and to install some programs other than Internet Explorer. To do this, use the Internet Explorer Administration Kit (IEAK) to customize any of the Setup configurations, or use additional switches with the standard Setup package in conjunction with the **/q** switch, as in the following example:

```
ie4setup /q /c:"ie4wzd.exe /x /q /m:0 /i:n /r:n /s:#e"
```

Switch	Description
/q	Quiet mode (applied to the Setup package)
/c:"ie4wzd.exe	Specifies the executable file to run after extraction
	(all following switches are for the wizard)
/q	Quiet mode (applied to the wizard)
/m:0	Installation option [0|1|2] (0 = browser only)
/i: [y|n]	Install the Integrated Desktop Update
/r: [y|n]	Reboot after installing
/s:#e"	Destination folder (default is #)

When IE4Setup.exe is run from a network share (such as: *server\share* \IE4Setup.exe) containing an IE4Setup.ini file, Setup will not look for a site list but will download all the .cab files from that share.

No Setup folder is created on the client computer when this installation method is used. Installing over the LAN is faster than using HTTP.

Using Debug Install

In Stepping mode (debug install), Setup will stop and present a status dialog box after each step. Stepping mode can be initiated by typing this:

```
ie4setup.exe /c:"ie4wzd.exe /s:#e /g:debug
```

or by creating this registry key prior to running Setup:

**HKEY_LOCAL_MACHINE\SOFTWARE\Microsoft\
Active Setup\"SteppingMode"="Y"**

Using Automatic Configuration

Automatic Configuration is an extension of the Automatic Proxy feature in Internet Explorer 3 that allows administrators to centrally control the default settings for all browser installations on a network. These settings are controlled using the IEAK Configuration Wizard and the IEAK Profile Manager. Settings, such as the browser title, Start page, Search page, Quick Links, and proxy settings, can be configured using these tools.

Administrators can use the IEAK to pre-configure an Automatic Configuration URL that Internet Explorer uses to update its own configuration settings. This file is checked each time Internet Explorer is launched.

The Automatic Configuration URL is stored in:

**HKEY_CURRENT_USER\Software\Microsoft\Windows\CurrentVersion\
Internet Settings\"AutoConfigURL"=**

If an Automatic Configuration URL has not been pre-configured, users can manually select one by using the following procedure.

▶ **To manually select an automatic configuration file in Internet Explorer**

1. On the **View** menu, select **Internet Options**.

2. In the **Internet Options** dialog box, click the **Connection** tab.

3. On the **Connection** tab, click the **Configure** button.

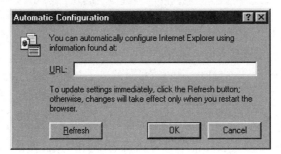

4. Type the URL to a Web page with a configuration script or .ins file, and click **OK**.

For more information, see Chapter 37, "Automatic Browser Configuration."

C H A P T E R   5

User Profiles

In this chapter

Understanding User Profiles

Internet Explorer 4 allows multiple users to use a single installation of Internet Explorer while retaining unique individual settings for each user.

In general, user settings are put in the **HKEY_CURRENT_USER** hive of the registry, and computer settings go under **HKEY_LOCAL_MACHINE**. Per-computer settings that might change when a laptop is in its docking station versus when it's undocked go under the **HKEY_CURRENT_CONFIG** hive.

When multiple users log on at a workstation, they each get their own profile. A profile is a folder for each user that contains user-specific files and configuration information, including the user's copy of the **HKEY_CURRENT_USER** registry hive in the form of a User.dat file. The name of the profile folder is the user name. It is a subfolder of C:\Windows\Profiles.

If a network is used, profiles can roam. This means the user's copy of User.dat is stored on a central server and downloaded to any workstation the user logs on to. This way, users can see the same environment no matter what workstation they use. It also allows administrators central control over individual user settings.

When a new user profile is added to the system, it is not simply a copy of the existing User.dat. A new User.dat is created for the new user with the same system defaults the original user saw after installing the operating system. This process of creating a new User.dat is handled by the operating system. The problem is that this process is not Internet Explorer-aware. Internet Explorer did not exist when these operating systems were written. After installing Internet Explorer, new user profiles created by the operating system have none of the user settings needed to run Internet Explorer.

There are two possible ways that a new User.dat can be updated with Internet Explorer settings: if the Windows Desktop Update is installed, Explorer.exe and Shdocvw.dll perform this task; if not, Loadwc.exe will do it. Loadwc.exe and Explorer.exe are always in memory.

When a new user profile is created, one of these components will compare the data in the following registry keys:

HKEY_LOCAL_MACHINE\SOFTWARE\Microsoft\ActiveSetup\ Installed Components

HKEY_CURRENT_USER\Software\Microsoft\ActiveSetup\ Installed Components

If the data matches, then no action is taken. If it does not match, then the two hives are synchronized.

A variable named StubPath is specified for most component keys in the aforementioned section of **HKEY_LOCAL_MACHINE**. The data of that variable provides instructions on what that setting in the new user profile should be. It points to an executable file or .inf files. For executable files, it commonly contains instructions, such as values and APIs. For .inf files, it will point to a specific section containing the data to be added to the User hive.

For each key that is not a match in both the User and Machine hives, the key is created in User (if it doesn't exist), and the StubPath is executed to set its variable. This results in the User keys being updated with the correct data.

Hive synchronization occurs in only one of the following scenarios:

- When a new user profile is created after Internet Explorer has been installed.
- The first time a user logs on after Internet Explorer has been installed on a computer that already has multiple profiles.
- When any user installs a newer version of one of the components.
- When a user on a multiuser system uninstalls Internet Explorer.

The method of configuring new user profiles works the same way in Windows 95 as in Windows NT.

Understanding Profile Structure

The settings in the **Personalized Items Settings** dialog box (for more information, see "Creating User Profiles" later in this chapter) corresponds to the types of files and settings that will be stored in a Users Profile folder.

In addition to containing a copy of the **HKEY_CURRENT_USER** hive (User.dat), an Internet Explorer profile contains subfolders for Cookies, Recent, History, Favorites, Desktop, and Application Data.

Understanding Roaming Profiles

Using the **Personalized Item Settings** dialog box to control the content and settings saved on a per-user basis is especially important when considering disk space or implementing roaming profiles. Allowing all the content in a profile to pass back and forth between the server and a client that the profile is using is not a realistic option. Though the server may have unlimited disk space to store the content, the impact on network traffic would be too great. Thus, when using roaming profiles, it is prudent to minimize the amount of data stored in the profiles:

- **Desktop folder and Documents menu.** If the Active Desktop is part of the corporate installation, this can be left on.
- **Start Menu and Program folders.** Since these are dependent on the programs installed in a standard corporate installation, this could be turned off.

- **Favorites folder.** This would be left on so that users could maintain a personal favorites list.

- **Downloaded Web pages.** This is the Temporary Internet Files folder, which contains Cookies and History. If strict size limitations are imposed, this could be left on, but in most cases this would be left off.

- **My Documents folder.** Network traffic would be minimized if this were turned off and a network share were used for document storage.

If roving profiles are already enabled on a computer, installing Internet Explorer will not automatically move the new folders to the profile. You will need to select the items from the User Profiles Manager in Control Panel.

Platform Dependence

Because roaming profiles are handled by the operating system, they are still bound by the differences between Windows 95 and Windows NT user profiles.

It is possible to log on to an Internet Explorer 4 roving profile using an Internet Explorer 3 system. Settings such as MRU, Start page, Search page, and Favorites are available from the Internet Explorer 3 browser. The main limitation will be orphaned links to Active Channels.

Home Directories

If profiles are enabled and the primary logon is a network logon such as NT or NetWare, Windows 95 will automatically try to roam your user profile to your home folder on a logon server. If accounts are not configured with valid home directories, logon/logoff may take a long time, or unexpected system policies may be applied. To prevent this default roaming behavior, create a DWORD value named UseHomeDirectory in **HKEY_LOCAL_MACHINE\Network\Logon**, and set it to 0.

Creating User Profiles

First, user profiles need to be enabled on the **User Profiles** tab of the **Passwords Properties** dialog box. (Click the Passwords icon in the Windows Control Panel.)

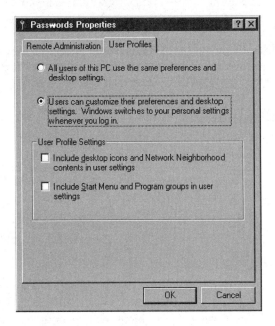

Simply log on using a user name that is new to the system (and therefore has no corresponding .pwl file). The system prompts you to confirm the new user password. Then you are asked if you would like to use global settings or per-user settings.

In addition to simply logging on with a new user name, there is a new way
to create a user profile. You will notice a Users icon in Control Panel. This
is a new interface and wizard for adding and configuring user profiles.
This is simply an alternative user interface for creating a new profile.

Users

The first time you click this icon, the wizard will run.

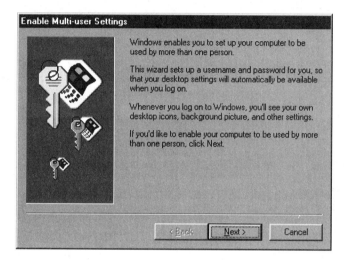

After clicking **Next**, you'll be prompted for a new user name and a password for that user. Here you specify the items to be included in the new profile:

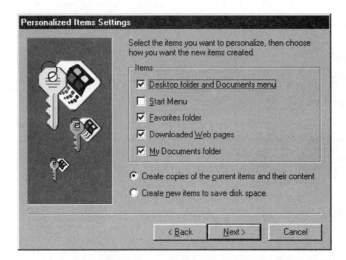

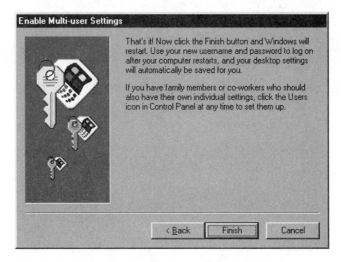

Profiles are now enabled. The user is prompted to reboot. The **Logon** dialog box
will appear with the name of the new user. You will see this message after the
reboot:

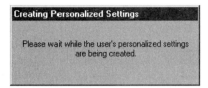

The User Profile Wizard only runs once. After that, the User List is displayed
when the Users icon in Control Panel is clicked and the correct supervisor
password is entered.

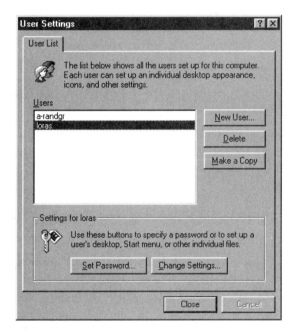

The **Change Settings** button brings up the **Personalized Items Settings**
dialog box.

Specifying the Profile Supervisor

The first user who launches the User Profile Wizard is automatically the administrator of all consecutive user profiles on that computer. On systems that have not enabled profiles, the profile supervisor will be the original user who installed the operating system. Non-administrators need the administrator's password to change the settings in their profiles. The prompt for the supervisor's password is displayed as soon as the Users icon in Control Panel is double-clicked.

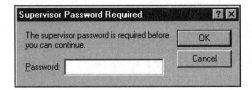

The supervisor is specified in:

HKEY_LOCAL_MACHINE\SOFTWARE\Microsoft\Windows\ Current Version\ProfileList\Supervisor

If the supervisor's Windows password in the .pwl file is null, then no supervisor key is created. By editing the above registry key, more than one supervisor can be specified or supervisor warnings can be disabled.

Understanding Advanced User Profile Functionality

Some functionality was added to the Internet Explorer Shlwapi.dll to make it easier to specify **HKEY_CURRENT_USER** settings for components. The following functions in Shlwapi.dll will retrieve user-specific registry settings that are normally stored in **HKEY_CURRENT_USER**:

- **SHRegOpenUSKey()** is equivalent to **RegOpenKeyEx()**
- **SHRegQueryUSValue()** is equivalent to **RegQueryValueEx()**
- **SHRegDeleteUSValue()** is equivalent to **RegDeleteValue()**
- **SHRegCloseUSKey()** is equivalent to **RegCloseKey()**
- **SHRegGetUSValue()** is the same as calling, **RegOpenKeyEx()**, **RegQueryValueEx()**, and **RegCloseKey()**.

These functions will look in **HKEY_LOCAL_MACHINE** if **HKEY_CURRENT_USER** is empty. This will fix problems for users who didn't install the product. Also, the functions have an optional default value parameter, which will be used if nothing is found in either **HKEY_CURRENT_USER** or **HKEY_LOCAL_MACHINE**. The functions will expand Windows NT environment variables. And a parameter will allow the caller to ignore the **HKEY_CURRENT_USER** value and use the **HKEY_LOCAL_MACHINE** value. This can be used for values that an administrator may not want a user to be able to customize (**SHRestricted**()).

If a local path is written under **HKEY_CURRENT_USER**, it may name a folder that does not exist on other computers (or even cannot exist, because it references a nonexistent drive letter). There are two things that can be done here. First of all, keys can be added to **HKEY_CURRENT_USER** to direct the operating system's user profile code to generate a per-user folder with a specific name and set a registry value under **HKEY_CURRENT_USER** to point to that path. This is how the **Desktop** and **Start** menu folders are made per-user. Secondly, it can store plain filenames and relative paths, wherever possible, and combine them with a per-user base path at runtime. For example, if the HTML template for the Control Panel is Control.htm, don't store C:\Windows\Web\Control.htm in the registry; store just Control.htm, call an API to get the per-user version of C:\Windows\Web, and combine the two.

If a path is stored in the per-user registry, it probably points to a folder with contents that are also per-user. You should consider whether these contents also should roam from one computer to another. Keep in mind that while any files can be made to roam, not all files should. Aside from the performance implications of copying large numbers of files to and from the user's logon server, there are security issues: a user may not want or expect sensitive documents to be copied to any workstation on which they log on and to remain there even after they log off.

Be particularly careful with hyperlinks to programs. They usually have hard-coded paths in them (such as a shortcut to C:\Program Files\Internet Explorer\ IExplore.exe), which may not roam well. If you want the contents of a folder full of shortcuts to roam, try to make sure the shortcuts don't have absolute paths in them.

There are actually several choices for how a folder setting behaves:

- **Not per-user.** The setting is the same for all users and does not follow the user to other computers.

- **Optionally per-user.** The user or network administrator can choose whether or not users get their own version of the setting. (To get even more complicated, it's possible for this optional configuration, to itself, be per-user. That is, either all users get their own version of the setting or none of them do, or some users get their own setting and others use the default.

- **Optionally both per-user and roaming.** Either all users get the same setting and the contents do not follow them from computer to computer, or users get their own settings and the contents do follow them. This is how the **Desktop** and **Start** menus work in Windows 95. Again, the determination of whether a particular user gets his own copy or just uses the default is done on a user-by-user basis.

- **Always per-user, optionally roaming.** All users on a computer get their own version of the setting, but the contents of the folder do not follow the user to other computers on the network. This is the way the WININET cache is expected to behave (several megabytes of cache would be far too much to copy all over the network).

- **Always per-user, always roaming.** Users each get their own content; their individual contents always follow them. This is the way ordinary per-user registry items work and is also how the user's Favorites, Cookies, and History folders is expected to work.

To keep the user interface simpler, the optional choices should only be used if there are good reasons why you would want a setting to be per-user or roaming and good reasons why you may want it not to be. If there are compelling arguments on both sides, make it optional. If the arguments on one side are weak or far-fetched, do not make it optional.

CHAPTER 6

Adding and Removing Components After Setup

Understanding the Add/Remove Dialog Boxes

There are two **Add/Remove** dialog boxes used by Internet Explorer, each with distinctly different functionality. The first dialog box is the traditional **Add/Remove Programs** applet in the Windows Control Panel. This is used to uninstall only Internet Explorer add-on components with corresponding .inf files containing uninstall information. This is not used to uninstall the Internet Explorer core files:

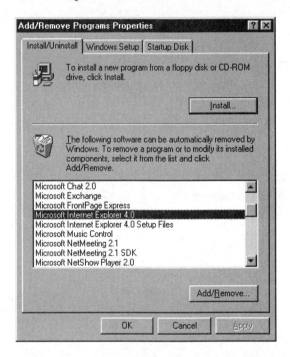

The second dialog box appears when the user selects **Microsoft Internet Explorer 4** from the software list in the **Add/Remove Programs** dialog box and then clicks the **Add/Remove** button.

This dialog box is displayed by Setupwbv.dll, which knows how to invoke maintenance mode ACME, call an .inf file uninstall, or launch Internet Explorer to download new components from the Web.

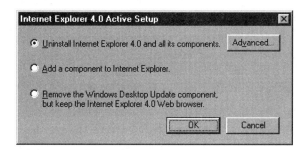

Removing Components

▶   **To remove a component**

1. In the Control Panel, double-click the Add/Remove Programs icon.

2. In the software list, click the component you want to remove, and then click the **Add/Remove** button.

When removing a component, its .cab file is always left in the Setup folder so that the user may reinstall it without downloading the .cab file again.

Deleting the Setup Folder

▶   **To remove the Setup Folder**

1. In the Control Panel, double-click the Add/Remove Programs icon.

2. In the software list, click **Microsoft Internet Explorer 4.0 Setup Files**, and then click the **Add/Remove** button.

This will remove the Setup folder and all the .cab files it contains. This procedure is no different than manually deleting the folder.

Warning   Unless you have a compact disc containing Internet Explorer, deleting this folder is not recommended, because you will not be able to perform a reinstall if Internet connectivity is lost for any reason.

For information on how to remove Internet Explorer core files or use the Uninstall Log, see Chapter 7, "Uninstalling Internet Explorer."

Adding Components

You can add optional components to Internet Explorer 4 from the Internet or from the Internet Explorer compact disc.

Adding Components from the Internet

▶ **To add or remove components from the Internet**

1. In the Control Panel, double-click the Add/Remove Programs icon.

2. In the software list, click **Microsoft Internet Explorer 4.0**, and then click the **Add/Remove** button. The resulting dialog box will present you with three options.

3. Select **Add a component to Internet Explorer**, and click **OK**.

Setup will automatically launch the browser (if it's not already running) and connect to one of the two sites below, depending upon the platform being used:

- **http://www.microsoft.com/ie/ie40/download/rtw/x86/en/ download/addon95.htm**

- **http://www.microsoft.com/ie/ie40/download/rtw/x86/en/ download/addonnt.htm**

Note The URLs to the add-on pages were moved from the IE4Setup.inf [AddonPagesW95.reg] and [AddonPagesWNT.reg] to the registry key:

HKEY_LOCAL_MACHINE\SOFTWARE\Microsoft\Internet Explorer\ Main\Addon-URL

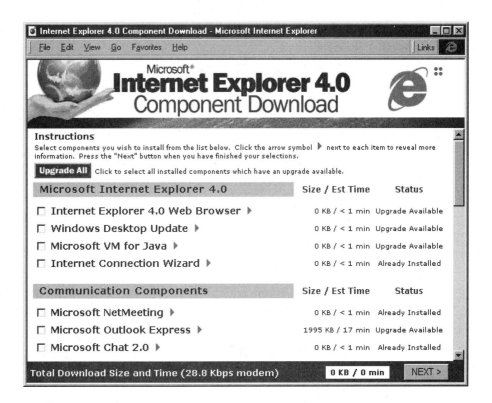

Tip You can also access this Web page by selecting **Product Update** from the **Help** menu in the Internet Explorer window. From the Download Area Web site, click the **Component Downloads** hyperlink.

These pages contain VBScript that will perform some system checking and determine what components are already installed on the system. The results of this check are displayed on the right side of the web page as **Not Installed**, **Already Installed**, or **Newer Version Available**. You simply check the boxes on the left side of the page that correspond to the components you want, then select the site from which the .cab files will download.

The **Upgrade All** button on the **Components Download** page can be used to reinstall all components that have a "Newer Version Available" result.

Some components available on the **Components Download** page are not included in any of the three installation options when installing Internet Explorer 4. Those components are:

- VRML
- Microsoft Agent
- Macromedia Shockwave Director

- Macromedia Shockwave Flash
- Supplemental Web Fonts
- Internet Explorer Sound Pack
- Task Scheduler
- Multi Language Support (Japanese, Korean, Pan-European, Chinese Traditional, Chinese Simplified)

Also, the Microsoft Script Debugger is available on the Site Builders Network (SBN) rather than as a component on the Internet Explorer 4 Component Download page.

Setup will go through trust, dependency, and CheckSum checks before downloading the .cab files and installing their contents. The .cab files are not downloaded to the Setup folder; instead they are stored temporarily in C:\Windows\Msdownld.tmp\Ase000.tmp.

For troubleshooting information about installing Internet Explorer components, see "Invalid Page Fault When Installing Additional Components" in Appendix B.

Adding Components from a Compact Disc

▶ **To add components from a compact disc**

1. Insert the Internet Explorer 4 compact disc into the drive, and the Autorun feature will display this screen:

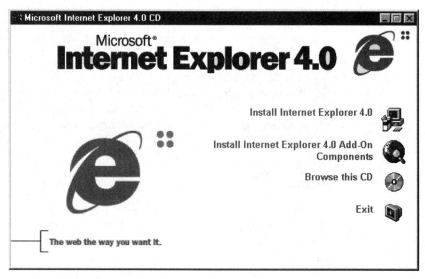

2. Click the **Install Internet Explorer 4.0 Add-On Components** hyperlink, which will open the add-on page from the compact disc:

[CD:]\EN\DownLoad\AddOn*xx*.htm

All add-on components are available on the compact disc, including the script debugger.

Reinstalling Components

If Internet Explorer 4 has been uninstalled or any of the components from its original installation have been removed, they can be reinstalled from the Setup folder—as long as the Setup folder has not been removed. When Setup is run in maintenance mode, it compares the installed components to the .cab files in the Setup folder. (If the Setup folder has been removed, you'll need to reinstall Internet Explorer 4 by repeating the steps of downloading from the Internet, as explained in Chapter 2, "Phase 1: Active Setup." Or you can follow the instructions for adding new components, as explained in the previous section.)

To reinstall Internet Explorer 4 or any of its components using your local Setup folder, run IE4Setup.exe from the Setup folder. Each time IE4Setup.exe is run in maintenance mode (after initial installation), you'll see the Welcome Screen, agree to the License Agreement, select an installation option, and confirm the Destination folder, as detailed in Chapter 2, "Phase 1: Active Setup."

When re-running IE4Setup.exe from the Setup folder, you are limited to the same installation option (or a subset thereof) that was selected during the original download. Cabinet (.cab) files for components added from either the Internet or compact disc add-on page will not exist in the Setup folder; they are not included in a local reinstallation.

If the Setup folder contains a .cab file for a component that is not currently installed, then the **Upgrade new items?** dialog box is displayed.

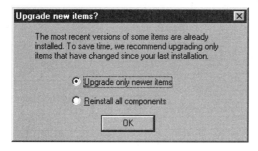

To reinstall components that have previously been removed, click the **Upgrade only newer items** option. This will install any .cab files in the Setup folder not already installed.

If the Setup folder contains no uninstalled .cab files, the **Reinstall all items?** message is displayed.

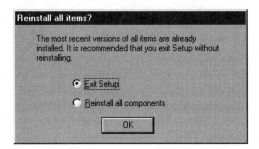

If, during a local reinstallation, all the components for the selected installation option are not installed and one of the .cab files needed to install a required component is missing from the Setup folder, this message is displayed:

Following those instructions, when IE4Setup.exe is run a second time, you will see the Welcome screen, the End-User License Agreement, the Smart Recovery screen, and, if you choose **Recover**, you will be prompted to choose a download site.

After the Preparing Setup screen is displayed, the Downloading Internet Explorer screen will show status information as the missing .cab files for the selected option are downloaded.

Using IExtract.exe

IExtract.exe is an MS-DOS-mode utility, found in the C:\Windows\Command folder, used to extract files from the IE4bak.dat file. It has the following syntax:

iextract [/w] [/l *folder*] *datafile* [*filename*]

- **/w.** Warn before overwriting a file. The default is to overwrite existing files.
- **/l.** Save extracted files to the following location. The default is current folder.
- ***datafile.*** Full qualified path to the backup information .dat file (required).
- ***filename.*** Name of the file to extract from the backup information file. You can use multiple file names (separated by blanks). The default is all files.

Here is an example:

```
iextract /w /l c:\windows\temp c:\windows\ie4bak.dat schannel.dll
```

This example will extract Schannel.dll from the IE4bak.dat file and place it in the Temp folder.

The Iextract.exe utility is particularly useful in troubleshooting problems resulting from a mismatch of shell or OLE files.

Adding and Removing the Windows Desktop Update

▶ **To add or remove the Windows Desktop Update**

1. In the Control Panel, double-click the Add/Remove Programs icon.

2. In the software list, click **Microsoft Internet Explorer 4.0**, and then click the **Add/Remove** button. The resulting dialog box will present you with three options. The third option allows you to add or remove the Windows Desktop Update (integrated browser). This dialog box changes depending on whether the Windows Desktop Update is installed or not:

For more information about the Windows Desktop Update, see Part 3, "True Web Integration."

The Integrated Browser.dat and Integrated Browser.ini are required for removing the Windows Desktop Update, and they are created when the Windows Desktop Update is added. During the uninstallation of the shell, the original System.1st is extracted from Integrated Browser.dat and overwrites C:\System.1st. This step will not take place if the creation of the new System.1st was skipped because of a low amount of disk space.

SoftBoot will attempt to simulate a reboot when the shell is being changed. For more information about System.1st and SoftBoot, see "Installing Internet Explorer 4 on Your Computer" in Chapter 3.

Updating Internet Explorer 4

Internet Explorer 4 comes with a Software Updates channel already listed in the Favorites menu. A subscription to this channel is already set up, so it's easy to check the Internet to see if a newer version of Internet Explorer has been posted for download. (For more information about Active Channels, see Chapter 16, "Managed Webcasting.")

The Internet Explorer Update Channel (linked to IEUpdate.cdf,) can be used to initiate the install of the newer version or to schedule an automatic upgrade.

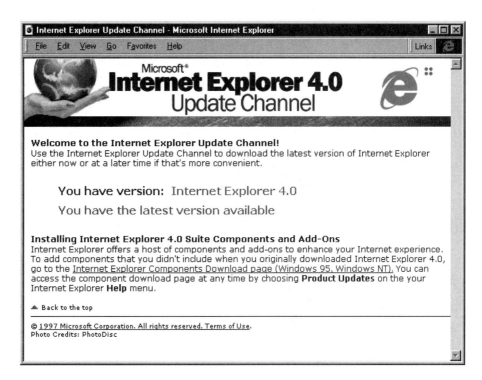

By default, you must go to the Update Channel to see if there is a newer version of Internet Explorer available, but the subscription can easily be changed from manual to automatic, which will give you automatic notification when a newer version has been made available. Then, when you sign on to Internet Explorer, if a new update is available, you'll be presented with a **Software Update Available** dialog box.

On this dialog box, the **Details** button reveals details about the currently installed version. The **Update Now** button will automatically connect to the Internet Explorer Update Channel, shown above. The **Don't Update** button allows you to postpone the update.

Using Product Update

The Product Update feature is not related to the Internet Explorer Update
Channel. It gives users an easy way to navigate to the Microsoft Download Area
Web site and the Download Components page to compare installed components
to those available. (For more information about the **Download Components**
page, see "Adding Components from the Internet" earlier in this chapter.)

This can be helpful if you have deleted your subscription to the Update Channel
or are between automated update checks.

C H A P T E R   7

Uninstalling Internet Explorer

In this chapter

Removing Internet Explorer Core Files

As explained in the previous chapter, there are two **Add/Remove** dialog boxes used by Internet Explorer, each with distinctly different functionality. The first dialog box is the traditional **Add/Remove Programs** applet in the Control Panel. This is used to uninstall only Internet Explorer add-on components with corresponding .inf files containing uninstall information. This is not used to uninstall the Internet Explorer core files. (For information on removing add-on components, see Chapter 6, "Adding and Removing Components After Setup.")

The second dialog box appears when **Microsoft Internet Explorer 4.0** is selected from the software list in the **Add/Remove Programs** dialog box, and the **Add/Remove** button is clicked. This dialog box is displayed by Setupwbv.dll, which knows how to invoke Maintenance-mode ACME, call an .inf file uninstallation, or launch Internet Explorer to download new components from the Web.

▶ **To uninstall Internet Explorer**

1. In the Control Panel, double-click the **Add/Remove Programs** icon.

2. In the software list, click **Microsoft Internet Explorer 4.0**, and then click the **Add/Remove** button. The resulting dialog box will present you with three options. The first of the three options is used to uninstall core files and any add-on components you select.

3. Select **Uninstall Internet Explorer 4.0 and all its components**, and then click the **Advanced** button.

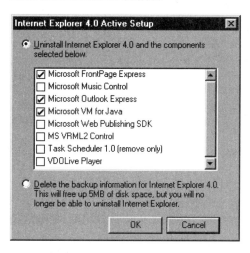

4. In the resulting dialog box, select **Uninstall Internet Explorer 4.0 and the components selected below**, and click the check boxes next to the components you want to uninstall.

For each component, the registry contains a minimum version and an Internet Explorer build number with which the component will work. For example, one component may work if Internet Explorer 3, build 1155, or greater, is installed. Another may only work if build 1300, or greater, is installed. Some only work if Internet Explorer 4 is installed. Setup recorded the previous browser version in the registry when Internet Explorer was installed. That value is compared to the version requirement of each component. If the previous version is less than the required version of the component, the component's box will be checked.

Warning In the **Advanced Uninstall** dialog box, if you select **Delete the backup information for Internet Explorer 4.0**, you will delete the IE4bak.dat, IE4Bak.ini, Integrated Browser.dat, and Integrated Browser.ini. files, which contain important uninstall information that you will need if you decide to reinstall and uninstall Internet Explorer again. It is recommended that you not delete these files. (For more information, see "Deleting Uninstall Files" in the next section.)

For troubleshooting information about removing Internet Explorer 4, see Appendix B.

Understanding the Uninstall Process

ACME Setup is used to uninstall Internet Explorer 4 core files, whereas the Internet Explorer add-on components use the standard .inf method of uninstallation, as per Windows 95 and Windows NT compatibility specifications.

ACME Setup relies on the following files:

- C:\Program Files\Internet Explorer\Setup\Setup.stf
- C:\Windows\IE4bak.dat
- C:\Windows\IE4bak.ini
- C:\Windows\IE4RegUn
- C:\Program Files\Internet Explorer\Uninstall\AINF0000
- C:\Program Files\Internet Explorer\Uninstall\Integrated Browser.dat
  (if the Integrated Browser is installed)
- C:\Program Files\Internet Explorer\Uninstall\Integrated Browser.ini
  (if the Integrated Browser is installed)

If, for some reason the .dat and .ini files are damaged or missing, the user may be able to get them from another system and successfully complete the uninstallation. Keep in mind that both systems must be running the same operating system, must have chosen the same Internet Explorer installation option, and must have had the same browser installed prior to installing Internet Explorer; and that the install path for each browser must be the same.

The registry information needed to uninstall is stored in the AINF0000 files. Installation instructions for each component includes the RegSave function, instructing Advpack.dll to move data from the registry into the AINF0000 files. During uninstallation the RegSaveRestore function is called, the AINF0000 files are loaded into the registry as hives, and the registry is updated with the original data. Similarly, an IE4RegUn file is created under the Windows folder, which contains backed-up registry information for the Internet Explorer core.

You should remove Internet Explorer 4 before performing any of the following actions:

- Installing an earlier version of Internet Explorer.
- Restoring a registry (System.dat or User.dat) that was created before you installed Internet Explorer 4. (This applies to Windows 95 operating systems only.)
- Using a Windows NT Emergency Repair Disk (ERD) that you created before you installed Internet Explorer 4. (This applies to Windows NT operating systems only.)
- Upgrading to a later release of Internet Explorer 4.
- Reinstalling your operating system (Windows 95 or Windows NT).
- Installing or uninstalling operating system upgrades (for example, Windows 95 Service Pack 1).

Uninstalling does not support the following versions or situations:

- The beta 2 version of Internet Explorer 4 installed over a previous version of Internet Explorer 4.
- The final version of Internet Explorer 4 installed over a previous version of Internet Explorer 4, other than beta 2.
- Internet Explorer 4 installed under multiple operating-system installations (Windows 95, OSR2, or Windows NT 4.0) on the same logical drive. If you need to run Internet Explorer in multiple operating systems, you must install each operating system to a separate logical drive letter.
- You have removed the Internet Explorer 4 backup files. If you removed these files, you cannot uninstall Internet Explorer 4 without reinstalling Windows to a different folder.

Uninstalling does not completely return your computer to its previous state. It leaves behind some files, registry entries, and shortcuts. Additionally, some user settings are not restored with the previous version of Internet explorer. System files such as Setupapi.dll are left behind to support other .inf file installs, or OLEAUT32 to prevent breaking OLE functionality in Office. For a complete list of files that uninstalling does not delete from the system, see Appendix A.

Because of the larger number of changes made to the system by Setup, a manual uninstall would require many, many steps and a great deal of time. Attempting a manual uninstall is not recommended.

For the latest list of issues you need to be aware of while running Setup and while uninstalling, check the Internet Explorer 4 Readme file.

Using Maintenance Mode ACME Setup

Uninstalling relies on the existence of this registry key:

**HKEY_LOCAL_MACHINE\SOFTWARE\Microsoft\Windows\
CurrentVersion\Uninstall\IE40 "C:\Program Files\Internet Explorer\
Setup\SETUP.EXE" /g C:\WINDOWS\IE4 Uninstall Log.txt**

This value launches maintenance-mode ACME Setup with hands-off operation.

Uninstalling also relies on the following back up files: IE4bak.dat, IE4bak.ini,
Integrated Browser.dat and Integrated Browser.ini. If these files are missing,
uninstall will fail. Note that the Integrated Browser files are only needed if the
Windows Desktop Update is installed at the time of uninstallation.

After maintenance mode, ACME Setup uninstalls Internet Explorer. The Setup
folder will remain on the system so that Internet Explorer may be installed again
without requiring connectivity to the Internet.

If the **User Profiles** option has been enabled, Setup will ask if you want to
remove Internet Explorer settings from your user profile (User.dat).

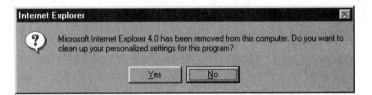

You can also run maintenance-mode Setup manually, by running Setup.exe from
the Setup folder in your Internet Explorer installation folder. To be in hands-off
mode or to create an uninstall log file (IE4unin.txt) you will need to specify the
following command line:

```
C:\program files\internet explorer\setup\setup /g C:\ie4unin.txt
```

Or, if you don't have long file-name support:

```
C:\progra~\intern~1\setup\setup /g C:\ie4unin.txt
```

Errors

If Shell32.dll and Explorer.exe are not successfully extracted from the Integrated Browser.dat, the newer versions of those files will still load, and you'll be presented with this message:

The SHLWAPI.dll made a bad call to Explorer.

To fix this, extract the original versions of Shell32.dll and Explorer.exe from your Windows CD-ROM and copy them to the system, overwriting the newer versions.

Files Used by Uninstall

There are several key files needed for a proper uninstall:

Setup.exe   Runs the ACME Setup program.

Setup.stf   Contains instructions for the ACME portion of Setup or uninstallation and calls IE4.dll.

IE4.dll   Custom Action Setup engine used for logging and for custom file or registry additions, changes, or removals.

IE4.inf   Contains instructions for IE4.dll.

Advpack.dll   Used for Internet Explorer Express cabpack extraction, and for .inf file parsing or execution while uninstalling programs installed with Internet Explorer Express. Used in combination with W9INF32.dll and W9INF16.dll on Windows 95 systems.

Setupapi.dll   Originally a Windows NT file, Internet Explorer uses this file in both Windows 95 and Windows NT for locating .cab file and .inf file installations.

Integrated Browser.dat   Contains Integrated Browser modes files, including the previous versions of Explorer.exe and Shell32.dll, and is used for installing or uninstalling the integrated browser mode. This file is called Integrated Browser NT.dat on the Windows NT operating system.

Integrated Browser.ini   Contains information about Integrated Browser.dat.

IE4bak.dat   Contains many of the files needed to uninstall Internet Explorer.

IE4bak.ini   Contains information about IE4bak.dat.

Setupwbv.dll   Used to control mode switching by parsing IE4Shell.inf and calling Advpack.dll for IE4shell.cab extraction.

IE4shell.cab   Contains new shell components and is used in mode switching and uninstall.

IE4shell.inf   Contains instructions for mode switching. Also contains the contents of IE4shell.cab.

IE4data.inf   Contains instructions for uninstalling data components.

IE4data.cab   Backup file for data components used during installation and uninstallation, and that rely on Internet Explorer (Task Scheduler, ActiveMovie, Multimedia Controls, etc.) This file is called by Advpack.dll.

There are several other uninstall .inf files; one exists for each external component. All are called using Advpack.dll.

Registry Entries Used by Uninstall

There are several registry keys that need to be present and populated for proper uninstalling:

HKEY_LOCAL_MACHINE\SOFTWARE\Microsoft\Windows\ CurrentVersion\Uninstall
contains entries for everything that shows up under Control Panel **Add/Remove Programs** and some that do not. Each item listed has its own method (command line) for launching an uninstall. Note that entries containing a **QuietUninstall** key refer to external components (.inf files) called during an Internet Explorer uninstallation.

HKEY_LOCAL_MACHINE\SOFTWARE\Microsoft\Windows\IE4\Options
contains location and other info for IE4bak.dat and 4bak.ini.

HKEY_LOCAL_MACHINE\SOFTWARE\Microsoft\IE4\SETUP
contains some miscellaneous file location information for various logs, etc.

HKEY_LOCAL_MACHINE\SOFTWARE\Microsoft\IE4\SETUP\History
contains information concerning previous browser information.

HKEY_LOCAL_MACHINE\SOFTWARE\Microsoft\IE4\SETUP\ IE4RegBackup
contains backup registry information saved by Setup. The 0 section contains the actual data, and the 0.map contains table-of-contents type tracking of the information in 0. In cases of reinstallation and upgrade, the *.map keys (starting with 3.map and incrementing by 1 per reinstallation) are created to track differences.

HKEY_LOCAL_MACHINE\SOFTWARE\Microsoft\ Advanced INF Setup\Integrated Browser\RegBackup
contains 0 and 0.map sections used to back up and track registry information used to uninstall the Integrated Browser. Map files are not created in this section, and the 0 and 0.map sections should be empty if Integrated Browser mode is not enabled.

Deleting Uninstall Files

If you delete the primary uninstall information (IE4bak.dat, IE4bak.ini, Integrated Browser.dat, Integrated Browser.ini), you will see this message if you reinstall:

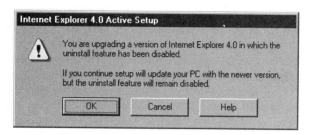

After the reinstallation is complete, you may have options disabled in the **Advanced Add/Remove** dialog box.

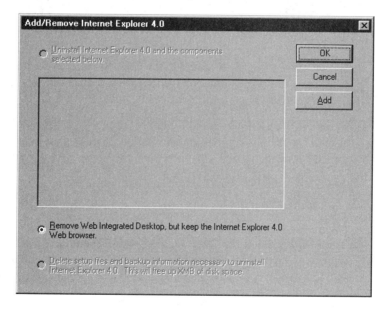

Understanding the Uninstall Log

The most important tool for troubleshooting an uninstallation is the uninstall log, called IE4 Uninstall Log.txt, located in the Windows folder. This log is very comprehensive. It covers the entire uninstallation process sequentially from beginning to end, including every file addition or removal; every registry addition, change, or removal; and any dialog boxes shown to the user. The log is divided into Passes which denote the different phases of an uninstall. Entries in the log also have an Object number—which corresponds to the line entry in Setup.stf. Lines without an Object number result from custom actions specific to Internet Explorer 4—and are contained in the IE4.inf file or in an .inf file from an external component uninstallation. The Uninstall Log is not created when IERemove.exe is run.

Understanding Emergency Uninstall: IERemove.exe

IERemove.exe is not a separate uninstall program. It is a forced removal of the Internet Explorer core. It should be used only in circumstances where the **Add/Remove Programs** applet in the Control Panel is unable to uninstall Internet Explorer, or if you absolutely have to replace a dead registry and have already tried System.1st or an updated Emergency Repair Disk (ERD).

A no-boot situation may be caused because of a problem with the new shell. To make the shell files compatible with the shell registry settings, boot to safe mode, run Task Manager, press CTRL+ESC, and then type the following:

```
c:\progra~1\intern~1\setup\ieremove /i:c:\progra~1\intern~1\
uninst~1\integr~1.dat
```

(Do not use the **/n:** switch.) IERemove will replace only the shell files, and the system will be bootable. Then you can run IE4Setup.exe out of your Internet Explorer 4 Setup folder (if you have one) to solve any problems. You will still need to reinstall programs installed after Internet Explorer was installed.

IERemove attempts to restore the system to the state it was in prior to installing Internet Explorer. This includes restoring the previously used browser. IERemove only replaces core files. It will not uninstall any additional components, even if they rely on the Internet Explorer core to function. Internet Explorer files with no original counterpart stored in the .dat files are not removed. Also, none of the folder structure associated with Internet Explorer will be removed, and **Start** menu items will remain. If the user had Internet Explorer 3 installed previous to Internet Explorer 4, IERemove will restore Internet Explorer 3 so that it works, although some settings may be lost.

IERemove.exe is found in the C:\Program Files\Internet Explorer\Setup folder. It is a Windows program. When it is run, an uninstall log.txt is created. SetupWbV.dll is not removed by IERemove, so the **Advanced Add/Remove** dialog box should still be available to users after they are able to boot.

IERemove relies on the backup files and will fail if the backup files are not present. The command-line switches listed below are not required. IERemove looks to the following registry keys for the locations of IE4bak.dat and its corresponding .ini file, and the Integrated Browser.dat and its corresponding .ini file, respectively:

HKEY_LOCAL_MACHINE\SOFTWARE\Microsoft\IE4\options

**HKEY_LOCAL_MACHINE\SOFTWARE\Microsoft\
Advanced INF Setup\Integrated Browser**

If you get an error such as the following when running IERemove.exe, it is likely that the registry keys mentioned above are absent:

Setup could only remove the shell integration option. Internet Explorer 4.0 was not completely removed.

To resolve this problem, use the command-line switches to specify the locations of the .dat and .ini files. Also, you can force IERemove to remove only the shell or only the core by using only one of the following switches:

- **/i:"*path*\integrated browser.dat"**
- **/n:"*path*\ie4bak.dat"**

Example:
```
ieremove /i:"C:\program files\uninstall information\
integrated browser nt\integrated browser nt.dat"
/n:"C:\windows\ie4bak.dat"
```

Or, if you don't have long file name support:

```
C:\progra~1\intern~1\setup\ieremove /i:C:\progra~1\intern~1\
uninst~1\integr~1.dat /n:C:\windows\ie4bak.dat
```

If IERemove runs on a computer that did not have Internet Explorer 3 previously installed, the user may not be able to successfully install Internet Explorer 3 because of version conflicts with Internet Explorer files left on the system. These files need to be renamed.

To find procedures for using IERemove.exe to uninstall Internet Explorer 4 for Windows 95 and Internet Explorer 4 for Windows NT, see Appendix B.

C H A P T E R   8

Configuring Connection Settings

Using the Internet Connection Wizard

The first time Internet Explorer is launched after Setup, the Internet Connection Wizard (ICW) runs. The ICW is a fully automated process that takes a user through the steps of setting up a connection to the Internet.

The following registry key is set to 0 when Internet Explorer is installed and indicates that the ICW has not yet run:

HKEY_CURRENT_USER\Software\Microsoft
Ineternet Connection Wizard\"Completed"="00 00 00 00"

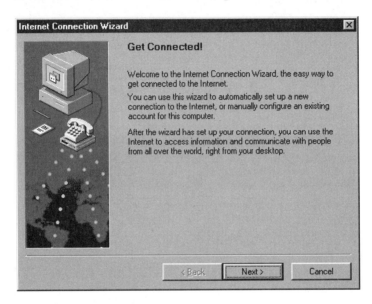

After the ICW has completed, it sets this registry key to 1:

HKEY_CURRENT_USER\Software\Microsoft
Ineternet Connection Wizard\"Completed"="01 00 00 00"

The ICW can also be launched from the **Start** menu or by selecting **Internet Options** from the **View** menu and clicking the **Connection** tab. The Internet Connection Wizard steps are described below.

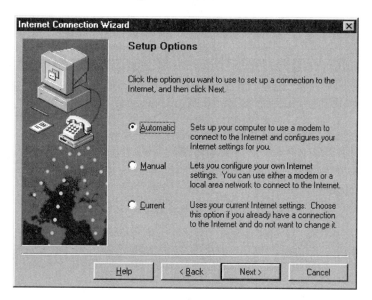

The first (automatic) option and second (manual) option lead the user through a similar process. The third option does nothing but take you to the end of the wizard; it accepts your current connection settings and does not check to see if the existing configuration is valid.

Choosing Manual Setup: Using an Existing Internet Account

The second option leads the user through the following screens. Users can choose a phone line or a Local Area Network, and they can choose whether to use Windows Messaging, an Internet mail client:

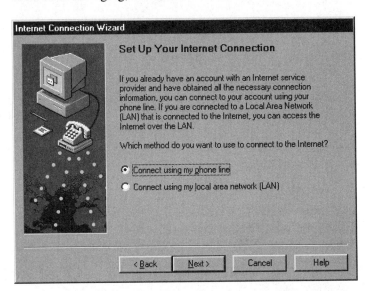

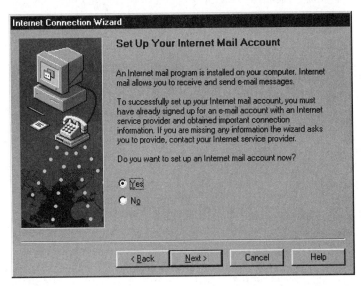

Both the manual and automatic options will install (or reinstall) Windows 95 networking drivers from the Windows 95 compact disc. No detection occurs to verify that these drives are already installed, but version conflict warnings will be displayed. TCP/IP and Dial-Up Networking (DUN) will be installed (or reinstalled), and the Install New Modem Wizard will run. The ICW checks that your modem is set up properly. If it's not, the Install New Modem Wizard is launched automatically so that you can configure a modem and dial-up settings.

Choosing Automatic Setup: Creating a New Internet Account

In addition to configuring the modem and a connection to an ISP, as described above, this option lets users create a new account with an ISP. However, the user must be using a modem; a LAN connection is not an option.

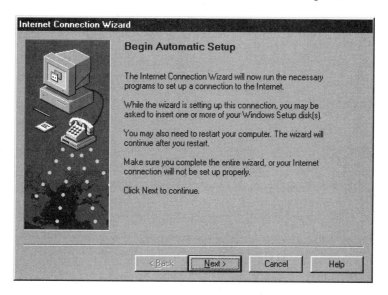

The ICW checks for an installed modem. If no modem is installed, it will launch the Modem Control Panel to begin modem detection. If not installed, TCP/IP and DUN will be installed. The user will be prompted for the Windows 95 compact disc.

If new drivers need to be added, the system is automatically rebooted after they are installed.

Users may receive this standard security warning:

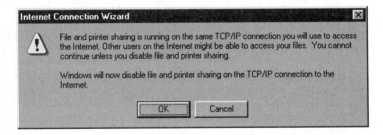

The Begin Automatic Setup screen is displayed, and then location information is gathered. (At this point, the user cannot use ALT+TAB to turn away from the wizard.)

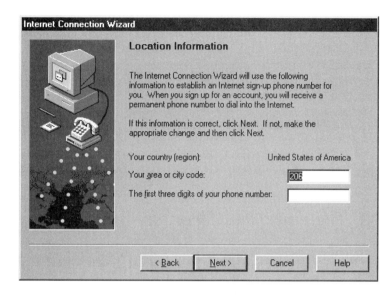

The browser then dials out to a Microsoft Referral Server.

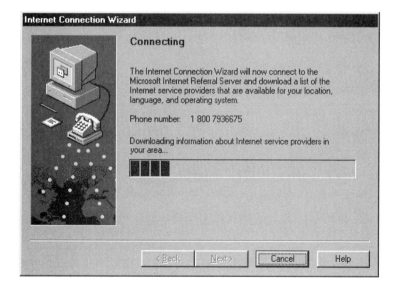

The browser is opened in kiosk mode to display a list of ISPs in your area that offer immediate accounts. The **Sign Me Up** button configures a DUN connectoid to the corresponding ISP.

Once you select an ISP, the ICW will attempt to connect to one of the ISP's servers to obtain further information for the sign-up process. If you have problems connecting to the ISP's server or finishing the sign-up after connecting, contact the ISP for support. To obtain the ISP's phone number, click the **More Info** hyperlink for the ISP on the Internet Referral Servers list of ISPs. (This is the first page you see after connecting to the Referral Server.)

If you have problems with the automatic option, Internet Explorer checks that the modem is working correctly and that the Dial-Up Adapter is installed and bound to TCP/IP. Otherwise, it treats the problem as a typical Dial-Up Networking problem until you connect to the Internet Referral Server.

If you have trouble connecting or maintaining a connection to the Referral Server, Internet Explorer tries to reduce the modem speed and configure it for a standard modem. If this fails, there may be a problem with the Referral Server, and you should try using the ICW at a later date.

After a user has signed up for an Internet account, the ICW will start a Setup program to install and configure the Internet software required by your service provider. For product support phone numbers in your area, refer to the file C:\Program Files\Internet Explorer\Support.txt.

Using Manual Configuration

A proxy server acts as an intermediary between your computer and the Internet. It is usually only used in a corporate intranet situation when users are connected to a LAN. It also acts as a security barrier between your internal network and the Internet. This helps secure important data, because it keeps other people on the Internet from gaining access to confidential information on your internal network. In addition, administrators can use this for proxy load balancing and site blocking. Proxies are becoming more advanced in their ability to reduce network traffic by caching content that is frequently requested by the browsers they serve.

Internet Explorer 4 includes a new dialog box with the most commonly used proxy settings on one tab and more detailed proxy settings on a separate tab. On the **View** menu, select **Internet Options**, and click the **Connection** tab.

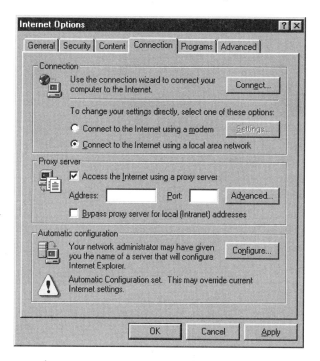

In the **Address** box, enter the name or IP address of the proxy server you want to handle requests from your browser. In the **Port** box, enter a port specified for passing Internet protocols. Typically, port 80, the reserved port for HTTP, is used.

A check box is available to bypass the proxy when connecting to intranet Web servers. This prevents requests for addresses with no period in the hostname string from being sent to the proxy server.

The corresponding registry settings can be found in:

HKEY_CURRENT_USER\Software\Microsoft\Windows\CurrentVersion\Internet Settings

> **"ProxyEnable"="01 00 00 00"**
>
> **"ProxyServer"="*data*"**
>
> **"ProxyOverride"="*local*"**

Clicking the **Advanced** button on the **Connection** tab of the **Internet Options** dialog box brings up the **Proxy Settings** dialog box.

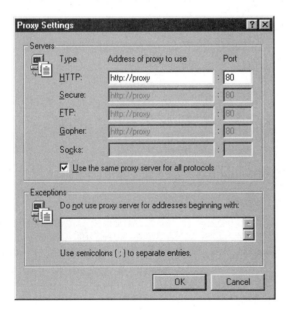

By default, the **Use the same proxy server for all protocols** check box is selected. All Internet protocols will use the same port. As soon as the user clicks the **Advanced** button on the previous dialog box, this setting is disabled, allowing the user to specify a separate proxy server and port number for each individual Internet protocol. Selecting the check box makes all the other entries unavailable and copies the proxy information in the HTTP setting into the other protocol settings. Selecting the check box also hides the information in the **Socks** setting.

The **Secure** settings are for HTTPS requests. Enter the proxy location and port number for the appropriate protocols.

Proxy locations that do not begin with a protocol (such as **http://** or **ftp://**) are assumed to be a CERN-type HTTP proxy. For example, the entry **proxy** would be treated the same as the entry **http://proxy**. For FTP gateways, such as the TIS FTP gateway and the WinGate Win95 Modem FTP proxy, the proxy should be listed with the protocol **ftp://** in front of the proxy name. For example, an FTP gateway FTP proxy should be entered as **ftp://ftpproxy**.

The proxy bypass list in the **Exceptions** section allows users to specify addresses that will bypass the proxy server and be accessed directly.

Using the Proxy Bypass List

Some network requests need to bypass the proxy. The most common reason to bypass the proxy is for local (intranet) addresses. Generally, these addresses do not contain periods in them. By selecting the **Bypass proxy server for local (intranet) addresses** check box on the **Connection** tab of the **Internet Options** dialog box, all addresses without a period will bypass the proxy and be resolved directly. To bypass more complex addresses, click the **Advanced** button on the **Connection** tab of the **Internet Options** dialog box, and use the **Proxy Settings** dialog box to enter the addresses in the **Do not use proxy server for addresses beginning with:** box.

A proxy bypass entry may begin with a protocol type. These may be **http://**, **https://**, **ftp://**, or **gopher://**. If a protocol type is used, the exception entry only applies to requests for that protocol. Note that the protocol value is case insensitive. Multiple entries should be separated by a semicolon (**;**).

If no protocol is specified, any request using the address will be bypassed. If a protocol is specified, requests with the address will only be bypassed if they are of the indicated protocol type. As with the protocol type, address entries are case insensitive. If a port number was added, the request is only processed if all previous requirements are met and the request uses the specified port number.

The **Exceptions** section of the **Proxy Settings** dialog box allows a wildcard (*) to be used in the place of zero or more characters. The following list contains examples showing how to use wildcards:

- To bypass servers, enter a wildcard at the beginning of an Internet address, IP address, or domain name with a common ending. For example, use ***.example.com** to bypass any entries ending in.example.com (such as some.example.com and www.example.com).

- To bypass servers, enter a wildcard in the middle of an Internet address, IP address, or domain name with a common beginning and ending. For example, the entry **www.*.com** matches any entry that starts with www and ends with com (such as www.someplace.com, www.almost.anywhere.com, and so on).

- To bypass servers, enter a wildcard at the ending of an Internet address, IP address, or domain name with a common beginning. For example, use **www.someplace.*** to bypass any entries that began with www.someplace. (such as www.someplace.com, www.someplace.org, and www.someplace.else.com).

- To bypass addresses with similar patterns, use multiple wildcards. For example, use **123.1*.66.*** to bypass addresses such as 123.144.66.12, 123.133.66.15, and 123.187.66.13.

Although wildcards are powerful, they must be used carefully. For example, the entry **www.*.com** will cause Internet Explorer to bypass the proxy for most Web sites.

If you need to bypass the proxy for a local domain, try using ***.domain.com**. This will not use the proxy for any computer name ending in .domain.com. You can use the wildcard for any part of the name.

Errors

Some features such as RealAudio and Secure Sockets Layer (SSL) may not work over a proxy server. Many of these features require special configurations on the proxy server.

PART 2

The Internet Explorer Browser

A powerful browser will help your organization reap the important benefits the Web has to offer. As the Internet increases in utility and complexity, more and more computer users have come to rely on Microsoft® Internet Explorer to help them make the most of it. Internet Explorer 4 contains a variety of improvements that make browsing the Web easier, faster, and more fun than ever before.

Ease-of-use innovations and enhanced personalization features in Internet Explorer 4 truly give users the Web on their terms, or "the Web the way you want it." Internet Explorer 4 also offers key underlying technologies for Web developers. Part 2 describes the new features, functionality, and technologies of the Internet Explorer 4 Web browser and explains how to use this browser to create the best Internet and intranet experience.

Chapter 9: Browser Features and Functionality

Having a great experience on the Web starts with the browser. Internet Explorer 4 contains a variety of improvements that make browsing the Internet and local intranets easier, faster, and more productive. For example, the Address bar in Internet Explorer automatically completes addresses for you, based on sites you've already visited. It also adds prefixes and suffixes to Internet addresses. Explorer bars for Search, Favorites, History, and Active Channels™, make it easier to find the sites you need, visit your favorite pages, return to the places you've been, and access the information you use most often. Administrators can customize Explorer bars and even create their own. Internet Explorer 4 also introduces the ability to browse offline. In addition, Internet Explorer 4 supports an open architecture that allows easy integration with third-party programs, offering users a flexible environment without loss of integration benefits.

Chapter 10: Browser Performance

As increased traffic on the Web continues to reduce browser responsiveness, Internet Explorer 4 has introduced enhanced features and implemented new technologies that improve the browser's ability to access Web sites more quickly. Internet Explorer 4 supports key technologies, including the latest HTML and HTTP standards, to make your browsing experience the fastest and most efficient on the Internet.

Chapter 11: The WebBrowser Control

The Internet Explorer WebBrowser Control allows developers to use the best of the Internet Explorer feature set in their own programs, offering a rich set of functionality in simple, reusable, ActiveX™ controls.

CHAPTER 9

Browser Features and Functionality

Ease of Use and Personalization Features

The features that distinguish Internet Explorer 4 as the best browser include the following:

- AutoComplete
- AutoDomain Searching
- Navigation history on **Back** and **Forward** buttons
- Explorer bars
- Full Screen mode
- Improved Favorites
- Movable Menu bar
- Improved Links bar
- Friendly user feedback
- Printing enhancements

AutoComplete

The Address bar in Internet Explorer 4 automatically completes addresses for you, based on sites you've already visited. By filling in long, complicated URLs automatically, AutoComplete makes it easier for you to type in URLs and reduces the opportunity for typographical mistakes. You can easily override the suggestions by typing over them. The functionality of AutoComplete will be familiar to many users, because it is based on the IntelliSense® technology implemented in Microsoft Office and is similar, for example, to the AutoFill feature in Microsoft Excel.

AutoComplete works by reading the information stored in the C:\Windows\History folder. This means that the AutoComplete feature becomes more effective over time, as you browse the Web and your History folder fills up with shortcuts. AutoComplete will work only if there are shortcuts in the History folder.

As an extension of the AutoComplete feature, Internet Explorer will offer you suggestions for the completion of partial URLs that you enter in the Address bar. Simply type the first few characters of a URL, then right-click in the Address bar, click **Completions** in the shortcut menu, and Internet Explorer will search your History file and list all the available completions of the URL you started to type.

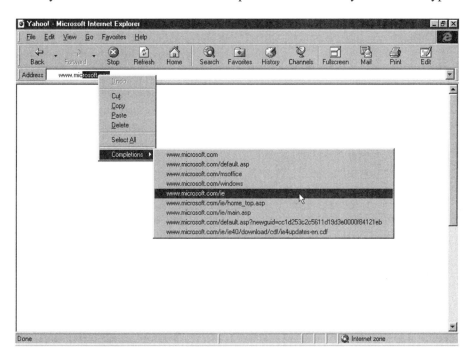

Internet Explorer 4 also makes it easier to get to Web sites by adding prefixes and suffixes to Internet addresses. Users can forego the common typing of "http://www." and ".com" before and after most URLs; just enter the site name and press CTRL+ENTER to add the prefix and suffix information. Internet Explorer will then navigate to that page.

To get the most of AutoComplete, you'll want to use the following features and shortcuts:

- Add to the string that has been automatically completed by pressing the RIGHT ARROW key and then typing the additional characters.

- Skip over separation characters in URLs (such as // and /) by pressing and holding CTRL, and then pressing the LEFT ARROW or RIGHT ARROW key.

- Search your History file by typing the beginning of an Internet address and right-clicking the Address bar to complete it. A shortcut menu appears; select **Completion** for a list of available URLs that match the address you started to type; press the DOWN ARROW on your keyboard to scroll though the list.

- Type a partial URL, then press CTRL+ENTER to add "http://www." before the entry and ".com" after it. For example, if you type "microsoft" in the Address bar and press CTRL+ENTER, the URL instantly becomes "http://www.microsoft.com/".

AutoDomain Searching

Internet Explorer 4 introduces a new feature called AutoDomain Searching. If you aren't sure of the exact address of a Web site, enter any word in the Address bar and Internet Explorer will search for the site. If it doesn't get a response from the DNS server for the name, it will use different prefixes and suffixes to try to find the site. For example, if you type the word Microsoft into the Address bar, Internet Explorer will search:

- http://www.microsoft.com
- http://www.microsoft.edu
- http://www.microsoft.org
- http://microsoft.com
- http://microsoft.edu
- http://microsoft.org

Using the Registry Editor, you can customize the way Internet Explorer searches for sites.

▶ **To add a new suffix to the default search routine**

1. Open the Registry Editor (type **regedit** in the **Run** dialog box), and go to the following registry key:

   **HKEY_LOCAL_MACHINE\SOFTWARE\Microsoft\
   Internet Explorer\Main\URLTemplate**

2. Right-click on any blank area in the right pane, and select **Add**, then **String Value**.

3. The Name of each entry is a numerical value representing the order in which each item will be searched. Type the next number in the sequence, and press **Enter** twice.

4. Type *%s.your suffix* as the Value Data (for example, %s.gov).

5. Repeat steps 2 to 4 to add additional suffixes. Notice that each suffix has two entries, one with www. preceding the wildcard, and one without.

6. Click **OK**, quit the Registry Editor and restart Internet Explorer to make the changes take effect.

Navigation History on Back and Forward Buttons

In Internet Explorer 4, the **Back** and **Forward** buttons have drop-down menus that display the navigation history of your current session. From that list, you can quickly go to the page you want. Simply click the drop-down arrow next to the **Back** or **Forward** button, or right-click either button, to view the menu. These navigation history menus save you from having to click the **Back** button multiple times to return to a page you have visited.

The **Back** and **Forward** buttons display only the sites visited in the current session (reading from the C:\Windows\History\Today folder). If you need to go further back in time, you can use the History bar to display all Web pages visited in the past 20 days (the default setting). See the following section for more information about the History bar.

Explorer Bars

The Explorer bar is an innovation exclusive to Internet Explorer 4 that makes it dramatically easier to navigate the Web. Explorer bars for Search, Favorites, History, and Active Channels make it easier to find the sites you need, visit your favorite pages, return to the places you've been, and access the information you use most often. When you select an Explorer bar by clicking its button on the Internet Explorer toolbar, a special pane slides in on the left side of Internet Explorer's content window. When you click a link in an Explorer bar, the corresponding page opens in the main content window, so that your links are still visible while the content is displayed. To dismiss the Explorer bar, simply click its close button. For more information, see "Using Explorer Bars," later in this chapter.

Full Screen Mode

Full Screen mode removes all toolbars, title bars, and scrollbars from the screen so that you can view Web pages in a larger area. You can toggle between Full Screen and normal modes by clicking the **Full Screen** button on the Internet Explorer toolbar.

Improved Favorites

Internet Explorer 3 took a big step forward with the way it handled Favorites. They weren't a list in an .ini file or an HTML file; they were actual shortcuts— just like any other shortcut in the system. This way, you could easily copy and paste them, send them to someone, or arrange them in your file system as you wanted. The **Favorites** menu has been updated in Internet Explorer 4 so that you can rearrange your favorites within the menu.

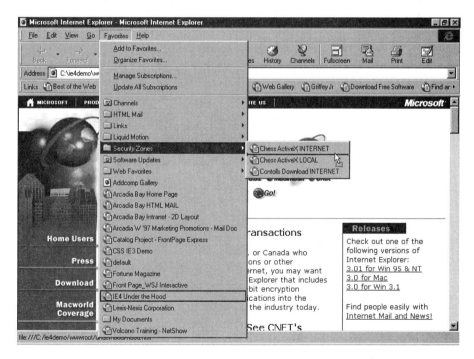

In addition, the **Favorites** menu has been opened up so that you can interact with the Favorites just as you would with any other file, with right-click functionality such as **Cut**, **Copy**, and **Paste**.

Movable Menu Bar

In Internet Explorer 4, the Menu bar has been implemented as a toolbar, so it can be moved and sized according to user preferences. This new feature helps you keep all your menu commands and toolbars available and still have a large area for browsing.

Improved Links Bar

Quick Links were introduced in Internet Explorer 3, but they had some limitations. For example, you were limited to five Internet shortcuts on the Links bar, and it was too difficult for most users to figure out how to customize them. In Internet Explorer 4, the Links bar allows you to drag URLs from the Address bar to create new Quick Links, and you can also drag buttons within the toolbar to rearrange your Quick Links. In addition, you can drag buttons off the Links bar to the Windows® desktop or other applications. Users can now have as many Quick Links as they want, and the Links bar provides scrolling arrows if your links run off the screen. You can also right-click on the Links bar to use shortcut menus to set properties or delete Quick Links buttons.

In Internet Explorer 3, the Links bar was limited to point to five sites on the Internet as specified in the registry. With Internet Explorer 4, any number of links can now be stored in the Links subfolder, within the Favorites folder. The default path depends on whether the User Profiles feature is turned on:

With User Profiles

C:\Windows\Profiles*username*\Favorites\Links

Without User Profiles

C:\Windows\Favorites\Links

Friendly User Feedback

With most Web browsers, you spend a long time waiting for pages to download, without being certain of the status of the process. Internet Explorer 4 provides improved user feedback, so you always know what the browser is doing. An improved Status bar provides visual feedback about whether you are online or offline, the download status of a specific page, and whether you are connected to the Internet, an intranet, or a local file system. When you have the Internet Explorer Sound Pack installed (available for free download), you can set two new Control Panel sound events, Start Navigation and Complete Navigation, to provide audible signals when the browser starts looking for a site and when loading has been completed. If Internet Explorer can't find a particular site that was entered into the Address bar, instead of displaying technical error messages, it will first search common domain names, such as .com, .edu, and .org. Then it will ask if you would like to search for the site.

Printing Enhancements

Internet Explorer 4 offers several printing enhancements that allow you to control how Web pages are printed. Frame-set improvements enable three options for printing frame sets: print frames as laid out on the screen; print all frames separately; or print only the selected frame. You can even configure Internet Explorer to print all linked documents for a print selection. Plus, support for style-sheet extensions allow Web-page designers to control placement of page breaks within a Web page, so users benefit from "smart page breaking."

Using Explorer Bars

Explorer bars make it easier for users to navigate the Web: they improve users' ability to find relevant information on the Internet during searches; they make working with Favorites simpler; they make it easier for users to identify what sites they have visited in their Web-browsing sessions so they can return to them again; and they improve the discoverability of Active Channels.

Explorer bars are implemented in a split-screen browser pane that is accessible at the same time as the user browses the Web. When you select an Explorer bar by clicking its button on the Internet Explorer toolbar, the Internet Explorer window divides into two panes—a navigation pane (the Explorer bar) on the left and a content pane on the right. When you click a link in the left pane, its content is displayed in the right pane. The Explorer bar takes advantage of the component architecture of Internet Explorer 4 and is not simply a frame, but a separate browser control. The Explorer bar has a title bar, a close button, and can be resized by the user.

The Explorer bar buttons on the toolbar are toggle buttons; when you click the button once, it will open the corresponding Explorer bar, and when you click the button a second time, it will close the Explorer bar. When the Explorer bar is closed, the content pane will fill the entire browser window.

There are four different Explorer bars:

- Search bar
- Favorites bar
- History bar
- Channel bar

Understanding the Search Bar

Finding information on the Web can be a frustrating experience. Not only do users commonly receive thousands of successful matches for a search query, but they then confront the difficulty of navigating from site to site. Internet Explorer 4 attempts to solve the navigation issue by displaying a Search bar when users click the **Search** button on the toolbar. The Search bar displays search results independent of the main browser area and remains visible until the user presses the **Search** button again.

Each time you open the Search bar, it displays a list of search engines from which you can choose. When you start a search, the results appear in the Search bar only. When you rest the pointer over a result, Internet Explorer also displays a summary of the site in a ToolTip.

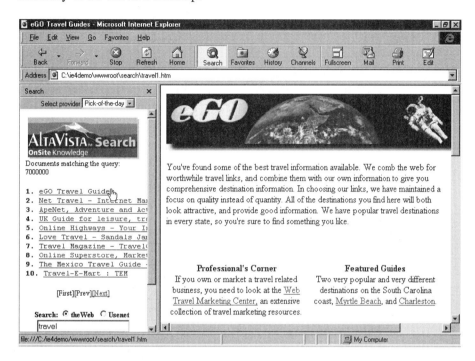

When you select a site from the results list, the site appears in the main browser area, keeping the Search bar available for future searches. The results remain in the Search bar, so if you need to visit a different site that the search engine revealed, you can easily move from result to result without repeatedly using the **Back** button to return to the search-results page. Internet Explorer 4 also preserves the state of the search, so if you click the **Search** button again during the same session, the results of the previous search are displayed. This way, you can move the Search bar out of the way and bring it back when you need it.

Configuring and Customizing the Search Bar

When you bring up the Search bar, Internet Explorer links to a default page at **http://home.microsoft.com/search/search.asp** that offers a Provider-of-the-day. (This is done so that the Search bar page code can be constantly updated and improved by Microsoft.) This Active Server Page also provides a drop-down menu that allows a different search site to be chosen. You can customize the Search bar to point to a search engine that is not on the default menu or to point to your own search site. There are two ways to do this:

If	Then
You have set up the Internet Explorer Administration Kit (IEAK) automatic browser configuration feature.	Use the IEAK Profile Manager. (For more information, see Chapter 37, "Automatic Browser Configuration."
You have not set up automatic browser configuration.	Use the Registry Editor.

Warning Using the Registry Editor incorrectly can cause serious problems that may require you to reinstall Windows 95. Microsoft cannot guarantee that problems resulting from the incorrect use of the Registry Editor can be solved. Use the Registry Editor at your own risk.

Note It is recommended that you make a backup copy of the registry files (System.dat and User.dat) prior to editing the registry. For information about how to edit the registry, see the Help menu in the Registry Editor (Regedit.exe).

▶ **To point to a different Search bar page using the IEAK Profile Manager**

1. From the IEAK Profile Manager, on the **File** menu, click **New**.

2. In the left pane, click **Start and Search Page**.

3. In the **Search pane URL** box, type the URL that you want, and then click **Test URL** to be sure it is correct.

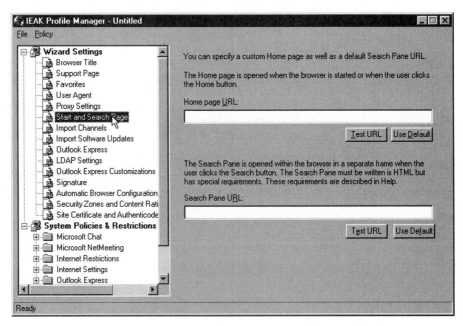

▶ **To point to a different Search bar page using the Registry Editor**

1. From the **Start** menu, click **Run**, type **regedit**, and then click **OK**.

2. In the Registry Editor, navigate to the following registry key:

   HKEY_CURRENT_USER\Software\Microsoft\Internet Explorer\Main

3. Click the **Main** registry key.

4. In the right pane of the Registry Editor, double-click **Search Bar** in the Name column. Then, under Value Data, type the complete URL or entire file path for the Search page you want to use in the Search bar.

5. If the value does not exist, complete the remaining steps.

6. Right-click a blank part of the right pane, click **New**, and then click **String**. The new value appears with a temporary name.

7. Type **Search bar**, and then press ENTER twice.

8. Under Value data, type the complete URL or entire file path you want for the Search page. This can be any address or a location on the local computer or network. For example:

   ```
   http://my server/my folder/my search page.htm
   ```

9. Close the Registry Editor, and then restart Internet Explorer 4.

Tip If you make a mistake that results in your computer not starting properly, it is possible to restore the registry. For instructions, see the Registry Editor Help topic, "Restoring the registry."

You can also make the **Find** menu (on the Windows **Start** menu) point to a different Search page when **On The Internet** is selected.

▶ **To make the Windows Find menu point to a different Search page**

1. In the Registry Editor, navigate to the following registry key:

   HKEY_CURRENT_USER\Software\Microsoft\Internet Explorer\Main

2. In the right pane, double-click **Search Page** in the Name column.

3. In the **Edit String** dialog box, replace the path under Value Data with the complete URL or entire file path you want for your Search page. This can be any address or a location on the local computer or network, for example:

   ```
   file://inetsdk/rtw-image/installed/help/default.htm
   ```

4. Close the Registry Editor, and then restart Internet Explorer.

Creating Your Own Search Bar

You can create your own custom search page for the Search bar in much the same way that you would create a Search page on an ordinary Web site. The following guidelines and tips will help you to get the most from your custom Search page:

- Result pages should include buttons for modifying the current search or running a new search. These buttons should be in the top 20 percent of the content area.

- The default size for the Search bar is 200 pixels wide by the current height of the browser window. Although the user can widen it, your page (including tables and elements) should fit within this area to avoid horizontal scroll bars.

- You can use Dynamic HTML, ActiveX technology, Java, and Cascading Style Sheets (CSS) to achieve dynamic effects and implement multimedia. Remember, however, that the space for the Search bar is limited.

- For direct links to the content area in the main browser window, you can:

    - Add the tag <Base Target="_main"> to the header of the Search page to direct all the links

        or

    - Add the attribute Target="_main" to the <A HREF> tag of each link, as you would reference a frame in a frameset.

- To make an exception to <Base Target="_main"> and direct all links to the contents area, add the attribute TARGET="_top" to the <A HREF> tag of the link, such as for a link to the next 10 searches. For example:

    ```
    <A HREF="URL" TARGET="_top">
    ```

- Use the TARGET=_self attribute for links that update the Search window.

- Any links on the page that don't target the main browser area should be used with caution. The Search bar has no visible navigation controls. If you change the content in the Search bar, you must provide your own navigation controls in your content, such as backward and forward links in the HTML of your new page.

Understanding the Favorites Bar

The best way to view the sites and files that you use most frequently is by using the Favorites bar. Click the **Favorites** button on the Internet Explorer toolbar to display a list of your favorite Web sites and files in the navigation pane in the browser window. From here, favorites can be easily accessed and organized. You can add sites to the Favorites bar by simply dragging a link into the bar. You can drag links or folders within the Favorites bar to rearrange the order of your list according to your preferences.

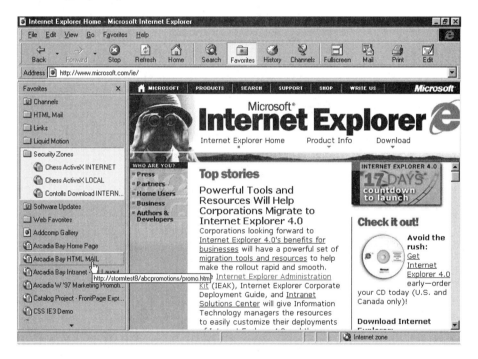

The path names used by the Favorites bar are stored in the C:\Windows\Favorites folder unless the User Profile feature is turned on; in that case, the Favorites folder is stored in your Profile folder. By default, Internet Explorer comes with the following Favorites folders:

- **Channels.** Includes Active Channels that are installed.

- **Links.** Includes a collection of Microsoft links.

- **Software Updates.** Contains a link to the Microsoft Channel Web site that checks for a new version of Internet Explorer or other Microsoft programs. Other programs can write .inf files to add themselves to this folder.

- **My Documents.** Opens the local My Documents folder.

Configuring Favorites

The list of favorites in the Favorites bar is the same list that is used in the **Favorites** menu on the browser and the **Favorites** menu on the **Start** button. Any changes to this list will be reflected in each place in which the favorites are displayed. You can add, rearrange, rename, or delete individual Favorites and favorites folders using the **Organize Favorites** dialog box.

▶ **To access the Organize Favorites dialog box**

- From the Favorites menu, select Organize Favorites.

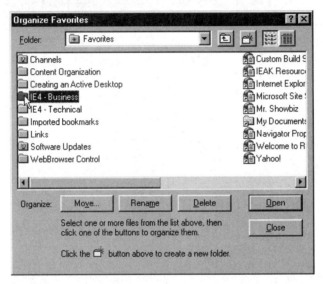

If you have set up the automatic browser configuration feature in the Internet Explorer Administration Kit (IEAK), you can change the default URLs that are included in the Links folder, or you can create an organization-wide standard set of favorites and distribute them to all users by using the IEAK Profile Manager. You can also use the Profile Manager to import a folder of existing Favorites. (For more information, see Chapter 37, "Automatic Browser Configuration.")

▶ **To edit favorites using the IEAK**

1. From the IEAK Profile Manager, on the **File** menu, click **New**.

2. In the left pane, click **Favorites**.

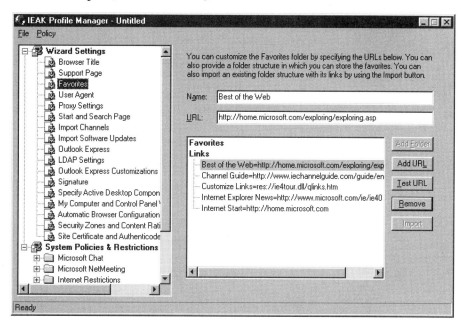

3. The URLs appear in the box at the bottom of the right pane. Here, you can:

   - Add a new URL or subfolder to the Favorites folder by selecting a subfolder and clicking **Add URL** or **Add Folder**. The new item will be added under the subfolder you select.

   - Edit an existing URL by clicking it and changing its path or friendly-name information in the text boxes above.

   - Remove an unwanted URL from the Favorites folder by selecting the URL and clicking **Remove**.

4. When you are finished editing, save the file in the subfolder within the IE4site folder that contains the installation package for your browser. In English versions, the folder is named En.

Understanding the History Bar

In previous browsers, it was difficult to make sense of the History directory, because it likely was filled with a dizzying array of .HTML, JPEG, .gif files, and other random information from the Web. In Internet Explorer 4, it's easy to see where you've been, because the browser automatically sorts your navigation history by date and then by site, displaying only useful shortcuts inside the History bar and ignoring other file types (such as graphics and cookies).

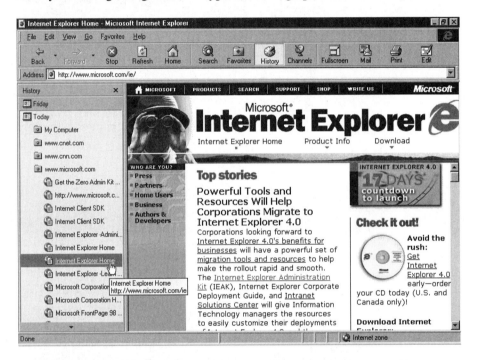

The History bar contains shortcuts for URLs and files that you have visited recently (within the last 20 days, by default). These are broken down according to when you last visited each page (the 3 previous weeks, the current week, and the current day). This information is stored in C:\Windows\History unless the User Profile feature is turned on; in that case, the History folder is stored in your Profile folder.

Note Internet Explorer still caches its complete file history in C:\Windows\Temporary Internet Files. This is useful if you need to see not only shortcuts but also every file that was downloaded in a past session.

To allow faster access, only the path names of recently visited sites are stored in the History folder. The actual contents of the sites or files you view are also downloaded as you view them, but these are saved in the Internet Explorer 4 cache, located at C:\Windows\Temporary Internet Files. In addition, you can find registry information about the History folder at:

**HKEY_LOCAL_MACHINE\SOFTWARE\Microsoft\Windows\
CurrentVersion\Internet Settings\Cache\Extensible Cache**

Configuring the History Bar

The only configurable feature of the History bar is the number of days the History list will retain its information.

▶   **To change the number of days pages will be saved in History**

1. From the **View** menu, select **Internet Options**. The **Internet Options** dialog box will appear.

2. On the **General** tab, in the **History** box, change the number next to **Days to keep pages in History**.

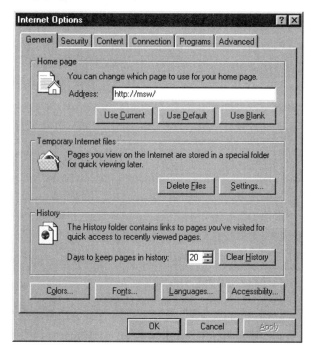

3. Click **OK**.

You can clear the entire history folder by clicking the **Clear History** button in the **Internet Options** dialog box.

Administrators can prevent users from modifying the History settings by checking the **Disable changing history settings** option in the IEAK Configuration Wizard or the IEAK Profile Manager. This option is located under **Internet Policies and Restrictions**, **Internet Restrictions**, **General**. (For more information, see Chapter 36, "Implementing the Deployment.")

Understanding the Channel Bar

The Channel bar displays the Active Channels currently available. When Internet Explorer is first launched, the cache is preloaded with a collection of channels that is stored in C:\Windows\Favorites\Channels. This is intended to introduce users to the concept of Active Channels by giving them the opportunity to sample from a variety of existing channels. For more information about Active Channels, see Chapter 16, "Managed Webcasting."

Configuring the Channels Bar

Administrators can deliver a custom collection of channels to their users by using the IEAK Configuration Wizard or the IEAK Profile Manager. This is done under **Internet Settings**, **Import Channels**. In addition, many subscription parameters can also be set in the IEAK tools under **System Policies and Restrictions**, **Subscriptions**. For more information, see Chapter 36, "Implementing the Deployment" and Chapter 37, "Automatic Browser Configuration."

▶   **To customize channels using the IEAK Profile Manager**

1. In the left pane of the IEAK Profile Manager, select **Import Channels**.

2. Customize the channels on the configuration machine. (Add new channels and remove unwanted ones.) These settings will be imported to the users in your workgroup.

3. Select **Import current channel configuration**.

4. When you are finished editing, save the file in the subfolder within the IE4site folder that contains the installation package for your browser. For example, in English versions, the folder is named En.

▶   **To restrict subscription settings using the IEAK Profile Manager**

1. In the left pane of the IEAK Profile Manager, select **Subscriptions** from the System Policies and Restrictions section.

2. Edit the subscription settings you want to change.

3. When you are finished editing, save the file in the subfolder within the IE4site folder that contains the installation package for your browser. In English versions, the folder is named En.

Creating a New Explorer Bar

You can create a custom Explorer bar to conveniently display a corporate folder, library, site map, or any other list or menu that members of your organization might frequently use to navigate the Internet or intranet. You might want to create several new Explorer bars containing sites that are specific to the task related to each department or workgroup in your organization.

You can create new Explorer bars in two ways: You can create a new name on the **View, Explorer bar** menu that points to an existing page, or you can program new components. To program new components for an Explorer bar, you should be familiar with OLE COM, Visual C++® programming, and component categories. For more information about creating an Explorer bar, refer to the "Band Objects" topic in the *Microsoft Internet Client SDK*.

Browsing Offline

When users want to go to a favorite site on the company intranet or on the Web, it's not always convenient to connect to the network or to their Internet service provider (ISP). With offline browsing, users can view sites without these connections. For example, users can browse offline while using their laptop computers at locations where Internet access is not available. Or users may find it helpful to browse offline at home when they don't want to tie up their only phone line. Some users may even prefer to browse offline at the office when server traffic is heavy and load time is slow. (Offline browsing is faster than browsing online.)

Internet Explorer 4 makes offline browsing possible by automatically caching every site you visit when online. All Web pages you access, as well as files related to those pages (such as graphics files), are stored on your hard disk, so they can be viewed later without an active Internet connection. To begin browsing offline, simply select **Work Offline** from the **File** menu in Internet Explorer and select any page from the History bar.

When browsing offline, if you hover over a link to a page that is not cached, the cursor will change, denoting that the content behind the link is not locally available. If you proceed to click on that link, a dialog box will offer the option of connecting to the Internet to access the page.

In addition, you can use the Webcasting technology in Internet Explorer to schedule your browser to automatically check a Web site for changes since your last visit and download any new or updated content, to ensure that you're always browsing the most up-to-date information, even when offline. For more information about Webcasting, see Part 4 "Information Delivery: Webcasting."

Understanding Offline Browsing

Internet Explorer 4 automatically caches every site you visit while browsing online and stores cached files in the C:\Windows\Temporary Internet Files folder. Each file in the cache is assigned an alphanumeric file name. This prevents Web developers from determining the relative path and file name of a file and attempting to execute it. If you view the contents of the Temporary Internet Files folder using Windows Explorer, you will see the original file names rather than the new file names. These names are mapped in the cache index (Index.dat). The Temporary Internet Files folder is invisible from the MS-DOS prompt. (Removing its attributes will not change this.) When you access one of the cached files, Internet Explorer checks the index to map the original file name to its new random file name, and the file is retrieved from the cache to the browser.

Understanding CD Caching

The new CD Caching utility in Internet Explorer 4 allows users to access part of the http namespace directly from a CD-ROM drive to avoid having to repeatedly connect and download frequently used content. The Cache Container Tool (**cdcache.exe**) is the AutoRun executable file that allows this. It associates selected HTTP content with a URL that the user specifies. When the user browses for this content, Internet Explorer first looks for the content on the CD-ROM drive. If it does not find the content there, Internet Explorer allows the user to look in the usual location. This tool can be found in the \bin folder of the *Microsoft Internet Client SDK*. For more information about creating your own cache container, see the "Cache Container Tool (**cdcache.exe**)" topic in the *Microsoft Internet Client SDK*.

Using Offline Browsing

To view Web content offline, it must first be downloaded from its online location, and offline browsing must be enabled.

▶ **To save a site or file to the hard disk**

- While Internet Explorer is online, browse to the desired site so that it gets saved in the cache.

  or

- Use Web site or Active Channel subscriptions to schedule the browser to download the latest content to your computer. (For more information, see Part 4, "Information Delivery: Webcasting.")

▶ **To enable offline browsing**

- On the **File** menu, click **Work Offline**.

    Internet Explorer will always start in Offline mode until you click **Work Offline** again to clear the check mark.

▶ **To open a site offline**

- Click the **History** button on the Internet Explorer toolbar and then select a shortcut from the History bar, or click the **Channels** button on the Internet Explorer toolbar; then, from the Channel bar, select a channel to which you have subscribed. You can also view any sites and files that are stored in the C:\Windows\Temporary Internet Files folder.

▶ **To check whether sites or files are saved on your hard disk**

1. On the **File** menu, click **Work Offline**.
2. Click the **History** button.
3. Move your mouse pointer over the History item you want to check. If the hand pointer appears, the item is saved on your hard disk and available for offline browsing. If a circle with a line through it appears, then you will not be able to view this content offline. Clicking that site brings up a dialog box asking you if you want to connect to the Internet.

Setting Advanced Browser Options

In Internet Explorer 4, the **Internet Options** dialog box is laid out in a more discoverable manner. Easy-to-access tabs have been updated for **General** options (including History and Cache settings), Security settings (including security zone configurations, Connections settings (for ISP and proxy configurations), and **Advanced** options (for browsing, multimedia, and other settings).

Some of the most important changes to the **Internet Options** dialog box are on the **Advanced** tab.

▶ **To configure Advanced browser settings**

1. On the **View** menu, click **Internet Options**.

2. Click the **Advanced** tab.

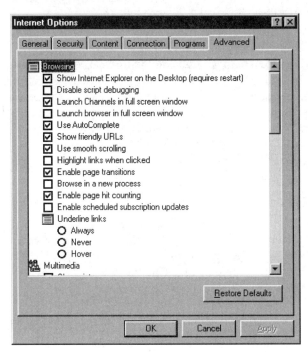

3. Click the check boxes to select or clear the options you prefer, as described in the table below.

Option	Description
Browsing	
Show Internet Explorer on the Desktop (requires restart)	Displays the Internet Explorer icon on the Active Desktop.™
Disable script debugging	Turns off the script debugger if installed.
Launch Channels in full screen window	Launches Active Channels in Full Screen mode.
Launch browser in full screen window	Automatically displays all Web pages in Full Screen mode.
Use AutoComplete	Automatically completes URLs as you type them in the Address bar, based on your navigation history.

Option	Description
Browsing *(continued)*	
Show friendly URLs	Shows the full URL for the current Web page on the Status bar at the bottom of the browser window.
Use smooth scrolling	Uses scrolling that will display content at a predefined speed.
Highlight links when clicked	Displays a thin border around selected hyperlinks.
Enable page transitions	Fades out the page you are leaving and fades in the new page as you move from one Web page to another.
Browse in a new process	Starts a new instance of Internet Explorer every time you open it (for example, if you click an HTML file in My Computer).
Enable page hit counting	Allows the tracking of page usage.
Enable scheduled subscription updates	Allows Webcasting technology to automatically perform subscription updates that you have scheduled (including downloading of new and changed content).
Underline links: Always	Underlines all links on pages.
Underline links: Never	Never underlines links.
Underline links: Hover	Underlines a link when your mouse pointer is "hovering" over it.
Multimedia	(For more information about how multimedia options affect browser performance, see the following chapter, "Browser Performance").
Show pictures	Includes graphical images when pages are displayed.
Play animations	Plays animations when displayed in Web pages.
Play videos	Plays video clips when displayed in Web pages.
Play sounds	Plays music and other sounds when included in Web pages. (If you have an audio player such as RealAudio installed, sounds may still play, even if this option is disabled.)
Smart image dithering	Smooths images so that they appear less jagged when displayed.

Option	Description
Security	(For more information about security options, see Part 7, "Security and Privacy.")
Enable Profile Assistant	Accepts sites' requests for Profile Assistant information and prompts you to choose which parts, if any, of your demographic information to share.
PCT 1.0	Sends and receives secured information through PCT (Private Communications Technology).
SSL 2.0	Sends and receives secured information through the SSL 2.0 (Secured Sockets Layer Level 2) protocol.
SSL 3.0	Sends and receives secured information through the SSL 3.0 (Secured Sockets Layer Level 3) protocol.
Delete saved pages when browser closed	Deletes saved (cached) pages that have been downloaded to your hard disk when the browser exits.
Do not save encrypted pages to disk	Prevents secured information from being saved to your hard disk.
Warn if forms submit is being redirected	Displays a warning when you send information using a Web-based form if the information will be sent to a location different than that of the form.
Warn if changing between secure and insecure mode	Displays a warning when you switch from Internet sites that are secure to sites that are not secure.
Check for certificate revocation	Checks certificates before accepting them as valid to see if they have been revoked.
Warn about invalid site certificates	Displays a warning when the URL in the digital certificate of an Internet site is not valid.
Always accept cookies	Accepts cookies without being prompted. A cookie is a file sent by an Internet site and stored on your computer; it stores information about your identity and preferences when you visit that site.
Prompt before accepting cookies	Displays a warning prompt before receiving a cookie from a Web site.
Disable all cookie use	Prevents cookies from being sent to your computer by Internet sites and prevents existing cookies on your computer from being read by Internet sites.

Option	Description
Java Virtual Machine (VM)	(For more information about Java VM and Java JIT, see the following chapter, "Browser Performance.")
Java JIT compiler enabled	Creates all Java applets automatically, using the Internet Explorer Java Just In Time compiler.
Java logging enabled	Creates a log of all Java program activity.
Printing	
Print background colors and images	Prints background colors and images when you print a page.
Searching	
Autoscan common root domains	Uses AutoDomain Searching to search for a URL using common root domains.
Search when URL fails: Never search	Disables searching for an accurate URL when the entered URL fails.
Search when URL fails: Always ask	Displays a prompt before searching for an accurate URL when the entered URL fails.
Search when URL fails: Always search	Always searches for an accurate URL when the entered URL fails.
Toolbar	
Show font button	Displays the **Font** button on the toolbar.
Small Icons	Displays the toolbar using Microsoft Office–style buttons without text descriptions.
HTTP 1.1 settings	(For more information about HTTP 1.1, see the following chapter, "Browser Performance.")
Use HTTP 1.1	Sets intranet connections to HTTP 1.1.
Use HTTP 1.1 through proxy connections	Sets proxy connections to HTTP 1.1.

Integrating Third-Party Programs

Internet Explorer 4 supports an open architecture for all non-HTTP clients. Third-party client software can be registered as Internet Explorer clients and included in the programs listed on the Internet Options **Programs** tab, for easy integration with Internet Explorer. You can use the **Programs** tab to select the default program used for:

- Mail
- News
- Internet call (Conferencing)
- Calendar
- Contact list (Address Book)

The default programs are launched when you click the corresponding menu option on the Internet Explorer **Go** menu. For example, if you select Outlook™ Express as your default mail and news client, Internet Explorer launches Outlook Express when, from the **Go** menu, you click **Mail** or **News**. Likewise, Internet Explorer launches the default Internet call, calendar, and contact list programs you specify as the defaults on the **Programs** tab.

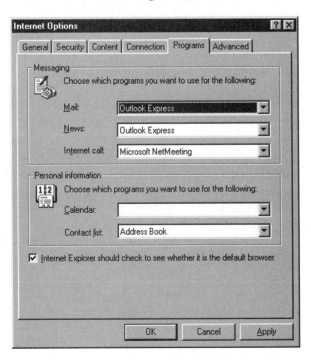

Client programs can register as Internet Explorer clients by creating subkeys in the registry at:

HKEY_LOCAL_MACHINE\SOFTWARE\Clients

The client subkeys are: **Calendar**, **Contacts**, **Internet Call**, **Mail**, and **News**.

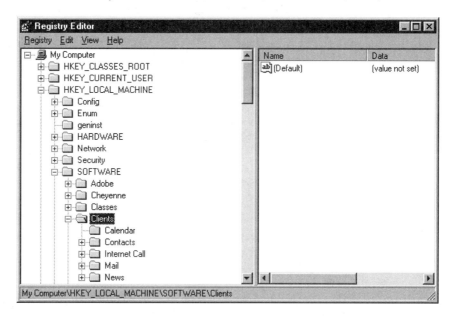

The following tables describe the Mail and News subkeys. (The other subkeys work the same way.)

Key	Description
HKEY_LOCAL_MACHINE\ SOFTWARE\Clients\Mail	Contains subkeys for registered mail clients; for example, Microsoft Outlook and Outlook Express.
HKEY_LOCAL_MACHINE\ SOFTWARE\Clients\News	Contains subkeys for registered news clients; for example, Microsoft Outlook and Outlook Express.

Subkeys for registered clients contain the following types of information:

Mail

Key	Description
HKEY_LOCAL_MACHINE\ SOFTWARE\Clients\Mail\ Outlook Express	Specifies friendly name for this client ("Outlook Express") that appears in the **Programs** tab, **Mail** selection list.
HKEY_LOCAL_MACHINE\ SOFTWARE\Clients\Mail\ Outlook Express\Protocols\ mailto	Specifies that Outlook Express is used as the mail client for mailto: URLs.
HKEY_LOCAL_MACHINE\ SOFTWARE\Clients\Mail\ clientname\shell\open\command	Specifies the path, program file, and command-line options that Internet Explorer uses to launch Outlook Express. For example, when the user clicks a mailto: URL, Internet Explorer runs the Outlook Express program with any specified command-line options.

News

Key	Description
HKEY_LOCAL_MACHINE\ SOFTWARE\Clients\News\ Outlook Express	Specifies friendly name for this client ("Outlook Express") that appears in the **Programs** tab, **News** selection list.
HKEY_LOCAL_MACHINE\ SOFTWARE\Clients\News\ Outlook Express\Protocols\news	Specifies that Outlook Express is used as the news client for Usenet news: URLs.
HKEY_LOCAL_MACHINE\ SOFTWARE\Clients\News\ clientname\Protocols\nntp	Specifies that Outlook Express is used for communications requiring the NNTP protocol.
HKEY_LOCAL_MACHINE\ SOFTWARE\Clients\News\ Outlook Express\Protocols\ snews	Specifies that Outlook Express is used for secure news (snews:) URLs.
HKEY_LOCAL_MACHINE\ SOFTWARE\Clients\News\ Outlook Express\shell\open\ command	Specifies the path, program file, and command-line options that Internet Explorer uses to launch Outlook Express to send news messages.

C H A P T E R   1 0

Browser Performance

In this chapter

Optimizing Browser Performance

Internet Explorer 4 includes a number of performance optimization features, as well as support for advanced protocols and technologies that deliver enhanced browser performance. At the most basic level, the rendering engine in Internet Explorer 4 has been greatly improved, allowing faster Web-page download on a local area network (LAN) or dial-up connection. Internet Explorer is fully integrated with the Windows shell to provide maximum performance of ActiveX controls. In addition, Internet Explorer supports the new HTTP 1.1 protocol, which compresses packets of data transferred via HTTP to boost performance as much as 50 to 100 percent over HTTP 1.0, for faster, more efficient downloads of Web content.

Internet Explorer also supports the Portable Network Graphics (PNG) specification, Dynamic HTML, and the Microsoft DirectX® multimedia extensions, which enable developers to design faster, more bandwidth-efficient graphics and interactive and animated Web content. (For more information about Dynamic HTML, see Part 6, "Authoring for Internet Explorer 4.") Plus, Internet Explorer includes the fastest Java Virtual Machine (VM) and Just In Time (JIT) compiler to provide optimum performance for Java applets.

Using HTTP 1.1

HTTP 1.1 provides enhanced Web performance between browsers and servers. Basically, browsers and servers communicate more efficiently using HTTP 1.1 than when using the older HTTP 1.0. Web communications using HTTP 1.1 require fewer delays and consume less bandwidth, and Web content downloads faster to the browser. By default, HTTP 1.1 communications are enabled in Internet Explorer to optimize browser performance when communicating with servers that support HTTP 1.1.

You can use the **Advanced** tab on the **Internet Options** dialog box to enable or disable HTTP 1.1. If HTTP 1.1 is disabled, all Web communications are transacted using the older and slower HTTP 1.0. The default settings for Internet Explorer do not allow HTTP 1.1 to be used through a proxy server. If you want to use HTTP 1.1 to communicate with Web servers through a proxy server, you'll need to select the **Use HTTP 1.1 through proxy connections** option. For more information about setting Advanced browser options, see "Setting Advanced Browser Options" in the previous chapter, "Browser Features and Functionality."

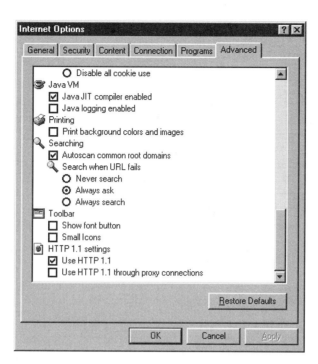

Using the Java Just In Time Compiler

Java applets are compiled into an intermediate form called byte code. The Java Virtual Machine (VM) included with Internet Explorer 4 translates the byte code into the machine code needed for the computing platform when it runs an applet. This translation process typically results in much slower performance for Java applets than for programs that are compiled in native machine language, such as standard Windows programs. The Java VM included with Internet Explorer 4, however, includes a Just In Time (JIT) compiler that significantly improves the performance of Java applets and offers the fastest Java experience available.

By default, the Java JIT is enabled to provide optimum performance for Java applets. You can use the Internet Options **Advanced** tab to disable the Java JIT compiler. For more information about setting Advanced browser options, see "Setting Advanced Browser Options" in the previous chapter, "Browser Features and Functionality."

Using Cached Content

The first time you connect to a Web page, Internet Explorer downloads the page and its supporting content to a cache stored in the Temporary Internet Files folder on your hard disk. By default, Internet Explorer uses the cached content instead of downloading new content when you return to browse a cached page. Using cached content provides faster performance when browsing Web sites, because the same content is not downloaded over and over again.

Each time Internet Explorer is restarted, however, it clears the cache and treats all Web pages you browse as new pages, downloading all the pages and their supporting content to the cache. During that session, Internet Explorer uses cached content whenever it is available until the next restart.

You can use the cache **Settings** dialog box to change the defaults and dictate when Internet Explorer downloads content when revisiting Web pages. For example, you can specify that Internet Explorer never clears its cache and always uses the stored content for a Web page, if available. Or you can require the browser to never use the cache and always download every Web page.

▶   **To configure the cache settings**

1. On the **View** menu, click **Internet Options**.

2. On the **General** tab, in the **Temporary Internet Files** box, click **Settings**.

3. Configure the cache options, as described in the table below.

4. Click **OK**.

Option	Description
Every visit to the page	Select to specify that Internet Explorer downloads Web-page content each time you browse a Web page. Choosing this option typically results in slower browsing, because content is always downloaded.
Every time you start Internet Explorer	Select to specify that Internet Explorer only downloads Web-page content the first time you visit a Web page in a given session. This option can speed up browsing, because cached content is reused rather than downloaded again. Internet Explorer downloads new content for this page only when you restart Internet Explorer. This is the default setting for Internet Explorer.
Never	Select to specify that Internet Explorer always uses cached content when you revisit Web pages. If you choose this option, you won't see updates or changes to cached Web pages.
Amount of disk space to use	Select to specify the percentage of disk space to use for the Temporary Internet Files folder.
	When you view a new page on the Web, Internet Explorer temporarily stores it (and some of its contents, such as graphics files) on your hard disk. This increases the speed at which previously viewed pages are displayed.
	The more disk space you allot to the folder, the more pages Internet Explorer can store on your hard disk. If you are low on disk space, however, you may want to set this option to a lower percentage.

Note No matter what cache settings you choose, you can always manually update the cache while browsing Web pages by clicking the **Refresh** button on the browser toolbar to see any changes to the page.

Configuring Multimedia Settings

By default, Internet Explorer shows or plays a wide range of standard multi-media content, including graphics, video, and audio. Internet Explorer also uses image-dithering technology to smooth images so they appear less jagged. However, multimedia content and dithering can cause Web pages to download and display slowly.

You can use the Internet Options **Advanced** tab to configure multimedia settings to allow Web pages with multimedia content to download faster. For example, you can specify that Internet Explorer not show graphics or play animations, videos, or sounds. You can also turn off image dithering to speed up image display time. Be aware, however, that when multimedia features are disabled, the pages will not display as intended, and you may miss some relevant content. For more information about setting Advanced browser options, see "Setting Advanced Browser Options" in the previous chapter, "Browser Features and Functionality."

Note When graphics, animations, or videos are turned off, Internet Explorer shows a small icon for the item in the browser window. You can selectively choose to display images or play animations and videos by right-clicking the icon for the image, animation, or video and clicking **Show Picture**.

CHAPTER 11

The WebBrowser Control

Understanding Browser Architecture

The Internet Explorer 4 program, Iexplore.exe, is basically a wrapper program for two browser ActiveX controls, Shdocvw.dll (also called the WebBrowser Control) and Mshtml.dll, which provide all of the functionality of the browser. These controls can be reused with any application that supports ActiveX controls to add HTML browsing functionality to the application. These controls provide the following features:

- **Hyperlink navigation and in-place hyperlinking.** In-place hyperlinking refers to the opening of documents in the same instance of the WebBrowser Control, rather than in a new window.
- **Uniform Resource Locator (URL) navigation.**
- **Favorites and History lists.**
- **Security.** (For more information, see Part 7, "Security and Privacy.")
- **Platform for Internet Content Selection (PICS) protocol.** This is the information exchange standard that allows you to control what content can be viewed in the browser. (For more information, see Chapter 30, "Content Advisor.")

The following diagram shows the basic architecture for Internet Explorer 4.

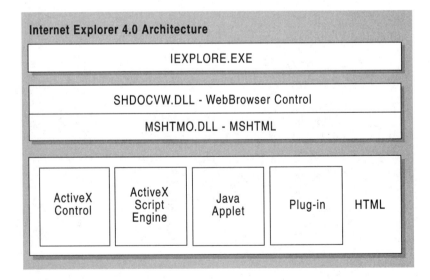

Internet Explorer uses ActiveX controls and Active Document interfaces to connect components. Iexplore.exe is a small program that hosts Shdocvw.dll, which in turn hosts Mshtml.dll. Shdocvw.dll, the WebBrowser Control, supplies the functionality associated with HTML navigation, in-place hyperlinking, Favorites and History management, and PICS support. Many companies, such as America Online, use Shdocvw.dll within their programs to provide Internet browsing. Shdocvw.dll can be found in the C:\Windows\System folder.

Although Shdocvw.dll provides navigation, Favorites, and History functionality, it cannot open, interpret, or render HTML pages. For that functionality, Shdocvw.dll calls on the following components, each of which is needed to create a rich, Internet experience:

- **Mshtml.dll** renders HTML pages.
- **Urlmon.dll** provides HTTP connectivity by processing URLs.
- **Wininet.dll** provides the Internet connection.
- **Java VM** runs Java applets.

Mshtml.dll is an Active Document (also known as an OLE document object) that exposes the HTML document through the Dynamic HTML Object Model and performs the HTML parsing and rendering in Internet Explorer 4. This component hosts the scripting engines, Java VM, ActiveX controls, and other objects that may be referenced in the HTML document that is loaded. Mshtml.dll implements the Active Document server interfaces, which allows it to be hosted using standard COM interfaces. This architecture is recursive in that Shdocvw.dll is in turn hosted by Mshtml.dll in a frameset situation. In this case, each instance of a frame is another instance of Shdocvw.dll hosting Mshtml.dll.

Earlier versions of Internet Explorer did not allow an ambient property, such as the ambient background color, to affect the OLE document objects. As an OLE-based architecture, Internet Explorer 4 does allow the ambient properties that are commonly used by ActiveX controls to be applied to its components. In this way, a host of the WebBrowser Control can set an ambient property that will filter down to all the frames and controls hosted in the loaded document.

Should I Reuse Shdocvw.dll or Mshtml.dll?

Developers can choose to use only Mshtml.dll in their programs or components. Hosting Mshtml.dll, however, is only recommended for specialized programs such as parsing HTML. Mshtml.dll does not support in-place hyperlinking, so clicking a hyperlink would run a new instance of the browser.

For the majority of programs, developers should use Shdocvw.dll, because it supports navigation and in-place hyperlinking and because it is very likely that the WebBrowser Control will already be loaded in memory. For more information about hosting Mshtml.dll, see the WalkAll sample in the *Microsoft Internet Client SDK* topic, "Samples List."

HTML Resources Within Shdocvw.dll and IE4tour.dll

Embedded within Shdocvw.dll and IE4tour.dll are several informational HTML pages. These pages are stored in this way to reduce the number of files actually included within the package and to prevent the need for Internet Explorer to maintain HTML files. These pages provide the Internet Explorer 4 Tour, seen the first time that Internet Explorer is opened, and provide any error messages that appear while using Internet Explorer.

To access the HTML pages, the **res://** command is used with the .dll file name and the name for the HTML page to be loaded. (The term "res" stands for *resource*.) The **res://** command will load an HTML resource from a specified .dll file. The following is a list of all the available resources. These URLs can be typed in the Run line or Address bar to open the resource.

Shdocvw.dll error messages

These messages are specified in the following registry key:

**HKEY_LOCAL_MACHINE\SOFTWARE\Microsoft\
Internet Explorer\AboutURLs**

- **res://shdocvw.dll/navcancl.htm**   An information page appears when the user gets a failed connection to a URL. The many types of connection errors include proxy server errors and invalid URLs.

- **res://shdocvw.dll/offcancl.htm**   An informational error appears when the user tries to view in offline mode a page that is not available in the cache.

IE4tour.dll Information Tour Resources

These resources are specified in the following registry key:

HKEY_CURRENT_USER\Software\Microsoft\Internet Explorer\Main

- **res://ie4tour.dll/channels.htm**   This resource loads the Channels tour demonstration page.

- **res://ie4tour.dll/tour.htm**   The Internet Explorer 4 tour of features and usability.

- **res://ie4tour.dll/welcome.htm**   The page that appears the first time Internet Explorer 4 is opened. This is the page with the three tour options: Tour, Channels, and Register.

Reusing the WebBrowser Control

The WebBrowser Control provides rich functionality for you to include in any program where you want to see elements of a browser interface or to have just HTML navigation, History and Favorites management, HTML parsing and rendering, and so on. Because Shdocvw.dll is registered as a control in the registry, you include it in your programs by adding **Microsoft Internet Controls** to the toolbox in your development program, such as Visual Basic.

▶ **To create your own Web browser using Internet Explorer 4 and Visual Basic 5**

1. Launch Visual Basic 5.

2. Choose **Standard EXE** from the **New Project** dialog box.

3. Right-click **Toolbox** on the left side of the screen, and click **Components**.

4. Check the box next to **Microsoft Internet Controls**, and click **OK**. Notice the two new icons in the toolbox for the WebBrowser Control and the ShellFolderViewOC.

5. Make your form a bit larger so that you have more room to work.

6. Select the **WebBrowser** control, and draw a box on your form covering approximately three-quarters of the bottom of your form. You have just created the area in your Web browser where the Web pages will be viewed.

7. To make an Address bar, select the **TextBox** control from the toolbox, and draw a rectangular box above the **WebBrowser** control on your form.

8. Add a button to your form by selecting the **CommandButton** control and placing it just next to your Address bar. You can change the caption Command1 to anything you want by typing a new caption.

9. Finally, to make this work, double-click the button you just created, and add the following line of code:

```
WebBrowser1.Navigate Text1.Text
```

10. Press the **Play** button or F5 to start your new Web browser. Type any URL in your Address bar, press the navigation button that you created, and the content appears below.

Your new Web browser contains all of the HTML rendering capabilities of Internet Explorer 4, because it is using Shdocvw.dll, which was described earlier in this chapter.

You can also use the Internet Explorer 4 object model to expose only the functionality you want your users to have. For example, you've just created a browser with no Forward, Backward, or Refresh button. If this suits your needs, this would be fine. To add this functionality, however, you only need to create a few more buttons on your form and add the following lines of code:

```
WebBrowser1.GoForward
WebBrowser1.GoBack
WebBrowser1.Refresh
```

You can experiment with the rest of the functionality inside Shdocvw.dll so that you can build the browser that fits your needs.

You can also make the following changes to Shdocvw.dll components in your programs:

- Change Error messages
- Customize WebBrowser Control functionality
- Add HTML resources

Changing Error Messages

To change the error messages that come with Shdocvw.dll, you must edit the registry.

Warning Using the Registry Editor incorrectly can cause serious problems that may require you to reinstall Windows 95. Microsoft cannot guarantee that problems resulting from the incorrect use of the Registry Editor can be solved. Use the Registry Editor at your own risk.

Note For information about how to edit the registry, see "Changing Keys and Values," a Help topic in the Registry Editor (Regedit.exe). You should make a backup copy of the registry files (System.dat and User.dat) before you edit the registry.

▶ **To change the Shdocvw.dll error messages**

1. From the **Start** menu, click **Run**, type **regedit**, and then click **OK**.

2. In the Registry Editor window, click the plus signs in the left pane to go to the following location:

   **HKEY_LOCAL_MACHINE\SOFTWARE\Microsoft\
   Internet Explorer**

3. Click the **AboutURLs** registry key.

4. In the right pane of the Registry Editor, double-click the error message you want to change in the **Name** column, and then, under Value data, type the complete URL. For example, type:

http://my server/my folder/my error message.htm

5. Close the Registry Editor, and then restart Internet Explorer.

Tip If you make a mistake that results in your computer not starting properly, you can restore the registry. For instructions, see the Registry Editor Help topic, "Restoring the Registry."

Customizing WebBrowser Control Functionality

You can customize WebBrowser Control functionality in your own programs by:

- **Overriding context menus, setting the 3-D border, or extending the Dynamic HTML Object Model.** You do these things by implementing the IDocHostUIHandler and IDocHostShowUI interfaces. These interfaces are obtained from the hosting program by either the WebBrowser Control or Mshtml.dll calling QueryInterface on the IOleClientSite interface.

- **Extending existing context menus.** You do this by changing registry settings.

- **Controlling what content is downloaded.** You do this by implementing the download control ambient property, which can restrict frames, images, Java, and so on.

- **Overriding security settings.** You do this by implementing the IInternetSecurityManager interface.

For more information about reusing the WebBrowser Control or Mshtml.dll, or controlling their functionality, see the *Microsoft Internet Client SDK* topic, "Reusing the WebBrowser Control."

Adding HTML Resources

Adding HTML to your program requires you to create your own .dll file that includes customized HTML pages as resources. With customized .dll files, you can control functionality, such as viewing the HTML source. You might also develop your own toolbar with your own set of features.

To create .dll file resources, you use the **ShowHTMLDialog** function to pass parameters to and receive parameters from an HTML dialog box. The HTML code also accesses the parameters that are passed into the dialog box and sets the return parameters from the dialog box using script.

To add the HTML as a resource, you include a file that contains nothing but the actual HTML in your application's resource script. This file is included as an HTML type resource. The following example shows how to include a file called MyHTML.htm as an HTML resource:

```
HTML_RESOURCE HTML "MyHTML.htm"
```

In this example, HTML_RESOURCE is the identifier of the resource. This can be either a string or a numerical identifier. HTML is the resource type. Visual C++ 5 will interpret this as the numeric value 23 and will substitute 23 for HTML when the resource file is opened for editing. MyHTML.htm is the file that contains the HTML source that will be added. The resource compiler adds this file as is and will not attempt to interpret the contents of the file.

You can specify the HTML resource in any function that will accept a res: protocol. **ShowHTMLDialog** is one example of how the res: protocol can use HTML from a resource. You can also use **FindResource** and **LoadResource** to obtain the HTML resource. In **FindResource**, specify the RT HTML value for **lpType** to find an HTML resource.

For more information on creating resources within a .dll file, see the HTMLDlg sample in the *Microsoft Internet Client SDK* topic, "Samples List," and the *Microsoft Windows SDK*.

Distributing Browser Controls with Applications

You can distribute Internet Explorer browser controls with your applications royalty free. However, you must first obtain a redistribution license for Internet Explorer 4 from Microsoft. You can obtain the necessary redistribution license as part of the license agreement for the IEAK. When you register for the IEAK and accept the licensing agreement, you are free to distribute the components of Internet Explorer to your customers or users within the terms of your licensing agreement. For more information, visit **http://www.microsoft.com/ie/ieak/**. For more information about how to obtain a redistribution license, see the Microsoft Customer Support Web page at **http://microsoft.com/Support/**.

P A R T   3

True Web Integration: Windows Desktop Update

Until now, business computer users got their information from two distinct worlds: the online world of the Internet and the "local" world of company networks and systems. But, as the Internet advances to permeate users' everyday computing experience, the integration of Web features and functionality with the desktop operating system is an idea that has become increasingly important and valuable.

For this reason, Internet Explorer 4 provides True Web Integration with the Windows® Desktop Update, a set of features that integrate the Internet into every aspect of personal computing—the desktop, file folders, the network, even the **Start** menu. The Windows Desktop Update provides users with a single metaphor for exploring and searching for information. Whether looking at a local hard disk, a LAN network drive, or a Web site on an HTTP server, the same navigation toolbar provides functionality for going backward and forward, marking favorite locations, and searching for desired information. Because the same menus and toolbar accomplish similar tasks in different scenarios, users need to learn only one navigational model, and the cost of training and supporting users is reduced. Plus, features such as auto-URL-completion and the convenient search-results pane make daily Web browsing easier and more efficient.

To add to the navigational benefits provided by the Web integration in Internet Explorer 4, the flexibility of the Active Desktop™ interface allows intranet administrators to use push and smart-pull technologies to make information and resources directly accessible from users' desktops and to customize that information for specific user groups. The Active Desktop turns users' desktops into dynamic, personalized, live Web "bulletin boards" that regularly update with the latest content, for quick access online or off.

Part 3 describes how True Web Integration works in Internet Explorer 4, details the features included in the Windows Desktop Update, and explains how you can use these features to create a richer, more streamlined, and more productive working environment in your organization.

Chapter 12: Start Menu and Taskbar

The **Start** menu and taskbar provide an anchor on the Windows desktop, giving users one center for starting and switching tasks.When using the Windows 95 and Windows NT® operating systems, users know they can use the **Start** button to access almost everything. Inside the Web browser, they know they can rely on their **Favorites** menu to get to their commonly used sites. In Internet Explorer 4, these ideas were combined and the **Favorites** menu attached to the **Start** button, so users can now get to their favorite sites quickly—without even launching the Web browser first. Following the same logic, the Internet Explorer 4 taskbar provides access to a wide array of Internet-focused functions, permitting users to get to the information they need, quickly and conveniently.

Chapter 13: Web View

In Internet Explorer 4, elements are extended to integrate Internet and intranet tasks into a user interface that today's users have already mastered. For example, an address bar allows users to enter any Web address or file path right from their Windows taskbar, eliminating the need to switch back and forth between the file folder window (Windows Explorer) and the browser window (Internet Explorer). This concept is called Single Explorer, and it offers consistent navigation at the same time as it provides flexible functionality.

Web View expands Web browser functionality to many parts of the standard Windows interface. Now it is possible to view files and Web content in the same window, regardless of file location (Internet, intranet, network, or local hard disk). Plus, it's easy to switch between Web View and the classic Windows interface, or to combine features of both. In Web View, folders can display Hypertext Markup Language (HTML) content, making the folders easier to use and enhancing the information they offer. Custom Web views can be designed for each folder on a system, making it possible to design complete solutions for distributing files on an intranet, local network, compact disc, or even a floppy disk.

Chapter 14: Active Desktop

The Active Desktop interface brings the Web right to users' desktops with HTML wallpaper, screen savers, and Active Desktop items. Now you can use a Web page as desktop wallpaper or as a screen saver, complete with graphics and links to your favorite files and URLs. ActiveX™ objects, JavaScript, and Visual Basic® Scripting Edition (VBScript) can be used to add even more functionality. Active Desktop items, which are essentially miniature Web pages that reside on the desktop, complement this functionality. They can be used to provide information such as news headlines, weather reports, traffic information, and stock quotes. For users, adding an Active Desktop item can be as simple as pointing and clicking. For system administrators, creating an Active Desktop item is as easy as creating a Web page. The Active Desktop can be designed to meet the unique needs of multiple workgroups, improving access to information for users of all levels. Such custom configurations can be easily managed using the Internet Explorer Administration Kit (IEAK).

True Web Integration Architecture

The key file that makes True Web Integration possible is Shdocvw.dll. As with Internet Explorer 3, this file is the Web browser control for Internet Explorer. It is an OLE-COM (ActiveX) application that, when hosted within a parent application, provides Internet browser functionality. Companies such as America Online use Shdocvw.dll within their proprietary applications to provide Internet browsing.

When Shdocvw.dll is loaded, it provides Internet functionality such as Web navigation, viewing of HTML pages, and linking to Favorites. All of the ability to open, interpret, and render HTML pages, however, is not within Shdocvw.dll. It calls upon other services such as Mshtml.dll to render HTML content, the Java run time to process Java applets, and so on. Each of these components is needed to get a rich Internet experience:

- Shdocvw.dll provides Internet functionality, such as Web navigation control. The Internet Explorer program Iexplore.exe is a host for the Shdocvw.dll file. Iexplore.exe is responsible for loading the .dll file and trapping errors for the application, but does not really perform any other tasks.
- Mshtml.dll is the HTML rendering engine.
- Urlmon.dll is used for HTTP connectivity.
- Wininet.dll processes ActiveX controls.
- VBScript.dll processes VBScript.
- Java VM runs Java applets.

Note   Shdocvw.dll can be found in the Windows\System folder.

When Windows Desktop Update is selected to be installed, Internet Explorer 4 replaces Explorer.exe and Shell32.dll during the installation process. These two files, along with Shdocvw.dll, make the Active Desktop and Web View functional.

Shell32.dll is needed to implement the updated layering model of the desktop and to fix some issues with the bounding outline in Active Desktop mode. Explorer.exe has been updated to be an OLE host for Shdocvw.dll. With this update, Internet Explorer can display HTML components on the desktop or provide full HTML support while a user is viewing local and network resources with either Internet Explorer or Windows Explorer.

C H A P T E R   1 2

Start Menu and Taskbar

In this chapter

Start Menu and Taskbar Overview

With Internet Explorer 4, the Windows **Start** menu and taskbar become Web savvy. They now contain many of the commands and functions that make sense in this more Web-centric world.

The Internet Explorer **Favorites** menu is now part of the **Start** menu, giving users easy access to their favorite URLs and channels.

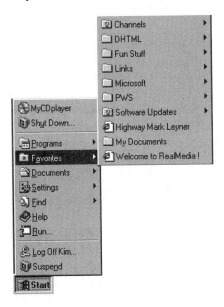

Just as users can rearrange the order of their favorites in the Favorites bar and
Favorites menu inside the browser, they can do the same in the **Favorites** menu
on the **Start** button. Internet Explorer 4 also adds this functionality to the
Programs menu, allowing users to rearrange the order of their applications
by dragging them where they prefer.

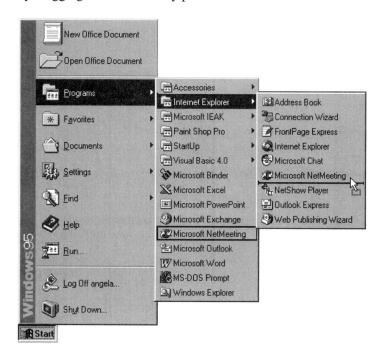

Chapter 18, "Outlook Express," describes support for Lightweight Directory Access Protocol (LDAP) directory services. Essentially, these services provide access to the Internet virtual white pages, which makes it easy to find anyone on corporate LDAP servers or on the Internet. In order to make finding e-mail addresses for individuals even easier, the **Find** command on the **Start** menu has a new **People** option, which enables users to perform LDAP searches directly from the **Start** button.

On the Internet is another new addition to the **Find** command. The **On the Internet** option will launch the Web browser and connect to your default search engine page, which is normally Allinone.htm.

The **Settings** command has also been integrated with Internet Explorer 4, so it is now possible to control settings for folders and icons, as well as the Active Desktop, directly from the **Start** menu. The Active Desktop can be easily activated, turned off, or updated directly from the **Start** button.

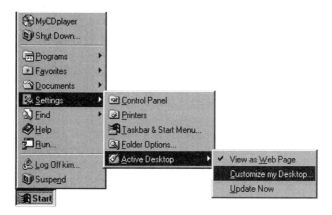

The **Folder Options** dialog box gives users a way to control how their local and network contents are displayed. In the Windows Desktop Update pane, users can choose to stay with the classic Windows 95 style of using their file system or have the computer look and act like the Web. For example, folders can now be displayed all in the same window or in multiple windows. Files can be launched with a Web-style single-click or remain with existing double-click action. Also, any custom combination of these settings can be applied. Changes are illustrated in the dialog box to provide a sample of the new user interface.

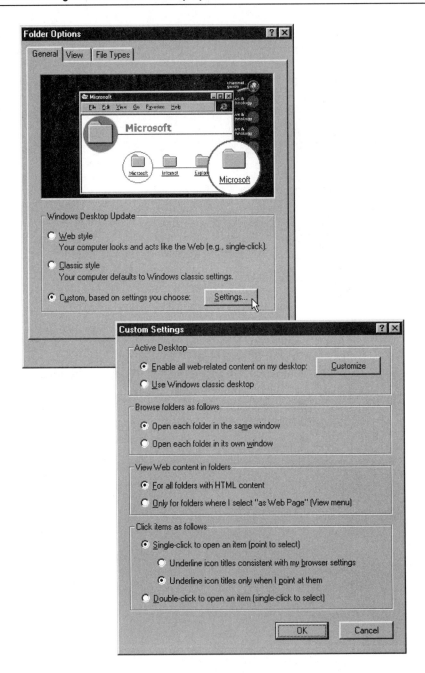

In Windows 95, the taskbar was simply the place where users could find the **Start** button, taskbar buttons for their open applications, the clock, and other utilities. With Internet Explorer 4, the taskbar has become extensible to support expandable, dockable, layered browser toolbars. Plus, custom toolbars can contain any sort of content, including application shortcuts or Web pages and support for full dragging functionality.

The new toolbars include:

- **Quick Launch toolbar**   A quick and easy place to launch commonly used applications and documents. Internet Explorer will provide a few default applications, but the Quick Launch toolbar can be customized simply by dragging any icon onto the toolbar. Also, any icon can be deleted by right-clicking the icon and choosing **Delete**. Notice the new **Show Desktop** button, which quickly hides everything so users can get instant access to the desktop. Pressing it again restores the applications to their previous state.

- **Address bar**   The address bar makes the Internet, intranet, and local network servers easily accessible at all times. Users can type in any URL before launching their Web browser, and Internet Explorer 4 will automatically take them to their desired location. It can even be used as a modified **run** command line as users enter UNC names or local content file names (C:\Windows) or URLs.

- **Quick Links bar**   The same Quick Links bar that is viewed inside Internet Explorer 4 can also be displayed on the taskbar. This makes it easy to get to the places that users visit most often, without launching the Web browser first.

- **Desktop bar**   This custom toolbar dynamically displays all icons that are present on the desktop. This way, if users have multiple applications open that are covering their desktop, they can still get access to those files or applications simply by clicking on the appropriate icon on the Desktop bar.

- **New Toolbar**   By using the **New Toolbar** command, users can generate their own custom toolbars simply by choosing a folder or entering a URL. If a folder is chosen, the contents of the folder will be displayed in the toolbar. If a URL is chosen, the toolbar will display the corresponding Web page.

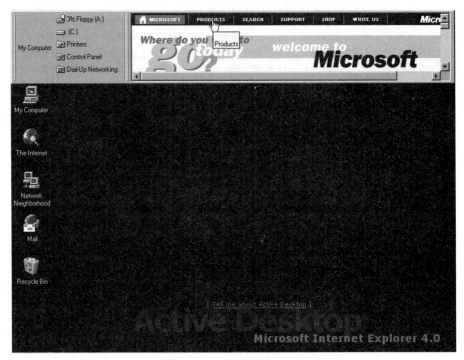

Any of these toolbars can be set up with **Always On Top** or **AutoHide** turned on. This prevents toolbars from taking up available space on the desktop, while still providing quick access to them.

Administrators can import custom toolbar settings to users' machines using the Internet Explorer Administration Kit (IEAK). Users can configure each of these options by right-clicking the taskbar and selecting the appropriate menu option, unless access has been restricted by the administrator.

For information about troubleshooting the **Start** menu and taskbar, see Appendix D.

Configuring the Start, Favorites, and Programs Menus

The Internet Explorer 4 Windows Desktop Update simplifies the process of customizing the contents of **Start**, **Favorites**, and **Programs** menus. System administrators can pre-configure custom settings for these menus and import them to user groups. To create custom menus for user groups, first configure the menus on the computer with the IEAK, and the settings will be carried over to users when the IEAK Configuration Wizard is run. Take note, however, that these settings cannot be adjusted in the IEAK Profile Manager.

When customizing the **Start, Favorites,** and **Programs** menus, the following points should be considered:

- Add the folders, documents, and applications that the workgroup uses most frequently to the **Start** menu. You also may want to add some of these items to the Windows taskbar, the Quick Launch toolbar, or to new toolbars that you create.

- Add all of the workgroup's custom program groups and applications to the **Programs** menu. Whenever a Windows 95–compatible program is installed on a computer, Windows creates a program group for that application on the **Programs** menu. However, you might want to create a program group called Inventory that contains only the inventory applications specific to the workgroup.

- If the workgroup accesses distributed applications that use the Distributed Component Object Model (DCOM), you might want to customize application shortcuts to point to the appropriate local component or to a component on a network server.

The **Start** menu reads the folder location out of the following registry key and displays the contents on the **Start** menu:

HKEY_USERS\.Default\Software\Microsoft\Windows\CurrentVersion\ Explorer\Shell Folders

If the folder specified in this registry entry is missing or corrupt, then the **Favorites** menu will be empty on the **Start** menu. The registry entry is tied to the Long File Name of the Favorites folder, so if this value does not match the registry, you lose the items on the **Start** menu.

▶   **To edit the contents of the Start and Programs menus**

1. Click the **Start** button, point to **Settings,** and then click **Taskbar & Start Menu**.

2. In the **Taskbar Properties** dialog box, click the **Start Menu Programs** tab.

   - Click **Add** or **Remove** to edit the contents of the **Start** menu.

   - Click **Advanced** to bring up the **Start** and **Programs** menus in Windows Explorer.

▶   **To edit the contents of the Favorites menu**

The contents of the Favorites folder can be edited from within Internet Explorer or from within the folder itself.

- **To edit Favorites from within Internet Explorer**

  1. Open Internet Explorer.

  2. Click the **Favorites** menu.

  3. Select **Add to Favorites** to add the current URL to the folder, or select **Organize Favorites** to edit the contents of the folder.

- **To edit the Favorites folder from within the folder itself**

  - Open **C:\Windows\Favorites**, and add or remove files, as desired.

    You will notice that Channels and Links are subfolders within the Favorites folder.

▶   **To reorder items on the Favorites and Programs menus**

1. Click the **Start** button, and then point to the folder you want to change.

2. On the folder's submenu, click the item you want to move, and drag it to the new location.

The location information is only saved at exit time, so you have to close Windows and log on again for changes to be written to the registry. If a crash occurs during a session, you may lose the location data.

The arrangement data is stored in the registry at:

HKEY_CURRENT_USERS\Software\Microsoft\Windows\ CurrentVersion\Explorer\Start Menu\Menu

Configuring the Taskbar and Toolbars

You can configure the taskbar to simplify a user's or workgroup's access to files, applications, and URLs. There are four ways to do this:

- **Customize the Quick Launch toolbar.** You can customize the default Quick Launch toolbar by adding files, folders, applications, and URLs.

- **Customize the default Windows taskbar.** You can customize the Windows taskbar by adding files, folders, applications, and URLs.

- **Creating new toolbars.** You can create new toolbars containing files, folders, applications, and URLs, and then add them to the Windows taskbar or the Active Desktop.

- **Add toolbars as windows on the Active Desktop.** You can add toolbars directly to the Active Desktop as toolbar windows that list the contents of the toolbar in a menu.

When customizing the Quick Launch toolbar, Windows taskbar, or creating new custom toolbars, an administrator should consider the following:

- Decide which files, folders, applications, and URLs the workgroup uses most frequently.

- Determine the best method of presentation for the workgroup. For example, if the workgroup consists of writers working on a specific Microsoft® Word document, you might want to create a shortcut to Microsoft Word or to that document on the Quick Launch toolbar. If the workgroup regularly accesses a folder of related files, applications, or URLs, you might want to create a toolbar containing the contents of that folder and place it on the Windows taskbar or as a floating toolbar on the Active Desktop.

- If you want to create new toolbars, group the files, applications, and URLs that the workgroup uses most frequently into one or more appropriately named folders. A new toolbar consists of the contents of a folder on a local or network drive, and the name of the toolbar will be the same as the name of the folder.

▶ **To customize the Quick Launch toolbar**

*   Drag a file, folder, application, or URL from My Computer or Windows Explorer to the Quick Launch toolbar, or add files directly to the Quick Launch folder in: <windir>\Application Data\Microsoft\ Internet Explorer\Quick Launch.

▶ **To add the Address toolbar**

1. Right-click the taskbar, and select **Toolbars,** then **Address**.

    The Address toolbar will appear in the taskbar.

2. You can drag the Address toolbar to another location on the desktop and resize it, as necessary.

▶ **To add and customize the Quick Links toolbar**

1. Right-click the taskbar, and select **Toolbars**, then **Links**.

    The Links toolbar will appear in the taskbar.

2. You can drag the Links toolbar to another location on the desktop and resize it, as necessary. Items can be added and removed by dragging them in and out of the toolbar.

▶ **To add and customize the Desktop toolbar**

1. Right-click the taskbar, and select **Toolbars**, then **Desktop**.

    The Desktop toolbar will appear in the taskbar.

2. You can drag the Desktop toolbar to another location on the desktop and resize it, as necessary. Items can be added and removed by dragging them in and out of the Desktop toolbar or the desktop itself.

▶ **To create a custom toolbar**

*   **To create a toolbar from the contents of a file folder**

    1. Right-click the taskbar, and select **Toolbars**, then **New Toolbar**.

        The **New Toolbar** dialog box will appear, showing a hierarchical display of the files on your machine.

    2. Create a file folder, and add the files, folders, and shortcuts you want its toolbar to contain.

    3. Select the folder, and click **OK**.

- **To create a toolbar from the contents of a Web page**

  1. Right-click the taskbar, and select **Toolbars**, then **New Toolbar**.

     The **New Toolbar** dialog box will appear, showing a hierarchical display of the files on your machine.

  2. Enter the URL in the text box, and click **OK**.

     The custom toolbar will appear in the taskbar. You can drag the new toolbar to another location on the desktop and resize it, as necessary. Items can be added and removed by dragging them in and out of the toolbar, or by changing the contents of the folder itself.

Importing Custom Toolbar Configurations for User Groups

System administrators can use the IEAK Configuration Wizard to import custom packages with pre-configured toolbar configurations for user groups. (For more information, see "Building Custom Packages" in Chapter 36. Administrators can also restrict users from changing custom toolbars.

▶ **To add custom toolbar settings to user group configuration**

- At the **Customize Desktop Toolbars** page of the IEAK Configuration Wizard, select **Import the current desktop Toolbar settings**.

  Your current desktop settings will be applied to the installation.

▶ **To lock down custom toolbars**

- **In the IEAK Configuration Wizard**

  1. At the **System Policies & Restrictions** page, expand the Active Desktop item.

  2. Scroll down to Desktop Toolbar Settings, and select the desired options. Check boxes will offer the option to **Disable dragging, dropping, and closing of ALL toolbars** and **Disable resizing of ALL toolbars**.

- **In the IEAK Profile Manager**

    1. In the left pane, in the System Policies and Restrictions hierarchy, select **Web Desktop**, and then click **Desktop**.

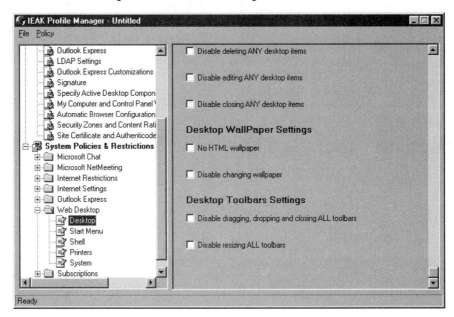

Note The IEAK Profile Manager is shown here, but the IEAK Configuration Wizard works similarly.

---

   2. In the right pane, under Desktop Toolbars Settings, select the desired options. Check boxes will offer the option to **Disable dragging, dropping and closing of ALL toolbars** and **Disable resizing of ALL toolbars**.

CHAPTER 13

Web View

In this chapter

Understanding Web View

Web View folders use Hypertext Markup Language (HTML) to display information in Windows Explorer. (Remember, Windows Desktop Update must be installed in order for Web View to work.) You can accept the Internet Explorer 4 default Web View, or system administrators can customize their own Web Views for the folders they choose. Standard HTML, Dynamic HTML, graphics, ActiveX objects, JavaScript, and VBScript can all be used to customize Web View folders, allowing you to leverage existing development resources.

A customized Web View can be used to give users a richer, more intuitive experience. Navigation can be vastly improved, and greater graphic consistency can be achieved. For example:

- A software download site on a network server can be simplified using Web View. Instead of being confronted with a confusing assortment of different files, users will see only links to things they can use.

- Crucial information can be prominently displayed in a folder, so it can't be missed by users.

- The appearance and functionality of Web View folders can be redesigned to match online resources, so users will have a consistent experience whether using file folders, Web pages on an intranet, or Web pages on the Internet.

For information about troubleshooting the Web View, see Appendix D.

Custom Web View Samples

The following samples illustrate some useful applications of Web View. The samples include solutions for three hypothetical scenarios and one stand-alone example. All samples can be run directly from the Internet Explorer 4 Resource Kit Compact Disc. To view the samples, simply click **Start**, then **Run**, and enter **D:\Samples** (substituting the letter of your CD-ROM drive if it is different than D). On the **View** menu, select **View as Web Page**.

- **Scenario #1: Arcadia Bay Travel Resources**

  Location: D:\Samples\travelpublic

  Many useful features of Web View have been incorporated into a special business-travel folder for this fictitious company. This example illustrates the potential for presenting information and resources in an intuitive manner while still retaining traditional Windows functionality. The FileList control has been used to make a file folder available to users in a familiar way.

- **Scenario #2: Acme Software Driver Floppy Disk**

  Location: D:\Samples\driverfloppy

  This example shows how Web View can transform an ordinary (and potentially confusing) floppy disk into an attractive one-click solution for a hardware driver installation. Try switching between Web View and the normal file views. Which view would you rather use?

- **Scenario #3: Software Installation Folder**

  Location: D:\Samples\products1

  This company has a potentially bewildering array of software available for its employees to install. In the days before Internet Explorer 4, users would have to hunt through a maze of cryptically named folders and then guess which installation option was the right one. Here, Web View and Dynamic HTML have been applied to help users find the software they want and get the information they need to know before installing it.

- **Media Preview Folder**

  Location: D:\Samples\preview

  This folder uses the ActiveMovie™ control to give a preview of sound and video files stored inside it.

Note The names of companies, products, people, characters, and/or data mentioned herein are fictitious and are in no way intended to represent any real individual, company, product, or event, unless otherwise noted.

Web View Architecture

To create the new, Internet Explorer 4 Web View, an extended view was added to the Windows Explorer default implementation of the **IShellView** interface (the shell code responsible for displaying files and folders in the shell's name space—the Large Icons, Small Icons, List, and Details views that you are already familiar with in Windows 95). To view a folder in the default Web View, all you have to do is select the **View as Web Page** option in the **View** menu. The default Web View for all folders is defined by the HTML in folder.htt. (.htt is the file name extension for HTML Template files.)

All Web content for Web View and Web/shell integration is stored in the C:\Windows\Web folder. These files are used to create the appearance and functionality of the Web/shell integration and maintain the user's desktop. The files that provide the main functionality are:

Mycomp.htt	HTML template file used to create the Web View for the My Computer folder.
Controlp.htt	HTML template file used to create the Web View for the Control Panel folder.
Deskmovr.htt	HTML template used to load the Deskmover.ocx file that controls the Active Desktop.
Folder.htt	The default HTML template for Web View in all folders. This file is duplicated when a folder is customized.
Printers.htt	HTML template file used to create the Web View for the Printers folder.
Safemode.htt	HTML template file that displays the Active Desktop Safe Mode (seen when Explorer.exe is shut down, then auto-restarted by the system).

Customizing Web View

Folders can be individually customized by opening the folder and selecting the **Customize This Folder** option in the **View** menu. When this option is selected, the Web View Wizard is launched. After the wizard is completed, two new files are created in the target folder: Desktop.ini and Folder.htt.

Desktop.ini

The Desktop.ini file is a standard .ini file, used to tell Internet Explorer that a folder has a customized Web View. Each customized folder has one Desktop.ini file. The shell reads the Desktop.ini, which directs the shell to host the MSHTML.dll component of Internet Explorer 4 and points it to the appropriate .htt file.

This is a sample Desktop.ini file:

```
[ExtShellFolderViews]
Default={5984FFE0-28D4-11CF-AE66-08002B2E1262}
{5984FFE0-28D4-11CF-AE66-08002B2E1262}={5984FFE0-28D4-11CF-
    AE66-08002B2E1262}
[{5984FFE0-28D4-11CF-AE66-08002B2E1262}]
PersistMoniker=file://folder.htt
[.ShellClassInfo]
ConfirmFileOp=0
```

Folder.htt

The Folder.htt file is a template that contains customized HTML content and an ActiveX control to display the normal directory listing. Each customized folder has one Folder.htt file. It is the same file referenced in the **PersistMoniker=file://folder.htt** desktop.ini setting earlier on this page. To create Folder.htt, the Web View Wizard launches your HTML editor with the <windir>\Web\Folder.htt template. If you save the default HTML provided by the wizard, the folder will appear the same as it did before you ran the wizard. The Folder.htt template file can be edited at any time, and it is liberally commented so you can find your way around in the file. A sample of an uncustomized Folder.htt file can be found in the <windir>\Web\directory.

The default Folder.htt page is a robust example of what can be done with Web View. Most of the functionality is provided by JavaScript and ActiveX controls. We recommend that you make changes to this file carefully and incrementally. Be sure to make a backup of the file before you begin editing.

Customizing a Folder with the Web View Wizard

When initially customizing Web View, we recommend that you use the Web View Wizard, since it automatically creates the Folder.htt and Desktop.ini files that will reside in the customized folder. After that, you can open and edit Folder.htt with the editor of your choice.

▶ **To customize a folder using the Web View Wizard**

1. Open the folder you want to customize.

2. On the **View** menu, select **Customize this Folder**.

3. Select **Create or Edit an HTML Document**, and then click **Next**.

   Your default HTML editor will start with the Folder.htt file open.

4. Insert the code for your custom HTML page.

5. Save and close the file.

6. Click **Finish**.

   The Folder.htt and Desktop.ini files will appear in the folder.

7. On the **View** menu, choose **View as Web Page** to test the new page.

Now, each time you run the wizard for that folder, it will automatically open that folder's Folder.htt file.

▶ **To remove customization from a folder**

After editing Folder.htt, you can remove customization to return the folder to its unedited state.

1. Open the folder you want to edit.

2. On the **View** menu, select **Customize this Folder**.

3. Select **Remove customization,** and then click **Next**.

4. Click **Next** again to proceed.

   The Folder.htt and Desktop.ini files will be removed from the folder.

Note To change the default Web View for *all* file folders, open the \Windows\Web folder and customize the master Folder.htt file. Afterwards, if you want to undo your customization of this master file, open the Windows\Web folder, and go through the standard process for removing customization from a folder; Folder.htt will be replaced by a backup file tucked away inside Webvw.dll.

Customizing the Default Folder.htt File

Folder.htt files may be edited in order to accomplish a variety of customization goals. For example, you may want to:

- Customize the file information that will be displayed in the folder's left pane when a file is selected.
- Add links to other files or URLs.
- Customize the header graphic.

To undo any edits you make to a Folder.htt file, follow the steps for removing customization from a folder, detailed in the previous section.

Customizing the Default Left Pane

The file information that is displayed in the left pane is controlled by a JavaScript function at the top of the Folder.htt file. The first few lines look like this:

```
// name
      text = "<b>" + fldr.GetDetailsOf(items, 0) + "</b>";
// type
      data = fldr.GetDetailsOf(items, 2);
      if (data != "")
          text += "<br>" + data;
```

This part of the JavaScript function is responsible for displaying the name and type of the file in the left pane. Notice the <b> tag that makes the name appear in bold, and the "if" statement that inserts a line break if the file property is null. If your files have additional properties, you can display these by adding new statements to this function, substituting the appropriate number for the property after "items" (items, x). File properties start at "0" (name) and increase by one for each column to the right. If you wish to prevent a property from being displayed, simply remove its section from the function.

Adding Links to the Default Left Pane

To add hyperlinks to the left pane, open Folder.htt, and search for the word "here." The following lines of text will be displayed:

```
<!-- HERE'S A GOOD PLACE TO ADD A FEW LINKS OF YOUR OWN -->
    <!-- (examples commented out)
    <a href="http://www.mylink1.com/">Custom Link 1</a>
            <br>
    <a href="http://www.mylink2.com/">Custom Link 2</a>
            <br><br>
    -->
```

Remove the comment, tags and replace the dummy link information with your own links.

Customizing the Default Header Graphic

The default header graphic is read from the Webvw.dll file. You can substitute it with a graphic of your choice by replacing this line in Folder.htt:

```
background: URL(res://Webvw.dll/folder.gif)
```

with something like this:

```
background: URL(%THISDIRPATH%\mylogo.gif)
```

Replace "mylogo.gif" with the name of your graphic. In this example, the graphic is in the same path as Folder.htt. You may need to modify some of the HTML code to adjust the positioning of the graphic.

You can point to a graphic stored in the template directory (C:\Windows\Web) by using %TEMPLATEDIR% in place of %THISDIRPATH%.

Replacing the Default Folder.htt with a Custom HTML Page

Rather than editing the default Folder.htt file, as explained above, you may prefer to replace it entirely with a new, custom HTML page. When you replace Folder.htt with a custom HTML page, you have the choice of reusing some of the code from the Folder.htt file or completely throwing it away and starting from scratch.

Note We do not recommend that you replace the My Documents folder with a custom Web page, due to the way this folder has been designed to interact with Windows. It is still possible, however, to customize the default Folder.htt file to add links and background graphics and to edit the information displayed in the folder's left pane.

The contents of Folder.htt can be replaced by any HTML code, scripts, or ActiveX objects. Although you will use the same tools and techniques as those used to develop traditional Web pages, keep in mind that Web View can incorporate functionality that is not used in the Internet environment. The following guidelines can help you make the most of Web View:

- Always save your custom file with the .htt file extension. This way, the .htt MIME filter will be activated to let you use things such as variable substitution strings. If you change the name of the file, be sure to update the PersistMoniker line in Desktop.ini to point to the new file. Some variable substitution strings that can be directly incorporated into the HTML code are:

  - **%THISDIRPATH%** (inserts the directory path of the folder).

  - **%THISDIRNAME%** (inserts the name of the folder).

  - **%TEMPLATEDIR%** (inserts the template directory path, usually C:\Windows\Web).

- When creating hyperlinks to files and subfolders, use the HREF tag, but omit the file-name extension for subfolders:

  For files: `<A HREF="filename.ext">`

  For subfolders: `<A HREF="foldername">`

- To display the contents of a folder, insert the FileList object:

```
<OBJECT ID="filelist" classid="clsid:EAB22AC3-30C1-11CF-A7EB-
0000C05BAE0B" width=150 height=470>
    <PARAM NAME="Location" value="%THISDIRPATH%\folder">
    <PARAM NAME="AlignLeft" value=1>
    <PARAM NAME="AutoSize" value=7>
    <PARAM NAME="AutoSizePercentage" value=100>
    <PARAM NAME="AutoArrange" value=1>
    <PARAM NAME="NoClientEdge" value=true>
    <PARAM NAME="ViewMode" value=3>
</OBJECT>
```

The parameter values of the FileList control affect the following settings:

- **Location** defines the path to the folder to be displayed.
- **AlignLeft/AlignRight** defines the alignment of the items when displayed.
- **AutoSize.** Leave this value set to 7.
- **AutoSizePercentage.** Leave this value set to 100.
- **AutoArrange.** A value of 0 allows items displayed in Large Icon or Small Icon views to be moved, while a value of 1 enforces autoarrange at all times.
- **NoClientEdge** defines whether or not the control will have a visible border.
- **ViewMode** defines the view in which the contents of the folder will be displayed (1=Large Icons, 2=Small Icons, 3=List, 4=Details).

Caution   When using this control, NEVER set the Location parameter value to the same folder that is hosting the control, as this could cause a looping VBScript error. Another important thing to keep in mind when using the FileList control is that whatever folder is referenced in the Location parameter will appear in Web View. Pointing the FileList control to uncustomized folders is the safest approach.

Customizing Printers.htt and Safemode.htt

You can customize the Web View of the Printers folder by modifying the Printers.htt file in the C:\Windows\Web directory. A nice addition to this folder might be contact information for technical assistance with printers and a link to an alias to report problems. The Printers.htt folder is set up similarly to Folder.htt, with a few minor differences.

The Safemode.htt HTML template file is displayed only when Explorer.exe is shut down and restarted by the system for any reason. It has a special control that is used to reset Active Desktop settings, along with instructions for what to do in this situation. This page could be modified to include additional support information for users. It is recommended that the reset object not be tampered with, to retain the functionality of this page. The reset object is identified by the following code:

```
<OBJECT ID="suih" width=0 height=0 classid="clsid:64AB4BB7-111E-
    11d1-8F79-00C04FC2FBE1">
```

Use caution when editing either of these folders, as they provide vital functionality to users.

Customizing Web View for My Computer and Control Panel

The My Computer and Control Panel folders must be edited differently than other folders. Since they are virtual folders, Desktop.ini and Folder.htt files cannot be created for them. The Web versions of these folders are controlled by registry entries that point to HTML files located in the Web folder (<windir>\Web\). They are called Controlp.htt and Mycomp.htt, respectively.

The registry settings for Control Panel are:

HKEY_LOCAL_MACHINE\Software\Classes\Clsid
\{21EC2020-3AEA-1069-A2DD-08002B30309D}
\shellex
\ExtShellFolderViews
\{5984FFE0-28D4-11CF-AE66-08002B2E1262}

Default value (Win95): "\Web\controlp.htt"</li>
Default value (WinNT): "%systemRoot%\Web\controlp.htt"</lt>

The registry settings for My Computer are:

HKEY_LOCAL_MACHINE\Software\Classes\Clsid
 \{20D04FE0-3AEA-1069-A2D8-08002B30309D}
 \shellex
 \ExtShellFolderViews
 \{5984FFE0-28D4-11CF-AE66-08002B2E1262}

Default value (Win95): "\Web\mycomp.htt"</li>
Default value (WinNT): "%systemRoot%\Web\mycomp.htt"</lt>

Selecting Thumbnail View in a Folder

With Internet Explorer 4, it is possible to create a thumbnail view of the content within any given directory. Thumbnails are a good way to get a quick snapshot of multiple Web sites or graphics files at the same time. When Thumbnail view is selected, the contents of graphics files, HTML files, and Office Documents are displayed in a 2 by 2-inch window. An icon is displayed for files that cannot display their contents in a thumbnail. A file called Thumbvw.dll controls the Thumbnail view. This feature is turned on in the **Properties** dialog box of each folder.

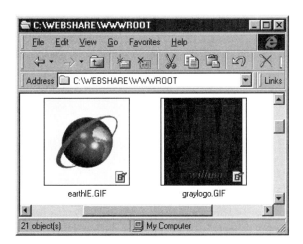

▶   **To enable Thumbnail view**

1. Right-click the folder for which you would like to enable Thumbnail view, and then select **Properties** on the shortcut menu.

2. On the **General** tab, select **Enable thumbnail view**.

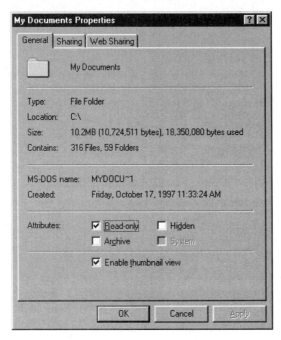

3. Click **OK** to add Thumbnails to the folder's view options.

4. Open the folder and, on the **View** menu, select **Thumbnails**.

   The contents of the folder will be displayed in Thumbnail view.

Note You cannot combine Thumbnail view and Web View for the same folder. Due to the complexity of each of these display options, they are mutually exclusive. If Thumbnail view is selected for a folder, Web View will automatically be turned off for that folder (although subfolders may still use Web View, as long as they don't also use Thumbnail view).

CHAPTER 14

Active Desktop

Understanding the Active Desktop

The Internet Explorer 4 Active Desktop interface is capable of hosting any Hypertext Markup Language (HTML) item, such as Web pages, Java applets, ActiveX controls, floating frames, and images. With this technology, users can create a highly customized environment that automatically brings their favorite Web content to their desktop. Web publishers can leverage their existing tools and production processes to enhance their Web content with Dynamic HTML support. The resulting desktop and Web integration benefits users through a richer and easier Web experience. Web publishers also benefit from the increased presence in the users' working environment.

Active Desktop technology for Internet Explorer 4 marries the best of the Internet to the Windows shell. It creates a unique opportunity to push and pull content and applications from internal and external Web sites, providing a powerful, customizable, information delivery architecture. Essentially, the Active Desktop allows users to place Web sites directly on their desktops, in the form of either Active Desktop items, wallpaper, or screen savers. You can also add an item from the Microsoft Active Desktop gallery, such as a Java clock or a stock ticker.

Historical Background of the Active Desktop

The seeds for integrating the Windows shell and browser were planted with the release of Internet Explorer 3, which componentized the Web browser as an ActiveX control so it could be embedded in a Visual Basic form or an HTML page. But to completely integrate the browser component with the container's frame, the browser piece would have to be extended further; it would need to become an Active Document server. (For more information, see the *Internet Client Software Development Kit.*) Active Documents make it possible to view non-HTML content without leaving the browser, and an Active Document server is simply an OLE Document server with additional interfaces that enable embeddable in-place objects to take over the entire document window. Active Documents thus unified the browsing model for applications, documents, and objects.

The brainstorm that drove design of the Active Desktop was to turn the Windows desktop into an ActiveX Document container. The Active Desktop doesn't include all of the browser's user interface elements, but as you will see, you can do quite a bit with an HTML view of the world.

Layers of the Active Desktop

The Active Desktop in Internet Explorer 4 is built from two separate layers. The desktop icon layer exposes all the user's existing desktop shortcuts, and the background HTML layer hosts the HTML wallpaper or screen saver and all Active Desktop items. The HTML layer is described by a single, local HTML file called Desktop.htm, which is created and edited automatically by Internet Explorer 4. This file contains the following:

- HTML tags that represent each Active Desktop item. Each Active Desktop item consists of a single HTML tag with arbitrary x- and y-positions. The HTML tag used for an Active Desktop item can be either an image (IMG tag) or a floating frame (IFRAME tag) and is generated automatically by Internet Explorer 4. The floating frame is the most commonly used approach, because it neatly encapsulates an entire arbitrary HTML document that can contain anything the publisher desires. In either case, a single URL points to the actual content.

- An ActiveX control that enables moving and resizing of the Active Desktop items and also helps manage the list of items.

- Any other static HTML that the user wants to have in the background. By default, this is just a reference to the user's chosen wallpaper, which is exposed as the background watermark for the HTML page.

Active Desktop items provide dynamic links from the desktop to Web content. An Active Desktop item can be an ActiveX control, a Java applet, an image, or an HTML document. Because these are all essentially things that you can put in an HTML document, they are no different from the HTML wallpaper, except that they live in a layer above it. You can see this by dragging a desktop item around your Active Desktop; it will always be drawn underneath the icons and on top of the wallpaper. Active Desktop items are hosted in an instance of the WebBrowser control. An Active Desktop item can act as a desktop shortcut or a quickly referenced source of regularly updated information. When combined with Web site subscriptions (explained in detail in Chapter 15, "Basic Webcasting.") you can present timely information to your users without requiring any effort on their part.

The Active Desktop is the part of the Windows shell that keeps track of Active Desktop objects. The persistent information about installed desktop items is located in the registry at

HKEY_CURRENT_USER\Software\Microsoft\Internet Explorer\Desktop

The desktop icon layer extends all the features of standard Web-page hyperlinks, such as single-click navigation and hot tracking, to your desktop icons. Plus, it extends this Web-like feel to the familiar features in the Windows 95 shell, such as click-through transparency, dragging, file-type associations, double-clicking, and more.

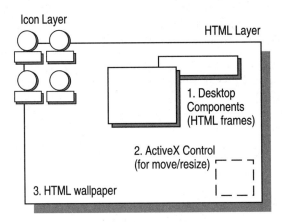

The Active Desktop and Webcasting

You can easily place any ActiveX control, Java applet, graphic, or HTML document on your desktop and leave it at that. To get the most from the Active Desktop, however, you'll want to utilize the Webcasting technologies that are available in Internet Explorer 4. Part 4, "Information Delivery: Webcasting," provides a complete explanation of these features, but a few ideas are important to understand now.

Active Desktop items and Active Desktop wallpaper are, essentially, Web sites that appear directly, in borderless frames, on users' desktops. Once a Web site is placed on the Active Desktop, the site's content is cached on the computer's hard disk, so it's always available for offline viewing. The user can then choose to "subscribe" to the Web site, and the Active Desktop item or wallpaper will be automatically updated at regularly scheduled times, so the content will always be up-to-date.

For optimum control of the update schedule and the type of content that is downloaded during these updates, Channel Definition Format (CDF) files can be used to create Active Channels. Again, Part 4 offers a complete explanation of Active Channels and CDF files. For our purposes now, it is only necessary to understand that CDF files can be used to create custom Active Desktop items and wallpaper and also to bring channel screen savers to the Active Desktop.

It's important to note that Webcasting is typically used to deliver Web content that appears in a subscriber's browser window, while Active Desktop items are used to deliver miniature Web pages that appear directly on subscribers' desktops. Desktop items live on the Windows desktop, alongside existing desktop shortcuts. A desktop item lets you create dynamic links to a workgroup's favorite Web content. Desktop items are typically designed to provide summary information in a small amount of screen space. Therefore, information in desktop items often includes hyperlinks or hot spots, so users can click a designated area to open a browser window and obtain the details they want.

You can configure individual update schedules for each Active Desktop item. For example, a user's Active Desktop can display three different desktop items: an inventory ticker that is updated every 15 minutes, a workgroup home page that is updated once a day, and a newsletter that is updated once a week. Internet Explorer 4 automatically refreshes the desktop item whenever the update occurs.

Customizing the Active Desktop

One of the best benefits of the Active Desktop for administrators is the ability to add custom HTML wallpaper, screen savers, and Active Desktop items for workgroups. This provides a way to display relevant, up-to-date information directly on users' desktops. HTML wallpaper and screen savers can be targeted to specific user groups, and Active Desktop items can be used to complement the information presented there.

For example, a company with many different departments can create a custom HTML page specific to each department. This page might include links to files, folders, and URLs of interest to the specific department, as well as company-wide resources such as organizational charts, a human resources intranet site, and the company's official Internet site. Active Desktop items could be created to alert employees of company news and events and provide a top-level summary of news feeds and trade-related information. A special Active Desktop item could be targeted to new employees that would make it easier to set up their computers and access company resources. Using Webcasting, the new user information could be automatically replaced after a specified period of time. A smaller organization might simplify this approach, by having one page for all employees.

To import a custom Active Desktop to user groups, first configure the Active Desktop on the computer with the Internet Explorer Administration Kit (IEAK), and the wallpaper, screen savers, and desktop items will be carried over to users when the IEAK Configuration Wizard is run. User access to Active Desktop settings can be restricted to prevent users from changing the configurations on their machines.

For information about troubleshooting the Active Desktop, see Appendix D.

Customizing Active Desktop Wallpaper

You can display any HTML page as the wallpaper on the Active Desktop. Remember that the page you select on your configuration machine will be the page seen by all users in the workgroup.

▶ **To use an HTML page as the default Active Desktop wallpaper**

1. Create the HTML page you want to use as wallpaper.
2. Right-click the Active Desktop to display the shortcut menu, and then click **Properties**.
3. Click the **Web** tab, and then select the **View My Active Desktop as a Web Page** check box.
4. Click the **Background** tab, and navigate to the location of the HTML file you created in step 1.
5. Select the file, and click **OK** to display the file.

Tip Try incorporating Dynamic HTML into your Web page to provide a more engaging experience for your users. For more information about Dynamic HTML, see: **http://www.microsoft.com/workshop/author/dhtml/**.

HTML Wallpaper Samples

These samples show how a company can create specialized HTML wallpaper to help meet the information needs of different workgroups. All samples can be run directly from the Internet Explorer 4 Resource Kit Compact Disc. Click **Start**, then click **Run**, and enter **D:\SAMPLES** (substituting the letter of your CD-ROM drive if it is different than D).

The HTML wallpaper samples are located in D:\Samples\desktops. You can view these samples in the browser window by double-clicking the HTML file in the Desktops directory; or, to view the samples directly on the desktop, copy D:\SAMPLES\DESKTOPS to your hard disk, and select the various HTML files as your wallpaper.

Here are two sample desktops that illustrate how custom wallpaper can be used effectively:

- **Corpdesk.htm** contains a floating frame that displays the current date and a short bulletin page. It also features an intranet search window (disabled for this demo).

- **Corpdesk1.htm** features a floating frame that displays current inventory data and a bar graph that displays various sales statistics. Although the information in this demo is read from a delimited text file, it can be easily adapted to interact with a database.

Adding Channel Screen Savers

You can configure the Active Desktop to use a screen saver provided by a subscribed Active Channel Web site, even if that usage is not specified in the Active Channel's CDF file. With a channel screen saver, a user can move the mouse and click objects on the screen without immediately dismissing the screen saver. Clicking a link on the screen saver opens a browser window and dismisses the screen saver.

In a corporate intranet, you might want to configure a channel screen saver that displays a stock ticker, broadcast bulletins, or an inventory counter. For more information about channel screen savers, see Chapter 16. Remember that the page you select on your configuration machine will be the page seen by all users in the workgroup.

▶ **To configure a channel screen saver**

1. Right-click the Active Desktop to display the shortcut menu, and then click **Properties**.

2. Click the **Screen Savers** tab, and then, in the **Screen Savers** dialog box, click **Channel Screen Saver**.

Configuring Active Desktop Items

You can add any graphic, URL, or HTML file to your desktop as an Active Desktop item. Adding a URL will automatically subscribe you to the site you selected. When you subscribe to a URL, site information is automatically cached on your computer for offline viewing, and Internet Explorer 4 will automatically update the desktop item on a schedule you choose. (For more information about Web subscriptions, see Part 4.)

▶ **To add an Active Desktop item**

1. Right-click the Active Desktop to display the shortcut menu, and then click **Properties**.

2. Click the **Web** tab; then click **New**.

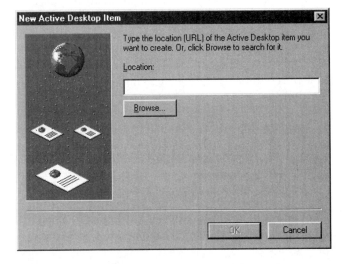

3. Enter the URL or path to the item, or click **Browse** to navigate to the file's location on your local or network drive.

4. Click **OK** to add the item to your desktop.

   Alternatively, you can add a desktop item by subscribing to an Active Channel that specifies a desktop component. For more information, see Chapter 16, "Managed Webcasting."

Note To download examples of Active Desktop items, visit the Active Desktop gallery at: **http://www.microsoft.com/ie/ie40/gallery/**.

▶   **To disable or delete an Active Desktop item**

1. Right-click the Active Desktop to display the shortcut menu, and then click **Properties**.

2. Click the **Web** tab.

   ▪ To disable an item, clear the check box next to the item. It will still be there if you want to use it again.

   ▪ To delete an item, select the item, and click **Delete**. This will permanently remove the item from your system.

3. Click **OK**.

System administrators can place Active Desktop items on users' desktops during configuration by setting them up on the configuration machine prior to running the IEAK Configuration Wizard. Users can be restricted from modifying, adding, and removing Active Desktop items by using the IEAK Configuration Wizard or the IEAK Profile Manager.

▶   **To lock down Active Desktop items**

In the IEAK Configuration Wizard or the IEAK Profile Manager, on the **System Policies and Restrictions** page, under **Web Desktop**, select the following options:

   ▪ **Disable all desktop items**

   ▪ **Disable adding any new desktop items**

   ▪ **Disable deleting any desktop items**

   ▪ **Disable editing any desktop items**

   ▪ **Disable closing any desktop items**

Developing Active Desktop Items

The process for developing a custom Active Desktop item is essentially the same as the process for developing an Active Channel. First, you design the desktop item (the Web page), and then you create its CDF file. In Chapter 16, the "Creating CDF Files" section offers a detailed explanation, with examples, of how to build CDF files, plus some special instructions for creating CDF files for Active Desktop items. Some additional information, specific to desktop items, is detailed below.

Designing Active Desktop Items

When first designing the Active Desktop item, there are some special guidelines to keep in mind. Again, Chapter 16 offers general guidelines for designing Web sites to be used as Active Channels, but if you want the channel to function with optimum effectiveness as a desktop item, also consider these guidelines and tips:

- **Try implementing Dynamic HTML in your Active Desktop item.** It is common for an Active Desktop item to cycle through a set of headlines or summary information. Dynamic HTML makes it possible to achieve this effect without using Java or ActiveX code.

- **The item must work offline.** Since most dial-up users don't have a constant connection to the Internet, an Active Desktop item should display some reasonable content in the absence of a connection. This is important, because the desktop is immediately visible when the user launches the operating system, even before the user has a chance to initiate a dial-up session. An Active Desktop item that displays a blank, gray square or an error message while the user is offline is neither useful or attractive.

  To avoid problems, any necessary data files the item requires should be configured to be cached on the user's computer. The Internet Explorer 4 subscription feature can be configured to cache any object referenced by an Active Desktop item by including it in the CDF file with the ITEM element. Subscriptions can be set to automatically download any images, sounds, objects, or applets, and also any number of HTML links n levels deep. It is important to note that Java applets cannot be pre-cached if the Java classes are not wrapped together in a .cab, .zip, or .jar file. If the classes are in separate files, Internet Explorer cannot determine the Java class dependencies and cache appropriately, because Java binds classes dynamically.

Java- and ActiveX-based desktop items should also be authored to give an error or informational message when not connected to the network, to prevent an empty, gray box from being displayed. Also, to read from the cache when not connected to the network, Java applets should call setUseCaches(TRUE) in their java.net objects. Active Desktop items can also specify individual subscriptions for any data files or objects they may reference. Please note that Java applets and ActiveX controls must be signed so they can access content from the offline cache. For more information about signing Java applets or ActiveX controls, see **http://www.microsoft.com/java/** or **http://www.microsoft.com/windowsdna/**.

- **Avoid using in-place navigation controls.** Active Desktop items are meant to be lightweight and therefore have no navigation controls available for the user to move backward and forward. By default, clicking a link inside an Active Desktop item creates a new browser window. The intended purpose of an Active Desktop item is to provide quick summary information and an easy browser-launching mechanism if the user wants more information. Therefore, authors shouldn't create in-place navigation controls, and they shouldn't depend on the Back and Forward commands being available to the item. Active Desktop item authors should not make any assumptions about the context in which the item is running.

- **Smaller is better.** An Active Desktop item needs to share the desktop space with any other icons or Active Desktop items the user has selected. Because this space is completely customizable by the user, Active Desktop items should be authored to be as small as possible to display their desired content. This gives Active Desktop users the maximum flexibility to arrange their desktop as they wish. A good benchmark is to make sure that the Active Desktop item takes up no more than one-sixth the area of the screen. By default, Internet Explorer lays out new Active Desktop items on a 3 by 2 grid. As more items are added to the desktop, they will start to overlap each other. For a desktop at a resolution of 640 x 480, allowing for reasonable spacing between items, this would translate into a maximum size of no more than 200×200 pixels. This size specification is merely a guideline. Internet Explorer 4 does not itself enforce any restrictions on the size of an Active Desktop item.

- **Avoid pop-up messages.** Today it is common for ActiveX controls, Java applets, and scripting content to notify the user of error messages or warnings by using modal dialog boxes that overlap the browser window. This is fine when the browser window is in the foreground. However, launching a modal dialog box from an Active Desktop item may confuse the user. If an Active Desktop item delivers a pop-up message to the user while the desktop is not in the foreground, the user may not be sure where the message came from or what to do about it. The typical situation to avoid is showing error messages when an Active Desktop item can't connect to the server. In these cases, the item should display some type of status message in the Active Desktop item itself, preferably with a hot spot or link that lets the user get more information and figure out how to proceed.

- **Use the default color palettes.** A large percentage of Internet Explorer 4 users have displays that are limited to 256 colors. For these users, Internet Explorer chooses a default palette that is intended to give a broad range of hues across the entire color spectrum. Therefore, when authoring an Active Desktop item, it is important to keep in mind exactly what the image colors will look like on a 256-color display.

- **Include a rating tag in your item.** Content Advisor is a feature in Internet Explorer that allows parents and supervisors to filter out Web content based on rating labels. This feature is based on the World Wide Web Consortium (W3C) standard for content ratings, known as PICS (http://www.w3.org/PICS/), or Platform for Internet Content Selection. (For more information about PICS, see Part 7.) Web publishers should include a rating tag in their HTML files because someone browsing with the Content Advisor turned on will not be able to see content that is not rated. For more information, see the *Microsoft Internet Client SDK*.

- **Handle expiration dates.** Web publishers can define an expiration date for time-sensitive desktop items. This information is specified by the EndDate attribute of the SCHEDULE element in the CDF file. For example, a typical desktop item schedule might look like this:

```
<SCHEDULE ENDDATE="1998.11.05T08:15-0500">
    <INTERVALTIME DAY="1" />
    <EARLIESTTIME HOUR="12" />
    <LATESTTIME HOUR="18" />
</SCHEDULE>
```

This schedule shows that on November 5, 1998, Internet Explorer will stop refreshing this desktop item's data from the source URL. The desktop item will remain on the user's desktop, but its content will become stale. A few days before the desktop item expires, Web publishers should use a notification page to replace the content to which the desktop item points. This page should explain to users that the desktop item is no longer valid and that they should either close it or get a new one. The actual desktop item should not be deleted from the HTTP server until after the expiration date, to avoid having broken desktop items on users' desktops.

Creating CDF Files for Active Desktop Items

The primary rule in creating Active Channels is that you are required to create a separate CDF file for each Active Desktop item or Active Channel you author. The basic syntax includes the ITEM and USAGE elements. (Remember, for a full explanation of how to create CDF files, see "Creating CDF Files" in Chapter 16.)

The CDF for an Active Desktop item must include at least one ITEM element under the top-level CHANNEL element, with a USAGE child element marked as "DesktopComponent" (see the example below). It is this USAGE element that tells Internet Explorer that the CDF file refers to an Active Desktop item, as opposed to another type of Active Channel. The CDF file should also include a SCHEDULE element to indicate when the item will be updated.

Since an Active Desktop item comprises a single HTML page, the only ITEM you need to include in the CDF file is the small Web page you want to embed in the user's desktop. This should be marked with the USAGE element as indicated in the example below. If you like, you can include additional ITEM elements for each page to which the Active Desktop item links. Including these as ITEMs in the CDF file has the additional benefit of keeping those pages "subscribed to" and available for offline viewing. The ITEMs, other than the actual Active Desktop item URL, are not exposed to the user. Note that this differs from Active Channels, which present a hierarchical list of ITEM tags to the user in the form of the Internet Explorer Channel Bar.

The following restrictions are placed on CDF files for Active Desktop items:

- If a CDF file has more than one ITEM element marked `<Usage VALUE="DesktopComponent">`, Internet Explorer uses the first one it encounters.

- Only the top-level CHANNEL element is valid. Nested CHANNEL elements have no effect, because these additional items don't correspond to any list or hierarchy that the user can access.

- USAGE elements set to anything other than "DesktopComponent" are ignored.

CDF Example for an Active Desktop Item

The following example shows a CDF file for an Active Desktop item.

```
<?XML VERSION="1.0"?>
<CHANNEL>

    <SCHEDULE ENDDATE="1998.11.05T08:15-0500">
        <INTERVALTIME DAY="1"  />
        <EARLIESTTIME HOUR="12"/>
        <LATESTTIME   HOUR="18"/>
    </SCHEDULE>

    <ITEM HREF="http://www.microsoft.com" LASTMOD="1996.11.05T08:15-
        0500">
        <Title>My News Ticker</Title>    <!-- Friendly name -->
        <USAGE VALUE="DesktopComponent"> <!-- Required -->
            <OPENAS VALUE="HTML"/> <!-- "HTML" (default) or "Image" -->
            <WIDTH  VALUE="200" />   <!-- Width in pixels        -->
            <HEIGHT VALUE="80"  />   <!-- Height in pixels       -->
            <CANRESIZE VALUE="Yes"/> <!-- Yes (default) or No     -->
        </USAGE>
    </ITEM>

    <!-- Other Item tags may go here.  IE4 won't display them anywhere,
        but -->

    <!-- will use them for site crawling and place them in the user's
        cache. -->

    <ITEM HREF="http://www.samplesports.com/topstories.html"
        LASTMOD="1996.11.05T08:15-0500" >
    </ITEM>

</CHANNEL>
```

Offering the Active Desktop Item to Users

Once you've designed your Active Desktop item and created its CDF file, you will need to make the CDF file available on your Web server. As with Active Channels, a link or button should be placed on any Web page that references the CDF file to allow users to subscribe to the new Active Desktop item. When the user clicks the link, Internet Explorer 4 automatically detects the USAGE element, which tells it that the CDF refers to an Active Desktop item.

Internet Explorer 4 then activates the Active Desktop item Subscription Wizard on the user's computer and allows the user to receive updated information about this Active Desktop item. As the content contained in the Active Desktop item is added, removed, or modified, Web publishers should update the CDF file to reflect the changes.

PART 4

Information Delivery: Webcasting

The information delivery architecture in Internet Explorer 4 enables new ways for Web content or applications to reach end users, using new push and pull technologies that are collectively referred to as *Webcasting*. Webcasting is the automated delivery of personalized, up-to-date information to users' desktops. Internet Explorer 4 provides a mechanism for end users to schedule recurring monitoring or crawling of Web sites and automatic downloading of updated information. These advanced features for pulling content allow online users to receive notification when content changes, and they allow mobile workers to view favorite Web content even when offline. The information delivery architecture further allows intranet administrators to set up servers that push content to corporate employees via bandwidth-efficient multicast protocols.

Why introduce a new model of information delivery on the Web? Because traditional Web browsing poses several problems for end users and the organizations that support them. Currently, most Internet and intranet sites require users to manually browse for useful information and then frequently revisit the sites for updates. This process is time-consuming for users and bandwidth-consuming for the network, as the same pages are repeatedly downloaded. For mobile workers, the problem is exacerbated by painfully slow dial-up connections.

To address these problems, Internet Explorer 4 provides three Webcasting options that allow you to take the best advantage of this new technology, based on your current business needs and technology investments. By automatically tracking updates to Web content, Webcasting can help minimize the time users spend searching the Web for up-to-date information, while ensuring that the latest information is automatically delivered to the people who need it. Plus, Webcasting can reduce the bandwidth necessary to deliver updated content on the Web, by reducing the amount of redundant information that is downloaded, and operating at off-peak network load periods, rather than the peak load periods often used with manual browsing.

Part 4 describes the three types of Webcasting and explains how to incorporate these information delivery technologies into your organization.

Chapter 15: Basic Webcasting

Using basic Webcasting, users can "subscribe" to any existing Web site and have Internet Explorer automatically visit and "crawl" the site on a scheduled basis to check for updated content. Internet Explorer will check the site up to three levels deep, and when content changes, notify users—either through a gleam on their Favorites lists or via e-mail. Internet Explorer can also automatically download updated content for offline use. Site subscription might be thought of as "smart pull" technology.

Chapter 16: Managed Webcasting

Similar to basic Webcasting, managed Webcasting also works through a subscription process, except users subscribe to publisher-specified Active Channels™, which deliver a defined range of Web content. This might be thought of as "programmed pull." Users can check for updates on specific types of content and can accept a publisher's predefined update schedule or specify a custom schedule. When channel content changes, Internet Explorer notifies the user of changes and can be set to download just the requested content for viewing offline.

Active Channels allow Web-site authors to optimize, personalize, and more fully control how a site is Webcast, and adding a Channel Definition Format (CDF) file is the only step required to convert any existing Web site into an Active Channel. Using CDF, it's easy to design Active Channels, Active Desktop™ items, or channel screen savers for your intranet to efficiently deliver business information to users' desktops.

Chapter 17: True Webcasting

True Webcasting, or "true push" technology, uses multicast add-ons, such as Microsoft NetShow™ 2.0, to deliver bandwidth-efficient multimedia information to users' desktops. Organizations can use true Webcasting to automatically push updated information to subscribers at scheduled periods.

C H A P T E R   1 5

Basic Webcasting

In this chapter

Understanding Basic Webcasting

Basic Webcasting with site subscriptions offers the following features and benefits:

- Automated visiting and crawling of sites on a scheduled basis to check for updated content reduces the time users spend on online browsing.

- Notification to users when updated Web content is available—with a red, asterisk-like gleam on updated favorites or via an e-mail message—helps users stay current easily.

- Automated download of subscribed content for dial-up users means remote workers and laptop users can browse their favorite sites even when offline, saving time and reducing online costs.

- Updates can be scheduled to take place during off-peak times, and only new or changed content is downloaded, so the burden on network bandwidth is reduced.

- Subscriptions work with any existing site that allows Web crawls, so Web site authors do not have to modify existing sites or their content to allow for subscriptions.

- Administrators can centrally lock down and manage a variety of subscription options for users.

Understanding Web Site Subscriptions

Internet Explorer 4 automatically enables Webcasting of any existing Web site without requiring modifications to the site. In order to Webcast content from a conventional Web site, Internet Explorer 4 performs a scheduled site-crawl of the site content, checking for updated content and optionally downloading information for offline use. Users initiate this process by subscribing to a Web site, using the **Favorites** menu in Internet Explorer. Users can also subscribe to Web sites while browsing the site. Once a user subscribes to a site, Internet Explorer periodically checks the site for updated content and notifies the user of changes. Users can configure a variety of subscription options using the Subscription Wizard and can later change configurations, using the tabs in the subscribed site's **Properties** dialog box.

Note Some sites disable Web crawls for selected pages or for the entire site. Site subscriptions won't work for Web pages that disable Web crawls.

Users can specify Web crawls up to three levels deep from a subscribed Web page. Internet Explorer crawls all Web links to the specified level and can optionally download and cache all linked Web pages to users' computers, including all linked images, audio and video, and ActiveX™ controls and Java applets.

When a user chooses to download updated content for offline access, Internet Explorer stores the updated content in a cache on the user's hard disk. Users can browse cached content offline when disconnected from the Web. When offline, if a user clicks on a link for content that is not cached, Internet Explorer queries the user whether to connect to the Web. Users can also complete and submit Hypertext Markup Language (HTML) forms when offline. Internet Explorer will cache the HTML forms and send the form data the next time the computer is connected to the Web.

System administrators can use the Internet Explorer Administration Kit (IEAK) Configuration Wizard and the IEAK Profile Manager to lock down subscription options for users. For example, you can restrict the number of subscriptions allowed at users' desktops or limit the depth level of site crawls.

For information about troubleshooting Webcasting, see Appendix E.

Link-Crawl Architecture

Basic Webcasting uses a general link-crawl process. Literally, Internet Explorer 4 will connect to a Web site, and given a starting Web page, will crawl each link on that page. If configured to do so, it will crawl multiple levels deep, or just look at the first page. During the link crawls, Internet Explorer can check to see if the page has changed, based on the current file size and date, and optionally download that page to the user's machine. Once the page has been checked, a notification of changes or content download is sent to the user.

- Webcheck.dll creates the subscription and launches the crawl at the scheduled time.

- Icmp.dll gets the HTTP header of the Web page to check if the page has changed.

- Shdocvw.dll is used to look for the META tags on the page.

- Mshtml.dll is used to download the page to the local cache and parse the content.

All subscriptions are stored in the registry at:

**HKEY_CURRENTUSER\Software\Microsoft\Windows\CurrentVersion\
NotificationManager\ScheduledItems**

This key contains a CLSID (or GUID) for each subscription. The data is primarily hexidecimal and binary, so is not readable. Deleting any entry from this key will completely remove the subscription. A subscription has no file components.

Link crawl uses the Scheduling Agent to perform its scheduling of downloads.

Web Crawling and the If_Modified_Since Header

The sitecrawler compares the date of a file in the Temporary Internet Files folder to the date of the same file on the Web server on which it resides. If the dates are different, it knows the page has changed. The file date from the server is sent in a special header field in an HTTP response.

The **If_Modified_Since** header field is used with the GET method to make it conditional: if the requested page has not been modified since the time specified in this field, an item will not be returned from the server; instead, a 304 (not modified) response will be returned without any message-body.

If_Modified_Since = "If_Modified_Since" ":" HTTP-date

An example of the field is:

If_Modified_Since: Sat, 29 Oct 1994 19:43:31 GMT

The purpose of this feature is to allow efficient updates of cached information with a minimum amount of transaction overhead.

It's also helpful to be aware of the following notes:

- The range-request header modifies the meaning of **If_Modified_Since**.
- **If_Modified_Since** times are interpreted by the server, whose clock may not be synchronized with the sitecrawler.

Subscribing to Sites

You can subscribe to a Web site while browsing the site, by using the **Add Favorite** dialog box.

▶   **To subscribe to a site while browsing the site**

1. On the **Favorites** menu, click **Add to Favorites**.

2. In the **Add Favorite** dialog box, select one of the following subscription options:

   ▪ **Yes, but only tell me when this page is updated** to subscribe but not download updated content to the cache.

   ▪ **Yes, notify me of updates and download the page for offline viewing** to subscribe and download updated content to the cache.

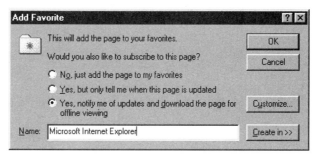

3. To customize subscription options, click **Customize**, and use the Subscription Wizard to configure subscription options. For more information, see "Customizing Subscriptions" next in this chapter.

4. Click **OK**.

You can subscribe to existing Favorites or unsubscribe from subscribed sites with the **Favorites** menu, either directly from the menu or using the **Subscription** tab in the site's **Properties** dialog box.

▶ **To open the Subscription tab**

1. On the **Favorites** menu (or on the **Organize Favorites** dialog box, available from the **Favorites** menu), right-click the site to which you want to subscribe, and click **Properties** on the shortcut menu.

2. Click the **Subscription** tab.

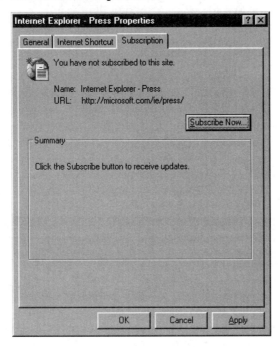

▶ **To subscribe to an existing site in the Favorites list**

1. Perform one of the following:

   ▪ On the site's **Subscription** tab, click **Subscribe Now**.

   ▪ On the **Favorites** menu, right-click the site to which you want to subscribe, and click **Subscribe** on the shortcut menu.

2. In the **Subscribe Favorite** dialog box, select one of the following subscription options:

   ▪ **Only tell me when this page is updated** to subscribe but not download updated content to the cache.

   ▪ **Notify me of updates and download the page for offline viewing** to subscribe and download updated content to the cache.

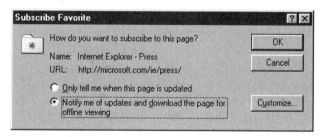

3. To customize subscription options, click **Customize**, and use the Subscription Wizard to configure subscription options. For more information, see "Customizing Subscriptions" next in this chapter.

4. Click **OK**.

▶ **To unsubscribe from a site**

   ● Perform one of the following:

     ▪ From the subscribed site's **Subscription** tab, click **Unsubscribe**.

     ▪ On the **Favorites** menu, right-click the site from which you want to unsubscribe and click **Unsubscribe** on the shortcut menu.

Customizing Subscriptions

You can customize most subscription options when you subscribe to sites by using the Subscription Wizard. After subscribing to a site, you can use the **Receiving** and **Schedule** tabs in the site's **Properties** dialog box to configure all subscription options.

Use the **Receiving** tab to specify the following options:

- Disable automatic download of updated content for offline viewing.
- Specify up to three levels of links—in addition to the subscription page— to download for offline viewing.
- Prevent images, sound and video, or ActiveX controls and Java applets from downloading during updates.
- Limit downloads to a specified number of kilobytes (KB) per update.
- Activate notification of updates by e-mail.
- Specify the user's e-mail address information.
- Specify a user name and password, if needed, to authenticate site logins.

▶ **To access the Receiving tab**

1. On the **Favorites** menu (or from the **Organize Favorites** dialog box, available from the **Favorites** menu), right-click the site to which you want to subscribe, and click **Properties** on the shortcut menu.

2. Click the **Receiving** tab.

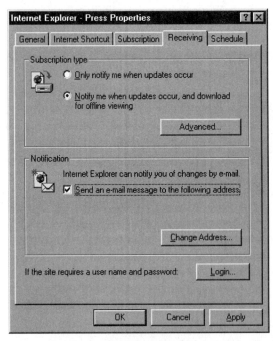

▶ **To configure advanced download options**

1. On the **Receiving** tab, click **Advanced**.

2. Configure the options.

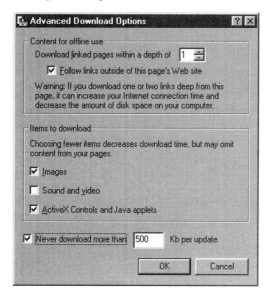

Option	Description
Follow links outside of this page's Web site	Select to specify whether you want Internet Explorer to download more than just the top-level page of the selected Web site.
Download linked pages within a depth of __	Select the depth level for Web crawls and downloads. Select **0** to crawl and download just the top-level subscribed page. You can specify that you want to download the specified Web site up to three levels deep. For example, if you specify two levels deep, the first page and all the pages to which the first page links will be downloaded. Specifying three levels will download all the pages linked to the second-level pages. Consider these levels carefully; automatic download of multiple site levels can fill your hard disk with large amounts of Web content.
Images	Clear to prevent downloading graphical images when Internet Explorer updates the selected Web site. If you choose not to download images, the Web site may appear incomplete or not display properly when browsed offline.

Option	Description
Sound and video	Clear to prevent downloading sound and video files when Internet Explorer updates the selected Web site. If you choose not to download these files, the Web site may not function properly when browsed offline.
ActiveX Controls and Java applets	Clear to prevent downloading ActiveX controls and Java applets when Internet Explorer updates the selected Web site. If you choose not to download these programs, the Web site may not function properly when browsed offline.
Never download more than __ Kb per update	Select this option, and enter a number of kilobytes to limit the maximum amount of information that Internet Explorer downloads to your hard disk from this Web site for each update.

3. Click **OK**.

▶ **To configure mail address options**

1. On the **Receiving** tab, click **Change Address**.

2. Configure the options.

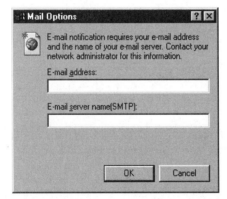

Option	Description
E-mail address	Enter the Internet e-mail address where you want to receive update notifications.
E-mail server name (SMTP)	Enter the name of your outgoing (SMTP) Internet e-mail server.

3. Click **OK**.

▶ **To configure login options**

1. On the **Receiving** tab, click **Login**.

2. Configure the options.

Option	Description
User name	Enter the user name necessary to authenticate logins to the site.
Password	Enter the password necessary to authenticate logins to the site.

3. Click **OK**.

Use the **Schedule** tab to specify the following options:

- Create a customized, automated update schedule.

- Disable automated updates. (User performs updates manually.)

- Permit updates only when the computer is idle.

▶ **To access the Schedule tab**

1. On the **Favorites** menu (or from the **Organize Favorites** dialog box, available from the **Favorites** menu), right-click the site to which you want to subscribe and click **Properties** on the shortcut menu.

2. Click the **Schedule** tab.

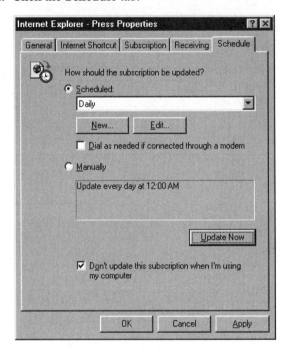

▶ **To create or edit a custom schedule**

1. On the **Schedule** tab, click **New** or **Edit**.

2. Configure the options.

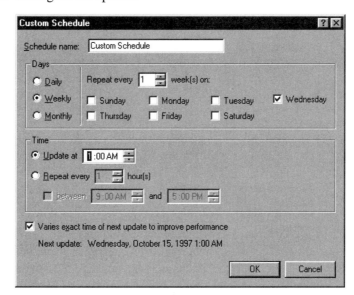

Option	Description
Schedule name	Enter a unique name for this schedule.
Daily	Select to specify an update interval based on days.
Every __ day(s)	Select this option, and enter an interval in days from 1 to 999 when automated updates are to occur. For example, enter **3** to specify updates every three days.
Every weekday	Select to update the site every weekday.
Weekly	Select to specify an update interval based on weeks.
Repeat every __ week(s) on	Enter an interval in weeks from 1 to 99, and select a day of the week (**Sunday** through **Saturday**) when automated updates are to occur. For example, you can enter **2** for **week(s)** and select **Wednesday** to specify biweekly updates on Wednesdays.
Monthly	Select to specify an update interval based on months.

Option	Description
Day __ of every __ month(s)	Enter the day of the month and an interval in months from 1 to 6 when automated updates are to occur. For example, you can enter **15** for **Day** and **2** for **month(s)** to specify updates to occur on the fifteenth day, every other month.
The __ __ of every __ month(s)	Select **first, second, third, fourth,** or **last** from the first selection list. Select **Sunday, Monday, Tuesday, Wednesday, Thursday, Friday,** or **Saturday** from the second selection list. Enter an interval in months from 1 to 6 when automated updates are to occur. For example, you can select **first** and **Saturday** and enter **1** for **month(s)** to specify updates to occur on the last Saturday of each month.
Update at __	Select this option, and enter the time of day when automated updates are to occur. For example, enter **1 A.M.** to update the site at 1 AM on the days of scheduled updates.
Repeat every __ hour(s)	Select this option and enter an interval in hours to repeat automated updates. Use this option only if you want updates on an hourly basis. This option overrides other update schedules. You can also use the **between __ and __** option to specify a range of time for repeating updates.
Between __ and __	Select this option and enter a range of time when repeated updates are to occur. Use this option if you want repeated updates to occur during a range of time each day. For example, enter **8 A.M.** and **5 P.M.** to specify repeated updates only during normal business hours. You must also select **Repeat every __ hour(s)** and enter the repeating interval in hours.
Varies exact time of update to improve performance	Select to vary automated updates by several minutes in actual start time for the next update. Selecting this option increases the likelihood of offsetting the demands other people may make at the same time for the same site and thus improve the efficiency of downloading from the Web.

3. Click **OK**.

▶ **To configure the Schedule tab options**

1. Configure the options.

Option	Description
Scheduled	Select this option, and then select a schedule from the selection list to specify the automated update schedule.
Manually	Select to disable automated updates and perform all updates manually.
Don't update this subscription when I'm using my computer	Select to permit updates to occur only when the computer is idle. Clear to enable updates to occur when you are using the computer.

2. Click **OK**.

Locking Down Subscriptions

System administrators can use the IEAK Configuration Wizard to lock down subscription options. After browsers are deployed, you can use the IEAK Profile Manager to lock down subscription options for user groups that have automatic browser configuration implemented. For more information, see "Building Custom Packages" in Chapter 36 and "Setting up Automatic Browser Configuration" in Chapter 37.

▶   **To lock down subscription options**

1. On the **System Policies and Restrictions** page of the IEAK Wizard or the IEAK Profile Manager, in the System Policies & Restrictions hierarchy, select **Subscriptions**, and then select the Subscriptions object.

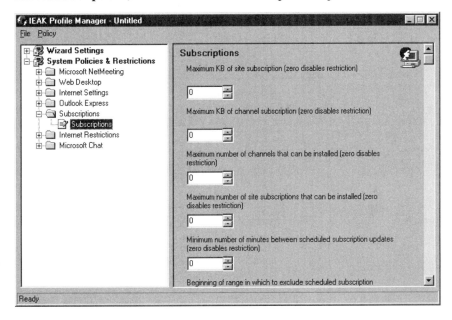

Note   The IEAK Profile Manager is shown here, but the **System Policies and Restrictions** page of the IEAK Configuration Wizard works similarly.

2. In the right pane, configure the following options:

Option	Description
Maximum KB of site subscription (zero disables restriction)	Enter the maximum kilobytes that can be downloaded per site update for each user. Users are prevented from downloading more than the specified number of kilobytes per site update.
Maximum number of site subscriptions that can be installed (zero disables restriction)	Enter the maximum number of site subscriptions that can be installed on users' computers. Users are prevented from subscribing to more than the specified number of sites locally.
Minimum number of minutes between scheduled subscription updates (zero disables restriction)	Enter the minimum number of minutes allowed between scheduled updates. Users are prevented from scheduling automated updates closer together than this number of minutes.
Beginning of range in which to exclude scheduled subscription updates. Measured in minutes from midnight (zero disables restriction)	Enter the starting time measured in minutes from midnight of a range of time when you want to exclude scheduled updates. Users are prevented from scheduling automated updates during this range of time. For example, you could enter **420** to start the range of time at 8 A.M. to exclude normal business hours.
End of range in which to exclude scheduled subscription updates. Measured in minutes from midnight (zero disables restriction)	Enter the ending time measured in minutes from midnight of a range of time when you want to exclude scheduled updates. Users are prevented from scheduling automated updates during this range of time. For example, you could enter **960** to end the range of time at 5 P.M. to exclude normal business hours.
Maximum site subscription crawl depth	Enter the maximum depth level allowed for site Web crawls and downloads to users' computers. Select **0** to restrict user crawls and downloads to just the top-level subscribed page. Users are prevented from specifying Web crawls and downloads deeper than the restriction you specify here.

3. In the System Policies & Restrictions hierarchy, select **Internet Restrictions**, and then select the **Channel Settings** object.

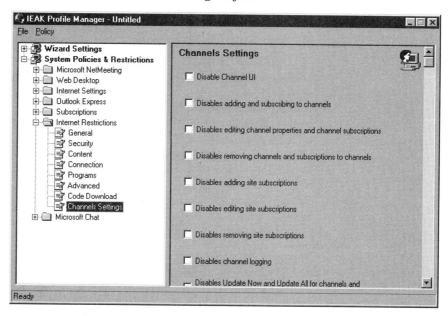

Note The IEAK Profile Manager is shown here, but the **System Policies and Restrictions** page of the IEAK Configuration Wizard works similarly.

---

4. In the right pane, configure the channel settings options.

Option	Description
Disables adding site subscriptions	Select to prevent users from adding site subscriptions.
Disables editing site subscriptions	Select to prevent users from using the **Properties** tab to change site subscription settings.
Disables removing site subscriptions	Select to prevent users from removing or unsubscribing to site subscriptions.
Disables Update Now and Update All for channels and subscriptions	Select to prevent users from manually updating channels or site subscriptions.
Disables all scheduled channel and site subscriptions	Select to prevent automated Web crawls and updates from users' computers.
Disables unattended dialing by subscriptions	Select to prevent automated dial-up connections to update channel and site subscriptions for users who have dial-up connections.

Option	Description
Disables password caching for channel and site subscriptions	Select to prevent users' authentication passwords from being stored and submitted automatically to channels and sites that require user authentication. When this option is selected, users will be prompted to enter the authentication password each time Internet Explorer connects to secure channels or sites.
Disable downloading of site subscription content—change notification will still work	Select to prevent the download of site content to the cache on users' computers. When this option is selected, users cannot browse the site offline.
Disables editing and creating of schedule groups	Select to prevent users from creating custom automated schedules for updates to subscribed channels and sites.

5. Save your changes to the auto-configuration (.ins) file or finish building the custom package, as appropriate.

Beyond Basic Webcasting: Addressing Site-Crawling Issues

While basic Webcasting offers several significant benefits, the technology that it employs, the sitecrawler, has some fundamental limitations and disadvantages that sometimes make it necessary to go beyond basic site subscriptions, namely:

- **Site crawling may be difficult for end users.** While it appears fairly easy to set up a subscription to any Web site, the user is left to make numerous choices, including schedules, process for content delivery, levels and amount of content, and more. This can be confusing for the general end user.

- **Too much information may be downloaded to the hard disk.** If the user wants to monitor a specific piece of information that is a couple levels down on a Web site, the sitecrawler will automatically download all the updated information down to the level the user requested, since the sitecrawler always starts from the top level of the Web tree.

- **Updates offer hit-or-miss usefulness.** With the sitecrawler, users cannot specify types of information; they only can grab all the new and updated information and then sift through it to determine what they need. Additionally, the Web site author has no way to offer organized groups of information to users. The HTML in conventional Web sites provides no cues to help a sitecrawler decide which links point to useful content and which point to useless content. Because no such cues exist, the crawler must rely on a set maximum number of levels and a disk-space limit, and hope that the content downloaded proves useful.

- **A need exists for smart scheduling and site-based control.** With the sitecrawler, the user sets the schedule for when new information should be retrieved, which may not coincide with the actual content updates of the Web site. Conventional Web sites do not advertise content-update schedules, and therefore, a scheduled site crawl may check for updates too often or not often enough. For example, if a Web site publishes updates every day at 3 P.M., but the user has the sitecrawler set to get updates at 2 P.M., the user will clearly miss key updates to the Web site. It would be better if the Web site could instruct the user's PC when to schedule updates.

- **Some Web sites disable site crawling.** Site crawling can cause a heavy load for the Web server, since the site will be entirely crawled by any user who has subscribed to it. Therefore, many Web sites simply do not allow crawling, which prevents basic Webcasting of their information.

- **Organizations have limited control over site subscriptions.** Organizations cannot use basic subscriptions to implement controlled information delivery solutions over the Web, and administrators cannot centrally schedule site updates to optimize intranet performance (although they can specify a block of time when automated site updates are *not* allowed).

To address these site-crawling limitations, Microsoft has introduced the next level of Webcasting—managed Webcasting, discussed in detail in the next chapter.

C H A P T E R   1 6

Managed Webcasting

Active Channels Overview

Managed Webcasting uses the Channel Definition Format (CDF) to create Active Channels, Active Desktop items, and channel screen savers to deliver information to subscribers' desktops. Managed Webcasting overcomes many of the limitations of basic Webcasting and allows Web publishers to optimize, personalize, and control the way sites are seen by subscribers. Managed Webcasting also provides organizations with a streamlined approach to information delivery that can be centrally controlled and fully managed using the Internet Explorer Administration Kit (IEAK).

Managed Webcasting with CDF provides many advantages over simple site subscriptions. By using managed Webcasting, you can:

- Define the subset of a Web site's pages that are actively monitored for changes (site-crawled), which can reduce the amount of network traffic required to monitor for new content.

- Provide a structured view of the content of a site to make user navigation easier and faster.

- Selectively control what subset of pages is downloaded and cached on subscribers' computers for offline viewing to deliver personalized content to individual users' desktops and use the minimal required amount of hard disk space.

- Smart-schedule the channel updates to coincide with scheduled Web site content updates or to take place during optimum network load times.

- Convert an existing Web site into an Active Channel without having to re-author the site or alter it in any way; all that is required is the addition of a CDF file.

Analogies

To understand the benefits that managed Webcasting offers, consider the following analogies. First, CDF offers the ability for users to select the specific content they wish to be downloaded, rather than simply pull large amounts of data from a Web site in the hope that some subset of that information is what they need. In this case, CDF is like a restaurant menu: users select the food (information) they want, and only the food they ordered is delivered to them. Browsing without CDF is like ordering everything on the menu and having to search through the many items on the table for the one dish you want to eat.

CDF also offers the ability to manage the amount of information delivered to users. In this case, CDF could be compared to an automatic sprinkler system that manages the scheduled flow of water to different parts of a lawn. Just as you wouldn't flood your yard to water a small area, users and corporate administrators want to control the "flood" of information to desktops. In this example, CDF is the brains of the sprinkler system (the Web site), which allows users and administrators to control the type and amount of water (information) delivered to the desktop on a scheduled basis.

Scenarios

System administrators can use managed Webcasting to provide a wide variety of information delivery solutions. Possible scenarios include:

- The channel screen saver from the Human Resources department alerts a user that the 401(k) open enrollment period ends in one week. Clicking on the screen-saver hyperlink takes employees directly to the Human Resources Web site.

- A corporate attorney subscribes to a fee-based Active Channel for a legal service. A list of tax-law news summaries displays in an Active Desktop item on the attorney's desktop. A click on a specific news item launches a browser window that provides detailed information about a change to the tax laws.

- A sales representative receives updated price lists on a laptop via one Active Channel, while another Active Channel provides an entire online catalog. In the evenings, a scheduled automatic dial-up connection updates the channel information and highlights changes on the sales representative's laptop. Because the browser downloads only new content, the update takes only a few moments. During the workday, the sales representative accesses the up-to-date information on the laptop while at customer sites.

- A purchasing agent gets notification of a supplier's special pricing programs through an Active Desktop item, which updates daily from the supplier's secured Internet site.

- A credit manager subscribes to an external (fee-based) Active Channel that provides a personalized desktop ticker that delivers news about significant changes in customer credit ratings. A click on the ticker launches a browser window that provides detailed information.

- An executive subscribes to Active Channels providing industry news. Some channels are supplied directly by news providers, while other channels are fed by several electronic news feeds, brought in-house, filtered and categorized, and published internally. When notified that something new has arrived, the executive can scan headlines and decide what to read first.

Understanding Active Channels

Active Channels are typically used to deliver Web content that appears in a subscriber's browser window, but they can also deliver information in two other, innovative ways—as Active Desktop items and as channel screen savers. Active Desktop items deliver miniature Web pages that appear directly on subscribers' desktops and usually contain summary information. Channel screen savers supply Web content that appears as screen savers on users' desktops when their computers are idle.

For information about troubleshooting Webcasting and for Frequently Asked Questions (FAQs) about Active Channels, see Appendix E and I, respectively.

Using Active Channels

Active Channels are Web sites that are defined by Channel Definition Format (CDF) files. Publishers can easily create a CDF file and turn existing Web sites into Active Channels. Active Channels can include any Web content supported by Internet Explorer 4, including Dynamic HTML, ActiveX controls, Visual Basic® Scripting Edition), Java applets, ECMA Script, and Active Server Pages.

The CDF file for an Active Channel typically specifies a channel hierarchy or table of contents for the Web pages that make up the Active Channel. When users subscribe to a channel, the channel appears in the Desktop Channel bar and the Internet Explorer Channel bar. The channel hierarchy defined in the CDF file appears in the Internet Explorer Channel bar. Channels can contain items that appear under the top-level channel in the Channel bar. When a user clicks the top-level channel, the lower-level items appear. Each item typically represents a Web page, but can represent any URL. When a user clicks an item in the Channel bar hierarchy, the corresponding Web page displays in the browser.

Channels can also include subchannels. Subchannels appear under the top-level channel, similar to items. Each subchannel, however, can also contain items. When a user clicks a subchannel, the items appear under the subchannel. Subchannels provide a good way to organize channels that contain a large number of Web pages.

When a user subscribes to an Active Channel, Internet Explorer reads and downloads the CDF file to the user's computer. All customization options available for site subscriptions are available for channel subscriptions, except users do not specify the depth levels for site crawls. Users can choose not to download any updated content, download all content specified by the publisher (in the CDF file), or download just the Web pages for the channel and subchannels (in which case Web content referenced by items is not downloaded). Downloaded Web content is cached, and users can browse the channel offline.

Channel updates use scheduled Web crawls. Users can accept the publisher's schedule (specified in the CDF file) for updates or specify a custom update schedule. When updated content is available for a channel, the red gleam appears in the left corner of the icon for the top-level channel. A red gleam does not appear for individual channel items or subchannels.

Users can also choose to be notified of updates by e-mail, and publishers can specify that the actual updated Web pages can be e-mailed to users. The updated Web pages display directly in mail programs that support HTML Mail and appear as attachments for mail programs that do not support HTML.

Using Active Desktop Items

Active Channels may be used as Active Desktop items, which appear directly in borderless frames on users' desktops. Desktop items can contain any standard Web content, including Dynamic HTML, ActiveX controls, VBScript, Java applets, ECMA Script, and Active Server Pages. Desktop items are typically designed to provide summary information in a small amount of screen space. Therefore, information items in desktop components often include hyperlinks or hot spots, so users can click a designated area to open a new browser and obtain the details they need. Possible desktop item applications include:

- **A ticker showing current stock quotes for a corporation.** An employee can click a hotspot to open a browser window that displays the home page for the corporation's employee stock option program.

- **A scrolling headline list of announcements or news stories.** When a user clicks a headline, a new browser window opens, displaying an executive summary of the news item or announcement with links to more detailed information, such as the full text of news articles.

- **A list of key employee services provided by an organization, such as help desk, payroll, and employee benefit services.** When a user clicks a list item, a new browser window opens displaying a page with relevant information and links for the appropriate service.

- **A scrolling list of available new software updates.** When a user clicks a list item, a new browser window opens, displaying a page with instructions for downloading the software update to the user's computer.

Desktop items should be designed to take up the minimum amount of desktop space necessary. For example, you could use scrolling lists to show a long list of items in a small amount of space.

Subscriptions to Active Desktop items work like regular Active Channel subscriptions. When updates for Active Desktop items are available, however, users are not notified by a gleam, because updated content automatically appears in the desktop frame.

For more information about the Internet Explorer 4 Active Desktop interface and desktop items, see Part 3, "True Web Integration: Windows Desktop Update."

Using Channel Screen Savers

The Internet Explorer 4 screen saver supports HTML pages. Screen-saver pages can use Dynamic HTML, ActiveX controls, VBScript, Java applets, or ECMA Script to provide a page that dynamically changes the content, style, and position of HTML elements on the screen. These pages are displayed on the full screen when the computer is idle. The Internet Explorer screen saver cycles through all enabled channel screen savers, allocating the same amount of display time to each one (by default, 30 seconds per channel).

Unlike many common screen savers, in a channel screen saver, the user can move the mouse and click objects without immediately dismissing the Internet Explorer screen saver. Clicking a link opens a new browser window and dismisses the screen saver. Clicking a point that is not an image, link, or object closes the screen saver. The user can also click the **Pause**, **Close**, and **Properties** buttons in the screen saver toolbar to change the current behavior.

Understanding CDF Files

Channel Definition Format files are standard text files. A bare-bones CDF file contains nothing but a list of URLs pointing to content. This type of file is easy to create and requires no changes to existing HTML pages. A more advanced CDF file can also include a schedule for content updates, a hierarchical organization of the URLs describing the Web site structure, and title/abstract information describing individual content items. Structured similarly to HTML files, CDF files are based on the open Extensible Markup Language (XML) standard.

CDF provides structured content indexing, independent of content format. It provides an index or map of a Web site that describes the type of information contained on the site. Specifically, CDF describes logical groupings of information (such as sports news versus financial information), providing hierarchical structure and category information about a site. Because this information is completely independent of content format, a CDF-based channel can include any kind of Web content or applications built on HTML, JavaScript, Java, or ActiveX technology. Because the CDF file defines what site content is included in the channel, but contains no Web content itself, a channel's CDF file can remain unchanged, even if the Web content changes regularly.

The CDF mechanism makes channel creation a simple, two-step process that does not require authoring of new content, does not require re-authoring of existing content, and does not require any programming—on either client or server. Creating a channel with CDF can be as simple as (1) writing a CDF file with a list of URLs pointing to existing content and (2) linking to this CDF file to make it discoverable.

CDF Link-Crawl Architecture

Channels add an extra dimension to the link-crawl process. The channel, using a CDF file, lets the content provider customize the content download; it's more like a programmed link crawl. Using CDF files, content providers can segment their data into specific types of content—without having to alter the Web site. A CDF file contains a list of HTML tags that reference specific Web pages on the site. A content provider would create one CDF file for each type of content he or she wants to designate on the site. For example, a news channel might have separate CDF files for sports, entertainment, politics, and so forth. Subscribers can choose to monitor specific CDF files and only download the pages pointed to by that file.

- Webcheck.dll creates the subscription and maintains the schedule of updates.
- Icmp.dll uses the page header to check whether the CDF file has changed.
- Msml.dll parses the CDF file. This file is also involved during the MIME download of the CDF.

- Cdfview.dll processes and applies the CDF file and updates the Channel bar for viewing purposes. It also makes registry entries for the channel.

- Shdocvw.dll and Mshtml.dll actually display the Web content in the browser and download the content to the local cache.

Other files are involved in the process, but these are the major items involved and their primary focus.

Creating CDF Files

The common tags used in a CDF file to create a channel are listed below, followed by two examples of code showing the tags in use. For a detailed CDF reference and guidelines for creating Active Channels, Active Desktop items, and channel screen savers, see the *Microsoft Internet Client SDK*.

For information about troubleshooting Webcasting and for Frequently Asked Questions (FAQs) about Active Channels, see Appendix E and I, respectively.

Define an XML document
<?XML VERSION=*"n.n"***?>**

This tag specifies that this file is an XML document and indicates the version of XML that this file supports. This header is required in every CDF file.

Create a channel
<CHANNEL> and **</CHANNEL>**

These tags note the beginning and ending of a channel or subchannel. The <CHANNEL> tag is used to specify the channel structure and can reference a URL, normally a Web page, that appears when the channel is clicked in the Channel bar. A channel can also include an unlimited number of <ITEM> tags. Items are used to reference URLs, such as HTML pages and other supporting Web content for the channel. Items can appear under the channel in the Internet Explorer Channel bar. When a <CHANNEL> tag is found within another <CHANNEL> tag, this is called nesting, and it creates a subchannel. A subchannel typically focuses on a specific area of content.

The CHANNEL element can include the following attributes:

- **HREF=**"*url*" where *url* specifies the Web page for the channel or subchannel.
- **BASE=**"*url*" where *url* specifies the base URL for the channel. A base URL can be used to resolve relative URLs specified in ITEM elements and subchannels contained within this channel.
- **LEVEL=**"*n*" where *n* specifies the number of levels or links deep that the sitecrawler crawls from this channel.
- **SELF=**"*url*" where *url* is used to specify the URL of this CDF file. This attribute is unnecessary and is only supported for backward compatibility.

  ```
  <CHANNEL HREF="http://www.samplesports.com/samplesports.htm">
  </CHANNEL>
  ```

Title of channel
```
<TITLE> and </TITLE>
```

These tags provide a text title for the channel.

```
<TITLE >SampleSports</TITLE>
```

Mouse-over ToolTip information
```
<Abstract> and </Abstract>
```

These tags mark text to be displayed as a ToolTip when the pointer is held over a particular item within the channel.

```
<ABSTRACT>The latest in sports and athletics from
SampleSports</ABSTRACT>
```

Automatic download scheduling of channel
<SCHEDULE>, **<EARLIESTTIME>**, **<LATESTTIME>**, **<INTERVALTIME>**, and **</SCHEDULE>**

Use these tags to let the content provider schedule the best time to check for changes to the channel. These can be overridden by the user.

```
<SCHEDULE ENDDATE="1994.11.05T08:15-0500">
<INTERVALTIME DAY="1" />
<EARLIESTTIME HOUR="12" />
<LATESTTIME HOUR="18" />
    </SCHEDULE>
```

Visual picture or logo
<LOGO>

This tag points to a graphic used as the logo of the Active Channel. The <LOGO> tag can have a style of IMAGE or ICON. The Image type defines the large image displayed on the Channel bar on the desktop and in Internet Explorer. The Icon type defines the image displayed in the **Favorites** menu.

```
<LOGO HREF="http://www.samplesports.com/images/logo.gif" STYLE="ICON" />
```

Channel content
<ITEM> and </ITEM>

These tags typically represent individual pages of content on the Web site to be displayed in the channel. ITEM elements can contain the following attributes:

- **HREF=**"*url*" where *url* specifies the Web page.
- **LASTMOD=**"*date*" where *date* indicate the last time the Web page was modified. You can use this attribute to report Web content updates to the sitecrawler, so the sitecrawler doesn't need to crawl the site, but just downloads content that has changed.
- **LEVEL=**"*n*" where *n* specifies the number of levels or links deep that the sitecrawler crawls from this item.
- **PRECACHE=**"Yes" | "No" where Yes or No specifies whether to download the Web page to the cache on users' computers. Specify No to prevent sitecrawlers from downloading the Web page to the cache.

An <ITEM> tag can point to any Web content, HTML pages, ActiveX controls, Java applets, ActiveMovie™ files, AVIs, animations, and so on.

```
<ITEM HREF="http://www.samplesports.com/articles/
a1.html" LastMod="1994.11.05T08:15-0500"></ITEM>
```

Usage of the channel

<USAGE VALUE="*UsageType*" />

A <USAGE> tag can follow an <ITEM> tag or the top-level <CHANNEL> tag to specify how the item or channel should be used. You can specify one or more USAGE elements per ITEM element. The *UsageType* can be one of the following:

- **"Channel"** to specify that an item appears in the Channel bar hierarchy. This is the default usage if now USAGE element is included.

- **"Email"** to specify that the Web page can be sent to users via e-mail to notify them of updated content. Users must enable e-mail notification for the channel before the Web page is actually sent via e-mail. Browsers that support HTML will view the Web page online; otherwise, the Web page is included as an attachment.

- **"None"** to specify that an item does not appear in the Channel bar hierarchy. You can use this value to include support content, such as ActiveX controls or Java Applets, you don't want to appear on the Channel bar.

- **"DesktopComponent"** to specify that a channel is a desktop item that appears directly in an invisible frame on the desktop instead of on the Channel bar. (Desktops items also require a closing tag: </USAGE>, as shown in the second example CDF file below.)

- **"ScreenSaver"** to specify that an item is used as a channel screen saver.

- **"SoftwareUpdate"** to specify that the channel is a software distribution channel and appears in the Favorites **Software Updates** folder instead of on the Channel bar.

  ```
  <USAGE VALUE="ScreenSaver" />
  ```

Logging user activities back to the Internet

<LOG> and <LOGTARGET>

These tags are used to specify that user actions get submitted back to the Web server. The <LOG> tag is used to specify which items need to be tracked, and the <LOGTARGET> tag specifies where to send the data and how.

<LOGTARGET HREF="http://www.samplesports.com/tracking"
METHOD="POST" SCOPE="OFFLINE" >

You can use the LOG and LOGTARGET elements to gather statistics on which Web pages users access on your Web site, even when you are offline. Statistics are logged when users browse cached Web pages offline, and the statistics are reported back to the Web server the next time users connect to the Internet.

Example of a CDF File

The following example shows a CDF file for a fictional news service named
Action News. When expanded, this channel appears in the Internet Explorer
Channel bar with the following structure:

Action News Channel
    The Market
        Business nirvana: low inflation, high growth
        Tech stocks soar on XYZ Corp. news

```
<?XML VERSION="1.0" ENCODING="UTF-8"?>
<CHANNEL HREF="home.htm"
    BASE="http://www.action.com/channel/" >
    <TITLE>Action News Channel</TITLE>
    <ABSTRACT>Description of the Action News Channel</ABSTRACT>
    <LOGO HREF="ActionLogo16x16.gif" STYLE="ICON"/>
    <LOGO HREF="ActionLogo32x80.gif" STYLE="IMAGE"/>
    <SCHEDULE STARTDATE="1997-10-17" ENDDATE="1997-10-17">
        <INTERVALTIME DAY="1"/>
    </SCHEDULE>

    <CHANNEL HREF="bus001.htm">
        <TITLE>The Market</TITLE>
        <ABSTRACT>"Summary of today's market news"</ABSTRACT>
        <LOGO HREF="marketLogo.gif" STYLE="ICON"/>

        <ITEM HREF="bus002.htm" LASTMOD="1997-10-17T11:12"
            PRECACHE="Yes" LEVEL="1">
            <TITLE>Business nirvana: low inflation, high growth</TITLE>
            <ABSTRACT>Best environment for business in 25 years due to
                convergence of factors.
            </ABSTRACT>
            <LOGO HREF="TopStoryLogo.gif" STYLE="ICON"/>
        </ITEM>

        <ITEM HREF="bus003.htm" LASTMOD="1997-10-17T11:15">
            PRECACHE="Yes" LEVEL="1">
            <TITLE>Tech stocks soar on XYZ Corp. news </TITLE>
            <ABSTRACT>XYZ Corp. showed unexpected growth this quarter,
                dragging up prices through the technology segment.
            </ABSTRACT>
            <LOGO HREF="TopStoryLogo.gif" STYLE="ICON"/>
        </ITEM>

        <ITEM HREF="control1.ocx">
            PRECACHE="Yes">
            <USAGE VALUE="None" />
        </ITEM>
    </CHANNEL>

</CHANNEL>
```

In this example CDF file:

- **CHANNEL HREF ="home.htm"** references the home page for Action News. When users click the top-level channel, the home page displays in the right pane of the browser.

- **CHANNEL HREF="bus001.htm"** is the top-level page for the news category "The Market." When users click the subchannel, this page displays in the right pane of the browser.

- **ITEM HREF="bus002.htm"** is a news article. When users click the item, the news article displays in the right pane of the browser.

- **LASTMOD="1997-10-17T11:12"** specifies the last time the page bus002.htm was updated. This notifies Internet Explorer when an update is available and a site crawl performed only to download updated content. Use this attribute to speed up updates and help reduce server load from Web crawls.

- **PRECACHE="Yes"** specifies that the news articles are downloaded to the users' hard disk cache for offline browsing. Use "No" to specify that the content for this item is not downloaded to the cache.

- **LEVEL="1"** specifies that Web crawls go one level deep from bus002.htm and download content to the cache. Use this attribute to specify additional content you want to be available for offline browsing. You can also use this attribute with the CHANNEL element. When this attribute is omitted, the default value is LEVEL="0" and Web crawls do not go deeper than the specified URL.

- **ITEM HREF="bus003.htm"** is a second news article. When users click the item, the news article displays in the right pane of the browser.

- **ITEM HREF="control1.ocx"** is an ActiveX control needed for offline browsing. This control is downloaded to the subscribers' cache so the channel will function properly when offline.

- **USAGE VALUE="None"** specifies that control1.ocx does not appear in the Channel bar hierarchy and is used only to download control1.ocx to the subscribers' cache for offline browsing.

In this example, you could easily add more subchannels and news items for more news categories. Although you can add an unlimited number of subchannels and items, you should limit subchannels and items to a manageable number. It's best to create a channel hierarchy that easily fits in the browser window when fully expanded. You should also limit the content that is downloaded to an appropriate amount to conserve bandwidth as well as subscribers' hard disk space.

Keep in mind that the Channel bar displays a navigable outline of the URLs you specify in a CDF file. The exposed hierarchy of the channel helps users efficiently navigate through a channel to find the content that most interests them.

Another Example of a CDF File

This example shows a CDF file for a desktop item. (Another example of a CDF
file for a desktop item and more information about creating desktop items is
available in the "Developing Active Desktop Items" section of Chapter 14,
"Active Desktop.")

```
<CHANNEL HREF="http://www.samplesports.com/samplesports.htm">
<SELF HREF="http://www.samplesports.com/channels/ch1.cdf"/>
<TITLE>SampleSports</TITLE>
<ABSTRACT>The latest in sports and athletics from
    SampleSports</ABSTRACT>
<SCHEDULE ENDDATE="1994.11.05T08:15-0500">
<INTERVALTIME DAY="1" />
<EARLIESTTIME HOUR="12" />
<LATESTTIME HOUR="18" />
</SCHEDULE>
<LOGO HREF="http://www.samplesports.com/images/logo.gif" STYLE="ICON" />
<ITEM HREF="http://www.samplesports.com/articles/a1.html"
    LASTMOD="1994.11.05T08:15-0500">
<TITLE>How to get the most out of your mountain bike</TITLE>
<ABSTRACT>20 tips on how to work your mountain-bike to the bone and come
    out on top. </ABSTRACT>
<LOG VALUE="document:view" />
</ITEM>
<CHANNEL>
<TITLE>SampleSports News</TITLE>
<ABSTRACT>Up-to-date daily sports news from SampleSports</ABSTRACT>
<LOGO HREF="http://www.samplesports.com/images/newslogo.gif"
    STYLE="ICON"/>
<LOGO HREF="http://www.samplesports.com/images/newslogowide.gif"
    STYLE="IMAGE"/>
<ITEM HREF="http://www.samplesports.com/articles/news1.html"
    LASTMOD="1994.11.05T08:15-0500" >
<TITLE>Michael Jordan does it again!</TITLE>
<ABSTACT>Led by Michael Jordan in scoring, the Chicago Bulls make it to
    the playoffs again! </ABSTRACT>
<LOG VALUE="document:view" />
</ITEM>
<ITEM HREF="http://www.samplesports.com/articles/news2.html"
    LASTMOD="1994.11.05T08:15-0500" >
<TITLE>Islanders winning streak ends</TITLE>
<ABSTRACT>The New York Islanders' 10-game winning streak ended with a
    disappointing loss to the Rangers"</ABSTRACT>
<LOG VALUE="document:view" />
</ITEM>
</CHANNEL>
<ITEM HREF="http://www.samplesports.com/animations/scrnsvr.html" >
<USAGE VALUE="ScreenSaver"></USAGE>
</ITEM>
```

```
<ITEM HREF="http://www.samplesports.com/ticker.html"
    LASTMOD="1994.11.05T08:15-0500" >
<TITLE>SampleSports News Ticker"</TITLE>
<ABSTRACT>The latest sports headlines from SampleSports"</ABSTRACT>
<USAGE VALUE="DesktopComponent">
<WIDTH VALUE="400" />
<HEIGHT VALUE="80" />
</USAGE>
</ITEM>
<LOGTARGET HREF="http://www.samplesports.com/tracking" METHOD="POST"
    SCOPE="OFFLINE" >
<PURGETIME HOUR="12"  />
<HTTP-EQUIV NAME="encoding-type" VALUE="gzip" />
</LOGTARGET>
</CHANNEL>
```

Item Usage

Not all tagged ITEM elements appear in the Channel bar. The ITEM elements can include the USAGE element to specify how the item is used. When the <USAGE> tag is omitted, the default is USAGE VALUE="Channel", which specifies that the referenced URL appears in the Channel bar hierarchy.

USAGE VALUE="Email" specifies that the referenced URL is sent as an e-mail to subscribed users whenever content is updated. However, users must choose the e-mail notification as a subscription option before an e-mail can be sent.

USAGE VALUE="None" specifies that the referenced URL does not appear in the Channel bar. The URL is downloaded to the subscribers' cache when PRECACHE="No". Use USAGE VALUE="None" to download Web content such as ActiveX controls or Java applets that you want to download to subscribers' caches to support offline browsing.

Publisher's Schedule

Publishers can specify a schedule using the SCHEDULE element as a child element in the first CHANNEL element. All subchannels and items in a CDF file are updated according to this schedule. It's a good idea to specify schedules that optimize network and server load. It's also helpful to randomize the time that subscribers update the channel, to prevent all subscribers from updating at the same time. The following sample schedule would cause the channel to be updated every day at a random time between 2 A.M. and 6 A.M.

```
<SCHEDULE>
    <INTERVALTIME DAY="1" />
    <EARLIESTTIME HOUR="2" />
    <LATESTTIME HOUR="6" />
</SCHEDULE>
```

Users can accept the publisher's schedule for updates or can specify a custom-update schedule. System administrators, however, can use the IEAK Configuration Wizard and the IEAK Profile Manager to lock down schedule options. For example, you can prevent users from changing the channel schedule and ensure that users use the publisher's schedule that you specify. For more information, see "Locking Down Active Channels and Desktop Items" later in this chapter.

Active Desktop Items

You can designate a specific URL as a desktop item by including the **USAGE VALUE="DesktopComponent"** attribute in the channel's CDF file. This must always be nested within the first ITEM element in the file. You also must close the usage section with a closing tag: **</USAGE>**, as shown in the following example.

```
<?XML VERSION="1.0"?>
<CHANNEL>
        <SCHEDULE ENDDATE="1998.11.05T08:15-0500">
        <INTERVALTIME DAY="1"  />
        <EARLIESTTIME HOUR="12"/>
        <LATESTTIME   HOUR="18"/>
</SCHEDULE>
    <ITEM HREF="http://www.XYZ.com/desktop.asp"
        LASTMOD="1996.11.05T08:15-0500">
        <TITLE>My News Ticker</TITLE>
        <USAGE VALUE="DeskopComponent">
            <OPENAS VALUE="HTML"/>
            <WIDTH VALUE="200" />
            <HEIGHT VALUE="80"  />
            <CANRESIZE VALUE="Yes"/>
        </USAGE>
    </ITEM>

        <ITEM HREF="control2.ocx">
            PRECACHE="Yes">
            <USAGE VALUE="None">
    </ITEM>
</CHANNEL>
```

Use the HEIGHT and WIDTH attributes to specify the size in pixels of the display frame on the user's desktop. By default, users can resize the frames on their desktops. However, you can specify the **CANRESIZE="No"** attribute to prevent users from resizing the frame.

Desktop items can contain unlimited ITEM elements that do not appear in the desktop frame. For example, extra items can reference support content, such as ActiveX controls or audio files, that needs to be downloaded to the cache on the subscriber's hard disk to enable offline use of the desktop item.

For more information about Active Desktop items, see Chapter 14.

Channel Screen Savers

You can designate specific URLs as screen-saver pages by nesting the **USAGE VALUE="ScreenSaver"** attribute within ITEM elements in the top-level channel.

```
<ITEM HREF="http://www.companyXYZ.com/screensaver.htm">
    <USAGE VALUE="ScreenSaver" />
</ITEM>
```

Note If **USAGE VALUE="ScreenSaver"** occurs within an ITEM element within a subchannel, the screen saver will be ignored.

Channel screen savers should download supporting content, such as ActiveX controls and Java applets, needed for the screen saver to function offline. Use additional ITEM elements with the PRECACHE="Yes" attribute and the USAGE VALUE="None" element to download support content to subscribers' caches.

Personalized Webcasts

You can personalize Webcasts by configuring your Web servers to dynamically generate CDF files and HTML pages for individual users or user groups. You need server software, such as Microsoft Internet Information Server, that supports generating dynamic CDF and HTML. You also need a way to identify users; you can use network user profiles or HTTP cookies to do this.

For example, when a user subscribes to a personalized channel, the Web server generates a CDF file based on predefined criteria and user preferences. An HTML form is used to query users for information and preferences during the subscription process. User information and preferences are then stored in a database on the server and in a cookie on the user's computer.

For an intranet news channel, you could configure the Web server so users in different departments receive different CDF files specifying news items related to their department. The URLs contained in the CDF file can also reference dynamically generated and personalized content. For more information about generating dynamic Web content, see the documentation for your Web server software.

In order for the dynamically generated CDF to be recognized, it must have the proper MIME/content type: **application/x-cdf.** To generate a CDF response from Internet Information Server Active Server Pages, the following line of code must be placed at the top of the page that generates the CDF:

```
<% Response.ContentType = "application/x-cdf" %>
```

Without this line, browsers will not perform the expected actions for CDF files. For example, the CDF file could be displayed as text in the browser window rather than launch the channel Subscription Wizard.

Example of a Personalized Channel

As an example, a software company could provide an Active Channel that would allow users to receive the latest information on software products, including support information on these products. In order to be effective, a personalized channel could be employed so that a user gets information only on products about which he or she is interested, rather than every product manufactured by that company.

The following steps illustrate how a software company, such as Microsoft, could create a personalized channel to provide product information, using Active Server Pages (ASP):

1. Create an .htm page that allows users to select the Microsoft products they want information about and save the file as Products.htm.

   Products.htm uses a form to query users which product they want information on. (For simplicity, this example includes only two of the Microsoft products currently available.)

```
<HTML>
    <TITLE>Microsoft Custom Subscription List</TITLE>
    <FONT FACE="VERDANA,ARIAL,HELVETICA" SIZE="2">
    <H1>Microsoft Custom Product Subscription List</H1>

    <FONT FACE="courier" SIZE="3">
    <PRE>
    <FORM METHOD="GET" ACTION="GenCDF.asp">
        <INPUT TYPE="checkbox" Name="IE4"     VALUE="1">Internet
            Explorer
        <INPUT TYPE="checkbox" Name="InetSDK" VALUE="1">Internet
            Client SDK
    </PRE>
    </FONT>
        <INPUT TYPE=SUBMIT Value="Subscribe" Name="Validate" >
    </FORM>
</HTML>
```

2. Create an .asp file that uses the information submitted from the form in Products.htm to dynamically generate the personalized CDF file. Save this file as Gencdf.asp.

   Gencdf.asp uses VBScript to generate the personalized CDF file for each user.

```
<%@ LANGUAGE=VBScript %>
<%
IE4 = Request ("IE4")
InetSDK = Request ("InetSDK")
%>
```

```
<% Response.ContentType = "application/x-cdf" %>

<?XML VERSION="1.0"?>
    <CHANNEL HREF="http://www.microsoft.com">
        <TITLE>Sample MS Custom Channel</TITLE>
    <ABSTRACT>Demo Channel on how to get a customized subscription
    using ASPs</ABSTRACT>

        <SCHEDULE>
            <INTERVALTIME DAY ="1" />
            <EARLIESTTIME HOUR="1" />
            <LATESTTIME HOUR="5" />
        </SCHEDULE>

<% If Not IE4 = 0 Then %>
    <CHANNEL HREF="http://www.microsoft.com/ie/ie40">
        <TITLE>IE4 Support Page</TITLE>
        <ABSTRACT>IE4 Product Page</ABSTRACT>
        <ITEM HREF="http://www.microsoft.com/iesupport">
        <ABSTRACT>This is where you can get all your questions on
          IE4 answered.</ABSTRACT>
    </ITEM>
    </CHANNEL>
<% End if %>

<% If Not InetSDK = 0 Then %>
    <CHANNEL HREF="http://www.microsoft.com/workshop/prog/inetsdk">
        <TITLE>Internet Client SDK</TITLE>
        <ABSTRACT>Internet Client SDK Product Page</ABSTRACT>
        <ITEM HREF="http://www.microsoft.com/support/inetsdk">
            <TITLE>Internet Client SDK Support Page</TITLE>
            <ABSTRACT>This is where you can get all your questions on
              IE4 programmability answered. </ABSTRACT>
        </ITEM>
</CHANNEL>
<% End if %>
</CHANNEL>
```

Again, note that CDF files that are dynamically generated through ASP
should have the following line inserted at the top of the CDF file (before
any CDF lines):

```
<% Response.ContentType = "application/x-cdf" %>
```

This ensures that servers return the MIME/content type "application/x-cdf." Problems with CDF files being displayed inside the browser as HTML text rather than presenting a Subscription Wizard are very likely caused by the server returning an incorrect MIME type of "text/html."

Note As an alternative for IIS 4.0 site authors, the CDF file can be created with a .cdx extension, instead of .asp, and the MIME content type line above can be omitted.

- For simplicity, the <LOGO> tags have been omitted in the sample CDF file. As a result, the default satellite dish logo is displayed in the Desktop Channel bar and in the Channel pane.

3. Place the Products.htm and Gencdf.asp files in the same directory on an IIS Server and then on he Internet Explorer address bar.

When users browse to the Web page (Products.htm), they fill out the form and submit the form to obtain the information they want for the specified product. The ASP page Gencdf.asp generates the personalized CDF file, and the Subscription Wizard opens so users can subscribe to the personalized channel. The personalized channel provides information on the product the user selected.

Design Guidelines for Active Channels

To take true advantage of the Webcasting mechanism available in Internet Explorer 4, channels should be as small as possible to minimize download time and provide compelling content and interactions when used offline. These guidelines will assist you in designing an effective Active Channel:

- Channels intended for offline use should consider the impact of bandwidth limitations. If the target user is a remote user dialing over a modem, the average amount of content delivered per update per channel should be no more than 500 KB to 1 MB, preferably smaller. Under ideal conditions, a megabyte of content can be downloaded via a 28.8K modem in about 6 minutes. In practice, however, depending on line and server conditions, downloading a megabyte takes about 10 minutes.
- Active Channels should be self-contained. The channel must deliver real value to the user while offline. It is likely that users will become annoyed with an offline channel that constantly forces online connections. This means that links to noncached resources should be minimized or hidden when the user is offline. Scripting can be used on an HTML page to determine when the user is offline and re-flow the page accordingly, using Dynamic HTML.

- Channels should be personalized whenever possible. A publisher can provide a personalized channel experience for each user by generating a custom CDF file for each user (based on user preferences stored in a cookie). Channels based on personalized CDF files can be more rapidly delivered, because content that is not important to the user will not be downloaded.

For design guidelines specifically related to Active Desktop items, see "Developing Active Desktop Items," in Chapter 14, "Active Desktop."

Subscribing to Active Channels and Desktop Items

You subscribe to an Active Channel or Active Desktop item by opening the URL for the channel's CDF file. Publishers of Active Channels and desktop items normally provide a link that you can click to subscribe.

▶ **To subscribe to an Active Channel**

1. While browsing the site, click the subscription link.

   (To get to the site, you can enter the URL and CDF file name directly into the Internet Explorer Address bar or, on the **File** menu, click **Open**, and enter the information in the resulting dialog box.)

2. In the **Add Active Channel** dialog box, select one of the following subscription options:

   - **Yes, but only tell me when updates occur** to subscribe, but not download, updated content to the cache.

   - **Yes, notify me of updates and download the channel for offline viewing** to subscribe and download channel content to the cache.

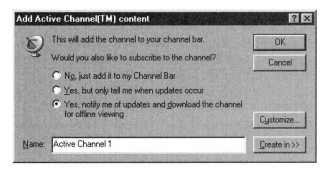

3. To customize subscription options, click **Customize** and use the Subscription Wizard to configure subscription options. For more information, see "Customizing Active Channels and Desktop Items" next in this chapter.

4. Click **OK**.

▶ **To subscribe to an Active Desktop Item**

1. While browsing the site, click the subscription link.

   (If you know the URL and the CDF file name, you can get to the site by entering the URL and file name directly into Internet Explorer's Address bar or, on the **File** menu, click **Open**, and enter the information in the resulting dialog box.)

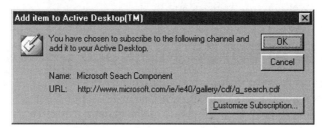

2. To customize subscription options, click **Customize Subscription**, and use the Subscription Wizard to configure subscription options. For more information, see "Customizing Active Channels and Desktop Items" next in this chapter.

3. Click **OK**.

Customizing Active Channels and Desktop Items

You can customize most Active Channel and Active Desktop item options by using the Subscription Wizard when you subscribe to sites. After subscribing to a channel or desktop item, you can use the **Receiving** and **Schedule** tabs in the channel's **Properties** dialog box to configure all subscription options.

Most of the customization options for channels are the same as the customization options for subscriptions. (For more information, see "Customizing Subscriptions" in Chapter 15, "Basic Webcasting.") However, the content download options for the **Advanced Download Options** dialog box are different for channels and are described below.

▶ **To configure advanced download options**

1. On the **Favorites menu**, click **Manage Subscriptions**.

2. In the **Manage Subscriptions** dialog box, right-click the channel or desktop item to which you want to subscribe, and click **Properties** on the shortcut menu.

3. Click the **Receiving** tab.

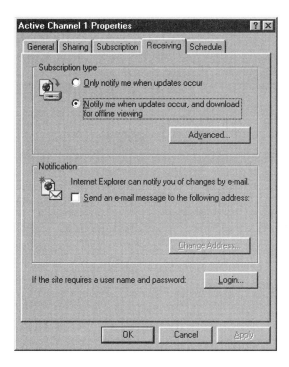

4. On the **Receiving** tab, click **Advanced**.

5. In the **Advanced Download Options** dialog box, configure the options.

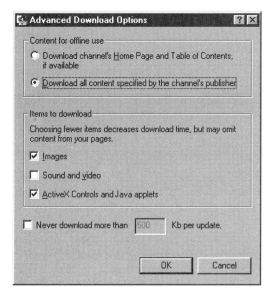

Option	Description
Download channel's Home Page and Table of Contents, if available	Select to download the top-level channel's home page and all subchannel pages as specified in the CDF file. When this option is selected, URLs referenced by ITEM elements are not downloaded, and the Web site may not function properly when browsed offline.
Download all content specified by the channel's publisher	Select to download all channels and items specified in the CDF file.
Images	Clear to prevent downloading graphical images when Internet Explorer updates the selected Web site. If you choose not to download images, the Web site may appear incomplete or not display properly when browsed offline.
Sound and video	Clear to prevent downloading sound and video files when Internet Explorer updates the selected Web site. If you choose not to download these files, the Web site may not function properly when browsed offline.
ActiveX Controls and Java applets	Clear to prevent downloading ActiveX controls and Java applets when Internet Explorer updates the selected Web site. If you choose not to download these programs, the Web site may not function properly when browsed offline.
Never download more than __ Kb per update.	Select this option and enter the number of kilobytes to limit the maximum amount of information that Internet Explorer downloads to your hard disk from this Web site for each update.

6. Click **OK**.

You can also accept the publisher's recommended update schedule using the channel's **Schedule** tab.

▶ **To accept the publisher's schedule**

1. On the **Favorites** menu, click **Manage Subscriptions**.

2. In the **Manage Subscriptions** dialog box, right-click the channel or desktop component to which you want to subscribe, and click **Properties** on the shortcut menu.

3. Click the **Schedule** tab.

4. Select **Scheduled**.

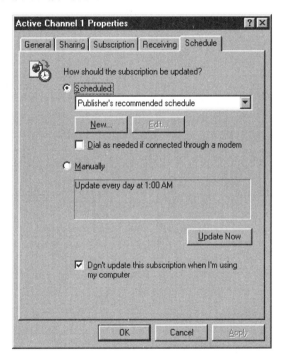

5. Select the publisher's schedule from the list of schedules.

6. Click **OK**.

Deploying Custom Packages with Predefined Channels for User Groups

System administrators can use the IEAK 4 Configuration Wizard to build custom packages with pre-configured Active Channels and Active Desktop items for their organizations. Using the IEAK, you can also build custom packages with specific settings for different user groups. (For more information, see "Building Custom Packages" in Chapter 36, "Implementing the Deployment.")

To create a custom package, you configure the Active Channels and Active Desktop items (components) on the computer running the IEAK Configuration Wizard and then import the channel and desktop item settings using the **Customize the Active Channel bar** and **Specify Active Desktop Components** pages of the wizard.

▶ **To import Active Channels**

1. On the **Customize the Active Channel bar** page of the IEAK Configuration Wizard, select **Import current channel configuration**.

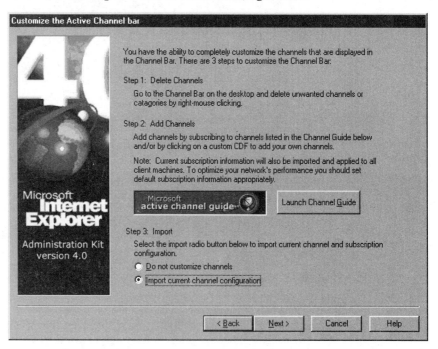

2. Click **Next**.

▶ **To import Active Desktop items (components)**

1. On the **Specify Active Desktop Components** page of the IEAK Configuration Wizard, select **Import the current Active Desktop components**.

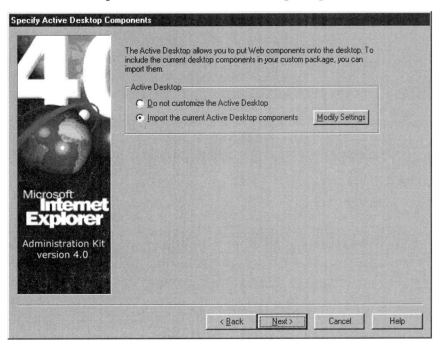

2. Click **Next**.

Finish building the custom package, as necessary.

The Active Channel and Active Desktop item configurations you imported from the current desktop are installed on users' desktops when the custom package is deployed. You can also lock down Active Channel and desktop item settings so users cannot modify the settings.

Locking Down Active Channels and Desktop Items

Once you've built your custom packages, you can use the IEAK Configuration Wizard to lock down channel options and restrict users from changing settings. After browsers are deployed, you can use the IEAK Profile Manager to lock down channel options for user groups that have automatic browser configuration implemented. (For more information about automatic browser configuration, see Chapter 37, "Automatic Browser Configuration.")

▶ **To lock down channel options**

1. On the **System Policies and Restrictions** page of the IEAK Configuration Wizard or at the IEAK Profile Manager, in the System Policies & Restrictions hierarchy, select **Subscriptions**, and then select the **Subscriptions** object.

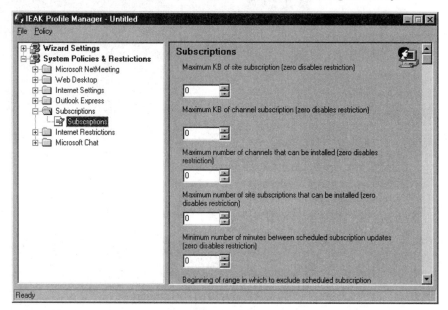

> **Note** The IEAK Profile Manager is shown here, but the **System Policies and Restrictions** page of the IEAK Configuration Wizard works similarly.

2. In the right pane, configure the subscription options.

Option	Description
Maximum KB of channel subscription (zero disables restriction)	Enter the maximum kilobytes that can be downloaded per channel update for each user. Users are prevented from downloading more than the specified number of kilobytes per channel update.
Maximum number of channel subscriptions that can be installed (zero disables restriction)	Enter the maximum number of channel subscriptions that can be installed on users' computers. Users are prevented from installing more than the specified number of channels locally.

3. In the System Policies & Restrictions hierarchy, select **Internet Restrictions**, and then select the **Channels Settings** object.

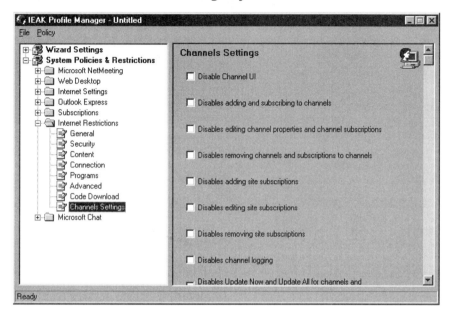

Note The IEAK Profile Manager is shown here, but the **System Policies and Restrictions** page of the IEAK Configuration Wizard works similarly.

4. In the right pane, configure the channels settings options.

Option	Description
Disable Channel UI	Select to prevent users from using the Active Channel interface. When this option is selected, users cannot add or subscribe to channels, delete or unsubscribe from channels, manually update channels, or change any subscription settings for the subscribed channels.
Disables adding and subscribing to channels	Select to prevent users from adding and subscribing to new Active Channels.
Disables editing channel properties and channel subscriptions	Select to prevent users from editing channel settings using the tabs in the channel's **Properties** dialog box.

Option	Description
Disables removing channels and subscriptions to channels	Select to prevent users from removing channels or unsubscribing from channels.
Disables channel logging	Select to prevent channel logging on users' computers. Publishers can specify channel logging in CDF files. The channel log file resides on subscribers' hard disks and logs information about how the channel is used, even when browsed offline. Select this option if you don't want log files residing on your users' computers.
Disables Update Now and Update All for channels and subscriptions	Select to prevent users from manually updating channels or site subscriptions.
Disables all scheduled channel and site subscriptions	Select to prevent automated Web crawls and updates from users' computers.
Disables unattended dialing by subscriptions	Select to prevent automated dial-up connections to update channel and site subscriptions for users who have dial-up connections.
Disables password caching for channel and site subscriptions	Select to prevent users' authentication passwords from being stored and submitted automatically to channels and sites that require user authentication. When this option is selected, users will be prompted to enter the authentication password each time Internet Explorer connects to secure channels or sites.
Disable downloading of channel subscription content-change notification will still work	Select to prevent the download of channel content to the cache on users' computers. When this option is selected, users cannot browse the channel offline.
Disables editing and creating of schedule groups	Select to prevent users from creating custom automated schedules for updates to subscribed channels and sites.

5. Save your changes to the auto-configuration (.ins) file, or finish building the custom package as appropriate.

Managing Channels for Deployed Browsers

To manage Active Channels and Active Desktop items for deployed browsers, you can use the IEAK Profile Manager in conjunction with automatic browser configuration. (For more information about automatic browser configuration, see Chapter 37, "Automatic Browser Configuration.")

To change Active Channels and desktop items for a group, configure the channels and desktop items on the machine running the IEAK Profile Manager, and then use the Profile Manager to import the configurations and save the new configuration settings to the auto-configuration files for the user group.

When automatic browser configuration is refreshed at users' computers, users' desktops are configured with the new Active Channel and Active Desktop settings you specify. You can also optionally remove previous Active Channel configurations from users' computers.

▶ **To change Active Channel and desktop-item configurations**

1. Use Internet Explorer to configure channels and desktop items for the current desktop.

2. Run the IEAK Profile Manager.

3. Open the auto-configuration (.ins) file for the user group.

4. In the left pane, select **Wizard Settings**, and then select **Import Channels**.

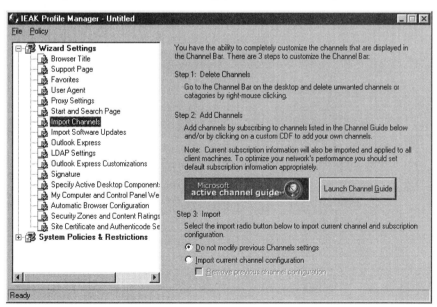

5. In the right pane, select **Import current channel configuration**.

6. If you want to remove previous channel configurations from users' computers, select **Remove previous channel configuration**.

7. In the left pane, select **Wizard Settings**, and then select **Specify Active Desktop Components**.

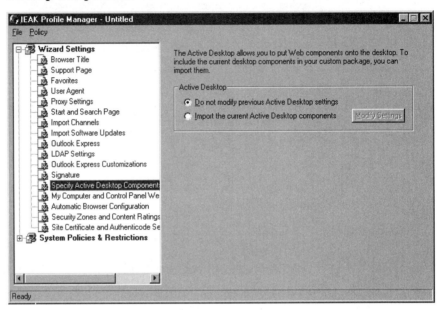

8. In the right pane, select **Import the current Active Desktop components**.

9. On the **File** menu, click **Save**.

Changes are made to users' configurations as scheduled by automatic browser configuration.

CHAPTER 17

True Webcasting

True Webcasting uses true push technology to deliver content to users' desktops while optimizing network bandwidth and performance. Users can subscribe to an information source, and the information is streamed from the server to the users' computers. Applications such as Microsoft NetShow can be used with Internet Explorer 4 to implement information delivery solutions that overcome the limitations of basic and managed Webcasting.

The Webcasting architecture in Internet Explorer 4 allows developers to create add-ons that define new URL transport protocols or provide an alternative delivery mechanism for Active Channels. For more information, see the *Microsoft Internet Client SDK*.

Microsoft NetShow uses the extensible architecture of Internet Explorer 4 to support Internet Protocol (IP) multicast or "true push." By taking advantage of special network hardware, multicast protocols provide bandwidth-efficient streaming of content throughout an intranet. If your network hardware supports multicast protocols, your organization can install and use NetShow servers and client software to deliver rich multimedia content to users' desktops with more bandwidth efficiency and better network performance than is possible using managed Webcasting. For more information about IP multicast technology and Microsoft NetShow, visit **http://microsoft.com/netshow/** and also see Chapter 19, "NetShow."

P A R T   5

Communication and Collaboration

Collaboration across the Internet has become one of the most exciting, avidly discussed topics today. The Microsoft® Internet Explorer 4 suite of applications provides solutions for all Internet-based communication needs users may have. Using its modular installation program or the Internet Explorer Administration Kit (IEAK), users and administrators can set up only the pieces they need or take advantage of the flexibility of the Internet Explorer suite and integrate it with their existing software solutions.

The Internet Explorer suite allows seamless integration from one application to the next, because the applications are all tightly integrated and have been developed with a common menu and toolbar. This simplifies training, because a user who learns one application in the suite already has a head start in learning the next one.

The Internet Explorer 4 suite contains these components for communication and collaboration across the Internet or local intranet:

- Outlook™ Express for e-mail and newsgroups
- NetShow™ for broadcasting
- NetMeeting™ for conferencing and application sharing
- FrontPage® Express for Web authoring
- Personal Web Server for Web publishing

An organization that uses the Internet Explorer suite does not need to discard its existing tools. For example, a corporation can use its existing messaging solution and still integrate with the Internet Explorer suite. In addition, Internet Explorer offers a scalable solution for users who need to move up to high-end applications. Microsoft Outlook can replace Outlook Express mail for those who need a richer mail client. While FrontPage Express is terrific for creating Web pages, Microsoft FrontPage is the full Web-site development platform. Then, for a true enterprise Web server, users can move from the Personal Web Server to Microsoft Internet Information Server, which has all the security, scalability, and power that a Web site needs for the Internet today. Internet Explorer 4 integrates with these high-end applications just as easily as it does with its built-in components.

Part 5 discusses each of the components in the Internet Explorer suite and explains how you can use it to improve communication and collaboration in your organization.

Chapter 18: Outlook Express

E-mail has become one of the most popular and effective ways for people to communicate, both in business and in their personal lives. Unfortunately, most e-mail has been limited to text-only messages, perhaps with attachments. Internet Explorer 4 allows an entirely new type of standards-based messaging, opening the door to greater richness and detail. Outlook Express supports full Hypertext Markup Language (HTML), so you can create e-mail messages with the color and functionality of Web pages, without knowing how to program HTML code. You can even send full Web pages from the Internet as part of your mail message.

Plus, Outlook Express provides users with powerful mail management features, more efficient e-mail and newsgroup use, enhanced security, and full support for Internet standards and technologies. Outlook Express is flexible enough to meet the diverse e-mail needs of users with dial-up Internet access through an Internet service provider (ISP) and users who work on a local area network based on Internet standards such as Simple Mail Transfer Protocol (SMTP), Post Office Protocol 3 (POP3), or Internet Mail Access Protocol 4 (IMAP4).

Chapter 19: NetShow

NetShow brings the power of broadcasting to the desktop. With NetShow, Web content comes alive with interactive content, including audio, illustrated audio (images and sound), and video. It includes both client and server components to add the power of traditional broadcasting systems—audio and video—to HTTP. NetShow harnesses Internet technologies and the power of Windows NT® server to transform Web communications into a richer and more effective medium: the network show.

Chapter 20: NetMeeting

Microsoft NetMeeting is a powerful tool that enables real-time communications and collaboration over the Internet or intranet, providing standards-based audio, video, and multipoint data conferencing support. From a Windows® 95– or Windows NT 4.0–based desktop, users can communicate over the network with real-time voice and video technology. They can share data and information with many people through true application sharing, electronic whiteboard, text-based chat, and file-transfer features. NetMeeting helps organizations communicate more effectively, thus increasing productivity for their users. Also, NetMeeting helps organizations reduce their support burden by providing real-time application sharing features, so that help-desk staff can remotely resolve user problems more quickly and efficiently.

Designed for corporate communication, NetMeeting supports international communication standards for audio, video, and data conferencing. With NetMeeting, people can connect by modem, ISDN, or local area network using the TCP/IP protocol, and communicate and collaborate with users of NetMeeting and other standards-based, compatible products. In addition, support for system policies in NetMeeting makes it easy for administrators to centrally control and manage the NetMeeting work environment.

Chapter 21: FrontPage Express

While HTML has made it possible for many people to become Web publishers, it is still not a particularly intuitive language. For this reason, Microsoft FrontPage Express has been included as a component of the Internet Explorer suite. Based on the full-featured Microsoft FrontPage 97 Web authoring and management tool, FrontPage Express features a graphical interface that makes creating HTML pages as easy as creating a document in a word processor. FrontPage Express allows users to create their own Web pages in a what-you-see-is-what-you-get (WYSIWYG) environment, without knowing HTML. FrontPage Express includes all the features of the FrontPage 97 editor, except for premium features such as Active Server Pages and some of the WebBot® components that rely on specific server extensions. WebBot components from FrontPage 97, such as Include, Search, and Time-Stamp, are still included, however.

Chapter 22: Personal Web Server

As millions of users flock to the Internet for information and entertainment, many decide that they also want to share information with the world. Personal Web Server offers a way for users and corporations to publish Web pages on their own servers, while the Web Publishing Wizard offers users the opportunity to publish Web pages on their own server or on a third-party server. The simplicity of these tools makes them perfectly designed for use by home users, schools, and corporate workgroups.

C H A P T E R   1 8

Outlook Express

Outlook Express Overview

Outlook Express offers a wide range of new features that make it easy to communicate more effectively with others, whether they're down the hall, across the city, or around the world. Important features include:

- Setup and migration tools
- Web integration
- Support for Lightweight Directory Access Protocol (LDAP)
- Support for Secure Multipurpose Internet Mail Extensions (S/MIME)
- Support for Internet Mail Access Protocol (IMAP4)
- The Outlook bar
- Newsgroup filters
- Subscription and channel delivery by e-mail
- Smart Reply
- Stationery
- Multiple e-mail and news server accounts
- Productivity features
- Integration with the Internet Explorer suite

Setup and Migration Tools

Users can get up and running easily with Outlook Express. The Internet Connection Wizard guides users through each step of establishing new mail, news, and LDAP accounts. Migration is simplified because Outlook Express automatically detects and offers the opportunity to import mail messages, news settings, and address books from Netscape Messenger, Eudora, and Internet Mail, on first boot. Users can also very easily import information from these products at their convenience. Of course, Outlook Express can also import information from Microsoft Exchange and Microsoft Outlook.

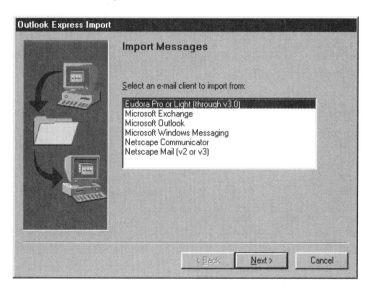

Web Integration

As the successor to Microsoft Internet Mail and News, Outlook Express further integrates e-mail with the Web by using the Internet Explorer Web browser control. Outlook Express supports full Hypertext Markup Language (HTML) as a native message format, so you can create messages in HTML and communicate using the richness of Web pages, without knowing how to program HTML code. In fact, with support for MIME HTML, users can send full Web pages from the Internet or intranet to each other. The **Insert HTML** command also lets users quickly and easily insert content from existing Web pages into messages. To maintain compatibility, messages created in Outlook Express are readable by both HTML-capable and non-HTML-capable e-mail clients. Outlook Express also doubles as a newsreader, so it is not necessary to switch between two separate applications for mail and news.

LDAP Support

Internet Explorer 4 has full support for Lightweight Directory Access Protocol
(LDAP) directory services, which provide access to virtual Internet white pages.
This makes it easy to find anyone on corporate LDAP servers or to use the built-in
support for Four11, InfoSpace, Bigfoot, Switchboard, and WhoWhere? to locate
anyone on the Internet. Internet Explorer also includes support for vCard, for
exchanging business card information.

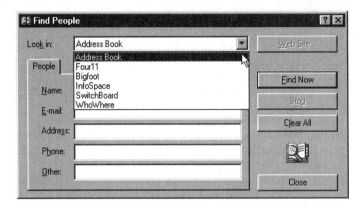

Security

Internet Explorer 4 features the latest in state-of-the-art technology for security.
Support for the Secure Multipurpose Internet Mail Extensions (S/MIME) standard
allows users to encrypt their messages, digitally sign messages, and certify
senders with digital certificates. Public key cryptography is used to facilitate the
encoding and decoding of encrypted messages. Outlook Express also incorporates
Internet Explorer security zones, which protect you as you access certain Web
sites and as you receive mail with Web content. (For more information about
security zones, see Chapter 27.)

Support for Internet Standards

Outlook Express provides full support for the following Internet standards:

- **SMTP (Simple Mail Transfer Protocol).** This protocol is a server standard for sending e-mail.

- **POP3 (Post Office Protocol 3).** This protocol is a server standard for receiving e-mail.

- **IMAP4 (Internet Mail Access Protocol).** IMAP4 is the next-generation standard for e-mail messaging. It allows users to access their mail from any computer on the network, by allowing messages to be stored on the server. For example, users can access their e-mail from work and from home. Support for IMAP4 also offers improved bandwidth utilization. For example, users can choose to download headers only. Plus, IMAP4 provides central mail-store administration, such as mail-store backup.

- **HTML Mail.** Users can send e-mail messages in HTML format. These messages retain their formatting, even if read by an e-mail client other than Outlook Express. Text and attachments can also be read by non-HTML e-mail clients.

- **MHTML (MIME HTML).** Users can embed images directly in their messages, which makes for richer e-mail content. This way, users are not required to connect to the Internet or intranet to view the message contents.

- **S/MIME (Secure MIME).** The security of a user's e-mail messages is ensured by allowing users to digitally sign and encrypt messages. Digital signatures verify the integrity of the sender, and encryption protects the contents of messages from being read by anyone except their intended recipient.

- **LDAP (Lightweight Directory Access Protocol).** LDAP allows users to easily find people on the Internet by searching Internet white-page services such as Four11 and WhoWhere?

- **NNTP (Network News Transfer Protocol).** This standard allows news clients to read and post to newsgroups. It also enables communication between news servers.

Outlook Bar

Outlook Express offers the same style of navigational tool that Microsoft
Outlook 97 introduced. The Outlook bar allows easy access to different folders
and modules and has been one of the most popular features of Outlook 97.

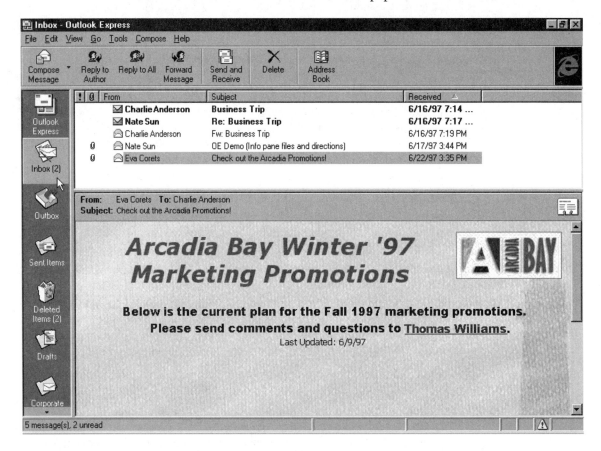

InBox Assistant

Users can develop e-mail rules for their mail to help them save time and stay organized. Filters can also be created to forward, move, or copy messages automatically. Plus, new rules can be applied to existing folders. Now you can use powerful queries to organize the messages that you've already received, in addition to your new incoming mail.

Newsgroup Filters

Users can create filters on an individual-newsgroup basis. Filters can be created to ignore messages based on sender, subject, date posted, or length of message.

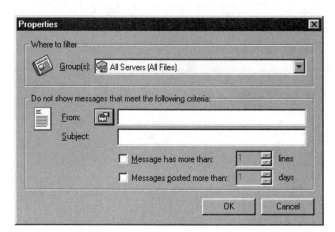

Subscription and Channel Delivery by E-Mail

Internet Explorer allows users to subscribe to Web sites in order to be notified of updated information. Users have the option of receiving notification of updated Web site subscriptions through e-mail. Users can also choose to have the updated content automatically delivered by e-mail. This way, when there is new information on a Web site to which you've subscribed, the actual Web page is delivered right to your Inbox. Because Outlook Express supports HTML, it simply displays the page instead of including it as an attachment. (For more information, see Part 4, "Information Delivery: Webcasting.")

Smart Reply

Outlook Express automatically replies to messages in the same format in which they were sent. For example, if you receive HTML mail, Outlook Express responds with HTML. If you receive the message in plain text, Outlook Express does not send HTML mail when replying to that message, and it remembers not to do so for future messages to that recipient.

Stationery

Because Outlook Express supports HTML as a format for its mail messages, you can use HTML stationery and professionally designed stationery from Greetings Workshop to give mail a personal touch.

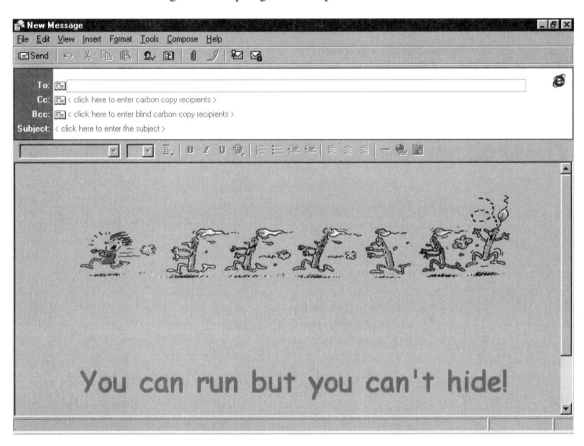

Multiple E-Mail and News Server Accounts

With Outlook Express, you can access and manage multiple e-mail and news accounts from a single client. You can also send and receive mail from numerous e-mail accounts. Outlook Express keeps track of which account an incoming message is using, so that when you reply to it, you can simply click **Send**, and Outlook Express sends your response back through the appropriate account.

Productivity Features

Numerous features have been added to make Outlook Express easier to use. Now you can do the following:

- Create multiple, hierarchical folders and drag them and their associated messages as needed.

- Easily save important e-mail addresses by using Address Book and the new Auto-Add feature, which automatically adds replied-to addresses to the Address Book.

- Enter a partial name of someone in the To: line, and Outlook Express compares it against your address book to fill in the rest of the name.

- Save e-mail messages in the Draft folder before they are sent, which makes it easy to keep track of messages in progress. This way, important messages won't get overlooked among the mail in your Inbox.

- Execute the **Send** and **Receive** commands separately, so you can spend your time online efficiently. For example, if you're on a slow link, you can choose to only send messages and not download large messages with attachments.

- Receive notification of unread messages and unfinished messages in your Draft folder when you start the application.

- Take advantage of several word processor-like features, including a built-in spelling checker (if Microsoft Office or another Microsoft application with spell checking is installed) and up to 150 levels of Undo.

Integration with the Internet Explorer Suite

Because Outlook Express is tightly integrated with the rest of the Internet Explorer applications, you can easily use them together and switch between applications seamlessly. Not only does Outlook Express share common menus and toolbars with the other suite components, it also lets you send a whole Web page to someone from a single click in the browser. The message embeds the entire page, not just a link to a Web site.

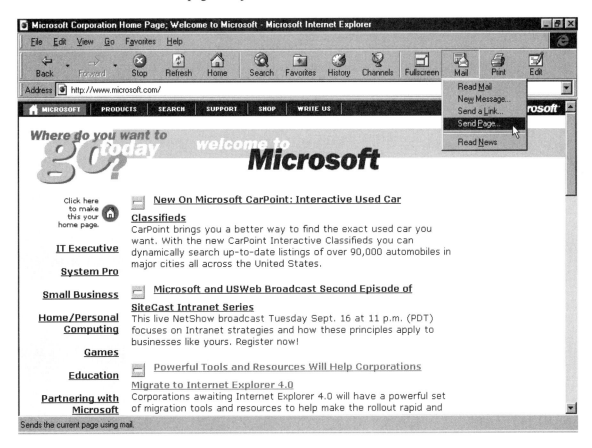

Understanding Outlook Express

Outlook Express is based on a very small, flat file system. When Outlook Express is installed, a .cab file named Mailnews.cab is copied to the Internet Explorer Setup directory. The .cab file is then extracted to give Internet Explorer the Outlook Express files and setup information.

Outlook Express Architecture

The main files used for Outlook Express are:

Wab32.dll	Windows Address Book (WAB) search engine
Msimnui.dll	Dialog boxes and other mail and news functions
Wab.exe	Windows Address Book; launches Wab32.dll
Wldap32.dll	LDAP support file for WAB and LDAP searches
Wabmig.exe	WAB import user interface
Msimnimp.dll	Internet Mail and News setting importer/exporter
Msimn.exe	Outlook Express main program; loads Msimnui.dll
Wabimp.dll	WAB import back end
Wabfind.dll	WAB search user interface
Inetcomm.dll	Parses MIME information
Msoeacct.dll	Account manager .dll file
Msoemapi.dll	Provides Simple MAPI support in Outlook Express
Msoert.dll	Run-time utility functions

To render HTML code in both the Preview pane and the Message window, Msimnui.dll uses the services of Mshtml.dll (the Internet Explorer WebBrowser Control).

Outlook Express Flat File Directory

When Outlook Express downloads mail messages and news articles, it stores them on the local hard disk. The path for Windows 95 varies slightly depending on whether the User Profiles feature is turned on or not. (For more information about user profiles, see Chapter 5.)

Without User Profiles:
Windows\Application Data\Microsoft\Outlook Express

With User Profiles (and on Windows NT):
%windir%\Profiles*username*\Application Data\Microsoft\Outlook Express

Within this directory are two folders, one for mail and one for news. The news folder has a subdirectory for each news account that is in use.

Outlook Express places data in two places in the registry. User accounts and LDAP services are stored in:

HKEY_CURRENT_USER\Software\Microsoft\Internet Account Manager\Accounts

Setting and configuration options are stored in:

HKEY_CURRENT_USER\Software\Microsoft\Outlook Express

Outlook Mail Data Directory

The Mail data directory has no subdirectories, only a collection of files used to manage mail accounts. The three types of files in the Mail directory are:

- **.mbx files**   These files contain the text of all messages stored on the system.
- **.idx files**   These files function as indexes for .mbx files. The .idx and .mbx files are always paired.
- **.nch files**   These files are used to retain the folder hierarchy.

Each .idx file has text pointers to each message that is stored in its companion .mbx file. The .mbx files store the content of each message, including the addressing information. For HTML messages, the raw HTML source code is visible in the .mbx file, but not on the HTML page.

Outlook News Data Directory

Inside the News data directory, a folder is created for each news account. Three types of files are used to manage newsgroups:

- **.nch files**   These files store a cache of articles downloaded from the server.
- **.dat files**   These files store two types of newsgroup lists. The names of all current newsgroups are stored in Grplist.dat, while the names of all subscribed newsgroups are stored in Sublist.dat.

Windows Address Book

The Windows Address Book directory service is a local resource provided by Wab.exe. The Wab.exe program creates and searches a local file *username*.wab found in the Application Data directory. The full path varies slightly, depending on whether the User Profiles feature is enabled or not. (For more information about user profiles, see Chapter 5.)

With User Profiles
%windir%**Profiles***username***Application Data\Address Book***username*.**wab**

Without User Profiles
%windir%**Application Data\Address Book***username*.**wab**

This file contains a list of people with whom the user has frequent communication. Data from previous address books is imported to the .wab file. The default name of the .wab file is the currently logged-on user's name with a .wab extension. This allows the Windows Address Book to easily support multiple users on the same machine and adds a level of privacy to the content.

When Windows Address Book is highlighted in the **Find People** dialog box, the current user's .wab file is searched for the address. The local .wab file is maintained by Wab.exe as well. The screen shot below shows the standard user interface.

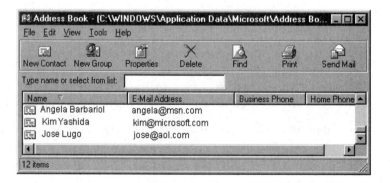

Configuring and Customizing Outlook Express

As the administrator, you can control a wide range of options during initial setup by using the Outlook Express interface and the IEAK Configuration Wizard, and after setup by using the IEAK Profile Manager. These options include:

- Specifying the type of incoming mail server (either IMAP4 or POP3).
- Specifying the name of the incoming mail server.
- Specifying the name of the outgoing mail server (SMTP).
- Specifying the name of the Internet news server (NNTP).
- Making Outlook Express the default mail and/or news client.
- Using Secure Password Authentication (SPA) to authenticate users when they log on.
- Importing messages and address book information.
- Specifying an LDAP server to provide Internet directory services for users.
- Setting rules with the InBox Assistant.
- Customizing the Outlook Express InfoPane.
- Creating a welcome message for new users.
- Appending a standard signature to all messages and news postings written in Outlook Express.
- Customizing the appearance of the Outlook Express window.
- Creating custom stationery.
- Configuring Internet security zones for mail and news.

For more information about deploying and maintaining custom packages using the IEAK Configuration Wizard and IEAK Profile Manager, see Part 9, "Deployment and Maintenance."

Specifying Mail and News Servers

When Outlook Express is launched for the first time, the Internet Connection Wizard automatically guides the user through the process of setting up Outlook Express for use with either an ISP or a POP3-based LAN or an IMAP4-based LAN, and an Internet news server. The user also has the option of making Outlook Express the default mail and/or news reader.

Administrators can pre-configure these settings for users by using the **Specify Internet Mail Servers, Domain, and News Server** page of the IEAK Configuration Wizard or the **Outlook Express** page of the IEAK Profile Manager. Pre-configuring these pages is optional, and they can be left blank to let users enter the information themselves when they run Outlook Express for the first time.

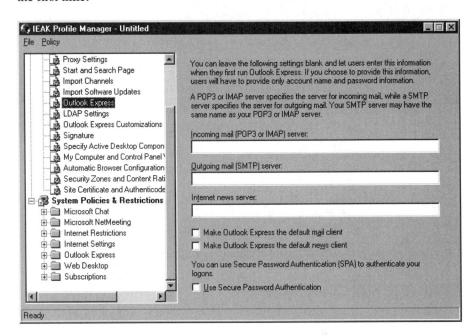

Importing Messages and Address Book Information

Once Outlook Express is set up, the first time users run Outlook Express and open the Inbox, Outlook Express automatically checks to see if they have another messaging application. If so, it immediately offers to import their address book and existing messages. Once that process has taken place, it is up to users to import their existing and future e-mail messages and address book information from the previous e-mail client. They can do so by selecting **Import** on the **File** menu. When messages are imported, the contents of the messages are saved into .mbx files in the Mail data directory. Address information gets copied into the user's Windows Address Book (.wab) file located in the Address Book directory.

▶   **To import address book information**

1. On the **File** menu, click **Import**, and then click **Address Book**. The **Address Book Import Tool** dialog box appears.

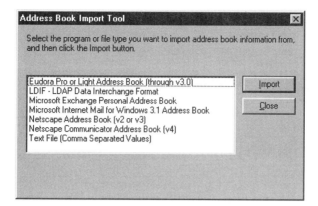

2. Select the format of the address information you want to import, and click **Import**. If you select Microsoft Exchange or Microsoft Internet Mail, you are prompted for a user profile. For other formats, Outlook Express either attempts to auto-detect the existing address book or prompts you for a path to the file's location.

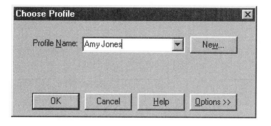

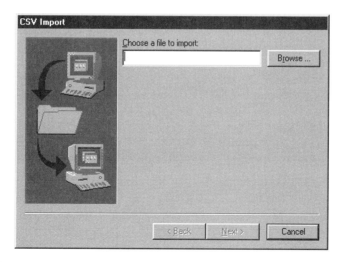

3. The address information is imported to your Windows Address Book file.

▶ **To import messages**

1. On the **File** menu, click **Import**, and then click **Messages**. The **Outlook Express Import** dialog box appears.

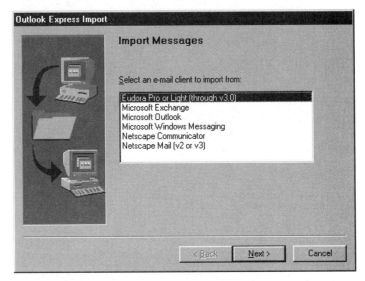

2. Select the e-mail client from which you want to import messages. If you select one of the Microsoft clients, you are prompted for a user profile. If you select any other client, you are prompted to enter the path to the current location of the message files.

3. Select a profile from the menu, or enter the path to the message file folder, and then click **OK**.

4. Select the message folders you want to import, and click **Finish** to import the messages to Outlook Express.

Configuring the LDAP Directories

The Address Book in Outlook Express supports LDAP for accessing Internet white-page services. These services give users a way to search for e-mail addresses and names. Profiles for each of these Internet directory search services are installed with Outlook Express:

- Four11
- InfoSpace
- InfoSpace Business
- Bigfoot
- Switchboard
- WhoWhere?
- VeriSign

Directory services maintain a search database of people around the world and information on how to contact them. Normally, if you know simple information, such as the name of a person, and some other piece of data, such as the city they live in, you can successfully search for people.

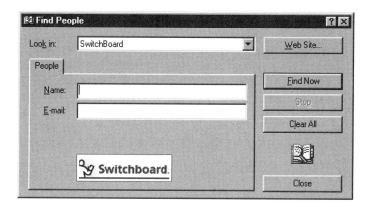

The LDAP search interface is controlled by Wabfind.dll. This .dll file provides a user interface for searching directory services on the Internet and in the local Windows Address Bookfound in the Windows directory.

You can specify one or more LDAP directories against which to check names and e-mail addresses. This is especially useful if your organization has its own LDAP server with a company-wide address book. Outlook Express checks address information against the user's personal address book first, and then against any LDAP servers that have been selected. If more than one LDAP server is specified, you can designate the order in which they must be checked.

▶ **To specify an LDAP directory for checking addresses**

1. On the **Tools** menu, click **Accounts**.

2. In the **Internet Accounts** dialog box, select the directory service you want to use for checking addresses, and click **Properties**.

3. Select **Check names against this server when sending mail**.

4. Click **OK**.

▶ **To set the order in which LDAP directory services are checked**

1. On the **Tools** menu, click **Accounts**.

2. In the **Internet Accounts** dialog box, click the **Set Order** button. The **Directory Services Order** dialog box opens.

3. Set the order of the listed directory services as desired, and then click **OK**.

Maintaining Directory Service Settings

Because the available directory services are constantly changing, being able to add and remove listings as needed is important. You can maintain your settings using the **Directory Service** tab.

▶ **To update directory services**

1. On the **Tools** menu, click **Accounts**.

2. Click the **Directory Service** tab. From here, you can:

   - Add a new directory service.

   - Remove an existing directory service.

   - Update the properties of an existing directory service.

   - Set the order of servers for checking names. (This option can be used only if you select the **Check Names against this Server** option in the **Directory Service Properties** dialog box.)

3. When you are finished making changes, click **Close**.

Tip You can access the **Directory Service** tab of the **Internet Accounts** dialog box directly from the **Find People** dialog box by right-clicking the **Look In** drop-down box and selecting **Directory Service**.

The configuration data for directory services is stored in the registry at:

**HKEY_USERS\.Default\Software\Microsoft\Internet\
Account Manager\Accounts**

You can specify an additional LDAP service for your users on the **Specify LDAP Server Settings** page of the IEAK Configuration Wizard or the **LDAP Settings** page of the IEAK Profile Manager. If your organization has an LDAP server, it is recommended that you set it up here so it will be available to your users immediately after they are set up.

Note Searching a directory service on the Internet requires the use of Windows Sockets. If your users connect to the Internet through a proxy server, Find People can be run only if a Web proxy client is installed.

Using the InBox Assistant

The Inbox Assistant helps users to manage the flow of incoming messages in several ways. Rules can be specified to move, copy, forward, or delete messages, or to send an auto-reply, depending on specified criteria. For example, a user may choose to move all mail received from a particular user to a different folder. The Inbox Assistant makes short work of managing multiple e-mail accounts by providing the ability to sort messages by account. A folder can be created for each separate account, preventing mix-ups. Rules can also be applied to entire folders at once, which is useful for managing messages that have already been received.

▶ **To use the Inbox Assistant**

1. On the **Tools** menu, click **Inbox Assistant**. The **Inbox Assistant** dialog box appears. It is blank until rules are added.

2. To add a new rule, click **Add** to bring up the **Properties** dialog box for the new rule.

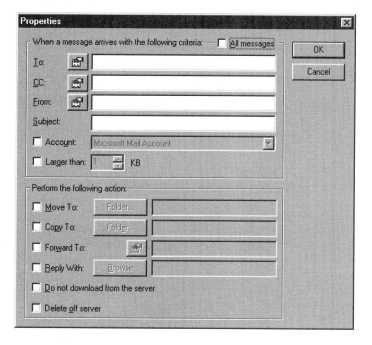

3. Create the rule by selecting message criteria and the desired actions to take.

4. Click **OK**.

▶ **To apply an inbox rule to a folder**

1. On the **Tools** menu, click **Inbox Assistant**. The **Inbox Assistant** dialog box appears.

2. Select the rule you want to apply to the folder.

3. Click the **Apply to** button. The **Select Folder** dialog box appears.

4. Select the folder to which you want to apply the rule, and click **OK**.

Data for Inbox Assistant rules is stored in the Registry at:

**HKEY_CURRENT_USER\Software\Microsoft\Outlook Express\
Mail\Inbox Rules**

Each rule has its own entry under Inbox Rules.

Customizing the InfoPane

The InfoPane is a one-inch pane that appears at the bottom of the Outlook Express window when you start the program. It is available only if you have customized Outlook Express with the IEAK. You can customize the InfoPane with an HTML file that is either a local file or an Internet address (URL). The InfoPane is a good place to include support numbers, links, FAQs, and other useful resources.

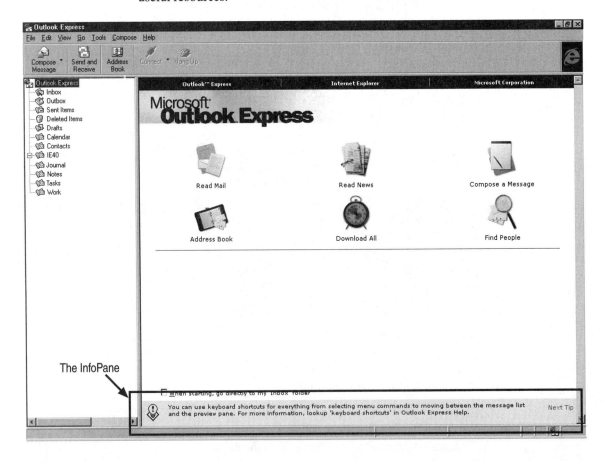

The InfoPane

▶ **To customize the InfoPane**

1. Create the HTML file that will go into the InfoPane. Keep in mind that you have a limited amount of space.

2. Save the file.

   ▪ Saving the file to a Web server lets you point to the file's URL. This makes it easy to update the file as needed.

   ▪ Saving the file to a local disk includes the file in your installation package. The files will be installed on users' machines when they install Internet Explorer.

The InfoPane customization options are found on the **Outlook Express Customization** page of both the IEAK Configuration Wizard and the IEAK Profile Manager. You can select an alternate InfoPane page using either administration tool.

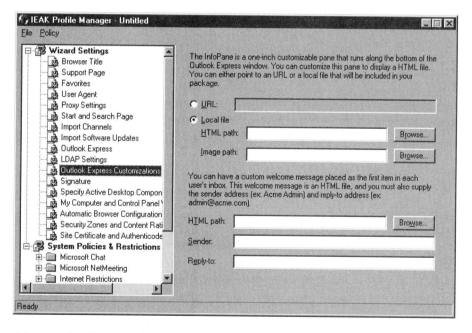

After configuring these options, the InfoPane path can be found in the registry at:

HKEY_CURRENT_USER\Programs\Microsoft\Outlook Express\bodybar

Creating a Welcome Message

You can create a welcome e-mail message that new users will see when they launch Outlook Express for the first time. This message can provide information that helps make it easier for new users to get started and directs them to resources they can use. The welcome message must be an HTML file. After the welcome message is created, you must specify it on the **Outlook Express Customization** page of either the IEAK Configuration Wizard or the IEAK Profile Manager.

Appending a Standard Signature

You can include a default signature or disclaimer that will appear in Outlook Express newsgroup or e-mail messages. For example, a disclaimer may be used to show that messages submitted by employees over the Internet do not represent official company policies. The maximum size of the signature is 1K. You can choose to append signatures to newsgroup messages only, to e-mail messages only, or to both. This is done on the **Include a Signature** page of the IEAK Configuration Wizard or the **Signature** page of the IEAK Profile Manager.

Customizing the Appearance of Outlook Express

Consistent with the rest of Internet Explorer, you can customize the toolbars in Outlook Express to display the most frequently used commands. Users can choose to position the toolbar on the top, right, or left side of the screen. These options can be selected by right-clicking the toolbar.

Administrators can further configure the view under **View Customization** on the **System Policies and Restrictions** page of both the IEAK Configuration Wizard and the IEAK Profile Manager. You can:

- Turn on the Outlook bar (it's off by default).
- Turn off the Folder List (tree view of folders).
- Turn on the Folder bar (horizontal line that displays folder names).
- Turn off the Tip of the Day.

Creating Custom Stationery

Stationery templates are files that allow users to personalize the look of the mail they send. Using HTML, stationery files define the background graphic and font colors and styles that appear in the message. Stationery can contain images, script, and other objects, which may be included with the message or referenced with a URL according to your needs. For example, a background graphic of 1K can easily be included with the message, while it would likely be preferable to use a URL to reference a larger image of 100K.

Note Style sheets, objects, and scripting that are referenced by URLs can be included only in stationery; they cannot be entered into the body text of Outlook Express messages.

Outlook Express comes with several user-modifiable default stationery templates, and you can create your own custom templates. Outlook Express reads stationery files and their associated graphics from:

C:\Program Files\Common Files\Microsoft Shared\Stationery

You can save your custom stationery templates and accompanying graphics in this folder, or you can create a subfolder in which to save them. Be sure to save any associated graphics in the same directory as the HTML files to which they belong. Because the path to Outlook Express stationery files cannot be customized, you must make any custom stationery files available for users to download to their computers.

When users create a message using stationery, Outlook Express loads the stationery template they select and inserts the message body directly into the HTML code. When the message is sent, the accompanying graphics are included by MHTML. If a message using stationery is sent to a mail client that is incapable of interpreting HTML, the message body will still be displayed properly, and other objects will be available as an attachment in a standard e-mail message.

A typical stationery file looks like this:

```
<HTML>
<HEAD>
<STYLE>
<!--
BODY {
margin-left: 4em;
color: "#427D64";
font-size: 12pt;
font-weight: regular;
font-family: "Arial";
}
-->
</STYLE>
</HEAD>
<BODY background="Ivy.gif">
 
</BODY>
```

The top of the file contains CSS styles, and the background graphic is defined in the <BODY> tag. Other graphics can be included, as well as scripts, objects, and text. Items that are referenced can be stored in the same folder as the stationery HTML file or in a different directory, as long as the stationery file references the correct path to the file. Stationery templates are created in exactly the same way as ordinary Web pages. They can be as complex or simple as your needs dictate. For more information about building Web pages, visit the Site Builder Workshop at **http://www.microsoft.com/workshop/**.

Tip When writing a message in HTML format, you can add formatting tags from within the New Message window by highlighting the text you want to format, clicking the **Style Tag** button in the toolbar, and choosing the desired style tag.

The integration of HTML with e-mail provides a range of possibilities that were not possible with traditional e-mail clients. Standard HTML, Dynamic HTML, input forms, scripting, and objects can all be incorporated into Outlook Express stationery. Now you can take ordinary messages and make them visually engaging as well as highly functional. The following screens show two examples of stationery that has been designed to gather input from users. Forms such as these could link to Active Server Pages or CGI scripts stored on your Web server.

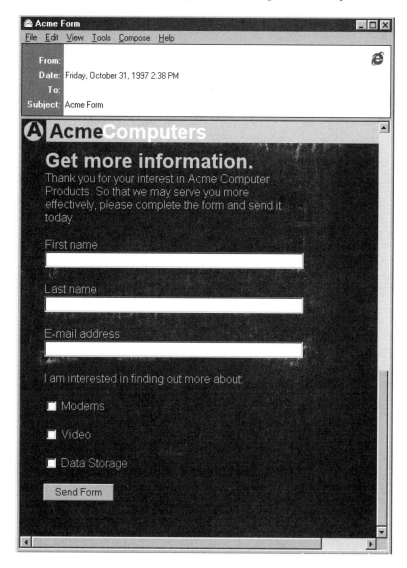

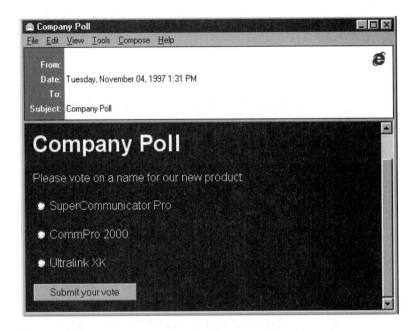

Understanding Security in Outlook Express

Outlook Express gives users the ability to use encryption and digital signatures for increased security when sending and receiving e-mail. Security is provided through the S/MIME version 2 specification and supports the following encryption algorithms: RC2 (40-bit and 128-bit), DES (56-bit), and 3DES (178-bit). The RC2 40-bit encryption algorithm is the only algorithm available in non-U.S./Canadian versions of Outlook Express. Outlook Express can decrypt 3DES (112-bit) and RC2 (64-bit) encrypted mail but cannot send messages using these algorithms.

Outlook Express uses SHA-1 as the hashing algorithm when signing messages. The bit length of your private key varies, depending on the Certificate Authority (CA) from which you obtain it. A CA that uses the Microsoft Enrollment Wizard generates private keys that are at least 512 bits in length.

By using digital IDs with Outlook Express, you can prove your identity in electronic transactions, a practice similar to showing your driver's license when you cash a check. You can also use your digital ID to encrypt messages to keep them private. A digital ID is composed of a "public key," a "private key," and a "digital signature." When you send your digital ID to others, you are actually giving them your public key so that they can send you encrypted mail, which only you can decrypt and read with your private key.

The private keys are stored on your computer and are only as secure as your computer. Private keys installed using Microsoft cryptographic system components are not transmitted to the CA that issues the digital ID; the keys are not stored in escrow with any government agency.

For more information about digital signatures, digital certificates, and security in Internet Explorer, see Part 7, "Security and Privacy."

Using Security Features in Outlook Express

The security features in Outlook Express allow you to associate your digital ID with a mail account, send and receive digitally signed mail, retrieve digital IDs for other people, send and receive encrypted mail, and configure security zone settings for Outlook Express.

Obtaining a Digital ID

Before encrypted mail can be sent or received, a digital ID must be obtained from an independent Certificate Authority. CAs are third-party companies that have a process for checking and verifying your identity. Once a digital ID has been obtained, it must be associated with the e-mail account for which you want to use it.

▶ **To obtain a digital ID for yourself**

- See the Microsoft Internet Explorer Digital ID Web site at **http://www.microsoft.com/ie/ie40/oe/certpage.htm**.

▶ **To associate a digital ID with a mail account**

1. In Outlook Express, on the **Tools** menu, click **Accounts**.
2. Select the mail account from which you want to send secure mail, and then click **Properties**.
3. On the **Security** tab, check **Use a digital ID when sending secure messages from**, and then click the **Digital ID** button.
4. Select the ID you want to use with this account.

▶ **To send your digital ID to others**

- Simply send them digitally signed e-mail (see below), and Outlook Express automatically includes your digital ID.

Sending and Receiving Signed Mail

Signed e-mail allows an e-mail recipient to verify your identity.

▶ **To send signed mail**

- On the **Tools** menu in your Message window, click **Digitally Sign** (or use the button on the Message toolbar).

  To send signed mail, you must have a digital ID of your own (see above).

Signed e-mail from others allows you to verify the authenticity of a message — that the message is from the supposed sender and the message has not been tampered with during transit.

▶ **To receive signed mail**

- Signed e-mail messages are designated with special, signed e-mail icons. You receive and read them as you would any other e-mail message. Any problems (described by Outlook Express security warnings) with signed e-mail that you receive could indicate that the message has been tampered with or was not from the supposed sender.

Sending and Receiving Encrypted Mail

Encrypting an e-mail message prevents other people from reading it when it is in transit. To encrypt an e-mail message, you need the digital ID of the person to whom you are sending the e-mail. The digital ID must be part of the person's entry in the Address Book. Outlook Express is the first e-mail program to allow you to retrieve digital IDs from directory services.

▶ **To retrieve a digital ID from someone else**

1. On the **Edit** menu, click **Find People**.

2. Select a directory service that has digital IDs (such as VeriSign), enter the recipient's name or e-mail address in the appropriate search field, and click **Find**.

3. Select a listing from the Results pane, and click **Add to Address Book**.

Tip Another way to get someone's digital ID is to have that person send you signed mail. To add the digital ID from a piece of signed mail to your Address Book, on the **File** menu, click **Properties**. Click the **Security** tab, and click the **Add Digital ID to Address Book** button.

Note When you add a digital ID to your Address Book, it has a trust status associated with it that indicates whether you trust the individual, group, or corporation to whom the digital ID was issued. If a digital ID owner warns you that he or she suspects that the digital ID's private key has been compromised, you may want to change the trust status to "Explicitly Distrust." For more information, look up "Trust Status of a Digital ID" in the Outlook Express Help Index.

▶ **To send encrypted mail**

1. Create your mail message as you would an ordinary piece of e-mail.

2. On the **Tools** menu in your Message window, click **Encrypt** (or click the button on the Message toolbar).

   When sending encrypted mail, you must have the recipient's digital ID in your address book (see above) so that they can decrypt the message when they receive it. Your e-mail address for replies must be the same as the account from which you're sending the digitally signed mail. Otherwise, message recipients won't be able to use the ID to reply with encrypted mail. (The e-mail address to which they reply won't match the address on the digital ID.)

When you receive an encrypted e-mail message, you can be reasonably confident that the message has not been read by anyone else.

▶ **To receive encrypted mail**

- Outlook Express automatically decrypts e-mail messages, provided that you have the correct digital ID installed on your computer.

For others to be able to send you encrypted mail, they need your digital ID.

Changing Security Zones Settings for Outlook Express

Outlook Express uses Internet Explorer's security zones technology to ensure that active Web content such as Java applets and ActiveX™ controls do not run inappropriately. Users can designate all incoming mail as part of the Internet zone (under which users are prompted before any active content runs) or the Restricted Sites zone (under which no active content can be run at all). In addition, for each security zone, you can choose a High, Medium, Low, or Custom security level setting. For more information, see Chapter 27, "Security Zones."

▶ **To change your security zone settings for Outlook Express**

1. On the **Tools** menu, click **Options**, and then click the **Security** tab.

2. You can select which security zone to use for mail and news. Click **Advanced** to change the security settings for zones. Changing the settings for the Internet zone or Restricted Sites zone also changes this setting for Internet Explorer, and vice versa.

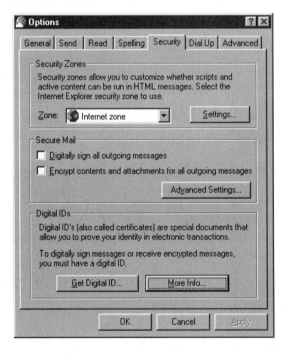

Administrators can set and lock down security options for users by using the **System Policies and Restrictions** and **Security Zones and Content Ratings Customization** pages in both the IEAK Configuration Wizard and the IEAK Profile Manager. For more information, see Part 7, "Security and Privacy."

C H A P T E R   1 9

NetShow

NetShow Overview

Microsoft NetShow 2.1 delivers a complete, high-performance system for broadcasting live and on-demand audio, video, and multimedia. NetShow is a platform for streaming multimedia over networks that range from low-bandwidth, dial-up Internet connections to high-bandwidth, switched local area networks (LANs). Using NetShow, organizations can offer new streaming content for applications such as training, corporate communications, entertainment, and advertising to users all over the world. NetShow is a powerful broadcast system that is easy to set up and operate. It empowers organizations to offer rich, high-quality interactive content over today's networks.

Only a few years ago, the business world was full of textual documents, and adding graphics to them was not easy. Now, the race is on to offer Web sites that attract and retain visitors through the latest in graphics and animation. Audio-enabled and video-enabled Web sites and applications are the next wave. The integration of audio and video into applications such as online training, corporate communications, customer and sales support, news and entertainment services, and product promotions will provide individuals and organizations with new and exciting ways to communicate.

Microsoft NetShow provides a complete platform for integrating audio and video into online applications, bringing the vibrant power of networked multimedia to the Internet and corporate intranets. With its leading-edge live and on-demand media-streaming technology, Microsoft NetShow allows users to receive audio and video broadcasts from their personal computers. It uses client/server archi-tecture and sophisticated compression and buffering techniques to deliver live and on-demand audio, video, and illustrated audio (synchronized sound and still images) to users of the NetShow Player. The NetShow Player continuously decompresses and plays the content in real time. Users can listen and watch live audio and video programs or navigate on-demand audio and video content.

Building upon the open, standards-based platform established with NetShow networked multimedia software version 1.0, NetShow 2.1 provides an easy, powerful way to stream multimedia content across intranets and the Internet. NetShow allows developers and Web professionals to add production-scale audio and video broadcasts to any Web application or site.

NetShow reduces the total cost of streaming multimedia, because of its tight integration with Microsoft Internet Information Server (IIS), the Microsoft Windows NT Server network operating system, and the Internet Explorer browser. Standard multimedia authoring and HTML programming tools can be used to create and host content.

Some of the important features and functionality of NetShow include:

- Streaming audio and video
- Rich, synchronized multimedia
- Compatibility with streaming technologies
- Live broadcast of audio and video
- Content scheduling
- Easy user access to broadcasts
- Multicast file transfer
- Multiple network transport protocols
- Server integration
- Scalability
- Distributed delivery of content streams
- Web-based administration
- Tools for monitoring and logging events
- Firewall support

Streaming Audio and Video

NetShow streams audio and video to users on demand, on an intranet or on the Internet, without waiting for content to download and without consuming the user's disk space. Streaming delivers content to the client as a continuous flow of data with little waiting time before playback begins, and data is never actually stored on the user's computer. NetShow provides an array of the best compression/decompression algorithms, or *codecs*, making NetShow the most comprehensive platform available today for delivering high-quality streaming multimedia content over a wide range of networks.

NetShow provides broadcast-quality audio and includes an audio codec from Fraunhofer Institut Integrierte Schaltungen that delivers mono and stereo audio at 28.8 kilobits per second (Kbps) and scales to near-CD-quality audio over ISDN, ADSL, cable modems, and LANs. In addition, NetShow includes several Voxware codecs, which are excellent for voice-only audio tracks and are able to compress audio smaller than any of the other codecs installed with NetShow. Plus, NetShow provides a premier implementation of the forthcoming, leading-edge, MPEG-4 video standard. Microsoft, working closely with the MPEG-4 standards committee, is implementing one of the first video codecs based on the emerging MPEG-4 video standard. At 28.8 Kbps, this codec produces market-leading video quality, that is becoming ever more impressive as network bandwidth increases. NetShow also includes Duck TrueMotion and Vivo video codecs.

For more information about streaming media in NetShow, see "Understanding Streaming Media," "Understanding Content Compression," and "Understanding Codec Independence" later in this chapter.

Rich, Synchronized Multimedia

Unlike most audio or video streaming products, NetShow enables content providers to generate sophisticated productions in which graphics, slides, photographs, and URLs can be synchronized with the audio and video stream. You can create multimedia programs that use live and on-demand streaming of audio, illustrated audio, and video synchronized with pictures (.jpeg, .bmp, and .gif files), as well as script (JScript™ and ActiveX script), URLs, and text. The result is a compelling mixed-media experience and the ability to deliver multimedia applications over low-bandwidth networks such as the Internet.

Compatibility with Streaming Technologies

NetShow supports the industry-leading Active Streaming Format (ASF) and the RealAudio and RealVideo formats by RealNetworks. By adding the ability to create, serve, and play live and on-demand ASF and RealAudio/RealVideo content, NetShow can now access more than 95 percent of the streaming media content on the Web, and content providers can use NetShow to provide streaming media for the majority of users on the Web. Thus, NetShow, coupled with industry efforts to establish ASF as the common streaming format, will help ensure the continued growth of the streaming media market. For more information about ASF, see "Understanding the Active Streaming Format" later in this chapter.

Live Broadcast of Audio and Video

NetShow 2.1 enables the delivery of live, real-time encoded audio, video, and illustrated audio content. By allowing many users to "tune into" a single broadcast transmission, network managers can dramatically reduce the load that would otherwise be placed on their networks when large numbers of users listen to or watch live events.

This represents a major improvement, as NetShow 1.0 only allowed the live delivery of audio over multicast-enabled networks, thus limiting the delivery of live events. NetShow 2.1 allows the delivery of live content, as well as on-demand content, over any network, independent of the transmission techniques and network transports used. This means that people using NetShow can broadcast live and on-demand content using either unicast or multicast techniques, depending on their needs and the available network infrastructure. To further facilitate delivery, NetShow can automatically switch from multicast to unicast to accommodate networks that are not multicast-enabled or to adjust to other delivery needs. For more information, see "Understanding Unicasting and Multicasting" later in this chapter.

Content Scheduling

NetShow 2.1 opens vast opportunities for Web-based broadcasts similar to the delivery of content over current television and radio stations. With NetShow, you can configure and schedule content streams for later delivery. You can also generate announcements to notify users of upcoming and in-progress sessions. This allows audio and video content to be organized into separate channels, each programmed with one or more individual programs. Each NetShow Server can have multiple channels.

Consider this analogy: A cable company manages multiple channels that are organized in a numeric sequence to make television surfing easy. For example, NBC might be channel 5, CNN channel 7, and so on. Each channel offers time-based programs, such as the 10:00 P.M. news, or a movie at 11:00 P.M. Users can easily find their favorite programs, because they know when and where to look. Following this analogy, NetShow makes it possible to organize audio and video content into separate channels, each of which has scheduled programs and announcements of current or upcoming sessions.

Easy User Access to Broadcasts

NetShow 2.1 brings the power of broadcasting to Microsoft Internet Explorer and other browsers such as Netscape Navigator, enabling browsers to receive a new class of innovative, interactive content and extending the browsers' strength for one-to-many communications. Because the NetShow Player is an integral part of browsers, users can easily view NetShow-hosted broadcasts. NetShow also adds NetShow Players for Windows 3.1, the Macintosh®, and UNIX operating systems.

Multicast File Transfer

NetShow supports multicast file transfer, which provides another way for network managers to save bandwidth when large quantities of data have to be simultaneously distributed to many users. Multicast file transfer provides a reliable mechanism to distribute any type of file. It can be used, for example, to dynamically change files on Web sites in order to broadcast a variety of Web content.

Multiple Network Transport Protocols

NetShow 2.1 supports a variety of network transport protocols, including IP multicast, RTP, UDP/IP, TCP/IP, and HTTP. As a result, NetShow users can distribute multicast audio to MBONE-compatible applications and can listen to MBONE multicasts (VAT-compatible on client and server). The broad range of network transport protocols supported by NetShow allows content providers to choose the protocol most effective for delivery of their content and the network infrastructure available.

NetShow is optimized to reduce content delivery losses due to changes or obstacles in the network infrastructure through its intelligent fail-over feature; it uses IP multicast on multicast-enabled networks and, if necessary, falls back to unicast UDP/IP traffic, then to unicast TCP/IP, and finally to HTTP traffic if unicast UDP/IP cannot be delivered.

The intelligent fail-over feature enables content providers to use NetShow to broadcast content, using either unicast or multicast techniques, without worrying about the nature of the available network infrastructure. Intelligent fail-over also allows content to be sent through firewalls, allowing intranet users to view NetShow content as easily as other users, without compromising the firewall security features.

Server Integration

NetShow and its streaming services are tightly integrated with Windows NT Server 4.0 to provide an efficient, reliable, scalable, and secure platform for delivering audio, illustrated audio, and video content over corporate intranets and the Internet. NetShow uses all key Windows NT Server administration features, including the graphical administration console, performance monitoring, the integrated directory and security model, and the event log.

NetShow also fully supports Windows NT connectivity, including network environments such as IP, IPX, 14.4/28.8 POTS, ISDN, Ethernet, and others. Sharing the same user interface, APIs, services, and tools means that end users and computer professionals don't have to learn different interfaces or tools. An integrated solution offers easier management, better connectivity, and lower support costs, and because NetShow and Microsoft IIS are designed to work together, they combine to deliver a complete, well-tested, and high-performance system for broadcasting multimedia.

Scalability

Broadcasts of audio and video on the Web need a server that can scale up to thousands of streams for enabling full-scale, one-to-many communication. The NetShow Server takes advantage of the scalability of Windows NT Server to provide both small-scale implementation and easy scaling to higher-performance systems. Thus, NetShow can easily adapt to an organization's growth.

NetShow scales to very high-performance, enterprise-class multiprocessor systems with many gigabytes of memory and terabytes of storage; it exploits the ability of Windows NT Server to run on leading-edge microprocessors such as Intel Corporation's Pentium and Pentium Pro and Digital Equipment Corporation's Alpha. Microsoft internal tests have shown that a NetShow Server can handle more than 1,000 streams of data at 28.8 Kbps on an industry-standard, Pentium Pro–based uniprocessor computer with 64 MB of RAM, with no impact on the quality of the content and services delivered to clients.

Distributed Delivery of Content Streams

With NetShow 1.0, all server components were installed on a single Windows NT Server. NetShow 2.1 allows the system to be divided into several components that can be installed on separate Windows NT Server computers. This increases the overall number of simultaneous streams that can be delivered, to provide services to an otherwise unserviceable number of clients. In addition, distributed delivery enables a geographically diverse distribution of NetShow servers, in order to optimize how content is distributed from the source to clients. The array of servers, in turn, can consist of many small, inexpensive computers, rather than just a few powerful but costly platforms.

Using Windows NT Server DNS, a cluster of NetShow servers can be configured to deliver content to a greater number of clients. For example, if you are broadcasting a live event, you can perform real-time encoding at the event site, using the NetShow Real-Time Encoder. The encoded content is transmitted in real time to a cluster of NetShow servers that then deliver the content to their respective connected clients.

Web-Based Administration

NetShow 2.1 administration is provided through the NetShow Administrator, an intuitive, Web-based interface that enables both local and remote administration of NetShow servers. Web-based administration allows administrators to centrally manage server installations and make configuration changes, without having to physically access each server.

Network managers can set the maximum content throughput per file and per server to control network bandwidth utilization and to monitor the state of all key NetShow Server services. The NetShow Administrator runs on both Windows NT and Windows 95 operating systems. Web-based administration enables faster deployment of information delivery solutions and reduces administrator training and support costs.

Tools for Monitoring and Logging Events

NetShow includes tools for monitoring and logging events. The Monitor Events Log is used to display events, and the NetShow Server Event Log is used to store events in a database. Both tools allow you to filter events by type: server, client, administrative, and alert. Server events indicate server status, such as whether a server is online or offline. Client events are logged, for example, when a client connects or disconnects. Administrative events are logged when configuration settings are modified, such as when the maximum number of clients or maximum bandwidth is modified. Alerts are logged when server configuration settings are exceeded, such as when the maximum number of clients is exceeded.

In addition, you can use all standard Windows NT Server administration features, such as the Windows NT Event Viewer and Performance Monitor, to monitor the number of streams sent from the server, the percentage of CPU time being taken by the NetShow services running, and other performance-related data.

Firewall Support

To prevent unauthorized access to their networks, corporations deploy firewalls. Most firewalls are based on packet filtering. In packet filtering, the computer examines the source and destination IP addresses of a packet and forwards only those packets for which access has been granted. The content streamed from Microsoft NetShow can stream through a number of firewalls from vendors such as Ascend Communications Inc., CheckPoint Software Technologies Ltd., Cisco Systems, Computer Software Manufacturer, Cycon Technologies, LanOptics Inc., Firewall System, Microsoft Corporation, Milkyway Networks, Secure Computing, and Technologic Inc. In addition, several other vendors are working to add NetShow support to their products. For a complete list of all firewall products that currently support NetShow, visit the NetShow Web page at **http://www.microsoft.com/netshow/**.

For firewalls that do not support streaming content from NetShow Server, you can stream NetShow content using an HTTP server. Firewalls can process HTTP streamed content; however, some of the functionality of ASF is not supported when streaming uses HTTP servers. For more information, see "Using HTTP Streaming" later in this chapter.

Components of NetShow

NetShow 2.1 includes the following software components:

- NetShow Player
- NetShow Server
- NetShow Administrator
- NetShow content authoring and production resources
- NetShow Software Development Kits (SDKs)
- NetShow Theater server

The NetShow components are available for free download from Microsoft. For more information about each of the NetShow components, visit the Microsoft NetShow Web page at **http://www.microsoft.com/netshow/**. To download components, visit **http://www.microsoft.com/netshow/software.htm**.

NetShow Player

The NetShow Player allows intranet and Internet users to play audio, illustrated audio (synchronized sound and still images), and full-motion video files. By simply activating a link to a file, the player launches automatically and begins playing the requested file. Within seconds, the content starts playing, with no download required. The player enables the same functions as a regular VCR, allowing the user to stop, pause, and start content.

The NetShow Player is provided as an optional component of the Internet Explorer 4 installation package. The NetShow Player is typically installed when you choose the Full Installation option during setup for Internet Explorer 4.

The NetShow Player comprises a stand-alone player and an ActiveX control that can be embedded in Web pages or in applications that support embedded controls. The stand-alone player can be used even if no browser is installed. NetShow Player can be run independently of the user's browser by launching it in a helper application that runs on top of the page. The advantage of playing content in the external player is that it can be launched by means of a small redirector in an e-mail message, launched from a shortcut to a location on a corporate network, or played in the background while the user surfs to other pages on the Web. The NetShow Player is available cross-platform, providing access to NetShow content for users of the Macintosh, UNIX, Windows 3.1, and Windows NT 3.51 platforms.

The ActiveX control allows you to embed the NetShow Player in Web pages to play NetShow content within the browser window of browsers that support ActiveX controls, such as Internet Explorer, versions 3 and 4. The ActiveX control also allows developers to embed NetShow content in applications that support ActiveX controls (including Visual Basic®, Visual C++®, and many third-party tools and applications).

The NetShow Player is also provided as a Netscape Navigator Plug-in, enabling users of Navigator to receive NetShow broadcasts directly within their browsers.

NetShow Server

The NetShow Server consists of a set of services running on Windows NT Server 4 that allow users to unicast and multicast audio, video, and other files to client computers. The NetShow Server can deliver both live and on-demand content. To deliver live, real-time content, the server works in conjunction with the NetShow Real-Time Encoder, which compresses the audio and/or video feed in real time and passes it to the NetShow Server for delivery to the network. Delivery of on-demand content requires that it be stored on a server's hard disk and passed to the network by the NetShow Server.

NetShow can restrict access and control client and server connections to the NetShow Server and the Real-Time Encoder based on the IP addresses of the clients or servers attempting to connect. Access is controlled by creating a list of addresses in the Windows NT registry. By default, all connections are allowed.

NetShow Administrator

The NetShow Server includes the NetShow Administrator, a set of documentation and tools that allow administrators to manage, configure, and monitor NetShow services. For example, you can use the NetShow Administrator to set the maximum number of concurrent streams the server can run, and you can limit the amount of data the server can send at one time. The NetShow Administrator also allows you to configure and set up channels and programs for multicasting content at specific times. The *NetShow Server Administrator Guide* provides detailed information on how to use the NetShow Administrator.

NetShow Authoring and Production Resources

Microsoft provides many resources to help you author both real-time (live) and on-demand (stored) NetShow content. The foundation for NetShow content creation is the Active Streaming Format (ASF). (For more information, see "Understanding the Active Streaming Format" later in this chapter.)

The NetShow authoring and production resources include:

- **Authoring tools for on-demand content.** NetShow provides simple ASF authoring tools to convert .avi and QuickTime® files to .asf or .wav files. Also provided is a simple ASF editor called the NetShow ASF Editor, which allows you to synchronize images to .wav audio files and add URL flip commands, markers, and script events. The NetShow tools also include the new NetShow Presenter, which allows a person giving a Microsoft PowerPoint® presentation to stream his or her video and slides to ASF.

- **Real-Time Encoder.** The Real-Time Encoder is a set of tools for encoding and authoring live multimedia streams. These tools allow content authors to encode live audio and video feeds and add them to dynamic mixtures of other media, such as audio, video, text, URLs, and script commands. These tools are used to indicate what media is to be injected into a live stream, and when. The appropriate media components are synchronized, compressed, augmented with error-correction information, and transmitted over a network.

- *NetShow Content-Creation Authoring Guide.* This HTML document provides detailed information and guidelines for creating live and on-demand ASF content. The document is updated frequently with new information. Be sure to download the latest version.

- **NetShow Encoder with RealVideo.** This tool converts video files into the RealVideo format for use in RealVideo programs.

NetShow Software Development Kits

Microsoft provides several SDKs for NetShow:

- *NetShow Client SDK.* This kit documents the interfaces to the player. This gives developers of Web pages and client applications all the information they need to integrate NetShow functionality into their products. Developers have complete control over audio and video rendering, along with the ability to interpret script commands transmitted as part of the NetShow stream.

- *NetShow Server SDK.* This kit documents the interfaces to the three administration controls. This gives application authors complete local or remote control over a network of NetShow Servers. For example, NetShow administration can be integrated into an overall, enterprise management system. The *NetShow Server SDK* supports the creation of NetShow Channel Manager administrative applications with the Channel Manager ActiveX control and the creation of NetShow unicast administrative applications with the Unicast ActiveX control. Independent software vendors and solution providers can build customized administration utilities using this SDK.

- *Real-Time Encoder SDK.* This kit documents the interfaces to the Real-Time Encoder itself. This gives application developers the ability to automatically insert script commands into the NetShow stream alongside audio and video. For example, a closed-caption or subtitling application can feed its output directly to the NetShow Real-Time Encoder by using these interfaces. The PowerPoint NetShow Presenter add-in for the PowerPoint presentation graphics program is an application written using the *Real-Time Encoder SDK.*

NetShow Theater Server

NetShow Theater Server adds a new streaming media engine to the NetShow Server capabilities. NetShow Theater Server is an optional feature of NetShow. It provides a powerful, scalable, and cost-effective solution for the delivery of MPEG-quality, full-motion, full-screen video across high-bandwidth corporate networks and dedicated video LANs.

NetShow Theater Server delivers a complete, high-performance system for streaming MPEG video that runs on the Windows NT Server platform. It's a distributed, fault-tolerant, real-time video server designed to provide MPEG video streams at a constant rate to large numbers of PC clients.

NetShow Theater Server's highly scalable and fault-tolerant architecture makes it ideal for video-on-demand applications that require large numbers of high-bandwidth video streams from 1 to 10 megabits per second (Mbps) or more.

Webcasting with NetShow

You can use NetShow 2.1 to provide true Webcasting solutions that push information to end users' computers. NetShow uses advanced streaming technology to deliver multimedia content optimized for network bandwidths from 14.4 Kbps to 6 Mbps.

True Webcasting can be used to overcome the limitations of basic Webcasting and managed Webcasting. For more information about basic Webcasting and managed Webcasting, see Part 4, "Information Delivery: Webcasting." For more information about using NetShow for true Webcasting, see the *NetShow Content Creation Authoring Guide*, the *NetShow Server Administration Guide*, and the NetShow SDKs.

True Webcasting Application Scenarios

Multimedia allows people to communicate more expressively and more effectively. The richer data structures of sound and moving images transcend the communicative power of text and graphics. NetShow provides a complete, true Webcasting platform for integrating audio and video into Web-based applications. These Web-based applications often deliver information solutions for training, corporate communications, advertising, and entertainment applications.

Training

Many organizations devote substantial resources to training. Using NetShow to extend the reach of professional instructors through intranets allows organizations to maximize the value of this investment. NetShow makes it easy for trainers to generate the content and for users to receive the training whenever and wherever they need it.

For example, a recorded speech in conjunction with the speaker's slides can form a NetShow broadcast. Training material can be provided for all divisions and subsidiaries of an organization so that all employees have the advantage of hearing the speech as it was delivered by the speaker.

Delivering multimedia information and presentations over the intranet or the Internet can help organizations save substantially on the costs required to distribute and maintain up-to-date training materials on hard copy or compact discs. It's easy to update NetShow content on the network and provide immediate, up-to-date information to users.

Corporate Communications

With NetShow, everyone in an organization, regardless of their geographic location, can hear important organizational briefings—such as internal presentations or presentations for the press or analyst—live. These same presentations can also be captured for later playback. The presentations can also grow into a library of available-on-demand information for reference and training. NetShow can reduce the burden of requiring all employees to fly into a central location for an announcement or training session, by allowing companies to send the content over the network to each employee's desktop or to a portable PC for those traveling.

Entertainment and Information

NetShow makes Web sites come alive with interactive audio and video content, from musical events and similar entertainment to news and other broadcasts. Organizations that already provide entertainment content on the Web can use NetShow to add visual content to their sites. When combined with products such as Microsoft Site Server, Enterprise Edition, organizations can offer NetShow-based entertainment content for fun and help justify its use by selling products over the Web, using the Site Server.

Advertising and Retailing

Advertising a product or service with audio and video can be much more compelling than doing it with static Web pages. For example, audio commentary can be used with images on a Web site to guide users through demonstrations of a product, a process, or the site itself. The synchronized sound and images of NetShow illustrated audio provide a rich environment for advertising and facilitate showing off a product or concept to best advantage, such as in a media catalog.

Organizations with external Web sites can promote and sell products on the Web using NetShow. Advertisers can use the NetShow streaming technology to deliver their messages without requiring users to wait for a movie or audio clip to download to their hard disks—which means users get the messages without frustrating delays.

Understanding NetShow Technology

NetShow provides a wide variety of features that allow customization of the system. How you use NetShow depends largely on the types of media you want to stream and the characteristics of the network used to deliver the data. Understanding the basic concepts discussed in this section will help you determine how to deploy NetShow for your particular application.

Understanding Streaming Media

Most of the audio and video content currently hosted on intranets and on Internet sites is downloadable. This means that the multimedia content must be copied to the user's local hard disk before it can be played. NetShow uses a client/server streaming architecture to deliver multimedia content to clients. *Streaming content* is digitized content that has been compressed or encoded into a format that the server can break down into packets and then stream across a network to a client player. Streaming is a significant improvement over the download-and-play approach to multimedia file distribution, because it allows content to be delivered to the client as a continuous flow of data, with little waiting time before playback begins. The content arrives, is buffered briefly, plays, and is discarded. It is never actually stored on the user's computer. NetShow users benefit by experiencing instant play, and they don't have the frustration of waiting for content to download before determining whether it meets their needs or interests. (For more information, see "NetShow Streams and Programs" later in this chapter.)

Understanding Network Bandwidth

Any computer network connection (Internet or intranet) has an upper limit on the amount of data that can pass through it in a given second. This data limit is called its *bandwidth*. The *data rate* (also *bit rate*) of an audio and video file is the amount of data that must transmit in a given second for the whole file to be heard or viewed in its entirety. To transmit a content file completely and smoothly, its data rate must be less than the available bandwidth of its target network.

Understanding Content Compression

Because today's networks are usually bandwidth-constrained, audio and video files must be compressed to reduce their data rates. To compress them, we apply mathematical compression/decompression algorithms called *codecs* that analyze the audio and video and decide what bits of data can be removed or merged with minimum impact on what the human ear can hear or eye can see. By nature, however, applying compression to an audio or video clip results in some loss of quality.

The level of quality and fidelity you can deliver in sound and video files depends primarily on how much bandwidth you have available and whether you have authored the content appropriately for that available bandwidth. For example, imagine that the bandwidth available is like an empty pipe. You decide to fill that pipe with audio only. If your pipe is large (that is, you are on a corporate network), you can author that audio to be only slightly compressed, so it has very high quality. If your pipe is small (you are targeting users on 28.8-Kbps dial-up connections), you have to use a codec to compress the audio to fit in such a small pipe, and as you would expect, it has a lower quality than audio authored for higher bandwidths. Now, imagine that you want to add images or video to that audio content. In order to make room in that pipe, you need to compress the audio even more. You also need to compress the images or video significantly. The end result is highly compressed multimedia that can play at bandwidths that previously supported only still images.

Understanding Codec Independence

The quality of streaming content for a given bit rate is largely determined by how good the codec is that you use to compress it. Advances in codec technology are happening practically monthly, and for this reason, NetShow was developed to be codec-independent. This means NetShow includes the best variety of codecs for creating content in a wide range of application and bandwidth scenarios. Content providers can choose the best compression scheme for their particular type of application and content, and users can decode without hassles.

NetShow offers the content author and end user a well-rounded suite of bundled and stand-alone third-party codecs for voice, music, images, and video, at a variety of bit rates. This gives you more options, more flexibility, higher-quality content, and faster innovation, because the codecs can be upgraded independent of NetShow. The codecs provided with NetShow include Microsoft MPEG-4, Vivo G.723 and H.263, Lernout and Hauspie (L&H), Fraunhofer Institut Integrierte Schaltungen (FhG) MPEG Layer-3, Voxware MetaSound, VDONet, and Duck TrueMotion RT. The inclusion of these new audio and video codecs makes NetShow 2.1 the most comprehensive platform available today for delivering high-quality, streaming multimedia content over a wide range of networks.

For more information, see "Using Codecs" later in this chapter, and visit **http://www.microsoft.com/netshow/codecs.htm**.

Understanding the Active Streaming Format

The foundation for all of the NetShow content-creation components is the Active Streaming Format. ASF is an open, standards-based file format that prepares multimedia content for streaming and adds error correction and other features necessary for streaming. ASF also enables the synchronization of different data types on a common timeline, enabling, for example, .jpg images, bitmaps, or .wav files to be synchronized with each other. Multimedia content must be converted to ASF before delivery over a network. ASF content can be hosted on a local hard disk, an HTTP server, or a specialized media server such as NetShow. This hosting flexibility gives extraordinary freedom to the content creator: the same content can be played locally from a compact disc or a hard disk, or played from a remote location hosted on an HTTP server or a specialized media server. ASF allows content and tool developers to work to a shared specification that supports the authoring, combining, archiving, annotating, and indexing of synchronized media objects, without regard to original media formats or underlying transports.

Multimedia content is stored in ASF as objects. Multimedia objects can include audio, video, still images, events, URLs, HTML pages, script commands, and executable programs. You can easily combine existing multimedia objects into a single ASF multimedia stream. ASF retains the form of each object's media (including audio and video compression), as well as optional synchronization information. Therefore, when the file is played over a network, users see and hear the file exactly as intended.

ASF data objects are stored within .asf files as packets. Each packet is designed to be directly inserted "as is" into the data field of data communication transport protocols. These packets are streamed across a network at a specific bandwidth or bit rate, so users can use, or "play," the multimedia data as it arrives. ASF supports a number of standard graphics, video, and audio file formats. You can easily convert other formats to a format that is supported by ASF.

ASF data can be tailored to satisfy a wide variety of differing network requirements. The data in each .asf file is optimized to stream at a distinct bit rate. You can specify ASF streaming bit rates from 14.4 Kbps to 6 Mbps. ASF content can thus be flexibly targeted for specific network environments with distinct capacity requirements.

For more information about ASF, see the Active Streaming Format white paper, available at **http://microsoft.com/netshow/about/whtepprs/**.

Understanding Error Correction and Masking

As files stream across a network, packets of information can be lost, particularly on the Internet. When packets are lost, users can experience choppy play, loss or gaps in the audio or video, and even loss of entire images. If packets stop being delivered, the NetShow Player stops rendering until it can rebuild its buffer.

To improve performance when packets of information are lost during transmission, you can use the NetShow error correction and masking feature of the ASF file format. For example, the ASF Editor and ASF Real-Time Encoder can optionally include redundant error-correction data in the stream, which enables the NetShow Player to correct for certain levels of packet loss. If packet loss is extreme (to the point where error correction is not possible), the player masks the errors. For audio masking, the player uses neighboring audio information to conceal the loss of data. For image masking, NetShow supports conversion of images into loss-tolerant .jpg images, which the NetShow Player can then use to minimize the loss of data packet, as opposed to discarding the entire image.

Understanding Unicasting and Multicasting

Unicasting refers to networking in which computers establish two-way, point-to-point connections. The bulk of the traffic on today's networks is unicast: A user requests a file, and a server sends the file to that client only. The disadvantage of unicasting is that each client that connects to the server receives a separate stream, which rapidly uses up network bandwidth. Networks also support *broadcasting*. When data is broadcast, a single copy of the data is sent to all clients on the network.

When the same data needs to be sent to only a portion of the clients on the network, both unicasting and broadcasting waste network bandwidth. Unicasting wastes bandwidth by sending multiple copies of the data. Broadcasting wastes bandwidth by sending the data to the whole network whether or not the data is wanted.

Multicasting avoids the weaknesses of both of these approaches. Multicasting sends a single copy of the data to those clients who request it. Multiple copies of data are not sent across the network, nor is data sent to clients who do not want it. Multicasting allows the deployment of multimedia applications on the network, while minimizing their demand for bandwidth. The following graph compares the network load per client, when unicasting and multicasting an 8 Kbps PCM audio stream, and shows how a multicast saves bandwidth.

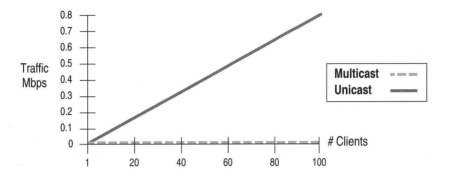

Unicast content is stored on a server, and users request the stream by opening a URL for the unicast. With unicasting, the content is sent over the network to each user on demand. When streaming multimedia over a network, the advantage of unicasting is that the client computer can communicate with the computer supplying the multimedia stream. With Microsoft NetShow, for example, the NetShow server can provide a unicast video stream to a client, and the client can take advantage of the VCR controls in the NetShow Player to ask the server to pause the stream or to skip backward or forward to a marker in the stream. As you can see, however, you pay a high price in bandwidth for this control.

Multicast content is broadcast from a server over the network, and users "tune in" to receive the content. With multicasts, the network bandwidth consumed is the same whether 1 user or 1,000 users receive the content stream. However, as with tuning in to a live television program, the user loses the ability to fast-forward and rewind.

Multicasting can provide bandwidth-efficient Webcasts when tens, hundreds, or thousands of individuals need the same information. For example, sales trends for the week can be presented to all regional sales managers by means of a multicast. Events such as a product introduction or an important press conference can also be multicast.

Multicasting follows a "push" model of communications. That is, like a radio or television broadcast, those who want to receive a multicast tune their machines to the channel they want to receive. In the case of multicasting, the user is simply instructing the computer's network card to listen to a particular IP address for the multicast. The computer originating the multicast does not need to know who has decided to receive it.

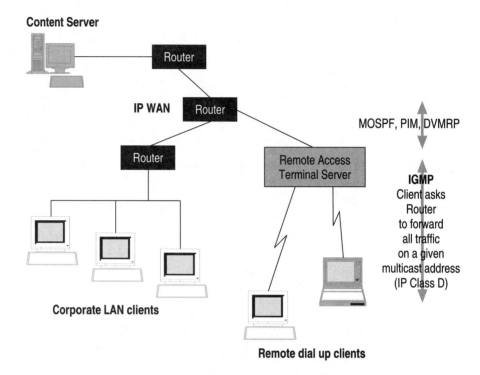

Content Server

IP WAN

Router

Router

Router

Remote Access Terminal Server

MOSPF, PIM, DVMRP

IGMP
Client asks
Router
to forward
all traffic
on a given
multicast address
(IP Class D)

Corporate LAN clients

Remote dial up clients

Multicast is sometimes called *IP multicast* because it requires a network with routers that support IP multicasting protocols. Two years ago, major router manufacturers began adding multicasting capability to their routers. Multicasting can be enabled on such routers by simply updating their software and adding memory.

Three multicast routing protocols are in use today: Distance Vector Multicast Routing Protocol (DVMRP), Multicast Open Shortest Path First (MOSPF) protocol, and Protocol-Independent Multicast (PIM). The task of these protocols is to create efficient multicast delivery paths through the network. Multicast routing protocols use varying algorithms to achieve efficiency.

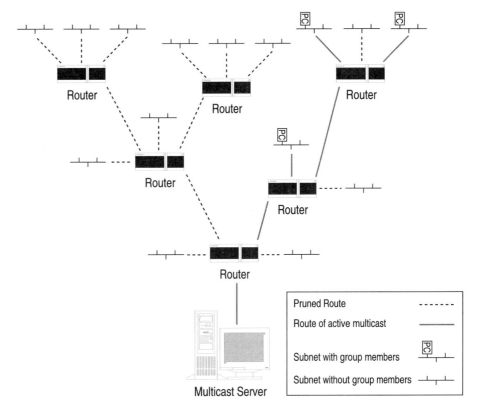

An efficient delivery path ensures that multicast data travels only to those users who want to receive it and takes the shortest path to those clients. If data travels elsewhere through the network, bandwidth goes to waste. You can visualize the network as a tree structure. The source of the multicast sends data through the branches of the tree. The routers are responsible for sending data down the correct branches to other routers and to the subnetworks, where members of a group are waiting for data. Routers prune off branches where no one wants data and graft branches back to the tree when a client in a new subnetwork joins the group. Routers can also stop data that is not wanted from traveling to their own subnetworks.

Multicasts can also support bidirectional communication. For example, individuals in widely dispersed locations can use Microsoft NetMeeting to set up a live conference that includes audio, video, and a whiteboard. For more information, see Chapter 20, "NetMeeting."

Understanding Unicasting and Multicasting with NetShow Server

NetShow Server is a service, similar to an HTTP server, that runs on a Windows NT Server. When NetShow Server is installed, a publishing point is established as the directory where the server will look to find the files that it will stream. When you place an .asf file on a NetShow Server for streaming, you must put that file in the NetShow publishing point; otherwise, NetShow Server won't know where to find the .asf file. When you enter a URL to access or play an .asf file, you specify the name of the NetShow Server and then the path to the .asf file. NetShow Server immediately begins looking in the NetShow publishing point for the requested .asf file. NetShow Server streams .asf files to NetShow Players.

To play an .asf file from a NetShow Server, you can open the .asf file using the stand-alone NetShow Player. You can also open .asf files using the browser, and the streamed content will automatically play using the integrated NetShow ActiveX control, which functions in the same way as the stand-alone player. For more information, see "Using the NetShow Player" later in this chapter.

NetShow Announcements

You can use a NetShow announcement (.asx) file to point users to a multicast channel or to the source of a unicast stream. The .asx file contains the information that NetShow Player needs to locate and play unicasts and multicasts.

There are two types of .asx files: those that are encrypted and those that aren't. Encrypted .asx files are used for multicasts. You use the NetShow Administrator Channel Manager to create .asx files for multicasts. Nonencrypted .asx files are used for unicasts. You can use a text editor to create .asx files for unicasts. For more information on creating .asf files, see the *NetShow Server Administration Guide* and the *NetShow Content Creation Authoring Guide*.

To notify users of a unicast or multicast, you can:

- Send .asx files to users by e-mail.
- Add the .asx file as a link reference in a Web page.
- Add the .asx file to a public directory on a network share.

The most common method for using an .asx file is as a link in a Web page. The following illustration shows what happens when a user clicks an .asx file on a Web page.

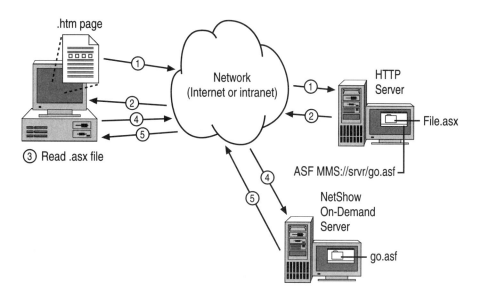

In this illustration, the user is browsing the Web page, clicks the .asx link, and the NetShow Player is called to play the .asf file. The basic process follows:

1. The user clicks the link—the .asx file.

2. The HTTP server sends the .asx file to the requesting browser.

3. The browser reads the .asx file and determines which NetShow server to contact and which .asf file to request.

4. The browser launches the NetShow Player to play the requested .asf file.

5. The browser contacts NetShow Server and requests the specified .asf file.

6. The NetShow Server begins streaming the .asf file to the NetShow Player.

HTTP Versus MMS

After you create .asf files, in order to stream them, you must place them on the NetShow Server or on an HTTP server. It is recommended that you place .asf files on the NetShow Server, because only there do you receive all the ASF functionality. HTTP servers can stream .asf files; however, an HTTP server cannot duplicate all the functionality of a NetShow Server.

In addition, when identifying the path to an .asx or .asf file, you must specify the protocol used to deliver the .asf file, either HTTP or the MMS protocol. For example:

```
mms://netshowserver/file.asf
```

```
http://webserver/file.asf
```

You normally want to use the MMS protocol when specifying URLs to stream .asf files to users. MMS streams content more reliably and delivers better streaming performance than HTTP. However, since some firewalls may not allow for streaming content that uses the MMS protocol, it may be necessary for some users to stream .asf files from an HTTP server. For more information, see "HTTP Streaming" later in this chapter.

NetShow Channels

When multimedia or files are multicast using NetShow, a channel is first set up. You use the NetShow Administrator Channel Manager to create and administer channels. The channel can be populated with programs, which are the content for that channel. Programs can be live feeds or on-demand content scheduled to be played at specific times. The channel establishes the communication between the server and the multicast clients. Much like television, what is seen on your screen may be live, or it may be played from a tape at a specific time. Also like television, you can't skip ahead or back; you get the broadcast and if you don't like it you either turn it off or change channels.

A NetShow channel specifies the destinations for ASF streams and provides the information that clients need to listen to the channel, including information on the IP address and port for the multicast and the format of the stream itself. NetShow channels are analogous to broadcast television channels. Just as television programs are assigned to channels, programs in NetShow are assigned to channels by specifying that the streams in the program use a particular channel.

Channels provide the flexibility to stream data using multicast and unicast methods to fit a variety of situations:

- To distribute streams by multicasting, specify a multicast address.
- To distribute streams by unicasting, specify a unicast server to which clients can connect. This allows clients that are not able to receive the multicast to receive the data.
- To distribute data to additional NetShow servers, set up a channel for distribution.

A channel is required when multicasting ASF streams. When unicasting ASF streams, using a channel is optional.

Although the primary use of a channel is to provide address and stream information to users, channels can also:

- **Roll Over to Unicast.** You can set up a channel so that clients unable to receive the multicast can automatically connect to the NetShow Server and receive a unicast of the same information. This feature can be used to reach clients who are behind a firewall.

- **Stream Distribution.** You can set up channels to supply secondary NetShow servers with streams, which they can, in turn, multicast. For example, you can distribute a stream to NetShow servers located on separate local area network segments. Each server can then multicast to clients on its segment. This feature is useful on intranets with routers that are not configured for multicasting.

You use the NetShow Administrator Channel Manager to create channels. After you create a channel, export the channel (.asc) file to a location where clients can reach the file. Typically, this is a publishing point on your HTTP server. However, it can also be a public share on your network.

NetShow Streams and Programs

A NetShow *stream* refers to the data transmitted across the network and to any properties associated with the data. A NetShow *program* consists of a group of one or more streams. You use the NetShow Administrator Program Manager to create and administer programs. You use a program to organize the streams you want to multicast. Starting a program starts the multicast of the streams in the program. A program plays its streams one at a time, in order. When you add streams to a program, you can specify how long each stream plays. Information about programs, such as what streams to play and how long to play them, is stored in program (.nsp) files on the NetShow Server.

The term *stream* also refers to the way in which data is transmitted across the network. When data is streamed across the network, clients can render the data as they receive it. For example, the client can play an audio stream as it arrives rather than storing it in a file and playing it only after the entire file has been received.

NetShow supports the following stream types:

- **Active Streaming Format (ASF).** ASF supports the greatest variety of data, including video, audio, images, URLs, and scripts. You can generate live ASF streams that contain audio and video using the NetShow Real-Time Encoder, or use the tools provided with NetShow or those from third parties to create and store ASF files that you can stream. An ASF stream can combine different types of data. For example, if you want to present a lecture that includes slides, you can stream audio while also streaming .gif files of the slides.

  By using NetShow channels, ASF provides the greatest flexibility for various network situations. NetShow can multicast or unicast ASF streams. When multicasting an ASF stream, you can also configure NetShow to provide a unicast source for the stream so that clients that are unable to receive the multicast can automatically receive it as a unicast.

- **RTP Live Audio.** RTP Live Audio streams audio that is fed into the server's sound card. NetShow supports RTP Live Audio multicasts, but not unicasts. Multicasts that stream RTP Live Audio are easy to set up. However, because channels do not support RTP Live Audio streams, connection information must be coded in the embedded control that clients use to receive and render the multicast.

- **RTP WAV Audio.** RTP WAV Audio streams audio recorded as .wav files. NetShow supports RTP WAV Audio multicasts, but not unicasts. Multicasts that stream RTP WAV Audio are easy to set up. However, because channels do not support RTP WAV Audio streams, connection information must be coded in the embedded control that clients use to receive and render the multicast.

- **File transfer.** File transfer supports the streaming transfer of directories and files. NetShow supports file transfer multicasts, but not unicasts. Multicasts that stream file transfers are easy to set up. However, because channels do not support file-transfer streams, connection information must be coded in an embedded ActiveX control that clients use to receive and render the multicast.

NetShow Multicast and Unicast Scenarios

You can set up and run NetShow 2.1 to provide a wide variety of true Webcasting solutions. The possibilities are nearly unlimited, but the following sections suggest some of the ways you can use NetShow to provide Webcasting solutions. (For more information about application scenarios, see "Webcasting with NetShow" earlier in this chapter.)

Multicasting Live ASF Streams

You can use ASF streaming to deliver live multimedia content to users' desktops. For example, you can multicast a CEO's speech over the corporate network to all employees. The only limitations on live ASF streaming are those presented by the network bandwidth.

You multicast audio and video by feeding the signal into the audio or video capture card on a server with the Real-Time Encoder. The Real-Time Encoder server delivers the encoded information to the NetShow Administrator Channel Manager on the NetShow Server, which multicasts a live ASF stream. As with .asf files, live ASF streaming must be restricted to the bandwidth of the network. In the case of live ASF streaming, the Real-Time Encoder uses codecs during the encoding process to make the outgoing ASF stream small enough to stream across the network.

The following illustration shows the Real-Time Encoder, NetShow Server, and HTTP server on separate computers. While all software can run on a single computer, in most cases you want to run the system as shown. Because the Real-Time Encoder places heavy demands on the processor, dedicating a computer to run it can ensure optimum performance.

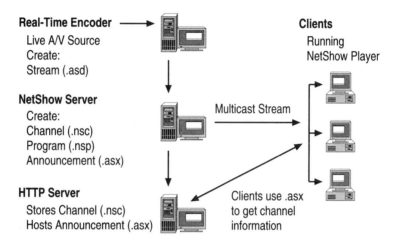

Real-Time Encoder
Live A/V Source
Create:
Stream (.asd)

Clients
Running
NetShow Player

NetShow Server
Create:
Channel (.nsc)
Program (.nsp)
Announcement (.asx)

Multicast Stream

HTTP Server
Stores Channel (.nsc)
Hosts Announcement (.asx)

Clients use .asx
to get channel
information

The Real-Time Encoder encodes live or stored audio and video into an ASF stream (a temporary .asd file), an .asf file, or both. The Real-Time Encoder is an extremely useful NetShow content-creation tool for two reasons: it is the only tool that can accept a live source, and it is the only tool that can compress the video source (live or stored) so that the resulting ASF stream or .asf file fits in a target bandwidth. All other tools require you to edit the video before you convert it to an ASF stream or .asf file. You can even use the Real-Time Encoder to convert .avi or .wav files into .asf files, without doing any preproduction work. Because the Real-Time Encoder can use video as a source, the encoder lets you set the size of the display window and choose a codec to compress the output ASF. Even if you are using live video and compact disc–quality audio as input, the ASF Real-Time Encoder can create an ASF stream with a 28.8-Kbps bit rate.

The Real-Time Encoder delivers the ASF stream that it creates to NetShow Server, which can then multicast or unicast the ASF stream over the network. If the Real-Time Encoder is used to create an .asf file, that file is saved to the directory that is specified during the configuration process. To play back an .asf file created by the Real-Time Encoder, you use NetShow Player to open the .asf file. For more information, see the *NetShow Server Administration Guide*.

The computer that houses the Real-Time Encoder must contain a sound card to encode live audio and a video capture card to encode video; you don't need either of these cards to encode an .avi or .wav file to an .asf file. The ASF Real-Time Encoder uses the inputs on the audio and video cards to receive the live source. For example, to multicast a live speech, you would plug the output from a video camera into the video card's input jack, and plug the output from the microphone into either the video card's audio input or the input on the sound card (whichever input the encoder is set to use). The encoder acknowledges these input sources, receives the input, and encodes the audio and video into an ASF stream that is then delivered to NetShow Server.

Multicasting Stored ASF Streams

You can multicast ASF streams stored as .asf files on your server. The following illustration shows how NetShow may be set up to multicast ASF streams.

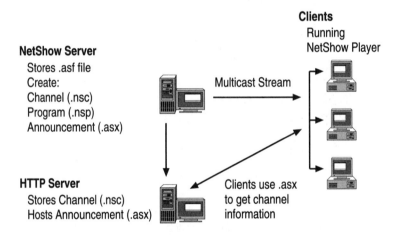

All software can run on a single computer; however, if you plan to use NetShow Server's unicast HTTP streaming, you must run your HTTP server on a separate computer.

Basically, you store the ASF files you want to stream in the publishing point on the NetShow Server. You generate a channel (.nsc) file for each stream and place the .nsc files at a location on the network where clients can reach the files. For example, if you are multicasting over a local area network to clients running the stand-alone NetShow Player, you can store the file in a public directory. If you are multicasting over an intranet or the Internet to clients running NetShow Player embedded in a Web page, you can store the file on the HTTP server.

You use the NetShow Administrator Program Manager to configure programs and create announcements (.asx files) for the programs. Announcements provide the information needed to locate the .nsc file that supplies channel information for the program. You can provide the announcement as a link on a Web page, or you can send the announcement to users in an e-mail message.

You use the Program Manager to start the program to begin the multicast. Users can now listen to the multicast, using their NetShow Player.

Unicasting a Live ASF Stream

You can also unicast a live ASF stream from the Real-Time Encoder. Setting up a unicast in this way allows users to receive one ASF stream. If you want clients to receive a series of streams, set up the unicast using a channel.

The following illustration shows the Real-Time Encoder, NetShow Server, and the HTTP server on separate computers. While all software can run on a single computer, in most cases you want to run the system as shown. Because the Real-Time Encoder places heavy demands on the processor, dedicating a computer to run it can ensure optimum performance.

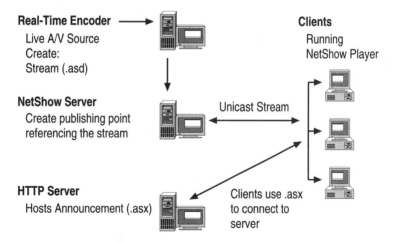

Real-Time Encoder ⟶
  Live A/V Source
  Create:
  Stream (.asd)

Clients
  Running
  NetShow Player

NetShow Server
  Create publishing point
  referencing the stream

Unicast Stream

HTTP Server
  Hosts Announcement (.asx)

Clients use .asx
to connect to
server

Unicasting a Stored ASF Stream

You can unicast an ASF stream stored as an .asf file on your server. When unicasting a stored ASF stream, users play only the one .asf file. If you want users to play a series of files, set up the unicast using a channel (as described in the next section).

The following illustration shows NetShow Server and the HTTP server on separate computers. All software can run on a single computer; however, if you plan to use NetShow Server's unicast HTTP streaming, you must run your HTTP server on a separate computer.

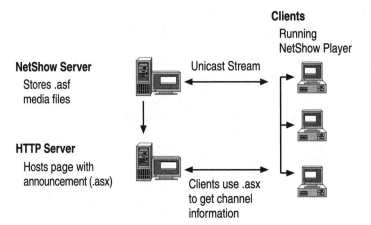

Basically, you store the .asf files you want to stream in the publishing point on the NetShow Server. You then create an announcement (.asx) file for users and store the .asx file where users can reach it. You can provide a link to the .asx file on a Web page. When users click the .asx link on the Web page, their browsers launch the NetShow Player to play the .asf file.

Unicasting Stored ASF Streams Using a Channel

You can use a channel to unicast a program that contains a series of ASF streams. The program can contain both live streams from the Real-Time Encoder and streams stored as files on your server.

The following illustration shows the Real-Time Encoder and NetShow Server on separate computers. If you are only unicasting stored streams, you do not need the Real-Time Encoder server.

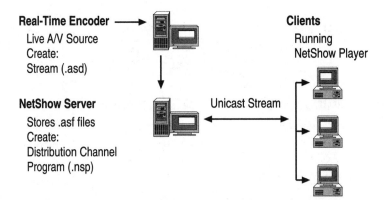

While all software can run on a single computer, in most cases you want to run the system as shown. Because the Real-Time Encoder places heavy demands on the processor, dedicating a computer to run it can ensure optimum performance.

Basically, you store the .asf files you want to stream on the NetShow Server. You generate a channel (.nsc) file for each stream and place the .nsc files at a location on the network where clients can reach the files. For example, if you are multicasting over a local area network to clients running the stand-alone NetShow Player, you can store the file in a public directory. If you are unicasting over an intranet or the Internet to clients running NetShow Player embedded in a Web page, you can store the file on the HTTP server.

You use the NetShow Administrator Manage Programs tool to configure programs and create announcements (.asx files) for the programs. Announcements provide the information needed to locate the .nsc file that supplies channel information for the program. You can provide the announcement as a link on a Web page, or you can send the announcement to users in an e-mail message.

You use the Manage Programs tool to start the program to begin the multicast. Users can now listen to the multicast using their NetShow Player.

Setting Up ASF Stream Distribution Servers

You can set up a NetShow Server to feed additional NetShow Servers. Such an arrangement can be useful when your network routers are not multicast-enabled. For example, you can set up NetShow Server to originate a live stream, unicast it to additional NetShow Servers located on subnetworks, and then multicast to the clients on those subnetworks.

The following illustration shows how you can set up a NetShow Server to feed a second NetShow Server, which provides a unicast stream to clients on a subnet.

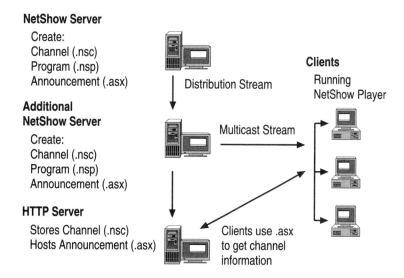

NetShow Server
 Create:
 Channel (.nsc)
 Program (.nsp)
 Announcement (.asx)

Distribution Stream

Clients
Running
NetShow Player

**Additional
NetShow Server**
 Create:
 Channel (.nsc)
 Program (.nsp)
 Announcement (.asx)

Multicast Stream

HTTP Server
 Stores Channel (.nsc)
 Hosts Announcement (.asx)

Clients use .asx
to get channel
information

On the second NetShow Server, in NetShow Administrator, you use the Configure Channels tool to create a channel for the stream. The channel must match the channel you created when setting up the first server, except that the IP address and port used for the multicast must be changed. You can create the new channel by importing the original channel's .nsc file and modifying it.

On the second NetShow Server, you use the NetShow Administrator Manage Programs tool to configure programs and create announcements (.asx files) for the programs. Announcements provide the information needed to locate the .nsc file that supplies channel information for the program. You can provide the announcement as a link on a Web page, or you can send the announcement to users in an e-mail message.

You use the Manage Programs tool to start the program on the second NetShow Server to begin the multicast. Users can now listen to the multicast from the second server using their NetShow Player.

Multicasting File Transfers

You can use NetShow multicasts for transfer of large files over the network. Multicast file transfer provides a reliable mechanism for distributing any type of file. With multicast file transfer, delivery is guaranteed only within the limits of the forward-error-correction scheme used in NetShow.

The following illustration shows NetShow Server and the HTTP server on separate computers. When multicasting files, all software can run on a single computer.

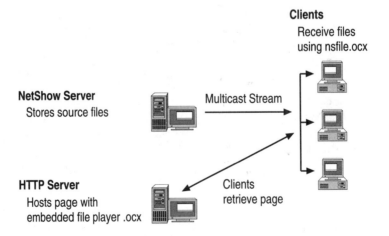

Basically, you store the files to multicast on the NetShow Server, and then use the NetShow Administrator Program Manager to create a program that organizes one or more media streams for multicast. You add a file to the program by specifying its file name and properties, such as the file location, the amount of bandwidth to use for the multicast, the destination IP address and port, and the scope of the multicast.

You must also create a Web page that includes the file-transfer control Nsfile.ocx and the multicast address where the client computer listens to receive the file. You store the Web page in the appropriate publishing point on the HTTP server to make it available to users. For more information, see the *NetShow Client SDK*.

You use the Program Manager to start the program on the NetShow Server to begin the multicast. Users can retrieve the Web page with the embedded Nsfile.ocx control to begin the multicast file transfer.

Using HTTP Streaming

You can unicast .asf files using the HTTP protocol with NetShow to stream content through firewalls that don't support MMS. Using HTTP streaming allows clients to receive streams across a network firewall; however, HTTP streaming does not perform as well as MMS streaming, and you cannot use certain features of the .asf file, such as jumping to markers.

Note   All server software can run on a single computer; however, if you use unicast HTTP streaming, you must run your HTTP server on a separate computer.

By default, HTTP streaming is disabled. To enable HTTP streaming, you must edit the Windows NT system registry to change the setting for HTTP streaming and then stop and restart the NetShow unicast service. You must also add two MIME types for the .asf and .asx extensions on the HTTP server computer.

Caution   Before editing the system registry, be sure to back up the registry. Incorrect changes or deletions made to the registry can damage the Windows operating system and prevent the system from running normally.

▶   **To enable HTTP streaming**

1. On the **Start** menu, click **Run**.

   The **Run** dialog box is displayed.

2. In the **Open** box, type **regedit**, and then click **OK**.

   Registry Editor starts.

3. In Registry Editor, use the tree view to navigate through the following path:

   HKEY_LOCAL_MACHINE\SYSTEM\CurrentControlSet\ Services\nsunicast\parameters

4. Click the **parameters** folder.

5. In the **Name** column, click **EnableHTTPStreaming**.

6. On the **Edit** menu, click **Modify**.

7. In the **Edit DWORD Value** dialog box, type **1** in the **Value data** box, and then click **OK**.

8. On the **Registry** menu, click **Exit** to close Registry Editor.

9. On the **Start** menu, point to **Settings,** and then click **Control Panel**.

10. In Control Panel, double-click the **Services** icon.

11. In the **Services** dialog box, click **NetShow Unicast Manager**, and then click **Stop**.

12. In the **Stopping** dialog box, click **OK**.

    Both the NetShow Unicast Manager service and the NetShow Program Manager service are stopped.

13. In the **Services** dialog box, click **NetShow Unicast Manager**, and then click **Start**.

14. In the **Services** dialog box, click **NetShow Program Manager**, and then click **Start**.

▶ **To set MIME types for Microsoft Internet Information Server**

1. On the **Start** menu, click **Run**.

   The **Run** dialog box is displayed.

2. In the **Open** box, enter **regedit**, and then click **OK**.

   Registry Editor starts.

3. In Registry Editor, use the tree view to navigate through the following path:

   HKEY_LOCAL_MACHINE\SYSTEM\CurrentControlSet\ Services\InetInfo\Parameters\MimeMap

4. Click the **mimemap** folder.

5. On the Edit menu, click **New**, and then click **String Value**.

6. In the right pane, enter **video/x-ms-asf,asf,,5** in the **mimemap** folder.

7. On the **Registry** menu, click **Exit** to close Registry Editor.

8. Restart the Internet Information Server.

▶ **To set MIME types for non-Microsoft HTTP servers**

1. Refer to your HTTP server documentation and follow instructions for adding the following:

   MIME type: video/x-ms-asf
   Extensions: asf,asx

2. If necessary, restart the HTTP server.

Developing Content for NetShow

Microsoft NetShow delivers live and on-demand multimedia content over intranets and the Internet. NetShow can transfer live multicast audio and files and can play on-demand streamed audio, illustrated audio, and video.

For more information about developing content for NetShow, see the *NetShow Content Creation Authoring Guide*, and visit the NetShow How-To Web page at **http://microsoft.com/netshow/howto.htm**.

A NetShow Scenario

Suppose that you work for ABX Compute Corporation, and your company is getting ready to release the newest version of your product, the Widget. ABX Compute is going to have a release party to promote the new Widget, and it is your job to design a way for all company employees, partners, and potential customers to share in the festivities, informational talks, and training that will go on.

At the party, the company president will give a keynote speech, and then several vice presidents will give demonstrations on how to use the Widget. ABX Compute always videotapes release parties. You decide to use NetShow, because you know that you can stream audio and images across the Internet; but your boss isn't quite convinced that it's the tool to use. He asks:

- *How do we deliver rich multimedia to Internet customers who are using 28.8-Kbps modems?*

   You explain that with NetShow, you can create and stream audio and video while controlling the bandwidth. NetShow is codec-independent, and because all NetShow installations include the VDONet VDOWave codec, you can compress the video for streaming over a 28.8-Kbps bandwidth network.

- *If lots of people around the company are running multimedia files across the network, won't that bog down all communications on the network?*

   Multicasting a file sends a single file to multiple users across the network. In the case of streaming files, a system administrator designates a maximum amount of data that can be streamed across the network at one time. This keeps the network from being bogged down or from interfering with other communication on the network.

- *How do we create the training and presentation files without spending a lot more money?*

   NetShow comes with several tools that allow you to turn various sources into .asf content. You can use the videotape to capture frames for illustrated audio .asf files and for Internet- and intranet-bandwidth video .asf files. You can use the existing video editing tools to capture frames and to edit the video.

- *ABX Compute has licensed a new video codec from Awesome Computers. Can we use this codec with NetShow?*

   NetShow is codec-independent. You can use any PCM/ACM codec for audio or video as long as the user's computer has the same codec.

- *All company employees are going to want to be part of the release party, even if they can't attend.*

   With NetShow, you can multicast the audio live from the release party to every employee, partner, or customer desktop. All any user needs to receive the multicast audio is the NetShow Player.

- *But what about viewing the demonstrations and training?*

   You can use the demonstration and training portion of the videotapes to create various NetShow .asf files. As opposed to forcing users to download huge video files, NetShow streaming allows users—even during peak viewing hours—to watch video files with no download time. The NetShow Player is free, so you don't have to worry about the user not having the player.

When streaming audio and video over a network, bandwidth is your most valuable resource, and knowing how to deal with it is your top priority. In most cases, you want to deliver the richest multimedia content possible, while using the minimum network bandwidth.

Developing Live NetShow Content

Because you don't have to convert any of your source material to a different format, it's easy to create live NetShow content. Just plug a compact disc player, tape player, audio output from a VCR or laser disc player, or any other audio source into the input on your NetShow Real-Time Encoder server's sound card.

In the case of ABX Compute Corporation, you would feed the live audio from the keynote speaker's microphone into the NetShow Real-Time Encoder server's sound card. The speech will be multicast to all listeners.

As long as you can input an audio source to your sound card through your computer's bus or input jack, you can multicast that audio. (Be sure you aren't violating any copyright or ownership laws.)

When choosing an audio source, be sure that you have complete access to the entire source. Using a live source is fine, but do not use a streaming or multicast audio file as your input source.

Developing On-Demand NetShow Content

NetShow on-demand content is provided in .asf files. You can deliver multimedia content such as audio, illustrated audio, or video at various data rates, including 28.8 Kbps. For more information, see "Adjusting Your Content for the Bandwidth Using Codecs" later in this chapter.

You can do more with .asf files than just deliver audio and video content. Within an .asf file, while it is playing, you can open Web pages and deliver scripting commands to the user's computer to create an entire user experience.

Using .asf files, you can, for example, deliver a training video, a PowerPoint presentation, or audio with synchronized images. With the ability to embed scripting commands, you can extend the ability of the .asf files so they can invoke URLs, process feedback from the user, and execute client-side commands.

NetShow streams .asf files, as well as RealAudio and RealVideo. You can place practically any type of video, image, or audio into an .asf file and then include URL and script commands.

Obtaining Content

Your first step in creating an .asf file is to obtain the video, image, and/or audio content you want to use. When creating .asf files, always start with the highest-quality source files. Then, as network bandwidth dictates, you can reduce the quality of your source files. In the ABX Compute Corporation example, you can use any videotape that was shot at the release party. If anyone used PowerPoint to create presentation slides, you can use the presentation files, too. The following sections briefly describe how to turn this content into .asf files.

Video

Video is an excellent source, because the audio and visual elements are already combined. To create a video source, convert (digitize) any beta, VHS, 8mm, Hi-8, laser disc, or other video content into .avi or .mov format. Once this is done, you can use the NetShow tools to convert the video source into .asf files.

For our example, let's say you've got the Widget release party speeches and presentations on VHS videotape. The first thing you must do is convert the video format from VHS tape to digital .avi or .mov format.

To digitize your video content and place it on a hard disk or network share, use a video editing tool such as VidEdit, VidCap, or Adobe Premiere. For this conversion, you need a computer that, along with the proper software, also contains a high-resolution video card with audio and video inputs, such as the Truevision Targa 1000 Pro, Miro Video DC20, or Digital Processing Systems Perception Video Recorder.

If you have digital video content that is not in .avi or .mov format, use a video conversion tool, such as those mentioned, to convert the video into .avi or .mov format. If you want to create illustrated audio, all you have to do is make a copy of the video's audio track and then synchronize frame captures to it.

Images

You can use any image in the .bmp, .dib, .rle, .jpg, or .gif format to create .asf files. Begin with a source image from a digital camera, video frame capture, PowerPoint slide, scanned image, or any other digital art. Once the image is in a digital format, use any image-processing software to convert it to one of the appropriate formats.

If you want to use video frame captures as images in an .asf file, you need the software and hardware discussed in the "Video" section above. If you already have your video in .avi or .mov format, use a video-editing tool such as VidEdit or Adobe Premiere to capture frames.

If the video is not in a file on a shared or local drive, use a video player to play the video into your video capture board, and capture and save the video frames in a usable format to your hard disk.

If you use Microsoft PowerPoint to create presentations, you can easily convert these slides into the JPEG (.jpg) format, using the Internet Assistant for Microsoft PowerPoint add-on tool. For information on how to download and use the tool, see **http://www.microsoft.com/powerpoint/Internet/IA/default.htm**.

Audio

Only .wav files can be used in an .asf file. The .wav file can use any ACM codec; that is, any .wav file you can play on your computer can be used in an .asf file. (Your Windows 95 or Windows NT operating system contains these codecs.)

If you want to convert live audio, a compact disc, or any other external source of recorded audio into a .wav file, use sound-editing software, such as SoundRecorder or Sonic Foundry's Sound Forge, to record the audio through your sound card's input or line-in jack, and then save it as a .wav file.

URLs

You can include any URL in an .asf file. The NetShow Player does not check, locate, or open the URLs. When the NetShow Player comes to a URL in an .asf file, it sends the URL to the default browser, which then opens the URL. If the computer that is playing the .asf file does not contain a browser or for some reason cannot access the URL, the URL is ignored.

Script Commands

Script commands are client-side code that you include in the .asf file. The NetShow Player does not run or execute script commands. Instead, as the NetShow Player receives the .asf file, the script commands are passed to a client-side application that handles the commands and executes the actions.

Selecting a Bandwidth

After you have your source, you need to decide for what size network bandwidth you are going to create the .asf file. Bandwidth limits the size of an .asf file. You can use NetShow tools to create an .asf file for any size bandwidth, but you may not be able to stream it across your network.

There are three classes of bandwidths: Internet, intranet, and specialized networks. Each class, and the type of .asf file that will stream across it, is briefly described in the following sections. In order to stream an .asf file over a limited bandwidth such as 14.4 or 28.8 Kbps, you need to reduce or compress your source files.

Internet (14.4-Kbps and 28.8-Kbps Modems or 64-Kbps ISDN Modem)

Internet bandwidth is equivalent to what most phone lines carry. 14.4-Kbps and 28.8-Kbps modem speeds are used by the majority of Internet computers, while only a few have access to ISDN modems. With a 14.4-Kbps modem, you can receive streaming audio with only a few images (if the streaming file is long). With a 28.8-Kbps modem, you can receive streaming audio and illustrated audio. With a 64-Kbps ISDN modem, you can receive extremely high-quality streaming audio, illustrated audio (with many more images than with a 28.8-Kbps modem), and reduced-quality video.

Intranet (100 to 200 Kbps or 128-Kbps ISDN Modem)

Intranet bandwidth of 100 to 200 Kbps is typical among business networks. With an intranet or a 128-Kbps ISDN modem, you can typically stream compact disc–quality audio, illustrated audio (with compact disc–quality audio and lots of images), and medium-quality video.

Specialized Networks (1 to 6 Mbps)

Many organizations are using new technology to upgrade their local area networks to support increased bandwidths from 1 to 6 Mbps. With 1 to 6 Mbps of effective bandwidth, a network can easily stream true video, as well as compact disc–quality audio.

Building the ASF File

After you have chosen source files and a bandwidth, you are ready to build .asf files. Because the source files used to create an .asf file are different, while you are creating the .asf file you need to make sure that all source files that will make up an .asf file can fit within the designated bandwidth. However, you may find that once you've built the .asf file, you don't like it. If so, edit and adjust the source files, and build it again. As you build .asf files, you will see that there are three main types: audio, video, and illustrated audio. The type that you build depends on the NetShow tool that you use.

Selecting a Tool

When you installed the NetShow tools, you installed everything that you need to convert audio, video, and illustrated audio into .asf files. Each of the tools described in the following sections is used to convert a specific file type or combination of file types into an .asf file.

For more information about content development tools, see "NetShow Authoring and Production Tools" earlier in this chapter.

WavToAsf

Use WavToAsf to convert .wav files to .asf files. The size of the .asf file that WavToAsf creates is directly proportional to the audio source. If you use a compact disc–quality .wav file to create an .asf file, you will get a compact disc–quality .asf file. Even though this may be what you think you want, realize that you will be streaming this file over a network. Many bandwidths cannot support the streaming of compact disc–quality audio. To build an audio-only .asf file for your chosen bandwidth, build the .asf file, and then test it to see whether it can stream over the network bandwidth. If it cannot, you need to compress the audio source and rebuild the .asf file.

The WavToAsf command-line tool is not an editor. If you need to do any editing or if you want to compress the .wav file, you need to use a third-party tool such as SoundRecorder or Sound Forge 4.0a to edit the audio source and then rebuild the .asf file. Even though you must run WavToAsf from the command line, WavToAsf allows you to create a full .asf file complete with markers, URLs, and script commands.

To return to the ABX Compute release party example, you can use WavToAsf to turn the multicast audio into a richer .asf file. Using WavToAsf, you can add script commands or invoke URLs at points in the audio where the additional Web page or .asf file information add to the audio-only .asf file.

VidToAsf

VidToAsf is a command-line tool that converts .avi or .mov files into .asf files. As with WavToAsf, VidToAsf is not an authoring or editing tool, it only converts video files into .asf files. The size of the video file that you use as a source directly correlates to the size of the .asf file. If you need to edit or compress the video source in any way before converting it to an .asf file, use a video editor. Use VidToAsf to turn the videotape from the ABX Compute release party into an .asf file.

When you run the command to convert the video source to an .asf file, you can also specify standard .asf options such as including markers, URLs, or script commands.

ASF Editor

ASF Editor is the most robust of the .asf creation tools. With ASF Editor, you can combine and synchronize audio, images, and script commands, and then output these into an .asf file.

To help you create .asf files that are suited for limited bandwidths, ASF Editor allows you to specify the bandwidth and also furnishes you with tools for resizing and compressing the audio and images.

In ASF Editor, you design the .asf files by placing the audio and image source files in a time line. ASF Editor gives you a graphic representation of how the source files fit in the specified bandwidth. From this representation, you will be able to tell whether your files can be built into an .asf file, whether you have attempted to put too much image or audio information into the bandwidth, or whether you have room left in the bandwidth for more information.

Unlike VidToAsf or WavToAsf, ASF Editor allows you to specify a bandwidth, which sets a limit on the size of your .asf file. Based on your chosen limit, as you build your .asf file, you may be forced to edit or discard some of the source files in order to correctly build an .asf file. If you want to edit the content of your audio or image sources, you need to use a third-party tool. If the image or audio won't fit in the bandwidth, use the ASF Editor compression tools to force the source into the designated bandwidth. If you like how the audio and image files fit together, build and then view your .asf file.

In the ABX Compute scenario, you can use ASF Editor to combine portions of the release party multicast audio, audio clips from the videotapes, frames captured from the videotapes, scanned pictures taken at the party, and slides taken from presentation files into an .asf file. You can determine the bandwidth that the .asf file will stream over.

NetShow Presenter

NetShow Presenter is a PowerPoint add-in tool that lets you synchronize a PowerPoint presentation into an ASF stream. You can use NetShow Presenter to output a PowerPoint presentation directly to an .asf file that's ready to stream. NetShow Presenter enables PowerPoint to:

- Connect with the Real-Time Encoder.
- Send URL script commands to the Real-Time Encoder.
- Export presentation slides.
- Create and control a PowerPoint presentation that remote users can watch over the network on their own desktop.

For example, suppose a company's CEO is giving a presentation to the heads of several companies. Because of time constraints and other commitments, many employees who would like to attend the presentation cannot. With NetShow and NetShow Presenter, the CEO can provide a live video feed of himself speaking along with synchronized images of his presentation slides. NetShow Server delivers the live video feed, and NetShow Presenter allows the CEO to synchronize the delivery of the presentation slides to specific points in the live video feed. Employees who wanted to watch the presentation can download the presentation Web page and receive the presentation as if they were in same room as the presenter.

ASFChop

ASFChop is a simple .asf file editor. Use ASFChop to delete pieces of an .asf file. ASFChop also makes an .asf file seekable; that is, if an .asf file is longer than 10 seconds in length, ASFChop creates an index for that file so that you can seek (similar to fast forwarding) through the file. This is a useful feature, because the Real-Time Encoder does not create seekable .asf files. You can use ASFChop to create an index in an .asf file without cutting any information.

Adjusting Your Content for the Bandwidth Using Codecs

What makes NetShow such an effective tool for creating streaming network multimedia files is its capability to adjust the source content files. NetShow is codec-independent. Other technologies use a proprietary codec, which means the codec can be used only by that one application, and other codecs cannot be applied.

NetShow lets the .asf author and end user use a well-rounded suite of bundled and stand-alone third-party codecs for voice, music, images, and video for various bandwidths. This results in a greater number of options, more flexibility, higher-quality content, and because the codecs can be upgraded independent of NetShow, faster innovation.

After choosing a bandwidth, reduce the size of your source content. You can reduce the size of your source content two ways: adjust the size (height and width) of the source of image or video files, or apply a codec. Most of the time you will want to apply a codec.

Adjusting Image Size

To adjust the size of an image or video file, use an image editor (Adobe Photoshop, CorelDRAW, or Microsoft Imager) or a video editor (AVIEdit, Adobe Premiere). You cannot adjust the size of an audio file without changing the content.

Using Codecs

When you install NetShow, you also install a variety of codecs designed specifically for image, audio, and video. These codecs reside on your computer and are available to the various editing tools that you will use to edit your audio, video, and image sources. Most codecs are designed for a specific purpose.

For example, VDONet VDOWave is a good video codec, but it is not good for compressing images. It's better to use JPEG compression for images. Before you build your .asf file, experiment with the various codecs to reduce the size of your source files.

Because the codecs are installed on your machine, you can use the codecs in any application that supports codecs. For example, to compress an .avi file, you can open Adobe Premiere on your computer and apply the VDONet VDOWave codec to the .avi file. Of the three NetShow tools (VidToAsf, WavToAsf, and ASF Editor) that are installed on your computer, only ASF Editor allows you to associate codecs with source files. You must use video or audio editing tools to associate codecs with the source files before using VidToAsf or WavToAsf to create .asf files.

Once you have the video content in .avi or .mov format, compress the files before you convert them to .asf. Because most compression algorithms are specifically designed for audio or video, you want to compress both the audio and video portions of your .avi file. Use tools such as Sonic Foundry's Sound Forge or Adobe Premiere to apply compression algorithms to the .avi.

NetShow supplies you with the codecs that you will want to use. For example, if you are creating a video .asf file of the ABX Compute release party for use over the Internet (28.8-Kbps bandwidth), you'll want to use the VDOWave codec for the video portion and the L&H codec for the audio portion. If you're creating a video .asf file for use over the ABX Compute internal network (100-Kbps band-width), you may want to use the Indeo 4.1 codec for the video and the Truespeech codec for the audio.

For more information about the codecs that are included with NetShow, see **http://www.microsoft.com/netshow/codecs.htm**.

Streaming the ASF File

After creating an .asf file, you will want to play it. You can double-click the .asf file to play it locally, but how do you enable others to stream the .asf file to their desktops? First, place the .asf file on a NetShow Server, and then create a way for others to access the .asf file.

Posting ASF Files on the NetShow Server

To post .asf files on a NetShow Server, simply copy the .asf files to the NetShow publishing point on that server.

Posting ASX Files on the HTTP Server

For users to play an .asf file on a Web page, the Web page must contain an .asx file (similar to a hypertext link that points to the .asf file), or the NetShow Player must be embedded as an OBJECT element in the Web page.

Active Stream Redirector (.asx) files are necessary for playing .asf files from a Web page that does not contain an embedded NetShow Player. An .asx file provides the information that the NetShow Player needs to connect to a server. An .asx file is a one-line text file whose contents look like this:

```
ASF protocol://servername/virtualdir/filename.asf
```

An .asx files specifies:

- The protocol used (either HTTP or MMS)
- The name of the server
- A virtual directory (if necessary)
- The .asf file

Only one .asf file can be specified per .asx file. Place your .asx files in a directory on an HTTP server. It is a good idea to create a virtual directory for the .asx files so that it is easy to create, remember, and possibly edit the path to these files.

For more information, see "NetShow Announcements" earlier in this chapter.

Using the NetShow Player

You can use the NetShow Player to listen and watch streaming multimedia programs. The NetShow Player can be used to play programs three ways:

- As a stand-alone player.
- Launched from the browser, using a link on a Web page.
- Embedded as an ActiveX control in a Web page, Visual Basic script application, or other ActiveX container applications.

You can also configure the NetShow Player for a variety of options. For more information, see Help for NetShow Player.

Using the Stand-Alone Player

When you use NetShow Player as a stand-alone application, you decide how you want to access the .asf files. If you play an .asf file locally, you are not streaming the file. NetShow Player reads the .asf file from the hard disk and then plays it. If you play an .asf file from a remote location, it streams to your computer.

When you play an .asf file, you must specify a protocol (either HTTP or MMS), a server, and an .asf or .asx file. The following instructions explain how to run NetShow Player and use it to play .asf files locally and from remote locations.

▶   **To open NetShow Player**

1. On the **Start** menu, select **Run**.

   The **Run** dialog box opens.

2. In the **Open** box, type **nsplayer.exe**.

3. Click **OK**.

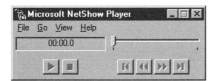

▶   **To open a local .asf file**

1. On the **File** menu, select **Open File**.

   The **Open** dialog box opens.

2. Type the file name, or browse and select the .asf file you want.

3. Click **OK**.

   The NetShow Player buffers the .asf file and then begins playing it.

▶   **To open an .asf file in a remote location**

1. On the **File** menu, select **Open Location**.

   The **Open Location** dialog box opens.

2. Enter the URL of the .asf or .asx file; for example:

   ```
   mms://XYZcompany.com/products/widgets.asx
   ```

3. Click **OK**.

   The NetShow Player buffers the .asf file and then begins playing it.

Launching the Player from a Web Page

To enable launching NetShow Player from a Web page, create a link in the HTML code as shown in the following example:

```
<A HREF=mms://server/file.asx>
```

When users click on the link from their browsers, the NetShow Player is launched to play the ASF stream. For more information about the process used to launch the NetShow Player and play the ASF stream, see "NetShow Announcements" earlier in this chapter.

Embedding NetShow Player in a Web Page

An easy way of providing the NetShow Player to people who don't already have it on their computers is to embed a NetShow ActiveX control (Nsplay.ocx) as an OBJECT element in a Web page. When a user accesses the page, the player is downloaded to the user's computer and used as an embedded control in the browser window. In the script commands that you use to embed the player, you can set the property that identifies the .asf file to play as well as how to play it. You can even set one of the player's properties to check the version of the player on the computer. If the player is outdated, the computer downloads the newest version of the player.

The Netshow player control is available on Microsoft's Web site, packaged as a .cab file (**http://www.microsoft.com/netshow/download/en/nsasfinf.cab**). The .cab file contains the .ocx file for the control, along with the codecs needed to support the control. An .inf file included in the cabinet specifies the files that need to be downloaded and performs the setup for the control to run.

The following example shows the OBJECT element used to embed the NetShow ActiveX control. This example would embed the control and show .asf content in the browser window for either Internet Explorer or Netscape Navigator.

```
<OBJECT ID="NSPlay"
    WIDTH=160 HEIGHT=128
    CLASSID="CLSID:2179C5D3-EBFF-11CF-B6FD-00AA00B4E220"

    <!--Code to go get NetShow player-->

    CODEBASE="http://www.microsoft.com/netshow/download/en/nsasfinf.cab#
        Version=2,0,0,912">

    <PARAM NAME="FileName" VALUE="http://server/path/myvideo.asx">

    <EMBED type="video/x-ms-asf-plugin"
        Src="http://server/path/myvideo.asx"
        FileName="http://server/path/myvideo.asx"

    PluginsPage="http://www.microsoft.com/netshow/download/player.htm"
        ControlType=1
        Width=290 height=250>
    </EMBED>
</OBJECT>
```

Use of the CODEBASE attribute is recommended, because it contains a URL pointing to where the Nsplayer.ocx control can be found if it is unavailable on a user's system. Besides the address of the player object, the CODEBASE attribute may also optionally specify a version number of the control.

How you set the parameters determines how the NetShow Player will work. For example, ControlType=1 specifies that the embedded control appears in the browser window with a full set of NetShow controls. The FileName parameter identifies the .asf file that will play. You set the value for this parameter to be a URL just as if you were going to play the .asf file from the **Open Location** option on the NetShow Player **File** menu.

When a user who doesn't have NetShow installed accesses the Web page, the player control downloads and is used to embed the player in the browser window and to play the .asf file (as specified by Myvideo.asx in the previous example).

For users who have downloaded and installed NetShow, the player control, Nsplay.ocx, is already located in the C:\Program Files\Microsoft NetShow\Player folder. Internet Explorer uses the installed version of the control unless a newer version is available. If a newer version of the embedded control exists, as indicated by the CODEBASE Version attribute, Internet Explorer installs and uses the newer version.

For more information about the NetShow ActiveX control and its properties, see the *Microsoft NetShow Client SDK*.

CHAPTER 20

NetMeeting

NetMeeting Overview

Microsoft NetMeeting conferencing software helps small and large organizations take full advantage of the global reach of the Internet or corporate intranet for real-time communications and collaboration. Connecting to other NetMeeting users is made easy with the Microsoft Internet Locator Server (ILS), which enables participants to call each other from a dynamic directory within NetMeeting or from a Web page. While connected on the Internet or corporate intranet, participants can communicate with both audio and video, work together on virtually any Windows-based application, exchange or mark up graphics on an electronic whiteboard, transfer files, or use the text-based chat program.

NetMeeting also provides an open development environment that supports international communications and conferencing standards and enables interoperability with products and services from multiple vendors.

NetMeeting 2.1 is fully compatible with NetMeeting 1.0 and 2.0, and with applications and solutions that use the *Microsoft NetMeeting Software Development Kit (SDK)* for the Windows 95 operating system. With its first release, NetMeeting 1.0 transformed the everyday telephone call into a richer and more effective tool. For the first time, people could use voice communication to interact and collaborate over the Internet using multipoint data conferencing capabilities based on the International Telecommunications Union (ITU) T.120 standard. NetMeeting 2.0 integrated a number of new features, as well as improving functionality and enhancing the user interface.

The following key features distinguish NetMeeting 2.1:

- Internet phone/H.323 standards–based audio support
- H.323 standards–based video conferencing
- Intelligent audio/video stream control
- Multipoint data conferencing
- The Internet Locator Server (ILS)
- Lightweight Directory Access Protocol (LDAP) standard support
- Support for Windows NT Workstation 4.0
- System policies
- User interface enhancements
- NetMeeting Mail extension
- The Software Development Kit
- Compliance with communications and conferencing standards

Internet Phone/H.323 Standards–Based Audio Support

Real-time, point-to-point audio conferencing over the Internet or corporate intranet enables you to make voice calls to associates and organizations around the world. NetMeeting audio conferencing offers many features, including half-duplex and full-duplex audio support for real-time conversations, automatic microphone-sensitivity-level setting to ensure that meeting participants hear each other clearly, and microphone muting, which lets users control the audio signal sent during a call. This audio conferencing supports network TCP/IP connections.

Support for the H.323 protocol enables interoperability between NetMeeting and other H.323-compatible audio clients. The H.323 protocol supports the ITU G.711 and G.723 audio standards and Internet Engineering Task Force (IETF) real-time protocol (RTP) and real-time control protocol (RTCP) specifications for controlling audio flow to improve voice quality. On MMX-enabled computers, NetMeeting uses the MMX-enabled audio codecs to improve performance for audio compression and decompression algorithms. This results in lower CPU use and improved audio quality during a call.

H.323 Standards–Based Video Conferencing

With NetMeeting, a user can send and receive real-time visual images with another conference participant using any video for Windows-compatible equipment. Participants can share ideas and information face to face, and use the camera to instantly view items, such as hardware or devices, that the user chooses to display in front of the lens. Combined with the audio and data capabilities of NetMeeting, a user can both see and hear the other conference participant, as well as share information and applications. This H.323 standard–based video technology is also complaint with the H.261 and H.263 video codecs.

NetMeeting video conferencing includes the following features:

- Participants can switch audio and video to another person during a meeting. This makes it easy for users to communicate with many different people.

- During a meeting, participants can remotely adjust the video image quality, balancing the need for higher quality or faster performance.

- Users can dynamically change the size of the video window to reduce or enlarge the image being sent to another person.

- In the NetMeeting main window, the video Preview and Receive windows are integrated on the Current Call window. Users can view these video windows from Current Call, or drag them to a different location on the desktop.

- Users can choose whether or not to transmit video immediately when a call starts. Also, they can pause or resume sending or receiving video by pressing a button in the video window frame.

- NetMeeting automatically balances the performance and quality of video during a meeting based on the speed of the network connection, thus providing the highest-quality, lowest-bandwidth video capabilities.

- Administrators can control access to video features using NetMeeting system policies. For more information about setting system policies, see "System Policies" later in this chapter.

- On MMX-enabled computers, NetMeeting uses the MMX-enabled video codecs to improve performance for video compression and decompression algorithms.

- Support for H.323 conference servers and gateways (currently being developed by leading vendors) enables NetMeeting users to participate in meetings with multiple audio and video connections.

Intelligent Audio/Video Stream Control

NetMeeting provides intelligent control of the audio and video stream, which automatically balances the load for network bandwidth, CPU use, and memory use. This intelligent stream control ensures that audio, video, and data are prioritized properly, so NetMeeting maintains high-quality audio while transmitting and receiving video and data during a call. Through system policy features, IS organizations can configure the stream control services to limit the bandwidth used for audio and video on a per-client basis during a meeting. For more information about limiting bandwidth usage, see Chapter 10, "Network Bandwidth Considerations," in the *Microsoft NetMeeting 2.1 Resource Kit*.

Multipoint Data Conferencing

Two or more users can communicate and collaborate as a group in real time. Participants can share applications, exchange information through a shared clipboard, transfer files, collaborate on a shared whiteboard, and use a text-based chat feature. Also, support for the T.120 data conferencing standard enables interoperability with other T.120-based products and services.

The following features make up multipoint data conferencing:

- **Application sharing.** A user can share a program running on one computer with other participants in the conference. Participants can review the same data or information in the program and see the actions as the person sharing the application works on the program (for example, edits content or scrolls through information). Participants can share Windows-based applications transparently, without any special knowledge of the application capabilities.

   The person sharing the application can choose to collaborate with other conference participants, and they can take turns editing or controlling the application. Only the person sharing the program needs to have the given application installed on his or her computer.

- **Shared clipboard.** A user can exchange the contents of a shared Clipboard with other participants in a conference, using familiar cut, copy, and paste operations. For example, a participant can copy information from a local document and paste the contents into a shared application as part of a group collaboration.

- **File transfer.** With the file transfer capability, a user can send a file in the background to one or all of the conference participants. When one user drags a file into the main window, the file is automatically sent to each person in the conference, who can then accept or decline receipt. This file transfer capability is fully compliant with the T.127 standard.

- **Whiteboard.** Multiple users can simultaneously collaborate using the whiteboard to review, create, and update graphic information. The whiteboard is object-oriented (versus pixel-oriented), enabling participants to manipulate the contents by clicking and dragging with the mouse. In addition, they can use a remote pointer or highlighting tool to point out specific contents or sections of shared pages.

- **Chat.** A user can type text messages to share common ideas or topics with other conference participants, or record meeting notes and action items as part of a collaborative process. Also, participants in a conference can use chat capabilities to communicate in the absence of audio support. A new "whisper" feature lets a user have a separate, private conversation with another person during a group chat session.

The Internet Locator Server

Replacing the NetMeeting 1.0 User Location Service (ULS), the ILS for NetMeeting 2.1 expands existing server technology to provide more advanced directory services, higher scalability, and better performance standards (LDAP). The ILS enables users to locate each other for conferencing. Users can view the ILS directory from within NetMeeting or a Web page and review a list of people currently running NetMeeting. Then, they can choose to connect to one or more of the listed users or select another user by entering the user's location information. For more information about the ILS, see the Web site at **http://www.backoffice.microsoft.com/**.

NetMeeting can detect whether a server is available and automatically attempt to log on in the background, without user intervention. If a user disconnects and then logs on again later, NetMeeting automatically logs on to the specified ILS.

LDAP Standard Support

The Lightweight Directory Access Protocol is an Internet standard that defines the protocol for directory access. NetMeeting uses LDAP to access the ILS and perform server transactions, including logging on and off, creating a directory listing of all available users, and resolving a particular user's address information, such as the Internet Protocol (IP) address. LDAP facilitates interoperability and allows organizations to implement compatible servers.

Support for Windows NT Workstation 4.0

Users of computers running the Windows NT operating system can communicate and collaborate with each other and with users of NetMeeting on Windows 95. The functionality of NetMeeting, including audio, video, and multiuser data conferencing for electronic whiteboard, text-based chat, and file transfer, is supported for Windows NT. Windows NT Service Pack 3 is required for a Windows NT user to share applications.

System Policies

Administrators can implement NetMeeting system policies to control user and computer privileges. Using system policies, they can predefine settings and restrictions, such as preventing the use of audio features and provide standard configurations for their user community. New system policies include the ability to limit the network bandwidth for audio and video streams. For more information about setting system policies, see "System Policies" later in this chapter.

User Interface Enhancements

One of the goals of NetMeeting is to enhance the existing user interface. Functions are easier to locate, view, and use. Enhancements focus on these areas:

- Call windows within the NetMeeting main window make it easy to connect to other users and participate in the current call. Four windows let users see a variety of information, such as the directory of all people currently logged onto the directory server and their audio/video capabilities, SpeedDial entries and their status, the users participating in the current call, or a history log of all received calls.

- Users can filter the directory entries to more easily find and connect with people. For example, users can filter the entries to identify only people currently participating in a call or only people with audio and video capabilities. Also, users can choose one of three user categories—personal, business, or adults-only—as an additional filter to show only people who selected the same user category.

- To more fully integrate with Internet Explorer, NetMeeting now includes a new **Go** menu for accessing Web-based directory information, as well as Internet Mail and News. Users can connect to other people from a Web-based directory view by entering the user's e-mail address, specifying the user's IP address, or entering the user's machine name.

- Refined NetMeeting Options tabs and wizards make it easier to set up and configure the NetMeeting environment. A new **Calling** tab lets a user choose directory and SpeedDial options. Additionally, an H.323 gateway calling option lets a NetMeeting user connect to a person by using a telephone number.

- A graphical interface similar to the one in Internet Explorer, including a common toolbar, makes it easier to move between applications that are part of the Internet Explorer suite. The toolbar is context-sensitive, displaying the most appropriate options based on the active window.

- The host computer lets the meeting originator hang up on one or more meeting participants, so people can be removed from the call more easily within conference groups.

- E-mail messaging gives users the option of sending e-mail to people who are not available for conferencing. NetMeeting uses MAPI to start a mail client of choice, automatically adds the subject information, and then includes a SpeedDial shortcut so that a person can easily call back later.

NetMeeting Mail Extension

NetMeeting includes a mail extension that works with Outlook and Exchange mail clients, which enables a user to place a call directly from a menu in the mail client based on entries in the mail address book. This feature gives people the flexibility to use their e-mail client to send a mail message or invoke a real-time meeting from the same mail address book. A NetMeeting system policy enables system administrators to specify the Exchange attribute for the NetMeeting address. For more information about setting this system policy, see "System Policies" later in this chapter.

The Software Development Kit

The *Microsoft NetMeeting 2.1 SDK* enables developers to integrate NetMeeting conferencing functionality directly into their applications or Web pages. Developers can extend the functionality of NetMeeting to add capabilities, such as a business card exchange, or to add conferencing functions to existing applications.

In addition, the *Microsoft NetMeeting 2.1 SDK* includes an ActiveX control for conferencing, allowing Web-site creators to integrate this functionality directly into their pages. Also, they can integrate the ActiveX control for conferencing with other ActiveX scripting solutions, such as JavaScript and Visual Basic Scripting Edition.

The *Microsoft NetMeeting 2.1 SDK* is available for download from the Web site at **http://www.microsoft.com/netmeeting/**.

Compliance with Communications and Conferencing Standards

NetMeeting is based on standards from the ITU, the same group that set standards for modems and the global telephone system. As a result, NetMeeting users can communicate with people using products on different platforms and from different vendors. In contrast, some Internet products are proprietary, and they leave their users stranded and able to talk only to people with the same product.

Broad support of standards ensures interoperability among solutions from different vendors. For example, the telephone industry uses a set of international standards to ensure that a person making a telephone call can connect to another person, regardless of what manufacturer produced either phone handset. Support for audio, video, and data conferencing standards provides the same transparent interoperability that customers expect.

NetMeeting supports the following industry standards that the ITU or IETF have ratified or proposed:

- **T.120.** ITU set of protocols for transport-independent, multipoint data conferencing. This standard also integrates with H.320 and H.324 protocols.
- **H.323.** ITU set of protocols for audio, video, and data conferencing over TCP/IP networks. This standard includes RTP and RTCP, and integrates with T.120, H.261, H.263, G.711, and G.723 protocols.
- **RTP/RTCP.** IETF packet format for sending real-time information across the Internet.
- **LDAP.** IETF set of protocols for directory access.

For more information about the standards that NetMeeting supports, see "Conferencing Standards" later in this chapter.

What's New in NetMeeting 2.1

As the leading Internet conferencing solution, NetMeeting has become the key building block for vendors of conferencing products and services. NetMeeting 2.1 is designed to support new technology featured in Windows 98, including DirectX® 5, universal serial bus (USB) video cameras, and the new video device driver model. NetMeeting 2.1 is packaged as part of Windows 98, but it is also designed to run as a stand-alone product on computers running Windows 95 and Windows NT 4.0 with Service Pack 3.

NetMeeting 2.1 includes the following enhancements:

- **Enhanced interoperability with H.323 devices.** Changes to the NetMeeting 2.1 infrastructure improve interoperability with new H.323 devices, including gateways and Multipoint Conferencing Units (MCUs). These changes include the ability to initiate a call using the H.323 calling model instead of the T.120 calling model.

- **Support for Windows 98 application sharing.** NetMeeting 2.1 enhances application-sharing functions to ensure support for Windows 98 device driver model changes and special multiple monitor support.

- **DirectX 5 support.** DirectX is a set of technologies that enable faster access to hardware in Windows. DirectX 5 is the latest version of DirectX. Installing the DirectSound® API component of DirectX 5 on your computer (with a compatible audio device) significantly reduces the latency of sending or receiving audio over the Internet using NetMeeting.

    DirectSound modifies the multimedia APIs in Windows 95, replacing your existing sound card driver with a new DirectX driver. The new DirectX driver supports DirectSound record and playback APIs (and also supports the existing driver functions). Users can install the DirectSound component of DirectX 5 from the NetMeeting Web site at **http://www.microsoft.com/netmeeting/**.

    Because DirectX drivers are often installed with games, many users may have DirectX capabilities already. Users must upgrade to DirectX 5, because older versions of DirectX do not support NetMeeting 2.1. To identify your DirectX version, double-click the **DirectX** icon in Control Panel.

Note Some DirectX sound drivers do not support full-duplex audio. When you upgrade your existing driver to a DirectSound driver, you may lose this capability. Removing DirectX restores your original configuration.

- **Outlook bar.** A new Outlook bar gives NetMeeting an appearance and functionality consistent with Microsoft Outlook 97 and Outlook Express. This Outlook bar provides easy access to frequently used NetMeeting functions, including Directory, SpeedDial, Current Call, and History.

NetMeeting Application Scenarios

NetMeeting is changing the way people communicate and collaborate on the Internet and corporate intranets by expanding the situations in which the PC is used. With its rich set of audio, video, and data conferencing features, this product has proven its effectiveness for management groups, developers, and user communities worldwide.

The following table describes several scenarios that demonstrate how you can use NetMeeting to work and communicate more efficiently.

In the past	Today, with NetMeeting
Virtual Meetings	
A problem with a part on a manufacturing line could have taken several days to resolve. An engineer might have needed to fly to the factory, inspect the part, and diagnose the problem.	*Participants can conference remotely or from different locations and conduct meetings as if everyone were in the same room.*
	Engineers and factory representatives can hold a conference without traveling to another location. They can view the part on camera, share engineering specifications, and discuss the problem.
	If an administrator disables audio features using NetMeeting system policies, other support engineers can participate in the conference using the company's existing PBX phone system for audio support.
Document Collaboration	
Negotiating a contract might have taken days, weeks, or even months, as companies faxed legal documents back and forth with their changes. Valuable time was spent as accounting, legal, and management representatives each provided their input to the negotiation.	*Two or more participants can work together and collaborate on documents or information in real time.*
	With application sharing, accounting, legal, and management representatives can instantly collaborate on the contract. Each person can provide input, update text, or graphics, and discuss contract details.
Customer Service	
If a customer wanted more information about a Web site but had only one telephone line, the customer would have to close the Internet connection before dialing.	*From a Web site, customer service representatives can communicate directly with their user community and share important information.*
	The ActiveX control enables developers to add conferencing directly to Web pages. With the click of a button, a customer can reach a service representative in person. The representative can share information about products and services and promote sales opportunities.

In the past	Today, with NetMeeting
Telecommuting	
On business travel to conferences and client sites, corporate managers who needed to convey vital information to their teams would have relied on telephone calls, faxes, and e-mail.	*While on the road or in remote locations, data conferencing capabilities enable users to extend beyond voice or e-mail.* A manager can participate in a virtual meeting, give a presentation, or share applications without being in the office. For example, a manager can remotely share a PowerPoint presentation. Because NetMeeting interoperates with other T.120 products, a manager can interact with team members at worldwide locations using existing T.120 MCUs.
Distance Learning	
For specialized training, an employee might have to travel to a corporate learning center or other distant location. Companies incurred the cost of traveling, training, and staff hours.	*Corporations can disseminate presentations or educational information over the Internet or intranets.* Students can participate in an interactive learning session. A teacher can present the class and then hold discussion groups or interact with individual students. Training can incorporate video instruction for complex processes and application sharing for additional class demonstration. To facilitate large conference groups, NetMeeting can also interoperate with standards-based conferencing bridges.
Technical Support	
A help-desk representative might have spent hours with a customer attempting to understand and diagnose a problem. The customer would have explained the symptoms, and the representative would have to duplicate the customer's scenario without actually "seeing" the problem.	*Support organizations can view a situation on a remote computer and correct a problem during the support call without traveling to a remote location.* Help-desk personnel can use the application-sharing features of NetMeeting to remotely observe a user's computer and take corrective actions in real time.

NetMeeting Architecture Components

NetMeeting is both a client and a platform. The NetMeeting client enables users to experience the benefits of a real-time, multipoint communication and collaboration program. The NetMeeting platform enables third-party vendors to integrate conferencing features into their own products and services. To support this dual purpose, Microsoft implemented NetMeeting capabilities using an open architecture of interworking components. Each component communicates with and passes data to and from the component layer above and below it. This open architecture means that vendors can easily develop products and services that build on the NetMeeting platform and interoperate with NetMeeting client conferencing features.

At the core of the NetMeeting architecture is a series of audio, video, and data conferencing and directory service standards. These standards work together with transport, application, user interface, and ActiveX conferencing components to form the NetMeeting architecture, shown in the following diagram.

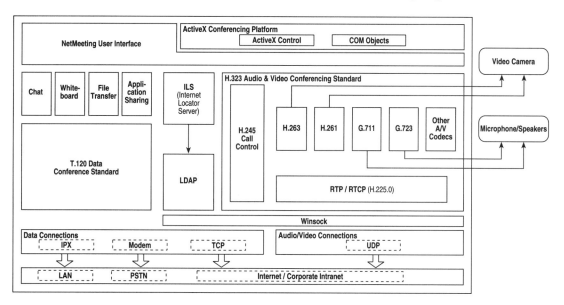

The following sections describe the key components that compose the NetMeeting architecture, beginning from the bottom of the diagram.

Transport Layer

At its lowest level, standards are responsible for translating, sending, and receiving NetMeeting information. The NetMeeting architecture includes protocols for null modem and network TCP/IP connections. The null modem protocol supports data-only conferencing connections; only TCP/IP connections support NetMeeting audio and video.

Information can be transported over the Internet or corporate intranet using transport control protocol (TCP) and user datagram protocol (UDP) connections. TCP is used primarily for data transport and call control, while UDP represents secondary connections for sending and receiving NetMeeting audio and video. Winsock provides the interface to the network stack and maps information between the applications and the network. The following diagram highlights this transport layer.

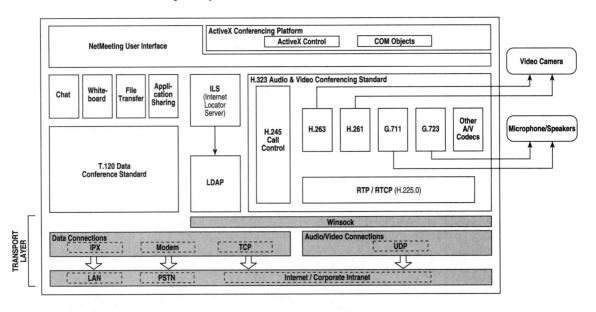

Core Standard and Application Components

The NetMeeting architecture is based on the following industry standards:

- The ITU T.120 standard for data conferencing
- The ITU H.323 standard for audio and video conferencing
- The IETF LDAP standard for directory services support

These standards provide the framework for managing NetMeeting connections, data conferencing, audio and video capabilities, and directory server access, highlighted in the following diagram. By supporting industry standards, NetMeeting enables audio, video, and multipoint data conferencing with standards-based products from other vendors.

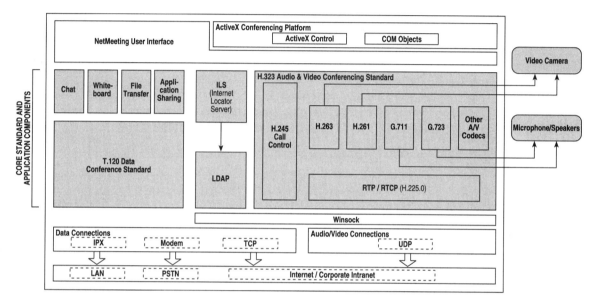

Each of these standards is summarized in the following paragraphs. For more detailed information, see "Conferencing Standards" later in this chapter.

T.120. NetMeeting contains a wealth of collaborative data capabilities, including chat, whiteboard, file transfer, and application sharing. At the heart of these capabilities is the ITU T.120 standard for multipoint data conferencing. T.120 provides the protocols for establishing and managing NetMeeting data flow, connections, and conferences.

H.323. NetMeeting includes audio and video codecs, as well as framing and call control protocols. H.323 codecs provide the format for audio and video that is transmitted over various connection rates. NetMeeting supports a suite of codecs appropriate for many different modes of Internet telephony.

ITU H.323. These protocols enable NetMeeting to send and receive audio and video information between NetMeeting and H.323-compatible nodes. A microphone, speakers, and video camera provide the necessary input/output devices for these audio and video capabilities.

LDAP. Directory services for NetMeeting use the LDAP standard. Internet Locator Servers use the LDAP interface to create directories of current NetMeeting users that people can call and communicate with over TCP/IP connections.

User Interface

NetMeeting audio, video, and data conferencing capabilities are available to end users through the NetMeeting user interface. This interface presents NetMeeting features in an easy-to-use and understandable format of visual icons, "hot" buttons, simple adjustment bars, and tabbed windows and call directories. The following diagram highlights this level of the NetMeeting architecture.

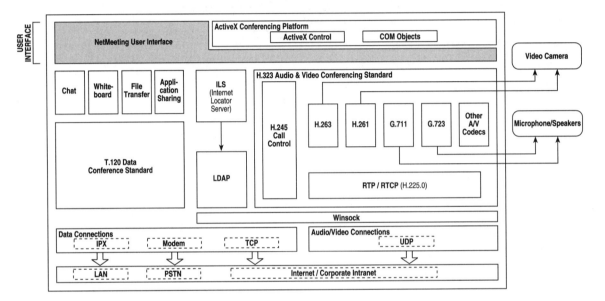

ActiveX Conferencing Platform

The NetMeeting platform enables developers to incorporate NetMeeting features, such as chat and whiteboard, in their applications and Web pages. This platform is based on ActiveX conferencing, which includes the following components:

- A set of objects based on the OLE Component Object Model (COM) for adding conferencing support to COM applications.

- A set of COM objects for building LDAP directory support into applications, including support for LDAP-based directories (ILSs) used by NetMeeting.

- ActiveX controls for adding conferencing support to Web pages, Visual Basic applications, and OLE-enabled documents and applications.

- A set of COM objects for installing custom audio and video codecs that NetMeeting can leverage during calls.

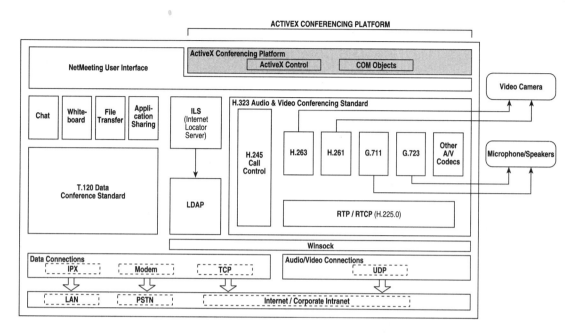

ActiveX conferencing is available in the *Microsoft NetMeeting 2.1 SDK.*

Understanding Conferencing Standards

Standards are critical to achieving the vision of NetMeeting: to create and popularize a new type of multimedia communications. To achieve this vision, a real-time communications and conferencing product must be developed with open standards so that users can connect with each other as easily and reliably as using a telephone. Consumers of this technology expect and demand that all products operate error-free and that every connection succeed. Standards ensure this experience.

With standards, a product from one vendor can provide a guaranteed level of compatibility with products from other vendors. Vendors can continue to build compatible add-on products that successfully interoperate with different real-time communications and conferencing products. Depending on the standards that these products support, users can potentially share applications and information, see each other with video, talk to one another, or perform all of these functions simultaneously.

Standards Organizations

The NetMeeting team is an active member of organizations that promote industry standards. The following organizations are at the forefront of standards development for communications and conferencing products:

International Telecommunications Union

Governments and the private sector coordinate global telecommunications networks and services through the ITU, which develops, regulates, and standardizes global telecommunications and organizes regional and world events. For more information about the ITU standards, including T.120 and H.323, visit the ITU home page at **http://www.itu.ch/**.

Internet Engineering Task Force

The IETF is the protocol engineering and development arm of the Internet. This organization is a large, open, international community of network designers, operators, vendors, and researchers concerned with the evolution of Internet architecture, as well as the smooth operation of the Internet. The IETF maintains working groups for research and technical study. For more information about the IETF standards, including drafts for LDAP specifications, visit the IETF home page at **http://www.ietf.org/**.

International Multimedia Teleconferencing Consortium

The IMTC is a nonprofit corporation founded to promote the creation and adoption of international standards for multipoint document and video teleconferencing. The IMTC provides a forum for its worldwide members to develop product specifications and educate others on standards-based development. The IMTC and its members promote a "Standards First" initiative to guarantee interoperability for all aspects of multimedia teleconferencing. For more information about the IMTC and to obtain information on standards, visit the IMTC home page at **http://www.imtc.org/**.

The T.120 Standard

The ITU T.120 standard is made up of a suite of communications and application protocols developed and approved by the international computer and telecommunications industries. These protocols enable developers to create compatible products and services for real-time, multipoint data connections and conferencing. T.120-based applications enable many users to participate in conferencing sessions over different types of networks and connections.

Depending on the type of T.120 product, they can make connections, transmit and receive data, and collaborate using compatible data conferencing features, such as application sharing, conferencing whiteboard, and file transfer. Microsoft and more than 100 other major companies support the development of products and services using the T.120 standard.

Benefits

The demand for standards-based products and services is based on the many benefits that standards provide to consumers. The following list describes some of the primary benefits of developing under the T.120 standard:

- T.120 ensures that many participants can send and receive data in real time without any errors in data transmission. Users can expect this reliability over many types of supported connections, including TCP/IP and null modem.

- For multipoint data conferencing, the T.120 standard supports a variety of common topologies, including star, daisy-chain, and cascaded connections. To learn more about these topologies, see "Topologies" later in this section.

- Developers can create applications with T.120 alone or in combination with other ITU standards, such as the H.323 standard for audio and video conferencing.

Interoperability

One of the most important features of the T.120 infrastructure is the interoperability of products and services that support the standard. This interoperability extends both to networking and applications. For more information about T.120 interoperability, see "Understanding Product Interoperability" later in this chapter.

T.120 Topologies

The T.120 architecture supports several topologies that define how users connect to a conference and transmit data during the conference. The following diagram illustrates three common topologies: star, daisy-chain, and cascaded. These topologies represent the types of connections typical of NetMeeting conferences.

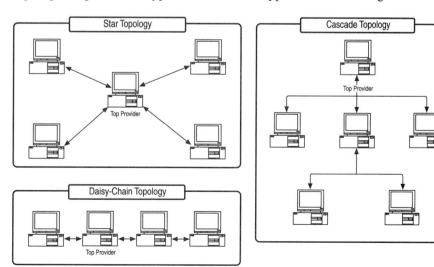

One of the participants in the conference is assigned as the top provider (conference host). The top provider's application is responsible for handling the global resources in the conference and also for sequencing data, if necessary. The top provider is determined within the initial connection between the first two participants. The location of the top provider and how the other participants are connected to the top provider differentiates the various topologies.

With NetMeeting, the person initiating the call is the top provider. The previous diagram illustrates the relationship of this top provider to other NetMeeting nodes in the various conference topologies; many other combinations of top provider and conference nodes are possible. NetMeeting actually initiates the call and determines whether a conference is already running. If no conference is running, NetMeeting creates one locally, with the person initiating the call as the top provider. If a conference is running, NetMeeting notifies the person, who then has the option of joining the remote conference. Also, NetMeeting provides a Host Meeting feature (**Call** menu), which determines the top provider automatically, based on the selected conference host rather than on the caller order.

Data flows according to the conference topology, which is determined by how each connection in the conference is established ("who calls whom"). For example, in the diagram, the following order of calls establishes the conference topology:

- A (top provider) initiates calls to B and C.
- Then, B calls D and E (or D and E each call B).
- C calls F and G (or F and G each call C).

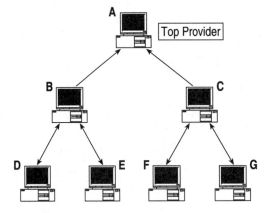

A conference can have only one top provider. After the top provider (A) is established, that computer remains the top provider throughout the conference. Note that two conferences cannot be joined together. Therefore, if C called F and G first, it would not be possible for them to join the conference with A, B, D, and E.

During data conferencing, if B shared an application with the other conference participants, data would flow simultaneously to the adjoining connections (A, D, and E). Then, data would continue to flow outward to the remaining connections. Also, any two connections within the conference can initiate audio and video conferencing. NetMeeting enables audio and video switching so that participants can switch the pair sharing audio and video.

If B hangs up or is removed from the conference, D and E are also removed. D and E may remain conferenced together, though, if they were connected with audio and video in the original session. D and E would not have data conferencing, however, because this function is removed when B hangs up.

How NetMeeting Uses the T.120 Standard

Microsoft developed NetMeeting data conferencing features based on the T.120 infrastructure, enabling NetMeeting to interoperate with other T.120 standards-based products. T.120 protocols are the building blocks for the following NetMeeting functions:

- **The ability to establish and maintain NetMeeting data connections.** Two or more participants can establish a NetMeeting connection. Within the conference, T.120 protocols manage the sequencing and flow of data transported by NetMeeting connections. T.120 ensures that data is accurately and reliably transmitted between conference nodes.

- **Built-in data conferencing applications.** NetMeeting conference participants can use T.120-based applications (which sit on top of T.120), such as file transfer based on the T.127 standard and application sharing based on T.128. Note that NetMeeting does not support T.126 currently; this support is expected in a future version of NetMeeting.

- **Support for multiuser conferences.** Many people can join a NetMeeting data conference for communication and collaboration. The conference host (top provider) in NetMeeting provides the node that manages participants and their applications.

- **Capability to interoperate across networks and platforms.** T.120 interfaces enable NetMeeting and other standards-based products to communicate across common networks using TCP/IP without platform restrictions.

Microsoft continues its efforts to enhance and extend the application of T.120 protocols. The standards groups that define T.120 are now working on the next generation of the protocols, and Microsoft is very active in these efforts.

The H.323 Standard

H.323 is an ITU standard that sets forth a specification for terminals (PCs), equipment, and services for multimedia communication over networks that do not provide a guaranteed quality of service. H.323 terminals and equipment can carry real-time audio, video, and data, or any combination of these elements. This standard is based on the IETF real-time protocol (RTP) and real-time control protocol (RTCP), with additional protocols for call signaling and data and audiovisual communications.

Products that use H.323 for audio and video enable you to interconnect and communicate with other people over the Internet, just as people using different makes and models of telephones can communicate over public switched telephone network (PSTN) lines. H.323 defines how audio and video information is formatted and packaged for transmission over the network. Standard audio and video codecs encode and decode input/output from audio and video sources for communicating between nodes.

Benefits

Leading the audio and video teleconferencing industry, H.323 products and services offer many benefits to consumers. The following list describes some of the benefits that distinguish H.323:

- Microsoft and more than 120 leading companies have announced their intent to support and implement H.323 in their products and services. This broad support establishes H.323 as the leading solution for audio and video conferencing over the Internet.

- Products and services developed by multiple vendors under the H.323 standard can interoperate without platform limitations. H.323 conferencing clients, bridges, servers, and gateways will support this interoperability.

- H.323 provides multiple audio and video codecs that format data according to the requirements of various networks, with different bit rates, delays, and quality options. Users can choose the codecs that best support their computer and network selections.

- The addition of T.120 data conferencing support to the H.323 specification means that products developed under H.323 can offer a full range of multimedia functions, with both data and audiovisual conferencing support.

Interoperability

Just as telecommunications standards enable people with telephones from different vendors to call anyone around the world, the H.323 standard will enable the same level of interoperability for audio and video conferencing on the Internet. For more information about H.323 interoperability, see "Understanding Product Interoperability" later in this chapter.

How NetMeeting Uses the H.323 Standard

Microsoft developed NetMeeting audio and video conferencing features based on the H.323 infrastructure, enabling NetMeeting to interoperate with other H.323 standards-based products. H.323 codecs and protocols are the building blocks for these NetMeeting functions:

- **The ability to establish and maintain audio and video connections.** Two participants can establish a NetMeeting conference with audio and video over a TCP/IP connection. H.225.0 enables multiple audio and video streams to transport inbound and outbound NetMeeting information. H.323 protocols enable NetMeeting to communicate with and transmit data to other compatible audio or video clients. Also, conferencing servers and bridges enable multiuser audio and video conferences between multiple NetMeeting clients, as well as other H.323-compatible products.

- **Audio and video codecs that optimize Internet connections.** NetMeeting supports a suite of codecs, operating between 4.8 Kbps and 64 Kbps, that support various computer and connection types.

- **Support for T.120 data communications.** NetMeeting creates the association between T.120 and H.323 during a NetMeeting conference. This association allows the NetMeeting call to be completed in two phases, one each for T.120 and H.323, but appear as a single call.

- **Support for H.323 Gateways.** Although Microsoft does not provide a gateway, NetMeeting will support third-party H.323 gateways when they become available. See "H.323 Conferencing Products and Services" later in this chapter.

- **Support for H.323 Gatekeepers.** NetMeeting does not support H.323 gatekeepers. Instead, NetMeeting uses system policies, Windows NT Domain Control, and LDAP-based directories to perform gatekeeper functions. This enables customers to leverage their investments on other standards-based management tools.

The standards groups that define H.323 are now working on the next generation of the protocols, and Microsoft is very active in these efforts. The H.323 group is incorporating its experience from the first generation of H.323 and is also adding new features, such as strong security and interoperability with streaming media servers.

The Lightweight Directory Access Protocol

The Lightweight Directory Access Protocol (LDAP), as its name implies, is a standard method by which application clients query for and access information stored on directory servers over TCP/IP connections. Typically, a published directory contains data about people or other entities that users can access. The most common examples of paper-based directories are the yellow and white pages of telephone books, which enable a customer to look up the telephone number for a person or company. An example of an electronic directory is a published e-mail address book, which enables an e-mail user to look up a person's e-mail address and other details, such as office location and internal phone extension.

LDAP Version 2 and Version 3

Most Internet applications currently support LDAP Version 2, which provides static directory services for storing user information that is constant. Traditionally, directories contain data that rarely changes. Telephone books are published once a year because customers do not change numbers frequently. E-mail directories are also very stable, typically requiring changes only when new users are added or outdated users are removed. One result is that a directory is read very often, but seldom written.

LDAP Version 3 is currently being developed. This version includes specifications for dynamic directory services, which store user information that changes frequently. Dynamic information can expire and must be updated periodically to remain up-to-date (for example, IP addresses through the dynamic host configuration protocol [DHCP]). Ratification of this new version is expected in the near future.

Benefits

LDAP has several benefits that give this standard an advantage over other directory server protocols:

- With LDAP, Internet clients, servers, and applications have a common method for accessing and using directory information.

- LDAP provides a simple search operation that reduces the amount of input and output processing. This is important for Internet implementations that favor more simplistic processing methods for slow Internet connections.

- By using TCP/IP connections, LDAP can be implemented relatively easily on most platforms.

- Directory servers developed under LDAP can support many users and their associated address information.

- With dynamic directory services, LDAP can track more volatile information that changes frequently and must be updated on a regular basis. This is a requirement for dynamic call directories that need to be continually updated to show the most current directory of users.

Interoperability

Many current servers use LDAP Version 2 technology, and developers can easily create new servers that provide dynamic directory services (required for NetMeeting). For more information about LDAP interoperability, see "Understanding Product Interoperability" later in this chapter.

LDAP Topology

The IETF Web site documents the LDAP architecture. For detailed information, visit **http://ietf.org/ids.by.wg/ldapext.html**. The following diagram illustrates the LDAP architecture. LDAP clients, such as e-mail programs, Web browsers, and external applications, can execute directory service transactions against the LDAP server. Directory services define the operations for locating and connecting people who want to join a conference. This capability may include simple search and update transactions, such as logging on and off, creating a directory listing of all available users, and resolving a user's address information.

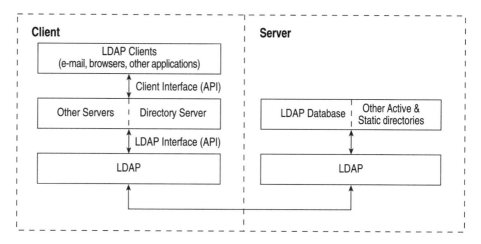

Through an LDAP interface, the server communicates with the LDAP database to retrieve directory information. LDAP servers can be multithreaded to support many LDAP databases simultaneously. The LDAP database stores and retrieves information based on a hierarchical structure of entries, each with its own distinguishing name, type, and attributes. The attributes (properties) define acceptable values for the entry. An LDAP database can store and maintain entries for a large number of users.

Databases can include static entries, dynamic entries, or both. A static entry contains information that remains accurate for a long period of time. On the other hand, dynamic entries (objects) and their attributes have a defined life expectancy and will expire if they are not updated by the client. The LDAP server is responsible for removing expired entries.

How NetMeeting Uses the LDAP Standard

Traditional static directories contain information that is presumed to have value until it is removed. In contrast, the NetMeeting directory information quickly degrades over time. Because NetMeeting is an IP-based conferencing application, the most important attribute is the computer's network or IP address. With the widespread use of DHCP, each time a user logs on to a LAN or ISP, his or her machine is assigned a different IP address, which means that the directory information needs to be frequently updated. Therefore, a traditional static database approach—to write seldom and read often—cannot be used.

NetMeeting directory requirements resulted in the Microsoft ILS, a new breed of LDAP-based *dynamic* directory services. ILS information can be updated as frequently as desired, because storage is not based on SQL or file-based databases; instead, the ILS stores directory data in memory to allow frequent changes. Even though the directory stores information differently, access to the information is still the same as traditional static directories. Therefore, NetMeeting uses the LDAP protocol to access the ILS.

NetMeeting and the ILS support the LDAP standard for the following functions and capabilities:

- **Using the LDAP Client/Server Infrastructure.** Based on the LDAP infrastructure, the ILS consists of both a client and a server. NetMeeting uses the client to access the server through an LDAP interface. The ILS provides a publishing mechanism that enables NetMeeting to publish information about its users for other people to view and search. For example, if NetMeeting publishes a user's name, online status, and audio/video capability, a potential caller can then identify the party to call, whether the user has video capability, and whether the user is currently on a call.

- **Support for Dynamic Objects (LDAP Version 3).** The ILS defines two dynamic object types: the **User** object and **MeetingPlace** object. The **User** object defines the properties of a NetMeeting user and is used to publish information about that user. The **MeetingPlace** object defines the properties of an ongoing conference. Each object consists of attributes, or properties. For example, the **User** object includes attributes, such as *First Name* and *Country*, and the **MeetingPlace** object includes attributes, such as *Attendee* and *Description*.

- **Dynamic Entry Expiration and Update Operations.** An important concept for dynamic directories is entry lifetime—each entry is valid only as long as the NetMeeting client is active. If the client computer goes offline (for example, the computer connection is terminated by another incoming call) the ILS entry is no longer valid and will be removed by the server as soon as possible. Each NetMeeting entry in the ILS directory has a lifetime, which is typically a specific number of minutes. NetMeeting regularly updates its entries in the ILS, maintaining only those entries that are still online and ready to accept a call. If a NetMeeting entry fails to update itself within the allotted time, the server removes the entry to keep the entire directory listing as accurate as possible.

NetMeeting and ILS 1.0 use LDAP Version 2, the most current, approved version of the LDAP specification. However, the concept of a dynamic entry lifetime and update is not defined in LDAP Version 2. Microsoft and other IETF members have proposed a dynamic entry lifetime and update for LDAP Version 3.

- **Developing Compatible Servers.** As described in this section, NetMeeting's unique capabilities impose new requirements for LDAP-based directory services that are unique to real-time conferencing applications. The ILS provides new services that were previously unavailable with LDAP Version 2. Because of this innovation, no other servers are currently compatible with NetMeeting.

  Compatible server products, though, can be engineered without a high development learning curve. The ILS uses the well-known industry standard LDAP for its access protocol, and these servers are close cousins of traditional static LDAP servers. ILS functionality and transactions are open and published; therefore, expertise in developing traditional LDAP directories can be easily applied toward building ILS-like directories. Because LDAP is the standard for directory protocols, any infrastructure or tools, such as proxy servers, firewalls, or networking monitoring tools, are completely applicable with it. Also, the ILS can easily be integrated with static directories that use a common LDAP protocol.

Understanding Product Interoperability

Product interoperability is important for several reasons:

- To instill customer confidence, products must be based on compatible rather than proprietary technologies.

- Particularly in the corporate environment, communication between local and remote locations is a necessity; to support these user communities, products must interoperate across platforms and networks.

- Products of varying levels of functionality must be able to communicate; standards enable compatibility of applications with a variety of functions and features.

- As more vendors develop standards-based products, customers benefit from competitive pricing, improved quality, and product upgrades.

The following sections describe the specific types of products and services, including clients, servers, and gateways, that interoperate with NetMeeting. Interoperability testing is described for two ITU standards that NetMeeting currently supports: T.120 for data conferencing and H.323 for audio and video conferencing. This discussion includes the elements that make T.120 and H.323 standards-based products interoperate.

Interoperability: The Big Picture

The following diagram shows how NetMeeting can interoperate with T.120- and H.323-compatible products over the Internet and corporate intranet using TCP/IP network connections. For corporate and home users, many interoperability scenarios are possible between NetMeeting and compatible, standards-based clients, servers, bridges, and gateways.

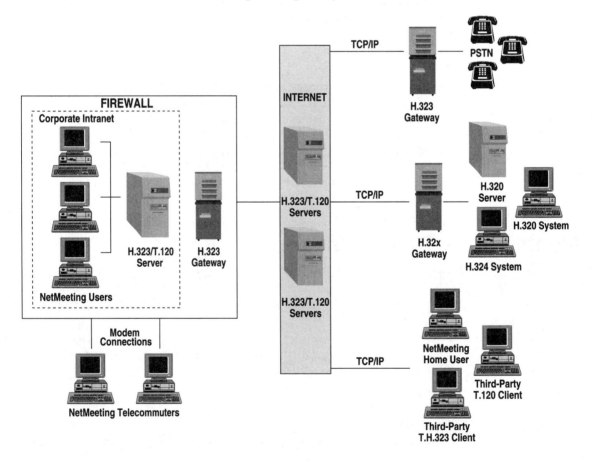

The diagram shows the following interoperability scenarios:

- Within an organization, NetMeeting users can connect with each other over the corporate intranet. A T.120 or H.323 conferencing server can provide inbound and outbound connectivity with compatible clients for data, audio, or video conferencing.

- An H.323 gateway can be used to bridge internal and external networks over a corporate firewall, supporting connections for audio and video conferencing.

- NetMeeting users can initiate multipoint connections with third-party T.120 clients. T.120 servers can provide administration services for this data conferencing scenario.

- NetMeeting users can initiate point-to-point connections with H.323 clients. T.120 data conferencing may be supported in conjunction with H.323 audio and video conferencing. H.323 servers can provide administration services for this conferencing scenario.

- Through an H.32x gateway, NetMeeting users can connect to H.320 and H.324 systems. Also, an H.320 server can be used for connectivity with multiple H.320 systems.

- An H.323 gateway also enables NetMeeting users to connect to people over PSTN lines.

Compatible Products and Services

For information about NetMeeting-compatible products and services from leading vendors, see the NetMeeting Web site at **http://www.microsoft.com/netmeeting/**. Some of these products are mentioned in the following sections.

Note Information in this directory has been submitted by third-party vendors. Microsoft has not tested or certified all the products and services for interoperability. Contact the appropriate vendor for more information.

T.120 Conferencing Products and Services

Because T.120 is purely a data standard, T.120-compliant products and services that operate with NetMeeting provide data conferencing and collaboration features rather than audio or video support. NetMeeting can potentially inter-operate with any T.120 product or service that uses the same TCP/IP transport. These products and services fall primarily into the following categories:

Data conferencing clients. The T.120 infrastructure gives products and services the ability to connect and send data. This means that NetMeeting is capable of connecting to any data conferencing client that supports ITU T.120. Also, these clients can potentially interoperate, depending on the compatibility of application layer protocols supported by the third-party product (any incompatibility in protocols would be at the application layer, and not with the T.120 protocols).

Conferencing servers or bridges. Otherwise known as multipoint control units, or MCUs, these central computing facilities host multipoint data conferences that might also be held in conjunction with audio or video conferencing. The MCU has the necessary components to handle multiple nodes from multiple computers in a single conference. For the MCU provider, conferencing services require an investment in server hardware, software, and technical support. Customers benefit from guaranteed performance and scalability that can cross platforms, vendors, and networks.

Note Using a bridge to host a meeting between computers with conferencing products from different vendors does not guarantee compatibility, particularly in the case of products that do not support the same application layer protocols. The conferencing bridge does not provide a compatibility layer that enables different products to interoperate.

Vendors provide multipoint bridging and management services that enable many sites to collaborate over the Internet. Also, these services enable users to schedule, create, administer, join, and track conferences all in one convenient place. Note that NetMeeting hardware requirements apply through a conferencing bridge, which limits the conference to the speed of the slowest connection.

H.323 Conferencing Products and Services

NetMeeting can potentially operate with any H.323 conferencing product or service over TCP/IP connections. H.323-compatible products and services fall primarily into these categories:

Audio and video conferencing clients. NetMeeting is capable of connecting to any audio or video conferencing client that supports the H.323 specification. Depending on the availability of compatible audio and video codecs (G.723.1, G.711, H.263, and H.261 are supported by NetMeeting), H.323 products can potentially interoperate and exchange audio and video information. For example, NetMeeting is fully interoperable with the Intel® Internet Video Phone, providing high-quality, face-to-face video and audio conferencing from a local desktop.

Conferencing servers and bridges. Conference servers and bridges can host multipoint audio and video conferencing for H.323-compatible products. Some servers and bridges may also host audio and video conferencing in conjunction with data conferencing. Service providers will offer an advanced network of audio, video, and data conferencing bridges, professional conference administrators, and special features such as password security. Connecting multiple sites in the United States or worldwide, these services will assist with equipment, reservation, scheduling, and customized reporting needs.

Gateways. Currently, several companies are developing H.323 gateways. These gateways will enable NetMeeting users to bridge to other types of networks, such as an H.320 ISDN video conference or a regular telephone on a public network.

Gatekeepers. NetMeeting does not support the gatekeeper function. Instead, NetMeeting uses system policies, Windows NT Domain Control, and LDAP-based directories to perform gatekeeper functions.

LDAP Conferencing Servers

ILS supports the IETF LDAP Version 2 standard for NetMeeting directory services. LDAP servers support the same LDAP protocol, but each server extends LDAP for a particular purpose. For example, ILS applies LDAP for use with dynamic records. LDAP Version 3 designers propose these dynamic directory services as part of the LDAP protocol. When Version 3 is finalized and implemented within NetMeeting, developers can access standards information from the IETF Web site for developing compatible servers. Currently, vendors can develop interoperable servers for NetMeeting by obtaining information about the LDAP extension from Microsoft.

In addition, many people use the ULS, developed for NetMeeting 1.0, for locating and connecting to other NetMeeting users. Third-party vendors have developed many interoperable ULSs, such as **uls.four11.com** and **uls.sitebuilder.net**, which users can log on to from NetMeeting.

Directory Servers

ILS, an optional component of the Internet Information Server, provides directory services that enable NetMeeting users to locate each other on the Internet or corporate intranets. These servers create a directory of NetMeeting users. From this directory, users can select participants for real-time conferencing and collaboration. The ILS product replaces ULS technology, which Microsoft originally developed for NetMeeting 1.0. ILS provides all of the ULS functionality, as well as introducing advanced server technology not previously available. Users can benefit from enhanced features and functions, better performance, and higher scalability to support more NetMeeting users.

Note The ILS is not required to use NetMeeting and connect with other users. You can connect directly with other people by entering their e-mail address in the NetMeeting Call window (although you must log on to the ILS for this connection method to work). Instead, the ILS simplifies the process of finding and connecting users by providing a directory listing of people who are running NetMeeting.

The Internet Locator Server

The ILS offers a standards-based, dynamic directory solution to the user location problem on the Internet. It provides organizations with a directory server for NetMeeting users. Like the ULS, the ILS provides a memory-resident database for storing dynamic directory information. This database enables users to find dynamic information, such as an IP address, for people currently logged on to an Internet service or site. The ILS database maintains the entries, which clients update periodically. This process ensures that clients can always access the most current information about each user's Internet location.

The following features distinguish the ILS:

Support for industry-standard protocols. The ILS provides both an LDAP interface for NetMeeting support and a proprietary ULP interface for legacy support of NetMeeting 1.0. Through these built-in protocols, the ILS provides directory server support for NetMeeting. These interfaces allow NetMeeting to access the server for dynamic directory information and facilitate point-to-point Internet communication sessions.

Note Other clients can access ILS through the LDAP interface; see the *Microsoft NetMeeting 2.1 SDK*. All client applications must migrate to LDAP to access dynamic directory information.

Performance monitoring. The ILS supports Windows NT Server administration features—including performance monitoring (Perfmon counters), Simple Network Management Protocol (SNMP) monitoring, and event logs—to measure activity and system performance. Operators enjoy administration features, such as transaction logs that collect usage statistics, track messages and transactions, and allow administrators to examine usage patterns. These tools enable administrators to proactively monitor server performance and identify potential problems.

Stable, robust server capabilities. This standards-based Internet directory server was designed to provide stable, robust directory services. The ILS uses thread pooling and connection management to enable more efficient handling of system resources. ILS users will experience better performance, because the ILS uses binary data packets to optimize performance. Also, the server uses a spanning tree architecture to support many concurrent users in a single server configuration.

Customization through Active Server Pages. With Active Server Pages, administrators can combine HTML and scripting components to customize their ILS interface. They can create scripts to display a specific group of NetMeeting users currently online, enable user searches, and initiate real-time communication sessions with other users. For example, administrators can create "buddy pages" that limit the directory to a list of specific users that share a common interest.

Easy setup and administration. The ILS provides a graphical setup program so that you can install server components quickly and easily. Then, administrators can set options for user logon, security, and server access through the Microsoft Internet Service Manager.

Microsoft product support. Microsoft provides worldwide product support through the Microsoft Support Network. ILS users can choose from standard or priority support.

For More Information

For information about setting up and implementing an ILS, refer to the *Microsoft Internet Locator Server Operations Guide* or to its companion, the *Microsoft Internet Locator Service Operations Reference*. Both documents are packaged with the product, or you can download the ILS and the accompanying documents from the Web site at **http://www.backoffice.microsoft.com/** (click **Product Information**, select the **Microsoft Commercial Internet System** product, and then click **Internet Locator Server**).

Firewall Configuration

Microsoft NetMeeting can be configured to work with most organizations' existing firewall security. However, because of limitations in most firewall technology, few products are available that allow you to securely transport inbound and outbound NetMeeting calls containing audio, video, and data across a firewall. You want to consider carefully the relative security risks of enabling different parts of a NetMeeting call in your firewall product. Especially, you must consider very carefully the security risks involved when modifying your firewall configuration to enable any component of an inbound NetMeeting call.

Components of a Secured System

A firewall is a set of security mechanisms that an organization implements, both logically and physically, to prevent unsecured access to an internal network. Firewall configurations vary from organization to organization. Most often, the firewall consists of several components, which can include a combination of routers, proxy servers, host computers, gateways, and networks with the appropriate security software. Very rarely is a firewall a single component, although a number of newer commercial firewalls attempt to put all of the components in a single box.

For most organizations, an Internet connection is part of the firewall. The firewall identifies itself to the outside network as a number of IP addresses—or as capable of routing to a number of IP addresses—all associated with domain name service (DNS) entries. The firewall might respond as all of these hosts (a virtual machine) or pass on packets bound for these hosts to assigned computers. The following diagram shows a firewall configuration.

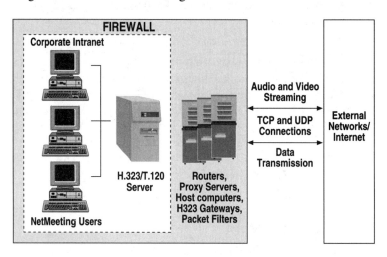

NetMeeting and Firewalls

You can configure firewall components in a variety of ways, depending on your organization's specific security policies and overall operations. While most firewalls are capable of allowing primary (initial) and secondary (subsequent) TCP and UDP connections, they might be configured to support only specific connections based on security considerations. For example, some firewalls allow only primary TCP connections, which are considered the most secure and reliable.

To enable NetMeeting multipoint data conferencing (application sharing, whiteboard, chat, file transfer, and directory lookups), your firewall only needs to pass through primary TCP connections on assigned ports. For NetMeeting to make calls with audio and video conferencing, your firewall must be able to pass through secondary TCP and UDP connections on dynamically assigned ports. Some firewalls can pass through primary TCP connections on assigned ports, but cannot pass through secondary TCP or UDP connections on dynamically assigned ports.

Note NetMeeting audio and video features require secondary TCP and UDP connections. Therefore, when you establish connections through firewalls that accept only primary TCP connections, you are not able to use the audio or video features of NetMeeting.

Establishing a NetMeeting Connection with a Firewall

When you use NetMeeting to call other users over the Internet, several IP ports are required to establish the outbound connection. If you use a firewall to connect to the Internet, it must be configured so that the following IP ports are not blocked.

This port	Is used for
389	Internet Locator Server (TCP)
522	User Location Service (TCP)
1503	T.120 (TCP)
1720	H.323 call setup (TCP)
1731	Audio call control (TCP)
Dynamic	H.323 call control (TCP)
Dynamic	H.323 streaming (RTP over UDP)

To establish outbound NetMeeting connections through a firewall, the firewall must be configured to do the following:

- Pass through primary TCP connections on ports 389, 522, 1503, 1720, and 1731.

- Pass through secondary TCP and UDP connections on dynamically assigned ports (1024-65535).

The H.323 call setup protocol (over port 1720) dynamically negotiates a TCP port for use by the H.323 call control protocol. Also, both the audio call control protocol (over port 1731) and the H.323 call setup protocol (over port 1720) dynamically negotiate UDP ports for use by the H.323 streaming protocol, which is the RTP. In NetMeeting, two UDP ports are determined on each side of the firewall for audio and video streaming, for a total of four ports for inbound and outbound audio and video. These dynamically negotiated ports are selected arbitrarily from all ports that can be assigned dynamically.

NetMeeting directory services require either port 389 or port 522, depending on the type of server you are using. ILSs, which support LDAP for NetMeeting, require port 389. ULS, developed for NetMeeting 1.0, requires port 522.

Firewall Limitations

Some firewalls cannot support an arbitrary number of virtual internal IP addresses or cannot do so dynamically. With these firewalls, you can establish outbound NetMeeting connections from computers inside the firewall to computers outside the firewall, and you can use the audio and video features of NetMeeting. Other people, though, cannot establish inbound connections from outside the firewall to computers inside the firewall. Typically, this restriction is due to limitations in the network implementation of the firewall.

Note Some firewalls are capable of accepting only certain protocols and cannot handle TCP connections. For example, if your firewall is a Web proxy server with no generic connection-handling mechanism, you will not be able to use NetMeeting through the firewall.

Security and Policy Concerns

Some organizations may have security or policy concerns that require them to limit how fully they support NetMeeting in their firewall configuration. These concerns might be based on network capacity planning or low confidence in the firewall technology being used. For example, security concerns might prohibit an organization from accepting any inbound or outbound flow of UDP data through its firewall. Because these UDP connections are required for NetMeeting audio and video features, disabling this function will exclude audio and video features in NetMeeting for calls through the firewall. The organization can still use NetMeeting data conferencing features—such as application sharing, whiteboard, and chat—for calls through the firewall by allowing only TCP connections on ports 522 and 1503.

A useful reference for firewall design, including policy and security considerations, is *Building Internet Firewalls* (D. Brent Chapman and Elizabeth D. Zwicky, 1995, Sebastopol, California: O'Reilly & Associates, Inc.).

System Policies and Restrictions

You can use the NetMeeting policies and restrictions to restrict most of the features that users can access within NetMeeting. For example, you can preset the NetMeeting work environment to control audio and video access, or to prevent users from sending files to or collaborating with other users during application sharing. You can also specify several NetMeeting settings, including the default directory server.

Issues to Consider Before Setting Policies

Before implementing system policies, you must consider the following issues:

- What types of restrictions and settings would you like to define and manage centrally? For example, do you want to limit access to NetMeeting file transfer, application sharing, or audio and video features?

- Do you want to use one set of standard system policies for all users and computers, or do you want to customize settings by groups of users? Also, do you want to maintain some individual settings for specific users and computers?

- Would it be useful to customize settings by groups, such as Accounting group and Marketing group? A small group of individuals, such as administrators, can have unique privileges set for their specific needs.

Customizing System Policies and Restrictions

You can use the Internet Explorer Administration Kit (IEAK) Configuration Wizard **System Policies and Restrictions** page to deploy Internet Explorer and NetMeeting to users with pre-configured system policy and restriction settings. For more information on how to use the IEAK Configuration Wizard to build custom packages, see "Building Custom Packages" in Chapter 36, "Implementing the Deployment."

When automatic browser configuration is enabled, you can use the IEAK Profile Manager to update and maintain users' system policies and restrictions for NetMeeting. For more information on automatic browser configuration, see Chapter 37, "Automatic Browser Configuration."

▶ **To change policies and restrictions for NetMeeting**

1. Perform one of the following:

   - Run the IEAK Configuration Wizard, and navigate to the **System Policies and Restrictions** page for the custom package you want to build.

   - Run the IEAK Profile Manager, and open the auto-configuration (.ins) file you want to change.

2. In the **System Policies & Restrictions** hierarchy, select **Microsoft NetMeeting**, and then select **NetMeeting Settings**.

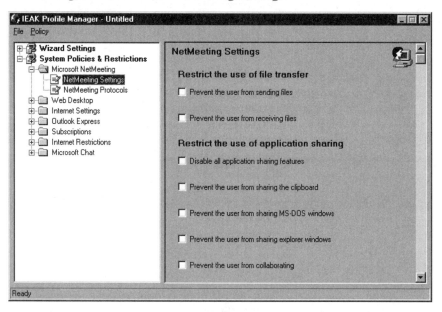

> **Note** The IEAK Profile Manager is shown here, but the **System Policies & Restrictions** page of the IEAK Configuration Wizard works similarly.

3. In the right pane, select the options you want.

   For more information, see the next two sections: "NetMeeting System Policies and Restrictions Options" and "Common System Policies and Restrictions Scenarios."

4. Save your changes to the auto-configuration (.ins) file, or finish building the custom package, as appropriate.

NetMeeting System Policies and Restrictions Options

The following table describes the available NetShow system policies and restrictions options.

Option	Description
Restrict the use of file transfer	
Prevent the user from sending files	Prevents the user from sending files to other participants in a meeting.
Prevent the user from receiving files	Prevents the user from receiving files from other participants in a meeting.
Restrict the use of application sharing	
Disable all application sharing features	Disables the **Share Application** option on the **Tools** menu and the **Share Application** button.
Prevent the user from sharing the clipboard	Prevents the user's Clipboard contents from being accessible to other participants in a meeting.
Prevent the user from sharing MS-DOS windows	Prevents the **MS-DOS windows** option from appearing on the **Share Application** menu.
	Note If you choose this option, you must also click **Prevent the user from sharing explorer windows**. These two options work only if they are both selected. If you do not choose **Prevent the user from sharing explorer windows**, the user will be able to share MS-DOS windows from Microsoft Explorer.
Prevent the user from sharing explorer windows	Prevents the **Microsoft Explorer windows** option from appearing on the **Share Application** menu.
Prevent the user from collaborating	Prevents a user from collaborating with other users with whom he or she is application sharing.
Restrict the use of the option dialog	
Disable the 'General' options page	Removes the **General** tab from **Options** (on the **Tools** menu) to prevent the user from changing general, network bandwidth, and file transfer features.
Disable the 'My Information' options page	Removes the **My Information** tab from **Options** (on the **Tools** menu) to prevent the user from changing user address and user category (personal, business, or adults-only) information.
Disable the 'Calling' options page	Removes the **Calling** tab from **Options** (on the **Tools** menu) to prevent the user from changing Directory features and SpeedDial options for automatically adding people and updating the SpeedDial list.

Option	Description
Restrict the use of the option dialog *(continued)*	
Disable the 'Audio' options page	Removes the **Audio** tab from **Options** (on the **Tools** menu) to prevent the user from changing general audio, microphone sensitivity, and H.323 gateway features.
Disable the 'Video' options page	Removes the **Video** tab from **Options** (on the **Tools** menu) to prevent the user from changing options for sending and receiving video, or from specifying send image size, video quality, and video camera properties.
Disable the 'Protocols' options page	Removes the **Protocols** tab from **Options** (on the **Tools** menu) to prevent the user from changing the selected TCP/IP or null modem protocol.
Prevent the user from answering calls	Prevents the user from being notified of incoming calls.
Prevent the user from using audio features	Prevents the user from using the audio features to talk to or hear other participants in a meeting. **Note** Disable the **'Audio' options** page is selected automatically when you choose this option.
Restrict the use of video	
Prevent the user from sending video	Prevents the user from transmitting video images to other participants in a meeting. **Note** Disable the **'Video' options** page is selected automatically when you choose both **Prevent the user from sending video** and **Prevent the user from receiving video**.
Prevent the user from receiving video	Prevents the user from receiving video images from other participants in a meeting. **Note** Disable the **'Video' options** page is selected automatically when you choose both **Prevent the user from sending video** and **Prevent the user from receiving video**.
Prevent the user from using directory services	Prevents the user from accessing all servers and server functions, including logging on, logging off, resolving addresses, and viewing directories. Users can still access Web directory services using the **Go** menu or using their Web browser. **Note** You may also want to choose **Disable the 'Calling' options** page.
Set the default Directory Server	
Directory Server	Sets the default Internet Location Server (ILS) to which the user logs on when starting NetMeeting.

Option	Description

Set Exchange Server Property for NetMeeting Address

Exchange Server Property	Specifies the Exchange attribute that the Exchange Extension looks at to determine the NetMeeting address. Press the DOWN ARROW, and select one of the listed Attributes.
	Note If you are unable to use one of the listed attributes, you must set the registry key manually.
	To set the registry keys manually, use the administration tool to set the attribute in Exchange. Export the following values from the address book: Object Class, Directory Name, Extension Attribute *number*, and SMTP or Exchange Address. Write a script to set the value of Extension Attribute *number* for each person (for example, *<servername>/<email address>*). Import the revised file into the address book. If you are specifying attributes for a large number of people, use several different servers. For additional information, see the Microsoft Exchange reference documents.

Preset User Information Category

Category	Identifies your category and purpose for using NetMeeting as either Personal, Business, or Adult. Category selections no longer appear in the IEAK Configuration Wizard and are dimmed on the **My Information** tab. Your name will be listed only in the directory for the category that you select.
	Note You can set this policy only prior to installing NetMeeting. If NetMeeting is already installed, you must remove the application, and then set the policy in order for it to take effect.

Select enabled set of T120 protocols

Enable TCP/IP T120 protocol	Enables a user to place and receive calls using a TCP/IP connection.

Set the NetMeeting home page

URL	Defines the specific URL for the Web page that users see when they select **Product News** (on the NetMeeting **Help** menu, click **Microsoft on the Web**, and then click **Product News**).

Set limit for audio/video throughput

Average audio/video throughput limit (in bps)	Sets the average bandwidth limit for combined audio and video throughput over the network. For example, if you are concerned about excessive audio and video bandwidth utilization over your network, you may set a limit to restrict the average throughput that is permitted. This limit applies to audio and video transmission only, and does not affect data.

Common System Policies and Restrictions Scenarios

Typically, organizations may want to implement several system policies and restrictions for their user communities. The following table lists some common scenarios and the associated system policy name that organizations would set.

If you want to	Set this system policy
Disable all audio features	1. **Prevent the user from using audio features**
	2. **Disable the 'Audio' options page**
Disable all video features	1. **Restrict the use of video**
	2. **Prevent the user from sending video**
	3. **Prevent the user from receiving video**
	4. **Disable the 'Video' options page**
Limit the network bandwidth used by audio/video	**Set limit for audio/video throughput**
Prevent access to ULS or ILS directory services	1. **Prevent the user from using directory services**
	2. **Disable the 'Calling' options page**
Specify the Web page that users see when they select **Product News**	**Set the NetMeeting home page**

Using NetMeeting on Intranet Web Pages

The NetMeeting platform enables third-party vendors to integrate conferencing features into their own products and services. The NetMeeting platform is available with the *Microsoft NetMeeting 2.1 SDK*, which includes the following components:

- A set of objects based on the OLE Component Object Model (COM) for adding conferencing support to COM applications. The COM interfaces are the same as the interfaces provided with NetMeeting 1.0.

- Online HTML Help files located in the \Nm21sdk\Doc\ folder, which is downloaded with the SDK. These Help files have been enhanced for NetMeeting 2.1.

- Sample files that demonstrate how to use the ActiveX control and COM objects, and detailed information about how to install and use each sample.

- A set of COM objects for supporting LDAP-based directories (ILSs) in your application.

- An ActiveX control for adding conferencing support to Web pages (using JavaScript-compatible languages or Visual Basic Scripting Edition), Visual Basic applications, and other OLE-enabled documents and applications.

- A set of COM objects for installing custom audio and video codecs that NetMeeting can leverage during calls.

- New tutorials and sample scripts that demonstrate how to use the *Microsoft NetMeeting 2.1 SDK*.

To download a copy of the *Microsoft NetMeeting 2.1 SDK*, see the NetMeeting Web site at **http://www.microsoft.com/netmeeting/** under Authors & Developers. Note that you must install NetMeeting 2.1 to use the *Microsoft NetMeeting 2.1 SDK*.

The NetMeeting ActiveX Control

With the ActiveX control, organizations can easily integrate the NetMeeting conferencing capabilities into their intranet Web pages. Web site creators can take advantage of established protocols for conferencing over the Internet and corporate intranet. They can create a Web page with NetMeeting conferencing support using JavaScript-compatible languages (JScript) or VBScript. Then, people can join a conference from the Web page.

The NetMeeting control runs on Windows 95 and Windows NT 4.0 platforms, using Microsoft NetMeeting 1.0, 2.0, or 2.1 (NetMeeting 2.0 or later is required for audio and video capabilities). The SDK provides sample HTML files for adding ActiveX control technology to Web pages. For more information, see the *Microsoft NetShow SDK*.

Note If you use Web pages with ActiveX conferencing, you must use a browser that supports ActiveX controls, such as Internet Explorer.

Alternatively, Web site creators can add a "callto" statement using the NetMeeting protocol handler so that people can place a NetMeeting call directly from a Web page. For more information, see the *Microsoft NetMeeting 2.1 SDK*.

Intranet Scenarios

NetMeeting expands the power of the corporate intranet as a tool for communication, information, and learning. Corporate users experience many benefits from these communication and collaboration tools; employees are more productive— they can find information quicker, resolve problems faster, and communicate more effectively. The following scenarios provide examples of how organizations can use the NetMeeting ActiveX control in the workplace.

Note In some cases, an alternative solution to using the NetMeeting ActiveX control would be to create NetMeeting SpeedDial numbers and add them to the intranet Web pages. The SpeedDial numbers enable people to connect using the NetMeeting application. This chapter, however, focuses on using the NetMeeting ActiveX control.

Help Desk: An Employee Needs Help with a Hardware or Software Problem

Scenario

An employee experiences a hardware or software problem and needs to reach a help-desk or PC repair representative within the company as soon as possible. The representative needs to resolve the problem quickly so that the employee can continue working with a minimum loss of productivity.

Solution

A company can use the NetMeeting ActiveX control to develop a PC Support page that provides an in-person response to hardware and software problems. An employee can go instantly to the page on the corporate intranet when they have a problem. In conjunction with NetMeeting support, the page can include a troubleshooting area. From this area, the employee can make selections that narrow down the type of hardware or software problem. For example, the employee may select an application, such as Microsoft Word, from a list. Then, he or she may select a specific problem area, such as Fonts, from a list of possible problem areas. Based on these selections, the server can connect the employee with an expert in the specific problem area.

After submitting the problem report, the server notifies the employee about how many other employees are also waiting for assistance and approximately how long it will be before an engineer can call back. The engineer then initiates a NetMeeting conferencing call with the employee to discuss the difficulty. The employee can use the NetMeeting application-sharing feature to share the Word application with the engineer, who can quickly locate the problem as the employee watches.

Virtual Meeting: A Manager Wants to Set Up a Conference with Employees at Local and Remote Locations

Scenario

A manager calls an emergency meeting with 10 team members who are located at both local and out-of-state offices. Team members need a simple, convenient method for meeting, because time does not permit traveling to a remote meeting location. Also, the manager needs to distribute pertinent information to all team members.

Solution

The NetMeeting ActiveX control makes virtual meeting setup simple. A company can create a Virtual Meeting page on its corporate intranet. The manager can send e-mail messages to attendees that gives the page URL and the time of the meeting. Attendees can then access the Web page prior to the conference to view the agenda, and download files pertinent to the meeting.

At the scheduled time, all the team members can open the intranet Web page and join the conference with data conferencing features, such as application sharing, chat, and file transfer. Attendees can follow along as the manager shares a presentation with the group using the NetMeeting application-sharing feature. During the meeting, one person takes notes and action items using the NetMeeting chat program. In addition, the manager can use the NetMeeting file transfer capability to send a copy of the presentation to each meeting attendee. The team completes the meeting's objectives successfully.

Group Collaboration: Employees at Different Locations Need to Collaborate for Information and Problem Solving

Scenario

Employees need an effective method for collaborating with each other, whether they are separated by a hallway, a building, or a continent. For example, within a manufacturing organization, engineering facilities, factories, and suppliers may need to coordinate their efforts to produce an assembled part. Delay in communication among these groups may slow the manufacturing process.

Solution

A company can use the NetMeeting ActiveX control to develop interactive Web pages for selected departments, such as Accounting, Engineering, and Human Resources. Using these intranet Web pages, the groups can quickly connect and communicate information and ideas with each other. If the factory needs to consult with an engineer because a part is not working correctly, and they cannot interpret the engineering blueprints, they can access an Engineering Web page from the factory floor. Then, they can initiate an ActiveX conferencing call with the appropriate engineer.

A series of events can occur, all made possible by the ActiveX control. The factory can show the part to the engineer, using a camera and NetMeeting video capabilities. The engineer can share the existing blueprints with the factory using the NetMeeting application-sharing feature. Then, the engineer can modify the part and call the supplier that builds the device. The engineer can use NetMeeting's file transfer capability to send the new blueprints to the supplier. The supplier can correct the problem and send the new part back to the factory, with only a minimum delay in the manufacturing process.

Benefits Information: Employees Want to Learn About Company Benefits

Scenario

Employees often have questions about the benefits provided by their company. "When can I enroll in the 401(k) plan?" "How do I purchase stock options?" They need a simple, easy method for locating benefits information and for contacting a human resources representative who can respond directly to questions.

Solution

Using the ActiveX control, companies can create a home page on the intranet where employees can go to learn more about benefits and policies. From the home page, employees can select options to get information about the 401(k) plan, medical and dental insurance, stock options, payroll, and vacation time. Employees can read fact sheets and responses to frequently asked questions about the selected benefit option. Then, they can click an icon to initiate a conference with a representative to get additional information. With the ActiveX control, the representative can transfer files with pertinent benefit information. Employees can easily stay informed about company benefits and policies.

Corporate Sales: Employees Want to Purchase Company Products and Services

Scenario

A company store or sales office may offer products and services for employee purchase. Employees need a simple method for getting product information and ordering a desired product or service that doesn't require time away from the office for ordering and delivery.

Solution

A company can develop a product and service catalog on the corporate intranet. Employees can access the Web catalog and select from a list of options to obtain the following types of information:

- Product specifications
- Availability of products
- Order forms to create and submit an order
- Payment information
- Delivery times and request forms

An employee can enter credit-card information directly on the intranet Web page. Optionally, the employee can click an icon to initiate ActiveX conferencing with a sales representative who can accept the payment details in person and also provide additional information about a product. By streamlining this process, employees can easily purchase company products and services from their desktops.

Discussion Groups: Employees with Common Interests Can Participate in Group Discussions

Scenario

An organization wants to provide a mechanism that enables employees to hold technology discussions and share other common interests from their local desktops.

Solution

Web pages with the ActiveX control can facilitate information sharing among employees. Employees with common interests can visit a Web page to share their knowledge and provide insightful information to other employees who want to learn about a new technology or topic. Organizations can build work-related communities based on these topics of interest.

For example, NetMeeting enthusiasts can go to a Web page and join a conference to talk with other NetMeeting users. During group discussions, experts can join the call to respond to questions or issues. Optionally, an employee can initiate a one-on-one discussion through ActiveX conferencing with a NetMeeting expert who is currently online.

C H A P T E R   2 1

FrontPage Express

In this chapter

FrontPage Express Overview

The features that distinguish FrontPage Express include the following:

- Flexible authoring environment
- Table creation and editing
- Forms creation
- Templates and wizards
- Support for Web technologies

Flexible Authoring Environment

FrontPage Express offers two ways to create and edit Web pages. The what-you-see-is-what-you-get (WYSIWYG) editor displays a graphical representation of what the Web page will look like when it's published. Users can type the contents directly onto the page and highlight text to change the color, size, and style. Things such as background colors and graphics, text and link colors, margins, and base location can be easily specified in the **Page Properties** dialog box. Generating tables is effortless with the Insert Table feature. FrontPage Express creates all the HTML code automatically, based on user input.

FrontPage Express also allows authors to view the actual HTML that is being generated. It adds color codes, indents, and formats to the HTML so it is easy to read. In fact, authors who are comfortable working with HTML can even edit in this mode and instantly see the results in the FrontPage Express application.

Table Creation and Editing

With FrontPage Express, it's easy to insert a table into a Web page and then edit either the entire table or individual cells. This feature also makes it easy to create nested tables without knowing the HTML that it normally requires.

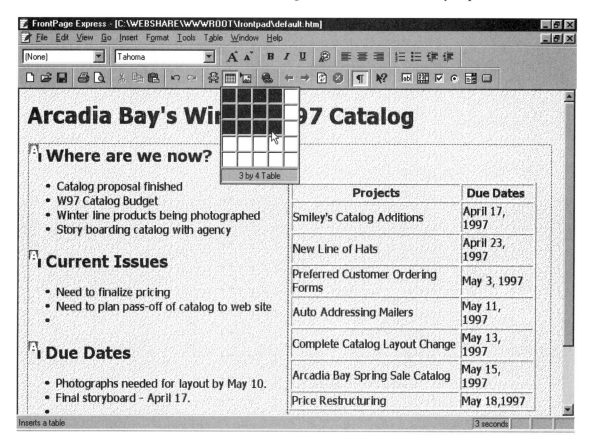

Forms Creation

You can add forms to your Web page that people can fill out and return. Your forms can include text boxes, drop-down menus, images, and more. You must be connected to a server running FrontPage server extensions to use these form-related features.

Templates and Wizards

If you're connected to a server running FrontPage server extensions, you can also use form-related templates and wizards in FrontPage Express. Templates are preformatted Web pages that can be used as a guide in creating your own pages and Web View folders. Wizards walk users through the step-by-step process of creating a Web page. Templates and wizards let you create the forms you want simply by selecting the types of information you need. You can also create a survey to collect information from readers and store it on your Web server. Or you can create a page to acknowledge that you have received the reader's input.

Support for Web Technologies

FrontPage Express supports top-standard Internet technologies to make your pages more engaging, without requiring programming knowledge. FrontPage Express supports the insertion of JavaScript, Java applets, VBScript, and ActiveX objects. Form elements, such as text boxes, buttons, and drop-down menus, can be added to pages directly from the toolbar, and users can easily edit their properties.

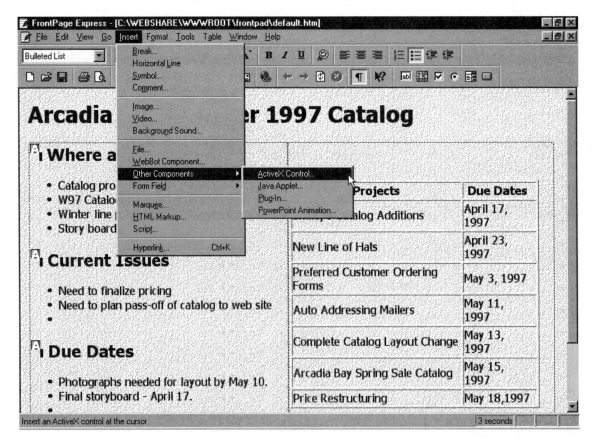

Using FrontPage Express

Creating and editing Web pages with FrontPage Express is easy. Its editing window shows you exactly what your page will look like, and all you need to do is add the text, links, graphics, and other elements to the page. After FrontPage Express is installed, an **Edit** button is added to the Internet Explorer toolbar so that you can launch FrontPage Express directly from the browser window to edit the current Web page.

Creating and Editing Web Pages

▶ **To start a new page**

1. Start FrontPage Express. A new blank page is displayed by default. You can start working on this page, or continue to step 2.

2. On the **File** menu, click **New**. The **New Page** dialog box appears.

3. Select a template or wizard from the menu. Selecting **Normal Page** gives you the same blank page that comes up when FrontPage Express is started.

4. Set the page properties by right-clicking anywhere on the page and clicking **Page Properties** on the shortcut menu. Here you can choose the background color or graphic, define colors for the various types of text on the page, set the margins, and specify header information.

5. To enter text, click your cursor on the page, and start typing. Editing the text is done the same way as with a word processor—just highlight the text you want to change, and choose the style from the toolbar or from the **Format** menu.

6. Use the **Insert** menu for inserting graphics, video clips, horizontal lines, scripts, and other items.

7. Click the **Save** button to save your new file.

▶ **To edit an existing page**

1. Start FrontPage Express.

2. On the **File** menu, click **Open**, navigate to the file you want to edit, select the file, and click **OK**. To open and edit a Web page from within Internet Explorer, click the **Edit** button on the Internet Explorer toolbar.

3. Make the desired changes to the Web page, and save your changes.

You can edit the registry to make Internet Explorer use a different HTML editor. The registry key that needs to be changed is:

HKEY_CLASSES_ROOT\htmlfile\shell\edit\command

The value for FrontPage Express is:

C:\Program Files\FPXpress\bin\fpexpress.exe %1.

For Notepad, this value can be changed to:

C:\Windows\Notepad.exe %1

For FrontPage 97 or FrontPage 98, this value can be changed to:

C:\Program Files\Microsoft FrontPage\bin\fpeditor.exe %1

When you open a Web page in FrontPage Express, it displays icons to represent certain items in the graphics display. Scripts, objects, and unrecognized HTML markup are each represented by their own special icon. These items can be edited by double-clicking the icon.

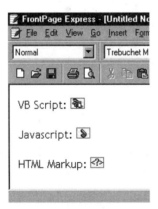

Note When you save a page in FrontPage Express, you can save the page as a file or add the page to a Web site using the Web Publishing Wizard. If you're using Microsoft Personal Web Server, save the page as a file to a location under Webshare\wwwroot. Use the Web Publishing Wizard to publish your Web files to an Internet service provider (ISP) or other file server. The Web Publishing Wizard is automatically activated unless you click the **As File** button in the **Save As** dialog box. For more information, see "Understanding the Web Publishing Wizard" in Chapter 22, "Personal Web Server."

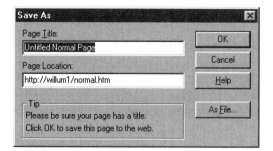

Creating a Custom Template

You can create your own custom page templates for use with FrontPage Express. This is useful if you frequently need to create a certain type of page. Template files are stored in the C:\Program Files\Microsoft FrontPage Express\Pages folder by default.

▶ **To create a custom template**

1. Open the Pages directory and create a new folder. When naming the folder, be sure to include a .tem file name extension so FrontPage Express recognizes it as a template folder. The template folder will contain two files: an .htm file that contains the template, and an .inf file that tells FrontPage Express what to display in the menu.

2. Create the HTML file for your template and save it in the Pages directory.

3. Use Notepad to create the .inf file. It should look something like this:

```
[info]
title=Normal Page
description=Create a blank Web page.
```

The title shows up in the menu of the **New Page** dialog box. The description shows up when a user clicks the template title in the **New Page** dialog box.

4. Store the HTML and .inf files in the .tem folder you created in the Pages directory. The next time you click **New** on the **File** menu, you will see your new template in the menu along with the default templates and wizards.

Inserting WebBot Components

WebBot components let you add functionality to your Web pages. FrontPage Express offers three WebBot components:

- The **Include** component lets you insert the body of another HTML page into the current page. This is useful for serial elements, such as headers and footers, that appear on multiple pages. Instead of having to edit every instance of a serial element, all you have to change is the included file.

- The **Search** component provides a convenient way to create a search page for users to search the contents of your Web site.

- The **Time Stamp** component automatically inserts the date and time a page was last updated.

▶ **To insert a WebBot component**

1. Position the blinking cursor where you would like the WebBot component to appear.

2. Click the **WebBot** button in the toolbar; or, on the **Insert** menu, select **WebBot Component**.

3. Select the WebBot component you would like to insert, and click **OK**. The **Properties** dialog box appears.

4. Enter the properties for the WebBot component, then click **OK**.

Inserting Scripts and Objects

Scripts and objects can help you bring your Web pages to life by adding a new level of functionality and interactivity. FrontPage Express makes it possible to insert client-side scripts, ActiveX objects, and Java applets directly into your Web pages.

▶ **To insert a script**

1. On the **Insert** menu, click **Script**. The **Script** dialog box appears.

2. Select the option for the type of script you are using, and paste the body of the script into the text window.

3. Click **Extended** to add attributes to the <SCRIPT> tag.

4. Click **OK** when you are finished. An icon representing the script appears on the screen. To edit the script at any time, double-click the icon.

▶ **To insert an ActiveX object**

1. On the **Insert** menu, click **Other Components**, then click **ActiveX Control**. The **ActiveX Control Properties** dialog box appears.

2. Select the control you would like to insert from the drop-down list box.

3. Under **Layout,** select the object's alignment, size, and border thickness. Click **Properties** to edit the properties of the control.

4. Click **OK** when you are finished.

C H A P T E R   2 2

Personal Web Server

In this chapter

Personal Web Server Overview

Microsoft Personal Web Server turns any Windows 95– or Windows NT 4.0–based computer into a Web server, enabling easy publication of personal Web pages. Easy to install and administer, Personal Web Server simplifies the sharing of information on corporate intranets or the Internet. Individual users can serve Web pages directly from their desktops, and workgroups can share information with each other or expose their projects to a wider audience.

Because Personal Web Server supports Active Server Pages, it can be used as a development and testing platform for Web sites. This lets Web developers test every aspect of a site directly on their local machine prior to posting it on an Internet or intranet server. Personal Web Server also includes support for all Internet Server API (ISAPI) extensions and CGI scripts, which offers the benefit of faster development. Personal Web Server is optimized for interactive workstation use and does not have the system requirements of a full Web server such as Internet Information Server (IIS).

The features and benefits that distinguish Personal Web Server include the following:

- Integration with Windows operating systems
- Ease of installation, use, and management
- Standards-based technology
- Expanded programmability features

Integration with Windows

Personal Web Server turns a Windows 95–based personal computer into a low-volume Web server, making it as easy to share HTML and FTP files over intranets and the Internet as it is to share and print document files over a network.

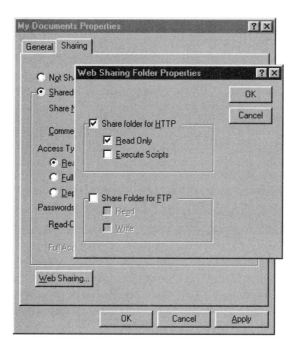

The software is fully integrated into the Windows 95 taskbar and Control Panel, allowing users to start and stop services whenever needed, administer the server, or change general options. Personal Web Server was designed to be complementary to larger Web server products such as Windows NT IIS and Peer Web Services included with Windows NT Workstation version 4.0.

Ease of Installation, Use, and Management

Personal Web Server installs in minutes and includes the Personal Web Manager, an intuitive, HTML-based administration utility that supports full remote administration. You can easily start and stop the service, view connection statistics, and manage virtual directories. The Home Page Wizard provides an easy way for novice users to get started creating Web pages, and the Publishing Wizard automates the process of publishing Web files to an Internet Service Provider (ISP). Personal Web Server supports both user-level and local security, ensuring flexible and effective protection of sensitive corporate information. Users can set up Personal Web Server to support Windows NT Challenge/Response encrypted-password transmission.

Standards-Based Technology

Personal Web Server 4 supports Active Server Pages and existing standards such as CGI, and includes the open ISAPI extension to the Win32® API, which is up to five times faster than CGI-based applications. This enables any user to take advantage of Active Server Pages, ISAPI, and CGI scripts.

Expanded Programmability Features

The following components can be installed to further extend the potential for developing Web-based applications using Personal Web Server:

- **Microsoft Transaction Server (MTS).** MTS is a component-based transaction processing system. It is used for developing, deploying, and managing high-performance, scalable, and robust server applications for the enterprise, Internet, and intranet. MTS defines an application programming model for developing distributed, component-based applications. It also provides a run-time infrastructure and a graphical tool for deploying and managing these applications. For more information about Microsoft Transaction Server, see the Personal Web Server online documentation, or visit **http://www.microsoft.com/transaction/**.

- **Microsoft Data Access Components.** These components facilitate database access with support for ActiveX Data Objects (ADO) and the Microsoft Access driver. Also included is Microsoft Remote Data Service (RDS), a fast and efficient data connectivity and data publishing framework for applications hosted on Internet Explorer. For more information about ADO, see the Personal Web Server online documentation, or see **http://www.microsoft.com/data/ado/**.

- **Microsoft Message Queue Server.** MSMQ makes it easy for application programs to communicate with other application programs quickly, reliably, and asynchronously by sending and receiving messages. The key features of MSMQ, such as ActiveX support, comprehensive security controls, powerful administration tools, an extensive feature set, and integration with strategic Microsoft products such as Internet Information Server and MTS, make MSMQ the message-queuing product of choice for applications running on Windows 95, Windows 98, and Windows NT operating systems. The Personal Web Server package includes the MSMQ Dependent and Independent Clients. For more information about MSMQ, see the Personal Web Server online documentation, or see **http://www.microsoft.com/ntserverenterprise/** (look under Product Guide, Features).

- **Internet Connection Services for Remote Access Systems (RAS).** This is a collection of software applications designed to help corporations and ISPs build comprehensive Internet access solutions, including dial-up Virtual Private Networks (VPN). Internet Connection Services for RAS let administrators quickly implement a custom remote access network. For more information about ICS for RAS, see the Personal Web Server online documentation.

Understanding Personal Web Server

When Personal Web Server is installed, a variety of files and directories are added to your computer. The C:\Inetpub directory is of primary concern to users, because its subdirectories store all files related to publishing on the site.

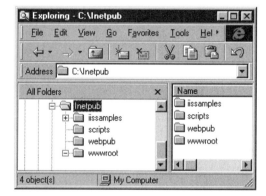

The subdirectories of C:\Inetpub are as follows:

- The Iissamples directory stores all of the Web files that are used by the Home Page Wizard.

- The Scripts directory stores all scripts used on the Web site.

- The Webpub directory stores all documents that are published on the site (for example, Word or Excel files). It effectively performs the same role as the FTP service in earlier versions of Personal Web Server.

- All Web files are served from the Wwwroot directory, which is the home directory by default. Users can add subdirectories to the Wwwroot directory as needed.

The URL for the server is taken from the **Identification** tab of the computer's Network control panel. For example, a computer named "Arnold" would have a URL of **http://Arnold/**. If the computer's name is changed, Personal Web Server automatically updates the URL to reflect the change.

Using Personal Web Server

By default, Personal Web Server runs automatically at startup with the HTTP service turned on. The Personal Web Server icon is visible in the taskbar when it is running. All Web server settings can be accessed through the Personal Web Manager.

▶ **To access the Personal Web Manager**

- Double-click the **Personal Web Server** icon in the taskbar, or right-click the icon and select **Properties**. The Personal Web Manager is started. The **Main** window of the **Personal Web Manager** dialog box tells you whether the server is running or not and lets you start or stop the Web server as needed. Connection statistics are displayed in the lower half of the window under **Monitoring**.

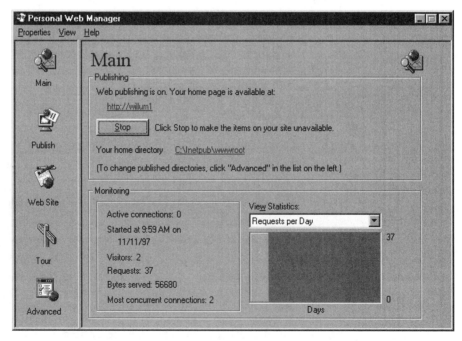

Administering Personal Web Server

Personal Web Server is administered on the **Advanced Options** page of the **Personal Web Manager**. Here, users can create or delete virtual directories, edit directory properties, and set directory browsing and logging options. Virtual directories are displayed in a tree-view menu.

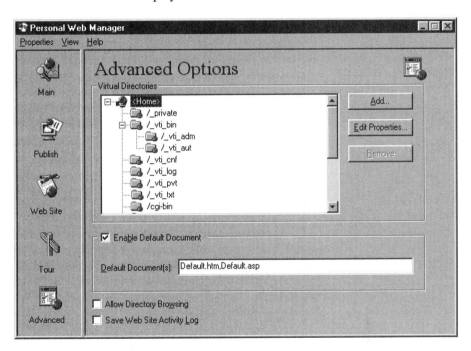

▶ **To Administer Personal Web Server**

1. Double-click the **Personal Web Server** icon in the taskbar, or right-click the **Personal Web Server** icon, and select **Properties**. The Personal Web Manager is started.

2. Click the **Advanced** icon in the left pane to open the **Advanced Options** window. From here, you can:

   ▪ Create, edit, and delete virtual directories. A virtual directory is a directory that is not physically contained within the home directory, but which appears as though it were to users who visit your Web site. Virtual directories give you the ability to publish information located on your hard disk. For example, if you created a virtual directory for C:\Documents\Reports and gave it an alias of /Reports, users could view the directory using **http://<*servername*>/Reports/**.

- Set the default document(s) for your Web site. Default documents are the first pages that users see when they access your site, or a subdirectory on your site. Each directory on your site can have a default document.

- Allow users to browse your site by directory. Directory browsing is an alternative way to provide navigation for visitors coming to your site. Instead of providing links on a home page to documents in the home directory, the default document is disabled, and a list of all files in the directory is presented. This is particularly useful if you intend to share documents in their native format.

- Save an Activity log for your Web site. This log file lists everyone who has visited your site and what files they accessed while they were there.

For more information, access the online documentation from the **Help** menu.

Adding Web Pages and Files

For files to be accessible through Personal Web Server, they must be stored in the home directory, or in a virtual directory that you create. You can add new Web files by copying them to the home directory, to a subdirectory of the home directory, or to a virtual directory.

Using the Publishing Wizard, you can publish other types of files (such as word-processed documents and spreadsheets) on your site. This allows users to view the files in their native format. Directory browsing must be enabled for this to work properly.

Using an ASP Redirect Page

An ASP redirect page can be used to redirect users to another location on your site. This can come in handy for certain situations. For example, if you need to take your site down for maintenance, you can redirect users to an alternate page (which is friendlier than just leaving them with a 404 error). Or, if most of the files you want to publish are stored in a certain directory, you can use an ASP redirect page to automatically send users to that directory, eliminating the need to change your default home directory.

▶ **To use an ASP redirect page**

1. Open the **Personal Web Manager**, click the **Advanced** icon, and create a virtual directory for the directory to which you would like to point.

2. Using Notepad, create the .asp file containing the redirect script, and save it to the root of the home directory. The contents of the file should look something like this:

```
<%@ LANGUAGE="VBSCRIPT" %>
<%
response.redirect "/<virtual directory alias>/default.htm"
%>
```

3. Go back to the **Advanced** page of the **Personal Web Manager**, and type the name of the .asp file in the **Default Document(s)** field. Use a comma to separate it from any other entries.

Now when users access your site, the ASP redirect script points them to the specified location.

Personal Web Server Scenarios

A Simple Document-Sharing Solution

Scenario

A construction company executive organizes the computer files by project. Each project contains building specification files, that the executive needs to share with the engineers. Each project also contains sensitive financial information to which the engineers should not have access. Because the project directories contain information the engineers should not access, the specification files must be copied to another directory. As changes are made to the specifications by customers, however, the copy available to the engineers must be updated.

Solution

Because the project directories contain information to which the engineers should not have access, the specification files are copied to the publishing directory. The engineers have the same software on their computers to view the files as the executive used to create the files; therefore, the documents do not need to be converted to HTML to be shared.

The executive creates a simple home page by using the Personal Web Server Home Page Wizard. He uses the Publishing Wizard to place copies of the files in the publishing directory. The wizard automatically adds links to the documents to the home page. The files can be easily updated by using the File Refresh feature built into the wizard. The executive sends the Web site address in an e-mail message to the engineers.

By using browsers such as Internet Explorer, the engineers are now able to view the specification files. The files are viewed in their native formats. The engineers are not able to view other documents in the project directories, because the project directories are not shared. Because the publishing directory folder has read permissions only, the files cannot be changed by the engineers.

A Custom Information-Exchange Solution

Scenario

The director of human resources at a small advertising firm wants to know how satisfied employees are with the current health-insurance carrier before spending time looking for potential new carriers. The director wants to keep the responses confidential, and doesn't want to compile results from a number of paper surveys. She would like to use an online survey; however, the entire graphic art department works on Macintosh computers, while the remainder of the employees have Windows-based computers.

Solution

Using the Home Page Wizard, the director builds an HTML-based Web page that includes a link to a survey form. She follows the cut-and-paste directions in the Personal Web Server documentation topic "Constructing an Interactive Form" to produce the survey form. She then sends out the Web address of the home page in an e-mail message.

Because the form is HTML-based, the employees are able to use their browsers to view and respond, regardless of the operating system they are using. The director has all the responses in a database file, which can be easily used to compile the results.

A Web Application-Testing Solution

Scenario

A Web application developer works as a private contractor, selling Web applications to various companies. He uses his home computer for much of the work and then sends the applications either to a company's Web server or to an Internet service provider. The present contract calls for the development and testing of a unique calendar component to include on a client's home page.

Solution

The developer has a choice of creating a calendar component using Microsoft Visual Basic or any other language program, or using an off-the-shelf, third-party component. Because the customer has requested something extraordinary, the developer elects to create a component using Visual Basic.

Once the component is finished, the developer registers it using the Microsoft Transaction Server Explorer. The component is then included when building the Web application, easily done with the Microsoft Visual InterDev™ Web development system.

As a final step, the developer loads the application on a sample Web site, hosted on Personal Web Server, and tests the calendar. When the developer is satisfied that the application is working properly, the page is sent to the company's Web server.

Understanding the Web Publishing Wizard

The Web Publishing Wizard (not to be confused with the Publishing Wizard feature of Personal Web Server) makes it easy to post Web pages on the Internet or an intranet by automating the process of copying files from your computer to a Web server or an ISP.

The Web Publishing Wizard can automatically post to a variety of Web servers and offers support for:

- Standard protocols: FTP, UNC, and HTTP Post.
- Third-party services, such as AOL, GNN, and Sprynet Primehost.
- System-independent protocols, such as CRS and FrontPage Extended Web.

The Web Publishing Wizard also supports the following ISPs:

- CompuServe
- America Online (AOL)
- Sprynet
- GNN
- America Online Primehost
- Microsoft FrontPage

ISPs that have their own protocol scheme for uploading files to their Web servers can write a custom WebPost Provider .dll file and distribute it from the Microsoft Web site at **http://www.microsoft.com/windows/software/webpost/**. For details on this procedure, send e-mail to **WebPost@lists.msn.com** expressing your interest in writing a provider .dll file. Code for a sample WebPost provider is included in the *Microsoft ActiveX SDK*.

The Web Publishing Wizard connects to the ISP, determines the protocol needed to copy the files, and then uploads the files to the appropriate directory on the ISP computer. Before publishing a Web site with the Web Publishing Wizard, users need to have the following information:

- The local path to the Web content that the user wants to publish (such as C:\WebFiles).
- The protocol used by the ISP to upload files. Users can choose from FTP, HTTP Post, or CRS. (FTP is the most commonly used protocol.)
- The URL to which files are to be uploaded (for example, **ftp://my_isp.com/** if the ISP requires users to post files using FTP).

- The URL for the user's root on the Web server. This is often the URL for the ISP, plus the username (for example, **http://www.my_isp.com/*username/***).

- The user name and password for the account.

The Web Publishing Wizard guides you through the steps of connecting to your ISP or intranet site and automatically uploads Web files from a directory you specify. Because it saves all the information that you enter, you won't be asked to enter it during subsequent publishing efforts, making future publishing efforts quick and convenient.

PART 6

Authoring for Internet Explorer 4

Microsoft Internet Explorer 4 supports a wide range of new features that publishers can use to create innovative and interactive Web pages based on the newest Internet technologies and standards. Using this set of technologies, Web authors can produce more attractive content while taking up less bandwidth. They can also develop consumer and business applications that deliver more value and create a unique, fun, and more rewarding Web experience.

Chapter 23: Dynamic HTML

Limitations of current browser technology often require authors using Hypertext Markup Language (HTML) to choose between interactivity and speed. Once a page is loaded, changing the display or content of the page typically requires that the entire page be reloaded. Or, depending on how extensive the changes are, additional pages may have to be retrieved from the server. To address that limitation, Internet Explorer 4 includes several new features collectively called Dynamic HTML. These features provide the client-side intelligence and flexibility to enable HTML authors to create interactive pages that dynamically change the display and content of a page entirely on the client machine, without requiring additional server resources. Dynamic HTML enables HTML authors to create innovative Web sites with interactive pages without having to pay a performance penalty. In addition, by reducing requests from the server, Dynamic HTML also reduces server load, thus improving performance.

Chapter 24: ActiveX

For those who need more power than Dynamic HTML offers, Internet Explorer 4 provides enhanced support for ActiveX™ controls. ActiveX controls are software components that provide interactive and user-controllable functions. Small and versatile, they open a wide range of opportunities for creating attractive and effective Web content. Internet Explorer 4 presents a set of new opportunities for control and script engine developers. Most notably, Internet 4 is an OC96-compliant host. Controls can now be faster, smaller, and more integrated than ever before.

Chapter 25: Java

You can also use Java to extend the capabilities of Dynamic HTML and create even more interactive, exciting Web content. While Internet Explorer 3 brought the fastest, most reliable, and fully compatible Java support to the market, Internet Explorer 4 goes even further, taking Java support to the next level. For example, you can use Microsoft Java multimedia class libraries to provide true multimedia effects in your Web pages. Java applets not only run faster than in Internet Explorer 3, but you can optimize Java applets to take full advantage of all the features and speed of the Windows® 95 and Windows NT® operating systems. Plus, Internet Explorer 4 introduces a Java security model that allows you to run powerful, interactive Java applications without harming your organization's computers or threatening its privacy.

Chapter 26: Active Scripting

With its support for active scripting, Internet Explorer 4 provides fast, comprehensive, language-independent script-handling capability. Users can view Web pages that use any popular scripting language, including Visual Basic® Scripting Edition (VBScript) and JScript™ development software. Internet Explorer scripting support allows authors to develop pages that can ask questions, respond to queries, check user data, calculate expressions, link to other programs, and connect to ActiveX controls, Java applets, or anything else you specify. In addition, Internet Explorer 4 complies with the new Internet scripting standard specified by the European Computer Manufacturers Association (ECMA). Compliance to Internet standards helps ensure that the Web content and active scripting you develop for Internet Explorer 4 will run seamlessly across a wide range of platforms and products.

C H A P T E R   2 3

Dynamic HTML

Dynamic HTML Overview

The most significant authoring innovation introduced by Internet Explorer is Dynamic HTML, a set of features that make it easy for developers to build interactivity into applications without burdening their servers. Dynamic HTML extends the Hypertext Markup Language (HTML) standard, giving developers the ability to control virtually anything on a Web page at any time.

You can use Dynamic HTML to create fast, compact, and interactive Web pages without the need to load new content from the server or use complex ActiveX controls and Java applets. Using only HTML and a few lines of script, you can change any element on a Web page based on user actions, and Internet Explorer will immediately display the changed content and reflow unchanged content as needed, without having to reload the page from the server. To optimize browser performance and speed, Internet Explorer redraws only those portions of the browser window that are affected by the change.

With previous browser technology, changing the display or content of a Web page typically required the entire page to be reloaded from the server. You could use scripts to change page display and content on clients, but only while the Web page loaded. Only a few, very limited elements in HTML could be changed after Web pages had loaded. When designing Web content, Web publishers had to choose between interactive pages and speed. Now, with Dynamic HTML, you can create dynamic, interactive pages without having to pay a performance penalty. You can also use Dynamic HTML to reduce Web server load and optimize server performance.

The following sections provide an overview of each of the key features of Dynamic HTML. Additional information about Dynamic HTML is available from a variety of resources, including:

- *Inside Dynamic HTML* (Microsoft Press, 1997) and the companion Inside Dynamic HTML Web page at **http://www.insidedhtml.com/**, which provide a comprehensive programmers reference for Dynamic HTML as well as online tips, articles, and samples showing how to use the full power of Dynamic HTML to create Web content.

- *Microsoft® Internet Client Software Developers Kit (SDK)*, which includes an extensive section on Dynamic HTML that provides a comprehensive Dynamic HTML language reference, design guidelines, and samples. The *Microsoft Internet Client SDK* is available at **http://www.microsoft.com/msdn/sdk/inetsdk/**.

- Microsoft Site Builder Network (SBN), which provides a wide range of resources to help you understand and use Dynamic HTML as well as other technologies for creating state-of-the-art Web sites. You can visit SBN at **http://www.microsoft.com/sitebuilder/** and join to become a member.

- SBN Workshop (**http://www.microsoft.com/workshop/**) provides technical workshops on authoring, designing, and programming Web sites. Each workshop provides links to tutorials, tools, and other resources available from Microsoft and from third parties. The workshops on authoring and design provide extensive information on creating and designing Web content using the features of Dynamic HTML.

- *Site Builder Magazine* (**http://www.microsoft.com/sitebuilder/columnists/**) provides up-to-date articles written by industry-leading experts on Web authoring, design, programming, and technology.

For information about troubleshooting authoring for Internet Explorer and for Frequently Asked Questions (FAQs) about Dynamic HTML, see Appendix G and I, respectively.

Dynamic HTML and Internet Standards

The implementation of Internet standards is crucial to enhancing the Web experience. Now, users can view and listen to real-time broadcasts, watch videos, run ActiveX controls and Java applets, and play interactive, multiplayer games over the Web. All of this can be experienced in Internet Explorer 4 due to the browser's extensive support for Internet standards and because it includes support for innovative, underlying technologies, such as Dynamic HTML, ActiveX, and Java.

Microsoft is committed to working with the World Wide Web Consortium (W3C) and other standards bodies to make the Web a better open environment for building efficient and interactive multimedia content. Microsoft is also committed to providing the best standards-based solutions. Dynamic HTML represents the next step in that commitment. Previously, Microsoft participated in the W3C's efforts to define and promote the use of the <OBJECT> tag as an extensible way for adding objects in an HTML page. That standard resulted in the use of ActiveX controls—objects that authors can insert in HTML pages and that users can view and run in a safe and seamless way. Microsoft is now working with the W3C to extend that paradigm to standard HTML.

Dynamic HTML is based on HTML extensions proposed for HTML 4.0 by the W3C, including the Document Object Model, positioning in Cascading Style Sheets (CSS), and Web font embedding. The extensions to HTML used for Dynamic HTML conform to the latest working drafts and recommendations of the W3C.

Microsoft worked closely with the W3C when developing Dynamic HTML and has submitted Dynamic HTML to the W3C for inclusion in HTML 4.0. The specification for HTML 4.0 is currently a work in progress and requires final ratification by the W3C. Microsoft is committed to providing future enhancements to Internet Explorer to conform to all specifications recommended by the W3C.

For more information about Internet standards, visit the Microsoft Specifications and Standards page at **http://www.microsoft.com/standards/** and the W3C home page at **http://www.w3c.org/**.

Since Dynamic HTML is an extension to the HTML standards, you can design Web pages for Internet Explorer 4 that offer rich, interactive content but that *gracefully degrade* in browsers that don't support the Dynamic HTML extensions. Graceful degradation ensures that older versions of browsers can display standard HTML elements while ignoring any Web page features that use Dynamic HTML. For more information about graceful degradation, see the *Microsoft Internet Client SDK*.

Understanding the Document Object Model

Dynamic HTML uses the Document Object Model, an open, language-independent object model for giving scripts access to all elements and attributes of standard HTML. The Document Object Model extends the object model used in Internet Explorer 3 to enable scripts to dynamically change the style, content, and structure of a Web page after the page has loaded. Basically, the Document Object Model exposes all HTML elements and browser window objects to scripts, so scripts can be used to manipulate everything that makes up the content displayed in the browser window. The Document Object Model also enables you to use events, such as user mouse clicks, to control dynamic changes to styles.

With previous object models for browsers, scripts could only be used to change a Web page as the content of pages was loaded. Now, using extensions to the Cascading Style Sheets and a few lines of script such as JScript or VBScript, you can design Web pages that change any element or attribute in an HTML file at any time, without loading any new content from the server. You can also control scripts based on a full set of bubble-up events; for example, when users click a hot spot or move the mouse cursor over an area of the page.

You can use extensions to Cascading Style Sheets and a few lines of script to change the entire makeup and appearance of a Web page, including changing HTML tags, the exact position of elements on the page, and the text that appears on the page. When Web pages change, the changes are rendered immediately in the browser window.

For more information about the Document Object Model, see "Document Object Model" in the *Microsoft Internet Client SDK*, and visit the W3C Document Object Model Web page at **http://w3c.org/DOM/**.

Using Dynamic HTML

Dynamic HTML is an umbrella term for several improvements in Internet Explorer 4. These enhancements fall into the following categories:

- Dynamic styles
- Font embedding
- Positioning
- Filter, transition, and animation controls
- Dynamic content
- Data binding
- Scriptlets

Using Dynamic Styles

Dynamic styles give you comprehensive control over the styles in Web pages. Dynamic HTML extends Cascading Style Sheets (CSS) to add several powerful new features. You can use dynamic styles to:

- Position HTML elements at absolute or relative positions on the page.
- Create multimedia-style effects using standard HTML elements with minimal or no graphics using filters and transitions.
- Create interactive Web features and dynamically change the appearance of HTML elements without needing to reload Web pages from the server or use complicated controls.

The following sections provide an overview of dynamic styles. For more information, see "Dynamic Styles" in the *Microsoft Internet Client SDK*.

Using Style Sheets

Cascading Style Sheets are design templates that help you control the presentation and layout of HTML elements. They allow you to separate the way you design information from the HTML content.

This section provides a brief look at how Cascading Style Sheets work. A number of good resources are available to help you understand and use style sheets. Two of the most comprehensive resources on style sheets are available on the Web:

- W3C Web Style Sheets site at **http://www.w3.org/style/**
- *Web Review* Style Sheets Reference Guide site at **http://style.webreview.com/**

Each of these Web sites provides a wealth of information on style sheets, including tutorials, online examples, book reviews, and lists of additional resources.

Using style sheets, you can create Web pages with minimal graphics, and therefore, much smaller downloads. Style sheets also provide you with a higher level of typographic control, and they enable you to make changes to an entire site through the use of linked style sheets.

You can specify the styles for any HTML element in three ways:

- Link the HTML file to external CSS files.
- Include STYLE element blocks within the HTML file.
- Include a STYLE attribute in individual HTML elements in the HTML file.

You can specify an external style sheet by including a LINK element in the Head section of the HTML file. The following example shows how you could use Sheet1.css to specify the default styles for the Web page.

```
<HEAD>
<LINK HREF="Sheet1.css" REL=Stylesheet>
</HEAD>
```

You can specify STYLE blocks that apply only to the current HTML file. The following example shows a STYLE block that specifies that the text for the P elements on the Web page should display using the 10-Point Verdana font, overriding the external style sheet, Sheet1.css.

```
<HEAD>
<STYLE>
<!--
    P    {font-family: Verdana;
          font-size: 10pt}
-->
</STYLE>
</HEAD>
```

You can specify styles for individual elements using the STYLE attribute. The following example shows how you could specify one instance of the P element to display as 12-point text, overriding the STYLE block.

```
<P STYLE="font-size: 12pt">This is 12-point text</P>
```

Styles are additive. For example, you can use a CSS file to specify the size of all P elements as 12 points; you can use a STYLE block to specify the font face for all P elements in the HTML file as New Times Roman; and you can use a STYLE attribute to specify that an instance of the P element is italicized. If styles conflict, the closest specification takes precedence, as in the previous examples.

The new Document Object Model enables you to access and change all style attributes in an HTML file. Using inline script events and scripts, you can change HTML style attributes based on user actions or *events* such as a mouse click or a response to an HTML form. You cannot use scripts to change the contents of external style sheets (CSS files), but you can use scripts to change all style attributes specified in the HTML file.

Creating dynamic styles is very easy. Once you understand CSS basics, all you need to know is some script syntax—and you can have any HTML tag change dynamically by applying CSS attributes to it.

For example, you can embed *inline script events* to dynamically change the style attributes of an HTML element when users touch it with the mouse (**onmouseover**) or move the mouse off of it (**onmouseout**), as shown in the following HTML code:

```
<H4 onmouseover="javascript:this.style.color= '#6633FF'"
    onmouseout="javascript:this.style.color='#000000'">
This headline will change to purple when the mouse touches it,
and back to black when the mouse moves off of it</H4>
```

When the mouse touches the headline (H4 element), it changes to purple. It also changes back to black when the mouse moves off of it.

Dynamic HTML also gives you several powerful new attributes that you can use to create dynamic content: absolute and relative positioning, and visual filters and transitions. You can now place HTML elements anywhere on a page, specify how the elements are layered, and create multimedia-style effects without having to load bandwidth-consuming controls or graphics files.

Using Font Embedding

The FONT element and the CSS font family attribute enable you to specify the exact font attributes to be used to display your Web pages. If the font is not installed on the user's computer, however, the browser displays the Web page using a default or secondary font face. To address this issue, Internet Explorer 4 supports font embedding, which gives Web designers total control over how their Web pages are displayed. Using font embedding, Web pages can link to compressed font objects, which Internet Explorer will download, decompress, and temporarily install. Thus, Web designers can specify fonts using Cascading Style Sheets or the <FONT FACE=> tag without having to worry about them not being installed.

Internet Explorer uses the Microsoft OpenType Font Embedding technology. Currently, the industry has no standard for font embedding. Microsoft has submitted the OpenType font-embedding technology for consideration by the W3C.

You can use the Microsoft Web Embedding Fonts Tool (WEFT) to embed fonts in your HTML files. WEFT analyzes HTML pages for you, creates an Embedded OpenType (EOT) font object file, and then adds the proper CSS font-embedding information to the HTML pages. For more information, visit the Microsoft WEFT Web page at **http://www.microsoft.com/typography/web/embedding/weft/**.

Font embedding is specified in HTML files using the @font-face definition and standard CSS syntax. The following example shows an HTML file STYLE block that was created using the WEFT. The tool also creates the associated EOT file (the font object), which is a subset of the font that will be temporarily installed on the user's computer to view your Web page.

```
<STYLE>
<!--
@font-face {
    font-family: Mistral;
    font-style: normal;
    font-weight: 700;
    src: url(MISTRAL.eot); }
-->
</STYLE>
```

Font download can be controlled in the **Custom Security Settings** dialog box, available from the **Security** tab of the **Internet Options** dialog box. (On the **View** menu, select **Internet Options**, click the **Security** tab, and then click the **Custom** button.)

TrueType fonts have embedding permissions encoded within them that determine how they can be used for embedding. There are four levels of embedding:

- **No-embedding** prevents fonts from being embedded. The creators of these fonts have decided not to allow embedding. Some foundries set their fonts to no-embedding but offer upgrades to embeddable versions. If you come across a no-embedding font that you would really like to use, contact the supplier and ask about an upgrade.

- **Print and preview** fonts can be embedded, but only in pages with static fonts. If you want to enable dynamic styles so the font can change, use **editable** or **installable**.

- **Editable** fonts can be embedded without the restrictions imposed on **print** and **preview** fonts. These fonts are installed in users' fonts folder.

- **Installable** fonts are treated as editable fonts by Internet Explorer 4, but installable fonts will not be installed in a user's fonts folder. This helps prevent users' fonts folders from becoming filled with fonts that they do not want.

You can use the WEFT to check the permission level of TrueType fonts installed on your system. You can also check the embedding permissions of fonts using the free Microsoft Font Properties Extension, which is available for download at **http://www.microsoft.com/typography/property/property.htm**.

Positioning HTML Elements

Dynamic HTML enables you to position HTML elements in the x- and y-coordinates as well as overlap elements in planes along the z-axis. You can place elements—DIV elements, images, controls, or text—exactly where you want them on the page. You can use positioning to help create 3-D effects. You can use scripts to change the position of elements and animate the page. Browsers that don't support positioning ignore the positioning and display the HTML in its natural flow.

You can also specify absolute and relative positions. Relative positions are measured from where the element would naturally appear on the page. The absolute position is measured from the upper-left corner of the browser window.

The following example shows how you could specify Graphic1.gif to appear starting at 100 pixels from the top of the browser window and 200 pixels from the left side of the browser window.

```
<IMG STYLE="position:absolute; top:100; left:200; z-index: -1"
    SRC="Graphic1.gif">
```

The **z-index** property can be used to layer objects on the page. By default, objects are layered bottom-to-top in the order that they appear in the HTML source. Higher-valued z-index objects are positioned above lower-valued z-index objects. Two elements with the same z-index are layered according to HTML source order. The z-index value can be any positive or negative integer. In the previous example, z-index: -1 ensures that the graphic appears below overlapping text that appears on the page.

The DIV element is often used with positioning because the DIV element can be used to enclose other HTML elements to define distinct areas on the page. Using the DIV element and positioning, you can create a wide variety of spectacular effects on Web pages.

You can use positioning to create 3-D effects by varying the x- and y-axis coordinates and the z-index property of objects. You can also use scripts to dynamically change the positioning of elements on Web pages to create spectacular animation effects. For more information, see "Positioning" in the *Microsoft Internet Client SDK*.

Using Visual Filters and Transitions

Dynamic HTML provides visual filters and transitions that you can use to apply multimedia-style effects to standard HTML elements, including divisions, text, and images. Browsers that don't support filters and transitions simply ignore the filters and transitions.

A *filter* is used to apply a special graphic transformation or effect to an element. For example, you can use a filter to create a mirror image or a drop shadow for an element. A *transition* is a type of filter that enables a transition from one visual state to another. For example, you can use a transition to make each slide in a slide show gradually fade in or out. You can use scripts and transitions to control the way that animated elements appear on the page.

The following example shows a filter that displays a vertical mirror image of Graphic1.gif.

```
<IMG STYLE="filter: flipv" SRC= "Graphic1.gif">
```

Transitions are divided into two types: blend and reveal. *Blend* makes the element gradually blend in or out of the surroundings, while *reveal* makes the element gradually appear or disappear in one of 23 predefined patterns. A primary difference between filters and transitions is that transitions must take place between two states, such as an invisible image and a visible one.

You can use a few lines of script combined with filters and transitions and positioning to provide spectacular animated and 3-D effects. For more information, see "Filters and Transitions" in the *Microsoft Internet Client SDK*.

Using Dynamic Content

Dynamic styles change the appearance of HTML elements on Web pages, but don't actually change the content of the HTML elements. You can use the dynamic content features of Dynamic HTML to change the content of most HTML elements. You can change an element to another element as well as change the text that appears in the element. For example, you could replace a text heading with new text or with a graphic.

The new Document Object Model enables scripts to change text content and HTML elements by manipulating four properties of most visible HTML elements: **innerText**, **outerText**, **innerHTML**, and **outerHTML**. The **innerText** and **outerText** properties specify plain text in elements (any HTML tags appear as verbatim text in the browser window and are not processed as HTML). The **innerHTML** and **outerHTML** properties specify text and HTML tags that are processed in the browser window as HTML. Scripts can also add new text content and new HTML elements to Web pages using the insertAdjacentText and insertAdjacentHTML methods that are supported by most visible HTML elements.

Most dynamic content needs can be met using the **innerText**, **outerText**, **innerHTML**, and **outerHTML** properties, and the insertAdjacentText and insertAdjacentHTML methods. However, you may want to perform advanced text manipulation using the **TextRange** object.

TextRange objects are an advanced feature of Dynamic HTML that you can use to perform useful tasks related to dynamic content, such as searching for and selecting text. **Text range** objects let you selectively pick out characters, words, and sentences from a document.

You can use the dynamic content features of Dynamic HTML to create a wide range of dynamic applications on your Web pages. For example, you could use a script to scan the elements of a page and use dynamic content to insert a table of contents at the beginning of the page. You can control the level of detail in the table of contents based on user actions such as mouse clicks or input from an HTML form. You could also use a script to create dynamic tables of data that a user can sort based on the user's preferences.

You can create many powerful interactive applications using dynamic content. For more information, see "Dynamic Content" in the *Microsoft Internet Client SDK* and visit the SBN Workshop at **http://www.microsoft.com/workshop/**.

Using Data Binding

Data-driven business applications are increasingly taking advantage of the Web, accessing data stored in server databases. These applications often require Web publishers to construct many Web pages for users to navigate through to view and manipulate the data. This can frustrate users as well as increase server loads.

Dynamic HTML provides data-binding features that you can use to integrate data with HTML elements on the Web pages downloaded to clients. You can use data binding with the dynamic content features of Dynamic HTML to create applications that display, sort, filter, and update data on the client with minimal visits to retrieve data from the server.

Dynamic HTML uses HTML tags to define a template that is populated with data on the client, and data source objects to supply data to the page. No specific data protocol or database management system (DBMS) is required to use these data-binding features.

Data source objects supply the data to the Web page. Data source objects can be either Java applets or ActiveX controls. The following data source objects are included with the standard installation of Internet Explorer 4:

- **Tabular Data Control.** The **Tabular Data Control** supplies data that is stored in a delimited text file to the page. The control uses a URL to locate the text file, enabling the data to be transmitted using standard Internet protocols. The file format is easily generated by most DBMS systems and applications. Since the text data files are cached on the client, the control can supply data in offline browsing scenarios.

- **Remote Data Service (RDS), previously known as Advanced Data Connector (ADC).** This data object enables publishers to access data from and transmit data to Open Database Connectivity (ODBC)-compliant databases. **RDS** provides direct, real-time access to server data. **RDS** also transmits data using the HTTP protocol, so **RDS** can work over the Internet and through firewalls.

- **JDBC Data Source Object.** This data source object is a Java applet that implements a JavaBeans-compliant interface. Data is retrieved through the Java Data Base Connectivity (JDBC) data source object and stored in a local cache implemented by the applet. Even though JDBC provides a forward-only cursor, the applet can provide random access to data when used with data binding.

- **Extensible Markup Language (XML) Data Source Object. XML** provides a standards-based way to represent structured data in a text format. The data-binding functionality of Dynamic HTML supports the display of **XML** data within a Web page by using a data source object that enables the **XML** data to be displayed in nested, repeated tables.

- **HTML Data Source Object.** In addition to using external components as data source objects, Web authors can define their data sets within an HTML document and use the Internet Explorer 4 HTML engine to provide read-only data to a page. This enables parts of one HTML document to be included in another HTML document, and all data processing takes place on the client rather than on the server.

As additional data source objects become available, Microsoft will add them to the Data Source Object Gallery at **http://www.microsoft.com/gallery/files/datasrc/**. You can also develop data source objects for use with data binding. For more information, see the *Microsoft Internet Client SDK*.

You specify the data source object to use for data binding by including an <OBJECT> tag in the HTML file. The data supplied by a data source object is bound to HTML elements within the page, using four new attributes that Microsoft has proposed to the W3C:

- DATASRC
- DATAFLD
- DATAFORMATAS
- DATAPAGESIZE

You can bind data to the following tagged HTML elements: <A>, <APPLET>, <BUTTON>, <DIV>, <FRAME>, <IFRAME>, <IMG>, <INPUT>, <LABEL>, <MARQUEE>, <OBJECT>, <SELECT>, <SPAN>, and <TEXTAREA>.

With data binding, you can present data as follows:

- **Repeated tables.** You can merge data with an HTML table on the client, which serves as a template. The content of the table is repeated once for each record in the data set, and headers and footers can be displayed as well. HTML elements within the cells of the table can then be bound to columns from the data set.

- **Current record binding.** You can merge data from the columns of the current record of the data source with HTML elements on the client. The current record can be moved through the data set by calling methods in the Active Data Objects (ADO) model, supplied automatically to every data source object.

For more information, see "Data Binding" in the *Microsoft Internet Client SDK*, and visit the SBN Workshop at **http://www.microsoft.com/workshop/**.

Using Scriptlets

A scriptlet is a Web page based on Dynamic HTML that you can use as a control in any application that supports controls. The scriptlet includes information that allows you to work with it as a control. You can get and set a scriptlet's properties, call its methods, and so on.

Before scriptlets, reusing HTML and script often meant cutting, pasting, and then customizing existing code. With scriptlets, you can author content once, using the HTML and script you know today, and then let others quickly reuse your content as scriptlets in their Web pages and applications. You create scriptlets by following simple conventions to expose well-defined interfaces. Through these scriptlet interfaces, others can customize and reuse existing Web content without having to understand the implementation details.

Since scriptlets consist only of HTML and script, they are easy to create and maintain. Scriptlets are small and efficient, and they quickly download and run on users' computers. Scriptlets can:

- Enable you to make optimal use of your existing knowledge of HTML and script to create reusable components.

- Make Dynamic HTML even easier to use. You need not understand scriptlet details, only the interfaces required to customize the scriptlet. You can take advantage of this existing content in other Web pages and in any application supporting the component object model (COM).

- Increase Web application performance because scriptlets download and run quickly and are stored in the cache on the end user's computer.

- Enable you to create reusable user interface components without having to harness the full power of C, C++, or other control-building environments.

- Enable you to change the appearance and behavior of Web pages from within the host environment. For example, you can use a Visual Basic application to read information from files and then write the information into a scriptlet that is used to change the Web page.

- Enable you to use the features built into Web pages in development environments that support ActiveX controls, such as Visual Basic and Visual InterDev. For example, you could use a scriptlet to provide the graphical and hypertext capabilities of a Web page as the visually rich interface for an application.

- Enable you to quickly prototype controls you intend to write in other environments. Since it's easy to put together a scriptlet, you can create scriptlets to validate your designs quickly. Then, after the design is validated, you can re-implement the control in another environment, such as C++, Visual Basic, or Visual J++™.

Creating Scriptlets

A scriptlet can be either an HTML page or an Active Server Page (ASP). You can use any HTML authoring environment to create a scriptlet, such as the Microsoft FrontPage® Web authoring and management tool or the Visual InterDev integrated Web application development system. Of course, if your authoring environment does not support scripting, you may have to manually insert the scripting code after first composing the HTML display elements.

You use scriptlets like a standard ActiveX control. In the scriptlet, you create any properties, methods, or events that you want by simply creating scripts in common active scripting languages such as JScript or VBScript. The scripts rely on the scripting capabilities of Dynamic HTML, which gives you a complete object model for the elements in the scriptlet.

For example, a scriptlet might be a Web page that contains animation based on Dynamic HTML that moves and resizes text on the page. You can write scripts to expose properties that allow another application to set the text, speed, and direction of the animation text, and to expose methods that allow another application to start, stop, and pause the animation.

You define the scriptlet interface using one of the following methods:

- Use an **ECMAScript Public_Description** object to define explicitly what properties and methods the scriptlet will make available. Any behavior that is not explicitly declared using the **Public_Description** object is not available. For more information, see "Creating a Public_Description Object" in the *Microsoft Internet Client SDK*.

- Use default interface descriptions. You do not explicitly declare properties or methods. Instead, any variables and functions that follow certain naming conventions become available as properties and methods This convention can be used to create scriptlet properties and methods in an active scripting language other than ECMAScript. For more information, see "Using Default Interface Descriptions" in the *Microsoft Internet Client SDK*.

Using a **Public_Description** object has several advantages. You can use any names for variables and functions that you want to expose as properties and methods, because you assign them public names in the **Public_Description** object. In addition, using the **Public_Description** object provides you with a convenient way to summarize and document the properties and methods that the scriptlet exposes.

In contrast, if you use the default interface descriptions, you must use the public_ prefix on any name that you want to expose. If a scriptlet already has a variable or function with the public_ prefix, it will be exposed, whether you want it to be exposed or not.

When you create the properties, methods, and events for the scriptlet, you can make full use of the Document Object Model to display text, animate HTML elements, change colors, or define any other behavior that you want the control to have. You can also use extensions to the Document Object Model to manipulate properties and methods that are unique to scriptlets. For more information, see "Scriptlet Model Extensions" in the *Microsoft Internet Client SDK*.

Support for scriptlets is built into Internet Explorer 4. Use the standard <OBJECT> tag to include the scriptlet in other Web pages.

Adding Scriptlets to Applications and Web Pages

You can use scriptlets in applications that support ActiveX controls and in Web pages.

Applications that support ActiveX controls

To use a scriptlet in applications that support ActiveX controls, you use a control called the *scriptlet container object,* which hosts the scriptlet. The host application, such as Visual Basic, uses the scriptlet container object to create a window for the scriptlet and provide a way for the host application to specify what scriptlet to use, where it displays, at what size, and so on. The scriptlet container object also provides the interface for you to set and get the scriptlet's properties, call its methods, and respond to its events. For more information, see "Adding Scriptlets to Your Application" in the *Microsoft Internet Client SDK*.

Web pages

To use scriptlets in Web pages, you insert an OBJECT element in the HTML file as shown in the following example:

```
<OBJECT width=200 height=123
    TYPE= "text/x-scriptlet"  DATA="Scriptlet.htm">
</OBJECT>
```

In this example, the OBJECT element references the scriptlet file **Scriptlet.htm**. Internet Explorer 4 recognizes the object as a scriptlet by the MIME type **"text/x-scriptlet"**. Note that there is no CLSID in the <OBJECT> tag. Internet Explorer 4 supports this MIME type on all platforms. Because of the open nature of the architecture, competing vendors will be able to implement support for scriptlets as well. Nothing in the nature of scriptlets restricts users to using Microsoft platforms.

Understanding Scriptlet Security

Scriptlets are as secure as Dynamic HTML and ECMAScript itself. A scriptlet recognizes when it is placed in a secure container, such as Internet Explorer, and obeys the security policies of its container.

In general, to operate correctly, a scriptlet must be loaded from the same Web server as its container page (the same as for Java applets). In a security-aware host application such as Internet Explorer, the scriptlet and any controls contained within it are subject to Internet Explorer 4 security.

Internet Explorer 4 uses the security settings for ActiveX controls to enforce security for scriptlets based on the zone of the server where the scriptlet originates. If the scriptlet contains controls that reside on a server in a more restrictive zone, the security settings for the more restrictive zone are enforced. For more information about security settings for ActiveX controls, see "Customizing Security Zones" in Chapter 27, "Security Zones."

For more information, see "Microsoft Scriptlet Technology" in the *Microsoft Internet Client SDK,* and visit the SBN Workshop at **http://www.microsoft.com/workshop/**.

CHAPTER 24

ActiveX

In this chapter

ActiveX Overview

ActiveX enables software components to interact with each other in a networked environment, regardless of the language in which they were created. Embracing both Java and Microsoft industry-standard component object model (COM) technology, ActiveX makes writing Internet applications as easy as writing applications for the operating system. You can create ActiveX components that provide standard application features and functions and then easily reuse the components in current networking and stand-alone applications.

The following sections describe how you can use ActiveX with Internet Explorer 4. For more information, see the *Microsoft Internet Client Software Developers Kit (SDK)* and visit the Microsoft Developer Network at **http://www.microsoft.com/msdn/** as well as the SBN programming workshop at **http://www.microsoft.com/workshop/**.

For information about troubleshooting authoring for Internet Explorer, see Appendix G.

Using ActiveX Controls

ActiveX controls are components (or objects) you can insert into a Web page or application to provide sophisticated formatting features and animation. ActiveX controls are small and versatile, and open limitless opportunities for creating spectacular Web content. ActiveX controls can be written in most programming languages, including Java, C++, and Microsoft Visual Basic. ActiveX controls can be easily reused by others in their Web pages and applications.

The open, component architecture of ActiveX enables you to create dynamic Web content and applications using proven COM technology, scripts, and software components (including Java applets). This architecture enables stand-alone applications to interact with each other. You can run ActiveX components in Internet Explorer that interact with other applications and components. For example, you could use a database access applet that interacts with a script to display multimedia graphics of data in Internet Explorer.

Because ActiveX controls are based on COM, the controls are language-independent. Java is an excellent programming language for both implementing and using COM objects, and Java and COM integrate seamlessly. COM makes Java a distributed language. Every public Java class is a COM object and can be called remotely just like any other COM object. COM gives Java direct access to native code. Any COM object appears to the programmer as a Java object. There is no need for large class libraries that wrap existing objects; the existing objects can be called directly.

Hundreds of ActiveX controls are available today with functionality ranging from a timer control (which simply notifies its container at a particular time) to full-featured spreadsheets and word processors. If you can imagine it, you can do it with an ActiveX control.

Optimizing ActiveX for Internet Explorer 4

Internet Explorer 4 complies with the OLE Controls 1996 (OC96) specification for host containers. Therefore, ActiveX control developers can now create faster, smaller, and more integrated controls that include:

- **Windowless controls.** These controls allow creation of transparent and nonrectangular controls, which combined with 2-D placement, enable Web publishers to overlap controls on a page. The multimedia controls included with Internet Explorer 4 are all windowless and take advantage of this functionality.

- **Apartment model controls.** Internet Explorer is a threaded container. For better performance, controls used inside Internet Explorer 4 should be marked as Apartment or Free Threaded.

- **Quick Activation.** The complex "QI Dance" that control writers needed to write is greatly simplified with Quick Activation. In most cases, a single call can initialize most controls.

- **SBindHost service.** Internet Explorer's support for the SBindHost service allows controls to download additional data asynchronously. This results in better performance for controls that download images or other complex data.

Controls written for previous versions of Internet Explorer work in Internet Explorer 4, but don't take advantage of these new OC96 enhancements. You can rewrite older controls to take advantage of the OC96 enhancements, but the control will not work in previous versions of Internet Explorer. Of course, you can always provide separate controls for browsers that don't comply with OC96.

With Internet Explorer 4, ActiveX controls have full access to the Document Object Model of Dynamic HTML. A control can now read its host page and modify all elements in the page at any time. Anything you can do in a script, you can do from an ActiveX control. You can use ActiveX controls to extend the capabilities of Dynamic HTML and create a wide range of interactive and animated Web page applications.

For example, you can apply filters and transitions to windowless controls, such as Microsoft DirectAnimation™ controls, to easily create spectacular multimedia effects. For more information, see "Multimedia Controls" later in this chapter.

Using ActiveX Controls in Web Pages

You can add ActiveX controls to your Web pages by using the standard HTML OBJECT element. The OBJECT element includes a set of PARAM elements that you use to specify which data the control should use and to control the appearance and behavior of the control.

To use an ActiveX control in a Web page, you refer to its Class ID Number as shown in the following example:

```
<OBJECT CLASSID="CLSIDXXXXXxxx…" ID="the name of the control"
  CODEBASE="URL of .ocx or .CAB file" #="version number">
<PARAM NAME="parameter name" VALUE="value">
<PARAM NAME="parameter name" VALUE= "value">
</OBJECT>
```

The CLASSID and version number of the control are generated when the control is compiled.

When downloading ActiveX controls is enabled in the security options, Internet Explorer 4 downloads controls and stores the controls on users' computers. Installed controls are used for Web pages that reference the control. Internet Explorer compares the version number of the installed control to the version number specified on the Web page. If a new version of a control is available, Internet Explorer downloads, stores, and uses the new version.

Listing and Removing ActiveX Controls

Internet Explorer 4 stores ActiveX controls in the following special Windows directory:

C:\Windows\Downloaded Program Files

You can open this directory using Windows Explorer to list installed ActiveX controls, to view information about the installed controls, to update the control with the latest version, or to remove controls.

Windows Explorer lists the following properties for installed controls:

- Program File
- Total Size
- Status
- Creation Date
- Last Accessed
- Version

You can use the control's **Properties** dialog box to view more detailed information about the controls.

▶ **To view detailed information about a control**

1. From Windows Explorer, perform one of the following:

   ▪ Select the control, and on the **File** menu, click **Properties**.

   ▪ Right-click the control, and then click **Properties**.

2. Select the **General**, **Dependency**, or **Version** tab to view information about the control.

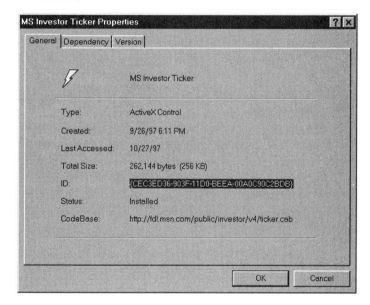

Option	Description
General Tab	
Type	Displays the type of control. If the type is Shortcut, you are viewing the properties for the shortcut to an item, not for the original item.
Created	Displays the date that the control was created.
Last Accessed	Displays the date that the control was last opened.
Total Size	Displays the size of the control files.
ID	Displays the Class ID (CLSID) for this control. This is the same ID that appears in the OBJECT element in the Web page.

Option	Description
General Tab *(continued)*	
Status	Displays whether the control is installed, damaged, or unplugged. Damaged means that one or more of the dependency files has been deleted. Unplugged means that an installation program has registered the .ocx file in a location different from where the code download installed it.
CodeBase	Displays the URL from which the control was installed. Internet Explorer uses this URL to update the control.
Dependency Tab	
File name	Lists the files on your computer, which this control requires to run. If any of these files are missing, the control will not work.
Package name	Lists any Java packages on your computer, which this object requires in order to run. If any of these packages are missing, the control will not work.
Version Tab	
Version	Displays the version number of this control. Internet Explorer compares this version number to the version number appearing in the OBJECT element in the Web page to determine if a more current version is available.
Description	Displays a description of the control.
Company	Displays the name of the publisher of the control.
Language	Displays the language version of the control.
Copyright	Displays the copyright information for the control.

▶ **To update a control**

- From Windows Explorer, right-click the control, and then click **Update**.

  Internet Explorer downloads the latest version of the control from the Web.

▶ **To remove a control**

- From Windows Explorer, perform one of the following:

  - Right-click the control, and then click **Remove**.
  - On the **File** menu, click **Remove Program File**.

  Internet Explorer removes the control and all dependency files.

Signing ActiveX Code

In Internet Explorer 4, you can set several security options for ActiveX controls and plug-ins to restrict the download of ActiveX controls for each security zone. For example, you can prevent the downloading of unsigned ActiveX controls from sites located in the Internet zone, but enable the downloading of unsigned ActiveX controls in the Local Intranet zone. For more information about setting security options for ActiveX controls, see "Customizing Security Zones" in Chapter 27, "Security Zones."

You should obtain a digital certificate from a Certificate Authority (CA) and digitally sign ActiveX controls consistent with your organization's security policy. You could decide not to sign controls for your Local Intranet zone, because you trust all of the sites. However, keep in mind that if you allow unsigned ActiveX controls to download automatically with no user intervention, you are also trusting any unsigned controls users may obtain from the Internet and reuse on your intranet. At a minimum, it is recommended that you sign ActiveX controls used for Web pages on the Internet to assure users of the integrity of your controls. For more information about digital certificates, see "Understanding Digital Certificates" in Chapter 28, "Digital Certificates."

You apply a digital signature to an ActiveX control at the time it is compiled. For more information, see "Signing Code with Microsoft Authenticode Technology" in the *Microsoft Internet Client SDK*.

Using Multimedia Controls

For Web publishers who want more multimedia effects than Dynamic HTML offers, Internet Explorer 4 includes the run-time version of the Microsoft DirectAnimation multimedia controls. A component of the DirectX® set of APIs, DirectAnimation provides unified, comprehensive support for such diverse media types as 2-D vector graphics, 3-D graphics, sprites, audio, and video, and a uniform time and event model.

Because DirectAnimation is a COM API with an underlying run-time engine, the DirectAnimation functionality can be accessed—in different ways—by a wide variety of programmers and authors:

- HTML authors can integrate animation using the DirectAnimation controls.

- Authors using VBScript or JScript, or Java applets, can program Web-page animation with Dynamic HTML.

- Programmers using Java, Visual Basic, and Visual C++® development systems can develop ActiveX controls or full applications that require multimedia support and interactive features.

The DirectAnimation run-time controls provide Internet Explorer 4 with access to many of the DirectAnimation scripting functions and libraries to implement additional multimedia and animation effects. The run-time controls allow you to deliver impressive vector graphics, image, and animation content over the Web with little code and short download times. The run-time controls include:

- **Sequencer.** Easily controls timing of events on pages.

- **Structured graphics.** Provides high-quality, lightweight, scalable, rotatable graphics. Internet Explorer 4 provides programmatic access so you can dynamically add new graphic elements through script. For example, you can create HTML applications that read values from a data-bound control and then create appropriate graphs.

- **Effects.** Alters any item on a Web page by applying a graphic filter. For example, you can add a glow filter and button bevel. The button bevel lets you dynamically create in/out beveled buttons from images and text.

- **Transitions.** Alters any item on a page, or the page itself, over time.

- **Behaviors.** Applies high-level behaviors to controls and Dynamic HTML elements.

- **Sprite.** Creates animated images.

- **Sprite buttons.** Creates animated multistate buttons.

- **Path.** Easily moves objects across a two-dimensional path.

- **Mixer.** Mixes multiple WAV files together dynamically.

- **Hot spot.** Establishes regions of the screen that can process mouse clicks.

All of these controls are transparent, windowless, and can be seamlessly integrated with Dynamic HTML. You can easily add DirectAnimation content to your Web pages by using the DirectAnimation controls as OBJECT elements and setting parameters (PARAM elements) on these controls—without programming at all.

Because DirectAnimation is integrated with Dynamic HTML, it is especially suited to adding compact animation effects to Web pages. For example, you can include DirectAnimation controls as windowless controls on the page (overlaying other elements such as text) and apply filters and transitions to DirectAnimation controls.

For more information, see the *DirectAnimation SDK* (included with the *Microsoft Internet Client SDK*), and visit the SBN Workshop at **http://www.microsoft.com/workshop/**.

CHAPTER 25

Java

Java Overview

Java is a programming language developed by Sun Microsystems and is a popular language for developing cross-platform-compatible Internet applications.

Internet Explorer 4 includes the Microsoft virtual machine for Java. It supports all functions of the Java Development Kit (JDK) Version 1.1, except for the following:

- **Java Native Interface (JNI).** Sun's proposed interface for linking Java code to platform-specific code.
- **Remote Method Invocation (RMI).** Sun's technology to allow Java objects to communicate over a network.
- **Digital signatures in Java Archive (.jar) files.** Sun's proprietary certificate format for digitally signing Java packages.

In Internet Explorer 4, Microsoft provides a native code interface called Raw Native Interface (RNI) as well as support for the component object model (COM) and the new J/Direct technology for native code access. COM and J/Direct make integration with native code significantly easier than either JNI or RNI. Overall, JNI is slower than RNI and requires more development work than J/Direct.

Developers looking for a robust, secure, high-performance solution for remote object interoperability should consider Distributed COM (DCOM), which is supported by Java today with the Microsoft virtual machine and allows both Java-to-Java communications and Java-to-non-Java communications.

Internet Explorer 4 does not support signed .jar files, because they are a Sun proprietary technology. However, Internet Explorer does support unsigned and compressed .jar files. Internet Explorer also supports .cab files, which offer significantly better compression than .jar files. Internet Explorer 4 allows the signing of Java .cab packages with industry-standard x.509v3 certificates. For more information, see "Signing Code with Microsoft Authenticode Technology" in the *Microsoft Internet Client SDK*.

Internet Explorer 4 makes it easier for developers to create more full-featured Java applications for the Web. Java performance has been improved, making Java applications run even faster than in Internet Explorer 3. In addition, the Java security model has been greatly expanded and improved.

The following sections describe significant Java improvements available for Internet Explorer 4. For more information, see the *Microsoft Internet Client SDK* and the *Microsoft SDK for Java 2.0*, and visit The Microsoft Java Technologies Web page at **http://www.microsoft.com/java/**, the Microsoft Developer Network at **http://www.microsoft.com/msdn/**, and the SBN programming workshop at **http://www.microsoft.com/workshop/**.

For information about troubleshooting for Internet Explorer and for Frequently Asked Questions (FAQs) about .cab files in Java, see Appendix G and H, respectively.

Java Improvements for Internet Explorer 4

The Java improvements for Internet Explorer 4 include:

- **Speed.** The Internet Explorer 4 Just in Time (JIT) compiler provides the fastest way to run Java applications.

- **Full component integration.** ActiveX controls can be accessed as Java Beans, and Java Beans accessed as ActiveX controls. (Java Beans is a specification for the creation of components referred to as "beans" in Java.) The Microsoft virtual machine for Java is the only virtual machine that has this automatic, seamless, bidirectional component support. In addition, debugging is seamless between VBScript, JScript, and Java.

- **New object model.** The Document Object Model is exposed through Java libraries. This allows Java developers to dynamically manipulate Web pages.

- **Improved Abstract Windows Toolkit (AWT).** The AWT has been improved to reduce overhead and improve performance.

- **New application foundation classes (AFC).** AFC provides the easiest way for Java developers to build rich, commercial-quality applications quickly. They are written entirely in Java and are intended to be compatible with all high-quality implementations of Java. The advantages of AFC include:

  - The GUI libraries include more than 30 prebuilt, extensible components for common UI features such as toolbars, tree controls, and dialog boxes.

  - The FX libraries include textures, support for wide-brush pens, and more. AFC is written in Java and runs on all standard Java platforms.

  - AFC provides a flexible look. Developers can use the standard Windows look, the look of another platform, or they can subclass to provide their own custom look.

  - AFC is available on all platforms for Internet Explorer 4, including Windows NT, Windows 95, Windows CE, Macintosh®, and select commercial versions of UNIX.

  - AFC Enterprise Libraries provide Java developers access to open, standards-based enterprise services, such as directory, management, database, distributed object, and transaction services.

- **New multimedia class libraries.** All the functionality of DirectX media and the DirectX foundation is provided as cross-platform Java class libraries, enabling developers to manipulate and animate a full set of media types.

- **Internationalization support.** Unicode support simplifies developing worldwide applications, because it supports multilingual display and input, and its easy resource format facilitates localization.

- **New Package Manager.** The Package Manager is a component of Internet Explorer 4 that manages the storage of Java class libraries. A database is used to associate properties and data with packages. When a component (the VM, development tool, and so on) wants to get class information, it calls a package manager API to get the information, instead of having to understand the complicated class path rules. The Package Manager works with .cab or .jar files to support the efficient download and storage of multiple .class files.

- **Complete Win32® integration.** With Internet Explorer 4, Java developers can leverage the power of the Win32 platform by utilizing the rich Win32 API set natively from their Java code.

- **Trust-based security for Java.** Internet Explorer 4 includes trust-based security for Java, which is a cross-platform security model for Java that provides fine-grained management of the permissions granted to Java applets and libraries.

How Java Works

Java is unlike other programming languages in that a program can be written without consideration for the platform on which it will be run. A Java applet can run on a variety of dissimilar platforms.

Java requires a client-side interpreter or virtual machine (VM) for running Java code. Platform-specific considerations are built into the virtual machine, thus allowing the Java applications to be platform independent.

Java uses classes to call functions that exist on the system in the form of Java class libraries. These libraries are installed when Internet Explorer is installed. System classes are always required to run Java applets. Without system classes, no Java applet could run on a system.

The Package Manager loads classes using the following registry key:

**HLM\Software\Microsoft\Code_Store_Database\
Java_Packages**

The class libraries are stored in the C:\Windows\Java\directory.

Because Java was developed by the UNIX industry, applets use case-sensitive syntax and long file name extensions such as .class (the 8.3 equivalent of .class is .cla).

Basically, you write Java code, perhaps using Microsoft Visual J++ development software, and then save the noncompiled Java source code as a file with a .java or .jav file name extension. You then compile the source code to byte code, and the file is renamed with a .class (.cla) file name extension. The end users' Java VM compiles the byte code .class (.cla) files into machine-specific code, so applets can run on the end users' computers.

Microsoft Virtual Machine for Java

The Microsoft VM for Java provided in Internet Explorer 4 is the Win32 Reference Implementation of Sun's Java VM. Microsoft's implementation of the VM provides a number of benefits, including:

- High-performance native code interface
- Separation of name spaces
- Integration between Java and COM
- Efficient, controllable garbage collection (GC)
- Efficient internal object model, allowing better performance (in the VM, GC, JIT, and so on)

The Microsoft VM for Java includes the following innovations:

- **Integrated debugging** and the industry's fastest Just-in-Time compiler for the fastest run-time performance of Java applets.
- **Cab file compression** using Microsoft's new, cross-platform, open, backward-compatible Cabinet (.cab) packaging technology, which allows Java applets to download faster than ever before and allows users to install class libraries locally, avoiding repeated downloads across the Internet.
- **COM integration**, which allows Java applets to communicate with the universe of existing software based on the industry-standard COM, including ActiveX, Automation, and Object Linking and Embedding.
- **Unicode support** for development of international applications.

Just In Time Compiler

The Microsoft VM for Java includes a new JIT that speeds up the Java compiling process, so Java applets run much faster in Internet Explorer 4 than in version 3. The JIT compiles the Java byte code to native code (platform-specific) during run time and ensures maximum speed and efficiency.

You can turn the JIT off by accessing the **Advanced** tab in the **Internet Options** dialog box in Internet Explorer 4. You can also use the **Advanced** tab to turn Java logging on, to record Java activity.

▶ **To change Java VM settings**

1. On the **View** menu, click **Internet Options**.

2. Click the **Advanced** tab.

3. Configure the **Java VM** options you want.

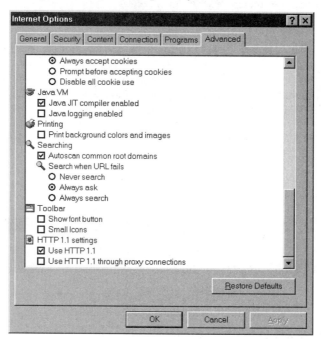

Option	Description
Java JIT compiler enabled	Clear to turn off the JIT compiler. The JIT is on by default.
Java logging enabled	Select to create a log of all Java program activity, which is useful for security and troubleshooting. Java logging is off by default.

J/Direct

A new feature of the Microsoft VM for Java, called J/Direct, allows Java code running on the Microsoft VM for Java to directly call Win32 functions. All you need to know is how to make the call in the C programming language.

The new Java packages and classes, such as AFCs and multimedia classes, that Microsoft provides in the *Microsoft SDK for Java 2.0* are one way to access the Win32 API. These new Java classes let you use Windows functionality from Java without writing any C code, but they do not cover all aspects of the Win32 API.

J/Direct, by providing a way to call functions exported from *any* Windows DLL, addresses the need of Java developers to access the full Win32 API directly from their Java code.

Using the Win32 API directly from Java, however, can cause sticky problems. Windows was written to be accessed from C, and because of the many fundamental differences between C and Java data types, it's tricky to build parameter lists and receive return values. There are compatibility problems: Java does not have pointers or a representation for unsigned numbers; Java strings don't look like C strings; and Java doesn't have an analog for the C structure data type. In addition, there are problems in calling conventions—such as how to invoke Win32 functions that use callbacks, or who allocates memory buffers. To help with these problems, J/Direct provides a set of guidelines and helper classes that outline the best ways to interact with the Win32 API from Java code.

If you need to access functionality provided by an existing Windows DLL, and you already know how to use that DLL, J/Direct lets you get the job done. J/Direct enables Java code to call functions exported from any Windows DLL. The code in the DLL does not need to be aware of the Java environment. You can use J/Direct to call Win32 APIs or APIs in third-party DLLs. J/Direct can speed up Java applications on Win32 platforms.

Java Security

Internet Explorer 4 introduces a new Java security model called trust-based Java security. The original Java security model limited Java applets to running in a "sandbox" that prevented applets from accessing a computer or network resources, but that also greatly restricted what applets could do.

Trust-based security for Java is a cross-platform security model for Java that provides fine-grained management of the permissions granted to Java applets and libraries. It uses Java Cabinet (.cab) signing technology to ensure that an applet can only perform actions for which it specifically requests permissions. With trust-based security for Java, developers can precisely limit the section of code where permissions have been granted, and administrators can have flexible control over the permissions granted to local classes. When combined with Internet Explorer zones, trust-based security can also simplify security decisions for end users.

For more information about trust-based security, see Chapter 29, "Trust-Based Security for Java," and visit the Microsoft Security Advisor Web page at **http://www.microsoft.com/security/**.

Using Java Applets in Web Pages

To use a Java applet in a Web page, you use the APPLET element as shown in the following example:

```
<APPLET CODE="loading class" CODEBASE="relative path to the file">
<PARAM NAME="parameter name" VALUE="value">
</APPLET>
```

Note If a Java applet is compressed as a .cab file, the OBJECT element can be used.

For more information about using Java applets in Web pages, see the *Microsoft Internet Client SDK* and the *Microsoft SDK for Java 2.0*.

C H A P T E R   2 6

Active Scripting

In this chapter

Active Scripting Overview

With the increasing popularity of Web applications, many Web developers are augmenting their HTML authoring skills by learning a scripting language. With the next generation of Web browsers, however, developers need to decide which scripting language to learn and which scripting features to take advantage of. Before making this decision, it is important to understand which scripting languages are supported by each browser and each browser's corresponding level of compliance with standards.

Internet Explorer 4 supports both JScript and Visual Basic Scripting Edition (VBScript). The modular script architecture of Internet Explorer is designed so that any third party can add scripting-language support to Internet Explorer using the Active Scripting interface. This enables developers to use the languages they know today to create Web pages and ensures that they have the most up-to-date and complete scripting language support available. For more information, see "ActiveX Scripting" in the *Microsoft Internet Client SDK*.

In addition, Microsoft is working with other industry leaders to ensure a broad level of scripting interoperability among third-party products. Consistent with this effort, Internet Explorer includes the JScript 3.0 scripting engine, the industry's first implementation of the new ECMA-262 specification.

For information about troubleshooting authoring for Internet Explorer and for Frequently Asked Questions (FAQs) about scripting, see Appendix G and I, respectively.

ECMAScript: The Internet Standard

The need for a scripting standard is clear. A scripting standard ensures that Web developers understand the direction of the industry and that they can write code consistent with this direction. It also allows developers to author script that will run seamlessly across a variety of products.

The European Computer Manufacturers Association (ECMA) scripting language committee was formed last year with the charter to standardize "the syntax and semantics of a general-purpose, cross-platform, vendor-neutral scripting language." Along with companies such as Borland, IBM, Netscape, and Sun Microsystems, Microsoft has participated actively in the development of the ECMAScript standard. A joint specification from Borland, Microsoft, and Netscape was recently ratified by the committee and published as the ECMA-262 specification.

With products such as Internet Explorer 4 and Internet Information Server 4.0, Microsoft is delivering JScript 3.0, the first scripting language to conform fully to ECMA-262. Microsoft is continuing to work with the ECMA scripting committee to ensure the advancement of the ECMA Internet Scripting Standard.

Basically, the ECMA-262 specification describes a Web scripting language that can enrich and enliven Web pages in a Web browser. More specifically, the ECMA-262 specification outlines an object-oriented programming language for performing computations and manipulating objects within a host environment, such as the browser. The complete ECMA-262 specification can be found at **http://www.ecma.ch/stand/ecma-262.htm**.

From a client perspective, a Web browser provides an ECMAScript host environment for client-side computations. These computations can include objects that represent windows, menus, pop-up menus, dialog boxes, text areas, anchors, frames, history, cookies, and input/output. In addition, the Web browser provides a means to attach scripting code to events such as change of focus, form submission, mouse actions, page and image loading, and others. The scripting code appears in-line with the HTML, and the rendered page is a combination of HTML elements and scripting engine computations.

JScript 3.0 in Internet Explorer 4

Microsoft JScript 3.0 is the first completely compliant industry implementation of the ECMA-262 specification. For more information about the feature/keyword syntax, visit the JScript Web site at **http://www.microsoft.com/jscript/**.

Microsoft has also submitted additional language functionality to the ECMA scripting committee for the next version of the ECMA specification. These features are being delivered in JScript 3.0, to provide the most advanced functionality for Web scripting available.

The following table describes the scripting features available in the ECMA-262 specification and Internet Explorer 4.

Category	Feature/*Keyword*
Array Handling	**Array** *object*, **join** *method*, **length** *property*, **reverse** *method*, **sort** *method*
Assignments	Assign (**=**) *operator*, Addition (**+=**) *operator*, Bitwise AND (**&=**) *operator*, Bitwise OR (**l=**) *operator*, Bitwise XOR (**^=**) *operator*, Division (**/=**) *operator*, Left Shift (**<<=**) *operator*, Modulus (**%=**) *operator*, Multiplication (***=**) *operator*, Right Shift (**>>=**) *operator*, Subtraction (**-=**) *operator*, Unsigned Right Shift (**>>>=**) *operator*
Booleans	**Boolean** *object*
Comments	**/* .. */** or **//** *statements*
Constants/Literals	**NaN** *property*, **null**, **true**, **false**, **Infinity** *property*, **undefined**
Control Flow	**break** *statement*, **continue** *statement*, **for** *statement*, **for...in** *statement*, **if...else** *statement*, **return** *statement*, **while** *statement*
Dates and Time	**Date** *object*, **getDate** *method*, **getDay** *method*, **getFullYear** *method*, **getHours** *method*, **getMilliseconds** *method*, **getMinutes** *method*, **getMonth** *method*, **getSeconds** *method*, **getTime** *method*, **getTimezoneOffset** *method*, **getYear** *method*, **getUTCDate** *method*, **getUTCDay** *method*, **getUTCFullYear** *method*, **getUTCHours** *method*, **getUTCMilliseconds** *method*, **getUTCMinutes** *method*, **getUTCMonth** *method*, **getUTCSeconds** *method*, **setDate** *method*, **setFullYear** *method*, **setHours** *method*, **setMilliseconds** *method*, **setMinutes** *method*, **setMonth** *method*, **setSeconds** *method*, **setTime** *method*, **setYear** *method*, **setUTCDate** *method*, **setUTCFullYear** *method*, **setUTCHours** *method*, **setUTCMilliseconds** *method*, **setUTCMinutes** *method*, **setUTCMonth** *method*, **setUTCSeconds** *method*, **toGMTStrong** *method*, **toLocaleString** *method*, **toUTCString** *method*, **parse** *method*, **UTC** *method*

Category	Feature/*Keyword*
Declarations	**function** *statement*, **new** *operator*, **this** *statement*, **var** *statement*, **with** *statement*
Function Creation	**Function** *object*, **arguments** *property*, **length** *property*
Global Methods	**Global** *object*, **escape** *method*, **unescape** *method*, **eval** *method*, **isFinite** *method*, **isNaN** *method*, **parseInt** *method*, **parseFloat** *method*
Math	**Math** *object*, **abs** *method*, **acos** *method*, **asin** *method*, **atan** *method*, **atan2** *method*, **ceil** *method*, **cos** *method*, **exp** *method*, **floor** *method*, **log** *method*, **max** *method*, **min** *method*, **pow** *method*, **random** *method*, **round** *method*, **sin** *method*, **sqrt** *method*, **tan** *method*, **E** *property*, **LN2** *property*, **LN10** *property*, **LOG2E** *property*, **LOG10E** *property*, **PI** *property*, **SQRT1_2** *property*, **SQRT2** *property*
Numbers	**Number** *object*, **MAX_VALUE** *property*, **MIN_VALUE** *property*, **NaN** *property*, **NEGATIVE_INFINITY** *property*, **POSITIVE_INFINITY** *property*
Object Creation	**Object** *object*, **new** *operator*, **constructor** *property*, **prototype** *property*, **toString** *method*, **valueOf** *method*
Operators	Addition (**+**) *operator*, Subtraction (**-**) *operator*, Modulus arithmetic (**%**) *operator*, Multiplication (*****) *operator*, Division (**/**) *operator*, Negation (**-**) *operator*, Equality (**==**) *operator*, Inequality (**!=**) *operator*, Less than (**<**) *operator*, Less than or Equal to (**<=**) *operator*, Greater than (**>**) *operator*, Greater than or Equal to (**>=**) *operator*, Logical And (**&&**) *operator*, Or (**ll**) *operator*, Not (**!**) *operator*, Bitwise And (**&**) *operator*, Bitwise Or (**l**) *operator*, Bitwise Not (**~**) *operator*, Bitwise Xor (**^**) *operator*, Bitwise Left Shift (**<<**) *operator*, Bitwise Right Shift (**>>**) *operator*, Unsigned Right Shift (**>>>**) *operator*, Conditional (**?:**) *operator*, Comma (**,**) *operator*, **delete** *operator*, **typeof** *operator*, **void** *operator*, Decrement (**--**) *operator*, Increment (**++**) *operator*
Objects	**Array** *object*, **Boolean** *object*, **Date** *object*, **Function** *object*, **Global** *object*, **Math** *object*, **Number** *object*, **Object** *object*, **String** *object*
Strings	**String** *object*, **charAt** *method*, **charCodeAt** *method*, **fromCharCode** *method*, **indexOf** *method*, **lastIndexOf** *method*, **split** *method*, **toLowerCase** *method*, **toUpperCase** *method*, **length** *property*

The following table describes those additional JScript 3.0 features submitted by Microsoft to ECMA but not included in the ECMA-262 specification.

Category	Feature/*Keyword*
Array Handling	**concat** *method*, **slice** *method*, **VBArray** *object*, **dimensions** *method*, **getItem** *method*, **lbound** *method*, **toArray** *method*, **ubound** *method*
Conditional Compilation	**@cc_on** *statement*, **@if** *statement*, **@set** *statement*, **@_win32** *variable*, **@_win16** *variable*, **@_mac** *variable*, **@_alpha** *variable*, **@_x86** *variable*, **@_mc680x0** *variable*, **@_PowerPC** *variable*, **@_jscript** *variable*, **@_jscript_build** *variable*, **@_jscript_version** *variable*
Control Flow	**do...while** *statement*, **Labeled** *statement*, **switch** *statement*
Dates and Time	**GetVarDate** *method*
Enumeration	**Enumerator** *object*, **atEnd** *method*, **item** *method*, **moveFirst** *method*, **moveNext** *method*
Function Creation	**Caller** *property*
Operators	Identity (**===**) *operator*, Nonidentity (**!==**) *operator*
Objects	**Enumerator** *object*, **RegExp** *object*, **Regular Expression** *object*, **VBArray** *object*
Regular Expressions and Pattern Matching	**RegExp** *object*, **index** *property*, **input** (**$_**) *property*, **lastIndex** *property*, **lastMatch** (**$&**) *property*, **lastParen** (**$+**) *property*, **leftContext** (**$'**) *property*, **multiline** (**$***) *property*, **rightContext** (**$'**) *property*, **$1...$9** *property*, **global** *property*, **ignoreCase** *property*, **lastIndex** *property*, **source** *property*, **compile** *method*, **exec** *method*, **test** *method*, **Regular Expression Syntax**
Strings	**concat** *method*, **slice** *method*, **match** *method*, **replace** *method*, **search** *method*, **anchor** *method*, **big** *method*, **blink** *method*, **bold** *method*, **fixed** *method*, **fontcolor** *method*, **fontsize** *method*, **italics** *method*, **link** *method*, **small** *method*, **strike** *method*, **sub** *method*, **sup** *method*

JScript 3.0 Availability

JScript 3.0 can be downloaded from the JScript Web site at **http://www.microsoft.com/jscript/**. JScript 3.0 will ship with the following Microsoft products:

- Microsoft Internet Explorer 4
- Microsoft Internet Information Server 4.0
- Microsoft Windows Scripting Host

Software developers can license JScript or Visual Basic Scripting Edition from Microsoft to use as the scripting language in their own applications. JScript and VBScript are available from Microsoft in two forms: as a ready-to-run (compiled) binary for several platforms or as source code. Licensing details can also be found at **http://www.microsoft.com/jscript/**.

Differences between JScript 3.0 and JavaScript 1.2

If you're designing Web pages that may be used by more than one type of browser, and you're using advanced technologies such as JScript and JavaScript, it's important to understand potential compatibility issues that may arise. For example, Netscape's JavaScript 1.1 served as the original basis for ECMA-262, although Netscape has yet to implement the ECMA-262 specification. In the latest releases of Netscape's Navigator software, JavaScript 1.2 does not comply with the ECMA-262 specification, and code written to JavaScript 1.2 works only with the version 1.2 scripting engine in Navigator.

As a result of Microsoft's standards support, code written using JScript 3.0 will work with other industry implementations of the ECMA-262 specification, including a future implementation from Netscape. In addition, Microsoft will ship the same JScript implementation in all versions of Internet Explorer 4, so developers can count on the same scripting behavior, regardless of the browser platform.

The following table details the support for the ECMA-162 Internet scripting standard offered by Microsoft Internet Explorer 4 and Netscape Navigator 4.0 and describes the corresponding behaviors in each browser. Developers can use this table as a tool to help during the migration process if scripting errors or anomalies arise with pages on your intranet.

Standard Feature or Behavior category	Microsoft Internet Explorer 4	Netscape Navigator 4.0
\u1234 used to specify unicode character	Fully supported	Not supported
Hexadecimal constants longer than 8 digits	Fully supported	Not supported
Octal constants that overflow 32 bits	Fully supported	Not supported
Negative Zero	Fully supported	Not supported
Date *object*	Fully supported	7th parameter (**ms**) not supported
Date.toUTCString	Fully supported	Not supported
Date.getFullYear	Fully supported	Not supported
Date.setFullYear	Fully supported	Not supported
Date.getUTCFullYear	Fully supported	Not supported
Date.setUTCFullYear	Fully supported	Not supported
Date.getUTCMonth	Fully supported	Not supported
Date.setUTCMonth	Fully supported	Not supported
Date.getUTCDate	Fully supported	Not supported
Date.setUTCDate	Fully supported	Not supported
Date.getUTCDay	Fully supported	Not supported
Date.setUTCDay	Fully supported	Not supported
Date.getUTCHours	Fully supported	Not supported
Date.setUTCHours	Fully supported	Not supported
Date.getUTCMinutes	Fully supported	Not supported
Date.setUTCMinutes	Fully supported	Not supported
Date.getUTCSeconds	Fully supported	Not supported
Date.setUTCSeconds	Fully supported	Not supported
Date.getMilliseconds	Fully supported	Not supported
Date.setMilliseconds	Fully supported	Not supported
Date.getUTCMilliseconds	Fully supported	Not supported
Date.setUTCMilliseconds	Fully supported	Not supported
NaN Dates	Fully supported	Not supported, set time to 0 (Jan 1, 1970 UTC) instead

Standard Feature or Behavior category	Microsoft Internet Explorer 4	Netscape Navigator 4.0
Full range of –100,000,000 days before Jan 1, 1970 UTC to 100,000,000 days after Jan 1, 1970 UTC	Fully supported	Not supported
Eval *method*	Fully supported	Supported, but often returns an incorrect value
== operator	Fully supported	Supported, but doesn't match standard specification
+ operator	Fully supported	Supported, but often returns incorrect results
Number formatting	ECMA standard behavior	Supported, but often returns incorrect results
Calling through a local function should pass the sglobal object as the "this" value	ECMA standard behavior	Passes activation object instead
Bind once to left operand on side-effect operators	ECMA standard behavior	Binds twice
Delete *operator*	ECMA standard behavior	Returns undefined
New *operator*	ECMA standard behavior	Grammar parsed incorrectly
Math.atan2 *method*	ECMA standard behavior	Does not implement many of the special cases listed in the standard specification

PART 7

Security and Privacy

Microsoft Internet Explorer 4 provides a full range of security features to help system administrators manage Internet and network security in their organizations. Internet Explorer 4 also provides features to help ensure user privacy. Part 7 describes the security and privacy features of Internet Explorer 4 and explains how these features can be used to help protect the individuals and information in your organization.

Chapter 27: Security Zones

Internet Explorer 4 introduces security zones, an innovative approach to secure browsing that offers greater management control and flexibility. Security zones allow users to divide the Internet and intranet into four groups of trusted (safe) and untrusted (unsafe) areas and to designate that specific Web content belongs to these safe and unsafe areas. This Web content can be anything from an HTML file, a graphic, an ActiveX™ control, a Java™ applet, or an executable program. Once zones of trust have been established, browser security levels can be set for each zone.

Chapter 28: Digital Certificates

To verify the identity of individuals and organizations on the Web and to ensure content integrity, Internet Explorer 4 uses industry-standard digital certificates and Microsoft Authenticode™ 2.0 technology. Together with security zones, these can be used to control user access to online content based on the type, source, and location of the content. For example, system administrators can use security zones in conjunction with certificates to allow users to have full access to Web content on their intranet but limit users' access to Web content from restricted sites located on the Internet.

Chapter 29: Trust-Based Security for Java

Internet Explorer 4 provides trust-based security for Java, which is a cross-platform security model for Java that provides fine-grained management of the permissions granted to Java applets and libraries.

Chapter 30: Content Advisor

System administrators can control the types of content that users can access on the Internet by using the Internet Explorer 4 Content Advisor. You can adjust the content rating settings to reflect what you think is appropriate content in four areas: language, nudity, sex, and violence.

Chapter 31: User Privacy

Internet Explorer 4 supports a wide range of Internet protocols for secure information transfers and financial transactions over the Internet or intranet. Internet Explorer 4 also provides a variety of features to help users assure the privacy of their information.

System administrators can use the Internet Explorer Administration Kit (IEAK) to pre-configure custom packages of Internet Explorer 4, giving them control over the security settings and content rating settings for user groups in their organizations. Once browsers are deployed, you can use the IEAK Profile Manager to manage security settings and content rating settings for user groups through the automatic browser configuration feature of Internet Explorer. You can also lock down security settings, certificates, and content rating settings to prevent users from changing settings.

Overview: Understanding Trust Management

Until recently, most people looked at browsing the Internet as a spectator sport. It didn't occur to them that they weren't just anonymously flipping through an online book; they were actively *exchanging* information and programs. Every visit to a Web site leaves a calling card, every animation fetches a program, and every hacker who becomes temporarily famous for demonstrating a security hole raises awareness that the bad guys are right behind us. Being wired has its price.

It follows that security and privacy in this new generation of the Internet has to be rethought. Traditional network security focuses on protecting valuable server resources from hostile clients. Now the problem also includes protecting valuable client resources from hostile servers. Information is flowing in both directions between publishers and consumers of Internet content, and comprehensive Internet security requires collaboration between both parties. This brings the issue of trust to the foreground.

The very fact that the Internet is open means that using it will remain somewhat dangerous. But not using it at all is not a practical solution. The right approach is to know the risks up front and make educated choices. Ultimately, the idea is not to avoid potentially dangerous operations, but to acknowledge that an action is potentially dangerous and provide the user with tools to make an informed decision about whether to allow it. Translated into Internet security terms, this is trust management.

Trust management is best compared to risk management. Insurance schemes of all kinds depend on managing risk, not avoiding it. Trust is a familiar concept. In its simplest form, it's an intuitive human construct based on three elements:

- Recognition
- Reputation
- Referral

Recognition is the most dependable element. It's one to one—a face, a voice, and by extrapolation and careful positioning, a brand. The problem with recognition is that it's not scalable. Reputation is better. It's indirect and scalable, but it can be unreliable: "great reputation, lousy food." It does, however, have the added property of capital. Reputation capital is important; companies build it based on delivering consistent quality. It's hard to get and easy to lose. Referral is the most complex form of trust because it's always transitive: "the doctor I trust says this is the best doctor for my condition." A combination of reputation and referral can be used to effectively establish trust in a digital world. The raw materials for digital trust come from public key cryptography: digital signatures, certificates, and encryption.

Establishing Trust on the Internet

Any trust proposition has to begin with a simple "Who am I dealing with?" The technical term is *authentication*, and it applies to both entities and to the origin of data. Strong authentication on the Internet relies on digital signatures and certificates.

A *digital signature* provides the cryptographic means to associate a message with its originator. Further, its use guarantees that a recipient of a signed document can verify that the signature is authentic and recover the message in a provably unmodified form. Signature verification is accomplished using an attached certificate.

A *digital certificate* is a computer-based record that provides an electronic means of confirming that individuals and organizations who communicate on the Web are who they claim to be. Essentially, a certificate is evidence of prior authentication, where authentication means providing some traditional form of proof, such as comparing a person's face to a picture on a driver's license or making sure he or she knows some secret that was sent to him or her in paper mail, and so forth. The sole purpose of authentication is to establish transitive trust.

For example, suppose Sam Shareware signs a document making an assertion that "My code contained herein is not intentionally malicious." The only way Sam (who is unknown to the user of his software) can be trusted is by referral. This starts with the fact that he went out and willingly submitted himself to a process that led to his being granted a digital certificate.

Still, the simplicity of Internet Protocol (IP) spoofing makes reading the URL insufficient evidence to authenticate a site. Requesting a site certificate by means of a secure protocol, such as SSL or IPSEC, provides a second level of assurance.

With Authenticode 1.0, a digital signature assures message integrity and can form the basis for a trust decision: Is execution allowed? Authenticode 2.0 allows a software publisher to additionally have its code "stamped" with a date. Certificates are generated using large cryptographic key pairs that have a practical life expectancy based on the amount of time in which their keys could be reasonably compromised. Expiration dates are applied to certificates to ensure that they expire long before then. Time-stamping guarantees that the signature was applied while the keys were good, and therefore the signature itself is valid.

Trusting Java

Authenticode 2.0 also includes finer-grained security for Java. While digital signatures can assure message integrity and authenticate publishers of mobile code, the only authorization decision presented is permission to execute—it's all or nothing. In practice, however, it's often more important to know what resources the mobile code needs than who published it. For example, while you may trust Microsoft, you may not want any code downloaded from the Internet to open any arbitrary file on your system.

Java originally defined a "sandbox" model for security, in which Java classes loaded from the network were granted extremely limited capabilities, and classes loaded from the local disk were given free reign to do virtually anything. Under this binary trust model, many interesting Web applications could not be written to run from the network, while unrestricted local classes could accidentally open arbitrarily bad security holes, either by themselves or when called from a malicious, untrusted applet.

Microsoft's Authenticode signing technology and Sun's JDK 1.1 added the ability to sign applets loaded from the network so that they could enjoy the same privileges as local applications. They did not, however, eliminate the all-or-nothing quality of Java security.

Authenticode 2.0 begins by adding intermediate levels of trust to the existing Java security model. It enhances the administrative options for the virtual machine to include fine-grained control over the capabilities granted to Java code, such as access to scratch space, local files, and network connections. This allows a system administrator to give an application some additional capabilities without offering it unlimited access to every capability in the system. Thus, only system classes with the highest level of trust can extend the model.

More important, the decision whether to trust an applet is presented before the applet is loaded. Two properties of Java (strong typing and the fact that it runs in a virtual machine) give it a security advantage. The developer can assert what resources his code needs and the virtual machine can enforce it. *Capability signing* allows an applet's signature to include a list of the capabilities requested by that applet. (This is in contrast to Netscape's model, which forces applets and class libraries to bury hard-coded capability requests in the Java source code.) Permissions requested for an applet (such as the hosts to which the applet is allowed to connect) are distinct from the code and can be expanded or reduced by an intranet administrator without having to recompile the applet. It also diminishes user interface "noise"—presenting the user with a trust dialog every time a new capability is requested while the code is running.

A new Package Manager allows the installation of local class libraries that are not fully trusted, using capability signing. This is especially important for Java Beans and class libraries. While it's desirable to allow these components to reside locally and to have some expanded capabilities, it's not prudent to give them unlimited power.

But, putting things into perspective, Java is but a component. What about the site itself?

Trusting Everything Else

Historically, the motive for discriminating on the basis of a site's content has been driven by a site's subject matter and the fact that some ideas and images are blatantly offensive to many people. In 1995, the World Wide Web Consortium Platform for Internet Content Selection (PICS) started to define an infrastructure for voluntary self-labeling, and more than a million sites are already labeled. While this is still an admittedly small fraction of the Internet, it's a good start. Internet Explorer 4 provides a Content Advisor with built-in PICS support, which can be used to control the types of content users can access on the Internet, based on the categories of language, nudity, sex, and violence.

Now there are new areas of concern relating to trusting Web content. While a site's subject matter may occasionally be an issue, it's more probable in a business setting that a content *feature*, such as whether the component wants to write to the hard disk, will be the cause of discrimination and will make the difference in whether to allow or disallow execution.

Unfortunately, the explosion of functionality available for the Web—Java with Capabilities, Scripting, ActiveX—has brought with it an explosion of complexity. What was previously a simple idea—"Don't let bad things happen to my machine"—has become a complex web of interrelated choices for the user.

Previous security schemes have depended on an end user or administrator making blanket security decisions for all Web sites and pages encountered. Java was always on or always off. ActiveX controls were always enabled or always disabled. This simplistic scheme is now a victim of the success of the Web.

Previously, all Web content was treated on an approximately level playing field. It really couldn't do much, so all content was given the same level of capability—virtually none. But corporations have recently realized that the combination of a Web browser and HTML can produce powerful internal applications. Systems that otherwise would have to be written in C++ or Visual Basic® programming language and then installed across the corporation can now be created quickly in HTML. With this technology, ongoing maintenance and installation costs are greatly reduced, and user interface is intuitive; it seems an ideal solution.

This solution raises new issues. Many Java applications need to perform application-like functions (such as writing to the disk, or network I/O), or they can use ActiveX controls to do the same thing. Blanket restrictions regarding Java and ActiveX are no longer practical; all content is no longer equal. You may trust active content in some situations, from some sources, but not trust it in other situations, from other sources.

One solution would be to ask users to make case-by-case judgment calls. But most users are not knowledgeable enough to be trusted with these decisions. For example, when browsing through a Web site, a user might be asked if the browser should allow the site to write to the disk, perform network operations, run ActiveX controls, script ActiveX controls, use more than 1 MB of memory, perform cross-frame operations, and so on. It's not likely that most users could adequately answer those questions.

To help simplify the decision-making process, Internet Explorer 4 has introduced *security zones,* a model of common security settings for related sites. Security zones do two things:

1. Group sets of sites together.
2. Assign security settings to that zone.

The security zone model breaks online content into four areas:

- The Internet
- The intranet
- Trusted Web sites
- Untrusted Web sites

Settings for ActiveX controls, downloading and installation, scripting, cookie management, password authentication, cross-frame security, and of course, Java capabilities can all be controlled based on the trust zone to which a site belongs. Users may accept the default zone settings or fully customize the zones and security levels to meet their needs.

The familiar High, Medium, and Low security levels are carried over from Internet Explorer 3, but with some significant changes. Users often questioned exactly what High, Medium, and Low security meant, and corporations requested additional control beyond these three settings. You can now see exactly what security options are disabled and enabled, and can have precise control of more than 50 options by choosing the new Custom setting.

If all of these choices are too much for an end user, an administrator using the IEAK can pre-configure the security options before the user installs Internet Explorer 4. Settings can also be locked down to prevent them from being altered by end users.

Thus, security zones reduce the number of intrusive and unanswerable dialog boxes that the end user encounters within a browsing session, while giving administrators fine-grained control over security options. Zones provide a means to express and enforce an organization's security rules or policies. And updates to zone membership and security settings can be automatically pushed to each user's desktop machine, so that administrators can manage security policy dynamically across all machines on their networks.

Summary

Any serious approach to Internet security must be comprehensive. And, ideally, it should bring order to the complex web of dangers, problems, and questions. Microsoft's Security Management Architecture acknowledges that it's not enough to provide assurances of component security. The problem is bigger than that, and it starts with trusting sites themselves. Trust is the unavoidable common denominator, and the decision whether to trust something or not must be based on fine-grained, but easy-to-understand choices.

Security zones and Authenticode 2.0 are two new tools that enable users to make good trust decisions. Zones give users and administrators a convenient means to specify Internet security policy based on origin. Authenticode 2.0 extends the digital shrink-wrapped software model to include time-stamping and signed Java capabilities. Together, they form the basis of a workable, extensible security scheme for the Internet.

CHAPTER 27

Security Zones

In this chapter

Security Zones Overview

Zone security is a system that allows the user or system administrator to divide into groups the Web content a browser can visit. This Web content can be anything from an HTML file, a graphic, an ActiveX control, a Java applet, or an executable file. Each group, or *zone,* then has a security level assigned to it. In this way, security zones control users' access to Web sites depending on the zone in which the site is located and the level of trust assigned to each zone. Internet Explorer 4 provides the following predefined security zones:

- **Local Intranet zone.** This zone includes all sites inside an organization's firewall (for computers connected to a local network). The Local Intranet zone is also home to Web applications that need access to the user's hard disk. The default security level is Medium.

- **Trusted Sites zone.** This is the zone where you specify Internet sites you know you can trust. These sites might include corporate subsidiaries or perhaps the Web site of a trusted business partner. The default security level is Low.

- **Internet zone.** All sites on the Internet that are not in the trusted or restricted sites zones are included in this zone. The default security level is Medium.

- **Restricted Sites zone.** This is the zone where you specify sites that you know you cannot trust. The default security level is High.

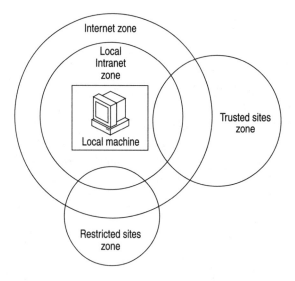

A fifth zone, Local Machine, exists but it is not included in the user interface and is not configurable through the security options. Local Machine can only be configured in the registry. Local Machine includes most content on the local disk, excluding cached classes in the Temporary Internet Files folder and classes that are signed with restricted privileges. This area forms a completely trusted zone, to which few or no security restrictions apply. System administrators can also exclude network and other drives by explicitly mapping them into other zones, if necessary.

Using security zones, it's easy to provide the appropriate level of security for the various types of Web content that users are likely to encounter. You can accept the default setting for each zone; change the setting to another of the preset High, Medium, and Low choices; or use the Custom setting for more precise control.

For example, it's likely that you fully trust sites on your company's intranet, so you probably want to allow all types of active content to run there. Simply set the Local Intranet zone to a low level of security. You probably don't feel as confident about sites on the Internet, so you can assign the entire Internet zone a higher level of security to prevent active content from being run and code from being downloaded to your computer. However, if there are specific sites you trust, you can place individual URLs or entire domains in the Trusted Sites zone. Other sites on the Internet are known to be sources of potentially harmful Web content, so you can choose to place the highest restrictions on those sites.

The default Low, Medium, and High security levels are detailed in the following table. You can accept the defaults or configure custom zone settings to meet your needs.

Security Option	Low Level	Medium Level	High Level
Script ActiveX controls marked safe for scripting	Enable	Enable	Enable
Run ActiveX controls and plugins	Enable	Enable	Disable
Download signed ActiveX controls	Enable	Prompt	Disable
Download unsigned ActiveX controls	Prompt	Disable	Disable
Initialize and script ActiveX controls not marked as safe	Prompt	Prompt	Disable
Java permissions	Low safety	High safety	High safety

Security Option	Low Level	Medium Level	High Level
Active scripting	Enable	Enable	Enable
Scripting of Java applets	Enable	Enable	Disable
File download	Enable	Enable	Disable
Font download	Enable	Enable	Prompt
User Authentication - Logon	Automatic logon with current name and password	Automatic logon only in intranet zone	Prompt for user name and password
Submit nonencrypted form data	Enable	Prompt	Prompt
Launching applications and files from an IFrame	Enable	Prompt	Disable
Installation of desktop items	Enable	Prompt	Disable
Drag and drop or copy and paste files	Enable	Enable	Prompt
Software channel permissions	Low safety	Medium safety	High safety

Administrators can also use the Internet Explorer Administration Kit (IEAK) Configuration Wizard and the IEAK Profile Manager to configure and manage security zones for custom packages to be deployed in user groups.

For more background information about security zones, see the "Trusting Everything Else" section of "Overview: Understanding Trust Management" at the beginning of Part 7.

Zone Architecture

When an HTML page is opened, a dynamic-link library called Urlmon.dll is used to determine from which zone it was loaded. To do this, two things happen. First, Urlmon.dll checks to see if a proxy server was used to get the HTML page; if so, Urlmon.dll automatically knows that the page is from the Internet. Next, it checks the registry to see if the page is from a designated Trusted or Untrusted location, and the security zone is set appropriately. If no proxy server is involved, the URL is then parsed to determine where the page comes from.

All of the zone security settings can be found in two registry keys:

- **HKEY_CURRENT_USER\Software\Microsoft\Windows\ Currentversion\Internet Settings\Zonemap**

  and

- **HKEY_CURRENT_USER\Software\Microsoft\Windows\ Currentversion\Internet Settings\Zones**

The **ZONEMAP** keys contain the list of Trusted and Untrusted (Restricted) Web sites, domains, and protocols. The **ZONES** key contains the actual zones and the security settings that apply to each zone.

Setting Up Security Zones

The options for setting and configuring security zones are the same whether you access them from Internet Explorer 4, the IEAK Configuration Wizard, or the IEAK Profile Manager.

▶ **To open the Security tab from Internet Explorer**

1. On the **View** menu, click **Internet Options**.

2. Click the **Security** tab.

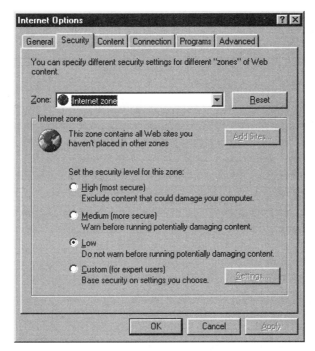

Note   Because security works differently in Internet Explorer 4, any existing Internet Explorer 3 settings are not preserved.

Designating the Sites Included in Zones

Users can specify the sites included in the Local Intranet, Restricted Sites, and Trusted Sites security zones. The Internet zone consists of all Web sites not included in any of the other zones.

Note   Web content can be addressed either by Domain Name System (DNS) name or by IP address. For sites that use both, it is important to configure both references to the same zone. In the common cases, the Local Intranet sites are identifiable by either local names or by IP addresses in the proxy bypass list. All other names and IP addresses would be mapped to the Internet zone. However, if a site name is entered into the Trusted Sites or Restricted Sites zone site list, but its IP address range isn't, then the site may be treated as part of the Internet zone if it is accessed by the IP address.

Local Intranet Zone

To be secure, it is imperative that the Local Intranet zone be set up in conjunction with the proxy server and firewall configurations. All sites in the zone should be inside the firewall, and proxy servers should be configured so that they do not allow an external DNS name to be resolved to this zone. Configuring the client zone security requires a detailed knowledge of the existing network configuration, proxy servers, and secure firewalls.

By default, the Local Intranet zone consists of local domain names and the addresses of any proxy exceptions specified in the **Proxy Settings** dialog box. (To access this dialog box, on the **View** menu, click **Options**, and then click the **Connection** tab.) You should confirm that these settings are indeed secure for the installation, or adjust the settings to be secure.

When setting up the zone, you can specify which categories of URLs should be considered. You can also add specific sites to the zone.

▶ **To set up sites for the Local Intranet zone**

1. On the **Security** tab, click **Add Sites**.
2. Select the sites to be included in this zone.

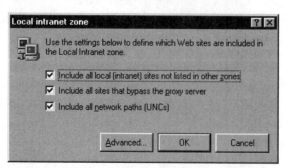

Option	Description
Include all local (intranet) sites not listed in other zones	Includes all sites not included in other zones. Intranet sites have names that do not include periods inside the URL (for example, http://local/). A site name such as http://www.microsoft.com/ is not local, because it contains periods. This site would be assigned to the Internet zone. The intranet site name rule applies to file: as well as http: URLs.
Include all sites that bypass the proxy server	Includes all sites that bypass the proxy server. Typical intranet configurations use a proxy server to access the Internet with a direct connection to intranet servers. This setting uses this kind of configuration information to distinguish intranet from Internet content for purposes of zones. If the proxy server is otherwise configured, this option should be cleared and other options should be used to designate intranet zone membership. In systems without a proxy server, this setting has no effect.
Include all network paths (UNCs)	Includes all network Universal Naming Convention (UNC) paths. Network paths (for example, \\local\file.txt) are typically used for local network content that should be included in the Local Intranet zone. If some network paths should not be in the Local Intranet zone, this option should be cleared, and other options should be used to designate membership. For example, in certain Common Internet File System (CIFS) configurations, a network path can reference Internet content.

3. Click **Advanced**.

4. In the **Local intranet zone** dialog box, enter the addresses of sites to include in this zone, and click **Add** after each site address you enter.

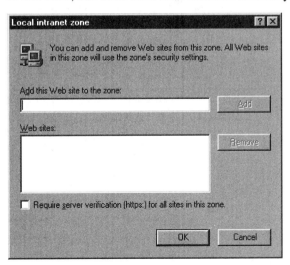

5. If you want to require all sites in this zone to use Hypertext Transfer Protocol Secure (HTTPS) server verification, select **Require server verification (https:) for all sites in this zone**.

6. Click **OK**.

Note If some parts of your intranet are less secure or otherwise not trustworthy, they can be excluded from this zone by assigning them to the Restricted Sites zone.

Once you have checked that the Local Intranet zone is secure, you may want to change the zone's security level to Low to allow a wider range of operations and make the Web pages more functional. You can also adjust individual security settings in the **Custom Settings** dialog box, which is explained in more detail later in this chapter.

Restricted and Trusted Sites Zones

The Restricted Sites and Trusted Sites zones are where you can assign specific Web sites that you trust more or less than those in the Internet zone or the Local Intranet zone.

The Trusted Sites zone is assigned a Low security level setting by default. It is intended for highly trusted sites, such as companies with which you frequently do business, and is sometimes known as an *extranet*. If you assign a site to the Trusted Sites zone, the site will be allowed to perform more powerful operations. Also, Internet Explorer will require the user to make fewer security decisions. Add a site to this zone only if you trust all of its content never to do anything harmful to the user's computer. For the Trusted Sites zone, it is strongly recommended that you use the HTTPS protocol or otherwise ensure that connections to the site are secure.

The Restricted Sites zone is assigned a High security level setting by default. This zone is designed for the rare case of a site you don't trust. If you assign a site to the Restricted Sites zone, the site will be allowed to perform only minimal, very safe operations. Due to the performance restrictions necessary for this extremely high level of security, some Web pages in this zone may not function properly.

▶ **To add sites to the Restricted Sites zone or Trusted Sites zone**

1. On the **Security** tab, in the **Zone** drop-down list, select **Restricted sites zone** or **Trusted sites zone**.

2. Click **Add Sites**.

3. In the **Trusted sites zone** dialog box, type the addresses of sites to include in this zone, and click **Add** after each site address you enter.

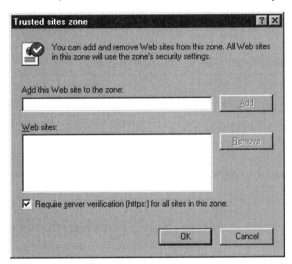

Note   The **Trusted sites zone** dialog box is shown here, but the **Restricted sites zone** dialog box is identical, except for the title.

Note   For the Restricted Sites zone, it is strongly recommended that you use the HTTPS protocol.

4. Click **OK**.

Changing Security Levels

If you choose not to accept the default security levels for the preset zones in Internet Explorer 4, you can easily assign a different level of security—High, Medium, or Low—to any zone.

▶   **To change security levels for a zone**

1. On the **Security** tab, in the **Zone** drop-down list, select a security zone.
2. Select a security level.

Security Level	Description
High (most secure)	Excludes content that could damage users' computers.
Medium (more secure)	Warns users and queries whether they want to run potentially damaging content.
Low	Runs potentially damaging content without notifying users.
Custom (for expert users)	Specifies custom settings for zones.

Note If you want to customize the security level for a zone, select **Custom (for expert users)**, and choose settings that suit your needs. For more information, see the next section.

3. Click **OK**.

Customizing Security Zones

The **Custom** option on the **Security** tab gives advanced users and system administrators additional control over security settings. Again, the options for customizing security zones are the same whether you access them from Internet Explorer 4, the IEAK Configuration Wizard, or the IEAK Profile Manager (with the exception of some Java controls, which will be explained later in this chapter).

Configuring Custom Settings

The custom security options for Internet Explorer are grouped into the following categories:

- ActiveX Controls and Plug-ins
- Java
- Scripting
- Miscellaneous

▶ **To customize security options**

1. On the **View** menu, click **Internet Options**.

2. Click the **Security** tab.

3. Select a security zone from the **Zone** drop-down list.

4. Select **Custom**, click **Settings**, and then select the options you want.

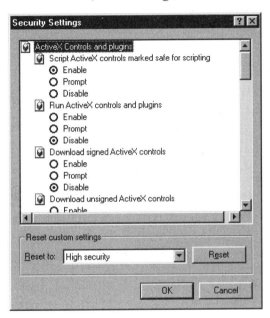

5. Click **OK**.

The following sections describe the security options for each security category.

ActiveX Controls and Plug-ins

These options dictate how ActiveX controls and plug-ins are downloaded, run, and scripted.

Note If an ActiveX control is downloaded from a site different from the page on which it is used, the more restrictive of the two sites' zone settings will be applied. For example, if a user is accessing a Web page within a zone that is set to enable a download, but the code is downloaded from another zone that is set to prompt a user first, the prompt setting is used.

Script ActiveX controls marked safe for scripting

This option determines whether an ActiveX control marked safe for scripting can interact with a script. The settings for this option are:

- **Enable**, to allow script interaction without user intervention.
- **Prompt**, to query users to choose whether to allow script interaction.
- **Disable**, to prevent script interaction.

Note that safe-for-initialization controls loaded with PARAM tags are unaffected by this option. This option is ignored when **Initialize and script ActiveX controls that are not marked safe** is set to **Enable**, because the setting bypasses all object safety. You cannot script unsafe controls while blocking the scripting of the safe ones.

Run ActiveX controls and plugins

This option determines whether ActiveX controls and plug-ins can be run on pages from the specified zone. The settings for this option are:

- **Enable**, to run controls and plug-ins without user intervention.
- **Prompt**, to query users to choose whether to allow the controls or plug-in to run.
- **Disable**, to prevent controls and plug-ins from running.

Download signed ActiveX controls

This option determines whether users may download signed ActiveX controls from a page in the zone. (For more information about digital signatures, see Chapter 28, "Digital Certificates.") The settings for this option are:

- **Enable**, to download signed controls without user intervention.
- **Prompt**, to query the user whether to download controls signed by publishers who aren't trusted, but still silently download code signed by trusted publishers. (For more information about trusted publishers, see Chapter 29, "Trust-Based Security for Java.")
- **Disable**, to prevent signed controls from downloading.

Download unsigned ActiveX controls

This option determines whether users may download unsigned ActiveX controls from the zone. Such code is potentially harmful, especially when coming from an untrusted zone. The settings for this option are:

- **Enable**, to run unsigned controls without user intervention.
- **Prompt**, to query users to choose whether to allow the unsigned control to run.
- **Disable**, to prevent unsigned controls from running.

Initialize and script ActiveX controls not marked as safe

This option determines whether ActiveX control object safety is enforced for pages in the zone. Object safety should be enforced unless all ActiveX controls and scripts that might interact with pages in the zone can be trusted. The settings for this option are:

- **Enable**, to override object safety. ActiveX controls are run, loaded with parameters, and scripted without setting object safety for untrusted data or scripts. This setting is not recommended, except for secure and administered zones. This setting causes both unsafe and safe controls to be initialized and scripted, ignoring the **Script ActiveX controls marked safe for scripting** option.

- **Prompt**, to attempt to enforce object safety. However, if the ActiveX control cannot be made safe for untrusted data or scripts, then the user is queried whether to allow the control to be loaded with parameters or scripted.

- **Disable**, to enforce object safety for untrusted data or scripts. ActiveX controls that cannot be made safe are not loaded with parameters or scripted.

Java

These options control the permissions that are granted to Java applets when they are downloaded and run in this zone. You can specify:

- The maximum permission level granted to signed applets downloaded from the zone.
- The permissions granted to unsigned applets downloaded from the zone.
- The permissions granted to scripts on pages in the zone that call into applets.

Note If a Java applet is downloaded from a different site than the page on which it is used, the more restrictive of the two sites' zone settings will be applied. For example, if a user is accessing a Web page within a zone that is set to allow a download, but the code is downloaded from another zone that is set to prompt a user first, then the prompt setting is used.

Java permissions

The settings for this option are:

- **Custom**, to control permissions settings individually. To view and change custom Java permissions for each security zone, use the Internet Explorer **Custom Java Security** dialog box. For more information, see "Configuring Custom Java Security" in Chapter 29, "Trust-Based Security for Java." You can also use the IEAK Configuration Wizard and Profile Manager to edit the advanced Java permissions for each security zone. For more information, see Customizing Java Permissions for User Groups" in Chapter 29.

- **Low Safety**, to enable applets to perform all operations.

- **Medium Safety**, to enable applets to run in their *sandbox* (an area in memory outside of which the program cannot make calls), plus capabilities like *scratch space* (a safe and secure storage area on the client computer) and user-controlled file I/O.
- **High Safety**, to enable applets to run in their sandbox.
- **Disable Java**, to prevent any applets from running.

Scripting

These options specify how scripts are handled by Internet Explorer.

Active scripting

This option determines whether script code on pages in the zone is run. The settings for this option are:

- **Enable**, to run scripts without user intervention.
- **Prompt**, to query users to choose whether to allow the scripts to run.
- **Disable**, to prevent scripts from running.

Scripting of Java applets

This option determines whether applets are exposed to scripts within the zone. The settings for this option are:

- **Enable**, to allow scripts to access applets without user intervention.
- **Prompt**, to query users to choose whether to allow scripts to access applets.
- **Disable**, to prevent scripts from accessing applets.

Downloads

These options specify how downloads are handled by Internet Explorer.

File download

This option controls whether file downloads are permitted from the zone. Note that this option is determined by the zone of the page with the link causing the download, not the zone from which the file is delivered. The settings for this option are:

- **Enable**, to allow files to be downloaded from the zone.
- **Disable**, to prevent files from being downloaded from the zone.

Font download

This option determines whether pages of the zone may download HTML fonts. The settings for this option are:

- **Enable**, to download HTML fonts without user intervention.
- **Prompt**, to query users to choose whether to allow HTML fonts to download.
- **Disable**, to prevent HTML fonts from downloading.

User Authentication

This option controls how HTTP user authentication is handled.

Logon

The settings for this option are:

- **Anonymous logon**, to disable HTTP authentication and use the guest account only for CIFS.

- **Prompt for user name and password**, to query users for user IDs and passwords. After a user is queried, these values can be used silently for the remainder of the session.

- **Automatic logon only in Intranet zone**, to query users for user IDs and passwords in other zones. After a user is queried, these values can be used silently for the remainder of the session.

- **Automatic logon with current user name and password**, to attempt logon using Windows NT® Challenge Response (also known as NTLM authentication). If Windows NT Challenge Response is supported by the server, the logon uses the user's network user name and password for logon. If Windows NT Challenge Response is not supported by the server, the user is queried to provide the user name and password.

Miscellaneous

These options control whether users can submit nonencrypted form data, launch applications and files from IFRAMEs, install Active Desktop items, drag files, or copy and paste files from this zone.

Submit non-encrypted form data

This option determines whether data on HTML forms on pages in the zone may be submitted. Forms sent with SSL (Secure Sockets Layer) encryption are always allowed; this setting only affects non-SSL form data submission. The settings for this option are:

- **Enable**, to allow information using HTML forms on pages in this zone to be submitted without user intervention.

- **Prompt**, to query users to choose whether to allow information using HTML forms on pages in this zone to be submitted.

- **Disable**, to prevent information using HTML forms on pages in this zone from being submitted.

Launching applications and files from an IFRAME

This option controls whether applications may be run and files may be downloaded from an IFRAME reference in the HTML of the pages in this zone. The settings for this option are:

- **Enable**, to run applications and download files from IFRAMEs on the pages in this zone without user intervention.
- **Prompt**, to query users to choose whether to run applications and download files from IFRAMEs on the pages in this zone.
- **Disable**, to prevent applications from running and files from downloading from IFRAMEs on the pages in this zone.

Installation of desktop items

This option controls whether users can install Active Desktop items from this zone. The settings for this option are:

- **Enable**, to install desktop items from this zone without user intervention.
- **Prompt**, to query users to choose whether to install desktop items from this zone.
- **Disable,** to prevent desktop items from this zone from being installed.

Drag and drop or copy and paste files

This option controls whether users can drag files or copy and paste files from a source within the zone. The settings for this option are:

- **Enable**, to drag files or copy and paste files from this zone without user intervention.
- **Prompt**, to query users to choose whether to drag or copy files from this zone.
- **Disable**, to prevent dragging files or copying and pasting files from this zone.

Software channel permissions

This option controls the permissions given to software distribution channels. The settings for this option are:

- **Low safety**, to allow users to be notified of software updates by e-mail, software packages to be automatically downloaded to users' computers, and software packages to be automatically installed on users' computers.
- **Medium safety**, to allow users to be notified of software updates by e-mail and software packages to be automatically downloaded to (but not installed on) users' computers.
- **High safety**, to prevent users from being notified of software updates by e-mail, software packages from being automatically downloaded to users' computers, and software packages from being automatically installed on users' computers.

Deploying Security Zones in User Groups

System administrators can use the IEAK Configuration Wizard to deploy and lock down security zone settings in their organizations. Using the IEAK, you can also build custom packages with specific security settings for different user groups. (For more information, see "Building Custom Packages" in Chapter 36.) Once custom settings have been deployed, you can use the IEAK Profile Manager to update those settings.

To specify security settings using the IEAK Configuration Wizard, use the **Security Zones and Content Ratings Customization** page. You can either accept the default security settings or customize the settings to meet your needs.

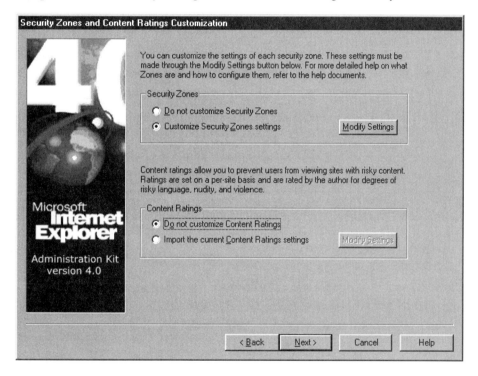

▶ **To customize security settings with the IEAK Configuration Wizard**

1. Select **Customize Security Zones settings**.

2. Click **Modify Settings**.

3. Use the **Security** dialog box and the **Security Settings** dialog box to customize the security settings for each security zone.

The dialog boxes for designating the sites included in security zones, changing security levels, and customizing security options are the same as the dialog boxes presented in Internet Explorer, described in the "Setting Up Security Zones" section earlier in this chapter.

Locking Down Security Options

Once you've built your custom security packages, you can also use the IEAK Configuration Wizard to lock down security options and restrict users from changing security configurations. After browsers are deployed, you can use the IEAK Profile Manager to lock down security options for user groups that have the automatic browser configuration implemented. (For more information, see Chapter 37, "Automatic Browser Configuration.") Again, the dialog boxes look the same in both the Configuration Wizard and the Profile Manager.

Using the IEAK, you can specify one or more of the following lock-down options:

- Lock down all security settings so users cannot change them. Security settings can be changed using automatic browser configuration, if implemented.

- Prevent users from changing settings for security zones. Users can still add sites to or remove sites from zones.

- Prevent users from adding sites to or removing sites from zones.

▶ **To lock down security options**

1. In the IEAK Wizard or the IEAK Profile Manager, navigate to the **System Policies & Restrictions** page.

2. In the **System Policies & Restrictions** hierarchy, select **Internet Restrictions**, and then select the **Security** object.

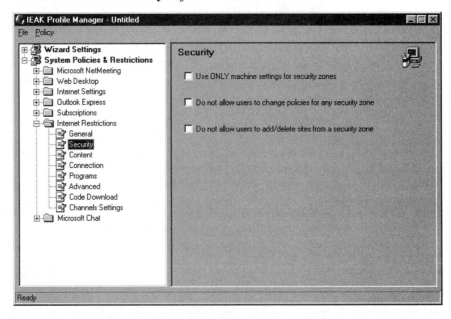

Note The IEAK Profile Manager is shown here, but the **System Policies & Restrictions** page of the IEAK Configuration Wizard works similarly.

3. In the right pane, select the options you want.

Option	Description
Use ONLY machine settings for security zones	Locks down all security settings. End users cannot change security settings specified for the zones. Settings can be changed using auto-configuration files and automatic browser configuration.
Do not allow users to change policies for any security zone	Prevents users from changing security settings for security zones.
Do not allow users to add/delete sites from security zone	Prevents users from adding sites to or deleting sites from security zones.

4. Save your changes to the auto-configuration (.ins) file or finish building the custom package, as appropriate.

Managing Security Settings for Deployed Browsers

To manage security settings for deployed browsers, you can use the IEAK Profile Manger in conjunction with automatic browser configuration. (For more information, see Chapter 37, "Automatic Browser Configuration.") You can update your security settings by opening the auto-configuration (.ins) file in the IEAK Profile Manager and selecting the **Security Zones and Content Ratings** object in the Wizard Settings hierarchy on the left pane.

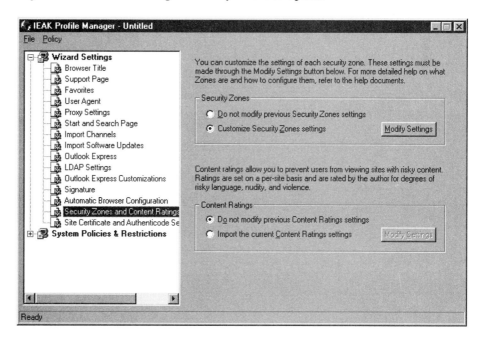

▶ **To customize security zones with the IEAK Profile Manager**

1. Select **Customize Security Zones settings**.

2. Click **Modify Settings**.

3. Use the **Security** dialog box and the **Security Settings** dialog box to customize the security settings for each security zone.

   The dialog boxes for designating the sites included in security zones, changing security levels, and customizing security options are the same as the dialog boxes presented in Internet Explorer, described in the "Setting Up Security Zones" section earlier in this chapter.

4. On the **File** menu, click **Save** to save changes to the auto-configuration (.ins) file.

   Changes are made to users' configurations as scheduled by automatic browser configuration.

You can also lock down security zone updates so users cannot modify the zone settings. For more information, see "Locking Down Security Options" earlier in this chapter.

C H A P T E R   2 8

Digital Certificates

Digital Certificates Overview

Digital certificates are electronic credentials that verify an individual's or an organization's identity on the Web. The identity of the digital certificate owner is bound to a pair of electronic keys that can be used to encrypt and sign digital information, assuring that the keys actually belong to the person or organization specified. (For more background information about digital signatures and certificates, see "Overview: Understanding Trust Management" at the beginning of Part 7.)

Digital certificates contain at least the following information:

- Owner's public key
- Owner's name or alias
- Expiration date of the digital certificate
- Serial number of the digital certificate
- Name of the certification authority that issued the digital certificate
- Digital signature of the certification authority that issued the digital certificate

Digital certificates may also contain other user-supplied information, including:

- Postal address
- E-mail address
- Basic registration information (country, postal code, age, and gender)

Digital certificates are authenticated, issued, and managed by a trusted third party called a Certificate Authority (CA). The CA must provide a combination of three essential elements: technology, such as security protocols and standards, secure messaging, and cryptography; infrastructure, including secure facilities, customer support, and redundant systems; and practices, including a defined model of trust and a legally binding framework for subscriber activities and disputes. In short, a CA must be a trusted online service operating 24 hours a day, 7 days a week, on a global basis. In addition to obtaining digital certificates from commercial CAs, you can also implement certificate servers such as Microsoft Certificate Server to provide certificate services for your Web infrastructure. Digital certificates form the basis for secure communication and client and server authentication on the Web. Digital certificates can be used to:

- Encrypt secure communication channels between client machines and the servers on the Web.
- Verify the identity (user authentication) of clients and servers for secure communication channels between clients and servers on the Web.
- Encrypt messages for secure Internet e-mail communications.

- Verify the authorship of Internet e-mail messages.

- Sign executable code to be downloaded on the Web.

- Verify the source and integrity of signed executable code downloaded from the Web.

You can install certificates and configure certificate settings for Internet Explorer to control secure e-mail communications, the downloading of active content, and user authentication for clients and servers. System administrators can use the Internet Explorer Administration Kit (IEAK) Configuration Wizard to specify certificate configurations for the custom packages of Internet Explorer they deploy in user groups. The IEAK Profile Manager can be used to manage certificate configurations for user groups through the automatic browser configuration feature of Internet Explorer.

Understanding Commercial Certificate Authorities

Commercial CAs issue digital certificates verifying the electronic identity of individuals and organizations on the Web. The CAs' primary responsibility is to confirm the identity of those seeking a digital certificate, thus ensuring the validity of the identification information contained in the digital certificate.

CAs do the following types of services:

- Provide, manage, and renew digital certificates.

- Authenticate the identities of individuals and organizations.

- Verify the registrations of individuals and organizations.

- Publish and maintain a Certificate Revocation List (CRL) of all digital certificates that have been revoked by the CA.

- Handle legal and liability issues for broken security.

Many commercial CAs offer certificate services for Microsoft products, as well as a wide range of other certificate services. For a current list of CAs who support Microsoft products, visit **http://www.microsoft.com/security/**.

Commercial CAs issue various types of digital certificates, such as:

- Personal certificates for individuals to digitally sign communications and assure secure transactions over the Internet and intranet.

- Client and server certificates for managing secure transactions between clients and servers.

- Software publisher certificates for individuals who digitally sign their software.

- Software publisher certificates for commercial software publishers who digitally sign their software.

CAs can also issue many other types of certificates. Each CA operates within the aegis of its Certification Practices Statement (CPS). It's a good idea to visit the CA's Web site and read the CPS to understand the certificates issued and the CA's operating procedures.

You should consider the following issues when choosing a Certificate Authority:

- Is the Certificate Authority a trusted entity operating a certification practice that can both meet your needs and operate efficiently in your region? Others should immediately recognize your Certificate Authority as a reputable, trustworthy organization. If you choose an authority with a questionable reputation, you run the risk of having users reject your server certificate.

- Is the Certificate Authority familiar with your organization's business interests? Look for a Certificate Authority from whom you can leverage technical, legal, and business expertise.

- What type of information will the authority require from you in order to verify your identity? Most Certificate Authorities will require detailed information, such as your identity, your organization's identity, and your official authority to administer the Web server for which you are requesting a certificate. Depending on the level of identification assurance required, a Certificate Authority may require additional information, such as professional affiliations or financial information, and the endorsement of this information by a notary.

- Does the authority have a system for receiving online certificate requests, such as requests generated by a key manager server? An online system can speed up processing of your certificate requests.

- With a commercial CA, you have less flexibility in certificate issuance and management. Some CA services and products may not integrate with your existing security model and directory services.

- Substantial costs can be associated with obtaining a server certificate, especially if you need a high degree of identification assurance.

Understanding Certificate Servers

Instead of obtaining all digital certificates from commercial CAs, you can implement a certificate server such as Microsoft Certificate Server to manage the issuance, renewal, and revocation of industry-standard digital certificates for your users. You can use these digital certificates in conjunction with servers that support SSL or PCT to build a secure Web infrastructure for the Internet or intranet. For large organizations with complex Web needs, certificate servers can offer many advantages over commercial CAs, including total control over certificate management policies and lower costs.

Depending on your relationship with your users, you can obtain server certificates from a commercial CA or you can issue your own server certificates. For services on your intranet, user trust is normally not an issue, and you can easily configure Internet Explorer to trust server certificates issued by your organization. For services on the Internet, however, users may not know enough about your organization to trust server certificates issued by you. Therefore, you may need to obtain server certificates issued by a well-known, commercial CA to ensure that users trust secure channels on your Internet sites.

Understanding Authenticode

Microsoft Authenticode 2.0 technology is used to identify the publisher of a piece of software and verify that it hasn't been tampered with. Software publishers who obtain a digital certificate from a CA can use Authenticode signing tools to digitally sign their software packages for distribution over the Web. (For more information, see the *Microsoft Internet Client Software Development Kit*.)

Authenticode is client-side software that watches for the downloading of ActiveX controls, .cab files, Java™ applets, or executable files, and then displays warnings to the user about possible security issues. In addition to these warnings, Authenticode displays certificate information, such as the name included in the digital signature, whether it's a commercial or personal certificate, and the date the certificate expires. This information is presented so that users can make a more informed decision before continuing with the download.

Authenticode works by looking for digital certificates (or the lack thereof) in the files being downloaded. The digital certificate is incorporated in a .cab or .ocx file at the time it is compiled. Part of a certificate is the digital signature—the name of the independent software vendor (ISV). A file containing a digital signature is referred to as *signed*.

If a piece of software has been digitally signed, Internet Explorer 4 can verify that the software originated from the named software publisher and that it has not been tampered with. Internet Explorer will display a verification certificate if the software passes the test.

A valid digital signature, though, does not necessarily mean that the software is without problems. It just means that the software originated from a traceable source that you may choose to trust and that the software has not been tampered with since publication. Likewise, an invalid signature does not prove the software is bad or dangerous, but just alerts users to potential dangers and problems.

When a digital signature fails the verification process, Internet Explorer reports the failure, reports why the signature is invalid, and queries users to choose whether to proceed with the download.

Internet Explorer can be configured to take different actions, depending on the status of digital signatures. A signature can be unsigned, signed using valid certificates, or signed using invalid certificates.

For signed or unsigned software, you can configure Internet Explorer to:

- Prevent downloading or running the software from a zone.
- Download and run the software without user intervention from a zone.
- Query users to make a choice whether to download or run the software from a zone.

How you configure Internet Explorer to respond to certificates will depend on various factors, such as the level of trust you have for the security zone where the content originated. If you are deploying Internet Explorer in an organization, you'll also want to consider the level of trust you have for the intended user group and the level of technical expertise the users have. For example, you might trust unsigned software from your intranet, but not trust unsigned active content from the Internet. In that case, you would configure Internet Explorer to automatically download unsigned active content from the intranet without user intervention and prevent the download of unsigned active content from the Internet. For more information about configuring security settings, see Part 7, "Security and Privacy."

Authenticode 2.0

Internet Explorer 3 browsers include Authenticode 1.0, but the client-side technology expired on June 29, 1997. Authenticode 2.0 not only renews security features for Internet Explorer users, but also brings new improvements.

Features

The new time-stamping feature of Authenticode establishes that a given piece of software was properly signed during the valid lifetime of a publisher's certificate. (The reason certificates have a limited lifetime is to prevent giving counterfeiters enough time to crack the code associated with the certificate.)

With Internet Explorer 4, Authenticode 2.0 delivers another new feature to protect Web surfers. Before downloading any potentially hazardous code, Internet Explorer 4 can automatically check to make sure a publisher's certificate has not been revoked. Publishers can have their certificates revoked if they abuse their code-signing agreement; for example, by creating malicious code that harms users' computers.

Plus, the valid-site-check feature verifies that the certificate is valid on the actual Web site where it resides. Based on security settings within the certificate, a certificate may be valid only on a specific site.

After Authenticode 1.0 Expiration

Users who don't upgrade to Authenticode 2.0 won't face new security risks, and signed code that has already been downloaded will continue to work; but users may start receiving warnings that some of the software found on the Internet is not safe to download—even if it has been properly signed by a reputable software publisher.

- **If security is set to High:** Even if the code has been properly signed and updated, you may be prompted that the code is not safe to download.
- **If security is set to Medium:** Even if the code has been properly signed and updated, you may be prompted that the certificate used to sign the code is out-of-date.

Upgrading to Authenticode 2.0

Microsoft Internet Explorer 4 will be shipping with Authenticode 2.0 support within the box. This upgrade to Authenticode supplies several new features that make running a signed ActiveX control more secure.

This technology can be introduced into Internet Explorer 3 using the Authenticode 2.0 patch made available in June 1997. To install the Authenticode 2.0 patch, users must be running the Windows® 95 or Windows NT® 4.0 operating system and Internet Explorer 3 or later on their computers.

Using Secure Client/Server Communications

Digital certificates can be used for secure communications and user authentication between clients and servers on the Web. With digital certificates, clients can be assured of a server's identity; the server proves its identity by presenting a certificate. A user who connects to a Web site that has a server certificate signed by a trusted authority can be confident that the server is actually operated by the individual or organization identified in the certificate. Similarly, digital certificates enable servers to be confident of a client's identity. When a user connects to a Web site, the server can be assured of the user's identity if the server receives the client certificate.

Secure Channels

The exchange of digital certificates between clients and servers is performed using a secure transmission protocol, such as Secure Sockets Layer (SSL) or Private Communications Technology (PCT). SSL 2.0 supports server authentication only. PCT 1.0 and SSL 3.0 support both client and server authentication. Secure transmission protocols can provide three basic security services:

- **Mutual authentication.** Verifies the identities of both the server and client through exchange and validation of their digital certificates.

- **Communication privacy.** Encrypts information exchanged between secure servers and secure clients using a secure channel.

- **Communication integrity.** Verifies the integrity of the contents of messages exchanged between client and server, which ensures that messages have not been altered en route.

Note Encrypting all traffic between clients and servers using secure channels places a high load on secure clients and servers because all information that is transferred must be encrypted and unencrypted. Therefore, secure channel encryption is normally used only for the transfer of small amounts of sensitive information, such as personal financial data and user authentication information.

Server Gated Cryptography

In situations that require the highest-possible level of security, such as online banking, Server Gated Cryptography (SGC) can be used to provide stronger encryption for the client, but only if the server is authorized to use SGC. A special certificate is required. SGC enables financial institutions with Microsoft Windows NT–based Internet servers to use 128-bit SSL encryption—the industry's toughest-to-crack code.

Some of the key benefits of SGC are:

- Banks and financial institutions can securely conduct financial transactions with their retail customers worldwide without requiring customers to change their standard Web browser or financial software.

- Microsoft's online banking solutions do not require any special client software. Customers can use standard, off-the-shelf, 40-bit exportable versions of Microsoft Internet Explorer to connect to an SGC server and conduct secure transactions with strong, 128-bit cryptography.

- SGC is fully interoperable with Netscape browsers and servers. This means that Internet Explorer users will be able to communicate at 128 bits with Netscape servers.

Enabling SGC

SGC works with standard, off-the-shelf export-version servers and client applications that use an updated Schannel.dll and have an SGC digital certificate. The updated Schannel.dll can be freely downloaded from the Microsoft Web site. End users can enable their Internet Explorer browser for SGC by simply downloading the exportable 128-bit SGC add-on. Banks can enable Internet Information Server (IIS) for SGC if they have the standard, off-the-shelf version of Microsoft IIS 3.0, which is part of Windows NT 4.0. They simply download and apply the patch that will update their Schannel.dll file for IIS 3.0. They can use the KeyManager in IIS 3.0 to generate a request for a certificate, which must then be submitted to an authorized Certificate Authority. Once the certificate has been issued and installed, IIS will be fully SGC enabled and will be able to communicate at 128 bits with SGC-enabled Microsoft and Netscape clients.

Implementing SGC

SGC builds on the standard SSL 3.0 protocol. If the server presents the special SGC certificate, then a 128-bit SSL session is set up; otherwise, a 40-bit session is set up. Just like a normal SSL session, the session keys are destroyed after the session is complete.

Two different implementations of SGC currently exist. Both are described below:

Microsoft's Implementation of Server Gated Cryptography Negotiates the SSL Connection Once.

- The client sends a normal export (40-bit) client hello to the server.

- The server responds with a *server hello,* selecting a 40-bit cipher supported by the client. The server certificate arrives with the *server hello.*

- The client examines the server certificate and determines that it is allowed to do "fast" SGC by checking the key usage extensions for the existence of the Microsoft Fast SGC key usage extension (1.3.6.1.4.1.311.10.3.2) and by verifying that the certificate chain is rooted with the Microsoft SGC Root or the VeriSign Class 3 CA.

- The client ignores the rest of the *server hello* up to the ServerHelloDone message.

- The client resets its handshake hashes and sends another *client hello,* containing all of the ciphers allowed in SGC (that is, 128-bit RC4, and so forth).

- The server receives the *client hello* and starts the handshake over again, completing the handshake with full-strength ciphers.

Netscape's Implementation of Server Gated Cryptography Negotiates the SSL Connection Twice.

- The client and server do a complete SSL handshake.

- The client then examines the server certificate to see if it should do SGC.

- The client then initiates a REDO by sending a *client hello* immediately after the SSL handshake has completed. The *client hello* contains the strong ciphers allowed in SGC (that is, 128-bit RCA, and so forth).

- The second SSL handshake completes with full-strength ciphers.

Details on SGC Certificates

Each server certificate may contain an extension listing key usage. Both Netscape and Microsoft clients look in these extensions to determine whether a server is certified for SGC.

If the certificate chain is rooted with the VeriSign Class 3 CA and it contains the Netscape key usage extension (OID 2.16.840.1.113730.4.1), then the client may do the Netscape method of SGC.

If the certificate chain is rooted with the Microsoft SGC certification authority and it contains the Microsoft SGC key usage extension SGC OID (1.3.6.1.4.1.311.10.3.2), then the client may do the Microsoft method of SGC.

To ensure interoperability, Microsoft will produce a special certificate signed by the Microsoft SGC certificate to chain to the VeriSign class 3 CA. This certificate will be installed in the Microsoft SGC solution (Schannel.dll). This will allow VeriSign to issue SGC certificates for use by Microsoft client and server software. Thus:

- If a Microsoft Internet Explorer client connects to a Netscape server with a VeriSign SGC Certificate, Internet Explorer will do Netscape's method of SGC. If Internet Explorer connects to a Microsoft Internet Information Server with a VeriSign SGC Certificate, it will do Microsoft's method of SGC.

- If a Netscape client connects to a Netscape server with a VeriSign SGC Certificate, or to a Microsoft Internet Information Server with a VeriSign SGC Certificate, it will do Netscape's method of SGC.

CryptoAPI 2.0

CryptoAPI provides the underlying security services for secure channels and code signing. Through CryptoAPI, developers can easily integrate strong cryptography into their applications. Cryptographic Service Provider (CSP) modules interface with CryptoAPI and perform functions including key generation and exchange, data encryption and decryption, hashing, digital signatures, and signature verification. CryptoAPI is included as a core component of the latest versions of Windows. Internet Explorer 4 will automatically provide this support for earlier versions of Windows.

Secure Networks

Socks Firewall Support

Many corporations provide their employees with access to the Internet through firewalls that protect the corporation from unwanted access. Socks is a standard protocol for traversing firewalls in a secure and controlled manner. Internet Explorer 4 is compatible with firewalls that use the socks protocol. Hummingbird Communications, a leading provider of firewalls, provided this support.

Windows NT Server Challenge Response

Corporations can take advantage of the Microsoft Windows NT Challenge Response (NTLM authentication) that might already be in use on their Windows NT Server network. This enables users to have increased password protection and security while remaining interoperable with their existing Internet information servers.

Configuring Certificates

You'll need to consider three areas of trust when installing and configuring certificates in Internet Explorer 4: root certificates for CAs, client certificates, and trusted publishers and CAs. The dialog boxes you'll use for configuration are the same whether you access them from Internet Explorer, the IEAK Configuration Wizard, or the IEAK Profile Manager.

From Internet Explorer, you access the certificates options from the **Content** tab.

▶ **To open the Content tab from Internet Explorer**

1. On the **View** menu, click **Internet Options**.

2. Click the **Content** tab.

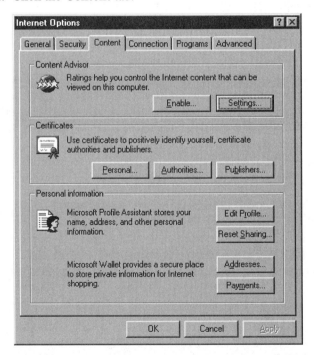

3. After you finish configuring certificates, click **OK** or **Apply** on the **Content** tab to save the changes to Internet Explorer.

If you're building custom packages to deploy in user groups, see "Deploying Browsers with Customized Certificates" later in this chapter. If you're using the IEAK Profile Manager to configure certificates, also see "Managing Certificates for Deployed Browsers" later in this chapter.

Root Certificate Authorities

Many CAs have their root certificates already installed in Internet Explorer. You can select any of these installed certificates as trusted CAs for server-user authentication, client-user authentication, secure e-mail, and software publishers.

Some CAs do not have their root certificates in Internet Explorer. If you want to use their services, you'll need to import their root public key into Internet Explorer. Each CA's Web site has instructions on obtaining their root certificate (public key). You can use the IEAK Configuration Wizard and the IEAK Profile Manager to import root certificates. For more information, see "Deploying Browsers with Customized Certificates" and "Managing Certificates for Deployed Browsers" later in this chapter.

To remove certificates or select trusted certificates for Internet Explorer, use the **Certificate Authorities** dialog box.

▶ **To configure root certificates**

1. On the **Content** tab, click **Authorities**.
2. In the **Certificate Authorities** dialog box, select an issuer type from the **Issuer Type** list.

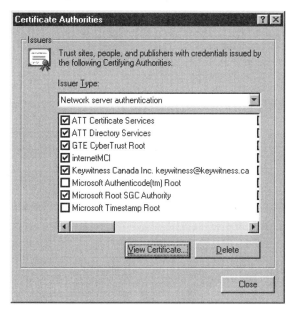

Issuer Type list:

- **Server user authentication**, to trust digital certificates from servers with digital certificates issued by the selected CAs.
- **Client user authentication**, to trust digital certificates from clients with digital certificates issued by the selected CAs.
- **Secure e-mail**, to trust transactions with other computers with digital certificates issued by the selected CAs.
- **Software publisher**, to trust downloads for software digitally signed by publishers with certificates issued by the selected CAs.

3. Select or clear check boxes for the listed CAs.

Note When you select a CA's root certificates as a trusted CA, you are trusting content from sites, people, and publishers with credentials issued by the CA.

---

4. Click **Close**.

Client Certificates

You may also want to install client certificates, which are used to authenticate users' computers as clients for secure Web communications. You can use the **Client Authentication** dialog box to install or remove client certificates for Internet Explorer.

▶ **To import client certificates**

1. In the **Content** tab, click **Personal**.

2. In the **Client Authentication** dialog box, click **Import**.

3. In the **Import Personal Certificates** dialog box, click **Browse**, and open the certificate file to import.

4. In the **Password** box, enter your certificate password.
5. Click **OK**.
6. Click **Close**.

Trusted Publishers and Certificate Authorities

To designate a publisher or CA as a trusted publisher or CA for Internet Explorer, use the **Security Warning** dialog box that appears when you download software from that publisher or CA. Active content that is digitally signed with a valid certificate by trusted publishers or CAs will download without user intervention, unless downloading active content is disabled in the security settings for the security zone. You can also use the **Authenticode Security Technology** dialog box to remove publishers and CAs from the list of trusted publishers and authorities.

▶ **To add a trusted publisher or CA**

1. Use Internet Explorer to download signed active content from the publisher or CA.
2. When the **Security Warning** dialog box appears, select **Always trust software from** *publisher or CA name*.
3. Click **Yes** to add the publisher or CA to the list of trusted publishers and CAs.

▶ **To remove a trusted publisher or CA**

1. On the **View** menu, click **Internet Options.**

2. In the **Content** tab, click **Publishers**.

3. In the **Authenticode Security Technology** dialog box, select a publisher or CA from the list of trusted publishers and CAs.

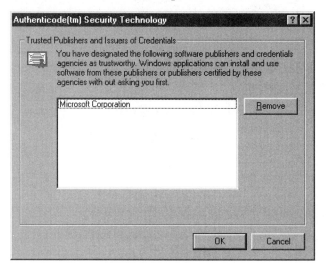

4. Click **Remove**.

5. Click **OK**.

Deploying Customized Certificates in User Groups

System administrators can use the IEAK Configuration Wizard to deploy certificate configurations in their organizations. Using the IEAK, you can also build custom packages with specific security settings for different user groups. (For more information, see "Building Custom Packages" in Chapter 36.)

To specify certificate settings using the IEAK Configuration Wizard, use the **Site Certificate and Authenticode Settings** page. You can either accept the default certificate settings or customize the settings to meet your needs. The options in the IEAK for configuring root certificates authorities, client certificates, and trusted publishers and CAs are similar to those presented in Internet Explorer 4, described in more detail in the "Configuring Certificates" section earlier in this chapter.

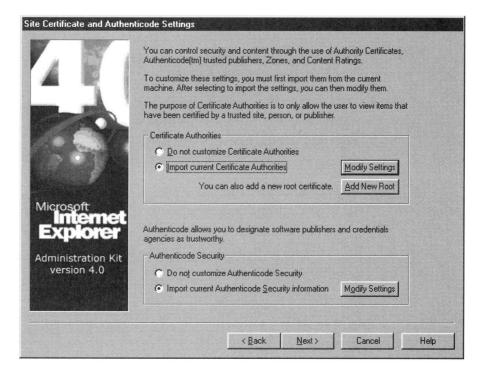

▶ **To accept the default settings in the IEAK**

1. Select **Do not customize Certificate Authorities**.

2. Select **Do not customize Authenticode Security**.

3. Finish building the custom package.

▶ **To add new root certificates**

1. Select **Import current Certificate Authorities**.

2. Click **Add New Root**.

3. From the **Browse** dialog box, select the *file name* of the root certificate file, and click **Open**.

▶ **To customize trusted certificates**

1. Select **Import current Certificate Authorities**.

2. Click **Modify Settings**.

3. Use the **Site Certificates** dialog box to remove certificates or to select trusted certificates for each **Issuer Type**.

▶ **To remove a trusted publisher or CA**

1. Select **Import current Authenticode Security information**.

2. Click **Modify Settings**.

3. Use the **Authenticode Security Technology** dialog box to remove certificates.

▶ **To add a trusted publisher or CA**

1. Use Internet Explorer to download signed active content from the publisher or CA.

2. When the **Security Warning** dialog box appears, select **Always trust software from** *publisher or CA name*.

3. Click **Yes** to add the publisher or CA to the list of trusted publishers and CAs.

Locking Down Certificates

Once you've built your custom certificate packages, you can also use the IEAK Configuration Wizard to lock down certificate configurations and restrict users from changing certificate settings. After browsers are deployed, you can use the IEAK Profile Manager to lock down certificates for user groups that have automatic browser configuration implemented. (For more information, see "Automatic Browser Configuration" in Chapter 37.)

▶ **To lock down certificates**

1. In the **System Policies & Restrictions** page of the IEAK Configuration Wizard or at the IEAK Profile Manager, in the **System Policies & Restrictions** hierarchy, select **Internet Restrictions,** and then select the **Content** object.

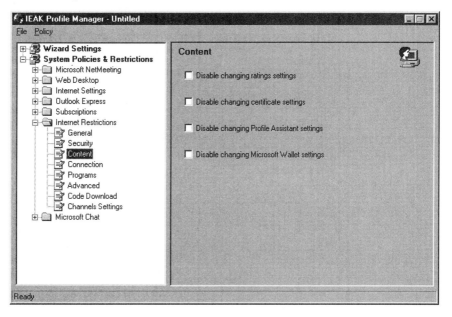

Note   The IEAK Profile Manager is shown here, but the **System Policies & Restrictions** page of the IEAK Configuration Wizard works similarly.

---

2. In the right pane, select **Disable changing certificate settings**.

3. Save your changes to the auto-configuration (.ins) file, or finish building the custom package, as appropriate.

Managing Certificates for Deployed Browsers

To manage certificates for deployed browsers, you can use the IEAK Profile Manager in conjunction with automatic browser configuration. (For more information, see "Automatic Browser Configuration" in Chapter 37.)

You can update certificate settings by opening the auto-configuration (.ins) file in the IEAK Profile Manager and, in the left pane, selecting the Wizard Settings hierarchy, and then selecting the **Site Certificates and Authenticode Settings** object.

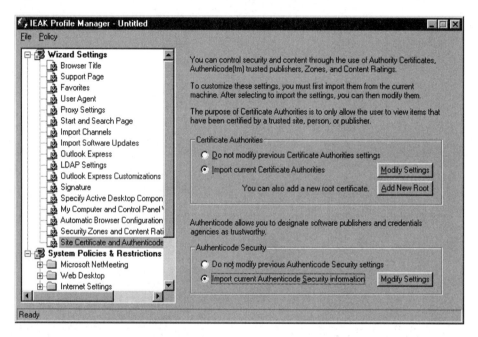

▶ **To add new root certificates**

1. Select **Import current Certificate Authorities**.

2. Click **Add New Root**.

3. From the **Browse** dialog box, select the *file name* of the root certificate file, and click **Open**.

▶ **To customize trusted certificates**

1. Select **Import current Certificate Authorities**.

2. Click **Modify Settings**.

3. Use the **Site Certificates** dialog box to remove certificates or to select trusted certificates for each **Issuer Type**.

▶ **To remove a trusted publisher or CA**

1. Select **Import current Authenticode Security information**.

2. Click **Modify Settings**.

3. Use the **Authenticode Security Technology** dialog box to remove certificates.

▶ **To add a trusted publisher or CA**

1. Use Internet Explorer to download signed active content from the publisher or CA.

2. When the **Security Warning** dialog box appears, select **Always trust software from** *publisher or CA name*.

3. Click **Yes** to add the publisher or CA to the list of trusted publishers and CAs.

▶ **To save changes to the auto-configuration (.ins) file**

• From the **File** menu, click **Save**.

Changes are made to users' configurations as scheduled by automatic browser configuration. You can also lock down certificates so users cannot modify the certificate settings.

C H A P T E R   2 9

Trust-Based Security for Java

Trust-Based Security for Java Overview

Trust-based security for Java is a cross-platform security model for Java that provides fine-grained management of the permissions granted to Java applets and libraries. It uses Java Cabinet (CAB) signing technology to ensure that an applet can only perform actions for which it specifically requests permissions. With trust-based security for Java, developers can precisely limit the section of code where permissions have been granted, and administrators can have flexible control over the permissions granted to local classes. When combined with Internet Explorer security zones, trust-based security can also simplify security decisions for end users. For more background information about trust-based security for Java, see "Trusting Java," in the "Overview: Understanding Trust Management" section, at the beginning of Part 7.

Understanding Trust-Based Security

Trust-based security for Java includes:

- **Security zones.** Administer related sites (such as all sites on a company intranet) as a group.
- **Permission model.** Integrate zones to provide fine-grained, parameter-based control over what Java classes can do.
- **Permission signing.** Specify the permissions used by a set of signed classes as a part of the signature itself, rather than through calls in the Java code.
- **Permission scoping.** Precisely limit the sections of code where a permission that has been granted to a class is actually activated and available for use.
- **Package Manager.** Flexibly control the permissions granted to local classes, unlike competing models, which allow only a few trust levels for local classes.
- **Trust User Interface.** Greatly simplify or eliminate the decisions that end users need to make regarding zones and permissions administration.

Trust-based security for Java comes with default settings that meet many organizations' needs without customization. Or, system administrators can use the Internet Explorer Administration Kit (IEAK) Configuration Wizard to specify custom Java security settings for user groups in their organization.

Security Zones

Security zones provide a new approach to secure browsing with Internet Explorer 4 by dividing the Internet and intranet into four groupings of trusted (safe) and untrusted (unsafe) areas and assigning a specific security level to each area. (For more information, see Chapter 27, "Security Zones.") Security zones interact with the trust-based security for Java permission model (explained in the following section) to create a configurable, extensible mechanism for providing security for users. Network administrators can configure three different sets of permissions for each zone for both signed and unsigned code:

- **Permissions granted without user intervention.** These are permissions available to applets from the zone without user intervention. They can be separately specified for signed and unsigned applets.

- **Permissions granted with user intervention.** Users are queried whether to grant these permissions to applets from the zone.

- **Permissions that are denied.** These are permissions that are considered dangerous and are therefore automatically denied to applets from the zone.

Applets that use only permissions granted without user intervention run automatically. If an applet uses any permissions that are denied, the applet will not run. If an applet uses permissions granted with user intervention, a dialog box will be displayed, listing all the permissions and their associated risk, and users are queried whether to trust the applet. If users choose not to trust the applet, the applet can continue to run with alternate and limited functionality, but is prevented from using the expanded set of permissions.

Permission Model

The permission model for trust-based security supports a rich set of permissions, which can be controlled by parameters such as storage (scratch) space size and network connections allowed. The following sets of permissions correspond to the standard Java sandbox:

- Allow thread access in the current execution context.

- Open network connections to the applet host.

- Create a top-level pop-up window with a warning banner.

- Access reflection to classes from the same loader.

- Read base system properties.

With trust-based security for Java, you can create sets of permissions that greatly expand permissions or restrict the sandbox. To view and change custom Java permissions for each security zone, use the Internet Explorer **Custom Java Security** dialog box. (For more information, see "Configuring Custom Java Security" later in this chapter.) You can also use the IEAK Configuration Wizard and Profile Manager to edit the advanced Java permissions for each security zone. (For more information, see "Customizing Java Permissions for User Groups" later in this chapter.)

Permission Signing

Trust-based permission signing extends the signed .cab file functionality provided by Internet Explorer 3. Under trust-based security, a signed .cab file can securely specify not only the identity of the signer, but also the set of permissions being requested for the signed classes. Because the system can determine all the permissions requested by a Java component by inspecting the signature, the Trust User Interface can present a single dialog box displaying all of the relevant trust questions before any of the code starts to run. Since the set of permissions are fully defined and understood by the Java virtual machine, the Trust User Interface can accurately warn users about the risk of each permission.

Java code may be signed with default capabilities of High, Medium, and Low Safety settings:

- **High Safety** is a restrictive set of capabilities that are the equivalent of "sandboxed" Java code. This setting allows the applet to:
  - Have thread access in the current execution context.
  - Create a top-level pop-up Window with a warning banner.
  - Access Reflection APIs for classes from the same loader.
  - Read system properties.
  - Open network connections to the host machine.

- **Medium Safety** includes the capability of High Safety and adds:
  - Storage (scratch) space.

- **Low Safety** includes the capabilities of High and Medium Safety and additionally allows the applet to:
  - Perform file I/O.
  - Execute other applications on the client.
  - Implement user-interface dialog boxes.
  - Provide thread group access in the current execution context.
  - Open Network Connections to machines other than the host.

- Load libraries on the client.

- Make native method calls.

- Determine whether an applet can make native method calls.

- Create a top-level pop-up window without a warning banner.

- Exit the virtual machine.

- Perform registry operations.

- Perform printing operations.

- Create a ClassLoader.

- Access Reflection APIs.

- Read system properties.

For more information about signing Java code, see the *Microsoft Internet Client Software Development Kit (SDK)* and the *Microsoft SDK for Java.*

Permission Scoping

Trust-based permission scoping prevents permissions granted to a trusted component from being misused (inadvertently or intentionally) by a less trusted component. Permission scoping allows a trusted class to precisely limit the range of code for which a granted permission is enabled for use. This is important because some methods that use enhanced capabilities are designed to be safely called by anyone, while other methods are only designed to be used internally by trusted callers and should not expose their permissions to less trusted callers.

For example, a trusted class might want to expose a **WriteEventLog** method. This method is safely callable by anyone and uses a public helper function called **WriteData** to actually write each log item to a file. The write permissions to the log file for **WriteData** should be enabled only when called from **UpdateEventLog** and other trusted functions, not when called directly by an untrusted caller (otherwise, the untrusted caller could use **WriteData** to store arbitrary data in the log file).

Trust-based security distinguishes between permissions that have been *granted* to a class and permissions that are actually *enabled* (and activated for use) at a particular time. The granted permissions are determined by the administrative options for a class's zone and the permissions with which the class was signed. The enabled permissions are determined by the permissions granted to other callers on the call stack and whether any explicit calls to the **activatePrivilege**, **disablePrivilege**, or **revertPrivilege** APIs have been made. If the call stack has less-trusted callers on it, the enabled capabilities can be more restrictive than the enabled permissions.

The first essential rule in trust-based security permission scoping is that permissions are never inherited from the caller. If a class has not been directly granted a permission, then it can never make use of that permission, regardless of what permissions its callers may have. This makes trust-based security invulnerable to luring attacks, in which an untrusted class "lures" a trusted class into calling it and is incorrectly allowed to make use of the expanded permissions of its caller.

The second essential rule is that even if a class has been granted a permission, its methods must explicitly enable that permission using the **activatePrivilege** method whenever there is a caller on the call stack that has not been granted that permission. The following pseudocode is a more precise description of this version:

```
CheckAccess(Privilege P)
{
Frame F = first_frame();
// start at the active frame

  while
  (F is not beyond the end of the stack)
  {
   if (P has not been granted to F)
    return FALSE;
     if (P has been activated on F)
      return TRUE;
       if (P has been disabled on F)
        return FALSE;

        F = next_frame(F);
    }
  return TRUE;
}
```

This says that a permission P is enabled only if P is granted in all of the stack frames from the active frame up to the earliest frame on the stack, or up to a frame that has called **activatePrivilege** on P, and if no intervening frame has called **revertPrivilege** on P.

In the example described earlier, the trusted class could allow the **WriteEventLog** function to be used from any caller by inserting a call to **activatePrivilege** at the beginning of the function and a call to **revertPrivilege** at the end of the function. (The raised permissions would terminate as soon as the **WriteEventLog** method returned, so the **revertPrivilege** call is not strictly necessary.) This allows the storage (scratch) space functionality to be accessed from untrusted callers only at well-defined places; for example, under the control of the **WriteEventLog** function, but not when an untrusted caller called **WriteData** directly.

Note that under trust-based security, *no* changes to the source code would be called if WriteEventLog did not need to be called from methods that hadn't been granted file write permissions. This would be the case, for example, if the method was part of a class in a stand-alone application.

For more information about permission scoping, see the *Microsoft Internet Client SDK* and the *Microsoft SDK for Java*.

Package Manager

Package Manager allows the installation of local class libraries that are not fully trusted, using permission signing. This is especially important for Java Beans and class libraries. It is desirable to allow these components to reside locally and to have some expanded permissions, but not to give them unlimited power.

System libraries are libraries that are both shared and have all possible security permissions available to them. These are the core of the Java system APIs and are the most privileged Java code. Most packages installed from nonsystem providers do not need this level of privilege, but Java has traditionally treated all local classes on the ClassPath as if they were system libraries.

Under trust-based security, classes from installed packages are not shared between applets or applications that use them. They also carry specific system permission identifiers that are approved by either the user or the system administrator when that package is installed on the user's system. These permission identifiers determine the maximum permissions that can be used by the classes in that package.

For more information about Package Manager, see the *Microsoft Internet Client SDK* and the *Microsoft SDK for Java*.

Trust User Interface

The Trust User Interface defined by trust-based security for Java shields end users from complicated trust decisions and reduces the number of dialog boxes they must answer. The integration of capabilities with security zones means that users only need to make a simple "Yes/No" choice when deciding whether to trust an application. The fine-grained decisions of which capabilities to allow have already been made by an administrator.

In addition, permission signing allows trust-based security to predetermine all the capabilities used by a class. When a package is installed, trust-based security for Java can use the signature to determine exactly the system permissions that it needs to provide, and a single trust dialog box can reliably present all of the capabilities required by an application before running any code. Since the default system permissions are well defined and static, their level of risk can be determined and refined over time, ensuring acceptable risk representation. All non-default system permissions should have a default risk level of Extreme.

For more information, see the *Microsoft Internet Client SDK* and the *Microsoft SDK for Java.*

Configuring Custom Java Security

To view and change custom Java permissions for each security zone, use the **Custom Java Security** dialog box. You can specify the way Java applet permission requests are controlled for both signed and unsigned applets.

Note This section describes the user interface for customizing Java permissions for Internet Explorer 4.01. The interface for Internet Explorer 4.0 differs, but it is similar to the advanced Java permissions editor dialog boxes described in "Customizing Java Permissions for User Groups," next in this chapter. For more information, see Help for Internet Explorer 4.

▶ **To access the Custom Java Security dialog box**

1. On the **View** menu, click **Internet Options**.

2. Click the **Security** tab.

3. In the **Zone** drop-down list, select a security zone to customize.

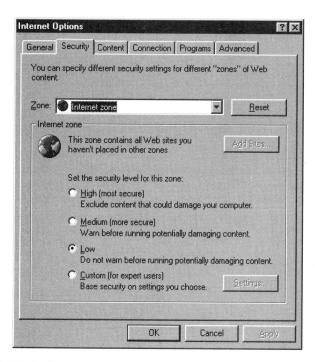

4. Under **Internet zone,** select **Custom (for expert users)**, and click **Settings**.

5. In the **Security Settings** dialog box, in the **Java** hierarchy, select **Java permissions**, and then select **Custom**.

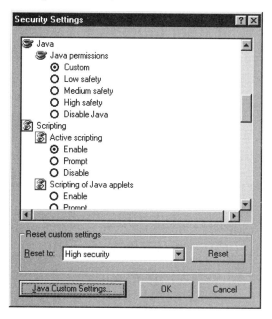

6. Click **Java Custom Settings**.

▶ **To view permissions at the Custom Java Security dialog box**

- Click the **View Permissions** tab.

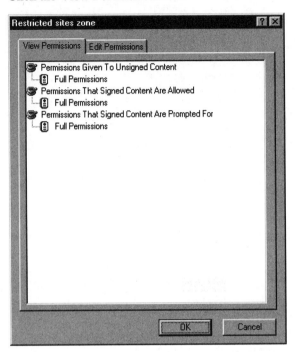

This tab displays permissions in a hierarchical tree, which you can expand and collapse. These permissions are set using the advanced Java permissions editor (see "Customizing Java Permissions for User Groups," next in this chapter). Permissions are organized into the following categories:

- **Permissions Given To Unsigned Content.** Unsigned Java applets that request these permissions can run without user query.

- **Permissions That Signed Content Are Allowed.** Signed Java applets that request these permissions can run without user query.

- **Permissions That Signed Content Are Prompted For.** Users are queried whether to allow signed applets to run when applets request these permissions.

▶ **To change custom Java permissions at the Custom Java Security dialog box**

1. Click the **Edit Permissions** tab.

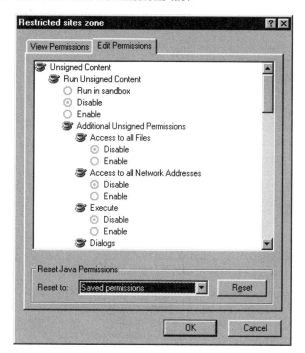

2. Configure the custom Java permissions options.

Option	Description
Unsigned Content—Run Unsigned Content	
Run in sandbox	Select to run unsigned Java applets for this zone in a Java sandbox that you specify. You can enable or disable individual options in **Additional Unsigned Permissions** by selecting **Disable** to disable and **Enable** to enable options.
Disable	Select to disable running unsigned applets for this zone. All options in **Additional Unsigned Permissions** are disabled and shaded.
Enable	Select to enable running unsigned applets for this zone. All options in **Additional Unsigned Permissions** are enabled.

Option	Description
Unsigned Content—Additional Unsigned Permissions	
Access to all files	Select **Enable** to allow unsigned applets to have read access to all files on your system. Select **Disable** to prevent unsigned applets from having read access to all the files on your system.
Access to all network addresses	Select **Enable** to allow unsigned applets to have access to network addresses. Select **Disable** to prevent unsigned applets from having access to network addresses.
Execute	Select **Enable** to allow unsigned applets to run other applications. Select **Disable** to prevent unsigned applets from running other applications.
Dialogs	Select **Enable** to allow unsigned applets to create file dialog boxes. Select **Disable** to prevent unsigned applets from creating file dialog boxes.
System information	Select **Enable** to allow unsigned applets to read system properties. Select **Disable** to prevent unsigned applets from reading system properties.
Printing	Select **Enable** to allow unsigned applets to access printer resources. Select **Disable** to prevent unsigned applets from accessing printer resources.
Protected scratch space	Select **Enable** to allow unsigned applets to use storage area on your hard disk. Select **Disable** to prevent unsigned applets from using storage area on your hard disk.
User-selected file access	Select **Enable** to query you whether unsigned applets can access selected files. Select **Disable** to prevent unsigned applets from accessing any files and to prevent querying you for permission.
Signed Content—Run Signed Content	
Prompt	Select to set individual options in **Additional Signed Permissions** to **Prompt**. You can select **Disable** to disable and **Enable** to enable each individual option.
Disable	Select to disable running signed applets for this zone. All options in **Additional Signed Permissions** are disabled and shaded.
Enable	Select to enable running unsigned applets for this zone. All options in **Additional Signed Permissions** are enabled.
Signed Content—Additional Signed Permissions	
Access to all files	Select **Prompt** to query you before signed applets can have read access to all the files on your system. Select **Enable** to allow signed applets to have read access to all files on your system. Select **Disable** to prevent signed applets from having read access to all the files on your system.
Access to all network addresses	Select **Prompt** to query you whether signed applets can have access to network addresses. Select **Enable** to allow signed applets to have access to network addresses. Select **Disable** to prevent signed applets from having access to network addresses.

Option	Description
Signed Content—Additional Signed Permissions *(continued)*	
Access to all network addresses	Select **Prompt** to query you whether signed applets can have access to network addresses. Select **Enable** to allow signed applets to have access to network addresses. Select **Disable** to prevent signed applets from having access to network addresses.
Execute	Select **Prompt** to query you whether signed applets can run other applications. Select **Enable** to allow signed applets to run other applications. Select **Disable** to prevent signed applets from running other applications.
Dialogs	Select **Prompt** to query you whether signed applets can create file dialog boxes. Select **Enable** to allow signed applets to create file dialog boxes. Select **Disable** to prevent signed applets from creating file dialog boxes.
System information	Select **Prompt** to query you whether signed applets can read system properties. Select **Enable** to allow signed applets to read system properties. Select **Disable** to prevent signed applets from reading system properties.
Printing	Select **Prompt** to query you whether signed applets can access printer resources. Select **Enable** to allow signed applets to access printer resources. Select **Disable** to prevent signed applets from accessing printer resources.
Protected scratch space	Select **Prompt** to query you whether signed applets can use storage area on your hard disk. Select **Enable** to allow signed applets to use storage area on your hard disk. Select **Disable** to prevent signed applets from using storage area on your hard disk.
User-selected file access	Select **Prompt** or **Enable** to query you whether signed applets can access selected files. Select **Disable** to prevent signed applets from accessing any files and to prevent querying you for permission.
Reset Java Permissions	
Saved permissions	In the **Reset to:** drop-down list, select and click **Reset** to restore all settings to the last saved permission. Initially, these settings are the settings set using the advanced Java permissions editor (see "Customizing Java Permissions" earlier in this chapter). Every time you change settings and click **OK**, a new set of saved permissions is saved.
High security	In the **Reset to:** drop-down list, select and click **Reset** to reset all permissions to High security level (most restrictive; applets run in safe mode).
Medium security	In the **Reset to:** drop-down list, select and click **Reset** to reset all permissions to Medium security level (applets run with some restrictions).
Low security	In the **Reset to:** drop-down list, select and click **Reset** to reset all permissions to Low security level (least restrictive; applets run with all permissions).

Customizing Java Permissions for User Groups

System administrators can use the IEAK Configuration Wizard to deploy custom Java permissions in their organizations. Using the IEAK, you can also build custom packages with specific Java permissions for different user groups. Once a custom browser has been deployed, the IEAK Profile Manager can be used to update Java permissions. (For more information, see "Building Custom Packages" in Chapter 36.)

Note This section describes the user interface for customizing Java permissions for Internet Explorer 4.01. The interface for Internet Explorer 4.0 differs, but it is similar to the advanced Java permissions editor dialog boxes described in this section. For more information, see Help for Internet Explorer 4.

To customize Java permissions for each security zone, use the advanced Java permissions editor dialog boxes. You can access the advanced Java permissions editor using the IEAK Configuration Wizard or the IEAK Profile Manager. Typically, end users cannot access the advanced Java permissions editor from Internet Explorer. However, when the IEAK is installed, and you run the IEAK Configuration Wizard or Profile Manager, access to the advanced Java permissions editor from Internet Explorer is turned on.

You can specify how applet permissions are handled for three classes of permission requests:

- Unsigned permission requests from unsigned applets.
- Trusted signed permission requests from signed applets.
- Untrusted signed permissions from signed applets.

You can specify the way applet permissions are controlled for:

- **Unsigned Permissions.** Grant these permissions to unsigned applets from the zone. Unsigned applets that request these permissions can run without user action. Unsigned applets that request additional permissions cannot run.

- **Trusted Signed Permissions.** Grant these permissions to trusted signed applets from the zone. Signed applets that request these trusted permissions can run without user action.

- **Untrusted Signed Permissions.** Grant these permissions to untrusted signed permissions from the zone. Signed applets that request these permissions are handled in one of the following ways:

  - Users are queried whether to allow the applet to run with these permissions.

  - Applets are prevented from running with no user query.

    You can optionally specify that all signed applet permission requests not specified as trusted or untrusted are treated as untrusted signed permissions.

End users can use the **Custom Java Security** dialog box to view and change custom Java permissions for each security zone. For more information, see "Configuring Custom Java Security" earlier in this chapter.

▶ **To access the advanced Java permissions editor**

1. Perform one of the following:

   ▪ Run the IEAK Configuration Wizard, and navigate to the **Security Zones and Content Ratings Customization** page.

   ▪ Run the IEAK Profile Manager and, in the **Wizard Settings** hierarchy, select the **Security Zones and Content Ratings Customization** object.

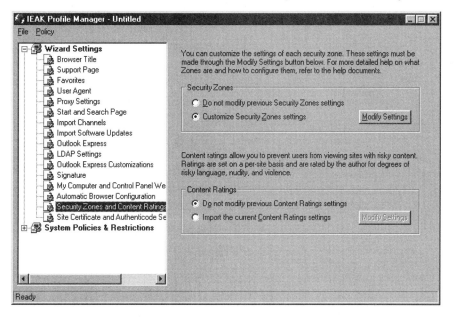

Note The IEAK Profile Manager is shown here, but the **Security Zones and Content Ratings Customization** page of the IEAK Configuration Wizard works similarly.

2. Select **Customize Security Zones settings**.

3. Click **Modify Settings**.

4. In the **Security** dialog box, select a security zone to customize from the **Zone** drop-down list.

5. Select **Custom (for expert users)**, and click **Settings**.

6. In the **Security Settings** dialog box, in the **Java** hierarchy, select the Java permissions **Custom** option.

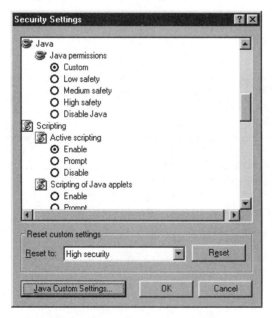

7. Click **Java Custom Settings**.

8. Click **Advanced Edit**.

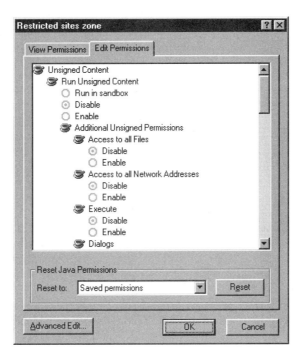

▶ **To customize advanced Java permissions**

    1. Use the **Edit Custom Permissions** dialog box to specify custom permissions.

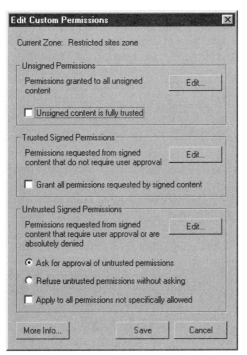

Option	Description
Unsigned Permissions	Click **Edit** to open the **Unsigned Permissions** dialog box and specify permissions granted to unsigned Java content for this zone. Unsigned Java applets that request permissions can run from this zone without user query, but unsigned applets that request permissions not granted cannot run from this zone. For more information, see "Specifying Unsigned and Trusted Signed Permissions" and "Specifying Untrusted Signed Permissions" later in this chapter.
Unsigned content is fully trusted	Select to trust all unsigned content from this zone. You should exercise caution before selecting this option, because it allows unsigned Java applets to run from this zone without user query and with full access to the user's computer and network resources. This option overrides any changes you make using the **Unsigned Permissions** dialog box.
Trusted Signed Permissions	Click **Edit** to open the **Trusted Signed Permissions** dialog box and specify the permissions granted to signed Java content for this zone. Java applets that request only these permissions can run without user query. For more information, see "Specifying Unsigned and Trusted Signed Permissions" and "Specifying Untrusted Signed Permissions" later in this chapter.
Grant all permissions requested by signed content	Select to trust all signed content from this zone. Selecting this option means signed Java applets can run with all requested permissions, without user query. This option overrides any changes you make using the **Trusted Signed Permissions** dialog box.
Untrusted Signed Permissions	Click **Edit** to open the **Untrusted Signed Permissions** dialog box and specify the permissions you do not want to be trusted for signed Java content for this zone. When signed Java applets request these permissions, either the user is queried to allow the applet to run, or permissions are denied and the applet cannot run, depending on whether **Ask for approval of untrusted permissions** or **Refuse untrusted permissions without asking** is selected. For more information, see "Specifying Unsigned and Trusted Signed Permissions" and "Specifying Untrusted Signed Permissions" later in this chapter.
Ask for approval of untrusted permissions	Select to query users whether to allow signed Java applets that request untrusted permissions to run. The applet can run only if the user approves the permissions.
Refuse untrusted permissions without asking	Select to prevent signed Java applets that request untrusted permission from running.
Apply to all permissions not specifically allowed	Select to control how signed Java applets are handled that request permissions not specified as trusted or untrusted in **Trusted Signed Permissions** and **Untrusted Signed Permissions**. When a signed applet requests permissions not specified as trusted or untrusted, either the user is queried to permit the applet to run, or the permissions are denied, depending on whether **Ask for approval of untrusted permissions** or **Refuse untrusted permissions without asking** is selected.

2. Click **Save** to save the changes as the default custom Java settings for user groups.

3. Save your changes to the auto-configuration (.ins) file, or finish building the custom package, as appropriate.

Specifying Untrusted Signed Permissions

You can use the **Unsigned Permissions** dialog box to specify custom permissions for untrusted signed Java applets. (The dialog boxes for **Unsigned Permissions** and **Untrusted Signed Permissions** are identical except for the title.) The dialog box is grouped into seven tabs, as detailed in the coming sections.

The effect of the permissions you assign here depends on whether you select **Ask for approval of untrusted permissions** or **Refuse untrusted permissions without asking**:

- If you select **Ask for approval of untrusted permissions**, users are queried whether to permit applets that request these permissions to run.

- If you select **Refuse untrusted permissions without asking**, applets that request these permissions cannot run.

▶ **To customize untrusted signed permissions**

1. In the **Edit Custom Permissions** dialog box, under **Untrusted Signed Permissions**, click **Edit**.

2. Click the appropriate tab, and customize the options as necessary.

Specifying Unsigned and Trusted Signed Permissions

You can use the **Unsigned Permissions** and **Trusted Signed Permissions** dialog boxes to specify custom permissions for unsigned and signed Java applets. The dialog boxes are grouped into seven tabs.

▶ **To customize unsigned or trusted signed permissions**

1. In the **Edit Custom Permissions** dialog box, under **Unsigned Permissions** or **Trusted Permissions**, click **Edit**.

2. In the resulting dialog box, click the appropriate tab, and customize the options, as necessary.

The following sections describe all customization options.

File tab

Use the **File** tab to specify files and file types that you will allow in this permission set for this zone. By default, all files are excluded, so you do not need to specify files to exclude, unless they are a subset of the files you are including. For example, if you include a multimedia file type (*.avi), you can exclude a specific file of that type (huge.avi). You can specify different permissions for Read, Write, and Delete access.

For example, for read access, you could type the following masks:

Include Files: C:\Windows*
Exclude Files: *.exe

These masks would result in read access to everything in the Windows directory, except for the .exe files in the Windows directory.

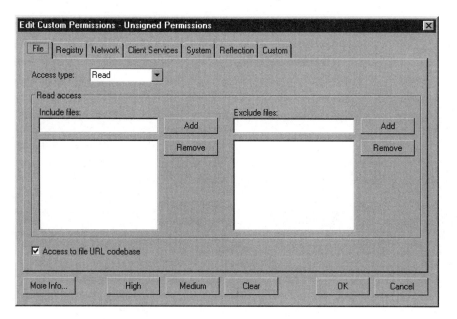

Option	Description
Access type	Select either **Read**, **Write**, or **Delete** to specify that applets can have read, write, or delete access to the included files for this zone.

Read access	
Include files	Enter the files to include for the selected access type.
Exclude files	Enter the files to exclude from the selected access type.
Access to file URL codebase	Select to allow access to the file URL codebase.

Security level	
High	Click to set the security level to High (most secure).
Medium	Click to set the security level to Medium.
Clear	Click to clear all options and settings on this tab.

Registry tab

Use the **Registry** tab to specify registry keys you will allow in this permission set for this zone. By default, all registry keys are excluded, so you do not need specify registry keys to exclude, unless they are a subset of the registry keys you are including. For example, if you include **HKEY_CURRENT_USER**, you can exclude a specific registry category underneath that key (**HKEY_CURRENT_USER\Network**).

You can specify different permissions for different types of access: read, write, delete, open, and create. Access can be specified either on a global basis or to specific portions of the registry using wildcard masks for either included keys or excluded keys.

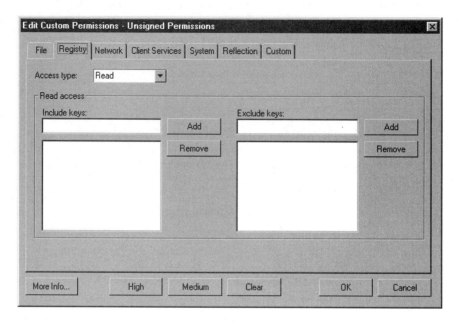

Option	Description
Access type	Select either **Read**, **Write**, **Delete**, **Create**, or **Open** to specify that applets can have read, write, delete, create, or open access to the included registry keys.
Read access	
Include keys	Enter the registry keys you want to include for the selected access type.
Exclude keys	Enter the registry keys you want to exclude from the selected access type.
Security level	
High	Click to set the security level to High (most secure).
Medium	Click to set the security level to Medium.
Clear	Click to clear all options and settings on this tab.

Network tab

Use the **Network** tab to specify the type of connections you will allow, and to which hosts and ports. By default, all hosts and ports are excluded, so you do not need to specify hosts and ports to exclude, unless they are a subset of the hosts and ports you are including. You can specify different permissions for different types of connections: connect addresses, bind addresses, multicast, and global ports.

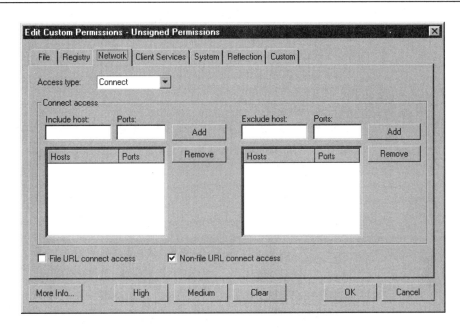

Option	Description
Access type	
Connect	Select to enable applets to have general communication to included hosts
Bind	Select to enable applets to connect to included hosts and ports.
Multicast	Select to enable applets to join specific multicast groups.
Global Ports	Select to enable applets to use communication settings that override the rules of the included ports.
Connect access	
Include host/Ports	Enter the hosts and ports that you want to enable applets to communicate with.
Exclude host/Ports	Enter the hosts and ports that you want to exclude from communicating with applets.
File URL connect access	Select to enable applets to connect to file:// URLs.
Non-file URL connect access	Select to enable applets to connect to non-file URLs.
Security level	
High	Click to set the security level to High (most secure).
Medium	Click to set the security level to Medium.
Clear	Click to clear all options and settings on this tab.

Client Services tab

Use the **Client Services** tab to specify which client resources and services Java applets can access for this permission set and zone.

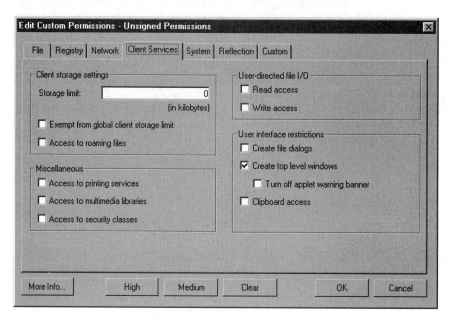

Option	Description
Client storage settings	
Storage limit	Enter the number of kilobytes of storage (scratch) space that applets can use on the client. Applets can access storage space determined by the size of the specified storage space and whether the storage space is private or global. Private storage space is encrypted and only available to the signed class or other classes signed by the same entity. Global storage space can be shared among arbitrary classes.
Exempt from global client storage limit	Select to enable applets to ignore the specified storage limits for all Internet files.
Access to roaming files	Select to enable roaming files to be created. Roaming files are created in the user's profile and are present on any computer the user is logged on to.

Option	Description
User-directed I/O	
Read access	Select to enable applets to read files on the client.
Write access	Select to enable applets to write to files on the client.
Miscellaneous	
Access to printing services	Select to enable applets to use the printing services.
Access to multimedia libraries	Select to enable applets to access the extended aspects of the DirectX™ APIs.
Access to security classes	Select to enable Java applets to access the JDK security classes java.lang.security.
User interface restrictions	
Create file dialogs	Select to enable applets to create file dialog boxes.
Create top level window	Select to enable applets to create a top-level window.
Turn off applet warning banner	Clear to display a warning when an applet requests to create a top-level window.
Clipboard access	Select to enable applets to use the client's clipboard to cut, copy, or paste information.
Security level	
High	Click to set the security level to High (most secure).
Medium	Click to set the security level to Medium.
Clear	Click to clear all options and settings on this tab.

System tab

Use the **System** tab to specify which operating system resources and services Java applets can access for this permission set and zone.

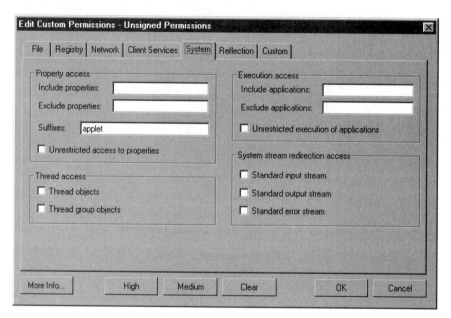

Option	Description
Property access	
Include properties	Enter the names of system properties that applets can access.
Exclude properties	Enter the names of system properties that you want to exclude applets from accessing.
Suffixes	Enter the suffixes of system properties that applets can access.
Unrestricted access to properties	Select to enable applets to have unrestricted access to system properties.
Thread access	
Thread objects	Select to enable unrestricted thread access for applets.
Thread group objects	Select to enable unrestricted thread group access for applets.

Option	Description
Execution access	
Include applications	Enter the names of applications that applets can run.
Exclude applications	Enter the names of applications that applets cannot run.
Unrestricted execution of applications	Select to enable unrestricted access for applets to run applications.
System stream redirection access	
Standard input stream	Select to enable applets to set the System.in stream.
Standard output stream	Select to enable applets to set the System.out stream.
Standard error stream	Select to enable applets to set the System.err stream.
Security level	
High	Click to set the security level to High (most secure).
Medium	Click to set the security level to Medium.
Clear	Click to clear all options and settings on this tab.

Note Java applets can read the system properties using the **System.getProperty** method. The following table lists the default system properties that can be read by applets.

Permission	Property
Java version	Java.version
Java vendor-specific string	Java.vendor
Java vendor URL	Java.vendor.url
Java class version number	Java.class.version
Operating System name	Os.name
User account name	User.name
User's home directory	User.home
User's current working directory	User.dir

Reflection tab

Use the **Reflection** tab to specify which Reflection APIs Java applets can access for this permission set and zone.

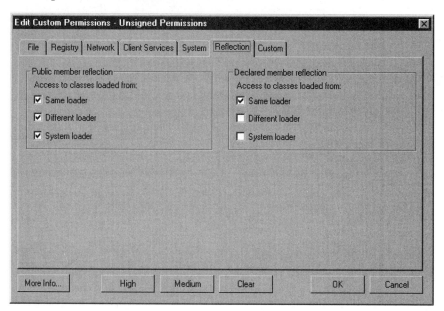

Option	Description
Public member reflection	
Same loader	Select to enable public reflective access to the reflection APIs for classes from the same loader.
Different loader	Select to enable public reflective access to the reflection APIs for classes from different loaders.
System loader	Select to enable public reflective access to the reflection APIs for classes from the system loader.
Declared member reflection	
Same loader	Select to enable declared reflective access to the reflection APIs for classes from the same loader.
Different loader	Select to enable declared reflective access to the reflection APIs for classes from different loaders.
System loader	Select to enable declared reflective access to the reflection APIs for classes from the system loader.
Security level	
High	Click to set the security level to High (most secure).
Medium	Click to set the security level to Medium.
Clear	Click to clear all options and settings on this tab.

Custom tab

Use the **Custom** tab to specify custom permission settings by class name and parameters. You can assign permissions to a Java class and specify what parameters are allowed.

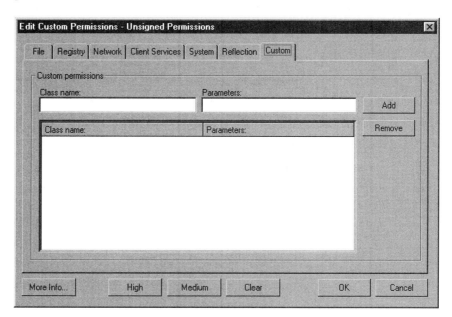

Option	Description
Custom permissions	
Class name	Enter the Java classes to include in this permission set.
Parameters	Enter the parameters that are allowed for the included Java classes.
Security level	
High	Click to set the security level to High (most secure).
Medium	Click to set the security level to Medium.
Clear	Click to clear all options and settings on this tab.

C H A P T E R   3 0

Content Advisor

In this chapter

Content Advisor Overview

Just as parents want assurances that children cannot visit Web sites that display inappropriate content, businesses often want to block the use of sites that offer no business value to their employees. To help meet these needs, the Content Advisor in Internet Explorer 4 can be used to control the types of content available through the browser. Parents or system administrators can adjust the content rating settings to reflect what they think is appropriate content in four areas: language, nudity, sex, and violence. Users can also subscribe to independent ratings bureaus and use third-party ratings to control access to Web content.

System administrators can use the Internet Explorer Administration Kit (IEAK) 4 Configuration Wizard to build and deploy custom packages with pre-configured Content Advisor settings for their user groups. Settings can also be locked down so they cannot be altered by end users. After browsers are deployed, administrators can use the IEAK Profile Manager to update Content Advisor settings through the automatic browser configuration feature of Internet Explorer.

Understanding Content Ratings

When you enable the Content Advisor, Internet Explorer 4 reads special tags placed in the HTML code of Web pages by content providers to determine whether that page meets your criteria for suitable content.

The most common content ratings are based on the Platform for Internet Content Selection (PICS) standard for defining and rating systems. PICS is an industry-developed technical standard that uses HTML meta tags to block access to Web pages based upon the values of the meta tags. For more information about PICS, visit **http://www.w3.org/PICS/**.

Internet Explorer 4 comes installed with the PICS-based RSACi content rating system. You can also subscribe to independent PICS ratings from other ratings bureaus. Or, you can import other content rating systems that meet your needs.

RSACi Content Ratings

RSACi is an open, objective, content rating system developed by the Recreational Software Advisory Council (RSAC), an independent, nonprofit organization. The RSACi system provides users with information about the level of sex, nudity, violence, offensive language (vulgar or hate-motivated) in software games and Web sites. For more information about RSAC and RASCi, see **http://www.rsac.org/**.

The following table shows the five levels of the RASCi rating system and describes the content *allowed* for each level in the four areas of content: language, nudity, sex, and violence. Level 0 is the most restrictive and level 4 the least restrictive.

Level	Violence Rating	Nudity Rating	Sex Rating	Language Rating
4	Rape or wanton, gratuitous violence	Frontal nudity qualifying as provocative display	Explicit sexual acts or sex crimes	Crude, vulgar language, or extreme hate speech
3	Aggressive violence or death to humans	Frontal nudity	Nonexplicit sexual acts	Strong language or hate speech
2	Destruction of realistic objects	Partial nudity	Clothed sexual touching	Moderate expletives or profanity
1	Injury to a human being	Revealing attire	Passionate kissing	Mild expletives
0	None of the above, or sports related	None of the above	None of the above or innocent kissing; romance	None of the above

You can set content ratings at any level from level 0 to level 4 in each of the four content areas. All content ratings are set at level 0 by default. When the Content Advisor is on and the PICS rating for a Web page exceeds the rating level you specify, users are prevented from accessing the page.

Web site publishers can obtain PICS content ratings from RSAC as well as a number of other nonprofit and fee-based ratings services. PICS ratings can be voluntarily added to Web sites by publishers.

You can also obtain independent PICS ratings from ratings bureaus. Ratings bureaus are typically fee-based and specialize in rating Internet sites. You can specify a ratings bureau for Internet Explorer to use to obtain PICS ratings for Web pages. Since Internet Explorer must contact the ratings bureau to obtain ratings, using ratings bureaus can slow down access to Web pages considerably.

You can configure Internet Explorer to prevent users from accessing Web pages without content ratings, or you can allow users to view unrated pages. For more information, see "Configuring Content Advisor" later in this chapter.

Other Rating Systems

Some Web publishers may rate their sites using rating systems that are not based on PICS. To use rating systems that are not based on PICS, you must subscribe to ratings services that support the non-PICS rating system and then import the rating system so Internet Explorer can use it to rate Web content. For more information, visit the Web sites of the ratings services and see "Configuring Content Advisor" later in this chapter.

Supervisor Password

The first time you turn Content Advisor on, you'll need to specify a supervisor password. The supervisor password allows administrators or supervisors to turn Content Advisor on or off and change Content Advisor settings for users.

In addition, you can configure Internet Explorer to allow users to display restricted Web pages by typing the supervisor password. When users attempt to access restricted content, the **Content Advisor** dialog box queries users to enter the supervisor password to optionally view restricted content. Or, you can also disable the option to enter the supervisor password to view restricted content. For more information, see "Configuring Content Advisor" later in this chapter.

Configuring Content Advisor

The Content Advisor is turned on and off by using the **Content** tab. You can use the Content Advisor **Ratings**, **General**, and **Advanced** tabs to configure the Content Advisor settings Internet Explorer uses to restrict user access to Web content.

▶   **To access the Content Advisor**

1. From the **View** menu, click **Internet Options**.

2. Click the **Content** tab.

▶ **To turn on Content Advisor**

1. On the **Content** tab, under **Content Advisor**, click **Enable**.

2. Enter the *supervisor password* when queried.

   The Content Advisor controls users' access to restricted Web content.

▶ **To turn off Content Advisor**

1. On the **Content** tab, under **Content Advisor**, click **Disable**.

2. Enter the *supervisor password* when queried.

   The Content Advisor no longer restricts Web content.

▶ **To configure content ratings**

1. On the **Content** tab, under **Content Advisor**, click **Settings**.

2. In the **Content Advisor** dialog box, on the **Ratings** tab, select the **Language**, **Nudity**, **Sex**, or **Violence** ratings category.

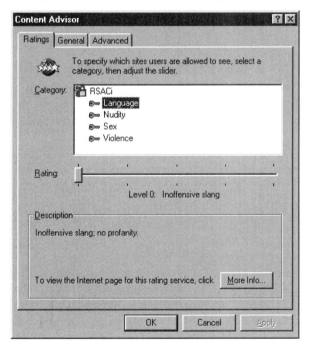

3. Click the **Rating** slider, and move the slider to the content level you want to allow users to access for the ratings category.

   The default settings for each content category is level 0, which is the most restrictive setting. Level 4 is the least restrictive setting. For more information about ratings levels, see "Content Ratings" earlier in this chapter.

▶ **To configure user options**

1. In the **Content Advisor** dialog box, click the **General** tab.

2. Select the **User options** you want.

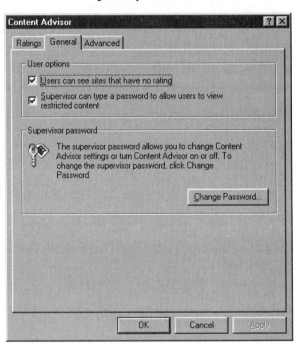

Option	Description
Users can see sites that have no rating	Clear to restrict access to Web pages that are not rated. Select to allow users to display Web pages that are not rated.
Supervisor can type a password to allow users to view restricted content	Clear to prevent users from optionally viewing restricted content by entering the supervisor password. Select to query users for the supervisor password when they attempt to view restricted content. When selected, users can display restricted content by entering the supervisor password at the **Content Advisor** dialog box.

▶ **To change the supervisor password**

1. In the **Content Advisor** dialog box, on the **General** tab, click **Change Password**.

2. In the **Old password** box, type the old supervisor password to verify that you are authorized to change Content Advisor settings.

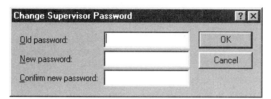

3. In the **New password** box, type the new password.

4. In the **Confirm new password** box, type the new password again.

5. Click **OK**.

▶ **To import new rating systems and ratings bureaus**

1. If necessary, install rating systems files following the directions provided by the ratings service.

2. In the **Content Advisor** dialog box, click the **Advanced** tab.

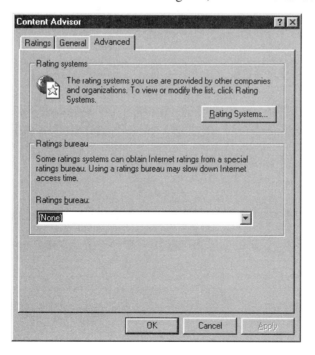

3. Click **Rating Systems**.

4. In the **Rating Systems** dialog box, select the rating system's rating (.rat) file from the list, and click **Add**.

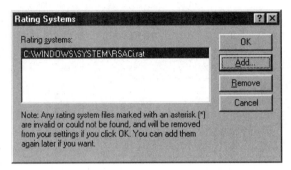

5. If this service uses a ratings bureau, select the ratings bureau from the **Ratings bureau** list.

6. Click **OK**.

You can now use the new rating system to set Web content restrictions following the instructions provided by the ratings service.

Deploying Content Advisor Settings to User Groups

Administrators can use the IEAK Configuration Wizard to build and deploy custom packages with pre-configured Content Advisor settings for user groups. (For more information, see "Building Custom Packages" in Chapter 36.)

You start by configuring the Content Advisor settings on the computer running the IEAK Configuration Wizard and then import the settings using the **Security Zones and Content Ratings Customization** page of the wizard. You can also open the Content Advisor and modify the settings from the **Security Zones and Content Ratings Customization** page.

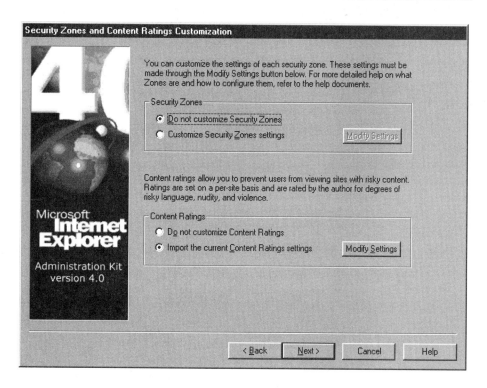

▶ **To import Content Advisor settings**

1. On the **Security Zones and Content Ratings Customization** page, select **Import the current Content Ratings settings**.

2. To modify the current Content Advisor settings, click **Modify Settings** and use the Content Advisor **Ratings**, **General**, and **Advanced** tabs to configure the Content Advisor settings. (For more information, see the previous section.)

3. Click **Next**.

4. Finish building the custom package.

The Content Advisor configuration you import from the current desktop will then be installed on users' desktops when the custom package is deployed. You can also lock down Content Advisor settings so users cannot modify the settings even if they know the supervisor password.

Locking Down Content Advisor Settings

You can use the IEAK Configuration Wizard to build and deploy custom packages and lock down Content Advisor settings so users cannot modify the settings even if they know the supervisor password. After browsers have been deployed, you can use the IEAK Profile Manager to lock down Content Advisor changes for user groups that have automatic browser configuration implemented.

To lock down Content Advisor options, perform the following steps at the **System Policies and Restrictions** page of the IEAK Wizard or at the IEAK Profile Manager:

1. In the **System Policies & Restrictions** hierarchy, select **Internet Restrictions**, and then select the **Content** object.

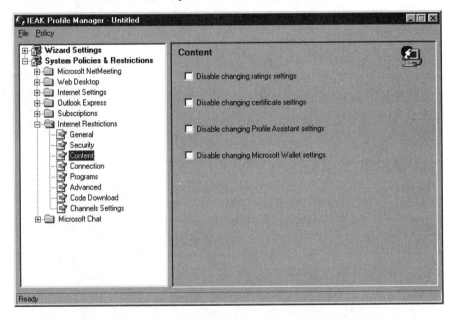

Note The IEAK Profile Manager is shown here, but the **System Policies and Restrictions** page of the IEAK Configuration Wizard works similarly.

2. In the **Content** pane, select **Disable changing ratings settings** to prevent users from changing Content Advisor settings even if they know the supervisor password.

3. Save your changes to the auto-configuration (.ins) file or finish building the custom package, as appropriate.

Managing Content Advisor Settings for Deployed Browsers

You can use the IEAK Profile Manager in conjunction with automatic browser configuration to update Content Advisor settings for deployed browsers. (For more information, see "Building Custom Packages" in Chapter 36.)

To change Content Advisor settings for a user group, you configure the Content Advisor settings on the machine running the IEAK Profile Manager and then use the Profile Manager to import the configuration. Then save the new configuration settings to the auto-configuration files for the user group. When automatic browser configuration is refreshed at users' computers, users' desktops are configured with the new Content Advisor settings you have specified.

▶ **To change Content Advisor settings for a user group**

1. Run the IEAK Profile Manager.

2. Open the auto-configuration (.ins) file for the user group.

3. In the left pane, select **Wizard Settings**, and then select **Security Zones and Content Ratings Customization**.

4. In the right pane, under **Content Ratings**, select **Import the current Content Ratings settings**.

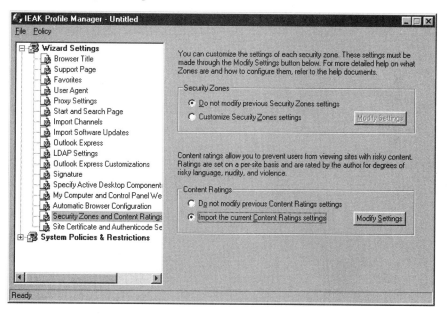

5. Click **Modify Settings**, and use the **Content Advisor Ratings**, **General**, and **Advanced** tabs to configure the Content Advisor settings. (For more information, see "Configuring Content Advisor" earlier in this chapter.)

6. On the **File** menu, click **Save** to save changes to the auto-configuration file.

Changes are made to users' configurations as scheduled by automatic browser configuration.

C H A P T E R   3 1

User Privacy

Understanding User Privacy

Internet Explorer 4 supports a wide range of Internet privacy standards and provides many features and options to help ensure user privacy on the Web. When you communicate over the Web, you want to know that what you send and receive cannot be intercepted or deciphered and that your passwords and other private information cannot be used by others. You also want to be sure that nobody can access information on your computer without your knowledge. Internet Explorer 4 protects your privacy in two key ways: it supports the latest Internet security and privacy standards; and it provides encryption and identification capabilities that ensure the Internet e-mail you send cannot be read or tampered with.

Secure Communications

Internet Explorer 4 supports the latest Internet security standards to block anyone from eavesdropping on your electronic communications. It supports the Secure Sockets Layer (SSL) and Private Communications Technology (PCT) protocols, so you can securely send information over the Internet. SSL and PCT protocols are used to create a secure channel that prevents anyone from eavesdropping on your communications over the Web.

When a Web site you are browsing supports SSL or PCT, Internet Explorer displays a lock icon in the browser's status bar at the bottom of your computer screen. When you see this lock, you know that you can safely send information over the Internet to the site you are browsing. You can configure Internet Explorer to allow SSL and PCT communications. For more information, see "Configuring User Privacy Security Options" later in this chapter.

In addition, Outlook™ Express (the e-mail and newsgroup program in Internet Explorer 4) also lets you encrypt your messages and use a personal digital signature to ensure that your identity is protected over the Internet. For more information on Outlook Express, see Chapter 18.

Zone-Based Password Security Protection

Internet Explorer prompts you before you transmit your user name or password to sites you haven't designated as Trusted in the security zones settings. For sites you do trust, you can configure security zones to send information without prompting you. For more information on security zones, see Chapter 27, "Security Zones."

Control over Cookies

An HTTP cookie is a small file that an individual Web site stores on your computer to provide customization features. For example, when you set custom settings on MSN™, The Microsoft Network, that information is stored in a cookie file on your computer. MSN then reads the cookie each time you visit the site. That's how MSN knows which options to display.

You can configure Internet Explorer to handle cookies in the following ways:

- Prevent cookies from being stored on your computer.
- Query you whether you want to accept cookies from the site.
- Allow cookies to be stored on your computer without notifying you.

For more information, see "Configuring User Privacy Security Options" later in this chapter.

Note Accepting a cookie does not give a Web site access to your computer or any personal information about you other than what you have specified in the customized settings for that site.

Profile Assistant

The Profile Assistant makes it easy for you to share registration and demographic information with Web sites that request this information, while maintaining your privacy and safety. The Profile Assistant saves you from having to repeatedly enter the same information, such as your name and e-mail address, every time you visit a new Web site. None of this information can be viewed on your computer or shared with others without your permission.

The Profile Assistant supports the Internet privacy model defined by the Platform for Privacy Preferences (P3), a World Wide Web Consortium (W3C) project. Basically, the P3 privacy model enables personal information to be exchanged between users and Web sites, while respecting the user's right to privacy. Users can store personal information in user profiles in secure, encrypted information stores on their computers and can choose whether to share the information upon request. Web sites can request information from users' profiles, but are not allowed to access profile information unless the users consent. Since the Profile Assistant complies with the Internet's P3 privacy standards, it can also work with other Internet programs and servers. (For information about how to write scripts to access Profile Assistant information, see the *Microsoft Internet Client SDK.*)

When a Web site requests information from your user profile, the **Profile Assistant** dialog box opens.

You can use the **Profile Assistant** dialog box to verify who is requesting information, choose which information (if any) to share, and understand how the Web site intends to use the information.

Option	Description
'*Requester name*' has requested information from you	Displays the name of the requester. This can be an individual or an organization.
Site	Displays the URL of the site requesting information from the user profile.
Profile information requested	Displays the list of information items requested. In the example shown: **First Name**, **Last Name**, **Email**, **Business Phone**, and **Fax (Business)**. Clear the check box for any items you don't want to send to the requester.

Option	Description
Always allow this site to see checked items	Select this option to add this site to a list of sites you allow to access your Profile Assistant information without notifying you. You can clear the list from the **Content** tab by clicking the **Reset Sharing** button.
Edit Profile	Click this button to open the **User Profile** dialog box where you can edit the profile information to be sent to this site. For example, you could change your fax number to send a new fax number to the site.
Privacy	Displays a message explaining whether the information you are sharing will be secure when it is sent over the Internet. It also displays a message describing how the requester intends to use this information.

Web sites can request up to 29 different items of information from your user profile. For more information, see "Configuring Profile Assistant" later in this chapter.

Microsoft Wallet

Microsoft Wallet is a software payment program that you can used to conduct secure financial transactions over the Web with sites that support the Wallet. You can use the Wallet to securely store private information, such as credit card account information, for making payments over the Internet. You decide what to put in Microsoft Wallet, who gets to see it, and who gets to use it. Once you've entered information into Microsoft Wallet, you'll never have to retype it.

The Wallet includes a protected storage area where your private information is stored. The information in the Wallet's protected storage area is encrypted and can only be accessed and viewed by you.

The Wallet supports all industry-standard payment methods, including Secure Sockets Layer (SSL) and Secure Electronic Transaction (SET), to enable the secure, electronic use of credit cards. The Wallet also supports add-on payment methods, such as digital cash and electronic checks, as required by merchants and financial institutions. Users obtain the payment method add-on and instructions on how to install and use the add-on from the appropriate merchant or financial institution.

The Wallet provides the **Address Options** dialog box and the **Payment Options** dialog box to store your address and payment information separately. You can use the **Address Options** dialog box to enter, store, and access addresses that can be referenced for shipping and billing during online order entry. Names, e-mail addresses, and telephone numbers of Wallet users can be viewed in the Address Book.

You can use the **Payment Options** dialog box to enter, securely store, and access various types of payment methods for making online purchases. This information is protected with a password you define. When you shop at an Internet store that supports the Wallet, the site may prompt you to select payment methods stored in the Wallet and authorize payment by typing your password.

For more information, see "Configuring Microsoft Wallet" later in this chapter.

Configuring Privacy Options

To configure the Internet Explorer privacy options, use the **Content** and **Advanced** tabs.

▶ **To open the Content tab**

1. From the **View** menu, click **Internet Options**.

2. Click the **Content** tab (or, when you're ready, click the **Advanced** tab).

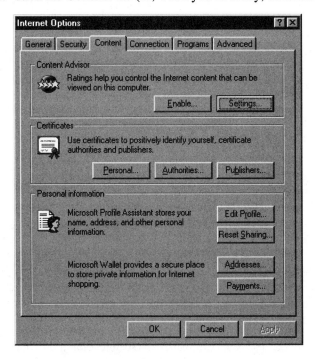

Configuring Profile Assistant

You can use the **User Profile** dialog box to configure your user profile to share with Web sites. The **User Profile** dialog box contains six tabs and is used by other Internet programs, including NetMeeting™ conferencing software and Outlook Express. The Profile Assistant uses information from the **Personal**, **Home**, **Business**, and **Other** tabs to create your user profile. You can access the **User Profile** dialog box from the **Content** tab.

▶ **To create or edit a user profile**

1. On the **Content** tab, click **Edit Profile**.
2. In the appropriate boxes on the **Personal**, **Home**, **Business**, and **Other** tabs, type the information you want to share.

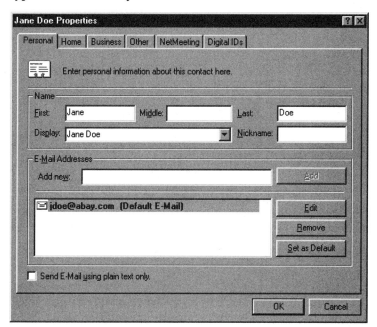

User profiles can include the following information:

Personal Tab	Home Tab	Business Tab	Other Tab
First name	Home street address	Company name	Notes
Middle name	Home city	Business street address	
Last name	Home state/province	Business city	
Display name	Home zip code	Business state/province	
	Home country	Business country	
Default e-mail address	Home phone	Business zip code	
	Home fax	Job title	
	Home cellular phone	Department	
	Gender	Office	
	Personal Web page URL	Business phone	
		Business fax	
		Business pager	
		Business Web page URL	

3. Click **OK**.

   The Profile Assistant creates your user profile using the information you specify and saves the profile in the protected information store.

You can use the **Advanced** tab to disable sites from requesting the information in the Profile Assistant. For more information, see "Configuring User Privacy Security Options" later in this chapter.

Configuring Microsoft Wallet

You can use the Microsoft Wallet **Address Options** and **Payment Options** dialog boxes to configure the information you can use for payments over the Internet. You can access the Wallet dialog boxes from the **Content** tab.

▶ **To add or edit addresses used for payments**

1. On the **Content** tab, click **Addresses**.

2. Click **Add** to add a new address or **Edit** to edit an existing address.

3. In the **Add a New Address** dialog box, type the Name and Address information, or click **Address Book** to select an existing address from the Address Book.

Note The **Add a New Address** dialog box is shown here, but the **Edit a New Address** dialog box is identical except for the title.

---

4. In the **Display name** box, type a display name to be used for this address.

5. Click **Home** to indicate a home address, or click **Business** to indicate a business address.

6. Click **OK**.

▶ **To add payment methods to the Wallet**

1. On the **Content** tab, click **Payments**.

2. On the **Payment Options** dialog box, click **Methods**.

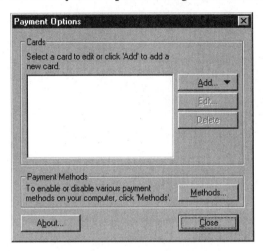

3. On the **Select Payment Methods** dialog box, from the **Installed Payment Methods** list, select the credit cards you want to be available to the Wallet.

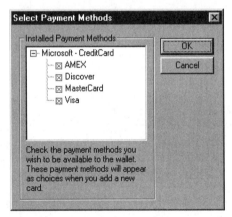

4. Click **OK**.

   These credit cards become available, so you can now use the **Payment Options** dialog box to add your personal account information to the Wallet.

▶ **To add personal credit card information**

1. In the **Payment Options** dialog box, click **Add** to add a credit card to the list of payment options.

2. On the list of credit cards, click the credit card you want to add and use the Add a New Credit Card Wizard to add the credit card.

You must provide your credit card account information and a password. You will need to enter this password before you can use the credit card to make a payment or edit the credit card information. This way, another person cannot sit down at your computer to make purchases on the Internet. Internet Explorer encrypts and stores this information in the Wallet's protected storage area.

Configuring User Privacy Security Options

You can configure a variety of user-privacy security options for Internet Explorer. These options appear in the **Advanced** tab, under the **Security** object.

▶ **To configure advanced security options**

1. From the **View** menu, click **Internet Options**.

2. Click the **Advanced** tab.

3. Select or clear options under the **Security** object.

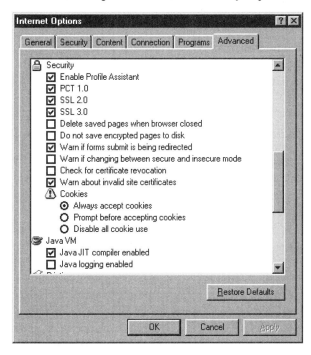

Option	Description
Enable Profile Assistant	Clear to prevent sites from requesting user profile information. When this check box is cleared, you will not be queried to provide information to Web sites.
PCT 1.0	Select if you want to send and receive secured information through PCT, a protocol developed by Microsoft that is significantly more secure than SSL 2. Note that some Web sites might not support this protocol.
SSL 2.0	Select if you want to send and receive secured information through SSL Level 2, the standard protocol for secure transmissions. All secure Web sites support this protocol.
SSL 3.0	Select if you want to send and receive secured information through SSL Level 3, a proprietary protocol that is intended to be more secure than SSL 2. Note that some Web sites might not support this protocol.
Delete saved pages when browser closed	Select to delete all secure Web pages from the Internet Explorer cache whenever you exit Internet Explorer. You cannot browse secure Web sites or Active Channel content offline after secure pages have been deleted from the cache.
Do not save encrypted pages to disk	Select to specify that secured information is not saved to your hard disk. This is useful if you are using Internet Explorer from a shared server and you do not want other people to see your secure information.
Warn if forms submit is being redirected	Select for Internet Explorer to query you whether to submit a Web-based form if the information is sent to a different Web location than the one on which the Web page form resides.
Warn if changing between secure and insecure mode	Select for Internet Explorer to warn you when you are switching between Internet sites that are and are not secure.
Check for certificate revocation	Select for Internet Explorer to check digital certificates from Web sites to see if they have been revoked before accepting certificates as valid.
Cookies	
Warn about invalid site certificates	Select for Internet Explorer to warn you when addresses (URLs) in digital certificates from Web sites are not valid.
Always accept cookies	Select if you want Internet Explorer to accept cookies without prompting you first.
Prompt before accepting cookies	Select for Internet Explorer to query you whether you want to accept a cookie from a Web site.
Disable all cookie use	Select to prevent cookies from being stored on your computer. When selected, Web site requests to store cookies are automatically denied without notifying you.

4. Click **OK**.

P A R T 8

Internet Explorer 4 Accessibility

Microsoft® Internet Explorer 4 introduces a number of advances that make the Web more accessible to computer users with disabilities. In particular, several features allow users to customize the appearance of Web pages to meet their own needs and preferences. Internet Explorer 4 also includes the best features of Internet Explorer 3, including the ability to navigate the Web using the keyboard. Users without disabilities may also be interested in many of these options as ways to customize colors and fonts to their own tastes or to save time using keyboard shortcuts. Part 8 describes the features in Internet Explorer that support enhanced accessibility and explains how to use them to accommodate different accessibility needs.

Chapter 32: Accessibility Overview

This chapter outlines the accessibility benefits offered by the new features in Internet Explorer 4 and lists some upgrade considerations for users transitioning from Internet Explorer 3. It also offers an outline of accessibility features and functions that are recommended for users with different types of disabilities, including users who are blind, have low vision, are deaf or hard-of-hearing, have physical impairments, have seizure disorders, or have cognitive or language impairments. In addition, this chapter provides an extensive list of other accessibility resources, including telephone numbers, postal addresses, and Web sites.

Chapter 33: Accessibility Features and Functionality

This chapters details procedures and shortcut keys for using keyboard navigation of the Internet Explorer browser, the Windows® Desktop Update, the Internet Explorer Help tool, and Web pages. Plus, it offers shortcut keys for the new AutoComplete feature. It details procedures for customizing the display of fonts, colors, and formatting on Web pages, the Help tool, and on the Windows Desktop Update. It also explains how to configure a wide range of advanced Internet accessibility options, such as disabling or enabling sounds, graphics, and animations; the use of smooth scrolling; and the treatment of hyperlinks. The last section discusses the accessibility features of NetMeeting™ and offers keyboard shortcuts.

Note Not all accessibility features were completed when Internet Explorer 4.0 first shipped. Internet Explorer 4.01 contains significant accessibility enhancements. The information presented in Part 8 assumes users are working with version 4.01. To find version information about your current copy of Internet Explorer, go to the **Help** menu, and select **About Internet Explorer**. If it says, "Version 4.72.2106.8," or later, then you are using Internet Explorer 4.01. Version 4.01 is available for free download at **http://www.microsoft.com/ie/ie40/download/**. For Active Setup information, to easily download just the updated files you need, see Part 1, Chapter 2, "Phase 1: Active Setup."

C H A P T E R   3 2

Accessibility Overview

Accessibility Benefits

Microsoft is committed to making computers easier to use for everyone, including individuals with disabilities. In recent years, Microsoft has established close relationships with users who have disabilities, organizations representing such individuals, workers in the rehabilitation field, and software developers who create products for this market. Internet Explorer 4 includes many new features that benefit users with disabilities. The most important new features allow users to:

- **Control how Web pages are displayed.** You can customize the colors of background, text, and hyperlinks based on your preference. You can control the size and typeface of fonts for all the Web pages you view by installing your own style sheet. Style sheets can also be used to make headings larger or to highlight italicized text with a different color. Any feature you choose for Web pages can also be used with the Active Desktop™ interface, Windows Explorer, and Internet Explorer Help. Users who like large fonts can also take advantage of the new scrolling menus, which prevent large menus from running off the screen.

- **Work better with screen readers and other accessibility aids.** Internet Explorer uses the new HTML 4 standard, which lets Web-page designers add additional information, such as the name of an image or control, that is useful to blind individuals who use screen readers. You can choose to turn off smooth scrolling and other effects that can confuse screen-reading utilities. The Dynamic HTML Object Model in Internet Explorer 4 makes possible exciting new classes of add-on utilities for Internet Explorer. Some, such as PowerToys, provide important features for users with disabilities. PowerToys offer the ability to zoom in on Web pages, view a framed page in its own frame, and conduct searches more easily. (For more information about PowerToys, visit **http://www.microsoft.com/ie/ie40/powertoys/**.)

- **Reduce the amount of typing required.** Using the AutoComplete feature, Internet Explorer 4 makes it easier for users to enter long or repetitive URLs. AutoComplete finishes typing URLs based on a cached history of sites you've visited before and an automatic domain-searching feature. Explorer bars for Search, History, Favorites, and Active Channels make it easier to find the things you need, things you've seen, or Web pages you use most often. The improved QuickLinks toolbar makes it even easier to return to the sites you visit the most.

- **Customize layout to make it easier to perform the tasks you need.** The Windows Desktop Update, an optional set of features of Internet Explorer 4, allows you to further customize your desktop, **Start** menu, and taskbar. Choose from a range of desktop toolbars, or create your own. Your Web **Favorites** menu can now be accessed from the **Start** menu, for faster access to the sites you choose. The new Address bar allows you to enter URLs directly from your Windows desktop, without having to launch the browser first. Shortcuts to the programs and folders you use the most can be set in a custom, dockable toolbar, for one-click access any time.

- **Have the information you need "pushed" to you.** The Webcasting features in Internet Explorer 4 allow you to spend less time searching and less effort navigating. Now you can subscribe to Web sites and be automatically notified of updates to the site. You can even schedule automatic downloads of updated information for easy, offline viewing. (For more information, see Part 4, "Information Delivery: Webcasting.")

- **Get better feedback.** Two new sound events, Start Navigation and Complete Navigation, have been added to the sounds list in Control Panel to signal when a Web page begins loading and when it finishes loading. These optional sounds can be helpful to users who are blind or have low vision. You can also set the appearance of hyperlinks to show when they are activated or rolled over with a mouse.

- **Use a mouse with greater ease.** With the Windows Desktop Update, you can choose to single-click instead of double-clicking to initiate common computer operations such as opening folders. And you can put the most commonly used commands and shortcuts on desktop toolbars where they are always one click away.

- **Communicate.** Microsoft NetMeeting delivers a complete Internet conferencing solution that can greatly enhance accessibility for users with a wide range of disabilities. NetMeeting users can experience the benefits of real-time, multipoint communication that allows them to collaborate and share information with two or more conference participants at the same time. NetMeeting offers a powerful set of data conferencing features, as well as audio and video conferencing.

In addition, features carried over from Internet Explorer 3 include the ability to:

- **Navigate with the keyboard.** Users can key through pages, panes, hyperlinks, toolbars, and other controls.

- **Replace images with textual descriptions.**

- **Turn off pictures, videos, and sounds.**

- **Use the High Contrast option.** This Windows option allows users to choose a simple color scheme and omit images that make text difficult for them to read.

Upgrade Considerations

Significant changes in architecture between Internet Explorer 4 and Internet Explorer 3 may affect the functionality of certain accessibility aids written for version 3. It is recommended that users test Internet Explorer 4 with their equipment to determine the specific places where its behavior differs from version 3. Also contact the vendor of your adaptive aids to find out how they work with Internet Explorer 4. The modular structure of Internet Explorer 4 makes it easy to customize the feature set by installing or uninstalling components based on the functionality that works best for you. Many features can also be turned on or off, according to your preferences.

Depending on each person's specific needs, different users may find challenges with different aspects of Internet Explorer 4, but the following list details a few general considerations when upgrading to version 4:

- Users who rely on keyboard navigation should be aware that the Help tool in Internet Explorer 4 works differently than in Internet Explorer 3. Most of the functionality is available through the keyboard, although some features, such as hyperlinks, are not accessible from the keyboard. All hyperlinked topics, however, are also listed in the Help Contents and Index, which are completely accessible from the keyboard.

- When navigating to a Web page, Internet Explorer 4 always sets the keyboard focus to the beginning of the page. When returning to a visited page, Internet Explorer 4 resets the keyboard focus to the beginning of the page. Internet Explorer 3 would allow you to continue navigating from the point of your last link—the last place you had visited on the page.

- Internet Explorer 4 allows you to navigate through links using the TAB key, just as you did in version 3. However, version 4 will also allow navigating to objects that are not currently visible on the screen. This may result in the keyboard focus seeming to "disappear" at times. Simply pressing TAB additional times will bring it back into view.

- The Windows Desktop Update in Internet Explorer 4 replaces the traditional **Start** menu with a scrolling **Start** menu that supports dragging, so that menu items can be rearranged. However, this type of menu limits the number of menu commands visible at one time to those that fit in a single column. Although long menu lists won't display all at once, all menu items are navigable by keyboard. Still, users who need to keep as many options as possible on the screen at one time and who currently have many commands on their **Start** menu may want to remove some commands from the **Start** menu and use the new desktop toolbar, the Quick Launch toolbar, or the custom toolbar feature to make those commands available from other places on the desktop. (See Part 3, Chapter 12, "Start Menu and Taskbar" for more information.)

- Users may have some difficulty reading the descriptions of images when the images are not displayed. Internet Explorer 3 allowed you to choose to display the entire description, whereas version 4 may cut off portions of those descriptions. Internet Explorer support for HTML 4, however, now allows you read the full descriptions of images while they are displayed.

- Internet Explorer 4 uses menus and check boxes that may not be described correctly by some blind-access utilities. If you choose the Windows Desktop Update option when installing Internet Explorer, these menus will also be used in Windows Explorer. It is recommended that you test these features with your adaptive aid to see if there any problems. Also contact the vendor of your aid to find out if there are any upgrades that may better support Internet Explorer 4.

Suggested Features for Different Types of Disabilities

The following lists are suggestions of features that may be useful to users with certain types of disabilities. These lists are not complete, as the needs and preferences of individuals vary, and many people have a combination of disabilities or differing abilities.

Features for Users Who Are Blind

Many users who are blind use screen readers—assisting software that provides a spoken or Braille description of windows, controls, menus, images, text, and other information that is typically displayed visually on a screen. Internet Explorer 4 provides improved functionality for screen readers and offers a range of other features and options that can be helpful to blind individuals.

The list below recommends specific settings and features that can benefit users who are blind. To learn about any of these features or for procedures that explain how to configure a certain setting, see the next chapter, "Accessibility Features and Functionality."

- Use keyboard navigation for Internet Explorer, Web pages, the Active Desktop, Internet Explorer Help, and NetMeeting.
- Use the Accessibility options on the **General** tab of the **Internet Options** dialog box to:
    - Ignore colors specified on Web pages.
    - Ignore font styles specified on Web pages.
    - Ignore font sizes specified on Web pages.
    - Format documents using your own style sheet.

- Use the **Advanced** tab on the **Internet Options** dialog box to:
    - Always expand alternate text for images.
    - Move the system caret with focus/selection changes.
    - Disable smooth scrolling.
    - Select not to show pictures in Web pages.
    - Select not to play animations in Web pages.
    - Select not to play videos in Web pages.
    - Disable smart image dithering.
- Use the **Sounds Properties** dialog box from Control Panel to:
    - Assign a sound to the Start Navigation event.
    - Assign a sound to the Complete Navigation event.

Features for Users with Low Vision

Common forms of low vision are color blindness, difficulty in changing focus, and impaired contrast sensitivity. Users with color blindness may have difficulty reading colored text on a colored background. Users who have difficulty changing focus or who experience eye strain with normal use of a video display may have difficulty reading small text, discriminating between different font sizes, or using small on-screen items as targets for the cursor or pointer. Users with impaired contrast sensitivity may have difficulty reading black text on a gray background. Individuals with low vision sometimes use magnification software or hardware, and as a result, may prefer to use keyboard shortcuts to make the selection of on-screen elements easier than it would be using the mouse.

The list below recommends specific settings and features that can benefit users who have low vision. To learn about any of these features or for procedures that explain how to configure a certain setting, see the next chapter, "Accessibility Features and Functionality."

- Use keyboard navigation for Internet Explorer, Web pages, the Active Desktop, Internet Explorer Help, and NetMeeting.
- Use the Accessibility options on the **General** tab of the **Internet Options** dialog box to:
    - Ignore colors specified on Web pages.
    - Ignore font styles specified on Web pages.
    - Ignore font sizes specified on Web pages.
    - Format documents using your own style sheet.

- Use the **Advanced** tab on the **Internet Options** dialog box to:
    - Always expand alternate text for images.
    - Move the system caret with focus/selection changes.
    - Disable printing of background color and images.
    - Select to show the **Font** button in the browser toolbar.
    - Select not to display small icons.
- Use the **Colors** options on the **General** tab on the **Internet Options** dialog box to:
    - Choose text and background colors for Web pages (or create custom colors).
    - Choose the visited and unvisited colors for Web links (or create custom colors).
    - Choose to display Web pages using the Windows High Contrast color scheme, which offers a simple color palette and omits images that make text difficult to read.
- Use the **Sounds Properties** dialog box from Control Panel to:
    - Assign a sound to the Start Navigation event.
    - Assign a sound to the Complete Navigation event.

Features for Users Who Are Deaf or Hard-of-Hearing

Sound cues in programs are not useful to users with hearing impairments or users working in a noisy environment. Users who are deaf may have sign language as their primary language and English as their secondary language, and as a result, they may have difficulty reading pages that use custom fonts, depart from typographical convention—such as mixing uppercase and lowercase letters—or use animated text displays.

The list below recommends specific settings and features that can benefit users who are deaf or hard-of-hearing. To learn about any of these features or for procedures that explain how to configure a certain setting, see the next chapter, "Accessibility Features and Functionality."

Note Users who are deaf and have sign language as their primary language and English as a second language may also be interested in the features recommended for users with cognitive or language impairments.

- Use the **Accessibility Properties** dialog box from Windows Control Panel to select SoundSentry, which generates visual warnings when your system makes a sound.

- Use the **Accessibility Properties** dialog box from Windows Control Panel to select ShowSounds, which displays captions for the speech and sounds the system makes.

- Integrate NetMeeting.

- Use the **Advanced** tab on the **Internet Options** dialog box to disable sounds in Web pages.

Features for Users with Physical Impairments

Some users are unable to perform certain manual tasks, such as using a mouse or typing two keys at the same time. Others may have a tendency to hit multiple keys, "bounce" fingers off keys, or be unable to hold a printed book. Many users need keyboards and mouse functions to be adapted to their requirements. Others rely exclusively on a single input device.

The list below recommends specific settings and features that can benefit users who have physical impairments. To learn about any of these features or for procedures that explain how to configure a certain setting, see the next chapter, "Accessibility Features and Functionality."

- Use keyboard navigation and shortcuts for Internet Explorer, Web pages, the Active Desktop, Internet Explorer Help, and NetMeeting.

- Use Explorer bars.

- Use Webcasting to subscribe to Web sites and Active Channels. (For more information, see Part 4, "Information Delivery: Webcasting.")

- Use the Accessibility options on the **General** tab of the **Internet Options** dialog box to:

  - Ignore font sizes specified on Web pages.

  - Format documents using your own style sheet.

- Use the **Colors** box on the **General** tab of the **Internet Options** dialog box to add hover colors to hyperlinks.

- Use the **Advanced** tab on the **Internet Options** dialog box to:

  - Always expand alternate text for images.

  - Move the system caret with focus/selection changes.

  - Choose to use AutoComplete.

  - Underline hyperlinks when hovering (rolling over them).

  - Select to show the **Font** button in the browser toolbar.

  - Select not to display small icons.

Features for Users with Seizure Disorders

Users with seizure disorders (such as epilepsy) may be sensitive to screen refresh rates, blinking or flashing images, or specific sounds.

The list below recommends specific settings and features that can benefit users who have seizure disorders. To learn about any of these features or for procedures that explain how to configure a certain setting, see the next chapter, "Accessibility Features and Functionality."

- Use the ESC key to immediately turn off animations.
- Use the **Advanced** tab on the **Internet Options** dialog box to:
  - Disable animation.
  - Disable video.
  - Turn off sounds.

Note   If RealAudio is installed, or if a movie is playing, sound might play, even if you clear the **Play sound** check box on the **Internet Options** dialog box.

Features for Users with Cognitive and Language Impairments

Cognitive impairments take many forms, including short-term and long-term memory loss, perceptual differences, and developmental disabilities. Language impairments, such as dyslexia or illiteracy, are also quite common. Even people learning the language used by their computer software as a second language can be considered to have a form of language impairment.

The list below recommends specific settings and features that can benefit users who have cognitive or language impairments. To learn about any of these features or for procedures that explain how to configure a certain setting, see the next chapter, "Accessibility Features and Functionality."

- Use keyboard navigation and shortcuts for Internet Explorer, Web pages, the Active Desktop, Internet Explorer Help, and NetMeeting.
- Use Explorer bars.
- Use Webcasting to subscribe to Web sites and Active Channels. (For more information, see Part 4, "Information Delivery: Webcasting.")
- Use the Accessibility options on the **General** tab of the **Internet Options** dialog box to:
  - Ignore colors specified on Web pages.
  - Ignore font styles specified on Web pages.
  - Ignore font sizes specified on Web pages.
  - Format documents using your own style sheet.

- Use the **Colors** options on the **General** tab on the **Internet Options** dialog box to:
  - Choose text and background colors for Web pages (or create custom colors).
  - Choose the visited and unvisited colors for Web links (or create custom colors).
  - Choose to display Web pages using the Windows High Contrast color scheme, which offers a simple color palette and omits images that make text difficult to read.
  - Choose a hover color for hyperlinks.
- Use the **Advanced** tab on the **Internet Options** dialog box to:
  - Always expand alternate text for images.
  - Move the system caret with focus/selection changes.
  - Choose to launch Active Channels and the browser in full screen mode, which removes all toolbars and scrollbars from the screen. This allows users with cognitive disabilities to have more information on the screen at one time or to remove distractions from peripheral controls.
  - Choose to use AutoComplete.
  - Choose to display friendly URLs.
  - Select to show the **Font** button in the browser toolbar.
  - Select not to display small icons.
  - Disable graphics.
  - Disable animation.
  - Disable video.
  - Select not to use smooth scrolling.

Accessibility Resources

For more information about Microsoft products and accessibility, see **http://www.microsoft.com/enable/**. This site also discusses how to design accessible Web pages that take advantage of new features in Internet Explorer 4. Plus, it offers information on new PowerToys, which make Internet Explorer even more accessible.

If you are deaf or hard-of-hearing, complete access to Microsoft product and customer services is available through a text telephone (TTY/TDD) service.

Customer Service

You can contact the Microsoft Sales Information Center on a text telephone by dialing (800) 892-5234 between 6:30 A.M. and 5:30 P.M. Pacific time.

Technical Assistance

For technical assistance in the United States, you can contact Microsoft Technical Support on a text telephone at (425) 635-4948 between 6:00 A.M. and 6:00 P.M. Pacific time, Monday through Friday, excluding holidays. In Canada, dial (905) 568-9641 between 8:00 A.M. and 8:00 P.M. eastern time, Monday through Friday, excluding holidays. Microsoft support services are subject to the prices, terms, and conditions in place at the time the service is used.

Microsoft Documentation in Alternative Formats

In addition to the standard forms of documentation, many Microsoft products are also available in other formats to make them more accessible. Many of the Internet Explorer 4 documents are also available as online Help, online user's guides, or from the Microsoft Web site. You can also download many Microsoft Press® books from the Microsoft Web site at **http://microsoft.com/enable/**.

If you have difficulty reading or handling printed documentation, you can obtain many Microsoft publications from Recording for the Blind & Dyslexic, Inc. Recording for the Blind & Dyslexic distributes these documents to registered, eligible members of their distribution service, either on audio cassettes or on floppy disks. The Recording for the Blind & Dyslexic collection contains more than 80,000 titles, including Microsoft product documentation and books from Microsoft Press. For information about eligibility and availability of Microsoft product documentation and books from Microsoft Press, contact Recording for the Blind & Dyslexic at the following address or phone numbers:

Recording for the Blind & Dyslexic, Inc.
20 Roszel Road
Princeton, NJ 08540

Phone: (609) 452-0606
Fax: (609) 987-8116

World Wide Web: **http://www.rfbd.org/**

Microsoft Products and Services for People with Disabilities

For more information for people with disabilities, contact:

Microsoft Sales Information Center
One Microsoft Way
Redmond, WA 98052-6393

Voice telephone: (800) 426-9400
Text telephone: (800) 892-5234

World Wide Web: **http://microsoft.com/enable/**

Computer Products for People with Disabilities

Microsoft provides a catalog of accessibility aids that can be used with the Windows and Windows NT® operating systems. You can obtain this catalog from the Microsoft Web site or by phone at the Microsoft Sales Information Center.

The Trace R&D Center at the University of Wisconsin-Madison publishes a database of more than 18,000 products and other information for people with disabilities. The database is available on their Web site. The database is also available on a compact disc, titled *CO-NET CD*, which is issued twice a year. The Trace R&D Center also publishes a book, titled *Trace ResourceBook,* which provides descriptions and photographs of about 2,000 products.

To obtain these directories, contact:

Trace R&D Center
University of Wisconsin
S-151 Waisman Center
1500 Highland Avenue
Madison, WI 53705-2280

Fax: (608) 262-8848

World Wide Web: **http://trace.wisc.edu/**

Information and Referrals for People with Disabilities

Computers and other assisting devices can help persons with disabilities to overcome a variety of barriers. For general information and recommendations on how computers can help you with your specific needs, you should consult a trained evaluator. For information about locating programs or services in your area that may be able to help you, contact:

National Information System
University of South Carolina
Columbia, SC 29208

Voice/text telephone: (803) 777-1782

Fax: (803) 777-9557

CHAPTER 33

Accessibility Features and Functionality

Using Keyboard Navigation

One of the most important accessibility features is the ability to navigate with the keyboard, because it is helpful to people with a wide range of disabilities. Keyboard shortcuts are also useful to anyone who wants to save time by combining key commands with mouse control for maximum navigational efficiency. This section discusses:

- Internet Explorer shortcut keys
- Keyboard navigation of Web pages
- AutoComplete shortcut keys
- Keyboard navigation of the Windows Desktop Update
- Keyboard navigation of the Help tool

Using Internet Explorer Shortcut Keys

You can use shortcut keys to move between screen elements, choose commands, and view documents.

To	Press
Move forward between links and the Address, Links, and Explorer bars	TAB
Move back between links and the Explorer, Links, and Address bars	SHIFT+TAB
Activate a selected hyperlink	ENTER
Display a shortcut menu for the page or hyperlink	SHIFT+F10
Go to the previous page	ALT+LEFT ARROW
Go to the next page (after having used ALT+LEFT to go backward)	ALT+RIGHT ARROW
Move forward between frames and the Address, Links, and Explorer bars	CTRL+TAB
Move back between frames and the Explorer, Links, and Address bars	SHIFT+CTRL+TAB
Scroll toward the beginning of a document	UP ARROW
Scroll toward the end of a document	DOWN ARROW
Scroll toward the beginning of a document in larger increments	PAGE UP or SHIFT+SPACEBAR
Scroll toward the end of a document in larger increments	PAGE DOWN or SPACEBAR
Move to the beginning of a document	HOME
Move to the end of a document	END
Refresh the current page	F5
Stop downloading a page and stop animation	ESC
Go to a new location	CTRL+O

To	Press
Open a new window	CTRL+N
Save the current page	CTRL+S
Print the current page or active frame	CTRL+P

For additional information about using Windows with the keyboard, see the *Microsoft Windows Keyboard Guide*, which is available at **http://www.microsoft.com/enable/**.

Using Keyboard Navigation of Web Pages

You can move forward and backward between the browser Address bar and hyperlinks using TAB and SHIFT+TAB. A one-pixel-wide border, or *focus box*, will appear around links, so you can see what is selected. When you press the TAB key, the selection rotates forward through the Web page in this order:

1. The current address (URL) in the Address bar

   - If the Address bar is not displayed, you may not see a focus box on your screen.

   - To display the Address bar, on the **View** menu, point to **Toolbars,** and then select **Address Bar**.

2. The Links bar

   - The Links bar is not displayed by default, so you may not see a focus box on your screen.

   - To display the Links bar, on the **View** menu, point to **Toolbars**, and then select **Links**.

3. The Explorer bar

   - If an Explorer bar is open, you'll see an entry highlighted on the bar.

   - To display an Explorer bar, on the **View** menu, point to **Explorer Bar**, and then select one of the Explorer bars. Or, simply click the **Search**, **Favorites**, **History**, or **Channel** icon on the browser toolbar. (For more information about Explorer bars, see Part 2.)

4. Hyperlinks on the page, moving left to right, then down

   - As links are highlighted, the link's URL appears on the message bar.

   - Press ENTER to activate the link.

   - Press SHIFT+F10 to open a shortcut menu for the link.

5. The Address bar.

Note Web-page designers may specify a different order for their links than the standard left-to-right and top-to-bottom order.

You can use SHIFT+TAB to move between the same areas, but in reverse order. However, the focus stops on the page as a whole before reaching the links on the page. When using SHIFT+TAB, the focus moves in the following order:

1. The current address (URL) in the Address bar

2. The page as a whole

3. Links on the page in right-to-left and then upward order

4. The Explorer bar

5. The Links bar

6. The Address bar

You can quickly skip to the next frame by pressing CTRL+TAB, or go to the previous frame by pressing CTRL+SHIFT+TAB.

Using AutoComplete Shortcut Keys

The Address bar in Internet Explorer 4 automatically completes site addresses and directory paths for you, based on recently visited sites or local files. It also adds prefixes and suffixes to Internet addresses. You can easily override the suggestions by typing over them. AutoComplete makes it easier for you to enter URLs and reduces the opportunity to make mistakes by filling in long URLs automatically. You turn AutoComplete on and off from the **Advanced** tab on the **Internet Options** dialog box. (For more information, see Chapter 9, "Browser Features and Functionality.")

AutoComplete also includes the following shortcuts:

- To add to the string that has been automatically completed, press the RIGHT ARROW key, and then enter the additional characters.

- To skip to break or separate characters in URLs (such as \), press and hold CTRL, and then use the LEFT ARROW or RIGHT ARROW keys.

- To search your history file, enter the beginning of an address, and then press the UP ARROW or DOWN ARROW keys to complete it.

- To add a prefix or suffix to a partial URL, press CTRL+ENTER to add "http://www." before the entry and ".com" after it.

If you install the Windows Desktop Update, AutoComplete will also work when you use the **Run** command from the **Start** menu.

Using Keyboard Navigation of the Windows Desktop Update

When you install Internet Explorer 4, you have the option of installing the Windows Desktop Update, a set of features that integrates the Web into every aspect of personal computing. For more information about the Windows Desktop Update, including descriptions of the new toolbars, see Part 3, "True Web Integration: Windows Desktop Update."

Press TAB and SHIFT+TAB to move forward and backward, respectively, between the **Start** button, the Quick Launch toolbar, the taskbar, desktop icons and items, and the desktop Channel bar. A 1-pixel-wide border appears around items, so you can see what is selected.

The selection rotates forward through the desktop elements in this order:

1. The **Start** button

2. The Quick Launch toolbar

   - One of the Quick Launch icons appears selected.

   - You can use the arrow keys to move among the toolbar icons. Once the focus is on an icon, press ENTER to launch the application, or press SHIFT+F10 to display the shortcut menu for the toolbar. (All the toolbars on the desktop share the same shortcut menu.)

   - The arrow keys wrap, so continuously pressing the RIGHT ARROW key will eventually bring it back to the leftmost icon.

3. The taskbar

   - A selection will not appear on the taskbar, but the focus is in fact there. Press SHIFT+F10 at this point to display the shortcut menu for the toolbar. (All the toolbars on the desktop share the same shortcut menu.).

   - Press the RIGHT ARROW key to select an application. You can press ENTER to display the selected application, or press SHIFT+F10 to display the shortcut menu for that application.

   - Use the arrow keys to move between the applications.

4. The desktop icons

   - An icon on the desktop appears selected.

   - Use the arrow keys to move between the icons on the desktop. You can press ENTER to open the application or document, or press SHIFT+F10 to display the shortcut menu for that icon.

   - Press CTRL+SPACEBAR to select or deselect the current icon. When no icon is selected, you can press SHIFT+F10 to display the shortcut menu for the entire desktop.

5. The Active Desktop items

   - A desktop item appears selected.

   - Use TAB to move forward through the hyperlinks in that item and on to the other items on the desktop. You can press ENTER to activate a hyperlink.

6. The desktop Channel bar

   - The topmost button on the Channel bar appears selected.

   - Use arrow keys to move between the icons on the Channel bar. Press ENTER to display a channel using Internet Explorer.

   - Note that you can only reach the Channel bar by pressing TAB. The Channel bar is skipped when you navigate in reverse order using SHIFT+TAB.

7. The **Start** button.

If you add other bars, such as the Address bar, QuickLinks toolbar, desktop toolbar, or a custom toolbar, you can also use TAB and SHIFT+TAB to navigate to these bars.

Using Keyboard Navigation of the Help Tool

The new Internet Explorer Help is based on a new Help tool called HTML Help, which displays Help information as Web pages. This new tool offers several significant accessibility advantages (explained in detail in the next section), but it also introduces a few changes and possible limitations in terms of keyboard navigation:

- Unlike in previous versions of Help, you cannot use TAB to navigate between buttons, links, or panes of Internet Explorer 4 Help. You can, however, use ALT+C, ALT+I, and ALT+S to navigate to and from the Contents, Index, and Search tabs, respectively, and press ENTER to move to the topic pane.

- The keyboard cannot be used to activate Help topic hyperlinks at this time. However, relatively few Internet Explorer Help topics contain hyperlinks, and all the hyperlink topics can also be accessed using Contents, Index, and Search.

- When you display a topic in the right pane, it continues to be displayed until replaced with another selection—by highlighting a selection and pressing ENTER. This can be confusing in navigation, because the topic name currently selected in the left pane may not match the topic shown on the right.

- The **Hide** button on the Help toolbar hides the left pane (used for Contents, Index, and Search). When the left pane is hidden, there is no way to navigate Help. The keyboard cannot be used to make the left pane visible again.

▶ **To use the Help Contents list**

1. On the **Internet Explorer Help** dialog box, click **Contents**.

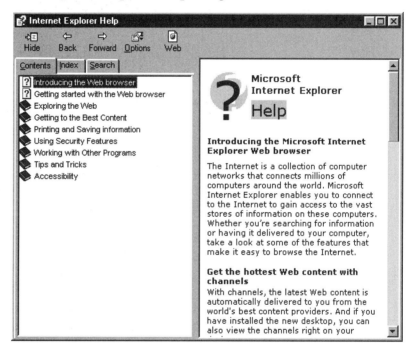

2. When Help is launched, the focus may be on the Help topic. To bring it back to the Contents pane, press ALT+I to toggle to the **Index** tab, and then press ALT+C to toggle to the **Contents** tab.

3. Use the UP ARROW and DOWN ARROW keys to move the selection in the Contents list. As you select parent topics, they will automatically open, indicated by the open-book icon and the expanded list of child topics. As you leave the last child page of an opened topic and move on to the next topic, the opened topic closes, collapsing the list and displaying a closed book icon.

4. Press ENTER to open and close topics indicated by book icons.

5. When you have highlighted the title of an available topic (indicated by a page icon), press ENTER to select the topic and display the information in the right pane. When the information in the right pane is replaced with a new topic, the keyboard focus moves to the Help topic. The string you searched for is highlighted wherever it appears in the topic.

   ▪ Use the arrow keys to scroll up and down or left and right.

   ▪ Press HOME or END to scroll the screen to the beginning or end of the topic.

   ▪ Use CTRL+F10 to display the shortcut menu for the topic.

6. To return to the Contents list, press ALT+C.

7. Press ALT+F4 to exit Help.

▶ **To use the Help Index**

1. On the **Internet Explorer Help** dialog box, press ALT+I to display the **Index** tab.

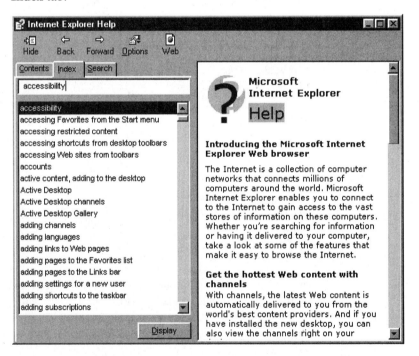

The **Index** tab has a text box where you can enter a term and a list box showing all available index entries. The keyboard focus will be in the text box. The first time you use this page, the text box is empty.

2. Use the arrow keys to scroll up and down the list of all topics. Topics will be highlighted as you scroll, and as they are highlighted they will appear in the text box. You may also enter the topic you want in the text box. The topic list will scroll to highlight matching topics as you type.

3. Press ENTER or ALT+D to display the highlighted topic information. Your topic will be displayed in the pane on the right, and the keyboard focus will move to the Help topic. The string you searched for will be highlighted wherever it appears in the topic.

   - Use the arrow keys to scroll up and down or left and right in the topic pane.

   - Press HOME or END to scroll the screen to the beginning or end of the topic.

   - Use CTRL+F10 to display the shortcut menu for the topic.

4. Use ALT+I to return to the Index to choose other topics, or ALT+F4 to close Help.

▶ **To search for a topic by keyword**

1. On the **Internet Explorer Help** dialog box, press ALT+S to bring the **Search** tab to the front. The keyboard focus will be in the keyword text box.

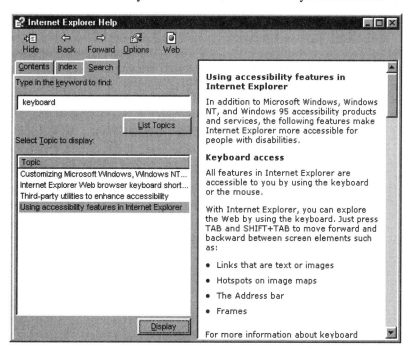

2. Enter the keyword you want.

3. Press ENTER or ALT+L. A list of topics pertaining to your keyword will appear in the **Topic** list box.

4. Press ALT+T and then the DOWN ARROW key to move the keyboard focus to the first item in the **Topic** list box. (The keyboard focus will not appear in the list box immediately after pressing ALT+T; it will appear after using the DOWN ARROW key.)

5. Use the UP ARROW and DOWN ARROW keys to highlight a topic.

6. Press ENTER or ALT+D to display the highlighted topic information in the pane on the right. The keyboard focus will move to the Help topic. The string you searched for will be highlighted wherever it appears in the topic.

   - Use the arrow keys to scroll up and down or left and right.

   - Press HOME or END to scroll the screen to the beginning or end of the topic.

   - Use CTRL+F10 to display the shortcut menu for the topic.

7. Use ALT+T to return to the **Search** tab to choose another topic, or ALT+K to begin another search

8. Use ALT+F4 to exit Help.

Customizing Display of Fonts, Colors, and Styles

When Web authors and designers create Web pages, they often specify particular font colors and sizes, typefaces, and background colors. These settings may be specified for each item as it is coded on the Web page, or they may be defined in a *style sheet*, which is a type of template for specifying how different styles should appear throughout a Web site. Internet Explorer 4 lets you override any or all of these settings. You can specify your own font and color preferences for all Web pages. You can also override formatting by using your own style sheet or by selecting the **High Contrast** option from the Windows Control Panel. If you're using the Windows Desktop Update, these font, color, and style options will also affect your Windows desktop and the presentation of your file folders.

In Internet Explorer 4, Help information is displayed as Web pages, which means that most of the accessibility features in the Internet Explorer browser are now also available for viewing Help topics. The new Internet Explorer Help is based on a new Help tool called HTML Help. HTML Help will be used by many applications in the future and was designed to replace the standard Windows Help. This holds great promise for people with disabilities. You can override and customize formatting and color settings, display text instead of images, disable animation, and even apply your own style sheet in order to have complete control over how Help is presented. When you adjust these and similar options in Internet Explorer and then restart Help, your settings will automatically apply to all Help topics you view.

Overriding Web-Page Formatting

> **Note** Because of the different ways Web pages can be formatted, some pages will not be affected by the procedures to customize options that are explained in this section. To change the appearance of such pages, you'll need to override the page formatting.

▶ **To override page formatting**

1. On the **View** menu, click **Internet Options**.

2. On the **General** tab, click **Accessibility**.

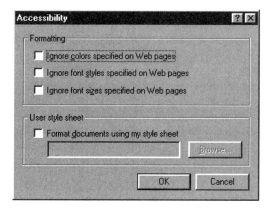

3. Select any of the following options:

   - **Ignore colors specified on Web pages**

   - **Ignore font styles specified on Web pages**

   - **Ignore font sizes specified on Web pages**

   - **Format documents using my style sheet**

4. Click **OK**.

Changing Font Size

When browsing a Web page, you can opt to immediately change the size of the displayed text.

▶ **To immediately display all text in a larger or smaller font size while viewing a page**

1. On the **View** menu, click **Fonts,** or click the **Font** button on the toolbar.

2. Choose the size you want. A check mark will appear next to your choice, and the change will immediately take effect.

If the **Font** button is not displayed on the toolbar, you can add it using the **Internet Options** dialog box.

▶ **To add the Font button to the toolbar**

1. On the **View** menu, click **Internet Options**.

2. Click the **Advanced** tab. A checklist of options appears.

3. Select **Toolbar** and **Show font** button.

4. Click **OK**.

Note The changes created by the **Fonts** menu option or **Font** button procedure will be active only for your current session. (To change the default font size: on the **View** menu, click **Internet Options**, and on the **General** tab, click **Fonts**; select a **Font Size** from the drop-down list.)

For more information about changing font sizes, see "Understanding Font Size Changes" later in this chapter.

Creating a Style Sheet

This section shows a sample style sheet that adjusts the display of Web pages and Help topics to be more easily read by users with certain types of low vision. In particular, it overrides normal formatting of all displayed pages in the following ways:

- Everything appears in high contrast, with a black background and brightly colored text. Body text is white, highlighted text is yellow, and links are brighter versions of their normal blue and purple.

- All text is displayed large and in a plain, sans-serif font. Body text is 24 point, and headings are 32 point.

- All bold, italics, and underlining, which can be difficult to read, are replaced by normal text with a single highlight color.

- The keyboard focus is emphasized by showing the active link in a bright, light green, sometimes called "low vision green."

These settings affect all pages viewed in Internet Explorer, as well as pages displayed by other programs (such as HTML Help) using Mshtml.dll.

▶ **To create a high-visibility style sheet**

1. Open Notepad.

2. Enter the following text into the new file:

```
<STYLE TYPE="text/css">
<!- -
BODY, TABLE {
    font-size: 24pt;
    font-weight: normal;
    font-family: sans-serif;
    background: black;
    color: white;}

B, I, U {color: yellow; font-weight: normal; font-style: normal;}
H1 {font-size: 32pt;}
H2 {font-size: 32pt;}
H3 {font-size: 32pt;}
H4 {font-size: 32pt;}
H5 {font-size: 32pt;}

a:visited {color: #FF00FF}
a:link {color: #00FFFF}
a:active {color: #B1FB17}
-->
</STYLE>
```

3. Save the file to the folder of your choice with a .css file name extension (for example, mystyle.css).

4. In Internet Explorer, on the **View** menu, click **Internet Options**.

5. On the **General** tab, click **Accessibility**.

6. Click **Format documents using my style sheet**.

7. Enter the path of the style sheet file you just created, or click **Browse** to navigate to the file's location.

8. Click **OK**.

Note The style sheet in the preceding example is just one possible solution for increasing the readability of the Web pages you view. By editing the style sheet, you can change the background color and the size, color, and style of the fonts to whatever works best for you.

Caution Use caution when experimenting with the **Format documents using my style sheet** option. Errors in style sheets can cause serious problems with Internet Explorer. It is best to use style sheets that have been created by professional designers. When trying out new style sheets, keep the style-sheet files on a floppy disk that can be removed in case a problem occurs.

Changing the Default Font

You can select the font you prefer to be used as the Internet Explorer default font.

▶ **To change the default display font**

1. On the **View** menu in Internet Explorer, click **Internet Options**.
2. On the **General** tab, click **Fonts**.
3. Select the character set of your choice. Fonts appear in the drop-down list boxes.
4. Select the fonts of your choice.
5. Click **OK**.

Changing the Color of Text and Backgrounds

You can select the colors you prefer for text and background on Web pages.

▶ **To change the color of text and backgrounds**

1. On the **View** menu, click **Internet Options**.
2. On the **General** tab, click **Colors**.

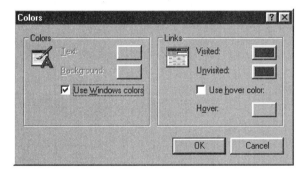

3. In the **Colors** box, click the **Use Windows colors** check box to clear it. Then click the **Text** or **Background** button.

4. In the **Color** dialog box, click the color of your choice from the color palettes. (To create custom colors, see "Creating Custom Colors" later in this section.)

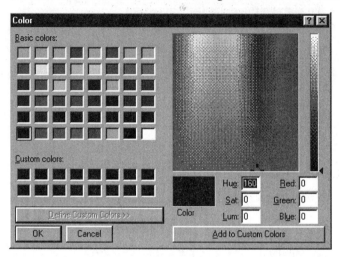

5. Click **OK**.

Changing the Color of Hyperlinks

You can select the colors you prefer for hyperlinks on Web pages.

▶ **To change hyperlink colors**

1. On the **View** menu, click **Internet Options**.

2. On the **General** tab, click **Colors**.

3. In the **Links** box, click the **Visited** or **Unvisited** button.

4. In the **Color** dialog box, click the color of your choice from the color palettes. (To create custom colors, see "Creating Custom Colors" later in this section.)

5. Click **OK**.

Setting Hover Colors

You can select the colors you prefer to be displayed when you are hovering on (rolling over) a Web object.

▶ **To customize hover colors**

1. On the **View** menu, click **Internet Options**.

2. On the **General** tab, click **Colors**.

3. In the **Links** box, select **Use hover color**. The **Hover** button will be enabled with the default color.

4. Click the **Hover** button.

5. In the **Color** dialog box, click the color of your choice from the color palettes. (To create custom colors, see "Creating Custom Colors" next in this section.)

6. Click **OK**.

Creating Custom Colors

You can create custom colors to be used for fonts, text background, links, and hovered objects.

▶ **To create custom colors**

1. On the **View** menu, click **Internet Options**.

2. On the **General** tab, click **Colors**.

3. In the **Colors** dialog box, click either the **Text**, **Background**, **Visited**, or **Unvisited** button to bring up the **Color** dialog box, which includes the Basics and Custom color palettes.

4. In the **Color** dialog box, click **Define Custom Colors**. The dialog box will expand.

5. Select a custom color using either of two methods:

   ▪ Enter the values of your choice in any of the Hue, Sat, Lum, Red, Green, or Blue boxes. The sample box changes color to reflect your choices.

   ▪ Click in the color box to select a color and drag the slider arrow (on the right) up or down to select the luminance level. The sample box changes color to reflect your choices.

6. Select **Add to Custom Colors**.

7. Click **OK**.

Selecting the High Contrast Color Scheme

Rather than creating your own, customized color scheme, you can choose to view your Web pages using the special, High Contrast color scheme offered by Windows.

▶ **To display Web pages in the High Contrast color scheme**

1. On the **Start** menu, point to **Settings**, and select **Control Panel**.

2. Double-click the **Accessibility Options** icon, and then click the **Display** tab.

3. Click the check box to set the **High Contrast** option. (For more options, click the **Settings** button.)

4. Click **OK** to close the **Accessibility Options** dialog box.

5. In Control Panel, double-click the **Internet** icon.

6. On the **General** tab, click **Accessibility**, select **Ignore colors specified on Web pages**, and then click **OK**.

7. On the **General** tab, click **Colors**, select **Use Windows Colors**, and then click **OK**.

8. Restart Internet Explorer to make the changes take effect.

Understanding Font-Size Changes

This section explains how font-size changes are applied in Internet Explorer. Listed below are the various factors affecting font size, listed in the order in which they are applied when the browser displays a page:

1. The Internet Explorer display defaults (for example, P is size 3, H1 is size 6).

2. A user-specified style sheet—if one is provided and **Format documents using my style sheet** is selected in the **Accessibility** dialog box.

3. Style sheet information in the document—unless **Ignore font sizes specified on Web pages** is selected in the **Accessibility** dialog box.

4. <FONT> tags in the document—unless **Ignore font sizes specified on Web pages** is selected in the **Accessibility** dialog box.

5. A scaling factor determined by the fonts options accessible from the **View** menu—except in those cases where the font is specified in an absolute size, such as 12 point.

The scaling factor used in step 5 can be set in either of two ways. Accessing the **Fonts** dialog box through the **Internet Options** dialog box on the **View** menu can change the default for current and future sessions, whereas accessing the **Fonts** menu directly from the **View** menu changes fonts for the current session only.

Font sizes can be specified in the <FONT> tag of an HTML page and in style sheets. Sizes can be specified three ways:

- As an index value (1–7)
- As a relative value (+1, +5)
- Using absolute size units (12pt, 32px)

Font sizes set using index values and relative values are affected by the **View** menu font options, while fonts set in absolute size units are not.

In order to have sizes in the user style sheet override those in the document, the **Ignore font sizes specified on Web pages** option must be selected in the **Accessibility** dialog box. The **Ignore font sizes specified on Web pages** option ignores all font sizes specified by <FONT> tags or style sheets, but it does not override relative sizes that are implied by structural tags. For example, a top-level heading (H1) will still be larger than body text, even when **Ignore Font Sizes** is turned on.

Configuring Advanced Internet Accessibility Options

Most accessibility features (other than customizing fonts and colors) are displayed in a checklist on the **Advanced** tab of the **Internet Options** dialog box.

1. On the **View** menu, click **Internet Options**.
2. Click the **Advanced** tab. You can either scroll through the checklist and make selections with your mouse, or:
   - Use the TAB key to move to the first option in the list.
   - Use the UP ARROW and DOWN ARROW keys to move through your selections.
   - Use the UP ARROW and DOWN ARROW keys to open or close groups of related options.
   - Use the SPACEBAR to select and clear the options you want.
3. Click **OK**.

Note   Using the SPACEBAR to select and clear options causes a beep, as if you had entered an incorrect keystroke.

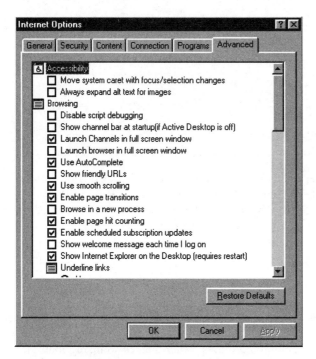

Useful Accessibility Options:

Move system caret with focus/selection changes

Specifies whether to move the system caret whenever the focus or selection changes. Some accessibility aids, such as screen readers or screen magnifiers, use the system caret to determine which area of the screen to read or magnify.

Always expand alt text for images

Specifies whether the image size should expand to fit all of the alternate text when the **Show Pictures** check box is cleared.

Useful Browsing Options:

Launch Channels in full screen window

Specifies whether to automatically display channels in full screen mode. This can be done more easily through the **View** menu. Use F11 to switch to full screen mode.

Launch browser in full screen window

Specifies whether to automatically display Web pages in a full screen whenever you start Internet Explorer. Full screen mode removes all toolbars and scroll bars from the screen to make more room for Web pages. This allows users with cognitive disabilities to have more information on the screen at one time or to remove distractions from peripheral controls. This mode is also useful if you are using large fonts or don't want to scroll as often. Use F11 to toggle out of full screen mode.

Use AutoComplete

Specifies whether you want Internet Explorer to automatically complete Internet addresses as you enter them in the Address bar. If you've visited the Web site before, the AutoComplete feature suggests a match as you type. Some users with cognitive disabilities may want to turn this off to avoid distractions, and some users of blind-access utilities may want to turn it off if their accessibility aid reads the suggestions as they appear, making typing difficult.

Show friendly URLs

Specifies whether you want Internet Explorer to show the full Internet address (URL) for a page on the status bar.

Use smooth scrolling

Specifies whether scrolling is used to gradually slide information up or down the screen when the user clicks on the scroll bar or presses navigation keys such as PAGE DOWN. Some users of blind-access utilities may want to turn this off if it causes timing problems. People with certain cognitive disabilities may want to turn it off because they find the motion distracting.

Underline links

Specifies how you want links on Web pages underlined. Select one of the following settings:

- **Always** to underline all links
- **Never** to not underline links
- **Hover** to underline links when your mouse pointer is over the link

  You may prefer to indicate whether or not a hovered link is indicated by a change in color (as explained earlier in this chapter). Older blind-access utilities rely on underlines to recognize links.

Useful Multimedia Options:

Show pictures

Specifies whether graphical images should be included when pages are displayed. Alt text (descriptive text) is displayed in place of the graphic if supplied by the page. When this check box is cleared, you can still display an individual image by right-clicking the icon that represents the graphic and then clicking **Show Picture**. (There is currently no keyboard equivalent for this.)

Turning off images will allow older blind-access utilities to read the textual description for these images aloud; however, newer utilities can use Microsoft Active Accessibility to identify and read these descriptions, even when the graphics are still displayed on the screen. Turning off images will speed up browser performance, although it may interfere with the functionality and effectiveness of some Web sites. If images are turned on or the textual description is cut off by space limitations, you can see the full description by moving the mouse over the image.

Play animations

Specifies whether animations can play when pages are displayed. Alt text is displayed in place of the graphic if supplied by the page. When this check box is cleared, you can still play an individual animation by right-clicking the icon that represents the animation and then clicking **Show Picture**. (There is currently no keyboard equivalent for this.)

As with users who are blind, users with seizure disorders may want to turn off animation (especially blinking). Users with cognitive disabilities may want to turn off animations or selectively download them to prevent distractions.

Play videos

Specifies whether video clips can play. When this check box is cleared, you can still play an individual video by right-clicking the icon that represents the animation and then clicking **Show Picture**. (There is currently no keyboard equivalent for this.)

As with users who are blind, users with seizure disorders may want to turn off video. Users with cognitive disabilities may want to turn off videos or selectively download them to prevent distractions.

Play sounds

If RealAudio is installed or if a movie is playing, sound might play, even if you clear this check box. As with users who are deaf or hard-of-hearing, users with seizure disorders may want to turn off sound. Users with cognitive disabilities may want to turn off sounds or selectively download them to prevent distractions. Users who are blind may want to turn off sounds or selectively download them so that they do not conflict with the screen reader when it is reading text aloud.

Useful Printer Options:

Print Background Colors and Images

Specifies that you want Internet Explorer to print background colors and images when you print a Web page. Users with low vision or those wanting to speed up print time may want to turn this off. You will also want to turn this off if you are preparing text to be scanned, for example, to provide it to a text reader.

Useful Toolbar Options:

Show font button

Specifies whether to display the **Font** button on the toolbar. You can use this button to immediately change the size of fonts displayed on a page you are currently viewing.

If the **Font** button does not appear on your toolbar when this setting is enabled, it may be off the right edge of the screen. The **Text Labels** option adds text labels to the toolbar buttons and makes the buttons larger, in some cases pushing some buttons off the screen. Without text labels, the toolbar buttons are smaller, and all fit on the toolbar. To hide the text labels, on the **View** menu, point to **Toolbars**, and then clear **Text Labels**.

Small icons

Specifies whether you want Internet Explorer to display the toolbar using Microsoft Office–style buttons. These buttons are smaller than the default buttons, and so users who prefer larger buttons should clear this option.

Using Accessibility Features in NetMeeting

Microsoft NetMeeting delivers a complete Internet conferencing solution that can greatly enhance accessibility for users with a wide range of disabilities. NetMeeting users can experience the benefits of real-time, multipoint communication that allows them to collaborate and share information with two or more conference participants at the same time.

Native application sharing allows you to share applications running on your computer with others in a conference. You can exchange graphics or draw diagrams with the electronic whiteboard. You can send messages or take meeting notes with the text-based chat program and send files to other conference participants with NetMeeting file transfer capability. Audio conferencing allows you to talk to friends, family, and business associates over the Internet or corporate intranet in real time. With a video capture card and camera, you can also send and receive video images for face-to-face communication. (You don't need a camera on your computer to see video that is sent by another user.) For complete information about NetMeeting, see Chapter 20, "NetMeeting," or visit **http://www.microsoft.com/netmeeting/**.

Using NetMeeting Keyboard Navigation and Shortcuts

You can use shortcuts to navigate in NetMeeting and to place calls.

To	Press
Place a call	CTRL+N
Send a file	CTRL+F
Start the Whiteboard	CTRL+W
Start Chat	CTRL+T
Toggle among the Directory, SpeedDial, Current Call, and History lists	CTRL+TAB
Refresh the Directory or SpeedDial list	F5
Stop loading the Directory list	CTRL+L
Open the folder list	CTRL+D
Toggle between the Audio toolbar and the main window, and, if open, the folder list	F6
Select check boxes (such as the **microphone** and **speaker** check boxes on the Audio toolbar)	SPACEBAR
Take control of a shared application	any key
Stop the collaboration of a person with whom you are sharing an application	ESC
When application sharing, toggle between open windows	ALT+TAB

P A R T 9

Deployment and Maintenance

The Microsoft® Internet Explorer Administration Kit (IEAK) provides tools that corporate administrators and information systems professionals can use to deploy custom versions of Internet Explorer 4 in their organizations. The IEAK also provides tools to centrally configure and maintain browser, application, desktop, and system settings on users' computers. Beginning with Internet Explorer 3, Microsoft has provided an IEAK to deploy and maintain the browser in organizations. With Internet Explorer 4, however, the deployment and maintenance capabilities of the IEAK have been greatly expanded. Organizations can now take advantage of the many new features of Internet Explorer 4 and the IEAK to exercise greater control over the deployment of Internet Explorer and over end-user desktop configurations.

Part 9 describes how to plan and implement successful deployments of Internet Explorer 4. It describes how to build and distribute custom versions of Internet Explorer to end users. It also describes how to centrally maintain end-user browser, application, and desktop configurations.

Chapter 34: Planning the Deployment

Planning is a key to successful deployment of Internet Explorer. Organizations need to: assign project teams; identify technical requirements, user needs, and migration issues; evaluate and choose deployment strategies; and then prepare project plans for the deployment.

Chapter 35: Validating the Deployment

To ensure a smooth deployment with minimum problems, organizations should test and refine their deployment plans in labs and in pilot programs before deployment to the whole organization. Feedback and lessons learned in the lab and during pilots provide valuable information for planning the final deployment.

Chapter 36: Implementing the Deployment

Organizations can use the enhanced features of the IEAK to build custom packages of Internet Explorer to distribute to user groups. These custom packages can be pre-configured with a wide range of browser, application, and desktop options and settings—giving corporate administrators a wide range of control over end users' browsers, applications, and desktops.

Chapter 37: Automatic Browser Configuration

Internet Explorer 4 provides enhanced capabilities for the automatic browser configuration feature introduced in Internet Explorer 3. Organizations can use the IEAK to deploy browsers that are set up for automatic browser configuration. System administrators can use the IEAK to centrally manage and maintain a wide range of browser, desktop, and system settings on users' computers.

Chapter 38: Software Distribution and Updates

Internet Explorer 4 introduces Active Channel™ technology, which can be used to automatically deliver new and updated Web content to users' computers. A software distribution channel is a special type of Active Channel that can be used to automate the distribution of new software and software updates to end users' computers.

Overview: The Deployment Process

The first three chapters of Part 9 contain information that network administrators and information systems professionals can use to plan and implement deployments of Internet Explorer in their organizations. To deploy Internet Explorer, you perform the following activities.

Develop the deployment plan	See **Chapter 34, "Planning the Deployment"** for information on how to perform the planning tasks.
▪ Assemble project teams.	
▪ Identify technical requirements for deployment.	
▪ Identify your organization's client/server configurations and end-user needs.	
▪ Identify migration issues and compatibility problems with previously existing systems.	
▪ Specify preferred distribution strategies.	
▪ Specify preferred custom-build configurations.	
▪ Develop the deployment project plan.	
Validate the deployment plan	See **Chapter 35, "Validating the Deployment"** for information on how to perform the validation tasks.
▪ Prepare the test plan and checklists.	
▪ Test the deployment process in the lab.	
▪ Plan the pilot program.	
▪ Conduct the pilot program.	
▪ Finalize the deployment project plan.	
Implement the deployment plan	See **Chapter 36, "Implementing the Deployment"** for information on how to perform the implementation tasks.
▪ Announce the deployment to the organization.	See also **Appendix J, "Custom-Build Checklist"** for information on how to complete the custom-build checklist.
▪ Provide user training and support.	
▪ Complete the custom-build checklist.	See also **Appendix L, "IExpress Configuration Wizard"** for information on how to build local packages that you can include with custom packages.
▪ Build custom packages.	
▪ Digitally sign custom package files.	
▪ Configure Active Setup installation options.	
▪ Implement a download site.	
▪ Produce distribution media.	See also **Appendix K, "IEAK FAQs"** for more information about the IEAK.
▪ Distribute Internet Explorer to users.	
▪ Monitor and assist user installation of the Internet Explorer browser, as needed.	

C H A P T E R   3 4

Planning the Deployment

Deployment Planning Overview

This chapter describes how to plan the deployment of Microsoft Internet Explorer in your organization. To plan the deployment:

- Assemble project teams.
- Identify technical requirements for deployment.
- Identify your organization's client/server configurations and end-user needs.
- Identify migration issues and compatibility problems with previously existing systems.
- Specify preferred distribution strategies.
- Specify preferred custom-package configurations.
- Develop the deployment project plan.

Assembling Project Teams

Typically, a project manager oversees the deployment of Internet Explorer in an organization. That project manager assembles the necessary teams of system administrators and other information systems (IS) professionals to help plan, test, implement, and support the deployment. Project teams can include:

- Planning teams that help plan the deployment and develop the project plan.
- Installation teams that set up the test lab and use it to test the deployment.

- Training teams that develop training plans and train the organization for deployment.
- Support teams that develop support plans and support users during and after the deployment.

The size and number of required project teams will vary depending on the needs of your organization. For small organizations, only a few people who perform the roles of all the teams may be involved.

Identifying Technical Requirements for Deployment

The project teams should study the technical documentation for Internet Explorer to identify the requirements for deployment in their organization. Sources of technical information include:

- This deployment guide.
- The Internet Explorer Web site at **http://www.microsoft.com/ie/**.
- The Internet Explorer Customer Support Center at **http://www.microsoft.com/iesupport/**.
- Internet Explorer Help.
- The Internet Explorer Administration Kit (IEAK) Configuration Wizard Help.

The following sections describe the system requirements to install and run Internet Explorer and the IEAK Configuration Wizard.

Requirements for Internet Explorer

The following table lists the minimum hardware and software system requirements to deploy Internet Explorer 4 on Windows® 95 and Windows NT® operating systems. For information about system requirements for other systems, see the Internet Explorer Web site at **http://www.microsoft.com/ie/**.

Requirements for Windows Operating Systems

	Windows 95	Windows NT
Service Pack	All	Service Pack 3 required
Processor	486/66	486/66
Memory	8 MB (16 MB with Windows Desktop Update)	16 MB (24 MB with Windows Desktop Update)
Disk Space	39 MB Minimal installation 51 MB Standard installation 70 MB Full installation	39 MB Minimal installation 51 MB Standard installation 70 MB Full installation

Disk space requirements depend on the suite of components installed. Internet Explorer 4 Setup offers three standard installation suites: minimal, standard, and full.

Internet Explorer Suite Components

Option	Includes
Minimal Installation (39 MB)	Internet Explorer, Java support, Microsoft ActiveMovie™
Standard Installation (51 MB)	Internet Explorer, Java support, Microsoft ActiveMovie, Microsoft Internet Connection Wizard, Microsoft Outlook™ Express, Microsoft Interactive Music control, Microsoft Wallet
Full Installation (70 MB)	Internet Explorer, Java support, Microsoft ActiveMovie, Microsoft Internet Connection Wizard, Microsoft Outlook Express, Microsoft Interactive Music control, Microsoft Wallet, Microsoft FrontPage® Express, Intel Indeo5 Codec, Microsoft NetMeeting™ 2.0, Microsoft Chat 2.0, Microsoft Visual Basic® 5.01 Run Time, Microsoft NetShow™, RealPlayer by Progressive Networks, Microsoft Publishing Wizard

In addition, you can use the IEAK Configuration Wizard to build custom packages of Internet Explorer that include up to 10 other custom components. You'll need additional disk space for the custom components to be included in the installations.

Requirements for the IEAK Configuration Wizard

The following table lists the requirements to install and run the IEAK Configuration Wizard, which you can use to build custom packages of Internet Explorer to distribute to your end users.

Note You must install Internet Explorer before running the IEAK Configuration Wizard. If Internet Explorer is not installed, the wizard may appear to run, but it will not build your customized package correctly.

Requirements for the IEAK Configuration Wizard

Item	Requirements
Processor	486/66
Operating System	Windows 95 or Windows NT 4
Memory	8 MB Windows 95 16 MB Windows NT 4
Disk Space	40 MB to 60 MB to install 40 MB to 100 MB per custom package
Connection	Must be connected to the Internet to run the wizard the first time.

The disk space required in the C:\Program Files\Ieak folder varies considerably, depending on the number of Microsoft components you plan to include in custom packages; for example:

- 43 MB for a standard installation (includes Internet Explorer, Outlook Express, and ActiveMovie).

- 50 MB for an enhanced installation (includes Internet Explorer, Outlook Express, FrontPage Express, and ActiveMovie).

- 60 MB for a full installation (includes Internet Explorer, Outlook Express, NetMeeting, FrontPage Express, Microsoft Wallet, NetShow, and ActiveMovie).

The disk space required for custom packages varies depending on the Internet Explorer components and custom components you plan to install, as well as the distribution method you use. If you plan to distribute Internet Explorer on compact discs or floppy disks, the custom packages include the distribution files for the compact discs or floppy disks. Therefore, compact-disc and floppy-disk packages require about twice as much disk space as packages that do not use compact discs or floppy disks.

Note You can specify a local drive or a network drive on which to install the custom builds.

Identifying Client/Server Configurations and End-User Needs

Gather information to identify the existing client/server hardware and software configurations and end-user needs for all groups targeted to migrate to Internet Explorer. Based on this information, you can determine the preferred deployment strategies for the Internet Explorer custom-package configurations, which are described in Chapter 36, "Implementing the Deployment." Use this information to evaluate migration issues, including the need for hardware and software upgrades to support migration.

Gather information by surveying and interviewing the appropriate group managers, system administrators, and users for the groups to be migrated. However, the information-gathering process can be tedious and time-consuming, especially for large organizations. Therefore, it's recommended that you use network-asset survey software to identify and report the client/server configurations whenever feasible.

Identifying Migration Issues

It's important to identify and solve migration issues such as compatibility problems before you attempt to migrate from previously existing systems to Internet Explorer. To identify migration issues:

- Identify end-user hardware configurations.
- Identify end-user operating systems and applications.
- Research migration and compatibility problems.
- Test the migration process in a lab environment, using the actual user configurations to identify problems.
- Identify solutions such as upgrades of noncompatible, previously existing systems.
- Add solution implementations to the deployment plan.

For more information about testing the migration in the lab, see "Testing the Deployment Process," in Chapter 35, "Validating the Deployment."

The following sections discuss some of the general migration issues you should consider. For more information about migration issues:

- See the *Internet Explorer 4 Release Notes,* included with the Internet Explorer software.

- Visit the Microsoft Internet Explorer Support Center at **http://www.microsoft.com/iesupport/**.

- Contact the manufacturer of the conflicting software or hardware.

Migrating from Internet Explorer 3

Internet Explorer 4 Setup installs over an installed version of Internet Explorer 3 and imports proxy settings, favorites, and cookies from the previous version. However, you must reinstall any add-ons that you want to keep.

Note   Users cannot have both Internet Explorer 3 and Internet Explorer 4 on the same machine unless they have created a dual-boot system, (a computer that can boot to either Windows 95 or Windows NT). With a dual-boot system, you can install Internet Explorer 3 under one operating system and Internet Explorer 4 under the other.

For more information, see Part 1, "Installing of Internet Explorer 4."

Migrating from Netscape Navigator 3

Internet Explorer 4 Setup imports proxy settings, bookmarks (called favorites in Internet Explorer), and cookies from Netscape Navigator 3. However, you must reinstall plug-ins. If you want helper applications to run when called by Internet Explorer, add the applications' Multipurpose Internet Mail Extension (MIME) types and file extensions to the list of Windows file-type extensions, and specify the program that opens files with those extensions. For more information on migrating e-mail information, see "Using Previously Existing Internet E-mail and News Programs," later in this section.

Coexisting with Netscape Navigator

Internet Explorer 4 can coexist safely with Netscape Navigator on the same machine. Since Netscape does not include support for ActiveX technology, the first thing Setup will do when upgrading Navigator is install ActiveX drivers on the system, so that Active Setup can run. If the Netscape ActiveX plug-in is installed, it makes no difference; it will not be used to support Active Setup.

If Netscape is installed when installing Internet Explorer, the Netscape plug-ins are copied to the Program Files\Internet Explorer\Plugins folder. The contents of this folder are loaded into memory each time the browser is launched.

Shdocvw.dll will call a plug-in to perform a rendering job if there is no native code for that task. However, at this time there is no Netscape plug-in that offers functionality beyond that offered by Internet Explorer's native code, so it is just a waste of memory to have them loaded. For this reason, a user may choose to delete files from the Plug-ins folder.

When installing Internet Explorer, Setup looks for an installed browser that is set to be the default browser. During Setup, the user-configurable settings, including proxy settings, dial-up connection, and favorites, are adopted from the current default browser. Some additional settings may also be adopted, if the corresponding optional components are installed, as indicated in the lists below.

Outlook Express Settings:

- SMTP server information.
- POP3 server settings (POP3 server name, POP3 user name).
- Identity information (name, e-mail address, reply address, organization, signature information).
- Personal address book.
- Internet telephone program, Web-based phone book.
- Send and post settings (8 bit chars. in headers, MIME compliance) if different from the Navigator default.
- Settings for check new message every x minutes if different from the Navigator default.

Web Publishing Wizard:

- Author name.
- Document template location.
- Publisher user name.
- Publisher password.

Using Previously Existing Browser Plug-Ins or Add-Ins

You can use most previously existing browser plug-ins and helper applications in conjunction with Internet Explorer 4 by including them as custom components when you build custom packages of Internet Explorer 4. For more information, see "Building Custom Packages" in Chapter 36, "Implementing the Deployment."

Keep in mind that some earlier plug-ins and add-ins may not be compatible with Internet Explorer 4. You may be able to obtain patches or updates to compatible versions from the software manufacturer.

Using Previously Existing Internet E-Mail and News Programs

You can configure Internet Explorer 4 to work with your previously existing e-mail and news applications in two ways. If the e-mail application is already on users' desktops, simply choose **Internet Options** from the **View** menu, and then click **Programs**. In the **Programs** tab, select the application you want to use for e-mail from the drop-down box. If you would like to introduce another e-mail or news application in conjunction with Internet Explorer, you can do so by including each application as a custom component when you build custom packages of Internet Explorer, and pre-configuring Internet Explorer to use each application. For more information, see "Building Custom Packages" in Chapter 36, "Implementing the Deployment."

You can also specify Outlook Express as your Internet e-mail and news program when you build custom packages of Internet Explorer. If Outlook Express is specified, Setup automatically imports folders from existing e-mail packages such as Netscape Mail, Eudora Light, and Eudora Pro into Outlook Express. Settings from Microsoft Exchange and Microsoft Outlook will also be imported into Outlook Express, if appropriate for your configuration.

Dealing with Compatibility Problems

Some previously existing software may not be compatible with Internet Explorer 4. In addition, Web pages that were developed for other Web browsers and for proprietary HTML or scripting extensions may not function the same way in Internet Explorer 4.

Compatibility problems with earlier software can often be corrected by obtaining upgrades or patches from the software manufacturer or by migrating previously existing applications to applications that are known to be compatible with Internet Explorer 4. To correct Web pages that do not function properly in Internet Explorer 4, however, you may need to redesign them to be compatible with Internet Explorer 4.

Test the Web pages on your intranet to see if there are any compatibility problems with Internet Explorer 4. For more information about third-party compatibility issues, see the *Internet Explorer 4 Release Notes,* included with the Internet Explorer software. For more information about scripting issues, see Part 6, Chapter 26, "Active Scripting."

Specifying Distribution Strategies

The IEAK Configuration Wizard is used to build custom packages of Internet Explorer 4 to distribute to end users. You can automate installations of Internet Explorer with preselected components and browser settings, so that no user action is required, or you can allow users to choose from up to 10 installation options during their installation.

You can distribute Internet Explorer from:

- Download sites on the Internet to end-user desktops.
- Download sites on your intranet to end-user desktops.
- Compact discs to end-user desktops.
- Floppy disks to end-user desktops.

The following sections discuss some of the factors to consider when you choose distribution strategies.

Meeting End-User Needs

Identify the needs of your end users. If your field personnel access your intranet through a remote-access modem pool at 28.8 Kbps, it can be time-consuming for them to download the Internet Explorer custom package from the Internet or their intranet. It also may unreliable due to poor phone connections. You can choose to distribute the custom package to field personnel on compact discs or floppy disks and distribute the custom package to the rest of your organization from download sites on your intranet.

Reaching Your End Users

Identify what's required to reach your end users. If some use stand-alone computers that are not connected to the network, you need either to distribute custom packages from the Internet or distribute custom packages on compact discs or floppy disks.

Assessing Size and Geographical Distribution of Your Organization

The size and geographical distribution of your organization will influence your distribution strategy. For example, a large organization may be able to produce compact discs at a volume discount and so can afford to distribute custom packages on compact discs. On the other hand, it may not be economical for a small organization to produce a small volume of compact discs; so that organization may decide to distribute custom packages over their intranet or the Internet. An organization with many offices worldwide may decide to distribute multiple-language versions of custom packages over the Internet.

Assessing Resources Available to Your Organization

The resources available to your organization will influence your distribution strategy. For example, if your organization doesn't have a wide-area network (WAN), you may decide to distribute custom packages to your worldwide user base over the Internet.

Assessing Network Performance and Bandwidth Issues

Your distribution strategies will affect network performance and the available bandwidth of your intranet. Choose distribution strategies that help optimize network performance and bandwidth. For example, if you distribute custom packages over the Internet to users on your intranet, it can cause excessive load on firewalls and proxy servers. If you distribute custom packages from only one download server in a large WAN, it can overload the server and cause traffic problems across the interconnecting routers and bridges of subnets and local area networks (LANs). You can usually achieve the best network performance by distributing custom packages from download servers that are located in multiple domains or subnets of your intranet.

Note   You can specify up to 10 download sites that Internet Explorer Setup will automatically switch between during installations. This provides optimum download performance, as well as distribution of load across the intranet.

Assessing Network Security Issues

The distribution strategies available to you depend on the security configuration of your intranet, as well as the level of Internet access that you allow your users to have.

You can distribute custom packages from the Internet to users on the intranet if you configure firewalls and proxy servers to allow users to download the Internet Explorer components. Internet Explorer components are authenticated when downloaded from the Internet. However, distributing custom builds over your intranet still provides maximum security and does not require firewalls and proxy servers.

If your organization does not provide the required level of Internet access to users, you do not have the option to distribute custom packages over the Internet. However, you still need to provide Internet access to the administrators who run the IEAK Configuration Wizard to build the custom packages. The IEAK Configuration Wizard must access the Internet to download the most current components of Internet Explorer from the Microsoft Internet-download site.

Specifying Custom Package Configurations

When you use the IEAK Configuration Wizard to build custom packages of Internet Explorer, you can specify a wide variety of configuration options. For example, you can specify the media and the Setup options used to distribute the custom package to end users. You can also specify the URLs of download sites and pre-configure browser settings, such as the security and proxy settings.

The following sections briefly describe the major configuration options that are available for building custom packages. For more information to help you specify custom builds, see the checklist in Appendix J, "Custom-Build Checklist," and "Building Custom Packages" in Chapter 36, "Implementing the Deployment."

Choosing Deployment Roles

When you enter your 10-digit customization code for Corporate Administrators, the following roles are available in the IEAK Configuration Wizard:

- Content Provider/Developer
- Service Provider
- Corporate Administrator

For the purposes of this internal Internet Explorer deployment, you should select the **Corporate Administrator** option. For more information about the Content Provider/Developer and Service Provider roles, see the IEAK Configuration Wizard Help and the Internet Explorer Web site at **http://www.microsoft.com/ie/**.

Deploying Language Versions

You must create and distribute a separate Internet Explorer custom build for each language you want to deploy.

Selecting Available Media for Distribution

You can distribute the Internet Explorer custom package files from download sites on the Internet or your intranet. You can also select one of the following optional distribution media:

- CD-ROM
- Multiple floppy disks

When you select **CD-ROM** or **Multiple floppy disks,** the CD-ROM or floppy disk distribution files are added to the custom package. You can then copy the distribution files to the compact disc or floppy disks. In addition, when you select **CD-ROM,** you can use the IEAK Configuration Wizard to create and use a custom CD-ROM Autorun screen. This screen will automatically appear, to help users with their installation, when users insert their customized Internet Explorer compact disc.

Selecting Version Synchronization Options

When you start the IEAK Configuration Wizard, Automatic Version Synchronization (AVS) is turned on by default. With AVS turned on, you can use the IEAK Configuration Wizard to:

- Select the Microsoft download site from which to download the Internet Explorer components.
- Download the most current versions of Microsoft components for the custom package.

You use AVS to keep custom packages up-to-date with the most current Internet Explorer components. The first time you run the IEAK Configuration Wizard to build a custom package, AVS is turned on and cannot be turned off because you must download the Internet Explorer components used to build custom packages. Later, if you do not want the IEAK Configuration Wizard to compare your packages with the software on the Microsoft Web site, you can turn off AVS.

Determining Internet Explorer Setup Appearance Options

The IEAK Configuration Wizard creates a custom build of the Internet Explorer Setup that you distribute to users. Users then run Setup to install Internet Explorer on their systems. You can use the IEAK Configuration Wizard to:

- Customize the CD-ROM Autorun screen (when **CD-ROM** is selected).
- Brand the Setup Wizard to include your organization's logo and name.

Specifying Component Installation Options

You can specify the components to be installed with the custom build, and you can specify various installation options. You can use the IEAK Configuration Wizard to:

- Select a silent installation, which doesn't give users any opportunity to change your custom installation settings.
- Specify up to 10 custom components that you provide for installation.
- Specify URLs for up to 10 download sites from which to distribute the custom build.
- Specify up to 10 installation options from which users can choose during the installation.
- Specify any combination of standard or custom components to be included in each installation option.
- Specify the version number and configuration identifier for the custom package.
- Specify the folder where Internet Explorer will be installed on end-user systems.
- Specify whether to integrate the Windows Desktop Update in the custom package.

Specifying Browser Branding Options

You can brand several browser features. You can use the IEAK Configuration Wizard to:

- Specify title-bar text and a toolbar background bitmap.
- Specify a logo.

Pre-Configuring Browser Settings

You can pre-configure a variety of browser settings. You can use the IEAK Configuration Wizard to:

- Specify browser start and search pages.
- Specify an online browser support page.
- Specify a default set of favorites.
- Specify a custom Internet Explorer welcome page and desktop wallpaper.
- Specify Active Channels for installation.
- Specify custom HTML files for My Computer and Control Panel Web views.
- Specify a user agent string to be appended to the default Internet Explorer string.
- Specify proxy settings.

Specifying Automatic Browser Configuration Options

You can set up the browsers in your organization to be managed from centrally located files, using the Internet Explorer automatic browser configuration. If you enable automatic browser configuration, you can use the IEAK Profile Manager to administer Internet Explorer configurations. The IEAK Configuration Wizard can:

- Enable automatic browser configuration for end users. This will force Internet Explorer to look at an auto-configuration URL each time the browser is launched, to see if there is a new configuration that the browser must apply.
- Specify the URL containing user Internet settings (.ins files).
- Specify the URL containing auto-proxy (.js or .pac files).
- Specify a schedule for when automatic configuration occurs, if more often than only when the browser is started.

Setting Browser Security

You can control user access to Web sites and content through site certificates, Authenticode™, trusted publishers, security zones, and content ratings. You can use the IEAK Configuration Wizard to:

- Specify site certificate and Authenticode settings.
- Specify security zones and content ratings.

Specifying Internet Mail and News Options

You can specify various settings and options for Internet mail and news. You can use the IEAK Configuration Wizard to:

- Specify Internet mail servers, domain servers, and news servers.
- Specify Outlook Express as the default mail and news client.
- Specify Secure Password Authentication (SPA) to authenticate users when they log on.
- Specify the Lightweight Directory Access Protocol (LDAP) settings.
- Specify the Infopane and welcome message for Outlook Express.
- Specify default signature files for e-mail and news messages.

Setting System Policies and Restrictions

You can specify numerous desktop, shell, and security settings across your organization. You can customize settings, for example, to allow users to delete printers or to prevent them from adding items to the new Windows Desktop Update. Be sure to understand the impact of the security settings on your users, especially if you have roaming users who share computers with other users.

You can use the IEAK Configuration Wizard to set system policies and restrictions for users in the following areas:

- Microsoft NetMeeting
- Active Desktop™
- Internet Properties
- Outlook Express
- Shell
- Channels and Subscriptions
- Microsoft Chat
- Internet Explorer Advanced Settings
- Internet Code Download

You can control, or *lock down,* features and functions in these areas. For example, you can use the **Colors** and **Fonts** options under **Advanced Settings** in Internet Explorer to specify browser colors and fonts that users cannot change. More important, you can prevent users from adding or deleting channels that you have preset, or from rearranging or adding Active Desktop items. You can use the Shell options to prevent Windows 95 users from restarting their systems in MS-DOS® mode. All Policies and Restrictions you set in the IEAK Configuration Wizard can be changed later by the administrator, using the IEAK Profile Manager.

Developing the Deployment Project Plan

Develop a project plan for the deployment. To develop a project plan:

- Establish deployment goals.
- Identify critical success factors.
- Identify tasks, resources, and tools.
- Identify task and resource dependencies.
- Budget resources needed to meet deployment goals.
- Assign task responsibilities and timelines for completion.
- Identify significant risks, and develop contingency plans.

The project plan includes the deployment tasks described in: Chapter 34, "Planning the Deployment"; Chapter 35, "Validating the Deployment"; and Chapter 36, "Implementing the Deployment." You should update the project plan continuously throughout the project and use a project management tool, such as Microsoft Project, to help plan and manage the deployment.

C H A P T E R   3 5

Validating the Deployment

Deployment Validation Overview

This chapter describes how to validate the deployment plan before you proceed to deploy Microsoft Internet Explorer to your entire organization. To validate the deployment, you need to:

- Prepare the test plan and checklists.
- Test the deployment process in the lab.
- Plan the pilot program.
- Conduct the pilot program.
- Finalize the deployment project plan.

Preparing the Test Plan and Checklists

Prepare a test plan and checklists for lab tests, and then use the test checklists to record satisfactory completion of tasks and note all problems with the process. Also, prepare a checklist to test each deployment and distribution strategy.

Test checklists tasks should include:

- Preparing custom packages for deployment:
  - Install and run the Internet Explorer Administration Kit (IEAK) Configuration Wizard.
  - Build custom packages containing the distribution files.
  - Configure browser auto-configuration (.ins, .js, .pac) files.
  - Configure download sites, and install the distribution files.
  - Copy distribution files to compact discs and floppy disks.
- Deploying custom packages to lab clients:
  - Run Internet Explorer Setup to install the custom package on each client.
  - Install, using each available user install option.
- Operating lab-client software after custom packages are installed:
  - Run Active Desktop to test all desktop features.
  - Run Internet Explorer to test all add-ins and features.
  - Run business applications to check for satisfactory operation.
- Restoring lab clients to their original state:
  - Uninstall Internet Explorer and add-ins.
  - Verify that Internet Explorer components have been removed.
  - Test the desktop and business applications.

Testing the Deployment Process

You should prepare a test lab and then test the proposed deployment strategies on lab computers that represent typical client/server configurations for your organization. If your organization is large or has groups with vastly different computing environments or needs, you may need to prepare multiple test labs and conduct tests at several different sites.

Preparing the Lab

Set aside a physical space for each lab, and acquire a mix of computers that accurately reflects your organization's hardware and software computing environment. If your organization uses portable computers that dial in from remote locations or you need to use additional servers or mainframe computers for business data, give the lab computers an analog phone line and appropriate access to the network.

Configure lab clients and servers to represent typical business and user configurations for your organization. Be sure to include all operating system and business-application configurations, as well as Internet and browser configurations. In addition, be sure to document the lab setup and maintain a record of any changes you make to the setup.

Conducting the Tests

To test the deployment in the lab:

- Perform all deployment tasks, using the test-plan checklists.
- Identify problems with the deployment process and migration issues.
- Revise the deployment plan based on test feedback.

Maintain a record of all issues and problems that you encounter. These records will help you design solutions to correct the problems you encounter. Be sure to follow the testing process described in this section when you test the solutions.

Planning the Pilot Program

Before you deploy Internet Explorer in your organization, plan a pilot program to further test and refine deployment strategies and configurations. The pilot program is a scaled-down version of the full deployment, using pilot groups that are representative of the users in your organization. To plan the pilot program:

- Select appropriate pilot groups.
- Document resources and tasks needed for the pilot program.
- Develop a user-support plan.
- Develop a user-training plan.

Selecting Pilot Groups

Identify and select pilot groups, and prepare them for the pilot program. If your organization is large or has groups with vastly different computing environments or needs, you may need to select several pilot groups. Locate groups that are representative of the users in your organization. Make sure participants have enough time in their schedules for the pilot and are willing to cooperate in the pilot program. Ask for volunteers for the pilot program—you don't want to ask people to participate who might be too busy meeting deadlines.

Documenting Resources and Tasks

Identify the tasks and resources you need to conduct the pilot, and add them to the project plan. Be sure to budget your resources to make sure those resources are available for the pilot program.

Developing the User-Support Plan

Develop a user-support plan that meets the needs of your users. Identify the support staff and resources necessary, and then budget to make sure those support staff and resources are available for the pilot program. User support may include providing online support for deployment through a Web page on your intranet, as well as providing support through your existing help desk.

This user-support plan is the basis for your final deployment user-support plan. You should revise the plan based on feedback from the pilot program and use it to support users during the final deployment.

Developing the User-Training Plan

Develop a training plan that meets the needs of your users. Identify the training staff and resources necessary, and then make sure the staff and resources are available for the pilot program. User training may include providing online Internet Explorer training through a Web page on your intranet, as well as presenting training information to groups to prepare them for the pilot.

This training plan is the basis for your final deployment user-training plan. You should revise the plan, based on feedback from the pilot program, and use it to train users for the final deployment.

Conducting the Pilot Program

You conduct the pilot program by preparing the pilot groups and then implementing the pilot-program plan.

Preparing Pilot Groups

Announce the start of the pilot program well in advance of the start date, and follow up your announcement with several reminders. Conduct meetings with the pilot group managers and with the entire group, to set their expectations and to answer any questions they have. Provide a deployment presentation that explains how users will install Internet Explorer. Explain any installation options that users may choose, and identify where users can go for support.

Conduct training on the new features of Internet Explorer 4. Encourage users to visit the Microsoft Internet Explorer Web site at **http://www.microsoft.com/ie/** for more information. If you implemented a Web page on your intranet for Internet Explorer training, use e-mail to broadcast the URL and a description of the training page to users. Be sure to explain how users can benefit from visiting your training page.

Implementing the Pilot-Program Plan

To implement the pilot-program plan:

- Prepare custom packages for deployment.
- Deploy custom packages to pilot users.
- Monitor and support users as they install Internet Explorer.

Preparing Custom Packages

Before you build custom packages, select a production computer that meets the system requirements for the IEAK Configuration Wizard. For more information, see "Requirements for the IEAK Configuration Wizard" in Chapter 34, "Planning the Deployment."

To prepare the custom packages:

- Install the IEAK on the production computer.
- Run the IEAK Configuration Wizard in the Corporate Administrator role.
- Build the required custom packages.
- Configure browser auto-configuration (.ins, .js, .pac) files.
- Configure download sites, and install the distribution files.
- Copy distribution files to compact discs and floppy disks (if necessary).

For more information on how to use the IEAK Configuration Wizard, as well as creating auto-configuration files and understanding the entire custom package preparation process, see Chapter 36, "Implementing the Deployment."

Deploying Custom Packages

Use the appropriate distribution methods to deploy the custom packages of Internet Explorer to pilot users. For example, you can send an e-mail message to users that directs them to the download site where they can follow instructions to download the custom package. Alternatively, you can include a batch file as an attachment in the e-mail message and instruct users to double-click the batch file to install the custom package. If you are using compact discs or floppy disks, you can distribute them to the users and provide e-mail instructions about how to install the custom package from the compact discs or floppy disks.

Monitoring and Supporting Users

The user support team can monitor the progress of the pilot program and provide user assistance, as necessary. Be sure to document all user trouble calls and problems, as well as the staff resources required to support users during the pilot. Use your experience during the pilot program to plan for the resources needed to support the final deployment.

Finalizing the Deployment Plan

Use the finalized deployment plan to deploy Internet Explorer in the rest of your organization. To finalize the deployment plan:

- Obtain feedback from all participants in the pilot, including end users.
- Document lessons learned during the pilot program.
- Incorporate lessons learned and participant feedback into the deployment project plan.

For information on how to conduct the final deployment, see Chapter 36, "Implementing the Deployment."

CHAPTER 36

Implementing the Deployment

Deployment Implementation Overview

This chapter describes how corporate administrators can deploy custom versions of Internet Explorer packages to user groups in their organization. To deploy Internet Explorer:

- Announce the deployment to the organization.
- Provide user training and support.
- Configure Active Setup installation options.
- Build custom packages.
- Implement a download site.
- Produce distribution media.
- Distribute Internet Explorer to users.
- Monitor and assist user installation of the Internet Explorer browser, as needed.

Announcing the Deployment

After you finalize the deployment plan, inform your users about it. You may want to announce the plan through an e-mail memo or face-to-face meetings. Either way, it's important to communicate the benefits of using Internet Explorer 4, the details of the overall plan, and how the process will be implemented by each department or group.

Providing User Training and Support

Both user training and user support are critical to the success of deployment. Time and resources spent in training will decrease the demand for user support. In general, it's best to provide initial training before Internet Explorer is deployed and to make user support available at deployment.

Setting Up User Training

Tailor user training to the backgrounds and skills of each group in the organization. Consider separately the groups that need to be trained, the best presentation methods, and the amount of information appropriate to each.

Consider these groups of users:

- Average Internet Explorer users
- Power users
- User-support personnel
- New hires after deployment
- Others

Consider covering only the basics required by "average" Internet Explorer users before the deployment, and following up with a program tailored to the subject matter most needed by users (possibly based on support calls).

Setting Up User Support

Internet Explorer provides an **Online Support** option on the **Help** menu. By default, when users click **Online Support**, the Microsoft Support Web page, at **http://support.microsoft.com/support/**, is displayed in the browser window.

However, it's recommended that you create a Web page to provide online technical support for users in your organization. You can build custom packages of Internet Explorer that substitute the URL for your support page as the link used by **Online Support**.

Other resources available to users include:

- Internet Explorer Help.
- The Microsoft Internet Explorer Web site at **http://www.microsoft.com/ie/**.
- Microsoft Press® books on Internet Explorer 4. For more information, see Microsoft Press online at **http://mspress.microsoft.com/**. Books include:
  - *Microsoft Internet Explorer 4 Step by Step*
  - *The Official Microsoft Internet Explorer 4 Book*
  - *Microsoft Internet Explorer 4 At a Glance*

Building Custom Packages

You use the Internet Explorer Administration Kit (IEAK) Configuration Wizard to build custom packages of Internet Explorer that are tailored to meet the needs of user groups in your organization. You can specify all end-user setup options and control most browser features, Outlook Express features, the Active Desktop, Active Channels, security zones, and much more.

After you build custom packages, you distribute the packages to the appropriate user groups, and they install the customized versions of Internet Explorer on their desktops. Internet Explorer is installed with the settings and options you specified when building the custom package.

You can also use the IEAK Configuration Wizard to set up automatic browser configuration. Then, once Internet Explorer is installed on users' desktops, you can use the IEAK Profile Manager to manage Internet Explorer settings centrally, and automatically update the configuration of end users' computers. For more information, see Chapter 37, "Automatic Browser Configuration."

Obtaining the Internet Explorer Administration Kit

To obtain the IEAK, you must visit the Microsoft IEAK Web site at **http://www.microsoft.com/ie/ieak/** and register to download the IEAK. After registering and accepting the licensing agreement, you'll receive additional instructions on how to download the IEAK and your 10-digit customization key. You need the customization key to unlock the IEAK Configuration Wizard before you can build custom packages.

Using the Custom-Build Checklist

The Custom-Build Checklist is the tool you'll use to assemble everything you need to create the custom packages. The checklist saves you both planning and creation time because it helps you focus on decisions you need to make, items you need to create, and other information you need to gather before you begin to use the IEAK Configuration Wizard.

For more information, see Appendix J, "Custom-Build Checklist."

Preparing to Build Custom Packages

Decide how you will be distributing your custom package (compact discs, floppy disks, or download). After the IEAK builds your package, you will need to move the files to the selected media. If you build a downloadable package, you must move the package to the appropriate places on your distribution servers.

Preparing Distribution Servers

If you decide to distribute your browser packages from servers on your intranet or the Internet, gather the path to the servers and the URLs from which the files can be downloaded. Then, create a folder, such as "CIE," on each server to publish all the files and folders associated with your custom browser. For example, if you create server paths of C:\Webshare\Wwwroot\Cie and C:\Webshare\Ftproot\Cie on the hard disks of servers on your intranet, the corresponding URLs would be http://*computername*/cie and ftp://*computername*/cie.

Note When you are creating a browser package, the IE4 folder site will be appended to your URL.

Create the following directory structure:

Folder Name	Description
\Cie	Parent root directory for all files
\Cie\Bitmaps	Optional custom bitmap files that you plan to use

Creating Any Custom Bitmaps You Want to Use

You have the option to customize the following bitmaps in your browser. Place the bitmaps in the \Cie\Bitmaps folder before you run the IEAK Configuration Wizard.

- The custom icon used for the Active Setup Wizard that your users will run when they install the browser

- The custom-toolbar bitmap (that displays as a background for the buttons and menus)

- The custom-background bitmap for the CD-ROM Autorun screen (if you create a compact-disc package)

- The custom image for the CD-ROM buttons (if you create a compact-disc package)

- The custom Channel bar graphics and icons (if you create Active Channels)

- The custom icon used for the Lightweight Directory Access Protocol (LDAP) service (if you provide your own LDAP server)

For more information on how to create these graphics, see "Creating Customized Graphics" and "Create a Bitmap for the Autorun Splash Screen" in the IEAK Help.

The IEAK includes a number of sample graphics files you can use for custom packages. These files reside in the directory: \Ieak\Reskit\ Graphics\Samples after you install the IEAK.

In addition, you'll need to convert any 24-bit images to the 256-color palette. For information about how to do this, see "Editing Your Graphic" in the IEAK Help.

Note Custom backgrounds and buttons are displayed only on computers with 256-color (8-bit) display capabilities. On computers with 16-color (4-bit) display capabilities, a standard low-resolution background bitmap and button set is displayed.

Gathering the URLs for Start, Search, and Support Pages

The start page, also called the home page, appears when the user clicks the **Home** button. Internet Explorer can show a default home page, or you can specify another URL, such as your organization's internal Web home page.

When users click the **Search** button on the toolbar, a default Search page appears on the Search bar in the pane on the left side of the browser window. The Search bar enables the user to see the search query and search results at the same time. The default page that appears in the Search bar comes with a choice of search engines. You can specify another search page to appear in the Search bar if you want.

You can create a user-support page that is linked to **Online Support** on the **Help** menu for Internet Explorer. You will be prompted for the start, search, and support page URLs when you run the IEAK Configuration Wizard. If you do not specify these URLs, Internet Explorer will install with default URLs.

Including Other Applications with a Custom Package

If you would like to include custom components inside the Internet Explorer installation process, such as a custom FTP client or communication software, the IEAK includes a utility called IExpress. IExpress is a tool that creates custom self-installing, self-extracting packages (or .cab files) of applications.

You use the step-by-step IExpress Configuration Wizard to package applications so that they can be installed by Active Setup along with Internet Explorer. This can make the rollout of multiple applications much easier, as they can all be done at the same time with Active Setup. The IExpress program resides in the directory: C:\Program Files\Ieak\Tools\Iexpress. For more information on how to use the wizard, see Appendix L, "IExpress Configuration Wizard."

Using the IEAK Configuration Wizard

You use the IEAK Configuration Wizard to create custom packages that install customized versions of Internet Explorer for user groups. The IEAK Configuration Wizard is a step-by-step process organized into five stages.

Important You should allow one hour to configure the first package from start to finish. It's best to do this in one session; otherwise, you may have to respecify some options. Once you configure a package, each subsequent package will require less time, because you can reuse some of the values you specified for a previous package.

Depending on the options you choose, some pages may not appear; however, each stage requires you to complete at least four wizard pages.

Starting the IEAK Configuration Wizard

▶ **To start the IEAK Configuration Wizard**

1. On the **Start** menu, click **Run**.

   The **Run** dialog box opens.

2. Type **ieakwiz.exe**.

3. Click **OK**.

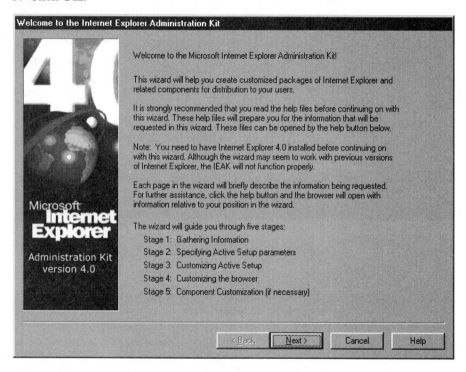

Navigating in the IEAK Configuration Wizard

To	Click
Display the next page, and accept the values on the current page	**Next**
Display any previous page (You may have to reenter some of the values you've entered.)	**Back**
Exit this package	**Cancel**

The following sections display all the wizard pages you can use to specify the custom package. Each page is followed by a table that describes the features and options available on that page.

Stage 1: Gathering Information

Before beginning to navigate the IEAK Configuration Wizard, be sure you have your completed Custom-Build Checklist available to speed up the configuration process. The checklist records all the information you need to supply as well as all the options you want to select. For more information, see Appendix J, "Custom-Build Checklist."

In Stage 1, you will:

- Provide your company name and 10-digit customization code. You received the customization code from Microsoft when you registered the IEAK.
- Select your role—Content Provider or Developer, Service Provider, or Corporate Administrator—based on your license agreement.
- Select the language of the browser package you are creating.
- Specify the destination folder for creating your browser package.
- Select any additional distribution methods you plan to use: compact disc, single floppy disk, or multiple floppy disks.

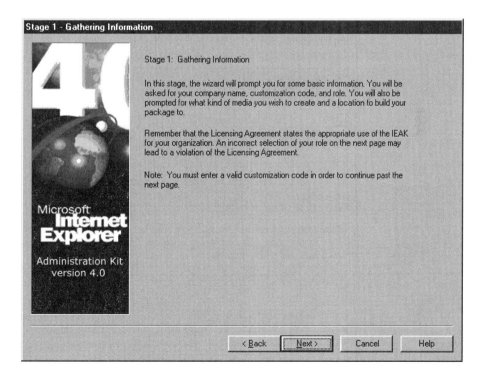

The IEAK Configuration Wizard pages in Stage 1 are:

- Enter Company Name and Customization Code
- Select a Language
- Select Media to Distribute Your Browser

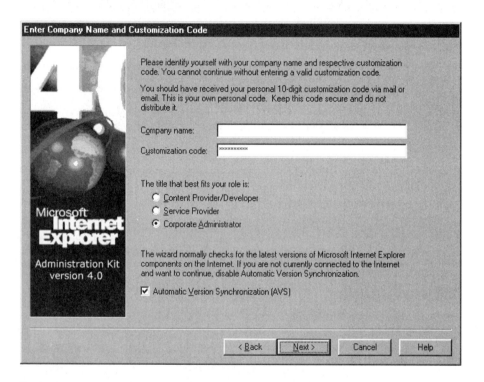

Option	Description
Company name	Type the name of your company. This information is put in the Registry for identification.
Customization code	Type the code you received from Microsoft when you registered your IEAK.
The title that best fits your role is	Select **Corporate Administrator**.
Automatic Version Synchronization (AVS)	This option is selected and shaded the first time you run the wizard to build a custom package, because you must download the components needed from the Internet. When you rebuild the custom package or build additional custom packages, you can clear this option if you don't want to connect to the Internet or update the components.

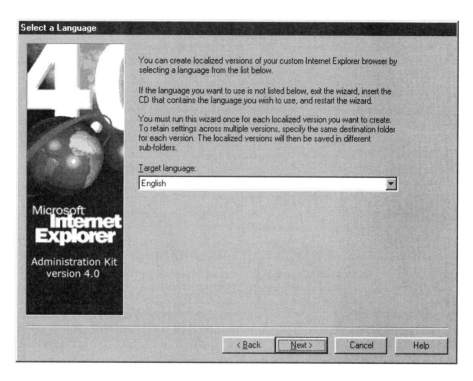

Option	Description
Target language	Type the name of the language for the Internet Explorer package you're creating.
	You need to run the wizard for each language you want to create.

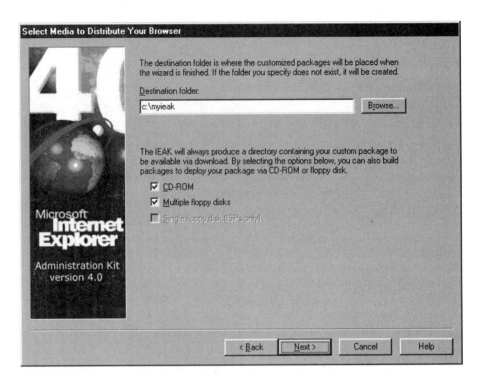

Option	Description
Destination folder	Type the name of the folder in which you want to place the customized package.
Deployment media	If you want to make the package available on compact disc and/or floppy disks, in addition to the destination folder, click one or both of these options.

Stage 2: Specifying Active Setup Parameters

Active Setup is a small, Web-based setup package that lets users install the latest Internet Explorer components directly from a Web site. It is small (about 400K), so it can be run from a single floppy disk or downloaded quickly over the Internet. Active Setup not only manages the entire installation process, but also can search to see what components are already installed, and alert users or administrators when there are newer versions available. When Active Setup downloads Internet Explorer 4, it breaks it up into several small segments. This makes it possible, in the event of a failure or dropped connection, to restart an installation from where it was interrupted, instead of having to start over from the beginning. For more information about Active Setup, see Chapter 2, "Phase 1: Active Setup."

In Stage 2, you will:

- Select the Microsoft download sites from which you receive your components.
- Download or update Microsoft components used to build the package.
- Select any custom components you want to include.
- Select the trusted publisher that signs your custom browser package. (For more information about trusted publishers, see Part 7, "Security and Privacy.")

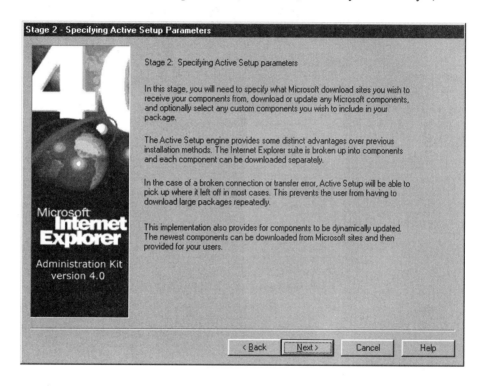

The IEAK Configuration Wizard pages in Stage 2 are:

- Select a Microsoft Download Site
- Automatic Version Synchronization (AVS)
- Specify Custom Active Setup Components
- Specify Trusted Publishers

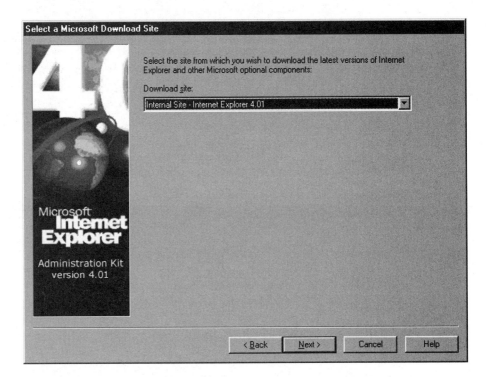

The IEAK automatically loads the list of sites from which you can choose.

Option	Description
Download site	Select the URL of the site—either HTTP or FTP—from which you will download the latest versions of Internet Explorer and other Internet Explorer components.

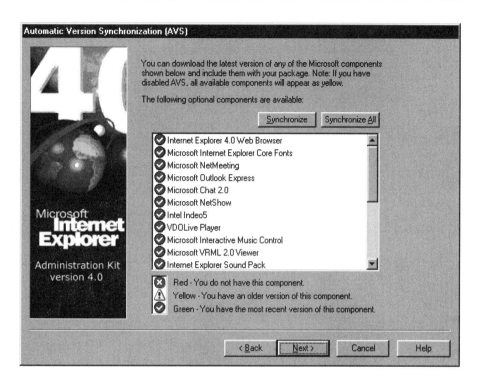

Option	Description
Synchronize	Select components, and click here to synchronize only the Internet Explorer components you want to update. The wizard downloads the latest versions of the selected components.
Synchronize All	Click to synchronize all the listed Internet Explorer components. The wizard downloads the latest version of all the Internet Explorer components.

With this wizard page, you can see quickly whether any updates have been posted for the Internet Explorer 4 components. A red signal means that you have not downloaded the component; a yellow signal means that a newer version is available; and a green signal means you already have the latest version.

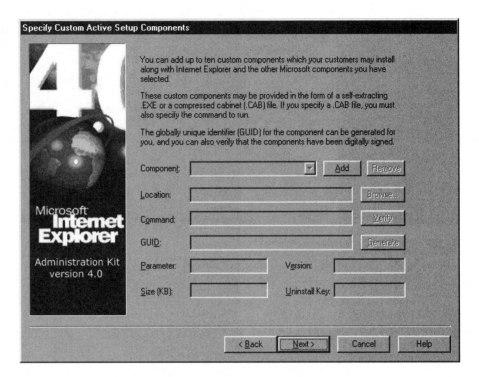

Here you can choose to add any custom components you may have built earlier with IExpress. You can add up to 10 custom components that your users can install at the same time they install the browser. These components can be self-extracting, executable (.exe) files or compressed cabinet (.cab) files.

It is recommended that you sign any custom code. Code-signing lets users know they can trust your code before they download it to their computers. The default settings in Internet Explorer will reject unsigned code.

Option	Description
Component	Type the name of your component in this box. This name will appear in the setup screen when users install your software.
Location	Click **Browse**, or type the path to the self-extracting .exe file or the .cab file for the component.
Command	*For .cab files only.* Type the command needed to run the .cab file.
GUID	If your program already has a globally unique identifier, or GUID, type it in this box. If your program doesn't have a GUID, then click **Generate** to assign a GUID. A GUID establishes a unique identity for programs, objects, and other items. For more information on GUIDs, see "What is a Globally Unique Identifier?" in the IEAK Help.

Option	Description
Parameter	*For .exe files only.* Type any command-line switches you want to run with the .exe file.
Size (KB)	Type the size of the program.
Version	Type a version number to help track versions of your program and to ensure that the latest version is installed.
Uninstall Key	If you want to allow users to uninstall this component, type the registry entry, including both the DISPLAYNAME and UNINSTALLSTRING values in **HKEY_LOCAL_COMPUTER/Software/ Microsoft Windows/CurrentVersion/Uninstall/**.

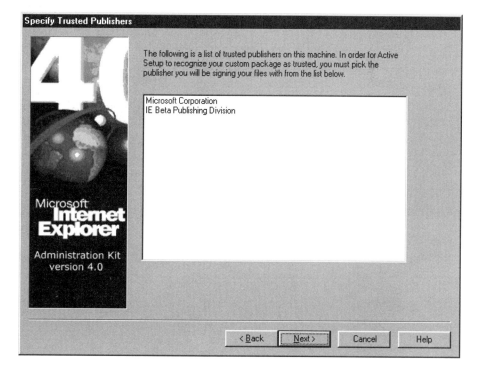

Option	Description
Publisher list	Select the publisher you will use to sign your files. For information about how to add a trusted publisher, see Part 7, Chapter 28, "Digital Certificates." For information about signing files, see the "Signing Your Programs" section of the IEAK Configuration Wizard Help.

The IEAK Configuration Wizard will display the list of trusted publishers installed on your machine. In order for Active Setup to recognize your custom package as trusted, you must select the publisher that will sign your files.

Stage 3: Customizing Active Setup

In Stage 3, you will:

- Specify an optional custom CD-ROM Autorun screen, if you are creating a CD-ROM package.

- Specify optional custom Active Setup Wizard title bar text and bitmap. These settings affect how Setup appears to the user.

- Choose whether to install the package "silently," with few or no prompts to the user.

- Specify up to 10 unique installation options, and determine which components are included with each option.

- Specify up to 10 sites from which your package will be downloaded.

- Specify a unique version number for your browser customizations.

- Specify the directory in which you want Internet Explorer to be installed on your users' computers.

- Specify whether you want to allow the Windows Desktop Update to be installed to integrate Web browser functionality into users' desktops and folders.

(For more information about Active Setup, see Part 1, Chapter 2, "Phase 1: Active Setup.")

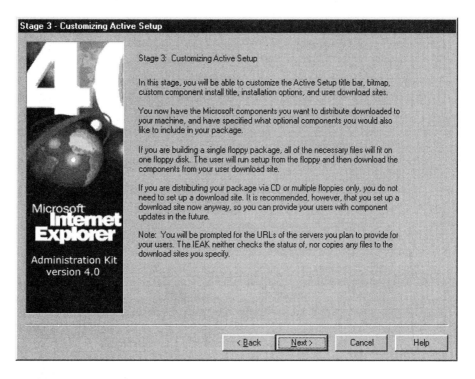

The IEAK Configuration Wizard pages in Stage 3 are:

- Customize the Autorun Screen for CD-ROM Installations
- Customize the Active Setup Wizard
- Custom Components Install Section
- Select Silent Install
- Select Installation Options
- Specify Download URLs
- Select Version Number
- Specify Where You Want to Install Your Browser
- Integrating the Web Desktop Update

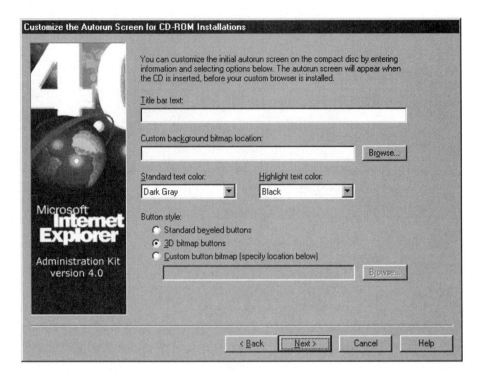

This wizard page displays only if you chose to distribute packages on compact disc (that is, you selected the **CD-ROM** check box in Stage 1 on the wizard page "Select Media to Distribute Your Browser").

Autorun is a technology that was introduced with Windows 95. The wizard creates an Autorun program and places it in the file system for the compact disc. Autorun will launch the appropriate startup screen when the user inserts the compact disc.

Option	Description
Title bar text	Type the text that you want to appear in the title bar of the user's Autorun page.
Custom background bitmap location	If you want a bitmap to appear behind the title bar text, type the path to its location here. Make sure that the background color doesn't conflict with the text color.
Standard text color	Select a color for text that isn't part of a link.
Highlight text color	Select a color for link text.
Button style	Click the button style to be used.
Custom button bitmap	*For Custom button bitmap only.* Click **Browse** to locate the path to the image.

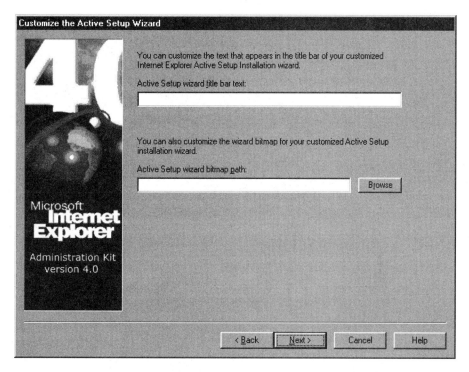

Option	Description
Active Setup wizard title bar text	Type the text you want to appear in the title bar of the end user's Active Setup Wizard.
Active Setup wizard bitmap path	Type the path to a bitmap, or click **Browse** to locate the path to the image.

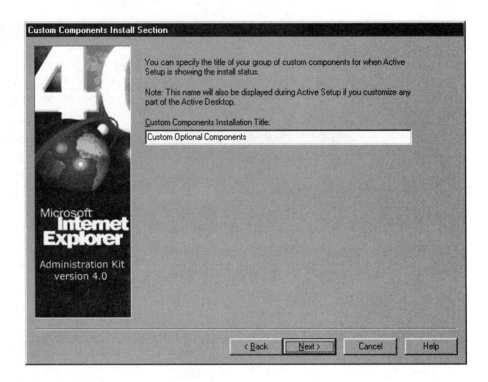

Option	Description
Custom Components Installation Title	Type the text you want to appear when Active Setup is installing your custom additions to the Internet Explorer package.

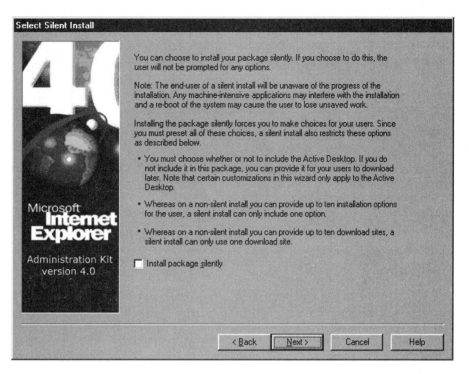

Option	Description
Install package silently	If you do not want end users to specify preferences during setup, select the check box.
	To allow end users to specify their preferences during setup, clear the check box.

Installing the package silently forces you, as administrator, to make choices for your users. Because the user is not presented with any choices, you must pre-configure each of the Internet Explorer installation options. A silent installation also restricts the options outlined below. For a silent installation:

- You must choose whether or not to include the Windows Desktop Update or Active Desktop functionality. If you do not include it in this package, you can provide it for your users to download later.

- You can provide only one installation option. With a regular installation, you can provide up to 10 installation packages for your users.

- You have only one site available for downloads. With a regular installation, you can provide up to 10 download sites.

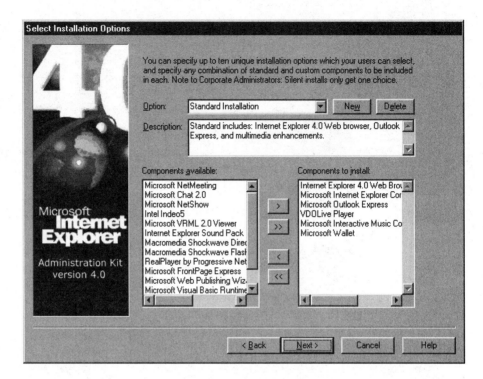

This wizard page enables you to do two things. First, you can customize the Minimal, Standard, and Full Installation packages to contain any components you want. Use the arrow keys to move the components back and forth to create customized packages. However, you aren't limited to just those three types of installations. You can create up to 10 installation packages that include whatever configuration you want, your name, and descriptions of those packages.

Option	Description
Option	Select the option you prefer, or click **New** to add a custom option.
Description	Type a description of this custom package that your end users will see when installing Internet Explorer. Provide enough information so that your users can make a decision about which software to install.
Components available	Lists the components that you made available on the Automatic Version Synchronization page. (To add additional components, click **Back** until you reach that page.)
Components to install	Lists the components to be included in this installation option.

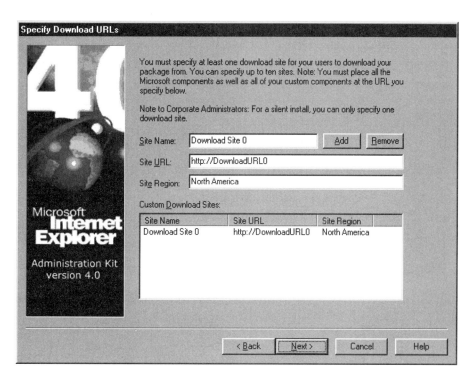

You must complete this wizard page for each download URL.

Option	Description
Site Name	Click **Add** to designate a download site. If you want, you can modify the name created by the wizard. Do not use commas in the name.
Site URL	Enter the URL for your HTTP or FTP server.
	IEAK appends the folder IE4site to the URL. Active Setup looks for this URL when installing Internet Explorer for this custom package.
Site Region	Enter the location of the site, such as the city, state, region, or country.
Custom Download Sites	Lists all the download sites.

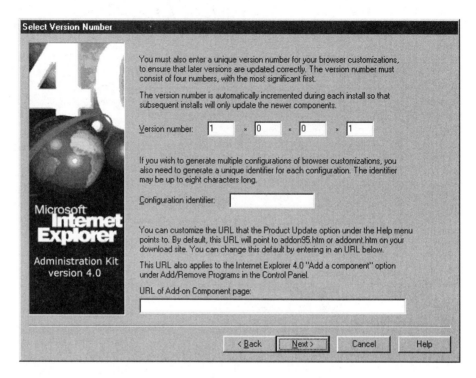

These options ensure that the latest version of each customized component and feature is installed every time.

Option	Description
Version number	If you want, you can revise the version number.
	The wizard increments this number each time you run the wizard. The first digit is the most significant; for example, 2 0 0 0 is newer than 1 0 0 6.
Configuration identifier	Type a unique number for this version.
	The configuration identifier is an 8-digit code that identifies your customized version of the browser. Using this code can prevent the user from installing a previous version over a newer version of your customized browser. For the configuration identifier to prevent an earlier version from being installed, the company name for both browsers must be the same. You specified the company name in Stage 1 of the IEAK Configuration Wizard.
URL of Add-on Component page	If you want to allow end users to update Internet Explorer from the **Help** menu, type the URL of addon95.htm.

When new versions of Internet Explorer become available, users will be able to select **Product Updates** from the **Help** menu in Internet Explorer 4 to update their Internet Explorer. To reach this page, users can also click the **Add/Remove Programs** icon in the Control Panel, click **Microsoft Internet Explorer 4.0**, and then click **Add/Remove**. If you want users to obtain software updates from another location that you have customized, specify that URL in the **URL of Add-on Component page** box.

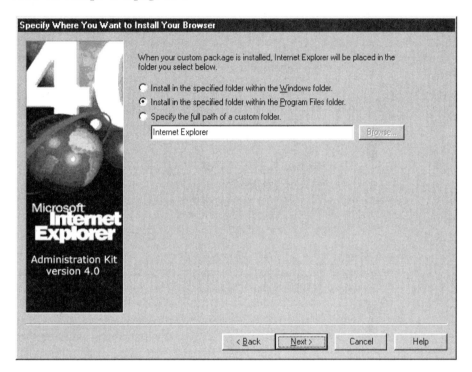

Option	Description
Install in the specified folder within the Windows folder	Click this option, and enter the name of the folder.
Install in the specified folder within the Program Files folder	Click this option, and enter the name of the folder or accept the default **Internet Explorer** option.
Specify the full path of a custom folder	Click and enter the path and folder name, or click **Browse** to locate it.

Active Setup installs Internet Explorer in the folder you specify on this wizard page. If the path you specify doesn't exist on the user's hard disk, Active Setup creates it.

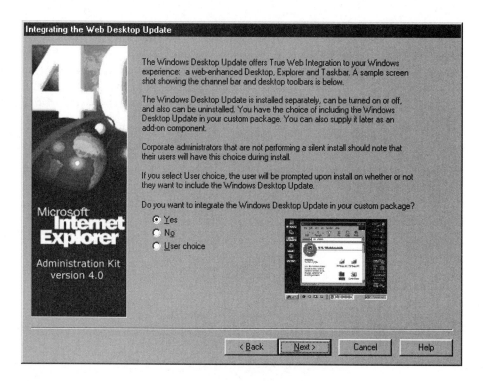

Option	Description
Yes	Click this option to install the Windows Desktop Update on users' computers.
No	Click this option if you don't want to install the Windows Desktop Update on users' computers.
User choice	Click this option to allow users to choose whether to install the Windows Desktop Update on their computers.

Stage 4: Customizing the Browser

In Stage 4, you will:

- Specify browser title bar text and a toolbar background bitmap.
- Specify start, search, and online-support pages for the browser.
- Specify favorites, Favorites folders, and links for the Links bar.
- Specify welcome messages and desktop wallpaper.
- Specify the Active Channels that appear on users' desktops.
- Specify software distribution channels to update software on user's computers.
- Specify the Active Desktop items that appear on users' desktops.
- Specify the desktop toolbars that appear on users' desktops.
- Specify custom folders for My Computer and Control Panel.
- Specify a custom browser user agent string.
- Specify automatic browser configuration settings.
- Specify Internet Proxy settings.
- Specify custom settings for site certificates and Authenticode Security.
- Specify custom settings for security zones and content ratings.

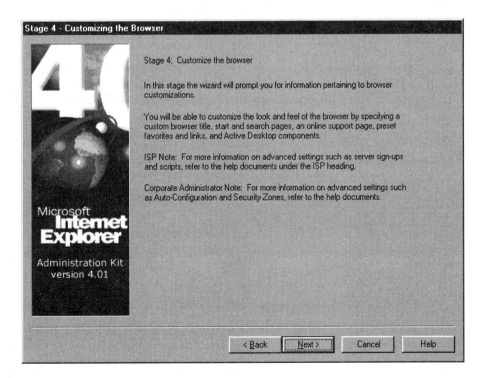

The IEAK Configuration Wizard pages in Stage 4 are:

- Customize the Window Title and Toolbar Background
- Customize the Start and Search Pages
- Specify an Online Support Page for Your Browser
- Favorites Folder and Links Customization
- Customize the Welcome Message and Desktop Wallpaper
- Customize the Active Channel bar
- Customize Software Update Channels
- Specify Active Desktop Components
- Customize Desktop Toolbars
- My Computer and Control Panel Webview Customization
- User Agent String Customization
- Automatic Browser Configuration
- Specify Proxy Settings
- Site Certificate and Authenticode Settings
- Security Zones and Content Ratings Customization

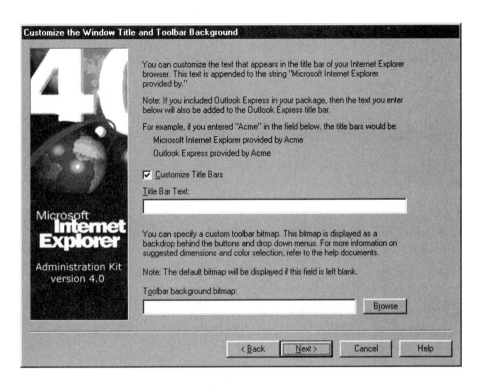

Option	Description
Customize Title Bars	Select this check box to customize the browser title bars (and Outlook Express, if included in the package).
Title Bar Text	Type the text that you want to follow the phrase: "Microsoft Internet Explorer provided by."
Toolbar background bitmap	Type the path and file name for the bitmap to be displayed in the background behind the Internet Explorer toolbar buttons, or click **Browse** to locate it.

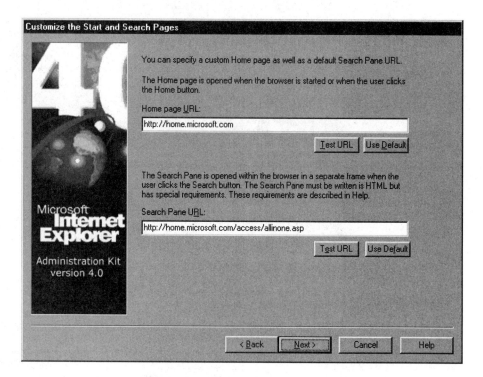

Option	Description
Home page URL	To use the default Internet Explorer home page, click **Use Default**. To use another home page, type the URL of the home page, and then click **Test URL** to ensure that the URL is correct.
Search Pane URL	To use the default Internet Explorer Search Pane, click **Use Default**. To use another Search bar, type the URL of the Search bar, and then click **Test URL** to ensure the URL is correct.

The Internet Explorer 3 Search-page functionality has been replaced with the Explorer Search bar—a pane that slides in on the left side of the screen. To load the Search bar, users simply click the **Search** button on the Internet Explorer 4 Standard toolbar. For more information about the Explorer Search bar, see "Explorer Bars" in Part 2, Chapter 9, "Browser Features and Functionality."

Important The Search bar lists search results in the Search bar pane, and when a user clicks a search-results link, the page is displayed in the main browser window, while the search-results list remains visible in the Search bar (until the **Search** button on the toolbar is clicked again). This functionality requires that special tags be included in the Search page. To learn more about creating a page for a custom Search bar, see "Explorer Bars" in Part 2, Chapter 9, "Browser Features and Functionality."

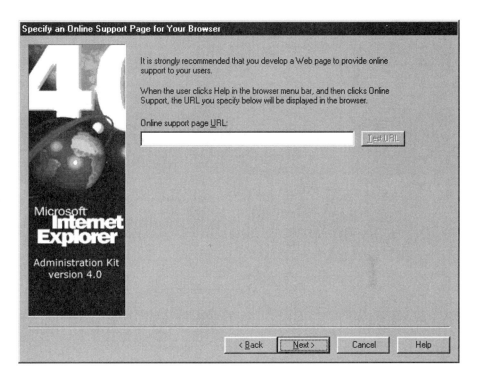

Option	Description
Online support page URL	Type the URL of the Web page that you created to offer technical support, and then click **Test URL** to ensure that the URL is correct.

This page will appear when your users click **Online Support** on the **Help** menu in Internet Explorer 4.

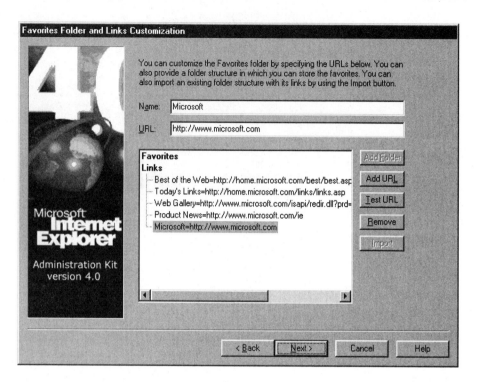

Option	Description
Name	Type a name for the Favorite or link.
URL	Type a URL for the Favorite or link.
Add Folder	To insert a hierarchical directory into the Favorites list, which can include more Favorites, click **Add Folder**.
Add URL	Select **Favorites** or **Links** or a folder, and then click **Add URL** to add its URL.
Test URL	You can click **Test URL** to ensure that the URL is correct.
Import	Select **Import** to point the IEAK to a link or a folder of links that you would like to import into the package.

The favorites you specify on this wizard page appear in the Favorites folder of end users' computers. For example, you could add key URLs for your organization, such as the Help Desk and the Human Relations Web pages.

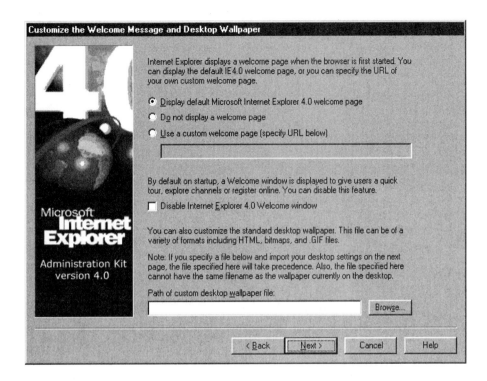

Option	Description
Display default Microsoft Internet Explorer 4.0 welcome page	Click here to choose the default Microsoft Internet Explorer 4 welcome page.
Do not display a welcome page	Click here if you don't want to display a welcome page. The first page that is displayed will be the home page.
Use a custom welcome page (specify URL below)	Click here, and type the URL for your custom welcome page.
Disable Internet Explorer 4.0 Welcome window	Click here to disable the Internet Explorer welcome window, which displays by default on the user's desktop when the Windows Desktop Update is installed.
Path of custom desktop wallpaper file	Type the URL for your custom desktop wallpaper, which can be a .bmp, .gif, or .htm file, or click **Browse** to locate the file.

Internet Explorer displays a Welcome page the first time the browser is launched. You can display the default Internet Explorer Welcome window, or you can specify the URL of your own custom welcome page. The welcome page is not the same as the home page, which is the page that opens each time you start your browser (after the first time) and when the user clicks the **Home** button.

By default, an Internet Explorer Welcome window displays on the user's desktop when the Windows Desktop Update is installed. The Welcome window provides a link to a quick tour of the features of Internet Explorer, as well as a link to explore Active Channels. It's recommended that you allow the Welcome window to appear, so new users can learn about the new features of Internet Explorer 4. Users can easily turn off the welcome tutorial by clearing the check box for **Show this next time you log in** on the Welcome window.

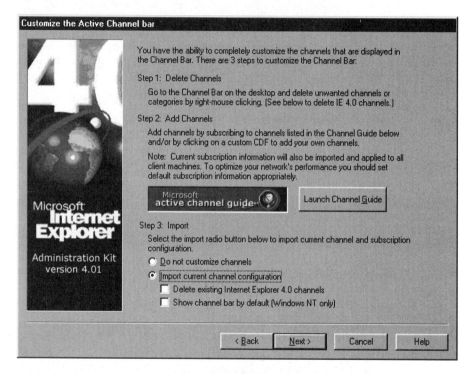

In order to insert a customized set of Active Channels into your IEAK packages, you must set them up on your computer the way that you want them to be configured on your users' desktops. The IEAK will import your current settings and distribute them to your users. If you want to prevent users from changing, adding, or deleting these channels once Internet Explorer is installed, you can specify this in Stage 5 of the IEAK Configuration Wizard using the System Policies and Restrictions page. For more information about setting up channels, see Chapter 16, "Managed Webcasting," in Part 4, "Information Delivery: Webcasting."

Option	Description
Launch Channel Guide	This is simply a shortcut to the Microsoft Channel Guide on the Internet, where you can easily subscribe to the channels and configure how they will appear on your users' Channel bar. You can also add channels from your intranet without going to the Microsoft Channel Guide. For more information, see "Understanding Active Channels" and Desktop Items" in Chapter 16, "Managed Webcasting."
Do not customize channels	Select if you do not want to install channels on end users' computers.
Import current channel configuration	Select to import the channels you have set up on your computer.
Delete existing Internet Explorer 4.0 channels	Select to delete any existing Active Channels on end users' computers.
Show channel bar by default	*For Windows NT only.* Select to show the Channel bar in the browser window by default.

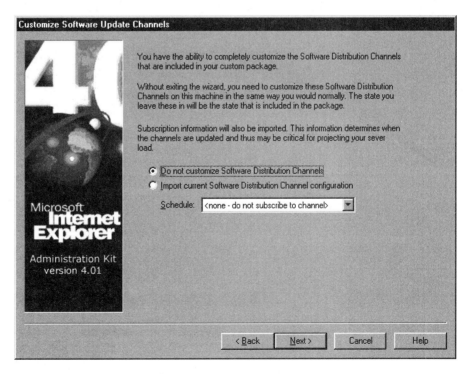

In order to insert a customized set of software distribution channels into your IEAK packages, you must set them up on your computer in the way that you want them to be configured on your users' desktops. The IEAK will import those settings and distribute them to your users. If you want to prevent users from changing their software distribution channel configuration once Internet Explorer is installed, you can specify this in Stage 5 of the IEAK Configuration Wizard, using the System Policies and Restrictions page. For more information about setting up software distribution channels, see Chapter 38, "Software Distribution and Updates."

Option	Description
Do not customize Software Distribution Channels	Select if you do not want to install software distribution channels on end users' computers.
Import current Software Distribution Channel configuration	Select to import the software distribution channels you have set up on your computer, and select a schedule option from the **Schedule** box.
Schedule Options	
<none – do not subscribe to channel>	Select to specify that all software distribution channels are imported, but not subscribed to, when the custom package is installed on users' computers. This is the default. Be careful you do not select this by mistake.
Auto	Select to specify that each software distribution channel uses the schedule information contained in the SCHEDULE section of its CDF file when the custom package is installed on users' computers
Daily	Select to specify that all software distribution channels are scheduled to be updated daily when the custom package is installed on users' computers.
Monthly	Select to specify that all software distribution channels are scheduled to be updated monthly when the custom package is installed on users' computers.
Weekly	Select to specify that all software distribution channels are scheduled to be updated weekly when the custom package is installed on users' computers.

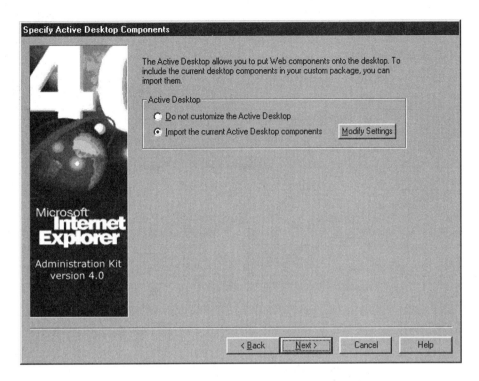

In order to insert a customized set of Active Desktop items into your IEAK packages, you must set them up on your computer in the way that you want them to be configured on your users' desktops. The IEAK will import those settings and distribute them to your users. If you want to prevent users from changing their desktop configuration once Internet Explorer is installed, you can specify this in Stage 5 of the IEAK Configuration Wizard. For more information about setting up Active Desktop items, see Chapter 16, "Managed Webcasting," in Part 4, "Information Delivery: Webcasting."

Option	Description
Do not customize the Active Desktop	Select if you do not want to customize the Active Desktop.
Import the current Active Desktop components	Select to import the desktop items you have set up on your computer.
Modify Settings	Click to open the **Display Properties** dialog box. Use the Web tab to specify or change settings for desktop items.

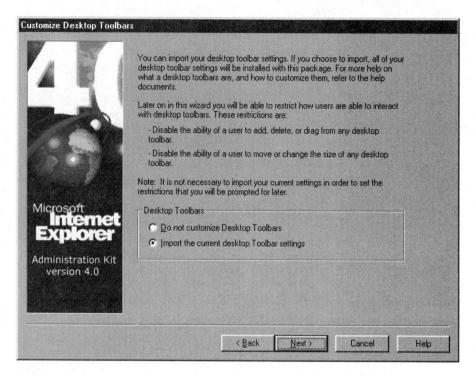

Option	Description
Desktop Toolbars	Click the option you want to use.

You can import your current settings by clicking **Import the current desktop Toolbar settings**. Click **Do not customize Desktop Toolbars** if you want users to have the default toolbar settings.

You can add the following four toolbars where you want them:

- The **Quick Launch** toolbar provides shortcuts to several often-used features of Internet Explorer 4: the desktop, the Web browser, Outlook Express, and channels.

- The **Address** toolbar enables you to enter a Web-page address (URL) without first opening the Internet Explorer browser.

- The **Links** toolbar provides shortcuts to important Web sites (for example, **http://www.microsoft.com/**) so that you can open them without first opening the browser.

- The **Desktop** toolbar contains all the shortcuts on your desktop and organizes them in one convenient location.

- In addition to the ready-made toolbars, you can create a toolbar from the contents of any folder.

For more information about these toolbars, see Part 3.

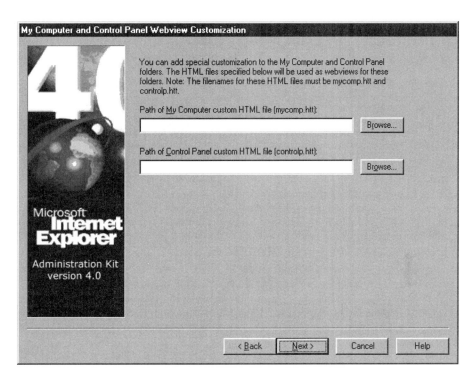

Option	Description
Path of My Computer custom HTML file (mycomp.htt)	Enter the path to the mycomp.htt file, or click **Browse** to locate it.
Path of Control Panel custom HTML file (controlp.htt)	Enter the path to the controlp.htt file, or click **Browse** to locate it.

You can customize how My Computer and Control Panel appear on your users' desktops by customizing the files that serve as templates for them: mycomp.htt (My Computer) and controlp.htt (Control Panel). If the user installs the Windows Desktop Update, My Computer and Control Panel can appear as Web pages in Web view. One reason to customize these folders is to provide your own instructions, a company logo, or links for support or corporate sites. For more information, see Part 3.

If you have installed the Windows Desktop Update on your computer, these files are located in the C:\Windows\Web or C:\Windows\NT folder. You can open them using a text editor, such as Notepad, or an HTML editor. It's recommended that you make a backup copy of these files before working with them, so you can restore them to their original state, if needed.

For more information about integrating Web views in the IEAK, see "Stage 4: My Computer and Control Panel Web View Customization," in the IEAK Help. For more information about development with **WebViewFolderContents** objects, see the *Internet Client SDK*.

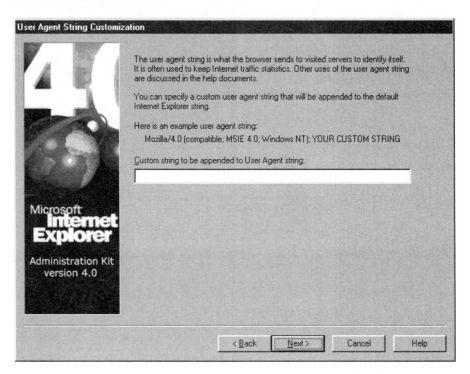

Option	Description
Custom string to be appended to User Agent string	Enter the text you want to append to the user agent string for user-group browsers.

The user agent string is what a browser sends to Web servers to identify itself. Web servers use the information to identify the browser type and version, and typically record the information in server usage logs. Many organizations use the user agent string information to track statistics about browser usage on their Web sites. For example, organizations can identify what percentage of users access Web pages using Internet Explorer and Netscape Navigator. Based on a browser's user agent string, some Web sites download Web pages that are tailored to the capabilities of the browser type and version.

You only need to customize the user agent string if you want to do any of the following:

- Track the browser usage of specific user groups, and differentiate user group browser statistics from your intranet or Internet sites.

- Provide custom Web content to user groups based on the custom user agent string. For example, you might want to set up your Human Relations Web site to provide different Web pages for managers, with content appropriate only for managers. Therefore, you build separate custom packages for managers and non-managers, and include the appropriate custom user agent string.

Be aware that other organizations that track site statistics will see the custom user agent string. The following example shows how the IEAK appends a custom string *CustomUserAgentString* to the default user agent string:

```
Mozilla/4.0(compatible;MSIE 4.0b1;WindowsNT);CustomUserAgentString
```

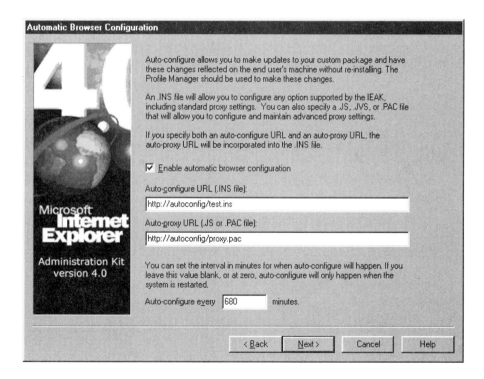

Option	Description
Enable automatic browser configuration	Click if you want to turn on automatic browser configuration for this custom package.
Auto-configure URL (.INS file)	Type the URL for the auto-configuration (.ins) file. This URL points to the auto-configuration (.ins) file for this custom package. You can create a different file for each user group in your organization. Use a unique file name for each group managed—for example, sysadm.ins for system administrators and grpman.ins for group managers. The URL includes the file name in the following format:
	http://path/file name
Auto-proxy URL (.JS or .PAC file)	Enter the path to the .js or .pac file. The URL includes this file name in the following format:
	http://path/file name
Auto-configure every __ minutes	Enter an interval, in minutes, when automatic configuration occurs. After deployment, Internet Explorer updates the auto-configuration information at the specified interval. If you leave the space for this interval blank or type "0," auto-configuration occurs only when users manually refresh the browser's automatic configuration or when Internet Explorer is restarted.

Automatic browser configuration is a feature of Internet Explorer 3 and Internet Explorer 4. You can set up Internet Explorer to periodically download auto-configuration files maintained on a central server. The contents of auto-configuration files are used to specify a wide variety of application, desktop, and shell settings for users. Internet Explorer 3 ignores any settings that apply only to Internet Explorer 4.

You typically create and maintain separate auto-configuration files for the different user groups in your organization. You can build custom packages configured to read auto-configuration files for each user group. You can then distribute the appropriate custom build to each user group. For more information, see Chapter 37, "Automatic Browser Configuration."

When the custom packages are deployed with automatic browser configuration enabled, Internet Explorer periodically downloads the auto-configuration files from the server. Each time the auto-configuration information is refreshed, the system checks to see if there are new changes and then updates user, application, desktop, and system settings, as necessary.

You can use automatic browser configuration to manage a wide range of settings for users' computers, including Internet Explorer settings, desktop settings, and system settings. You can use the IEAK Profile Manager to create and modify auto-configuration files to change most of the settings and options you specified using the IEAK Configuration Wizard. You can also use the Profile Manager to update and manage system policies and restrictions and to lock down settings to prevent your users from changing the settings you specify. For example, you can prevent users from changing automatic browser configuration settings in their **Internet Options** settings. For more information, see Chapter 37, "Automatic Browser Configuration."

You can use the auto-proxy (.js or .pac) files to configure proxy settings dynamically for user groups. Using auto-proxy files is optional. You may want to specify proxy settings for each user group, using the Specify Proxy Settings page, which displays next. For more information about creating auto-proxy files, see Chapter 37, "Automatic Browser Configuration," and "JavaScript or JScript Auto-Proxy Example Files" in the IEAK Help.

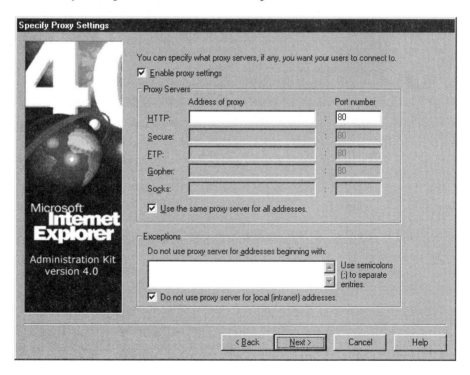

Option	Description
Enable proxy settings	If you do not use proxy servers, clear this check box. You should clear this check box if you use auto-proxy files.
HTTP	Type the URL of the proxy server for HTTP and its port number.
Secure	Type the URL of the secure proxy server and its port number.
FTP	Type the URL of the proxy server for FTP and its port number.
Gopher	Type the URL of the proxy server for Gopher and its port number.
Socks	Type the URL of the socks proxy server and its port number.
Use the same proxy server for all addresses	To use different proxy servers for different URLs, clear this check box.
Exceptions	Type the path(s) or domain(s) that do not require the use of proxy servers.
Do not use proxy server for local (intranet) addresses	To use proxy servers for local intranet URLs, clear this check box.

For more information about configuring proxy settings, see Chapter 8, "Configuring Connection Settings."

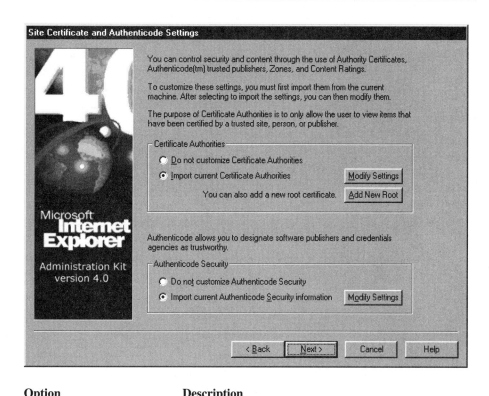

Option	Description
Do not customize Certificate Authorities	Select to accept the default Certificate Authorities settings.
Import current Certificate Authorities	Select to import the certificate settings you have set up on your computer.
Modify Settings	Click to modify Certificate Authority settings. Use the **Certificate Authorities** dialog box to remove certificates or to select trusted certificates for each **Issuer Type**.
Add New Root	Click to add a new root certificate. Use the **Browse** dialog box to add the *file name* of the root certificate file.
Do not customize Authenticode Security	Select to not install trusted publishers and authorities on your users' computers.
Import current Authenticode Security information	Select to import the trusted publishers and authorities you have set up on your computer.
Modify Settings	Click to remove trusted publishers and authorities. Use the **Authenticode Security Technology** dialog box to remove certificates for trusted publishers and authorities.

Internet Explorer 4 uses industry-standard digital certificates and Microsoft Authenticode technology to verify the identity of individuals and organizations on the Web and to ensure content integrity. Together with security zones, these can be used to control user access to online content based on the type, source, and location of the content. For example, you can use security zones in conjunction with certificates to allow users to have full access to Web content on your intranet, but limit the access to Web content from restricted sites located on the Internet. For more information, see Part 7, "Security and Privacy."

You can either accept the default certificate settings or customize the settings to meet your needs. For information on how to configure certificates, see Chapter 28, "Digital Certificates."

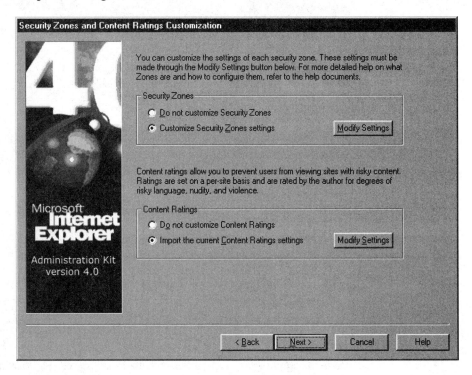

Option	Description
Do not customize Security Zones	Select to accept the default security zone settings.
Customize Security Zones settings	Select to import custom security zone settings you have set up on your computer.
Modify Settings	Click to customize security zone settings. Use the **Security** dialog box to specify the security levels assigned to the security zones.
Do not customize Content Ratings	Select to install browsers on users' computers with default settings and with content ratings disabled.
Import the current Content Ratings settings	Select to import custom content rating settings you have set up on your computer.
Modify Settings	Click to customize content rating settings. Use the **Content Advisor** dialog box to specify the custom content ratings.

You can manage security zones and content ratings for your company and customize the settings for each security zone. For more information, see Chapter 27, "Security Zones." You can configure security zone settings to control how users can access Web content from sites located on the intranet, Internet, trusted sites, and restricted sites.

You can also control the types of content users can access on the Internet. You can adjust the content rating settings to reflect what you think is appropriate content in four areas: language, nudity, sex, and violence. For more information, see Chapter 30, "Content Advisor."

Stage 5: Customizing Components

In Stage 5, you will:

- Specify your users' Outlook Express news and mail settings.
- Specify any LDAP server settings to provide Internet directory services to your users.
- Specify the Outlook Express welcome e-mail message to welcome users and customize the InfoPane that appears when users start the program.
- Specify default signatures to provide a corporate disclaimer or signature in Internet newsgroup or e-mail messages.
- Specify system policies and restrictions settings and lock down a wide range of browser, application, and system settings.

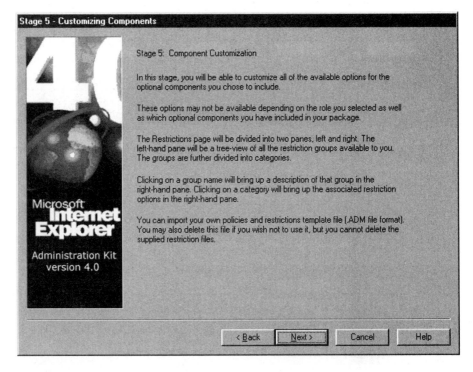

The IEAK Configuration Wizard pages in Stage 5 are:

- Specify Internet Mail Servers, Domain, and News Server
- Specify LDAP Server Settings
- Outlook Express Customizations
- Include a Signature
- System Policies and Restrictions

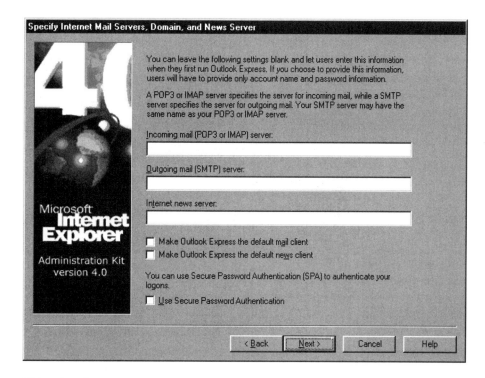

This wizard page appears only when you have chosen Outlook Express as an Internet Explorer component. It's optional because end users can provide this information when they run Outlook Express. This is a good way for administrators to pre-configure server settings that their users may not have.

Option	Description
Incoming mail (POP3 or IMAP) server	Type the server name, domain name, and subdomain for handling incoming mail.
Outgoing mail (SMTP) server	Type the server name, domain name, and subdomain for handling outgoing mail. This may be the same as the incoming mail server.
Internet news server	Type the server name of which Network News Transfer Protocol (NNTP) to use.
Make Outlook Express the default mail client	If you want Outlook Express to be the default mail client, select this check box.
Make Outlook Express the default news client	If you want Outlook Express to be the default news client, select this check box.
Use Secure Password Authentication	If you want Secure Password Authentication to authenticate users when they log on, select this check box.

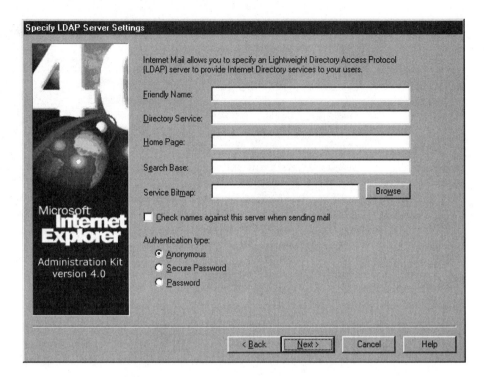

Directory services are powerful search tools that help your users find people and businesses around the world. The Address Book supports LDAP for accessing directory services, and it comes with built-in access to several popular directory services. You can specify the LDAP services for your users.

Option	Description
Friendly Name	Type the name of the LDAP server.
Directory Service	Type the directory service.
Home Page	Type the URL of the home page that Internet Explorer displays when the end user requests the LDAP Web site.
Search Base	Type the root or scope for the hierarchical level at which to search the LDAP server: base, one, or sub.
Service Bitmap	Type the path to the location of the bitmap, or click **Browse** to locate it.
Check names against this server when sending mail	If you want Outlook Express to check names before sending mail, select this check box.
Authentication type	Select the authentication type: Anonymous, Secure Password, or Password.

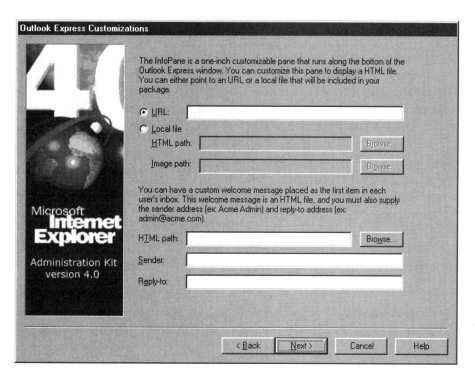

Option	Description
URL	Click to specify a URL for the Outlook Express InfoPane.
Local file	Click to use an HTML file for the Outlook Express InfoPane.
HTML path *(InfoPane)*	Type the path to the InfoPane file, or click **Browse** to locate it.
HTML path *(custom welcome message)*	Type the path to the custom welcome message file, or click **Browse** to locate it.
Sender	Type the user's name.
Reply-to	Type the user's e-mail address.

You can give Outlook Express a custom look and welcome new users with an e-mail message.

The Outlook Express InfoPane contains helpful information and links. You can customize this pane with support numbers, Frequently Asked Questions (FAQs), and information about your company.

The InfoPane appears as a window at the bottom of Outlook Express when you start the program. You can customize the InfoPane with an HTML file that is either a local file or an Internet address (URL).

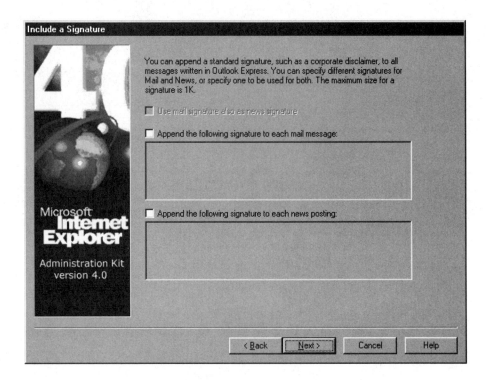

Option	Description
Use mail signature also as news signature	To use the e-mail signature for posting news, select this check box.
Append the following signature to each mail message	Type the signature to append to each e-mail message.
Append the following signature to each news posting	Type the signature to append to each news posting.

You can include a default signature or disclaimer that will appear on Outlook Express newsgroup or e-mail messages. A disclaimer is often used to show that messages submitted by employees over the Internet do not represent official company policies. The maximum size of the signature is 1K. You can choose to append signatures to newsgroup messages only, to e-mail messages only, or to both types of messages.

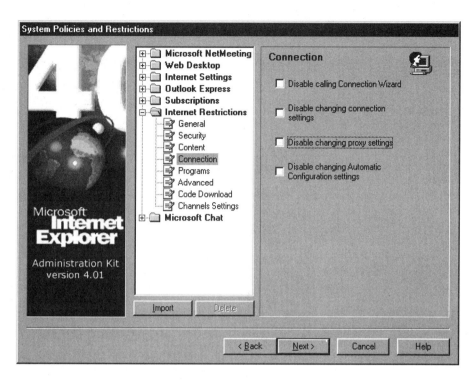

Option	Description
Left pane	Select the subject for which you want to change policies and restrictions.
Right pane	Specify the policies and restrictions you want for the subject.

For more information on the System Policies and Restrictions page, see Chapter 37, "Automatic Browser Configuration." Also, for a complete list of all the options on this page, see Appendix J, "Custom-Build Checklist."

Generating the Package

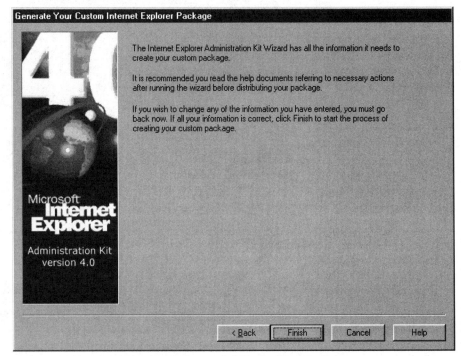

After finishing Stage 5, the IEAK Configuration Wizard displays this page to give you a last chance to make changes. Once you click **Finish**, the wizard creates the package as you specified.

Signing Custom Package Files

Digital signatures identify the source of programs and guarantee that the code hasn't changed since it was signed. Depending on how users' browser security levels are configured, users could be warned not to download files that aren't signed, or could be prevented from downloading them. Therefore, you should digitally sign the .cab files created by the IEAK Configuration Wizard and any custom components you include.

Signing .cab files and custom programs requires two steps: obtaining a digital certificate—from a Certificate Authority (CA) such as VeriSign or GTE—and signing the code. For more information, see Chapter 28, "Digital Certificates," "Signing Your Programs" in the IEAK Help, and "Signing Code with Microsoft Authenticode Technology" in the *Internet Client SDK*.

Producing Distribution Media

This section covers the downloading and distributing of custom browser packages.

Designating Distribution

If you created the browser package on an Internet or intranet server, you need to set up your Web site so that users can download the files. For example, you can create a page where you post download information and a link to the install engine, IE4Setup.exe.

The IEAK Configuration Wizard places IE4Setup.exe in a directory at the URL you entered in the **Destination folder** box on the **Select Media to Distribute Your Browser** page during Stage 1. For example:

```
C:\Webshare\WWWroot\CIE\Download\Win95_NT\En\IE4setup.exe
```

Note The IEAK Configuration Wizard creates the directory structure using a convention that indicates the language version (English: En) and the platform (Windows 95 and Windows NT: Win95_NT) for the custom package.

If you created the browser package on your hard disk or network drive, you need to move the distribution files from the \IE4site folder on your hard disk or network drive to the \IE4site folder on the an Internet or intranet server at the URL you specified for your distribution servers.

The \IE4site folder contains the .cab files of the language version you are posting and the folder contents. For example, the English version is located in \IE4site\En. You need to move the \IE4site*Language version* folder and the files it contains to the URL you specified for download sites. For example, move files in C:\Cie\IE4site\En to C:\Webshare\Wwwroot\Cie\IE4site\En.

Active Setup uses the \IE4site\IE4sites.dat file to locate the files Active Setup needs to install the custom package on users' computer. You need to move the file \IE4site\IE4sites.dat to the URL for the download site (or sites) you specified when you ran the IEAK Configuration Wizard. For example, move IE4sites.dat from C:\IE4site\IE4sites.dat to C:\Webshare\Wwwroot\Cie\IE4site\IE4sites.dat.

Designating Other Distribution Media

For packages on compact discs or floppy disks, make sure to produce a sufficient volume of the chosen distribution media to meet end-user needs.

If you distribute your custom browser on compact discs for Windows 95 users, a splash-screen Autorun program appears when the user inserts the compact disc. This program offers users the choice to install your custom browser or view more information. If the current version of Internet Explorer is already installed, the Autorun program detects it. The browser appears in what is known as Kiosk mode, with the Start.htm file loaded.

The IEAK Configuration Wizard will also enable you to distribute your custom browser on multiple 1.44-MB floppy disks.

Distributing Internet Explorer

Depending on the media in which you distribute the custom packages, you can use one or more of the following methods to distribute Internet Explorer to end users:

- From download Web or FTP sites on the Internet
- From download Web or FTP sites on your intranet
- From compact discs
- From floppy disks

For each of these methods, end users run the Active Setup program, IE4setup.exe, to install the custom build of Internet Explorer.

Using Compact Discs and Floppy Disks

For distribution from compact discs and floppy disks, IE4Setup.exe is included on the distribution media. Users install Internet Explorer by running IE4Setup.exe from the AutoRun splash screen of the compact disc or from Disk 1 of the floppy disk set. Active Setup installs the appropriate files from the distribution media. You can provide written instructions to guide users through the installation process. You can include the instructions in an e-mail message to users or as hard-copy instructions packaged with the distribution media.

Using Distribution Sites on the Intranet or Internet

From distribution sites on the intranet or Internet, you can deliver IE4setup.exe directly to end users as an e-mail attachment, if your network bandwidth and load can support sending multiple copies of IE4Setup.exe, which is about 420K. You can also direct users where to go to download the IE4Setup.exe. For example, you could send an e-mail message with instructions and a link to a download Web page. The download Web page could provide instructions on how to download Internet Explorer.

Running Active Setup

When users run IE4.Setup.exe, Active Setup installs Internet Explorer from the distribution media as follows:

- IE4Setup.exe extracts the setup files into a temporary directory.

- IE4Setup.inf looks at the [String] section for the URL location of the IE4site.dat file.

- Active Setup goes to the file IE4site.dat, which points to the location of the download .cab files and then displays the download options to the end user.

- Active Setup downloads the .cab files, which are placed in the specified directory; for example, C:\Program Files\Internet Explorer.

- Active Setup extracts the .cab files.

- Active Setup installs Internet Explorer and each component for the specified installation package.

After Internet Explorer is installed, Active Setup prompts the user to restart the computer. After the computer restarts, Active Setup completes configuring the user's desktop and opens the Welcome splash screen to introduce the user to Internet Explorer 4.

Troubleshooting Active Setup

For troubleshooting Active Setup:

- Review the Active Setup Log.txt file in the Windows directory. Each installation creates a log file, which collects information about that particular installation. If an Active Setup Log.txt file exists when an installation is started, Active Setup renames the existing log as a .bak file and creates a new log file. (For more information about the Active Setup Log.txt file, see Part 1, "Installing Internet Explorer 4.")

- Make sure that the download URL in the file IE4Setup.inf is exact.

- Refer to Appendix B, "Troubleshooting Installation and Uninstallation."

Assisting Users During Installation

The user support team should monitor the progress of the pilot program and provide user assistance, as necessary. It's recommended that you provide an online support Web site that can provide users with help resources to solve common problems.

You should use your experience from pilot programs to provide the types of information and help your typical users need. As solutions are developed to solve users' problems during the deployment process, you should update the support Web site to provide solutions to problems.

You could integrate the online support site with your help desk and provide mechanisms to escalate unusual or difficult problems to user support specialists.

C H A P T E R   3 7

Automatic Browser Configuration

In this chapter

Automatic Browser Configuration Overview

This chapter describes how to set up Internet Explorer and servers on the network to enable automatic browser configuration and how to use the automatic browser configuration feature of Microsoft Internet Explorer 4 to centrally manage desktop configurations. This chapter also explains how to use the Internet Explorer Administration Kit (IEAK) Profile Manager to create and manage separate configuration files for different user groups in your organization.

The information provided here will help you to:

- Understand the automatic browser configuration feature.
- Set up computing systems for automatic browser configuration.
- Use the IEAK Profile Manager to maintain configuration files.

Understanding Automatic Browser Configuration

Automatic browser configuration is a feature of Internet Explorer 3 and Internet Explorer 4. You can set up Internet Explorer to periodically download auto-configuration files maintained on a central server. The contents of auto-configuration files are used to specify a wide variety of application, desktop, and shell settings for users. Internet Explorer 3 ignores any settings that apply only to Internet Explorer 4.

You typically create and maintain separate auto-configuration files for the different user groups in your organization. You can build custom packages configured to read auto-configuration files for each user group. You can then distribute the appropriate custom build to each user group.

When the custom packages are deployed with automatic browser configuration enabled, Internet Explorer periodically downloads the auto-configuration files from the server. Each time the auto-configuration information is refreshed, the system checks to see if there are new changes, and then updates user, application, desktop, and system settings, as necessary.

Note Some auto-configuration changes require the system to be restarted before changes to the system registry can take effect.

You can use automatic browser configuration to manage a wide range of settings for users' computers, including Internet Explorer settings, desktop settings, and system settings. You can use the IEAK Profile Manager to create and modify auto-configuration files to change most of the settings and options you specified using the IEAK Configuration Wizard. You can also use the Profile Manager to update and manage system policies and restrictions, and to lock down settings to prevent your users from changing the settings you specify. For example, you can prevent users from changing automatic browser configuration settings in their **Internet Options** settings.

Setting Up Automatic Browser Configuration

You should set up automatic browser configuration when you deploy Internet Explorer. With automatic browser configuration enabled on all desktops in your organization, you can make configuration settings centrally, without having to touch the individual computers again. You can still set up automatic browser configuration after deployment, but then it requires some additional steps.

To set up automatic browser configuration before deployment:

- Set up custom packages for automatic browser configuration.
- Lock down automatic browser configuration.
- Create user-configuration files.
- Digitally sign auto-configuration cabinet files.
- Create optional auto-proxy files.
- Configure central auto-configuration servers.

To set up automatic browser configuration after deployment:

- Set up automatic browser configuration for deployed browsers.
- Update distribution files with the new custom-package files.

Setting Up Custom Packages

You use the IEAK Configuration Wizard to set up automatic browser configuration when you build custom packages. When the custom packages are deployed, Internet Explorer is installed with automatic browser configuration enabled.

To build custom packages, you need to run the IEAK Configuration Wizard and specify the custom package. For more information, see "Building Custom Packages" in Chapter 36, "Implementing the Deployment."

To set up automatic browser configuration, perform the following steps at the **Automatic Browser Configuration** page:

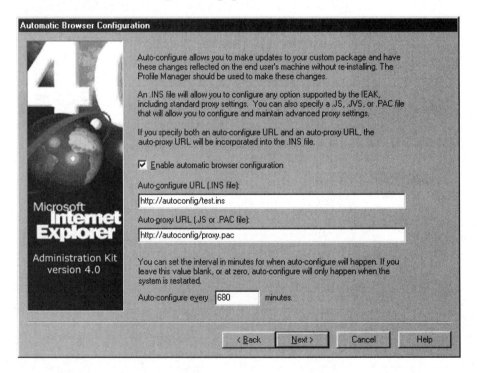

1. Select **Enable automatic browser configuration**.

2. Type the URL for the *user-configuration file* in the **Auto-configure URL (.INS file)** box.

3. Type the URL for the *auto-proxy file* in the **Auto-proxy URL (.JS or .PAC file)** box.

4. Type the *auto-configuration interval* in the **Auto-configure every _____ minutes** box.

The information you need is explained in the table below.

Information Needed	Explanation
URL for the user-configuration file	This URL points to the auto-configuration (.ins) file for this custom package. You can create a different file for each user group in your organization. Use a unique file name for each group managed—for example, sysadm.ins for system administrators and grpman.ins for group managers. The URL includes the file name in the following format:
	http://path/file name
URL for the auto-proxy file	You can use the auto-proxy (.js or .pac) file to configure proxy settings dynamically. The URL includes this file name in the following format:
	http://path/file name
auto-configuration interval	This interval is the time, in minutes, during which automatic configuration occurs. After deployment, Internet Explorer updates the auto-configuration information at the specified interval. If you leave the space for this interval blank or type "0," auto-configuration occurs only when users manually refresh the browser's automatic configuration or when Internet Explorer is restarted.

5. Finish building the custom package.

To specify automatic browser configuration, the IEAK Configuration Wizard places the following entries in the [URL] section of the install.ins file:

```
AutoConfig=1
AutoConfigURL=http://URL/user-configuration file name
AutoConfigJSURL=http://URL/auto-proxy file name
AutoConfigTime=auto-configuration interval
```

Locking Down Automatic Browser Configuration

You can use the IEAK Configuration Wizard to lock down automatic browser configuration and prevent users from changing automatic browser configuration in their **Internet Options** settings. After browsers are deployed, you can use the IEAK Profile Manager to lock down automatic browser configuration for user groups that have automatic browser configuration implemented.

▶   **To lock down automatic browser configuration**

1. Go to the **System Policies and Restrictions** page of the IEAK Configuration Wizard.

2. In the System Policies & Restrictions hierarchy, select **Internet Restrictions**, and then click **Connection**.

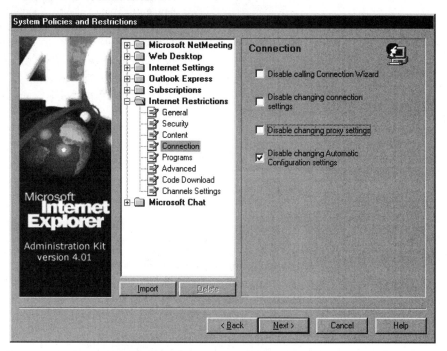

Note The IEAK Configuration Wizard is shown here, but the **System Policies and Restrictions** section of the IEAK Profile Manager works similarly.

---

3. In the right pane, click **Disable changing Automatic Configuration settings**.

4. Finish building the custom package.

When Internet Explorer is installed on end users' computers, the **Automatic Connection** option on the **Connections** tab of the **Internet Options** dialog box appears dimmed, preventing users from opening the **Automatic Configuration** dialog box to change settings.

Creating User Auto-Configuration Files

You use the IEAK Profile Manager to create and maintain user auto-configuration files. The Profile Manager generates the auto-configuration .ins file and companion .cab files that are needed to configure users' systems.

You can create user auto-configurations for each user group in your organization. You use the Profile Manager to specify the configurations and save them as *usergroup*.ins files, where *usergroup* is a unique name for each user group. The Profile Manager automatically generates the companion .cab files. For example, you could specify a user-group configuration for system administrators and save the configuration as sysadmin.ins. The Profile Manager would then generate the necessary companion .cab files.

A .cab file stores compressed files in a library. Cabinet files are used to organize installation files that are downloaded to users' systems. The cabinet files that the Profile Manager generates contain information (.inf) files that are automatically unpacked on users' systems.

The *usergroup*.ins file is used by Internet Explorer to change browser customization settings corresponding to the Wizard Settings section of the Profile Manager. For more information, see "Changing Wizard Settings" later in this chapter. Internet Explorer processes the contents of the *usergroup*.ins file and makes any changes specified. For example, if proxy settings have changed in *usergroup*.ins, Internet Explorer updates the user's Internet proxy settings. Internet Explorer also downloads and unpacks the companion .cab files for Windows to process. The unpacked auto-configuration .inf files are used by Windows to change system policies and restrictions corresponding to the System Policies and Restrictions section of the Profile Manager.

Each .inf file contains version information. When you modify user configurations, the Profile Manager changes the affected .inf files, updates the version information, and repackages the companion .cab files. When the auto-configuration .cab files are downloaded to a user's system and unpacked, the system checks the version of the .inf files and only updates system settings using new versions of the .inf files.

Signing Auto-Configuration Cabinet Files Digitally

Digital signatures identify the source of programs and guarantee that the code hasn't changed since it was signed. Depending on how users' browser security levels are configured, users could be prevented from downloading .cab files that aren't signed. Therefore, you should digitally sign the companion (.cab) files created by the IEAK Profile Manager.

Signing .cab files requires two steps: obtaining a digital certificate—from a Certificate Authority such as VeriSign or GTE—and signing the code. For more information, see Chapter 28, "Digital Certificates," "Signing Your Programs" in the IEAK Help, and "Signing Code with Microsoft Authenticode Technology" in the *Internet Client SDK*.

Creating Auto-Proxy Files

You can use a text editor to create auto-proxy (.js or .pac) files that dynamically assign browser proxy settings based on the location of hosts. Auto-proxy files are JScript files. When an auto-proxy file is specified, Internet Explorer uses the auto-proxy script to determine if it should connect directly to a host or use a proxy server. You can use auto-proxy files to configure users automatically to use different proxy servers for different domains.

The following example shows an auto-proxy function that checks to see whether the host name is a local host, and if it is, whether the connection is direct. If the host name is not a local host, the connection is through the proxy server, named proxy1.

```
function FindProxyForURL(url, host)
    {
        if (isPlainHostName(host))
            return "DIRECT";
        else
            return "PROXY proxy1:80";
    }
```

The *isPlainHostName()* function checks to see if there are any dots in the host name. If there are, it returns false; otherwise, the function returns true. For more examples of JScript auto-proxy files, see Help in the IEAK Configuration Wizard.

Note Using auto-proxy files is optional. You may want to specify proxy settings for each user group that uses the IEAK Configuration Wizard or the IEAK Profile Manager. You can also lock down the proxy-settings option. For more information, see "Using the IEAK Profile Manager" later in this chapter.

Configuring Central Auto-Configuration Servers

You need to configure servers on your intranet to support automatic browser configuration. To configure central management servers:

- Install Web-server software, such as Microsoft Internet Information Server.
- Install the auto-configuration and auto-proxy files on the server at the URLs necessary for automatic browser configuration.

The number of automatic browser configuration servers you need will vary depending on the size and demands of your organization. If your organization is large, you could configure automatic browser configuration servers for each domain. For example, you specify automatic browser configuration for user groups in domain 1:

- http://domain1_server/autoconfig/*usergroup*.ins
  http://domain1_server/autoconfig/proxy1.pac

You would install a Web server at http://domain1_server/ and install the *usergroup*.ins and *usergroup*.cab files and proxy1.pac on the server at http://domain1_server/autoconfig/. When users in domain 1 start Internet Explorer, it reads the appropriate auto-configuration files and the auto-proxy file residing at http://domain1_server/autoconfig/.

Setting Up Auto-Configuration in Previously Deployed Browsers

Clearly, it is advantageous to use the IEAK to customize Internet Explorer 4 so that automatic configuration is enabled before you deploy the browser. If that is not possible, users will have to perform a simple procedure to turn on automatic configuration. Once they have performed these steps, you can use the IEAK Profile Manager to lock down these settings, so your users will not be able to change these settings.

▶ **To set up Internet Explorer 4 for automatic configuration**

1. From the Internet Explorer window, on the **View** menu, choose **Internet Options**.

2. Select the **Connection** tab.

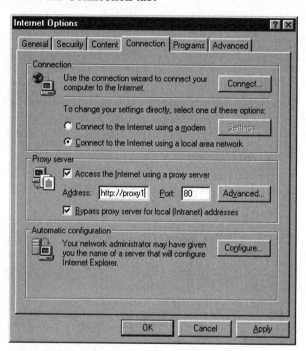

3. Select **Configure**.

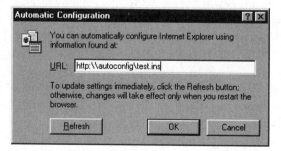

4. Type the *URL/auto-configuration file name* in the URL box.

5. Select **Refresh** to refresh auto-configuration information.

Note Some auto-configuration changes require the system to be restarted before changes to the system registry will take effect.

When automatic browser configuration is turned on, the **Connection** tab displays a caution: "Automatic configuration set. This may override current Internet settings."

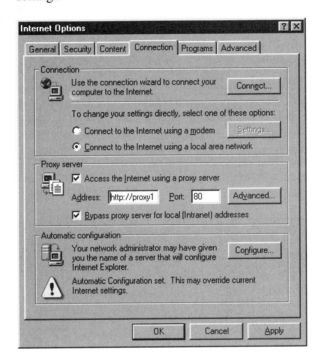

Updating Distribution Files

If you deployed Internet Explorer with automatic browser configuration disabled, you should update distribution files from new custom package builds that are enabled for automatic browser configuration. This ensures that new-user installations of Internet Explorer are enabled for automatic browser configuration.

Be sure to update all download sites. If you distribute custom packages using compact discs or floppy disks, you'll also need to produce new compact discs or floppy disks for distribution.

Using the IEAK Profile Manager

You can use the IEAK Profile Manager to create and maintain the auto-configuration files. With the Profile Manager you can specify a wide range of browser, user, desktop, and system settings and restrictions.

Starting the IEAK Profile Manager

▶   **To start the IEAK Profile Manager**

1. On the **Start** menu, click **Run**.

   The **Run** dialog box opens.

2. Type **profmgr.exe**.

3. Click **OK**.

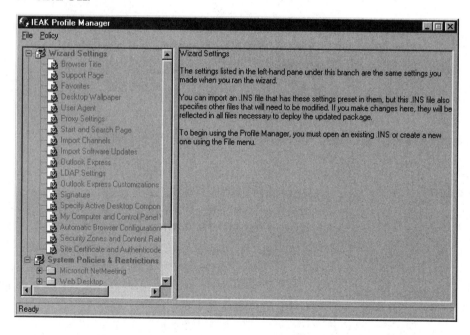

The Profile Manager is organized into a left pane showing a hierarchical tree of objects and a right pane showing the options. When you select an object in the tree in the left pane, the options and settings for that object appear in the right pane. You can change options or specify settings as necessary to manage automatic browser configurations.

The IEAK Profile Manager provides two categories of settings that you can specify: **Wizard Settings** and **System Policies & Restrictions**.

Changing Wizard Settings

In the left pane, the Wizard Settings object and its subobjects correspond to settings you can also specify using the IEAK Configuration Wizard. You can select an object and change the corresponding options and settings. For example, you can select the Browser Title object and change the **Browser Title Bar** and **Toolbar background bitmap** options.

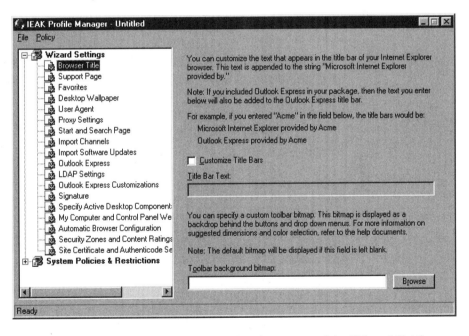

The following table briefly describes each subcategory of the **Wizard Settings** section of the IEAK Profile Manager.

Area	Description
Browser Title	Specifies the text that appears in the title bar of Internet Explorer and in a custom toolbar bitmap.
Support Page	Specifies the online-support page that appears when users select Online Support on the **Help** menu in Internet Explorer.
Favorites	Specifies the default favorites that appear on the **Favorites** menu in Internet Explorer.
Desktop Wallpaper	Specifies a custom wallpaper file to be used for the desktop background.
User Agent	Specifies a custom user agent string that will be appended to the default Internet Explorer string.
Proxy Settings	Specifies the proxy settings that Internet Explorer uses.
Start and Search Page	Specifies the start page that appears when users click **Home** and the search page that appears when users click **Search**.
Import Channels	Specifies custom Active Channels on users' desktops.
Import Software Updates	Specifies software distribution channels on users' desktops.
Outlook Express	Specifies Outlook Express Internet mail and news settings.
LDAP Settings	Specifies a Lightweight Directory Access Protocol (LDAP) server to provide Internet directory services to users.
Outlook Express Customizations	Specifies a custom InfoPane and welcome message for Outlook Express.
Signature	Specifies a standard signature line, such as a corporate disclaimer, to be appended to Outlook Express mail and news messages.
Specify Active Desktop Components	Specifies custom Active Channels on users' desktops.
My Computer and Control Panel Webview Customization	Specifies custom Web views for the My Computer and Control Panel folders.
Automatic Browser Configuration	Specifies automatic browser configuration settings.
Security Zones and Content Ratings Customization	Specifies security and content rating settings.
Site Certificate and Authenticode Settings	Specifies digital certificate and Authenticode trust settings.

For more information about specific Wizard Settings options, see "Building Custom Packages" in Chapter 36, "Implementing the Deployment."

Changing System Policies and Restrictions

In the left pane, the **Systems Policies & Restrictions** object and its subobjects correspond to the same settings available on the IEAK Configuration Wizard **System Policies and Restrictions** page. You can select an object and change the corresponding policies and restrictions. For example, you can expand the Web Desktop tree and select the **Desktop** object to specify Desktop options, such as **Disable Active Desktop**.

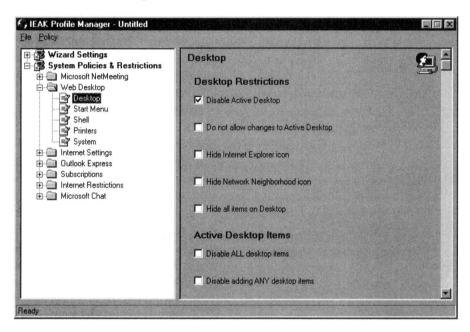

The IEAK uses a default set of Windows policy templates (.adm) files to define the rules for the wide range of policies and restrictions that appear in the **System Policies & Restrictions** hierarchy. You can also use your own custom .adm files to add policies and restrictions to the hierarchy.

Policies and restrictions that you specify using the IEAK are saved to information (.inf) files, which are packaged into the auto-configuration companion cabinet (.cab) files for download to user's systems. When unpacked, the .inf files are used to change policies and restrictions on users' systems.

The first time the IEAK Configuration Wizard is run, the policy template (.adm) files in the C:\Program Files\Ieak\Policies directory are created. The following table briefly describes each of the default areas for which you can specify system policies and restrictions.

Area	Description
Microsoft NetMeeting	Specifies policies to control user and computer-access privileges for your NetMeeting community.
Web Desktop	Restricts users from adding, accessing, modifying, or deleting various portions of the desktop.
Internet Settings	Specifies a variety of Internet settings for users.
Outlook Express	Specifies restrictions to help reduce Internet mail and news-support costs.
Subscriptions	Specifies restrictions for subscriptions.
Internet Restrictions	Specifies and locks down settings for Internet Explorer **Internet Options** settings, code download, and channel settings.
Microsoft Chat	Restricts access to Chat features and functions.

You can specify a wide variety of Internet Explorer, application, desktop, and operating system settings across your organization. You can customize settings, ranging from whether users can delete printers to whether or not they can add items to the new Windows Desktop Update.

You can lock down features and functions. For example, you could use the **System** options, under the **Web Desktop** category, to prevent Windows 95 users from restarting their systems in MS-DOS mode. You could also use the **Security** option under **Internet Restrictions** to prevent users from changing any of the security settings on the **Security** tab in Internet Explorer. When features are locked down, they either don't appear, or they appear dimmed on the user's desktop.

Before changing system policies and restrictions, you should understand the impact of the security settings on your users, especially if you have roaming users who share computers with other users. For example, what are the implications of removing icons from the desktop or not allowing users to change their security settings? Make sure that your users understand which features they have access to and which features need to be configured by your IT organization.

Using Custom Policy Templates

Those who are familiar with Windows policy template (.adm) files can create their own templates to define additional restrictions. Policies and restrictions and .adm files are standard in Windows 95 and Windows NT. For more information, see your Windows documentation.

You can choose **Import** on the **Policy** menu in order to import custom .adm files. You should choose **Check Duplicate Keys** on the **Policy** menu to check for duplicate registry keys in the templates, then delete any duplicates from your templates. Always test your templates thoroughly in the lab before using them to make changes to users' systems.

When you use custom policy templates, the IEAK Profile Manager generates an .inf file, using the file prefix for the imported custom template. For example, if you import custom.adm, a custom.inf file will be generated and added to the companion .cab files.

Using Auto-Configuration File Templates

You should use the install.ins file for each custom package as a template to create your auto-configuration files.

▶   **To use install.ins as a template**

1. On the **File** menu, click **Open**, and then open the appropriate install.ins file.

2. On the **File** menu, choose **Save As,** and save the file as *usergroup*.ins (where *usergroup* is the name of the user group).

3. Change and save any new options or settings you want for the user group configurations.

4. Copy the file to the appropriate auto-configuration directory on the central management server.

When you first create the *usergroup*.ins file, the companion .inf files are generated and packaged as .cab files.

Maintaining Auto-Configuration Files

You maintain auto-configuration files by opening the *usergroup*.ins file in the Profile Manager, changing settings, and saving the *usergroup*.ins file. The Profile Manager keeps the companion files current, each time you save the *usergroup*.ins file.

For example, if you add more proxy servers to your network and you don't use auto-proxy files, you'll need to update users' settings by selecting the Proxy Settings object in the Wizard Settings hierarchy in the left pane of the IEAK Profile Manager. You would use the IEAK Profile Manager to modify the proxy settings for the affected user groups. Automatic browser configuration then updates the users' proxy settings at the specified auto-configuration interval or when Internet Explorer is restarted.

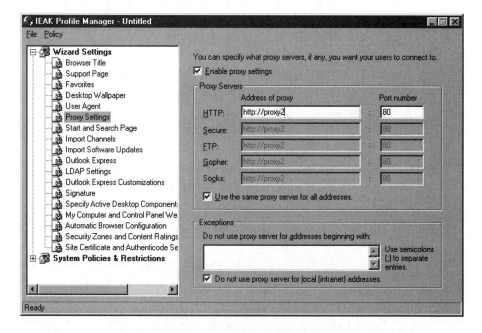

Caution You should not maintain files directly on the production server. You should copy *usergroup*.ins files and their companion files to a working directory, modify the files as necessary, and test auto-configuration in a lab to verify that auto-configuration changes work as intended. After changes have been validated, update the auto-configuration files on the production server.

CHAPTER 38

Software Distribution and Updates

Software Distribution Overview

This chapter describes how to implement a software distribution system using Active Channels in Microsoft Internet Explorer 4. It describes how software distribution channels work. It also details how to configure software distribution channels and deploy custom packages of Internet Explorer, including the software distribution channels for your users.

This chapter provides information to help you:

- Understand software distribution channels.
- Implement software distribution channels.
- Manage software distribution channels.

Understanding Software Distribution Channels

Internet Explorer 4 users can subscribe to Active Channels, which are Web sites designed to deliver content from the Internet or intranet to subscribing computers. Subscribers receive updated information from Active Channels on demand or at scheduled intervals. You can turn any Web site into an Active Channel by creating a Channel Definition Format (CDF) file to define the channel. For more information on Active Channels, see Chapter 16, "Managed Webcasting" and the *Internet Client Software Development Kit (SDK)*.

Software distribution channels are a special type of Active Channel. The CDF files for software distribution channels contain Open Software Distribution (OSD) elements that specify the software distribution settings and options. You can schedule a software distribution channel to update subscribers' computers at an interval of time such as daily, weekly, or monthly. Each time the channel is updated, the latest version of the CDF file is downloaded to subscribers' computers. When the OSD section of the CDF file indicates that a new version of the software is available, subscribers' computers can be instructed to do one of the following:

- Download the installation files to users' hard disks so that users can manually install the update.
- Install the update automatically.

You specify the update process to be used in the OSD section of the CDF file for the channel. You can also notify users and provide instructions for installation of the updates.

Implementing Software Distribution Channels

You can use software distribution channels to distribute software updates over your intranet or the Internet to end-user desktops. To implement software distribution channels:

- Identify software distribution requirements.

- Select software distribution strategies.

- Configure Web servers for software distribution channels.

- Build custom packages of Internet Explorer with pre-configured software distribution channels and automatic browser configuration enabled.

- Deploy the pre-configured custom packages to end users.

The following sections describe the process for implementing software distribution channels. Detailed technical information is provided in the following resources:

- For more information about the CDF and OSD specifications, see the Microsoft Site Builder Network specifications and standards page at **http://www.microsoft.com/standards/**.

- For detailed information about how to use CDF files and OSD files to create software distribution channels, see the *Internet Client SDK*. To obtain the Internet Client SDK, see **http://www.microsoft.com/msdn/sdk/inetsdk/asetup/**.

- For information on how to use sample CDF templates to set up software distribution channels for updating Internet Explorer 4, see the section named "Updates with Software Distribution Channels" in the Internet Explorer Administration Kit (IEAK) Help.

Identifying Software Distribution Requirements

Before selecting strategies for software distribution, identify the software distribution requirements for your organization. Begin by surveying the user groups in your organization and identifying the software packages they use. Be sure to note special requirements for each group, such as language requirements and any custom applications they use. For example, you would note that a graphics design group uses a suite of professional illustration applications that are not used by other groups in your organization.

After all user groups are surveyed:

- Identify the applications you want to support.
- Identify the user groups you want to provide with pre-configured software distribution channels.
- Group common applications into functional categories such as office-productivity applications and Internet applications.
- Group specialized applications by function or by the user groups that use them.

You'll use this information to help specify software distribution strategies for each user group that you want to support.

Selecting Software Distribution Strategies

The strategies you choose depend on various factors, including the size of your organization and the types of applications you need to distribute to your users. Select strategies for each of the following:

- Number of distribution sites
- Types of software distribution channels
- Software distribution channel-update schedule
- Installation methods
- Notification methods

Determining the Number of Distribution Sites

Small organizations may need only one distribution Web site. Large organizations may need to provide multiple, mirrored software distribution Web sites to distribute network load and to meet the needs of diverse groups of users. For example, an organization with large operations in North America, Europe, and Asia could implement mirrored distribution sites in each major region of North America, Europe, and Asia.

Determining the Types of Channels

The types of software distribution channels you include in custom packages of Internet Explorer will depend on the number and types of applications you plan to support, as well as the design limitations of CDF and OSD.

Depending on the contents of the CDF file, each software distribution channel can:

- Appear in the Channel bar or in the Software Updates folder on the **Favorites** menu in Internet Explorer.

- Include an unlimited number of software packages or SOFTPKG update items that specify software packages you can update.

- Define the installation of multiple languages, processors, and operating systems for each SOFTPKG update item.

Note   Each user can configure Internet Explorer to enable e-mail notification. If a user has configured a channel to enable e-mail notifications, a notification page for each SOFTPKG update item can be automatically sent by e-mail to the user when the channel is updated.

When the channel appears in the Software Updates folder:

- Updates are indicated by a red gleam in the upper-left corner of the channel, and users can select the channel to view the notification Web page in the browser window. This Web page typically contains information briefly describing all available updates, and hyperlinks to pages providing more information on each update.

- Each channel can include an unlimited number of SOFTPKG update items, but only the top-level channel notification page will appear in the browser. Users are notified of individual updates only if they enable e-mail notification in Internet Explorer.

- Only the top-level channel can contain the SCHEDULE element, so all SOFTPKG update items will be updated on the subscribers' computers at the same time.

When the channel appears on the Channel bar:

- The top-level channel and all SOFTPKG update items appear as a hierarchical tree on the Channel bar.

- Updates are indicated by a red gleam in the upper-left corner of the top-level channel and users can select the top-level channel to view the notification Web page in the browser's right pane. This Web page typically contains information briefly describing all available updates, and hyperlinks to pages that provide more information on each update.

- Each SOFTPKG update item appears under the top-level channel without a red gleam. However, users can select each item to view the corresponding notification page in the browser's right pane. Users are notified of individual updates only if they enable e-mail notification in Internet Explorer.

Note A SOFTPKG item with **USAGE VALUE="None"** does not appear in the channel hierarchy.

- Only the top-level channel can contain the SCHEDULE element, so all SOFTPKG update items will be updated on the subscribers' computers at the same time.

Since only the top-level channel shows the update gleam, you should use top-level notification pages to provide a summary of all available updates. The top-level notification page is the Web page users see when they click on the top-level Channel bar. By default, notification pages appear in the browser window and can also be sent to users via e-mail (when users enable e-mail notification). The summary page could provide a brief description of available updates and provide hyperlinks to the corresponding notification page for each update.

In addition, you can create an Active Desktop item that displays a summary page of available software components. An Active Desktop item is simply a Web page that displays in a floating, borderless frame on the user's desktop. Custom Active Desktop items require special CDF files. For more information, see Chapter 14, "Active Desktop," and Chapter 16, "Managed Webcasting."

When you deploy custom packages of Internet Explorer to end users, you should have enough pre-configured software distribution channels to meet your organization's needs. If automatic browser configuration is enabled for your user groups, however, you can use the IEAK Profile Manager to add or delete software distribution channels for deployed browsers.

You can also easily add SOFTPKG update items to CDF files for existing software distribution channels. Likewise, you can also easily delete SOFTPKG update items if an application is discontinued.

When you pre-configure custom packages for user groups, you should only provide the software distribution channels that each user group needs. For example, you could provide a software distribution channel for office-productivity applications to all user groups, but you wouldn't pre-configure the channels for users in the human resources department to include a software distribution channel for software-developers' applications.

Specifying Distribution Schedules

Specify the schedule for updates by using the SCHEDULE element in CDF files. You can specify daily, weekly, or monthly update frequencies as well as the time of day and the interval during which updates can occur. You can override the default CDF schedule, using the IEAK Configuration Wizard or the IEAK Profile Manager to specify different schedules for each custom package you build. Assigning user groups to different schedules, such as alternating days or weeks, can help distribute network load. All SOFTPKG update items use the same schedule as the top-level channel.

Schedule software downloads for times of low network load—especially for large software packages. To avoid heavy load on your distribution servers when all subscribers update the software distribution channel, you should randomize the time that Internet Explorer updates the channel. For example, you could schedule updates for a channel to occur between 1 A.M. and 5 A.M. one day a week. On the specified day, each subscribed Internet Explorer updates the download channel at a random time between 1 A.M. and 5 A.M.

Choosing Installation Methods

Use any of the following installation methods:

- Notify users by e-mail when new software updates are available. Provide instructions and hyperlinks so they can download the software manually.

- Download the installation files to users' hard disks, notify users, and provide instructions and hyperlinks so they can run the installation program manually.

- Install the updates on users' computers automatically, and notify users that the updates were made.

Use the installation methods that meet your needs, but be cautious about specifying large software packages to download or install automatically. Thoroughly test installation methods in the lab before implementing them as a production solution.

Choosing Notification Methods

Users do not receive e-mail notification on updates automatically. They can receive notification if they enable e-mail notification for each software distribution channel using the **Internet Explorer Software Distribution Channel Receive property** page. Also, even though Active Channels provide a top-level update gleam and you can provide a summary page to describe the available updates, users may not view the Internet Explorer Channel bar or the Software Updates folder on the **Favorites** menu for long periods of time—if ever. For this reason, consider multiple ways to notify your users, such as sending e-mail notices and instructions to all users for each new software update.

Configuring Software Distribution Channels

Software distribution channels are Web sites dedicated to software distribution. The content of the Web sites must support the software distribution strategies you select.

To configure software distribution channels:

- Create the Web content to support the channels.
- Create the CDF files to configure the channels.
- Create the OSD files for Microsoft Internet Component Download (MSICD) distributions.
- Create the software distribution packages.
- Sign the software distribution packages.
- Configure the Web servers to support the channels.

Creating Web Content

You can provide notification Web pages for each CDF file. You can also provide optional Channel bar graphics images for use by Internet Explorer.

The notification Web page is used to describe, briefly, all updates available and typically provides users with hyperlinks to the individual update-notification pages for more details. The summary page could be an HTML page or an Active Server page. The notification page is specified in the CDF file for the CHANNEL element HREF attribute—for example, HREF="http://webserver/*filename*.htm" where *filename* is the name of the summary page. When users select the channel on the Channel bar or in the **Favorites** menu, the summary page appears in the browser's right pane. If USAGE VALUE="E-mail", a notification page is sent via e-mail to users who have enabled e-mail notification.

You can create two optional graphics images in either .gif or .jpg format that are used by Internet Explorer to display in the desktop Channel bar and in the browser Channel bar. You can also create an optional .ico image for use in the browser window Channel bar hierarchy. The .ico image will appear to the left of each item in the Channel bar hierarchy. You can use a different icon for each SOFTPKG item in a CDF file.

- **Desktop Channel bar logo.** 32 pixels high by 80 pixels wide and a black background.

    CDF entry: <LOGO HREF="*filename*.gif" STYLE="Image">
- **Browser Channel bar logo.** 32 pixels high by 194 pixels wide and a color background.

    CDF entry: <LOGO HREF="*filename*.gif" STYLE="Image-Wide">

- **Browser Channel bar icon.** 16 pixels high by 16 pixels wide, with different images, colors, or shapes to indicate whether an item is a container for other items or is actual content.

  CDF entry: <LOGO HREF="*filename*.ico" STYLE="Icon">

You can use the Channel bar logo for the browser window logo, and the extra area will be filled in with the same color as the rightmost top pixel. Animated .gif files are not supported. Images are displayed with a fixed 256-color palette regardless of the monitor color depth. Therefore, you should use the Windows halftone palette.

Note The Channel bar provides users with a 14-pixels-high by 14-pixels-wide red gleam to indicate when channel content has been updated. The gleam is a triangular overlay applied to the upper-left corner of the Channel bar logos. When creating Channel bar logos, do not place critical text or visual elements in this area. A 7-pixels-high by 7-pixels-wide gleam is also applied to the upper-left corner of icons to indicate when item content has been updated.

Creating the CDF Files

Create a CDF file for each software distribution channel to be installed on users' desktops. An unlimited number of subchannels or SOFTPKG items can be nested in the CDF file, but they will all have the same schedule as the top-level channel.

This section describes the elements of CDF that are used to define software distribution channels. For more information about CDF files, see "Understanding CDF Files" in Chapter 16, "Managed Webcasting."

The following shows an example CDF file that, when subscribed to, appears on the **Favorites** menu in the Software Updates folder. This CDF file specifies the download of software package 1 to users' hard disks.

```
<?XML version="1.0"?>
<!DOCTYPE Channel SYSTEM "http://www.w3c.org/Channel.dtd">
<CHANNEL HREF="http://ie4support/softdist/product1_info.htm" >
    <TITLE>Software Distribution Channel 1</TITLE>
    <ABSTRACT>This is the abstract for the channel.</ABSTRACT>
    <USAGE VALUE="SoftwareUpdate" />
    <SCHEDULE>
        <INTERVALTIME DAY="7" />
        <EARLIESTTIME HOUR="1" />
        <LATESTTIME HOUR="5" />
    </SCHEDULE>
```

```
<SOFTPKG NAME={D27CDB6E-AE6D-11CF-96B8-444553540000}"
    VERSION="2,33,608,0" AUTOINSTALL="No"
    STYLE=" " PRECACHE="Yes">
    <IMPLEMENTATION>
        <OS VALUE="win95" />
        <CODEBASE HREF="http/download/Pkg1_95.cab" />
    </IMPLEMENTATION>

    <IMPLEMENTATION>
        <OS VALUE="winnt" />
        <CODEBASE HREF="http/download/Pkg1_NT.cab" />
    </IMPLEMENTATION>
    </SOFTPKG>
</CHANNEL>
```

In this example:

- **CHANNEL HREF="http://ie4support/softdist/product1_info.htm"**
  provides the notification page for this channel.

- **<USAGE VALUE="SoftwareUpdate" />** specifies that this channel
  appears in the **Software Update** folder on the **Favorites** menu and not on
  the Channel bar.

- **INTERVALTIME DAY="7"** specifies the interval as weekly. Use "1"
  for daily or "28" for monthly (every four weeks).

- **EARLIESTTIME HOUR="1"** and **LATESTTIME HOUR="5"** specifies
  that subscribed Internet Explorer browsers refresh the channel at random times
  between 1 A.M. and 5 A.M. Use a 24-hour scale starting with Midnight = "0."

- **HREF="http://ie4support/softdist/package1.htm"** is the notification page
  that appears in the browser's right pane when users click this software update
  channel. You can provide installation instructions and hyperlinks on this page.

- **VERSION="2,33,608,0"** specifies the major, minor, build, and custom
  version numbers of the update. You change this for each new version and
  the system looks for update instructions.

- **AUTOINSTALL="No"** specifies that the software update is not automatically installed by the system. Use "Yes" to specify automatic installation
  of the update without user action. AUTOINSTALL overrides the PRECACHE
  element.

- **STYLE="MSICD"** specifies that the user's computer should use the MSICD
  to download the distribution package and look at the OSD file for processing
  instructions. Use "ActiveSetup" to specify that the user's computer should use
  Active Setup to install the package.

When STYLE="ActiveSetup," the CODEBASE HREF does not specify a .cab file and an OSD file is not used. Instead, Active Setup looks for the Internet Explorer update-distribution package by checking the IE4site.dat file. For example, the IMPLEMENTATION section for an Internet Explorer 4 update channel could specify the location of IE4site.dat as follows:

```
<IMPLEMENTATION>
    <OS VALUE="win95" />
    <CODEBASE HREF="http/ie4support/ie4site/ie4site.dat" />
</IMPLEMENTATION>
```

- **PRECACHE="Yes"** specifies that the software update is downloaded to the user's hard disk. Use "No" to specify that the update is not downloaded.
- **OS VALUE="win95"** and **CODEBASE HREF="http/download/Pkg1_95.cab"** specifies an implementation for Windows 95–based computers. Windows 95–based computers install this package.
- **OS VALUE="winnt"** and **CODEBASE HREF="http/download/Pkg1_NT.cab"** specifies an implementation for Windows NT–based computers. Windows NT–based computers install this package.

You can specify an OS VALUE element for each operating system you need to support. In addition, you can specify other attributes for the IMPLEMENTATION element, including the LANGUAGE and PROCESSOR attributes to further differentiate implementations. You can add IMPLEMENTATION sections that provide software packages for each of your platforms and operating systems.

Many other OSD elements and attributes can be used to specify software distribution channels. For example, you can use the DEPENDENCY element to specify a software component that needs to be present on the user's computer for the software distribution package to install successfully. For more guidelines on how to create CDF files for software distribution and a detailed reference on CDF and the OSD extensions, see the *Internet Client SDK*.

Creating OSD Files

The OSD file is similar to the OSD section of the CDF file. This file contains the information that users' computers need to download the MSICD distribution package from the server.

Note   You do not create OSD files if you use Active Setup to install a software package.

The following example OSD file specifies a download location for the Windows 95 version of software package 1.

```
<?XML version="1.0" ?>
<!DOCTYPE SOFTPKG SYSTEM
"http://www.microsoft.com/standards/osd/osd.dtd" >
<?XML::namespace href="http://www.microsoft.com/standards/osd/msicd.dtd"
as="msicd"?>

<SOFTPKG NAME="{D27CDB6E-AE6D-11CF-96B8-444553540000}" VERSION="2,0,0,0"
STYLE="MSICD">
    <TITLE>Update for Product 1</TITLE>
    <ABSTRACT>This distribution contains package1.
    </ABSTRACT>

    <msicd::NATIVECODE>
        <CODE    NAME="diagnose.ocx"
                 CLASSID="{D27CDB6E-AE6D-11CF-96B8-444553540000}"
                 VERSION="2,33,608,0" >
            <IMPLEMENTATION>
                <OS VALUE="win95" />
                <CODEBASE HREF="http/download/Pkg1_95.cab" />
            </IMPLEMENTATION>
        </CODE>
    </msicd::NATIVECODE>
</SOFTPKG>
```

The OSD file is packaged in the Pkg1_95.cab file, and the system uses the OSD file information to properly install the distribution package. You create an OSD file for each implementation of the software package that you install. For more information, see the *Internet Client SDK*.

Creating Software Distribution Packages

Create the software distribution packages you need to support your software distribution channels. Active Setup distribution packages and MSICD software distribution packages contain files that are compressed using the .cab compression format. For more information on .cab, see the *CAB SDK*, which is provided as a self-extracting executable file (Cab-Sdk.exe) in the \bin directory of the *Internet Client SDK*.

For Active Setup, each .cab file contains an .inf file that specifies how the .cab file should be installed. To locate the .cab files for the update, Active Setup reads the information in the ie4site.dat file specified by the CODEBASE HREF="http/ie4support/ie4site/ie4site.dat" entry in the OSD section of the CDF file.

You can use Internet Express (IExpress) to create software packages that can be installed with Active Setup. IExpress is included in the IEAK 4. For more information, see Help for the IEAK.

For MSICD, the .cab files contain the OSD file that specifies how the .cab files should be installed. The MSICD CAB can be packaged three ways:

- Only the OSD file in the .cab file
- The OSD file and application files in the .cab file
- The OSD file and another .cab file in the .cab file

Having only the OSD file in your .cab file is the smallest distribution package possible. The OSD file would indicate the URL of the resource containing the software update in the CODEBASE HREF="http://download/*filename*.cab" element of the OSD file.

The simplest case is to package the OSD file with the application files into the .cab file. In this case, the OSD file does not need the CODEBASE element in it. When no CODEBASE element is given, the user's system automatically checks the same .cab file in which the OSD file was found to locate the application files.

When multiple program files are involved, and especially when the application files are separated into multiple subdirectories, it is easier to organize the distribution package by creating a .cab file that contains the OSD file and another .cab file that contains the application files.

Signing Software Distribution Packages

Digital signatures identify the source of programs and guarantee that the code hasn't changed since it was signed. Depending on how users' browser security levels are configured, users could be prevented from downloading .cab files that aren't signed. Therefore, you should digitally sign .cab, .exe., or .ocx files before distributing software to users' computers.

Signing software package files requires two steps: obtaining a digital certificate—from a Certificate Authority (CA) such as VeriSign or GTE—and signing the code. For more information, see Chapter 28, "Digital Certificates," "Signing Your Programs" in the IEAK Help, and "Signing Code with Microsoft Authenticode Technology" in the *Internet Client SDK*.

Configuring Web Servers

Configure enough Web servers to support your distribution channels, as well as the volume of software you distribute. You can include multiple channels on each Web server.

To configure Web servers:

- Install Web-server software, such as Microsoft Internet Information Server.
- Configure file systems for each software distribution channel.
- Add the notification pages, graphics files, and distribution packages.

Building Custom Packages With Pre-Configured Channels

Build custom packages with software distribution channels pre-configured for each user group in your organization. You should also enable automatic browser configuration, so you can add and manage software distribution channels after browsers are deployed.

When the IEAK Configuration Wizard adds software distribution channels to custom packages, it imports the Internet Explorer software distribution channel configurations from the computer running the wizard. You import the current software distribution channel configuration and specify schedule options.

You can also use the IEAK Configuration Wizard to lock down software distribution channels and prevent users from adding, deleting, or modifying the channels that you specify.

Configuring the Current Computer

Configure the current computer's Internet Explorer to incorporate your software distribution channels before running the IEAK Configuration Wizard. To configure the computer for software distribution channels, you subscribe to each of the software distribution channels you want to include for this user group.

▶ **To subscribe to a software distribution channel**

1. Run Internet Explorer 4.
2. On the **File** menu, click **Open**, and enter http://*server/path/filename*.cdf.

   Where *server/path/filename* is the Web server, path, and file name in which the CDF file is located.

   An **Add Active Channel** or an **Add Software Distribution Channel** dialog box appears.

3. At the dialog box, select **OK** to subscribe to the channel.

Repeat this process for each software distribution channel.

Importing the Software Distribution Channels

To import the software distribution channels, use the IEAK Configuration Wizard.

▶ **To import the software distribution channels**

1. Run the IEAK Configuration Wizard, and navigate to the **Customize Software Update Channels** page:

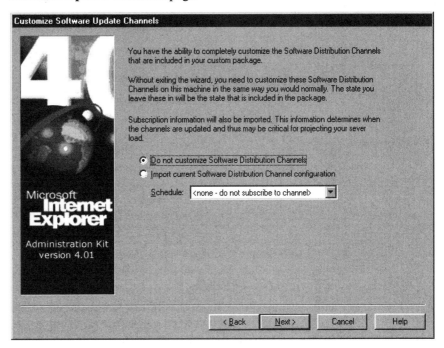

2. Select **Import current Software Distribution Channel configuration** to import the software distribution channel configurations.

3. Select one of the following options from the **Schedule** selection box.

Option	Description
<none – do not subscribe to channel>	Specifies that all software distribution channels are imported, but not subscribed to, when the custom package is installed on users' computers. This is the default. Be careful you do not select this by mistake.
Auto	Specifies that each software distribution channel uses the schedule information contained in the SCHEDULE section of its CDF file when the custom package is installed on users' computers.

Option	Description
Daily	Specifies that all software distribution channels are scheduled to be updated daily when the custom package is installed on users' computers.
Monthly	Specifies that all software distribution channels are scheduled to be updated monthly when the custom package is installed on users' computers.
Weekly	Specifies that all software distribution channels are scheduled to be updated weekly when the custom package is installed on users' computers.

4. Select **Next** to use the current channel configuration for the custom build.

5. Finish building the custom package.

Locking Down Software Distribution Channels

You can use the IEAK Configuration Wizard to lock down software distribution channels for the custom packages that you build. After browsers are deployed, you can use the IEAK Profile Manager to lock down software distribution channels through automatic browser configuration.

Software distribution channels use the same settings as Active Channels. For more information on how to lock down Active Channels, see "Locking Down Active Channels and Desktop Items" in Chapter 16, "Managed Webcasting."

Deploying the Custom Packages

Deploy custom packages to your user groups with the appropriate software distribution channels pre-configured. When custom packages are deployed and installed, you can manage software distribution and updates for each user group using the software distribution channels. For more information about how to deploy custom packages, see "Building Custom Packages" in Chapter 36, "Implementing the Deployment."

You could also add subscription links for the CDF files to your Web pages, so users who do not have pre-configured software distribution channels can visit your Web pages and click on the links to subscribe to the channels.

Managing Software Distribution Channels

To manage software distribution channels for deployed browsers, you can use the IEAK Profile Manager in conjunction with automatic browser configuration. (For more information about automatic browser configuration, see Chapter 37, "Automatic Browser Configuration.")

To change software distribution channels for a group, you configure the channels on the machine running the IEAK Profile Manager and then use the Profile Manager to import the configurations and save the new configuration settings to the auto-configuration files for the user group.

When automatic browser configuration is refreshed at users' computers, users' desktops are configured with the new software distribution channel settings you specify. You can also optionally remove previous software distribution channel configurations from users' computers.

▶   **To change software distribution channel configurations**

1. Use Internet Explorer to configure software distribution channels for the current desktop.

2. Run the IEAK Profile Manager.

3. Open the auto-configuration (.ins) file for the user group.

4. In the left pane, select the **Wizard Settings** hierarchy, and select the **Import Software Updates** object.

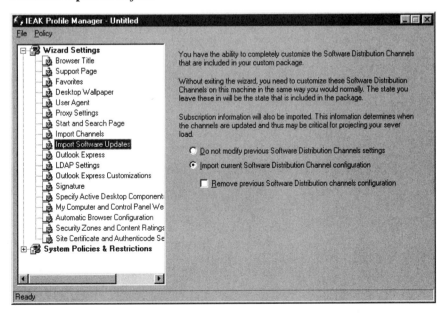

5. In the right pane, select **Import current Software Distribution Channel configuration** to import the software distribution channel configurations.

6. If you want to remove previous channel configurations from users' computers, select **Remove previous Software Distribution channels configuration**.

7. On the **File** menu, click **Save**.

   Changes are made to users' configurations as scheduled by automatic browser configuration.

A P P E N D I X   A

Switches, Keys, and Files in Internet Explorer 4 Setup

This appendix details the following switches, keys, and files for Internet Explorer Setup:

- WExtract command-line switches for IE4Setup.exe
- Other setup registry keys
- Command-line switches for Active Setup AutoUpdate
- Command-line switches for ACME Setup
- The sections of the SoftBoot.inf
- Files left in the system after uninstalling Internet Explorer

To learn more about Setup, see Chapters 2 and 3.

WExtract Command-Line Switches for IE4Setup.exe

The command-line switch **/c:*program command*** specifies the command to execute, which overrides the command defined in running WExtract at authoring time. If the command is blank, WExtract just extracts files to the defined temporary folder and leaves files there without executing a command or deleting any files.

If there is no blank **/c:** switch (user does not request to keep the extracted files), WExtract adds the RunOnce entry **wextract /d:*subfolder path*** before the RunCommand phase, in case the RunCommand phase never returns (failed install). This way, the next reboot will clean up the leftover files in the temp folder from the failed process.

If the RunCommand phase returns, WExtract will clean up the temp subfolder and delete the RunOnce entry entered earlier. Otherwise, if the RunCommand phase never returns to WExtract, RunOnce will call WExtract with the **/d** option at reboot time to clean up the process.

Switch	Purpose	Description
/q	Quiet mode	The difference between User and Admin quiet mode has to do with the amount of user-interface dialog boxes that are presented. User quiet mode will still present some user-interface dialog boxes, whereas Admin quiet mode will not show any user interface dialog boxes.
/qu -	User quiet mode	
/qa -	Admin quiet mode	
/t:*folder path*	Change target folder	Provides a target path. Failure to use a colon will return user to command help (/?). If the folder specified does not exist, WExtract will create it and remove it after using the files, if the /c switch is not also used. By default, without the /t: switch, WExtract will extract files to a unique, randomly created subfolder under C:\Temp or to the current folder if C:\Temp does not has enough space.
/c	Extract only	Prevents the execution of a Setup process after the extraction is complete.
/c:*path to exe*	Change Setup.exe	Specifies the path to .exe to run instead of the default .exe after file extraction.
/r:n	Never reboot	Never reboot.
/r:i	Reboot if necessary	Reboot if necessary.
/r:a	Always reboot	Always reboot.
/r:s	Silent reboot	Silent reboot.
/n:g	Do not run GrpConv	Do not run GrpConv.
/n:e	Do not extract files	Do not extract files.
/n:v	No version checking	No version checking. Enables you to install over anything.
/i:y	Integrated shell mode	Install integrated shell mode.
/i:n	Browser-only mode	Install browser-only mode.
/q	Batch mode	Install batch mode with no user interface dialog boxes.
/m:*mode*	Specify installation option	Used to select the installation option (**Full**, **Standard**, **Enhanced**), exact syntax not known.
/s:*installation path*	Target location	Chooses the location to install Internet Explorer.
/u:*download path*	Download location	Chooses the location to download the Internet Explorer files.

Other Setup Registry Keys

The following is a list of other registry keys—not mentioned in Chapter 2—that Setup uses before the download phase is complete:

HKEY_CURRENT_USER\Software\Microsoft\Active Setup\jobs

HKEY_CURRENT_USER\Software\Microsoft\Active Setup\jobs\job.IE4

**HKEY_CURRENT_USER\Software\Microsoft\Active Setup\jobs\job.IE4\
Internet Explorer 4.0**

**HKEY_CURRENT_USER\Software\Microsoft\Active Setup\jobs\job.IE4\
Communication Components**

**HKEY_CURRENT_USER\Software\Microsoft\Active Setup\jobs\job.IE4\
Multimedia Components**

**HKEY_CURRENT_USER\Software\Microsoft\Active Setup\jobs\job.IE4\
Web Authoring Components**

**HKEY_CURRENT_USER\Software\Microsoft\Active Setup\jobs\job.IE4\
Additional ActiveX Controls**

**HKEY_CURRENT_USER\Software\Microsoft\Active Setup\jobs\job.IE4\
CustomOptionalComponents**

HKEY_LOCAL_MACHINE\SOFTWARE\Microsoft\Active Setup

**HKEY_LOCAL_MACHINE\SOFTWARE\Microsoft\
Active Setup[VALDWORD]"TrustValueSet"="3"**

**HKEY_LOCAL_MACHINE\SOFTWARE\Microsoft\Active Setup\
Installed Components**

**HKEY_LOCAL_MACHINE\SOFTWARE\Microsoft\
Active Setup\Component Progress**

**HKEY_LOCAL_MACHINE\SOFTWARE\Microsoft\
Active Setup\Component Progress\IE4**

**HKEY_LOCAL_MACHINE\SOFTWARE\Microsoft\
Active Setup\InstallInfo**

**HKEY_LOCAL_MACHINE\SOFTWARE\Microsoft\
Active Setup\InstallInfo\"Setup option"="6"**

**HKEY_LOCAL_MACHINE\SOFTWARE\Microsoft\
Internet Explorer\Security**

**HKEY_LOCAL_MACHINE\SOFTWARE\Microsoft\
Internet Explorer\Security\Basic**

**HKEY_LOCAL_MACHINE\SOFTWARE\Microsoft\
Internet Explorer\Security\
Basic[VALSTR]"SecurityName"="Basic Authentication"**

**HKEY_LOCAL_MACHINE\SOFTWARE\Microsoft\
Internet Explorer\Security\Basic[VALSTR]"DLLFile"="WININET.dll"**

**HKEY_LOCAL_MACHINE\SOFTWARE\Microsoft\
Internet Explorer\Security\Basic[VALSTR]"SchemeList"="Basic"**

**HKEY_LOCAL_MACHINE\SOFTWARE\Microsoft\
Internet Explorer\Security\Basic[VALBINARY]"Flags"="00000000"**

Command-Line Switches for Active Setup AutoUpdate

The following is based on Trigger.exe, now renamed to Actsetup.exe:

Switch	Description
/j:	Specifies "Job" branch to use under ActiveSetup for baseURL and .cif file name.
/u:	URL used to override job, no site switching.
/s:	URL of site list location.
/q	No user interface for any of the session.
/I:	GUID ID to install.
/c:	CIFCAB:.cif file name.

When a user runs Actsetup.exe with a job name, the .exe will look in the branch under the registry key

HKEY_LOCAL_MACHINE\SOFTWARE\Microsoft\Active Setup\Job

for the job name. Stored there will be the following values:

- SitelistURL
- Region
- baseURL
- alternate URLs
- .cif
- .cif .cab name

Then Actsetup.exe will look at the InstalledComponents branch and queue up all the items in the list by creating a temporary job. The job will then be passed to Jobexec.dll for processing. If the **/u:** is specified, only one URL will be used and will override the job settings. If **/s:** is used, Actsetup.exe will get the list and first try the URLs in the job list. If none are found, it will display to the user a list of sites similar to the user interface in the base Internet Explorer setup. The selected URLs should also be written back to the "job" branch under ActiveSetup, if possible.

If **/I:** is passed, only that GUID will be used for the update. Priorities for installed items will be based on entries in the CIF file. Priority = x (larger numbers being higher priority). Actsetup.exe will not set up any of the priorities in the job it creates. If not set in the .cif file, there will be no priorities for the session.

Command-Line Switches for ACME Setup

Switch	Purpose	Description
s/a	Administrator mode	Only available from original media (not from an image or flat).
/b *<digit>*	Always suppress AppMainDlg by preselecting one big button.	Always suppresses AppMainDlg by preselecting one big button. *<digit>* is the 1 based index into the button list in the data field of the AppMainDlg object. Invalid digit == noop.
/c *<COA>*	Specify OEM PID	Enters and validates the 20-character Product ID from the OEM Certificate of Authorization, replacing user dialog box. Example: /C 12345OEM123456712345 (OEM must be in caps.)
/f	No LFNs	Suppresses long file names and uses FAT compatible 8.3 names.
/g "*<path\file>*"	Generate logfile	Generates the log file that provides details of the install. Requires a fully qualified path.
		Note: When logging is turned on for Debug builds, any Assertion Failures will be sent directly to the log file without displaying a message box.
/g# "*<path\file>*"	Debug only	Debug only: dumps all error messages to log.
/gc "*<path\file>*"	Debug only, including all calls and returns from custom actions	Like **/g**, but includes all calls and returns from custom actions. This can get very big.

Switch	Purpose	Description
/g+ "_\<path\file>_"	Append log entries to existing log file	Appends log entries to existing log file.
/g#c+ "_\<path\file>_"		Can use any permutation or combination of **/g** parameters
/h		Reserved for BiDi Help file specification.
/i		Reserved for BiDi Help file UI interface choice.
/k "_\<CD key>_"	Specify PID	Enters and validates the 10- or 11-digit key from the compact-disc sticker, replacing the user dialog box that would appear. Example: **/k** "1234567890" (key size depends on whether trigger is being used).
/l _\<lst file>_	Specify Setup.lst file	Specifies the file that lists files bootstrapper copies to the temporary directory. Defaults to Setup.lst. Not seen by Acmsetup.exe.
/m [#]	Bypass anti-piracy limits	Bypasses anti-piracy limits. When used with a number, such as **/m50**, it specifies the additional licenses to be activated by an MLP purchaser.
/n ""		Uses Win.ini. Copies Disincentive Name if it exists; otherwise, prompts the user. Not useful with **/a**.
/n "_\<name>_"		Uses Win.ini. Copies Disincentive Name if it exists; otherwise, uses the _\<name>_ value. Not useful with /A.
/o ""		Uses Win.ini. Copies Disincentive Org if it exists; otherwise, prompts the user.
/o "_\<org>_"		Uses Win.ini. Copies Disincentive Org if it exists; otherwise, uses the _\<org>_ value.
/p _\<script file>_	Debug only	Debug only: List of forced checkpoint failures.
/q[0|1|T]	Quiet install mode	Batch mode: no UI. Normally, the exit dialog box is still displayed (**/q** or **/q0**). /Q1 will suppress the exit dialog box, /QT will suppress all UI, including the background frame window and the copy gauge. Assert failures will still show up in debug mode, however.
		Note: An administrator can modify the check box State fields in the .stf file to generate a customized batch mode Setup. (See table.txt for more detail.)

Switch	Purpose	Description
/qn[1lt]	Quiet mode with reboot suppressed	Not valid with **/q0**. Warning: Chaining together several installs with suppressed reboots may have unpredictable results.
/r	Reinstall the application	
/s *<src dir>*	Specify alternative source files	Specifies the location of source files to be installed. Overrides the default source (where ACME was launched from, or the source specified in the maintenance mode .stf file). Provided automatically by the bootstrapper if ACME is bootstrapped.
/t *<table file>*	Specify alternative table files	Specifies table file to use (default is *<base>*.stf, where *<base>* is the "8" part of your .exe file's 8.3 file name).
/u [a]	Uninstall the application	Uninstalls the application. If **/q** is also specified, the user will not be prompted about removing shared components. **/u** will not remove shared components by default. **/ua** will always remove shared components without prompting the user.
/v	Don't bind executable files	Doesn't bind .exe files that are marked as bindable. This gives you a back door if binding turns out to be a problem.
/w *<stf file>*	Specify alternative stf files	Used to indicate that the bootstrapper is running on a previously installed .stf file. Not seen by Acmsetup.exe.
/x "*<path\file>*"	Create a network install log file.	Creates a network install log file for tracking the number of installs from an admin image. Overrides the value (if any) specified in the .stf file. See doc\table.txt for a description of Network Log Location.
/y	Do not copy files	Does not copy files. Useful when trying to track down problems that occur after the (time-consuming) step of copying the files.
/z		Optional UI hook .dll for replacement dialog boxes (consumer).
/#	Force reserialization of the PID	Forces reserialization of the Product ID. This is to be used in the rare case that two installations from the same original media have received the same generated PID.
/?	Usage message	
/##		## or other invalid parameter yields a better usage message.

Notes about command-line switches:

- The ACME command-line arguments are case insensitive.
- The /a and /q flags are mutually exclusive.
- The /u and /r flags are mutually exclusive and only make sense when running maintenance mode.

The Sections of the SoftBoot.inf

`[W95_NoKillProgs]`

SoftBoot will not close these programs/processes.

`[NT_NoKillProgs]`

SoftBoot will not close these programs/processes.

`[W95_SafeKillProgs]`

These programs will be terminated safely, i.e., a WM_ENDSESSION message will be sent to them.

`[NT_SafeKillProgs]`

These programs will be terminated safely, i.e., a WM_ENDSESSION message will be sent to them.

`[16BitDLLs]`

When programs/processes are terminated, their 16-bit DLLs are not freed up. This section specifies the 16-bit DLLs that need to be freed up explicitly.

`[KeepDLLs]`

Do not process the entry in the Wininit.ini that says to replace these files.

`[OkIfDelFileFails]`

During uninstall time, if SoftBoot cannot delete these files, don't flag this condition as requiring a hard reboot.

`[KnownApps]`

We do not care if these programs/processes are running. If these are running, the user will not be prompted to close programs.

Files Left in the System After Uninstalling Internet Explorer

Windows\Dooflop.exe

Windows\MSImgSiz.dat

Windows\FpXpress.ini

Windows\RaUninst.exe

Windows\MSMusCtl.ini

Windows\Active Setup Log.txt

Windows\IE4 Setup Log.txt

Windows\IE4 Uninstall Log.txt

Windows\JavaInst.log

Windows\Reg Restore Log.txt

Windows\Soft Boot Log.txt

Windows\Bind List Log.txt

Windows\RunOnceEx Log.txt

Windows\WpLog.txt

Windows\INF\IE4Setup.inf

Windows\INF\ICW95.inf

Windows\INF\INFD132.pnf

Windows\INF\INFD324.pnf

Windows\INF\CChat2.inf

Windows\INF\Setup.pnf

Windows\INF\MSImn.inf

Windows\INF\IR50_32.inf

Windows\INF\MSDXMIni.inf

Windows\INF\VdoLive.inf

Windows\INF\FPXpress.inf

Windows\INF\CabPayIE.inf

Windows\INF\ChlEn-US.pnf

Windows\INF\MSImn.pnf

Windows\INF\INFD0F1.pnf

Windows\System\IEJava.cab

Windows\System\ChatSock.dll

Windows\System\ILS.dll

Windows\System\MSSCMC32.dll

Windows\System\L3CodeCa.acm

Windows\System\WLDAP32.dll

Windows\System\ViVOG723.acm

Windows\System\IR50_32.dll

Windows\System\IR50_QC.dll

Windows\System\NSFile.ocx
Windows\System\IVVideo.dll
Windows\System\IR50_QCX.dll
Windows\System\HomePage.inf
Windows\System\IE4Files.inf
Windows\System\UniD192.tmp
Windows\System\IE4Uinit.exe
Windows\System\IE4Uinit.inf
Windows\System\MSVCRT.dll
Windows\System\AsycFilt.dll
Windows\System\CFGMgr32.dll
Windows\System\CkCNV.exe
Windows\System\MSAPSSPC.dll
Windows\System\IERnOnce.dll
Windows\System\LoadWC.exe
Windows\System\SetupAPI.dll
Windows\System\SoftBoot.exe
Windows\System\SoftBoot.inf
Windows\System\Cabinet.dll
Windows\System\VdK32119.acm
Windows\System\UniD1B4.tmp
Windows\System\UniD204.tmp
Windows\System\InetComm.dll
Windows\System\MSOEMAPI.dll
Windows\System\MSOERt.dll
Windows\System\MSOEAcct.dll
Windows\System\VdK3211W.dll
Windows\System\VdK32116.dll
Windows\System\VdoWave.drv
Windows\System\VdoDEC32.dll
Windows\System\DECVW_32.dll
Windows\System\ClrVidDD.dll
Windows\System\TR2032.dll
Windows\System\UNAXA.exe
Windows\System\IAC25_32.ax
Windows\System\IVFSrc.ax
Windows\System\SetDefEd.exe
Windows\System\MSDatSrc.tlb
Windows\System\MSR2C.dll
Windows\System\MSR2CENU.dll
Windows\System\MSVBVM50.dll
Windows\System\WLTUnins.exe

Windows\Help\MSMusCtl.hlp

Windows\Help\SignIn.hlp

Windows\Help\InetComm.hlp

Windows\Help\Conn_OE.hlp

Windows\Help\Conn_OE.cnt

Windows\SendTo\Mail Recipient.MAPIMail

Windows\Fonts\WebDings.ttf

Windows\Java\Security.txt

Windows\Cursors\Globe.ani

Windows\Temporary Internet Files\OAVI1SGX\Desktop.ini

Windows\Temporary Internet Files\ULCRMVYH\Desktop.ini

Windows\Temporary Internet Files\C1QL8AWK\Desktop.ini

Windows\Temporary Internet Files\4JDTB8SW\Desktop.ini

Windows\Recent\PreIE4US.txt.lnk

Windows\Recent\WithUS1712.2.txt.lnk

Windows\Application Data\Microsoft\Internet Explorer\Desktop.htt

Windows\Downloaded Program Files\Microsoft XML Parser for Java.osd

Windows\Downloaded Program Files\Internet Explorer Classes for Java.osd

Windows\Downloaded Program Files\DirectAnimation Java Classes.osd

Recycled\Desktop.ini

Program Files\Common Files\MSCreate.dir

Program Files\Common Files\Microsoft Shared\MSCreate.dir

Program Files\Common Files\Microsoft Shared\Stationery\Baby News.htm

Program Files\Common Files\Microsoft Shared\Stationery\
    Balloon Party Invitation.htm

Program Files\Common Files\Microsoft Shared\Stationery\Chess.htm

Program Files\Common Files\Microsoft Shared\Stationery\Chicken Soup.htm

Program Files\Common Files\Microsoft Shared\Stationery\Formal Announcement.htm

Program Files\Common Files\Microsoft Shared\Stationery\For Sale.htm

Program Files\Common Files\Microsoft Shared\Stationery\Fun Bus.htm

Program Files\Common Files\Microsoft Shared\Stationery\Holiday Letter.htm

Program Files\Common Files\Microsoft Shared\Stationery\Mabel.htm

Program Files\Common Files\Microsoft Shared\Stationery\Running Birthday.htm

Program Files\Common Files\Microsoft Shared\Stationery\Story Book.htm

Program Files\Common Files\Microsoft Shared\Stationery\Tiki Lounge.htm

Program Files\Common Files\Microsoft Shared\Stationery\Ivy.htm

Program Files\Common Files\Microsoft Shared\Stationery\One Green Balloon.gif

Program Files\Common Files\Microsoft Shared\Stationery\Baby News Bkgrd.gif

Program Files\Common Files\Microsoft Shared\Stationery\Chess.gif

Program Files\Common Files\Microsoft Shared\Stationery\Chicken Soup Bkgrd.gif

Program Files\Common Files\Microsoft Shared\Stationery\
    Formal Announcement Bkgrd.gif

Program Files\Common Files\Microsoft Shared\Stationery\For Sale Bkgrd.gif

Program Files\Common Files\Microsoft Shared\Stationery\FunBus.gif

Program Files\Common Files\Microsoft Shared\Stationery\Holiday Letter Bkgrd.gif

Program Files\Common Files\Microsoft Shared\Stationery\MabelT.gif

Program Files\Common Files\Microsoft Shared\Stationery\MabelB.gif

Program Files\Common Files\Microsoft Shared\Stationery\Running.gif

Program Files\Common Files\Microsoft Shared\Stationery\Santa Workshop.gif

Program Files\Common Files\Microsoft Shared\Stationery\Soup Bowl.gif

Program Files\Common Files\Microsoft Shared\Stationery\Squiggles.gif

Program Files\Common Files\Microsoft Shared\Stationery\StoryBook.gif

Program Files\Common Files\Microsoft Shared\Stationery\Tiki.gif

Program Files\Common Files\Microsoft Shared\Stationery\Christmas Trees.gif

Program Files\Common Files\Microsoft Shared\Stationery\Ivy.gif

Program Files\Common Files\Microsoft Shared\Stationery\
    Balloon Party Invitation Bkgrd.jpg

Program Files\Common Files\Microsoft Shared\Stationery\Technical.htm

Program Files\Common Files\Microsoft Shared\Stationery\Tech.gif

Program Files\Common Files\System\MSAdC\MSAdCo.dll

Program Files\Common Files\System\MSAdC\MSAdCor.dll

Program Files\Common Files\System\MSAdC\MSAdCe.dll

Program Files\Common Files\System\MSAdC\MSAdCer.dll

Program Files\Common Files\System\AdO\MSAdEr15.dll

Program Files\Common Files\System\AdO\MSAdOr15.dll

Program Files\Common Files\System\OLE Db\MSDAdC.dll

Program Files\Common Files\System\OLE Db\MSDAPS.dll

Program Files\Common Files\Services\Bigfoot.bmp

Program Files\Common Files\Services\Four11.bmp

Program Files\Common Files\Services\WhoWhere.bmp

Program Files\Common Files\Services\InfoSpce.bmp

Program Files\Common Files\Services\SwtchBrd.bmp

Program Files\Common Files\Services\VeriSign.bmp

Program Files\Common Files\Services\InfoSpBz.bmp

Program Files\Internet Explorer\Setup\MSCreate.dir

Program Files\Internet Explorer\Signup\Install.ins

Program Files\Internet Explorer\Plugins\NpsMlVdo.dll

Program Files\Outlook Express_ISetup.exe

The entire contents of the Internet Explorer 4 Setup folder

APPENDIX B

Troubleshooting Installation and Uninstallation

This appendix reviews some of the issues related to Microsoft® Internet Explorer 4 installation and uninstallation that may require troubleshooting and explains procedures for solving installation and uninstallation problems. Topics include:

- Cannot install Internet Explorer 4 after download
- Windows Desktop Update not enabled after installing Internet Explorer
- Problems installing 128-bit server gated cryptography
- Problems reinstalling Windows® 95 with Internet Explorer 4
- Invalid page fault when installing additional components
- Problems installing Service Pack 3 after Internet Explorer
- Cannot uninstall Internet Explorer 4 using the Add/Remove Programs tool
- Cannot view Internet properties after uninstalling
- Problems returning to an earlier version of Internet Explorer
- Removing Internet Explorer 4 for Windows 95 using IERemove.exe
- Removing Internet Explorer for Windows NT® 4.0 using IERemove.exe

To learn more about these topics, see Part 1.

Important This section contains information about editing the registry. Before you edit the registry, you should first make a backup copy of the registry files (System.dat and User.dat). Both are hidden files in the Windows\System folder.

Warning Using Registry Editor incorrectly can cause serious problems that may require you to reinstall your operating system. Microsoft cannot guarantee that problems resulting from the incorrect use of Registry Editor can be solved. Use Registry Editor at your own risk.

Troubleshooting Installation

There are a variety of problems you may encounter during or after installation of Internet Explorer 4.

Cannot Install Internet Explorer 4 After Download

During download of Internet Explorer 4, Active Setup determines the version of the operating system running and automatically downloads the files appropriate for that operating system. Because these files are unique to the operating system, you cannot download the Internet Explorer installation files using one operating system and then install it to another operating system.

If you attempt to install Internet Explorer from files that were downloaded using a different operating system than the one you are currently running, the following error message may display:

The Internet Explorer files on your computer are not the correct files for your operating system. To continue, you must download the correct files from the Internet. Do you want to continue?

If you click **No**, Active Setup quits. If you click **Yes**, Internet Explorer continues with Active Setup and attempts to download the appropriate files from the Internet.

Note You must be connected to the Internet for the download to continue.

▶ **To resolve this installation issue, use any of the following methods:**

- Download the installation files using the same operating system on which you intend to install Internet Explorer.

- Download the installation files for both operating systems in one session.

Windows Desktop Update Not Enabled After Installing Internet Explorer

After you install Internet Explorer with the Windows Desktop Update, the Windows Desktop Update (and Active Desktop™) may be disabled. This problem occurs when you are running different language versions of Internet Explorer and Windows 95 or Windows 95 OEM Service Release. For example, Windows Desktop Update would be disabled if you installed the English version of Internet Explorer 4 on a computer running a non-English version of Windows 95. As a result, Web sites and pictures are not displayed on your desktop, and the **Desktop** tab does not appear in the **Display Properties** dialog box.

To correct this problem, uninstall Internet Explorer, and then install the same language version of Internet Explorer as the version of Windows 95 or OEM Service Release installed on your computer. For more information about installing Internet Explorer 4, see Chapter 2, "Phase 1: Active Setup."

Problems Installing 128-Bit Server Gated Cryptography

If you install the English-language, exportable 128-bit Server Gated Cryptography (SGC) add-on for Internet Explorer 3 on a computer with Internet Explorer 4 installed, the following message may display:

Microsoft Internet Explorer SGC 128 update

Your computer already has a newer or 128-bit version of this product. Installation will exit.

▶ **To enable 128-bit strong encryption in Internet Explorer 4, use either of the following methods:**

- Install the 128-bit strong encryption version of Internet Explorer 3 before you upgrade to Internet Explorer 4.

- After you install Internet Explorer 4, download the 128-bit strong encryption upgrade for Internet Explorer 4 from the following Web site:

  http://www.microsoft.com/ie/download/?/ie/download/128bit.htm

To learn more about SGC, see Chapter 28, "Digital Certificates."

Problems Reinstalling Windows 95 with Internet Explorer 4

Before you reinstall any version of Windows 95, you should uninstall Internet Explorer 4. If you do not uninstall Internet Explorer 4 before reinstalling Windows 95, you may be unable to start Windows or run Internet Explorer or related components. To avoid these problems, uninstall Internet Explorer, reinstall Windows 95, and then reinstall Internet Explorer.

If you already reinstalled Windows 95 without uninstalling Internet Explorer 4 first and are having problems, read the following information, and select one of the methods explained below. To select the correct method for recovery, you must determine the version of Windows 95 you are running.

▶ **To determine the version of Windows 95 you are running**

1. In the Windows Control Panel, double-click the System icon.

2. On the **General** tab, locate the version number under the System heading, and then match that number to the version of Windows 95 in the following table:

Version number	Version of Windows 95
40.950	Windows 95
40.950A	Windows 95 plus the Service Pack 1 Update, or OEM Service Release 1
40.950B	OEM Service Release 2 (OSR2)

If you are running OEM Service Release version 2.1, you will see the version number 40.950B (the same as OSR2). To determine whether you are running OSR 2.1, check for "USB Supplement to OSR2" in the list of installed programs in the **Add/Remove Programs Properties** dialog box. Then, check for version 43.1212 of the Ntkern.vxd file in the Windows\System\Vmm32 folder.

Windows 95 may have been preinstalled on your computer. These installations are referred to as original equipment manufacturer (OEM) installations.

▶ **To determine whether you have an OEM installation of Windows 95**

1. In the Control Panel, double-click the **System** icon.

2. On the **General** tab, locate the Product ID number under the Registered To heading. This number typically contains 20 digits. If digits 7, 8, and 9 contain the letters "OEM," you have an OEM installation of Windows 95. For example:

```
12345-OEM-6789098-76543
```

If you are using an OEM installation of Windows 95, you should contact your computer's manufacturer for Windows 95 support.

The methods outlined below are specific to the version of Windows 95 you are running and whether you selected **Yes** or **No** in all **Version Conflict** dialog boxes that displayed while you reinstalled Windows 95.

Version of Windows 95	Response to version conflicts	Use this method
Windows 95 or A	Yes	1
Windows 95 or A	No	2
Windows 95B	Yes	3
Windows 95B	No	4

Method 1

You do not need to make any changes to your current configuration. Reinstalling Windows 95 with Internet Explorer 4 installed and answering **Yes** to all file version conflicts does not cause any problems.

Method 2

Windows 95 works properly, but you may need to reinstall Internet Explorer to resolve browser problems. Reinstalling Internet Explorer 4 should resolve any file version conflicts resulting from reinstalling Windows 95.

Method 3

Windows 95 works properly, but you may experience problems running Internet Explorer 4, because Windows 95 reinstalls Internet Explorer 3. To resolve this problem, reinstall Internet Explorer 4.

Method 4

If you are using the Windows Desktop Update component, the following error messages may occur:

- When you start your computer:

  Error loading Explorer.Exe. You must reinstall Windows.

- When you click **OK**:

  Error Starting program: The Explorer.Exe File is Linked to Missing Export SHLWAPI.DLL:ShopenRegstreamA

In addition, the following may occur:

- Your computer stops responding (hangs) or shuts down.

- If you did not have the Windows Desktop Update installed, you may be able to start Windows 95, but you cannot run Internet Explorer, and your desktop icons cannot be moved.

▶   **To resolve these issues**

1. Restart your computer. When the "Starting Windows 95" message appears, press the F8 key; then choose **Command Prompt Only** from the **Startup** menu.

2. Type the following line, and press ENTER to change to the Uninstall folder:

   cd *uninstall folder* where *uninstall folder* is the location of the uninstall folder for Internet Explorer 4. For example:
   cd C:\Progra~1\Intern~1\Uninst~1.

3. Type the following line, and press ENTER to view the hidden files:

   attrib -s -h -r *.*

4. Type the following lines to restore the files necessary to start Windows 95:

   iextract integr~1.dat

5. Type the following lines to place the files in their proper folders:

   copy explorer.exe c:\windows

   copy shell32.dll c:\windows\system

6. Restart the computer.

7. Uninstall Internet Explorer 4, and then reinstall it.

Invalid Page Fault When Installing Additional Components

When you try to install additional components from the Internet Explorer Components Download page, an invalid page fault may occur in Kernel32.dll. As a result, you may not be able to properly restart your computer. This problem can occur if you do not have enough free hard disk space to install the selected components. To correct this problem, free some hard disk space, and try to install the additional components again.

Note The Components Download page does not indicate the amount of hard disk space needed to install the selected components. Instead, the Web page lists the total size of the components.

Problems Installing Service Pack 3 After Internet Explorer

When you try to reapply or uninstall Windows NT 4.0 Service Pack 3 after installing Internet Explorer 4, the following warning message may appear:

Update.exe

This program may not run correctly because of the new features in Internet Explorer 4. You may need to obtain an updated version of this program. For information about obtaining an updated version, click **Details**. If you want to try running this program, click **Details** to determine whether it will cause other problems. Then, if running this program will not cause other problems, click **Run Program**.

The warning dialog box includes a **Run Program** button (runs the program normally), a **Cancel** button (stops the program from running), and a **Details** button.

This warning occurs for the following reasons:

- Reapplying Service Pack 3 has rendered the Internet Explorer 4 shell (and other components) inoperable and invalidated your Service Pack 3 Uninstall folder.

- Uninstalling Service Pack 3 has rendered the Internet Explorer 4 shell (and other components) inoperable.

You can reapply Service Pack 3 by clicking **Run Program** on the warning dialog box and choosing the following options while you're reapplying Service Pack 3:

- Select **No, I do not want to create an Uninstall directory**.
- Select **No** whenever you are prompted to replace newer files.

If you're trying to uninstall Service Pack 3, click **Cancel** on the warning dialog box and uninstall Internet Explorer 4 before uninstalling Service Pack 3.

Windows NT 4 Service Pack 3 is required to run Internet Explorer 4. If you don't have Service Pack 3 installed when you install Internet Explorer 4, the following error message displays, and Setup cannot continue:

Windows NT 4 Service Pack 3 must be installed before Internet Explorer 4 installation can continue.

If you click **Details** on the warning dialog box, the following message appears:

Do not uninstall Windows 95 Service Pack 1. Doing so will render the Internet Explorer 4 shell inoperable.

This message should read as follows:

Do not uninstall Windows NT 4 Service Pack 3. Doing so will render the Internet Explorer 4 shell inoperable. If you are reapplying Service Pack 3, you can safely click Run Program if you choose the following while you are reapplying Service Pack 3:

Note To prevent the warning from being displayed when you run this program in the future, select the **Don't display this message in the future** check box.

Troubleshooting Uninstallation

There are a variety of problems you may encounter during or after uninstallation of Internet Explorer 4.

Cannot Uninstall Internet Explorer 4 Using the Add/Remove Programs Tool

If you cannot uninstall Internet Explorer 4 using the Add/Remove Programs tool in the Control Panel, it is probably because you have deleted the uninstall information by removing the necessary Setup files (IE4bak.dat, IE4bak.ini, Integrated Browser.dat, and Integrated Browser.ini). The Internet Explorer **Advanced Uninstall** dialog box offers the option to uninstall this backup information, but doing so will prevent you from uninstalling Internet Explorer in the future. (For more information, see "Deleting Uninstall Files" in Chapter 7.)

If you attempt to reinstall Internet Explorer after deleting these files, the following message will display:

You are upgrading a version of Internet Explorer 4 in which the uninstall feature has been disabled. If you choose to continue, Setup will update your PC with the newer version, but the uninstall feature will remain disabled.

Cannot View Internet Properties After Uninstalling

After you remove Internet Explorer 4, the following may occur because you have an incorrect version of the Inetcpl.cpl file installed on your computer:

- The **Internet** icon may not be present in the Control Panel.
- You may not be able to access the **Internet Properties** dialog box.
- When you are running Internet Explorer 3, and you select **Options** on the **View** menu, nothing happens.

▶ **To install the correct Inetcpl.cpl file**

1. Delete the Inetcpl.cpl file in the Windows\System folder.
2. Install (or reinstall) Internet Explorer 3. To download Internet Explorer 3, see **http://www.microsoft.com/ie/**.

Problems Returning to an Earlier Version of Internet Explorer

If you install Internet Explorer 4 and then decide that you want to return to an earlier version of Internet Explorer, you should uninstall Internet Explorer 4 before installing the earlier version.

If you attempt to install an earlier version of Internet Explorer on a computer with Internet Explorer 4 installed, the following error message appears:

Internet Explorer 3 cannot be installed on a system that has Internet Explorer 4 installed.

If you click **OK**, the following message appears:

There was an error during the Setup process. Either the user pressed Cancel or there was not enough disk space. Installation failed.

To correct this problem, install Internet Explorer 4 again, and then uninstall it. You can then safely install an older version of Internet Explorer. For information on how to reinstall Internet Explorer 4, see "Reinstalling Components" in Chapter 7. (The process for reinstalling Internet Explorer is the same as the process for reinstalling its components.)

Removing Internet Explorer 4 for Windows 95 Using IERemove.exe

This section describes how to remove Internet Explorer 4 for Windows 95 using the IERemove.exe tool and a registry (for example, System.1st) that was created before you installed Internet Explorer 4.

Use this procedure for the following situations:

- You tried to uninstall Internet Explorer 4, but were unsuccessful.

- With Internet Explorer 4 installed on your computer, you restored a registry that was created before you installed Internet Explorer 4.

Do *not* use this procedure for the following situations:

- You have not tried to uninstall Internet Explorer 4 by using the **Add/Remove Programs** applet in the Control Panel.

- You have removed the Internet Explorer 4 backup files. If you removed these files and are unable to uninstall Internet Explorer using the standard procedure (see Chapter 7), you cannot remove Internet Explorer without reinstalling Windows 95 to a different folder.

For more information about IERemove.exe, see "Understanding IERemove.exe," in Chapter 7.

Note IERemove.exe is a command-line executable file designed to remove Internet Explorer 4 and its components. IERemove.exe cannot remove Internet Explorer without using command line options. For information about the command-line options available for IERemove.exe, type **ieremove /?**.

▶ **To remove Internet Explorer 4 by using the IERemove.exe tool and a registry that was created before you installed Internet Explorer 4**

If you have not already done so, restore the registry that was created before you installed Internet Explorer 4.

Note During the Internet Explorer 4 installation, the original System.1st file is replaced with a copy of the registry. The original System.1st file is saved in the Integrated Browser.dat file (Integr~1.dat).

---

1. To extract the original System.1st file from the Integr~1.dat file, type the following command at a command prompt and press ENTER:

   cd *path***\uninst~1** where *path* is the path to the folder where Internet Explorer is installed.

2. Type the following line, and press ENTER:

   attrib integr~1.dat –h

3. Type the following line, and press ENTER:

   iextract /L *dir* **integr~1.dat system.1st** where *dir* is the folder in which the extracted file will be saved.

4. Restart the computer. When the "Starting Windows 95" message appears, press the F8 key, and then choose **Safe Mode Command Prompt Only** from the **Startup** menu.

5. Type the following commands, pressing ENTER after each command:

   cd *path***\uninst~1**

   attrib integr~1.dat -h

   iextract integr~1.dat

   copy shell32.dll c:\windows\system

   copy explorer.exe c:\windows

   where *path* is the path to the folder where Internet Explorer is installed.

6. Restart the computer.

7. From the **Start** menu, select **Run**, and then type the following command in the **Open** box (with quotation marks):

   "*path1*\ieremove.exe" /i:"*path2*\integrated browser.dat"/n:"*path3*\ie4bak.dat"

   where **path1** is the full path to the IERemove.exe file, **path2** is the full path to the Integrated Browser.dat file, and **path3** is the full path to the IE4bak.dat file. For example, if the IERemove.exe file is in the C:\Windows\System folder, the Integrated Browser.dat file is in the C:\Program Files\Internet Explorer\Uninstall Information folder, and the IE4bak.dat file is in the C:\Windows folder, you would type the following command (with quotation marks):

   "c:\windows\system\ieremove.exe" /i:"c:\program files\internet explorer\uninstall information\integrated browser.dat"/n:"c:\windows\ie4bak.dat"

8. Click **OK**, click **Yes**, then restart your computer after the IERemove.exe tool is finished running.

9. Reinstall Internet Explorer 4, and then uninstall it. This step is necessary to ensure that the additional components included with Internet Explorer 4 are removed.

Removing Internet Explorer for Windows NT 4.0 Using IERemove.exe

This section describes how to remove Internet Explorer 4 for Microsoft Windows NT by using the IERemove.exe tool and the Emergency Repair Disk (ERD).

Use this procedure for the following situations:

- You tried to uninstall Internet Explorer 4, but were unsuccessful.

- You created an ERD before you installed Internet Explorer 4, and then you used the ERD while Internet Explorer 4 was installed on your computer.

Do *not* use this procedure for the following situations:

- You have not tried to uninstall Internet Explorer 4.

- You have removed the Internet Explorer 4 backup files. If you removed these files and are unable to uninstall Internet Explorer using the standard procedure (see Chapter 7), you cannot remove Internet Explorer without reinstalling Windows NT to a different folder.

For more information about IERemove.exe, see "Understanding IERemove.exe," in Chapter 7.

Note IERemove.exe is a command-line executable file designed to remove Internet Explorer 4 and its components. IERemove.exe cannot remove Internet Explorer without using command-line options. For information about the command-line options available for IERemove.exe, type **ieremove /?**.

Before proceeding, locate the "Integrated Browser NT.dat" and the IE4bak.dat files.

▶ **To locate the "Integrated Browser NT.dat" and IE4.bak files**

1. From the **Start** menu, select **Find** and then **Files Or Folders**.

2. In the **Named** box, type **"Integrated Browser NT.dat"** (with quotation marks), and then click **Find Now**.

3. Note the path for the "Integrated Browser NT.dat" file in the In Folder column.

4. Repeat steps 1 to 3 for the IE4bak.dat file.

5. From the **File** menu, select **Close**.

To remove Internet Explorer 4, use the IERemove.exe tool and an ERD that was created before you installed Internet Explorer 4. The following steps guide you through uninstalling the Windows Desktop Update component (if it has been installed) and Internet Explorer. You should uninstall the Windows Desktop Update component before you uninstall Internet Explorer 4.

▶ **To uninstall the Windows Desktop Update component using IERemove.exe**

1. Use the ERD that was created before you installed Internet Explorer 4 to repair your Windows NT installation.

2. Restart your computer and log on to Windows NT.

3. Press CTRL+ALT+DELETE to open the **Windows NT Security** dialog box, and then click **Task Manager**.

4. On the **File** menu, select **New Task (Run)**, and type the following command in the **Open** box (with quotation marks):

   "path1\ieremove" /i:"path2\integrated browser nt.dat" where ***path1*** is the full path to the IERemove.exe file and ***path2*** is the full path to the "Integrated Browser NT.dat" file.

   For example, if Windows NT is installed in the C:\Winnt folder, the IERemove.exe file will be in the C:\Winnt\System32 folder, and the "Integrated Browser NT.dat" file will be in the C:\Program Files\Plus!\Microsoft Internet\Uninstall Information folder. In this case, you would type the following command (with quotation marks):

   "c:\winnt\system32\ieremove" /i:"c:\program files\plus!\microsoft internet\uninstall information\integrated browser nt.dat"

5. Click **OK**.

6. Minimize the Task Manager window.

7. At the Internet Explorer 4 Uninstall prompt, click **OK**.

8. Click **Yes**, and then click **OK**.

9. Close Task Manager, and restart your computer.

▶ **Uninstall Internet Explorer using IERemove.exe**

1. From the **Start menu**, select **Run**.

2. In the **Open** box, type the following command (with quotation marks):

   "path1\ieremove" /n:"path2\ie4bak.dat" where ***path1*** is the full path to the IERemove.exe file and ***path2*** is the full path to the IE4bak.dat file.

   For example, if Windows NT is installed in the C:\Winnt folder, the IERemove.exe file will be in the C:\Winnt\System32 folder, and the IE4bak.dat file will be in the C:\Winnt folder. In this case, type the following command (with quotation marks):

   "c:\winnt\system32\ieremove" /n:"c:\winnt\ie4bak.dat"

3. Click **OK**, and then click **OK** again.

   After the IERemove.exe tool has uninstalled Internet Explorer 4, reinstall Internet Explorer 4, and then uninstall it normally. This step is necessary to ensure that the additional components included with Internet Explorer 4 are removed.

A P P E N D I X   C

Troubleshooting the Browser

This appendix reviews some of the issues related to the Microsoft® Internet Explorer browser that may require troubleshooting and explains procedures for improving and configuring browser performance. Topics include:

- Font size change is not saved
- Determining your previous version of Internet Explorer
- Slow connections and inability to view non-Microsoft sites
- Restoring functionality to the downloaded program files folder
- Changing the download location for ActiveX files

To learn more about the browser, see Part 2.

Important This section contains information about editing the registry. Before you edit the registry, you should first make a backup copy of the registry files (System.dat and User.dat). Both are hidden files in the Windows folder.

Warning Using Registry Editor incorrectly can cause serious problems that may require you to reinstall your operating system. Microsoft cannot guarantee that problems resulting from the incorrect use of Registry Editor can be solved. Use Registry Editor at your own risk.

Font Size Change is Not Saved

When you change the font size in Internet Explorer by using the **Fonts** command on the **View** menu or the **Fonts** button on the toolbar and then restart Internet Explorer, your change is lost.

Note This behavior is by design. The **Fonts** command on the **View** menu and **Fonts** button on the toolbar are designed to immediately change the font size for the current session only. The **Internet Options** dialog box enables you to change the default font size for future sessions.

▶ **To change the default font size for viewing Web pages**

1. On the **View** menu, click **Internet Options**.

2. On the **General** tab, click **Fonts**.

3. Select a font from the **Font Size** box.

4. Click **OK,** then **OK** again.

Because of the different ways Web pages can be formatted, some pages will not be affected by the above procedure. To change the appearance of such pages, you'll need to override the page formatting.

▶ **To override page formatting**

1. On the **View** menu, click **Internet Options.**

2. On the **General** tab, click **Accessibility.**

3. Select any of the following options:

   - Ignore Colors specified on Web pages
   - Ignore font styles specified on Web pages
   - Ignore font sizes specified on Web pages
   - Format documents using my style sheet

4. Click **OK.**

For more information, see "Customizing Display of Fonts, Colors, and Styles" in Chapter 33, "Accessibility Features and Functionality."

Determining Your Previous Version of Internet Explorer

To determine your previous version of Internet Explorer after installing Internet Explorer 4, view the PreviousIESysFile value under the following registry key:

HKEY_LOCAL_MACHINE\SOFTWARE\Microsoft\IE4\Setup

The following table lists the possible values for the PreviousIESysFile registry value and the version of Internet Explorer that corresponds to each:

Value	Version
4.70.0.1155	3.0
4.70.0.1158	3.0
4.70.0.1215	3.01
4.70.0.1300	3.02
4.71.<xxxx>	4.0

Note   The Internet Explorer 4 Uninstall feature returns your computer to a pre-Internet Explorer 4 browser. As a result, the PreviousIESysFile value cannot be used to determine if you upgraded to Internet Explorer 4 over an earlier, beta version of Internet Explorer 4.

The PreviousIESysFile value is used by the Internet Explorer 4 Uninstall program to determine which components should be removed when Internet Explorer 4 is removed. The registry contains a RequiredIESysFile value for each component. If the RequiredIESysFile value for a particular component is equal to or less than the PreviousIESysFile value, the component is not removed when you remove Internet Explorer 4. If the RequiredIESysFile value for a component is greater than the PreviousIESysFile value, the component is removed when you remove Internet Explorer 4.

Slow Connections and Inability to View Non-Microsoft Sites

When you use Internet Explorer version 3 or 4 with a proxy server and Novell NetWare 32-bit client software to browse the Internet, you may experience the following:

- Slow connections.
- Inconsistent downloads.
- An inability to view non-Microsoft sites.

To resolve these problems, verify that you are using the Novell NetWare 32-bit client and that you are connecting to the Internet using a proxy server.

▶ **To verify that you are using the Novell client**

1. On the **Start** menu, point to **Settings**, then click **Control Panel**.
2. Double-click the **Network** icon, and click the **Configuration** tab.
3. Verify that **Novell 32** appears in the box labeled **The following network components are installed**.

▶ **To verify that you are connecting using a proxy server**

1. On the **View** menu, click **Internet Options**, then click the **Connection** tab.
2. Verify that the **Access the Internet Using a Proxy Server** check box is checked and that the **Address** box contains entries. This indicates that Internet Explorer is set up to connect to the Internet through a proxy server.

▶ **To add DontUseDNSLoadBalancing to the Internet settings registry key**

If you are using the Novell NetWare 32-bit client and are connecting to the Internet using a proxy server, use the following information to add to the registry key:

1. Create a new binary value named:

    DontUseDNSLoadBalancing under the following registry key:

    HKEY_CURRENT_USER\Software\Microsoft\Windows\ CurrentVersion\Internet Settings

2. Set the value to:

    01 00 00 00

3. Restart your computer.

Note The Novell NetWare 32-bit client is not manufactured by Microsoft. Microsoft makes no warranty, implied or otherwise, regarding this product's performance or reliability.

For more information about configuring proxy server settings, see Chapter 8, "Configuring Connection Settings."

Restoring Functionality to the Downloaded Program Files Folder

The Download Program Files folder contains functionality that enables you to easily uninstall ActiveX controls. When this folder is deleted, a new Downloaded Program Files folder is created the next time Internet Explorer downloads new program files. However, the newly created folder does not contain the functionality to easily uninstall ActiveX controls. This section describes how to restore this functionality to the new folder.

▶ **To restore the ability to easily uninstall ActiveX controls**

1. From the **Start** menu, point to **Programs**, then click **MS-DOS Command Prompt**.

2. Type **cd**, and then press ENTER.

3. Type the following command, and then press ENTER:

    cd *windows***\system**
    where *windows* is the folder in which Windows is installed.

4. Type the following command, and then press ENTER:

    regsvr32 /i occache.dll

5. Type **exit**, and then press ENTER.

6. From the **Start** menu, select **Shut Down**, click **Restart**, and then **OK**.

Controls that were deleted with the original folder are listed with a status of Damaged. These controls should be removed because the associated files have already been deleted.

Changing the Download Location for ActiveX Files

ActiveX .ocx and .inf files are installed in the Windows\Downloaded Program Files folder by default.

▶ **To change the location of ActiveX files**

1. Use Registry Editor to change the ActiveXCache value to the location you want in the following registry key:

   HKEY_LOCAL_MACHINE\SOFTWARE\Microsoft\Windows\ CurrentVersion\Internet Settings

2. Use Registry Editor to change the 0 value to the location you want in the following registry key:

   HKEY_LOCAL_MACHINE\SOFTWARE\Microsoft\Windows\ CurrentVersion\Internet Settings\ActiveXCache

---

Note The values you enter in steps 1 and 2 must match.

The new value can be a folder on a local hard disk, a Universal Naming Convention (UNC) name, or a mapped network drive. Storing ActiveX files on a network server may reduce Internet Explorer performance, because the ActiveX files must be delivered over the network.

APPENDIX D

Troubleshooting the Active Desktop

This appendix reviews some of the issues related to the Microsoft® Internet Explorer Active Desktop™ that may require troubleshooting and explains procedures for solving problems that may occur in this area. Topics include:

- Pointing to desktop icons causes text to disappear
- Changing to single-click mode using the registry
- Images copied to the desktop are saved as Active Desktop items
- **Find on the Internet** command appears twice on the Start menu
- Active Desktop items stop working when offline .
- System properties do not show that Microsoft Plus! is installed
- Internet Explorer cannot find the Active Desktop
- Do not use Web pages with frames as your desktop wallpaper

To learn more about the Active Desktop, see Part 3.

Important This section contains information about editing the registry. Before you edit the registry, you should first make a backup copy of the registry files (System.dat and User.dat). Both are hidden files in the Windows folder.

Warning Editing the registry incorrectly can cause serious problems that may require you to reinstall your operating system. Microsoft cannot guarantee that problems resulting from the incorrect editing of the registry can be solved. Edit the registry at your own risk.

Pointing to Desktop Icons Causes Text to Disappear

If your computer is running Internet Explorer 4 and the Windows Desktop Update and you point to an icon on the desktop, the text under the icon may disappear. This behavior occurs when selected items and desktop are configured to use the same color in the **Display Properties** dialog box. To resolve this problem, either configure Windows® 95 so that selected items and the desktop are not configured to use the same color, or configure Windows 95 so that you must double-click to open an object.

▶ **To configure Windows 95 so that selected items and the desktop are not configured to use the same color**

1. From the **Start** menu, point to **Settings**, then click **Control Panel**.

2. Double-click the **Display** icon.

3. Click the **Appearance** tab, click **Selected Items** or **Desktop** in the list of items, then select a different color.

4. Click **OK**.

▶ **To configure Windows 95 so that you must double-click to open an object**

1. Double click the **My Computer** icon on the desktop, then click **Options** on the **View** menu.

2. Click the **View** tab, then click **Double-Click To Open Any Item**.

3. Click **OK**.

Changing to Single-Click Mode Using the Registry

If the Windows Desktop Update is installed, administrators can configure Internet Explorer so that instead of double-clicking to open an item, users single click, and rather than using a single-click to select an item, users point to select. Users can select this Web-style option for themselves (by selecting **Folders and Icons** from the **Settings** menu on the **Start** menu), but administrators may find it helpful to implement this option without user intervention. To do this, you must create a registry file.

▶ **TO create the .reg file**

1. Using any text editor, such as Notepad, create a file with the following content:

   regedit4[HKEY_LOCAL_MACHINE\SOFTWARE\Microsoft\Windows\ CurrentVersion\explorer]"IconUnderline"=hex(0):03,00,00,00

[HKEY_USERS\.Default\Software\Microsoft\Windows\CurrentVersion\ Explorer]"ShellState"=hex:1c,00,00,00,41,08,00,00,00,00,00,00,00,00,00,00, 00,00,00,00,\00,00,00,00,09,00,00,00"IconUnderline"=hex(0):03,00,00,00

2. Save this file as Single.reg and place it on a server.

▶ **To run the .reg file**

• Add the following command to users' login scripts:

regedit *path to file***single.reg –s**

The **-s** switch makes the command run silently, so that no user intervention is required. After the command is carried out, restarting the computer or refreshing the screen activates the option to single-click to open an item (point to select).

Images Copied to the Desktop Are Saved as Active Desktop Items

When have the Windows Desktop Update installed and attempt to save an image file to the desktop by dragging the image from a Web page to the desktop, you may receive the following prompt:

Security Alert
Do you want to add a desktop item to your Active Desktop?

When you click **Yes**, the Subscription Wizard starts to set up a subscription for updating the image. When the wizard is finished, the image appears as an Active Desktop item, rather than as a file icon. This only occurs when you drag Web-based content to the desktop. You can drag items from My Computer or Windows Explorer to the desktop and the file is copied normally.

To work around the Active Desktop process, you can manually save the image.

▶ **To manually save the image**

1. Right-click the image to be copied, and then, on the pop-up menu, click **Save Picture As**.

2. Double-click your Desktop folder, then click **Save**. (By default, the Desktop folder is C:\Windows\Desktop in Windows 95 and C:\Winnt\Profiles*name*\Desktop in Windows NT®.)

You can also avoid this situation by uninstalling the Windows Desktop Update component. For the procedure to uninstall the Windows Desktop Update, see Chapter 6, "Adding and Removing Components after Setup."

"Find on the Internet" Command Appears Twice on the Start Menu

When you click **Start** and then point to **Find**, you may see two **On The Internet** commands, and one of the commands may not work correctly. This can occur when both Internet Explorer 4 and FindX PowerToy are installed on your computer.

Windows PowerToys are a suite of tools available for free download from the Microsoft Web site. Microsoft Technical Support does not support the installation or usage of PowerToys or any of their components. FindX is a Windows 95 PowerToy that you can use to add your own custom commands to the **Find** menu, including a built-in **On The Internet** command.

To resolve this issue, remove FindX PowerToy from your system.

▶ **To remove the FindX PowerToy**

1. Click **Start**, point to **Settings**, then click **Control Panel**.
2. Double-click the **Add/Remove Programs** icon.
3. On the **Install/Uninstall** tab, click **Find... Extensions** in the list of installed programs.
4. Click **Add/Remove** to remove FindX.

Active Desktop Items Stop Working When Offline

Active Desktop items that host Java programs may stop working when Internet Explorer 4 is offline. This can occur if the Java program is removed from the Temporary Internet Files folder. Also, if the Java program is not packaged into a .cab, .zip, or .jar file, it may not get cached at all.

Active Desktop items are retrieved from the cache when Internet Explorer 4 is offline. If the cache reaches its maximum size, Java programs may be automatically removed from the cache to make room for current downloads. If an Active Desktop item hosts a Java program that has been removed from the cache and Internet Explorer 4 is offline, the Active Desktop item stops working.

▶ **To activate Active Desktop items for offline use**

Empty the Temporary Internet Files folder or increase the amount of hard disk space it uses, by using the appropriate method:

- Empty the Temporary Internet Files folder by following these steps:
    1. In Internet Explorer, on the **View** menu, click **Internet Options**.

2. On the **General** tab, in the **Temporary Internet Files** box, click **Delete Files**.

3. Click **OK** when you are prompted to delete the files, and then click **OK** again.

4. Connect to the Internet.

5. Right-click an empty area on your desktop, point to **Active Desktop**, and then click **Update Now** to update the Active Desktop items.

- Increase the amount of hard disk space the Temporary Internet Files folder uses by following these steps:

  1. In Internet Explorer, on the **View** menu, click **Internet Options**.

  2. On the **General** tab, in the **Temporary Internet Files box,** click **Settings**.

  3. Move the **Amount of disk space to use** slider to the right.

  4. Click **OK**, then click **OK** again.

  5. Connect to the Internet.

  6. Right-click an empty area on the desktop, point to **Active Desktop**, then click **Update Now** to update the Active Desktop items.

System Properties Do Not Show That Microsoft Plus! Is Installed

If you install Microsoft Plus! and then install Internet Explorer 4, the **System Properties** dialog box may indicate that Microsoft Plus! isn't installed. The information line no longer shows:

Microsoft Plus! for Windows 95

Instead, this line reads:

IE 4.0 *7-digit build number*

The opposite behavior may also occur. If you install Microsoft Plus! after installing Internet Explorer 4, the **System Properties** dialog box line no longer shows:

IE 4.0 *7-digit build number*

Instead, this line reads:

Microsoft Plus! for Windows 95

This behavior is solely cosmetic; it does not affect your ability to run installed Microsoft Plus! or Internet Explorer.

Internet Explorer Cannot Find the Active Desktop

When you make changes to the Active Desktop, the following error message may occur:

Internet Explorer cannot find the Active Desktop HTML file. This file is needed for your Active Desktop. Click OK to turn off Active Desktop.

This occurs when the Windows\Web folder has been moved or renamed, because Internet Explorer needs to write to certain files stored within that folder.

To solve the problem, use Windows Explorer to create a new Windows\Web folder, or remove and reinstall Internet Explorer to re-create the folder. For the procedures to uninstall and reinstall Internet Explorer, see Chapter 7, "Uninstalling Internet Explorer" and Chapter 6, "Adding and Removing Components After Setup," respectively. (The process for reinstalling Internet Explorer is the same as the process for reinstalling its components.)

Do Not Use Web Pages with Frames as Your Desktop Wallpaper

If you use a Web page as your desktop wallpaper and it contains frames, some desktop items may stop working. For example, you may find that the Channel bar is removed from the desktop.

The Active Desktop cannot display desktop wallpaper with frames. Such pages are actually several separate pages tied together with links. If a frame set is copied to a computer, it is not usable as wallpaper, even if all related pages are copied.

A P P E N D I X   E

Troubleshooting Webcasting

This appendix reviews some of the issues related to Webcasting in the Microsoft® Internet Explorer 4 that may require troubleshooting and explains procedures for solving problems with Web-site and channel subscriptions. Topics include:

- Unattended dial-up does not work without user intervention
- E-mail notification is not sent for updated web sites
- Red gleams do not appear on channel bar when site content updates
- Subscription images are downloaded even if images are disabled

Unattended Dial-Up Does Not Work Without User Intervention

If you configure an unattended dial-up connection in Internet Explorer 4 or Outlook™ Express, you may receive the following message when the modem attempts to connect:

You are currently using NetWare servers, which will be inaccessible if you establish this connection.

Click OK to continue dialing. Click Cancel if you do not want to dial at this time.

The unattended dial-up connection does not continue until you click **OK**. This can occur if the Microsoft Client for NetWare Networks™ is installed on your computer and the Inter-network Packet Exchange/Sequenced Packet Exchange (IPX/SPX)-compatible protocol is bound to the Dial-Up Adapter. To resolve this problem, disable the IPX/SPX protocol for the Dial-Up Adapter.

▶ **To disable the IPX/SPX protocol in the Dial-Up Adapter**

1. From the **Start** menu, point to **Programs**, point to **Accessories**, and then click **Dial-Up Networking**.

2. Right-click the connection you are using for the unattended dial-up, and then click **Properties**.

3. Click **Server Type**, and then click the **IPX/SPX Compatible** check box to clear it.

4. Click **OK**, and then click **OK** again.

You can use unattended dial-up in the following situations:

- You configure Internet Explorer to perform an unattended dial-up connection when it updates Web-site and channel subscriptions.

- You configure Outlook Express to automatically dial when it checks for new messages.

E-Mail Notification Is Not Sent for Updated Web Sites

Despite the fact that <USAGE VALUE="Email" /> has been specified for a parent ITEM element in a CDF file, the subscribed user may not receive e-mail notification when a content update occurs. This problem may occur for one of two reasons: when the user subscribed to the channel, he or she did not specifically ask to receive e-mail notifications for content update, or the SMTP server was not specified correctly.

For channel e-mail notifications to be sent, the following three conditions must be met:

1. <USAGE VALUE="Email" /> must be specified in the CDF file, as in this example:

```
<CHANNEL HREF="http://example.microsoft.com">
   <ITEM HREF="http://example.microsoft.com/emailthis.htm">
   <USAGE VALUE="Email" />
   </ITEM>
   </CHANNEL>
```

2. When subscribing to the channel, the user must select one of the two **Yes** options on the **Add Favorite** dialog box, then click the **Customize** button and select **Yes, send an e-mail notification to the following address** when asked if he or she wants to be notified in an e-mail message when the page has changed.

3. When prompted for an e-mail address, the user must click the **Change Address** button and specify the correct SMTP server name. If you do not know the correct server name, ask your Internet service provider (ISP) what server name to specify.

If all three conditions above are met, an e-mail notification is sent to the subscribed user in this format:

```
Subject:  Internet Explorer Notice: <web site title>
Message:  <site URL> Your subscription to <web site title> has been
updated. To view the subscription offline, click here: <site URL>
This message was sent by the Internet Explorer 4.0 Information Delivery
Agent.
```

If your e-mail client is HTML-aware, then the e-mail received is the actual Web page specified in the <ITEM> tag in the CDF file.

Red Gleams Do Not Appear on Channel Bar When Site Content Updates

When you subscribe to a channel Web site, a gleam may not appear on that channel's icon on the Channel bar, even though the contents of the subscribed Web site have changed.

When Internet Explorer checks a subscribed channel for updated information, it only checks the actual subscribed CDF file (that is, the specific type of information requested by the user during the subscription setup). If the subscribed file changes, a red gleam appears on that channel's icon. If the subscribed file does not change, no gleam appears on the subscription's icon. This is true whether or not any other content in the subscribed channel has changed.

Subscription Images Are Downloaded Even If Images Are Disabled

When you disable image downloading in an Active Desktop™ item's subscription properties, images may still be downloaded and displayed when the desktop item's subscription is updated. To prevent images from being downloaded when an Active Desktop item's subscription is updated, you must disable image downloading in both the subscription and in Internet Explorer.

▶ **To disable image downloading for desktop items**

1. In Internet Explorer, on the **Favorites** menu, click **Manage Subscriptions**.

2. In the **Subscriptions** dialog box, right-click the subscription for which you want to disable image downloading, and then click **Properties**.

3. Click the **Receiving** tab, then click **Advanced**.

4. In the **Items To Download** box, click the **Images** check box to clear it, then click **OK**, and click **OK** again.

5. On the **File** menu, click **Close** to close the Subscriptions window.

6. In Internet Explorer, on the **View** menu, click **Internet Options**, and then click the **Advanced** tab.

7. Under **Multimedia**, click the **Show Pictures** check box to clear it, and then click **OK**.

If image downloading is disabled in Internet Explorer 4 only, images are still downloaded when the desktop item's subscription is updated, but these images are not displayed in the desktop item.

A P P E N D I X   F

Troubleshooting Outlook Express

This appendix discusses some of the issues related to Microsoft Outlook™ Express that may require troubleshooting and explains procedures for solving problems that may occur. Topics include:

- Problems changing the default mail client for Internet Explorer
- Cannot import address book in Outlook Express
- Preview pane does not display news messages when enabled
- Error message: **The command failed to execute.**
- Internet mail and news files renamed by Outlook Express

For more information about Outlook Express, see Chapter 18.

Problems Changing the Default Mail Client for Internet Explorer

▶ **To change the default mail client in Internet Explorer**

1. In Internet Explorer, on the **View** menu, click **Internet Options**.
2. Click the **Programs** tab.
3. In the **Mail** drop-down list and in the **News** drop-down list, click the programs you want.
4. Click **OK**.

In Internet Explorer, these changes modify the URL:MailToProtocol registered file type that is listed when you follow these steps:

1. In My Computer, on the **View** menu, click **Folder Options**, and then click **File Types**.

2. Click **URL:MailToProtocol**, click **Edit**, click **Open** in the **Actions** box, and then click **Edit**.

   The command line that controls the program that is used to open a MailTo Uniform Resource Locator (URL) appears in the **Application used to perform action** box.

Some programs may modify this setting without updating the list of programs available in Internet Explorer. For example, the Eudora Internet mail client changes the URL:MailToProtcol registered file type to the following:

C:\<EudoraFolder>\Eudora.exe /m

You can also change the default program back to **Internet Mail** or **Windows Messaging** in the **Mail** box on the **Programs** tab.

Selecting **Internet Mail** in the **Mail** box changes the URL:MailToProtcol registered file type to:

rundll32.exe C:\WINDOWS\SYSTEM\mailnews.dll,Mail_RunDLL

Selecting **Windows Messaging** in the **Mail** box changes the registered file type to:

rundll32.exe url.dll,MailToProtocolHandler %l

▶ **To specify Microsoft Outlook 97 as the program you want to open MailTo URL addresses**

1. In My Computer, on the **View** menu, click **Folder Options**, and then click **File Types**.

2. Click **URL:MailToProtocol**, click **Edit**, click **Open** in the **Actions** box, and then click **Edit**. Click the **Application used to perform action** box and press **DELETE** to delete the data in the box.

3. Type the following (including quotation marks) for the **Application used to perform action** box for the **Open** command:

   "C:\Program Files\Microsoft Office\ Office\Outlook.exe" -c IPM.Note /m "%1"

4. To save the changes, click **OK** until you return to My Computer.

▶ **To specify Microsoft Outlook Express as the program you want to open MailTo URL addresses**

1. In My Computer, click **Folder Options** on the **View** menu, and then click **File Types**.

2. Click **URL:MailToProtocol**, click **Edit**, click **Open** in the **Actions** box, and then click **Edit**. Click the **Application used to perform action** box, and press **DELETE** to delete the data in the box.

3. Type the following (including quotation marks) for the **Application used to perform action** box for the **Open** command:

   "C:\Program Files\Outlook Express\Msimn.exe" /mailurl:%1"

4. To save the changes, click **OK** until you return to My Computer.

Specifying Older Mail Programs

The list of mail programs that you can choose under the Internet Explorer options is made up of registry keys, which outline the behavior of the program you want to use. Modifications that need to be made to the registry are detailed and very specific. Most programs either self-register upon usage or have an option to become the default program. If these options are not available, please contact the manufacturer about how to make its program the default mail client.

Cannot Import Address Book in Outlook Express

When you attempt to import an address book in Outlook Express version 4, the address book may not be imported and you may not see an error message. This occurs when the Wabmig.exe file is missing or damaged.

If the Wabmig.exe file is damaged, rename the file, and then reinstall Outlook Express.

▶ **To rename the Wabmig.exe file**

1. From the **Start** menu, point to **Find**, and then click **Files Or Folders**.

2. In the **Named** box, type **Wabmig.exe**, and then click **Find Now**.

3. Right-click the file, and then click **Rename**.

4. Rename the file to Wabmig.*xxx*.

5. Reinstall Outlook Express.

Preview Pane Does Not Display News Messages When Enabled

While you are reading news messages in Outlook Express, you may receive the following message in the preview pane even though the preview pane is already enabled:

Press <Space> to display the selected message. You can also choose to automatically show messages in the preview pane from the Options command.

If you press SPACEBAR, the message reappears. If you double-click the news message to open it, you receive the following error message:

There was an error opening the message.

This occurs when there is not enough free space on your hard disk to open the news message. Increase the amount of free space on your hard disk by using one or more of the following methods:

- Remove any unnecessary files from the hard disk.
- Empty the Recycle Bin.
- Delete the Internet Explorer 4 Setup folder, or remove unnecessary files from the folder. Deleting this folder does not affect the performance of Internet Explorer, but it is important to note that without this folder, you will not be able to reinstall Internet Explorer or its components from the hard disk; you will have to download another copy from the Microsoft Web site.

Warning The Setup folder contains important backup files that are necessary for uninstalling Internet Explorer. IE4bak.dat and IE4bak.ini and, if Windows Desktop Update is installed, Integrated Browser.dat, and Integrated Browser.ini. are critical files. It is recommended that you not delete these files. (For more information, see "Deleting Uninstall Files" in Chapter 7.) If you need to make more disk space available, it is recommended that you leave these files and delete other files in the folder.

Error Message: The Command Failed to Execute

When you attempt to save a mail attachment to your hard disk in Outlook Express, you may receive the following error message:

The command failed to execute.

This occurs when there is not enough free disk space on your hard disk to save the attachment.

Increase the amount of free space on your hard disk by using one or more of the following methods:

- Remove any unnecessary files from the hard disk.
- Empty the Recycle Bin.
- Delete the Internet Explorer Setup folder. (Important: Note the warnings and information about removing the Setup folder, above.)

After you free some hard disk space, try to save the attachment again.

Internet Mail and News Files Renamed by Outlook Express

When you install Internet Explorer 4, the Windows®Address Book files used by Internet Mail and News 1 for Windows® 95 and Windows NT® 4.0 are renamed. This is because Outlook Express is installed as an upgrade to Internet Mail and News.

The following files in the Windows\System or Winnt\System32 folder are renamed:

File Name	Renamed To
Wab32.dll	Wab32.ie3
Wabfind.dll	Wabfind.ie3
Wabimp.dll	Wabimp.ie3

The following files in the Windows folder are renamed:

File name	Renamed to
Wab.exe	Wab.ie3
Wabmig.exe	Wabmig.ie3
Username.**wab**	*path\Username*.wab.ie3

where *path* is one of the following paths:

- Windows\Profiles*Username*\Application Data\Microsoft\Address Book
- Program Files\Internet Explorer\Outlook Express*Username*\Address Book
- Program Files\Common Files\Microsoft Shared\Address Book

When the *Username*.wab file is moved and renamed, a new copy of the *Username*.wab file is used by Outlook Express. The Windows Address Book files are restored, however, if you uninstall Internet Explorer 4.

A P P E N D I X   G

Troubleshooting HTML Authoring

This appendix reviews some of the issues related to Microsoft® Internet Explorer 4 HTML authoring that may require troubleshooting and explains procedures for resolving these authoring problems. Topics include:

- Text doesn't wrap in text boxes
- Background images are not displayed
- Internet Explorer browser is not automatically redirected
- Frames not displayed in web pages
- Permission denied when scripting across frames

For more information about HTML authoring for Internet Explorer 4, see Part 6.

Text Doesn't Wrap in Text Boxes

When you enter text in a text box created using the <TEXTAREA> tag on a Hypertext Markup Language (HTML) page, the text may not wrap correctly. In this case, the text continues to flow to the right side of the text box without breaking or wrapping. This is because the HTML page does not contain the parameters that activate text wrapping in a text box.

▶ **To wrap text in a text box, use one of the following methods:**

- Use the WRAP attribute of the <TEXTAREA> tag with either the Physical or Virtual value to enable word wrapping.

  The non-wrapping <TEXTAREA> tag might look like:

  ```
  <TEXTAREA NAME="Name" ROW99S=6 COL99S=40>
  </TEXTAREA>
  ```

- To enable wrapping, insert WRAP=Physical, as in the following example:

  ```
  <TEXTAREA NAME="Name" ROW99S=6 COL99S=40 WRAP=Physical>
  </TEXTAREA>
  ```

When you are typing in the text box, manually insert line breaks by pressing ENTER to wrap the text.

Background Images Are Not Displayed

Pages created with the Data Form Wizard by Visual InterDev™ may not display background images in Internet Explorer 4. If this occurs, it is likely due to the fact that Internet Explorer 4 adheres more closely to the HTML 3.2 specification than does Internet Explorer 3. In the Cascading Style Sheet (CSS) spec, CSS tags take precedence over HTML tags. Pages created using the Data Form Wizard reference a CSS; the CSS has a tag for the background image of Transparent, thus overriding any value in the body tag of the ASP file.

▶ **To display background images**

- Delete the "background: transparent" line from the BODY property of the CSS.

Internet Explorer Browser Is Not Automatically Redirected

When you load a Web page that contains the <meta http-equiv="refresh"...> HTML tag, the browser may not be automatically redirected to another Web page. This may occur for one of the following reasons:

- The author of the page did not place the <meta http-equiv="refresh"...> tag in the <HEAD> section of the HTML source code.

- The syntax of the <meta http-equiv="refresh"...> HTML tag is incorrect.

To resolve this issue, update the Web page using the appropriate method:

- If the <META> tag is not located in the <HEAD> section

  Modify the HTML source code to place the <META> tag in the <HEAD> section of the Web page. This may require adding the <HEAD> and </HEAD> tags to the Web page.

- If the syntax of the <META> tag is incorrect

  Modify the HTML source code to correct the syntax of the <META> tag. For example, a <META> tag might look like this:

```
<meta http-equiv="refresh" content="n;url=http://www.domain.com/
    pagename.htm">
```

  where n is the number of seconds the browser program pauses before loading the new Web page.

For information about the HTML 3.2 Specification Reference, see **http://www.w3.org/TR/REC-html32.html**.

Frames Not Displayed in Web Pages

When you're using Internet Explorer 4 to view a Web page, a blank page may display instead of a defined set of frames. If you right-click an empty area of the Web page and then click **View Source**, or right-click an empty area of the Web page, click **Properties**, and then click **Analyze**, the following message may display:

This document might not display properly because there is a <FRAMESET> within the <BODY> of the document.

This behavior is by design and occurs when the Web author puts the <FRAMESET> tag after the <BODY> tag in the main or "framing" HTML document. All <FRAMESET> tags and underlying instructions should precede any <BODY> tags.

▶ **To resolve this problem**

1. Remove the <BODY> tag.
2. Remove any additional HTML code between the <HEAD> of the document and the <FRAMESET>.

The framing HTML document defines the frame regions that display in the browser and the documents or objects that initially appear in the frames. For information about the HTML syntax for frames, see **http://www.w3.org/pub/WWW/TR/WD-frames-970331.html**.

Permission Denied When Scripting Across Frames

Script code that attempts to access a script or an object in a different frame may result in the following script error message:

Permission denied: 'Parent.RemoteFrame.RemoteObject'

Internet Explorer 4 implements cross-frame security. A script or an object in one frame is not allowed to access scripts or objects in another frame when the documents referenced by the frames' SRC attribute specify Web servers in different second-level domains. This corresponds to the *domain-name.xxx* portion of the full server-name syntax *server.domain-name.xxx*.

The Internet Explorer Dynamic HTML object model allows a certain subset of safe actions to be scripted. For example, the *window.location* property of a remote server's frame can be set to allow navigation, but it cannot be read to prevent one frame from snooping on the contents of another frame.

For example, it is valid for a document retrieved from **http://test.microsoft.com/** to manipulate another document retrieved from **http://test.microsoft.com/**. It is not valid for a document retrieved from **http://server1.some-domain-name.org/** to manipulate a document retrieved from **http://server2/** or **http://server3.microsoft.com/**.

The intention of cross-frame security is to prevent a Web-page author from misusing or snooping on the trusted objects authored by another Web page author. Only pages hosted in the same domain can be trusted to safely script the contents of a particular page. Cross-frame security should also prevent unwanted communication between documents on opposite sides of a corporate firewall. Please refer to the *Microsoft Internet Client Software Development Kit (SDK)* for more information.

To allow two documents hosted on the same second-level domain to interact, both documents must set the *document.domain* property to their shared second-level domain. For example, one document on **http://example.microsoft.com/** could script and access another document on **http://test.microsoft.com/** if both documents used the following line of script code:

```
<SCRIPT LANGUAGE="VBScript">
document.domain = "microsoft.com"
</SCRIPT>
```

Given the following FRAMESET:

```
<FRAMESET COLS="50%, *" FRAMEBORDER=1>
<FRAME SRC="http://server1/server1.html" ID="Server1Frame">
<FRAME SRC="http://server2/server2.html" ID="Server2Frame">
</FRAMESET>
```

Script in the "Server1Frame" frame is not permitted to access script or objects in the "Server2Frame" frame, and vice versa.

The following example script code in server1.html causes the "Permission Denied" error, given that **RemoteTextBox** is an object created on the server2.html document:

```
<!-- From server1.html -->
<SCRIPT LANGUAGE="VBScript">
Sub CommandButtonLocal_Click()
Parent.Server2Frame.RemoteTextBox.Text = "Changed Text"
'Server2Frame has SRC on different server
end sub
</SCRIPT>
```

A P P E N D I X   H

Frequently Asked Questions About Cabinet Files in Java

This appendix covers some of the Frequently Asked Questions (FAQs) about cabinet (.cab) files. For other Java-related FAQs visit: **http://www.microsoft.com/support/java/content/faq/default.htm**.

Where do I get the Code Sign Kit?

You can find the Code Sign Kit on the Visual J++™ CD-ROM, *Microsoft® ActiveX® Software Development Kit (SDK)*, or "Java Signing Tools" in the *Microsoft SDK for Java 2.0 Beta 2* or newer. The *Microsoft ActiveX SDK* is available at **http://www.microsoft.com/Intdev/sdk/**. The *Microsoft SDK for Java 2.0 Beta 2* is available at **http://www.microsoft.com/java/sdk/**.

Where can I get the *CAB Developers Kit* or the *CAB Resource Kit*, and what are they used for?

The *CAB Developers Kit* has been incorporated into the *Microsoft SDK for Java*, which is available at **http://www.microsoft.com/java/sdk/**. It's also available stand-alone at **http://www.microsoft.com/workshop/prog/cab/default.htm**. It will give you all of the tools you need to build cabinet files. The latest version includes cabarc.exe, a new tool that makes it easier to create cabinet files directly from the command line.

The *CAB Resource Kit* provides the information necessary to help the tool development community understand and work with cabinet files. It includes the compression and decompression application programming interfaces (APIs), documentation on their interfaces, and sample applications using these APIs. Soon, there will be more information on the cabinet file format. The updates provided on January 13, 1997, featured multithread and multicontext support and allow use in MFC-based applications.

When programmatically creating a .cab file from a Java application, can I reserve space in the .cab for signing?

The Java CAB API currently does not support the creation of reserved areas. The command-line tools, Cabarc.exe and Diamond.exe, support this functionality. The latest version of the Signcode.exe utility that is available in the *Microsoft SDK for Java 2.0 Beta 2* and newer does not require space to be reserved in the .cab file for a digital signature. It will automatically create space in the .cab when it is signed.

Can I sign a Java class file for use with Internet Explorer?

Although it is possible to digitally sign a Java class file and verify the signature using the trust check utility, Internet Explorer does not recognize the class as signed and does not present a certificate to the user at runtime. Furthermore, the class is not considered trusted by the Microsoft VM for Java. Presently, you need to place the classes within a .cab file, which can then be signed.

Will the Microsoft Virtual Machine for Java support the .jar file format?

Jar support is the same as .zip. .jar = .zip + manifest. So Microsoft will support uncompressed and compressed .jar files, but not signed .jar files. If you need Java security (beyond sandbox) in Internet Explorer 4, you need to use a signed .cab file. This applies to all fine-grained Java security (including running in a sandbox on the local machine using the Package Manager).

Can my applet that is inside a .cab file use class files from outside the .cab that are not installed in the local machine's CLASSPATH?

Class files from a Web server cannot be used by classes in a .cab file with the Microsoft VM for Java, build 1517 and earlier. With build 2057 of the VM, from the *Microsoft SDK for Java 2.0 Preview*, you can use classes from outside of the .cab file.

When I run signcode.exe on my .cab file, I get the following error:

Unable to sign the program <.cab file>. (80004005)

You did not reserve space in your .cab file. Recreate the .cab file using the **-s** 6144 option to Cabarc.exe. This space must be reserved in the .cab file to allow room for the digital signature. Note: it is not necessary to use the **-s** switch with the signing tools included with the *Microsoft SDK for Java 2.0 Beta 2* or newer. The Signcode.exe utility will now create the necessary space for the certificate at the time the .cab file is signed.

Unable to sign the program <.cab file>. (80030070)

You did not reserve enough space in your .cab file. Recreate the .cab file using the **-s** 6144 option to Cabarc.exe. Note: it is not necessary to use the **-s** switch with the signing tools included with the *Microsoft SDK for Java 2.0 Beta 2* or newer. The Signcode.exe utility will now create the necessary space for the certificate at the time the .cab file is signed.

Unable to sign the program <.cab file>. (80070005)

Your .cab file is marked read-only.

Unable to sign the program <.cab file>. (80070057)

Your .cab file is corrupt.

When do I use the -s option for Cabarc.exe?

The **-s** 6144 option reserves unnecessary space in most situations. With the 'test' certificate, you can typically get by with 1K of reserved space in the .cab. A good estimate of the space required is slightly larger than the size of the .spc file with which you are signing. Also note, it is possible that the certificate will require more than 6144 bytes. Note: it is not necessary to use the **-s** switch with the signing tools included with the *Microsoft SDK for Java 2.0 Beta 2* or newer. The Signcode.exe utility will now create the necessary space for the certificate at the time the .cab file is signed.

When do I use the -i option for Cabarc.exe?

The **-i** switch is used to insert a version number, SET ID, into a .cab file. The version number will be displayed when viewing a .cab file with the following command-line statement: **cabarc L <.cab file>.** Diamond.exe uses the ID number when spanning multiple .cab files.

How do I install a Java package on the user's machine?

You can use a setup information (.inf) file in a .cab to install Java libraries and packages on the local machine. The .inf file defines which files to extract from the .cab and where to place them on the user's system. There is an example .inf file called Master.inf included in the *Microsoft SDK for Java*. Place all the Java libraries and packages in a .cab file. In a second signed .cab file, place the unsigned .cab file and the .inf file. Reference the signed .cab file with an <OBJECT> tag in your HTML page.

For distributing trusted applets on my intranet, is there a more elegant solution than using a test certificate?

Currently, the only solution is to relax the security in Internet Explorer by placing the classes on the user's machine in the CLASSPATH or distributing the files in a signed .cab file. You can obtain a certificate for use within the company or use the test certificate and have the users run the Wvtston.reg file to enable test certificates on their machines.

Can I include .gif, .jpg, or .au files used by my applet in a .cab file?

Yes, the .cab file serves as a single, compressed repository for all .class, audio, and image files required by the applet. When creating the .cab file, be sure to use the **-r** and **-p** options to Cabarc.exe to recurse and preserve directory structure if any of the files in the .cab are in subdirectories. The **cabarc.exe -l** command can be used to confirm the directory structure was preserved.

Image and audio clips stored in the .cab can be retrieved by the applet code via the java.lang.applet.getImage and java.lang.applet.getAudioClip methods. Note that in order for Internet Explorer to find an image file or audio clip from within the .cab file, the URLs passed to these methods must be based upon the applet's codebase. For example, if the following code is found within an applet loaded from a .cab file, the image file picture1.gif and the audio clip sound1.au will be loaded from the .cab file (assuming that they are in the .cab). If an image or audio clip file is not within the .cab file, Internet Explorer will look for them on the server.

```
Image img = getImage(getCodeBase(),"picture1.gif");
AudioClip clip = getAudioClip(getCodeBase(),"sound1.au");
```

Why doesn't Internet Explorer display the certificate from a signed .cab file on some machines?

The two most common reasons for this behavior are the following:

If the .cab file was signed using a test certificate, you must enable test certificates for the local machine. Otherwise, the signature is not considered valid. You can do this by running the Wvtston.reg file included with the code signing kit.

You have accepted a software publisher as Always Trusted. To verify this, in Internet Explorer, on the **View** menu, click **Internet Options**. Click the **Content** tab, then click the **Publishers** button to ensure the publisher does not appear in the list box. If so, you can use this dialog box to remove it.

A P P E N D I X I

Internet Client SDK FAQs

This appendix covers some of the most Frequently Asked Questions (FAQs) about developing with the *Microsoft Internet Client Software Development Kit (SDK)* for Microsoft® Internet Explorer 4. These FAQs are also available on the Microsoft Web site at **http://www.microsoft.com/support/inetsdk/content/faq/**.

Setup

What are the system requirements for installing the SDK?

To download and use the *Microsoft Internet Client SDK*, you need the following:

- Internet Explorer 4.
- Windows NT® 4 or Windows® 95.

Active Channels

For more information about Active Channels™ and CDF files, see Part 4, "Information Delivery: Webcasting."

What MIME type do I specify in my dynamically generated CDF file?

A CDF file that is dynamically generated through Active Server Pages (ASP) should insert the following line at the top of the file (before any CDF lines):

```
<% Response.ContentType = "application/x-cdf" %>
```

This ensures that servers return the correct MIME (Multipurpose Internet Mail Extensions) /content type "application/x-cdf."

Problems with CDF files being displayed as HTML text inside the Internet Explorer browser, instead of invoking the Subscription Wizard, may be caused by the server returning the incorrect MIME type of "text/html" instead of the desired "application/x-cdf."

When dynamically generating a CDF file from an Active Server Pages (ASP) page, is the ASP file the one to which the user needs to subscribe?

Yes. Assuming that the correct CDF MIME type is specified in the ASP page, as illustrated in the FAQ above, double-clicking on a link to the ASP file should bring up the CDF Subscription Wizard appropriately.

I cannot use the ampersand character in my CDF file title. Do I have to specially treat certain characters when working with CDF files?

CDF supports encoding of ASCII characters with the format *&#nnn*. The ampersand character, therefore, could be encoded with its ASCII decimal value of 38 by using the string &#038.

To specify "Peaches & Cream," for example, your <TITLE> tag would look like this:

```
<TITLE>Peaches&#038;Cream</TITLE>
```

Is it necessary to specify the <!DOCTYPE> tag in my CDF file?

No. Internet Explorer 4 does not use the <!DOCTYPE> tag.

Is http://www.w3c.org/channel.dtd a valid URL for a <!DOCTYPE> tag?

No. This URL (Uniform Resource Locator) is only an example, does not actually exist, and is best not used in actual CDF files.

Is there a difference between the subscription cache and the regular cache that Internet Explorer maintains?

All subscription information goes into the same cache maintained by Internet Explorer. The subscription content in the cache, however, is specially marked so that it does not get deleted when a user clears the cache.

If the user is browsing a subscribed channel while connected to the Internet, is content pulled from the cache, or does Internet Explorer query the server again?

Internet Explorer looks at the Expires HTTP header returned by the server when the page was retrieved and checks to see if the cached page is still valid. If it is, content is pulled from the cache; otherwise, Internet Explorer queries the server again for the content. Note that with the latter, when Internet Explorer re-queries the server for content, in most cases, Internet Explorer will issue an HTTP GET request with an If_Modified_Since header, which helps reduce the server load.

Does the actual download of the HTML page occur upon subscription to the site or only during a subscription update?

Actual download occurs during subscription update. However, users can manually update a subscription any time they want.

From a CDF file, is there a way to specify items to be cached, without having the items appear in the Channel bar's item list? For example, can I specify a WAV file to be downloaded as part of the subscription update, so that it gets cached and is available when the user browses offline?

Yes, here's the correct way to do this:

```
<ITEM HREF="http://example.microsoft.com/sound.wav">
<USAGE VALUE="NONE"></USAGE>
</ITEM>
```

Note that in XML, an element that does not have child elements can be represented in a more compact format. For example, the above <USAGE> line could be written more compactly in the manner shown below. (Note the final / at the end of the tag.)

```
<USAGE VALUE="NONE" />
```

Also, when listing multiple items that are to be cached but not viewed in the Channel bar, instead of marking each one with a <USAGE VALUE="NONE" />, it is better to place them all in one subchannel that is marked with a usage tag, as illustrated in the example below:

```
<CHANNEL>
<USAGE VALUE="NONE" />
<ITEM HREF="http://example.microsoft.com/sound1.wav"/>
<ITEM HREF="http://example.microsoft.com/sound2.wav"/>
<ITEM HREF="http://example.microsoft.com/sound3.wav"/>
</CHANNEL>
```

Is it possible to specify multiple schedules for updates in one CDF file?

No. Only one schedule can be specified per CDF file in Internet Explorer. Also, a desktop item cannot be bundled with a channel in one CDF file. They have to be two separate CDF files to work correctly.

Is it possible to specify a global time for the <SCHEDULE> tag, so that my channel updates occur between certain times, regardless of the time zone?

Currently there is no way to specify local or global time in a CDF file. Information specified in the <EARLIESTTIME> and <LATESTTIME> tags is considered local and ignores any time zone information specified in the <STARTDATE> and <ENDDATE> tags.

How do I keep Internet Explorer from opening a new window when a user clicks on a link from a desktop item?

The way to do this is to specify a TARGET="_top" with the <A HREF> tag.

I haven't been able to get my desktop item to work unless I put it on a separate CDF file from the rest of my channel. Is this how it's designed to work?

Yes. Desktop items have to be in a separate CDF file from the rest of the channel.

HTML

For more information about HTML and Internet Explorer 4, see Part 6, "Authoring for Internet Explorer 4."

Why are my HTML pages with frames not showing up in Internet Explorer 4? They used to work fine in Internet Explorer 3.

Unlike Internet Explorer 3, Internet Explorer 4 does not support <FRAMESET> tags embedded within <BODY> tags. This was done in Internet Explorer 4 to ensure compatibility with Netscape Navigator. To work around the problem, move the <FRAMESET> outside the <BODY> tags.

In some cases, a <NOFRAMES> element is specified within the <FRAMESET> tags, as in the example below:

```
<BODY>
<FRAMESET>
<NOFRAMES>Sorry, your browser does not support frames! </NOFRAMES>
</FRAMESET>
</BODY>
```

Although Internet Explorer 4 supports frames, when the above HTML code is displayed in Internet Explorer, the content specified within the <NOFRAMES> tag is displayed. Moving the <FRAMESET> outside the <BODY> tags causes the page to display correctly.

Why doesn't Internet Explorer 4 close the <PLAINTEXT> container as Internet Explorer 3 did?

The <PLAINTEXT> tag is designed to render all of a Web page's subsequent text without parsing any tags, including its own </PLAINTEXT> tag. Internet Explorer 4 supports this tag as it is defined by the HTML DTD. This element is not recommended, as different browsers may not support it consistently. Instead, use the <PRE> tag, and display all reserved characters (such as brackets) with their corresponding HTML character entities.

Dynamic HTML

For more information about Dynamic HTML and Internet Explorer 4, see Part 6, "Authoring for Internet Explorer 4."

Is there a way to implement a custom ToolTip over anchors in Internet Explorer 4 (the same way you can use the ALT attribute in an <IMG> tag)?

By default, Internet Explorer renders the URL of the HREF attribute as a ToolTip, which may not always be the desired behavior. Yes, the way to do this is to specify the ToolTip in the TITLE attribute of the <A> tag, as in this example:

```
<a href="file.htm" TITLE="ToolTip goes here">some text</a>
```

How can I change the HTML or text associated with an element? I used to be able to do this using the rangeFromElement method, but now I keep getting the error "Object does not support this property or method." Have things changed?

Yes, the **rangeFromElement** method has been removed. Use innerHTML/outerHTML and innerText/outerText to manipulate text or HTML.

How do I determine the client width and height?

There are new properties on the body object, **clientWidth,** and **clientHeight,** which can be used for this purpose.

How do I change the current cursor being used as mouse pointer?

There is a cursor Cascading Style Sheet (CSS) attribute that can be used. Refer to the *Microsoft Internet Client SDK* documentation under the Dynamic HTML\HTML and CSS Reference section for more information.

Why do I get the error "Wrong number of arguments" in my event handlers?

Events do not have parameters (arguments). All information can be retrieved using the **window.event** object.

I'm finding that IFRAMES within a relatively positioned <DIV> tag causes Internet Explorer 4 to crash every time. This makes it difficult to relatively position IFRAMES. Is this a known problem, and is there a workaround?

Yes, the workaround is to put the positioning on the <IFRAME> directly.

WebBrowser Control

For more information about the WebBrowser Control, see Part 2, "Configuring the Browser."

In the Web browser documentation for developers of Visual Basic, the Navigate and Navigate2 methods look identical. Is there a difference?

The only difference is that the URL parameter is packaged as a VARIANT in Navigate2 instead of a BSTR. (You could verify this in the Web browser documentation for developers of C and Visual C++®.) Unlike a C++ application, a Visual Basic® application is not able to use the WebBrowser Control to navigate into special folders in the shell namespace like "My Computer." Currently, the shell does not expose an object that provides a PIDL, which a Visual Basic application can then use in a Navigate2 call.

I have an application that uses the WebBrowser Control. Is it possible to install just the WebBrowser Control without installing Internet Explorer 4?

No, there is no way to do this. The minimal installation will install the browser. Also, note that Internet Explorer 3 and 4 cannot coexist on the same machine. More information on redistributing Internet Explorer can be found on the IEAK page at **http://www.microsoft.com/ie/ieak/**.

Component Packaging

What version of the MFC .dll files will come with Internet Explorer 4? I'd like to know so I don't have to worry about packaging the MFC .dll files with my ActiveX® control.

Any component should be careful not to rely on the presence of any MFC .dll files with the currently installed browser, because Internet Explorer 4 and future versions of Internet Explorer may include alternative versions or may not include any MFC .dll files at all. A component that uses the MFC .dll files as dependencies should package the MFC .dll files accordingly.

I've written an ActiveX control that I've marked as Safe for Scripting, and I'm having trouble getting it to work when running off a page on a local hard disk. What am I doing wrong?

The problem may be due to any of the following reasons:

- A missing dependent .dll file
- Necessary security level set on the wrong zone
- A control that is not marked as "safe for scripting and initialization" will not be loaded if the page that references the control is being accessed from the local hard drive.

For more information on marking ActiveX controls as "safe for scripting and initialization," please refer to the *Microsoft Internet Client SDK* documents on "Safe Initialization and Scripting for ActiveX Controls" in the Component Development/ActiveX Controls section.

Control Development

How can I improve performance in my ActiveX control?

For better performance, make your control an apartment-model control. Internet Explorer 4 uses multiple threads and may host the control in a secondary thread. If the control is not created as apartment-model aware and marked as such, it is created and executed in the context of the calling application's primary thread, requiring calls on the control's methods to be marshaled between threads. This can cause a performance hit and can be very prominent if there are many non-apartment-model controls in an HTML page. To make a control apartment model, the control needs to be marked as such in the registry and has to be written so that it is apartment-model safe.

Scripting

How do I determine from a script if the Internet Explorer browser is running offline or not?

Currently, there is no way to determine this from a script. Although the IWebBrowser2 interface provides a get/put_Offline method that indicates whether the WebBrowser is reading from the cache, there is no way to get this information from the WebBrowser object model up to the script level. If desired, you could write an ActiveX control that gets this information from the WebBrowser object model and expose it as a property or method, which can then be accessed from a script.

Why do I get a Permission Denied error whenever I try to access a frame's document from a script written in another frame's document? The same code runs fine in Internet Explorer 3.

This is due to a cross-frame security feature that is implemented in Internet Explorer 4, but not in Internet Explorer 3. A frame running on one server is not able to access another frame's document running on another server. Similarly, with the introduction of security zones in Internet Explorer 4, a script cannot access pages across zones.

Why do I get a Permission Denied error whenever I try to access a frame on a different first-tier domain, but on the same second-tier domain?

This is another side effect of the Internet Explorer 4 cross-frame security feature described above. A frame running on example1.microsoft.com cannot access a frame on example2.microsoft.com.

The correct way to do this is to set the domain property on both pages to the common substring domain. In this case, set the domain to microsoft.com, as illustrated below:

```
<SCRIPT>
document.domain = "microsoft.com"
</SCRIPT>
```

From a client-side script, how do I check for the browser version so my application can degrade gracefully if the browser does not support the new Internet Explorer 4 features?

You can use the JScript™ function below, from a client-side script, to determine the version of the browser on which it is running. The function returns the major version number for any Microsoft Internet Explorer browser, and zero (0) for others. Use of this function ensures that the script is compatible with future versions of Internet Explorer.

```
// This function returns Internet Explorer's major version number,
// or 0 for others. It works by finding the "MSIE " string and
// extracting the version number following the space, up to the
// decimal point, ignoring the minor version number
<SCRIPT LANGUAGE="JavaSCRIPT">
function msieversion()
{
var ua = window.navigator.userAgent
var msie = uA:indexOf ( "MSIE " )

if ( msie > 0 ) // If IE, return version number
return parseInt (uA:substring (msie+5, uA:indexOf (".", msie )))
else    // If another browser, return 0
return 0
}
</SCRIPT>
```

Is there a way to detect the browser's support for the new Internet Explorer 4 features from a server-side script?

The Browser Capability component that comes with ASP provides your scripts with a description of the capabilities of the client's Web browser by comparing the User-Agent HTTP Header with the entries in the Browscap.ini file. In order for an ASP application to detect the browser's support for the new Internet Explorer features, copy the latest Browscap.ini from **http://www.microsoft.com/iis/usingiis/developing/updates.htm** to your \Windows\System32\Inetsrv\Asp\Cmpnts directory and execute a server-side script similar to the example described in article Q167820 in the Microsoft Knowledge Base.

Miscellaneous

Is it possible to have Internet Explorer 3 and Internet Explorer 4 coexist on the same machine?

No. There are no plans to support the coexistence of these two Internet Explorer versions at this time. Internet Explorer 3 and Internet Explorer 4 share system components that cannot exist in multiple copies on the same machine.

What is the difference between ADO and ADOR, and which should I be using on my Web pages?

The Active Data Object (ADO) components ship in two forms—one for a Web server and another for the client. The ADO component installed with Internet Explorer 4 is the ADO Recordset (ADOR). ADOR provides an object model for script access to data supplied by a data source object (DSO) embedded in a Web page. It does not, however, provide ADO Connection or Command objects. These are provided only as part of the server installation.

Included with the *Microsoft Internet Client SDK,* in self-extracting archives, is the full set of ADO components. When building applications using ADO for Internet Explorer, your client-side scripts should depend only on the availability of the **Recordset** object. The full ADO interfaces are intended for use with ASPs and custom business objects that run on a Web server. Refer to Mdac.txt in the Inetsdk\Bin folder for more details.

APPENDIX J

Custom-Build Checklist

The following tables are designed to help administrators prepare for the Microsoft® Internet Explorer Administration Kit (IEAK) Configuration Wizard. The information below outlines all the configuration options that will be presented in the IEAK. By preparing this information in advance, you can speed up your custom package generation. It is also recommended that you run through the IEAK Configuration Wizard yourself, in order to get acquainted with its features.

Stage 1—Gathering Information	
Enter Company Name and Customization Keycode	
Company Name	
IEAK Keycode	
Automatic Version Synchronization Support	Yes No
Select a Language	
Target Language	
Select Media to Distribute Your Browser	
Path of Destination Folder	
Select Media	
CD-ROM	Yes No
Multiple Floppy Disks	Yes No

Stage 2—Specifying Active Setup Parameters	
Select a Microsoft Download Site	
Download Site	
Automatic Version Synchronization (AVS)	
Microsoft Internet Explorer 4 Web Browser	
Microsoft Internet Explorer Core Fonts	
Microsoft NetMeeting™	
Microsoft Outlook™ Express	
Microsoft Chat 2.0	
Microsoft NetShow™	
Intel® Indeo™5	
VDOLive Player	
Microsoft Interactive Music Control	
Microsoft Internet Explorer Sound Pack	
Macromedia Shockwave Director	
Macromedia Shockwave Flash	
RealPlayer by Progressive Networks	
Microsoft FrontPage® Express	
Microsoft Web Publishing Wizard	
Microsoft Visual Basic® Run Time	
Microsoft Wallet	
Task Scheduler	
Microsoft Internet Explorer Supplemental Fonts	
Specify Custom Active Setup Components (up to 10)	
Components	
Locations	
Commands	
Global Universal Identifiers (GUIDs)	
Parameters	
Versions	
Sizes	
Uninstall Keys	
Specify Trusted Publishers	
Specify Trusted Publishers	

Stage 3—Customizing Active Setup	
Customize the Autorun Screen for CD-ROM Installations	
Title Bar Text	
Custom Background Bitmap Location	
Text Colors	
Button Styles	Standard 3-D Custom
Customize the Active Setup Wizard	
Active Setup Wizard Title Bar Text	
Active Setup Wizard Bitmap Path	
Custom Components Install Section	
Custom Components Installation Title	
Select Silent Install	Yes No
Select Installation Options (up to 10)	
Option Names	Minimal Standard Full Custom
Option Descriptions	
Component Combinations	
Specify Download URLs	
Site Names	
Site URLs	
Site Regions	
Select Version Number	
Version Number	
Configuration Identifier	
Product Update URL	
Specify Where You Want to Install the Browser	Windows Program Files Custom
Integrating the Web Desktop Update	Yes No User Choice

Stage 4—Customizing the Browser	
Customize the Window Title and Toolbar Background	
Title Bar Text	
Toolbar Background Bitmap Path	
Customize the Start and Search Pages	
Start Page URL	
Search Page URL	
Specify an Online Support Page for Your Browser	
Online Support Page URL	
Favorites Folder and Links Customization	
Add URLs	
Test URLs	
Import URLs	
Customize the Welcome Message and Desktop Wallpaper	
Display Welcome Page	Default Page No Page Custom Page
Disable Internet Explorer 4 Welcome Window	Yes No
Path of Custom Desktop Wallpaper File	
Customize the Active Channel Bar	
Delete Channels	
Add Channels	
Import Channels	
Do Not Customize Channels	
Import Current Channel Configuration	
Delete Existing Internet Explorer 4 Channels	Yes No
Show Channel Bar by default (Windows NT® only)	Yes No

Stage 4—Customizing the Browser *(continued)*	
Customize Software Update Channels	
Do Not Customize Software Distribution Channels	
Import the Current Software Distribution Channel Configuration	
Schedule	None Auto Daily Weekly Monthly
Specify Active Desktop Components	
Do Not Customize the Active Desktop™	
Import the Current Active Desktop Components	
Background HTML Settings	
Web (Desktop Item Settings)	
Customize Desktop Toolbars	
Don't Customize	
Import the Current Desktop Toolbar Settings	
My Computer and Control Panel Web View Customization	
Path of My Computer (Mycomp.htt)	
Path of Control Panel (Controlp.htt)	
User Agent String Customization	
Custom String to Be Appended to User Agent	
Automatic Browser Configuration	
Enable automatic browser configuration	Yes No
Auto-configure URL (.ins file)	
Auto-proxy URL (.js or .pac file)	
Auto-configure Every *n* Minutes	

Stage 4—Customizing the Browser *(continued)*

Specify Proxy Settings

Enable Proxy Settings	Yes No
HTTP	
Secure	
FTP	
Gopher	
Socks	
Use Same Proxy for All Addresses?	Yes No
Exceptions to Proxy Server	
Do Not Use Proxy Server for Local (intranet) Addresses	Yes No

Site Certificate and Authenticode Settings

Import Certificate Authorities	
Import Authenticode™ Security	
Add New Root Certificate	

Security Zones and Content Ratings Customization

Security Zone Modifications	
Zones	
Local Intranet Zone Setting	High Medium Low Custom
Trusted Sites Zone Setting	High Medium Low Custom Add Sites
Internet Zone Setting	High Medium Low Custom

Stage 4—Customizing the Browser *(continued)*	
Restricted Sites Zone Setting	High Medium Low Custom Add Sites
Settings	
High	
Medium	
Low	
Custom Security	
ActiveX® Controls and Plug-ins	
Java	
Scripting	
Downloads	
User Authentication	
Miscellaneous	
PICS Content Advisor	
Ratings	
Language	0 (none) to 4 (explicit)
Nudity	0 (none) to 4 (explicit)
Sex	0 (none) to 4 (explicit)
Violence	0 (none) to 4 (explicit)
General	
User Options	
Users Can See Sites That Have No Rating	Yes No
Supervisor Can Type a Password to Allow Users to View Restricted Content	Yes No
Supervisor Password	
Advanced	
Rating Systems	
Ratings Bureau	

Stage 5—Component Customization

Specify Internet Mail Servers, Domain, and News Server

Incoming (POP3 or IMAP) Server	
Outgoing Mail (SMTP) Server	
Internet News Server	
Make Outlook Express the Default Mail Client	Yes No
Make Outlook Express the Default News Client	Yes No
Use Secure Password Authentication	Yes No

Specify LDAP Server Settings

Friendly Name	
Directory Service	
Home Page	
Search Base	
Service Bitmap	
Check Names Against This Server When Sending Mail	Yes No
Authentication Type	Anonymous Secure Password Password

Outlook Express Customizations

Customize InfoPane	
URL	
Local File Path	
Custom Welcome Message	
HTML Path	
Sender	
Reply-to	

Include a Signature

Append to Mail Messages	Yes No
Append to News Postings	Yes No

Stage 6—System Policies and Restrictions

Microsoft NetMeeting Settings

Restrict the Use of File Transfer	
Prevent the User from Sending Files	Yes No
Prevent the User from Receiving Files	Yes No

Restrict the Use of Application Sharing	
Disable All Application Sharing Features	Yes No
Prevent the User from Sharing the Clipboard	Yes No
Prevent the User from Sharing MS-DOS® windows	Yes No
Prevent the User from Sharing Explorer windows	Yes No
Prevent the User from Collaborating	Yes No

Restrict the Use of the Options Dialog	
Disable the General Options Page	Yes No
Disable the My Information Options Page	Yes No
Disable the Calling Options Page	Yes No
Disable the Audio Options Page	Yes No
Disable the Video Options Page	Yes No
Disable the Protocols Options Page	Yes No
Prevent the User from Answering Calls	Yes No
Prevent the User from Using Audio Features	Yes No

Stage 6—System Policies and Restrictions *(continued)*	
Restrict the Use of Video	
Prevent the User from Sending Video	Yes No
Prevent the User from Receiving Video	Yes No
Prevent the User from Using Directory Services	Yes No
Set the Default Directory Server	
Set Exchange Server Property for NetMeeting Address	
Preset User Information Category	
Microsoft NetMeeting Protocols	
Disable TCP/IP	Yes No
Disable null modem	Yes No
Web Desktop Settings	
Desktop	
Disable Active Desktop	Yes No
Do not allow changes to Active Desktop	Yes No
Hide Internet Explorer icon	Yes No
Hide Network Neighborhood icon	Yes No
Hide all items on Active Desktop	Yes No
Active Desktop Items	
Disable All Desktop Items	Yes No
Disable Adding Any Desktop Items	Yes No
Disable Deleting Any Desktop Items	Yes No
Disable Editing Any Desktop Items	Yes No
Disable Closing Any Desktop Items	Yes No

Stage 6—System Policies and Restrictions *(continued)*

Desktop Wallpaper	
No HTML Wallpaper	Yes No
Disable Changing Wallpaper	Yes No
Desktop Toolbars Settings	
Disable Dragging, Dropping and Closing All Toolbars	Yes No
Disable Resizing All Toolbars	Yes No
Start Menu	
Remove Favorites from Start Menu	Yes No
Remove Find from Start Menu	Yes No
Remove Run from Start Menu	Yes No
Remove Documents from Start Menu	Yes No
Do Not Keep History of Recently Opened Documents	Yes No
Clear History of Recently Opened Documents	Yes No
Disable Logoff	Yes No
Disable Shut Down	Yes No
Disable Changes to Printers and Control Panel Settings	Yes No
Disable Changes to Taskbar and Start Menu Settings	Yes No
Disable Context Menu (right-click) for Taskbar	Yes No
Hide Custom Programs Folders	Yes No
Hide Common Program Groups in Start Menu (Windows NT only)	Yes No

Stage 6—System Policies and Restrictions *(continued)*

Shell Settings	
Enable Classic Shell	Yes No
Disable File Menu in Shell Folders	Yes No
Do Not Allow Customization of Folders in Web View	Yes No
Disable Context Menu in Shell Folders	Yes No
Only Allow Approved Shell Extensions	Yes No
Do Not Track Shell Shortcuts During Roaming	Yes No
Hide Floppy Drives in My Computer	Yes No
Disable Net Connections/Disconnections	Yes No
Printer Settings	
Hide General and Details Tabs in Printer Properties	Yes No
Disable Deletion of Printers	Yes No
Disable Addition of Printers	Yes No
System	
Run only specified Windows applications	
Do not allow computer to restart in MS-DOS mode	Yes No
Internet Settings	
Colors	
General Colors	
Background Color (0,0,0 through 255,255,255)	
Text Color (0,0,0 through 255,255,255)	
Use Windows Colors	Yes No

Stage 6—System Policies and Restrictions *(continued)*

Link Colors	
Link Color (0,0,0 through 255,255,255)	
Visited Link Color (0,0,0 through 255,255,255)	
Use Hover Color	Yes No
Hover Color (0,0,0 through 255,255,255)	
Fonts	
Font Size (0 smallest – 4 largest)	
Languages	
Choose the Default Language Preferences	
Modem Settings	
Dial-up Networking Connection	
Enable Autodialing	Yes No
Number of Times to Attempt Connection	
Number of Seconds to Wait Between Attempts	
Connect Without User Intervention	Yes No
Disconnect If Idle After Specified Number of Minutes	Yes No
Minutes to Wait Before Disconnecting	
Perform System Security Check Before Dialing	Yes No
Programs	
Program to use for Calendar	
Program to use for Contacts	
Program to use for Internet Call	
Browsing	
Disable Script Debugger	Yes No
Launch Channels in Full Screen Mode	Yes No
Launch Browser in Full Screen Mode	Yes No

Stage 6—System Policies and Restrictions *(continued)*	
Use Autocomplete	Yes No
Show Friendly URLs in Status Bar	Yes No
Enable Smooth Scrolling	Yes No
Enable Page Transitions	Yes No
Browse in a New Process	Yes No
Enable Page Hit Counting	Yes No
Enable Scheduled Subscription Updates	Yes No
Underline Links	Always Never Hover
Multimedia	
Show Pictures	Yes No
Play Animations	Yes No
Play Videos	Yes No
Play Sounds	Yes No
Smart Image Dithering	Yes No
Security	
Enable Profile Assistant	Yes No
Delete Saved Pages When Browser Is Closed	Yes No
Do Not Save Encrypted Pages to Disk	Yes No
Warn If Forms Submit is being Redirected	Yes No

Stage 6—System Policies and Restrictions *(continued)*	
Warn If Changing Between Secure and Insecure Mode	Yes No
Cookies	Always accept Prompt Disable
Java VM	
JIT Compiler Enabled	Yes No
Java Logging Enabled	Yes No
Printing	
Print Background Colors and Images	Yes No
Searching	
Autoscan Common Root Domains	Yes No
Search When URL Fails	Always Search Always Ask Never Search
Toolbars	
Show Font Button	Yes No
Small Icons	Yes No
HTTP 1.1 Settings	
Use HTTP 1.1	Yes No
Use HTTP 1.1 Through Proxy Connections	Yes No
Outlook Express Settings	
General Settings	
Mail and News Security Zones	
Put Mail and News in the Restricted Sites Zone (instead of the Internet Zone)	Yes No

Stage 6—System Policies and Restrictions *(continued)*	
HTML Mail and News Composition Settings	
Mail: Make Plain Text Message Composition the Default for Mail Messages (instead of HTML mail)	Yes No
News: Make HTML Message Composition the Default for News Posts (instead of plain text)	Yes No
View Customization	
Folder and Message Navigational Elements	
Turn On Outlook Bar	Yes No
Turn Off Folder List (tree view of folders)	Yes No
Turn On Folder Bar (horizontal line displaying folder names)	Yes No
Turn Off the Tip of the Day	Yes No
Channels and Subscriptions Settings	
Maximum KB of Site Subscriptions (zero disables restriction)	
Maximum KB of Channel Subscriptions (zero disables restriction)	
Maximum Number of Site Subscriptions That Can Be Installed (zero disables restriction)	
Minimum Number of Minutes Between Scheduled Subscription Updates (zero disables restriction)	
Beginning of Range in Which to Exclude Scheduled Subscription Updates. Minutes from Midnight (zero disables restriction)	
End of Range in Which to Exclude Scheduled Subscription Updates. Minutes from Midnight (zero disables restriction)	
Maximum Site Subscription Crawl Depth	
Internet Explorer Properties	
General Tab Settings	
Disable Changing Home Page Settings	Yes No
Disable Changing Cache Settings	Yes No
Disable Changing History Settings	Yes No

Stage 6—System Policies and Restrictions *(continued)*

Disable Changing Color Settings	Yes No
Disable Changing Link Color Settings	Yes No
Disable Changing Font Settings	Yes No
Disable Changing Language Settings	Yes No
Disable Changing Accessiblity Settings	Yes No
Security Tab Settings	
Use Only Machine Settings for Security Zones	Yes No
Do Not Allow Users to Change Policies for Any Security Zone	Yes No
Do Not Allow Users to Add/Delete Sites from a Security Zone	Yes No
Content Tab Settings	
Disable Changing Ratings Settings	Yes No
Disable Changing Certificate Settings	Yes No
Disable Changing Profile Assistant Settings	Yes No
Disable Changing Microsoft Wallet Settings	Yes No
Connection Tab Settings	
Disable Calling Connection Wizard	Yes No
Disable Changing Connection Settings	Yes No
Disable Changing Proxy Settings	Yes No
Disable Changing Automatic Configuration Settings	Yes No

Stage 6—System Policies and Restrictions *(continued)*	
Programs Tab Settings	
Disable Changing Messaging Settings	Yes No
Disable Changing Calendar and Contact Settings	Yes No
Disable Changing Internet Explorer Default Browser Settings	Yes No
Advanced Tab Settings	
Disable Changing Settings on Advanced Tab	Yes No
Code Download	
Internet Search Path*	

* This is the CodeBaseSearchPath. The default is **CODEBASE; http://activex.microsoft.com/objects/ocget.dll**

When Internet Component Download is called to download code, it traverses the Internet Search Path to look for the desired component. This is a list of Object Store servers that will be queried every time components are downloaded using GoGetClassObjectFromURL. This way, even if an <OBJECT> tag in an HTML document does not specify a CODEBASE location to download code for an embedded OLE control, the Internet Component Download will still use the Internet Search Path to find the necessary code.

Stage 6—System Policies and Restrictions *(continued)*	
Channels Settings	
Disable Channel User Interface	Yes No
Disable Adding and Subscribing to Channels	Yes No
Disable Editing Channel Properties and Channel Subscriptions	Yes No
Disable Removing Channels and Subscriptions to Channels	Yes No
Disable Adding Site Subscriptions	Yes No
Disable Editing Site Subscriptions	Yes No
Disable Removing Site Subscriptions	Yes No

Stage 6—System Policies and Restrictions *(continued)*	
Disable Channel Logging	Yes No
Disable Update Now and Update All for Channels and Subscriptions	Yes No
Disable All Scheduled Channel and Site Subscriptions	Yes No
Disable Unattended Dialing by Subscriptions	Yes No
Disable password caching for all channel or site subscriptions	Yes No
Disable Downloading of Channel Subscription Content (change notification will still function)	Yes No
Disable Downloading of Site Subscription Content (change notification will still function)	Yes No
Disable Editing and Creating of Schedule Groups	Yes No
Microsoft Chat Settings	
Chat Server List (separated by semicolons)	
Default Chat Server	
Default Chat Room	
Default Character	
Default Backdrop	
User Profile String	
Show Only Registered Rooms in Room List	Yes No

A P P E N D I X   K

Internet Explorer Administration Kit (IEAK) FAQs

This appendix covers some of the most Frequently Asked Questions (FAQs) about the Microsoft® Internet Explorer Administration Kit (IEAK) 4. For more information about using the IEAK, see Part 9.

What are some of the new features in the IEAK 4?

Brand the setup as well as the browser

The IEAK 4 now allows you to brand the entire user experience. With the IEAK 4, you can specify title elements and graphics to be used during the setup process. With the IEAK 3.2a, you could only brand the browser.

Create and/or delete channels in the Internet Explorer 4 Channel Guide

With the IEAK 4, you can add your own Active Channel™ to the Internet Explorer Channel bar. You can also use the IEAK 4 to delete competitors' channels. Please note that the IEAK 4 license agreement limits you to deleting only channels of competing Internet access providers.

Import Active Desktop items

The IEAK 4 enables you to specify which Active Desktop™ items appear on your end users' computers. You can add desktop views of Web pages, or you can display custom controls that link directly to your Web site.

Import Desktop toolbar settings

With the IEAK 4, you can import toolbar settings that will be applied when your end users install Internet Explorer 4. These settings are taken directly from the settings specified on the machine you used to build your Internet Explorer installation packages.

Specify more than five links on the Internet Explorer Links toolbar

Now you can specify more than five links to appear on the Internet Explorer 4 Links toolbar.

Create a package with up to 10 different installation options

With previous versions of the IEAK, you could only build a package with one installation option. Using the IEAK 4, you can build a package with up to 10 different installation options from which the user can choose.

Customize user agent string

Now you can customize the user agent string of your browser packages, so you can track the number of hits that are generated by your customized browser and distinguish between various distribution programs. Here's an example of a user agent string that would appear in your Web server log:

```
Mozilla/4.0 (compatible; MSInternet Explorer 4.0; Windows NT); your
       custom string
```

Create a custom welcome page

Present end users with your own custom page when they start up Internet Explorer for the first time.

Customize the Internet Explorer 4 Search bar

With IEAK 4, you can fully customize the new Internet Explorer Search bar.

Change toolbar background bitmap

Now you can customize the look of Internet Explorer by changing the background bitmap on the Internet Explorer toolbar. Use this feature with caution, however; using background bitmaps with dark colors can make the toolbar unreadable.

10 user-specified components

You can now build installation packages to include up to 10 user-specified components. The IEAK 3.2 allowed you to add just 2 user-specified components.

Specify up to 10 download sites

You can specify up to 10 download sites for each installation package you build with the IEAK 4.

Security zones and other security enhancements

Internet Explorer 4 adds a new security feature called security zones. Security zones break up the Internet and intranet sites to allow for greater manageability. Internet Explorer includes four default zones: Local Intranet, Trusted Sites, Internet, and Restricted Sites. As the system administrator, you can preset these settings. You can apply different security settings (high, medium, low, or custom) to each of these.

System policies and restrictions management

As the system administrator, you can manage system policies and restrictions with an easy-to-use interface in both the IEAK Configuration Wizard and the Profile Manager. Some of these restrictions include Active Desktop and shell feature lock-downs, as well as component settings (such as not allowing users to place calls from NetMeeting).

Improved Profile Manager

The improved Profile Manager (formerly known as the INS Editor) includes a tree-view pane that gives you easy access to all the options available in the IEAK Configuration Wizard. You can reach each option quickly, and the interface for making changes is as simple to use as the IEAK. The Profile Manager also has incorporated the System Policies and Restrictions management capabilities that are available at the end of the IEAK Configuration Wizard.

What optional components are available in the Internet Explorer 4 suite?

Here is a quick overview of the components included with the IEAK 4.

Microsoft Outlook™ Express

Outlook Express is a highly versatile tool for exchanging e-mail and newsgroup messages with individuals and groups. You can use the new HTML functionality to add graphics, animation, and even multimedia files to your e-mail messages.

Microsoft NetMeeting™

With NetMeeting, the Internet's premier conferencing tool, you can hold video and voice conversations and collaborate with groups of people in real time by sharing software applications, chatting, and sharing a whiteboard.

Microsoft Chat 2.0

Get online and communicate with others, using Microsoft Chat. This new kind of chat program lets you decide how to display your message—choose text only or a combination of text and graphical features.

Microsoft Web Publishing Wizard

This wizard steps you through the process of posting your Web site to almost any Web server available.

Microsoft FrontPage® Express

FrontPage Express makes it easy to create and edit Web pages that you can post on the Internet or intranet.

Microsoft Interactive Music Control

Internet Explorer 4 introduces the new Interactive Music control, an ActiveX® control that composes and plays music in response to a user's actions. The Interactive Music Control thus creates a soundtrack of the user's actions—for instance, in a computer game or guided tour of a Web site—all without using WAV or MIDI files that require time to download.

Microsoft Interactive Music Control with Synthesizer

The Microsoft Interactive Music Control with Synthesizer adds the Microsoft Synthesizer and support for DLS. DLS is an industry standard format for packaging instrument sounds in a way that can be recognized and used by hardware (like a soundcard) or software synthesizers.

Microsoft VRML 2.0 Viewer

With the Microsoft VRML 2.0 Viewer, Internet Explorer users can view engaging virtual 3-D worlds.

Microsoft Agent

Microsoft Agent is a set of software services that supports the presentation of software agents as interactive personalities within the Microsoft Windows interface. These agents can be developed to provide assistance to users by speaking to them as they use your applications of Web sites.

Macromedia Shockwave Director

With Director, you can create a variety of multimedia productions, including business presentations, Web content, interactive advertising pieces, kiosk productions, and CD-ROM titles.

Macromedia Shockwave Flash

Flash brings Web pages to life without the wait. Vector-based Flash movies offer compact, interactive Web interfaces, animations, buttons, advertising banners, logos, maps, cartoons, and more.

Microsoft Script Debugger

Microsoft Script Debugger for Internet Explorer is a debugging environment that extends Internet Explorer by allowing Web developers to browse, edit, and debug HTML pages that contain Visual Basic® Scripting Edition (VBScript) or JScript™ (the Microsoft implementation of JavaScript). The Microsoft Script Debugger is the first environment that allows users to debug scripted HTML. This tool gives developers a seamless way to combine HTML and script development.

Microsoft NetShow™

NetShow broadcasts high-impact, low-bandwidth video and more to computer desktops for entertainment, training, sales, event coverage, and more.

Microsoft Internet Explorer Supplemental Fonts

The IEAK provides a set of TrueType® fonts that can be used with Internet Explorer. If users install these, they will be able to read Web-page text that was designed to be viewed with the following TrueType fonts: Arial, Comic, Courier, Impact, and Times New Roman.

Microsoft Visual Basic Run Time

Microsoft Visual Basic Run Time makes it possible for you to distribute ActiveX controls with your Internet Explorer 4 installation packages.

Intel® Indeo™5

Indeo video is the Intel digital video capture, compression, and decompression codec—a software driver used to compress digital video data for storage and to decompress it for playback on a multimedia computer. The latest version of Indeo video, designed for Intel MMX technology, allows software-only playback of high-quality video on desktop multimedia computers.

VDOLive Player

The VDOLive Player takes advantage of streaming technology to deliver high audio and video quality over limited bandwidth.

Microsoft Internet Explorer Sound Pack

The Internet Explorer Sound Pack provides a collection of sounds for use with the Internet Explorer to help users know when pages have started and finished loading. It also alerts users when a site has been found.

RealPlayer by Progressive Networks

You can use RealPlayer to play different media types, including animation, audio, video, 3-D images, MIDI, presentations, and text.

Can an IEAK 3 .ins file be used in the IEAK 4?

The .ins files are backwards compatible. Sections and entries that existed in the IEAK 3 .ins files have not changed, but there are new sections and entries for the new features added to the IEAK 4. To take advantage of all the new features included in the IEAK 4, it's recommended that you create a new .ins file with the IEAK Configuration Wizard.

What are the requirements for running the IEAK Configuration Wizard?

Internet Explorer 4 must be installed on the build machine before the IEAK Wizard can be used. Before starting the wizard, calculate how much disk space is required for the components you want to install. If you plan to install all the components of the Internet Explorer suite, you will need approximately 50 MB in the Program Files folder and 50 MB on the destination drive.

What type of distribution media will the IEAK 4 support?

The IEAK 4 will support download from an intranet or the Internet, compact disc, and single and multiple floppy disks.

How can I offer a customized browser that takes advantage of 128-bit encryption?

U.S. regulations regarding encryption technology require a separate licensing process for users who wish to redistribute 128-bit encryption with Internet Explorer 4. According to federal regulations, licensees must be located in the U.S. or Canada only and must agree to distribution restrictions described in an addendum to the IEAK Licensing Agreement.

For more information, see the "Server Gated Cryptography" section of Chapter 28, "Digital Certificates," or see the Microsoft IEAK Licensing Agreement Web page at **www.microsoft.com/ie/ieak/license.htm**.

How can I uninstall components that were installed with Internet Explorer 3?

To remove the components installed with Internet Explorer 3, select the **Add/Remove Programs** icon in Control Panel, and then uninstall the appropriate component.

What are the bitmap dimensions for the Active Setup bitmap, and are there any sample bitmaps?

The dimensions for the Active Setup bitmap are 120 pixels wide by 239 pixels high. It needs to be a BMP file, and it must be 256 colors or fewer. No sample bitmaps are included with the IEAK.

What are the dimensions for the toolbar bitmap?

The toolbar bitmap can use any dimensions. It must be a BMP file, and it must be 256 colors or fewer. When creating a toolbar bitmap, however, be careful not to use colors that are too dark, or text will be difficult to read and graphics hard to see.

Is there a way to control the order of the channels in the IEAK?

There is no way to preset a custom channel order.

Can existing channels be removed?

Yes, you can remove channels in the IEAK. You can also use the Profile Manager to prevent users from adding or deleting the channels that you have pre-configured.

Are there any technical specs on how the Channel Definition Format (CDF) file is created and where it resides?

The CDF specification is located at **http://www.microsoft.com/standards/cdf.htm** and can also be found in the *Microsoft Internet Client SDK* at **http://www.microsoft.com/workshop/prog/inetsdk/**.

How does a CDF file get pushed to customers when they visit a Web site?

The CDF file itself does not get pushed to users who visit your Web site. The file resides on the server, and you must provide an HTML link to it. When the visitor clicks that link, it will activate the Channel Subscription Wizard that steps the user through the process of subscribing to a channel. Of course, you can pre-configure your own custom CDF files to be built into Internet Explorer using the IEAK. In that case, users won't have to do anything since the channels will already be present in their Channel bar. For more information about creating CDF files, see Chapter 16, "Managed Webcasting."

How do you configure Outlook Express to support multiple user scenarios?

Outlook Express uses Windows profiles to address the multiple user scenarios. Users can log into their respective profiles and access their mail. To switch from one user profile to another, users select the **Log Off** option from the **File** menu in Outlook Express or from the **Start** button on the Windows taskbar. Alternatively, they can restart Windows if they already have a profile set up. If users don't have a profile set up on their computer, the **Enable Multi-user Settings** dialog box will appear and guide users through the steps to set up a profile. Once the new profile is set up and new users log into Windows and then Outlook Express, they can set up their own account and use their own mail store. For more information about user profiles, see Chapter 5, "User Profiles."

What importing options does Outlook Express support?

Outlook Express ships with migration tools to convert mail messages, address books, and account settings from the following mail packages: Eudora Light and Eudora Pro, Netscape Mail, Communicator, Windows Messaging, Outlook, Exchange, and Internet Mail and News. In addition, Outlook Express offers conversion of LDIF-LDAP and comma-separated address books. For more information about Outlook Express, see Chapter 18.

Can I configure the Outlook Express AutoReply option with the IEAK?

By default, Outlook Express replies to messages in the format in which they were sent. For example, if a user sends you a message in plain text, you will respond in plain text, even though your default is HTML. This cannot be configured through the IEAK, but users have the option to turn it off. In addition, the IEAK does allow you to designate the default message format for users. You can write an .adm file that will turn this feature off by default in your users' version of Outlook Express. For more information about Outlook Express, see Chapter 18.

What is the "InfoPane" in Outlook Express?

You can use the IEAK to customize a 50-pixel-high HTML pane across the bottom of the Outlook Express screen. You have two options for customizing the InfoPane. First, you can download a local HTML file to your users' computers and have the InfoPane display this file. You can use this file to provide links to account information, support sites, training information, your home page, and other sites or images. The second option is to point the InfoPane to any URL on the Web. When users are online, they will see the contents of that site inside the InfoPane. When they are not online, the InfoPane will be blank. Note that users will always have an option to turn the InfoPane off.

Whichever option you choose, we suggest that you design your HTML content for 640 pixels wide by 50 pixels high.

Does the installer wait for custom components to finish?

Yes, Active Setup will not proceed until your custom components have finished installing. For more information about Active Setup, see Chapter 2.

Is there an installation option that allows users to select the individual components they want to install?

Yes, the IEAK does not offer a check box for each component, but there is an option for users to choose from 10 possible installation options. It is up to the IEAK administrator to create applicable packages. If you do not wish to include these components in your distribution package, you can provide them by a component add-on Web site.

Will there be a way to customize the Readme.txt?

No.

How do I create versions of Internet Explorer for Windows 3.1?

The IEAK 4 currently does not build packages for 16-bit platforms. Once Internet Explorer 4 for Windows 3.1 has been released, Microsoft will make available an IEAK that will generate packages for the 16-bit platform.

How do I import a collection of favorites arranged inside folders?

When you import a collection of favorites, the IEAK imports the contents of the folder but not the folder itself. To import an entire directory structure, select the top-level folder that contains all of the subdirectories you want to import. This will import all favorites and their folders.

Does the IEAK 4 support the creation of a single self-installing, executable (.exe) file (vs. the .cab files used by Active Setup)?

No.

What is Active Setup?

Active Setup is new in Internet Explorer 4. Active Setup is a small, Web-based setup package that enables your users to install the latest Internet Explorer components directly from your Web site or intranet. Active Setup can be run from a single floppy disk and over the Internet.

The Active Setup engine provides significant advantages in usability for both download and floppy-disk installations. For a download installation, it divides the download into several smaller segments, making it possible to restart in the event of a failure. For a floppy-disk installation, it enables Internet Service Providers (ISPs) to produce and distribute packages with a single floppy disk.

You can specify up to 10 download sites when you build your package(s), making it easy for your users to download and install Internet Explorer and its components.

Active Setup also detects which installed components need to be updated, so your users don't have to download an entirely new package just to update one of the components. For more information about Active Setup, see Chapter 2.

Are there any Setup switches for Internet Explorer 4?

There are two .exe files that actually run: IE4Setup.exe and IE4wzd.exe.

The IE4Setup.exe is just an application that wraps around Internet Express (IExpress), and most of the installation wizard code is in IE4wzd.exe. Since IE4Setup.exe is just the IExpress wrapper, typing /? does not reveal all the correct command-line switches. (For more information about IExpress, see Appendix L.)

This is the command line you can use to run IE4Setup.exe in batch mode (hands-free mode—so you don't need to click Next or press the ENTER key) to go to the next wizard page.

```
IE4Setup.exe /c:"ie4wzd.exe /q /u:""http://webserver/
    directory/cab"" /s:#e"
```

–Or–

```
IE4Setup.exe /c:"ie4wzd.exe /q /u:""file://\\netlocation\
    directory\cab"" /s:#e"
```

Other switches of interest in IE4wzd.exe are:

- /S:#e—Location of calling .exe (Usually will be IE4Setup.exe, not required but helps softboot work)
- /U—Location for installation .cab files (not used on CD-ROM)
- /M:1,2,3—0 = standard install(default), 1 = enhanced, 2 = full
- /I:Y,N—Whether you want integrated desktop or not. Default is "Y"
- /R:N—To disable hardboot/softboot

For more information about Active Setup and ACME Setup, see Chapters 2 and 3, respectively. For more information about Setup command-line switches, see Appendix A.

Where can I get more information about Internet Explorer 4?

For more information, see the following Web sites.

- For information about Internet Explorer 4:

  http://www.microsoft.com/ie/ie40/

- For information about the IEAK, including licensing:

  http://www.microsoft.com/ie/ieak/

- For Microsoft Internet Explorer Press (for news regarding Internet Explorer and the IEAK):

  http://www.microsoft.com/ie/press/

- For CDF specification:

  http://www.microsoft.com/standards/cdf.htm

- For information about developing content for Internet Explorer 4, such as Dynamic HTML and Active Channels:

  http://www.microsoft.com/workshop/

A P P E N D I X   L

IExpress Configuration Wizard

If you want to include custom components inside the Internet Explorer installation process, such as a custom FTP client or communication software, the Microsoft® Internet Explorer Administration Kit (IEAK) includes a utility called Internet Express (IExpress) for this purpose. IExpress is a tool that creates custom, self-installing, self-extracting packages (or .cab files) of applications. The IExpress program resides in the directory C:\Program Files\ieak\tools\iexpress.

Using the IExpress Configuration Wizard

You can use the step-by-step IExpress Configuration Wizard to package applications so that they can be installed by Active Setup along with Internet Explorer. This can make the rollout of multiple applications much easier, as they can all be done at the same time.

Starting the IExpress Configuration Wizard

▶ **To start the IExpress Configuration Wizard**

1. On the **Start** menu, click **Run**.

   The **Run** dialog box opens.

2. Enter **IExpress.exe**.

3. Click **OK**.

Navigating in the IExpress Configuration Wizard

To	Click
Display the next page, and accept the values on the current page	**Next**
Display any previous page You may have to retype some of the values you've entered.	**Back**
Exit this package	**Cancel**

The following section displays all of the IExpress Configuration Wizard pages you need to navigate to specify packages. Each page is followed by a table that describes the features and options available on that wizard page.

Creating the Package

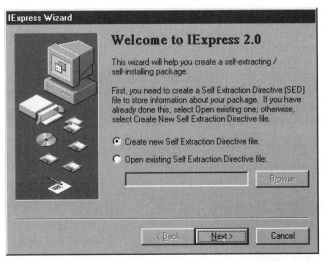

You can create a Self Extraction Directive (SED) file to store information about this application package.

Option	Description
Create new Self Extraction Directive file	To create a completely new SED file for an application, click this option.
Open existing Self Extraction Directive file	To modify an existing SED file or to use an SED file to create another, click this option. Then enter the path and file name, or click **Browse** to locate it.

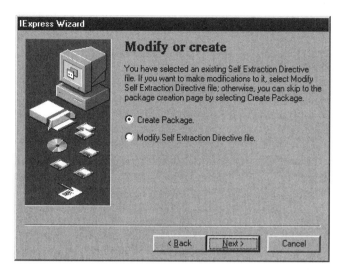

This page appears only when you open an existing SED file from the Welcome page.

Option	Description
Create Package	Select this option to create a package, just as you would at the end of this process.
Modify Self Extraction Directive file	Select this option to modify the SED.

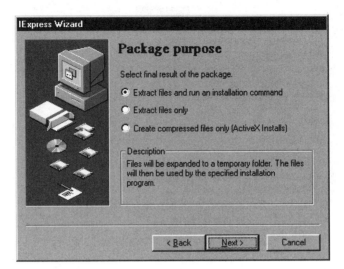

Option	Description
Extract files and run an installation command	Select this option if you want the package to consist of compressed files and an installation program.
Extract files only	Select this option if you want only files compressed.
Create compressed files only (ActiveX® installs)	Select this option if you want the files to be compressed into a .cab file.

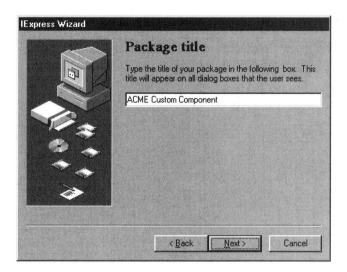

Option	Description
Type Package title	Type the title that you want to appear on all of the dialog boxes.

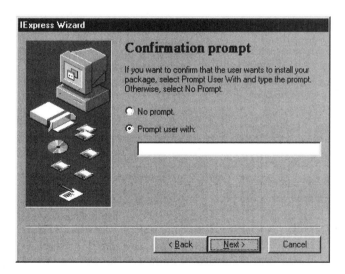

Option	Description
No prompt	Select this option when you do not want end users to see a confirmation prompt.
Prompt user with	Select this option to display a confirmation prompt, then enter the text you want the end user to see.

Option	Description
Do not display a license	If the software in this package does not need to be licensed to the end user, select this option.
Display a license	When the software in the package needs to be licensed to the end user, select this option. Then, enter the full path and file name for the license agreement, or click **Browse** to locate it.

Option	Description
Enter filename and path	Click **Add**, then select the files you want in the package.
	To remove a file from the package, click **Remove**.

This page appears only if you have chosen **Extract files** and then run an installation command on the second screen of this wizard (**Package Purpose**).

Option	Description
Install Program	Select the program or .inf file that you want this package to launch.
Post Install Command	If you want to execute a command after this package's launch is complete, enter the command or select it.

Option	Description
Default	Click this option to display the installation's window to the end user.
Hidden	Click this option to hide the installation's window from the end user.
Minimized	Click this option to display a minimized window to the end user.
Maximized	Click this option to display a maximized window to the end user.

Option	Description
No message	Click this option if you do not want to display a message that tells the end user that the installation is finished.
Display message	Enter a message that you want displayed to the end user after the installation is finished.

Option	Description
Enter target path and filename	Enter the path and file name of the file to which the application should be installed on the end-user's computer, or click **Browse** to locate the path and file.
Hide File Extracting Progress Animation from User	If you do not want to display progress indications to the end user, select this check box.
Store files using Long File Name inside Package	If you want to use long file names in this package, select this check box.

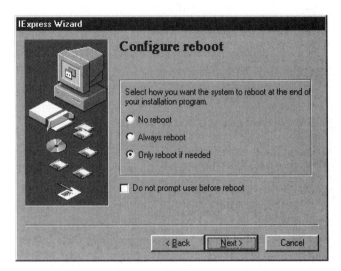

This page appears only if you have chosen **Extract files** and then run an installation command on the second screen of this wizard (**Package Purpose**).

Option	Description
No reboot	Click this option if you do not want the computer to be restarted after the installation.
Always reboot	Click this option if the computer must be restarted after the installation.
Only reboot if needed	Click this option if the computer may or may not need to be restarted after the installation.
Do not prompt user before reboot	Select this check box if you do not want to inform the user that the computer will be restarted.
	You should select this option whenever the end-user's installation is silent.

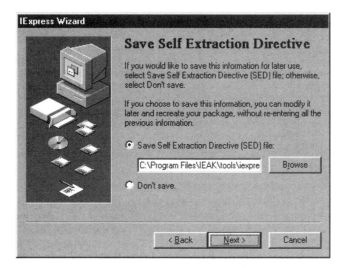

Option	Description
Save Self Extraction Directive (SED) file	To save the SED file, click this option. Then enter the full path and file name, or click **Browse** to locate it.
Don't save	To abandon this SED file, click this option.

The IExpress Configuration Wizard displays this page to give you a last chance to save the package you've created. Once you click **Next**, the IExpress Configuration Wizard creates the package files as you specified.

Signing Package Files

Digital signatures identify the source of programs and guarantee that the code hasn't changed since it was signed. Depending on how users' browser-security levels are configured, users could be warned not to download files that aren't signed, or could be prevented from downloading them. Therefore, you should digitally sign the .cab files created by the IEAK Configuration Wizard and any custom components you include.

Signing .cab files and custom programs requires two steps: obtaining a digital certificate—from a Certificate Authority (CA) such as VeriSign or GTE—and signing the code.

Now that you have created the package, you must sign it; otherwise, Active Setup will not install it. For more information about signing your files, please see the "Signing Your Programs" section of the IEAK Help.

Index

W

X

/x switch (ACME Setup) 713
XML (Extensible Markup Language)
  Data Source Objects 408
XML tags *See* individual tag names
<XML VERSION=> tag 216

Y

/y switch (ACME Setup) 713
Yes, but only tell me when this page is updated
  (site subscription setting) 193
Yes, notify me of updates and download the page for
  offline viewing (site subscription setting) 193

Z

/z switch (ACME Setup) 713
z-index property 405
zones *See* security zones
zone security *See* security zones

This is how
Microsoft
Windows NT
pros become
incredibly
resourceful.

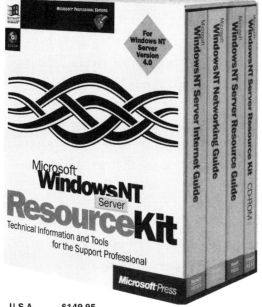

This three-volume kit provides the valuable technical and performance information and the tools you need for handling rollout and support issues surrounding Microsoft Windows NT Server 4.0. You get a full 2500 pages—plus a CD-ROM—loaded with essential information not available anywhere else. For support professionals, MICROSOFT WINDOWS NT SERVER RESOURCE KIT is more than a guide. It's a natural resource.

U.S.A.   **$149.95**
U.K.   £140.99 [V.A.T. included]
Canada $199.95
ISBN 1-57231-344-7

Microsoft Press

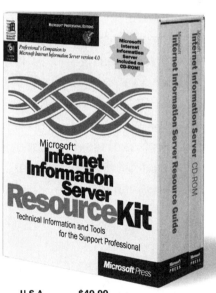

Create *vivid,* *interactive* *Web content* with Microsoft **Internet Explorer 4!**

Here's the indispensable volume for site builders, Webmasters, multimedia authors, and anyone else who wants to discover all the technologies that make Microsoft® Internet Explorer 4 a major breakthrough. Inside is a rich exploration of Dynamic HTML, Cascading Style Sheets, the Internet Explorer 4 object model, scripting, multimedia effects and controls, and data binding. You'll discover Dynamic HTML as a multimedia authoring tool for Web, network, or CD-ROM–based productions. And you'll work with plenty of helpful examples on the enclosed CD-ROM. In short, if you want to do great things with Dynamic HTML, you want DYNAMIC HTML IN ACTION.

U.S.A.	**$39.99**
U.K.	£37.49 [V.A.T. included]
Canada	$57.99
ISBN	1-57231-820-1

Microsoft®*Press*

6. **U.S. GOVERNMENT RESTRICTED RIGHTS.** The SOFTWARE PRODUCT and documentation are provided with RESTRICTED RIGHTS. Use, duplication, or disclosure by the Government is subject to restrictions as set forth in subparagraph (c)(1)(ii) of the Rights in Technical Data and Computer Software clause at DFARS 252.227-7013 or subparagraphs (c)(1) and (2) of the Commercial Computer Software—Restricted Rights at 48 CFR 52.227-19, as applicable. Manufacturer is Microsoft Corporation/One Microsoft Way/Redmond, WA 98052-6399.

7. **NOTE ON JAVA SUPPORT.** The SOFTWARE PRODUCT may contain support for programs written in Java. Java technology is not fault tolerant and is not designed, manufactured, or intended for use or resale as online control equipment in hazardous environments requiring fail-safe performance, such as in the operation of nuclear facilities, aircraft navigation or communication systems, air traffic control, direct life support machines, or weapons systems, in which the failure of Java technology could lead directly to death, personal injury, or severe physical or environmental damage.

MISCELLANEOUS

If you acquired this product in the United States, this EULA is governed by the laws of the State of Washington.

If you acquired this product in Canada, this EULA is governed by the laws of the Province of Ontario, Canada. In such case, each of the parties hereto irrevocably attorns to the jurisdiction of the courts of the Province of Ontario and further agrees to commence any litigation which may arise hereunder in the courts located in the Judicial District of York, Province of Ontario.

If this product was acquired outside the United States, then local law may apply.

Should you have any questions concerning this EULA, or if you desire to contact Microsoft for any reason, please contact the Microsoft subsidiary serving your country, or write: Microsoft Sales Information Center/One Microsoft Way/Redmond, WA 98052-6399.

LIMITED WARRANTY

NO WARRANTIES. Microsoft expressly disclaims any warranty for the SOFTWARE PRODUCT. The SOFTWARE PRODUCT and any related documentation is provided "as is" without warranty or condition of any kind, either express or implied, including, without limitation, the implied warranties or conditions of merchantability, fitness for a particular purpose, or noninfringement. The entire risk arising out of use or performance of the SOFTWARE PRODUCT remains with you.

NO LIABILITY FOR DAMAGES. In no event shall Microsoft or its suppliers be liable for any damages whatsoever (including, without limitation, damages for loss of business profits, business interruption, loss of business information, or any other pecuniary loss) arising out of the use of or inability to use this Microsoft product, even if Microsoft has been advised of the possibility of such damages. Because some states/jurisdictions do not allow the exclusion or limitation of liability for consequential or incidental damages, the above limitation may not apply to you.

Si vous avez acquis votre produit Microsoft au CANADA, la garantie limitée suivante vous concerne :

GARANTIE LIMITÉE

EXCLUSION DE GARANTIES. Microsoft renonce entièrement à toute garantie pour le LOGICIEL. Le LOGICIEL et toute autre documentation s'y rapportant sont fournis « comme tels » sans aucune garantie quelle qu'elle soit, expresse ou implicite, y compris, mais ne se limitant pas aux garanties implicites de la qualité marchande, d'adaptation à un usage particulier ou d'absence de violation des droits des tiers. Le risque total découlant de l'utilisation ou de la performance du LOGICIEL est entre vos mains.

ABSENCE DE RESPONSABILITÉ POUR LES DOMMAGES. Microsoft ou ses fournisseurs ne pourront être tenus responsables en aucune circonstance de tout dommage quel qu'il soit (y compris mais non de façon limitative les dommages directs ou indirects causés par la perte de bénéfices commerciaux, l'interruption des affaires, la perte d'information commerciale ou toute autre perte pécuniaire) résultant de l'utilisation ou de l'impossibilité d'utilisation de ce produit, et ce, même si la société Microsoft a été avisée de l'éventualité de tels dommages. Parce que certains états/juridictions ne permettent pas l'exclusion ou la limitation de responsabilité relative aux dommages indirects ou consécutifs, la limitation ci-dessus peut ne pas s'appliquer à votre égard.

La présente Convention est régie par les lois de la province d'Ontario, Canada. Chacune des parties à la présente reconnaît irrévocablement la compétence des tribunaux de la province d'Ontario et consent à instituer tout litige qui pourrait découler de la présente auprès des tribunaux situés dans le district judiciaire de York, province d'Ontario.

Au cas où vous auriez des questions concernant cette licence ou que vous désiriez vous mettre en rapport avec Microsoft pour quelque raison que ce soit, veuillez contacter la succursale Microsoft desservant votre pays, dont l'adresse est fournie dans ce produit, ou écrire à : Microsoft Customer Sales and Service, One Microsoft Way, Redmond, Washington 98052-6399.